The Dispossessed Majority

ALSO BY WILMOT ROBERTSON
Ventilations

The Dispossessed Majority

Wilmot Robertson

HOWARD ALLEN   CAPE CANAVERAL

To my co-author. No other title adequately describes your inestimable assistance.

NEW 1981 EDITION

First paperback printing

International Standard Book Number: 0–914576–16–X
Library of Congress Catalog Card Number: 71–167649

Printed in the United States of America

In order to possess what you do not possess
You must go by the way of dispossession.

—T. S. ELIOT, *Four Quartets*

Contents

PART IV
The Minority Challenge

PART V
The Cultural Clash

PART VI
The Political Clash

PART VII
The Economic Clash

PART VIII
The Legal Clash

PART IX
The Foreign Policy Clash

PART X
Prospects and Perspectives

Preface

THE MOST TRULY disadvantaged are those who are hated for their virtues, not their vices, who insist on playing the game of life with opponents who have long ago abandoned the rules, who stubbornly go on believing that a set of highly sophisticated institutions developed by and for a particular people at a particular point in time and space is operational for all peoples under all circumstances.

The intent of this book is to supply members of this discomfited and threatened group—here provisionally defined as the American Majority—with a systematic diagnosis of the diseases and debilities that have laid them low and a probative regimen for their recovery.

So many liberals having become minority racists and so many conservatives having become rootless cranks, so much religion having become social science and so much social science having become intellectual sleight-of-hand, the thoughtful Majority member has nowhere to turn but to himself. This, however, may be his salvation. In isolation the critical faculty cuts deeper. Only now is it possible to understand the tragic and humiliating fate of the American Majority because only now are a few Majority minds, deepened by decades of solitary contemplation and sharpened by the grim chronicle of events, finally tuning to the emergency wavelength of collective survival.

On the surface America appears lost. But the animalization of the body and the brutalization of the spirit, the desecration of the environment, the venality of politics, the drug and homosexual plagues, the taste-destroying shock waves of pornography, the

ghetto savagery, the degeneration of the military, the torrents
of illegal immigrants, the apostasy of the professors and journalists, the mindlessness of the students, the phobic materialism and
Babbittry of their parents—all these, perhaps, are not the irreversi-
ble regressions they seem but merely short-term roadblocks or
detours on the Great Trek to a higher and more luminous life
form. In the sequence of organic rebirth, what is to be done must
first be undone. Unthinking must precede rethinking. According
to the sine curve of human action, degeneration alternates with
regeneration. Quite possibly, the present phase is one of *reculer
pour mieux sauter.*

On the hopeful side, the chromosomal material, the first and
fundamental requirement for an American resurgence, is still in
abundant supply. Life scientists and those few social scientists
worthy of the name are seething with insights and breakthroughs
that cannot help but unbait some of the dogmatic traps that have
been deliberately set for the more active Majority intellects. From
the raked-over ashes of burnt-out historicism flashes a spark or
two of authentic history. There is even the glimmer of a new
religion (or the rejuvenation of the old) in the Promethean utterances and riddles of the new ontology.

At all events, the Majority will soon be out of limbo. There is
nowhere for it to go but up—or all the way down. It is really a
matter of timing, a race between the encroaching jungle and the
ripening harvest. The moon walk may turn out to be the last
mile, or the crossing of the Rubicon.

PART I

Racial Dynamics

CHAPTER 1

The Concept of Race

NOTHING HAS RAISED man to higher peaks of creativity or lowered him to greater depths of destructiveness than the dual notion of human similarity and dissimilarity.

Every man is like every other man in that he belongs to the same species, *Homo sapiens.* The seven-foot Watusi and the four-foot Pygmy, the milk-white Swede, the coffee-colored Latin American mestizo, and the almond-eyed and almond-tinted Oriental are all capable of interbreeding. The idea of human likeness consequently has biological origins. But so does the idea of human unlikeness. Every man differs physically and mentally from every other man, which accounts both for human individuality and group differences.[1] As Shakespeare wrote:

> "Strange is it that our bloods,
> Of colour, weight, and heat, pour'd all together,
> Would quite confound distinction, yet stand off
> In differences so mighty." [2]

The average person probably starts life as a similarist and ends as a dissimilarist. The child grows older and wanders from the family hearth, only to find that all fathers do not look like his

---

1. Even identical twins differ slightly in height, weight, head length, and head width. L. C. Dunn and Theodosius Dobzhansky, *Heredity, Race and Society,* New American Library, New York, 1960, p. 27. "Deux jumeaux identiques, provenant du même oeuf, possédant la même constitution génétique, manifestent chacun une personnalité différente." Alexis Carrel, *L'homme, cet inconnu,* Librarie Plon, Paris, 1935, p. 336.

2. *All's Well that Ends Well,* act 2, sc. 3.

3

father, all mothers are not like his mother, all children not like his brothers and sisters. As he strays farther afield, he discovers noticeable physical and cultural differences among the populations of big cities and foreign countries.[3] Inevitably he recognizes that some human beings have a set of physical and cultural characteristics similar to his own while others do not. With or without the help of father, mother, teacher, book, or television, he has separated one group of people from another. Whether he likes it or not, whether he knows it or not, he has subscribed to the concept of race.

The belief that every man belongs to a distinct human breed is a persistent one—and the despair of physical anthropologists. For more than a century they have been trying to eradicate such "loose thinking" by developing more rigorous definitions of race. So far their efforts have been concentrated on the accumulation and classification of biometrical data and have produced as much controversy as agreement. Even if they eventually succeed in establishing the physiological component of race on firm scientific ground, they will still be faced with the mysteries and complexities of the psychological component. Race, as every American politician is well aware, goes far beyond the realm of the physical.

Unfortunately for those anthropologists who work with tape measures and computers, the concept of race leans as heavily on the *awareness* of blood relationship as it does on the *fact* of blood relationship. The physical anthropologist will only permit biological factors to enter into the determination of race. The statesman, poet, and prophet take a less scientific approach. They know the immense power that feelings of kinship exert in human affairs and the vast political and social transformations that take place when these feelings are kindled or rekindled in large numbers of human hearts. When men cannot appeal to anthropology to justify the existence of a race, they will often appeal to history. "The device of myths to establish a common ancestry for an ethnic

---

3. One social scientist, George Murdock, has found 73 elements common to all cultures, among them: courtship, dancing, division of labor, education, family, folklore, games, hair styles, hospitality, law, magic. *The Science of Man in the World Crisis,* edited by Ralph Linton, Columbia University Press, New York, 1945, p. 124.

group," sociologist E. K. Francis noted, "is a very ancient one." [4]

Ethnic group is a favorite term of those anthropologists and biologists who wish to drain race of its emotional content and subjectivity. Even more anemic is population group. But changing man's vocabulary does not necessarily change his thinking. Ethnic group, population group, cline, *Formenkreis,* and the like are handy labels for classifying certain segments of mankind with minimal friction, but they by no means tell the whole story.

There are other, less watered-down synonyms for race, a few of the more common being stock, breed, and nationality. They still hit rather wide of the mark. More descriptive, though rather awkward, are such sociological neologisms as we-feeling and we-group. William Graham Sumner, a pillar of the almost extinct conservative school of sociology, had a particular fondness for ethos, the Greek word for the collection of ideas, standards, and habits that differentiated one human group from another.[5] Ethos, however, leaves much to be desired because it almost ignores the physical stratum.

Perhaps the word which most closely approximates race is people, either modified by a possessive (my, your) or as Oswald Spengler defined it when he wrote, "The Roman name in Hannibal's day meant a people, in Trajan's time nothing more than a population." [6] More highly charged expressions for race are the crude but communicative blood brother and soul brother, which Negro store owners sometimes paint on their windows during ghetto riots to escape the wrath of black arsonists and looters.

So meaningful and at the same time so meaningless, the concept of race encompasses so many facts and fancies, so much love and hate, so much reason and unreason that it is more easily sensed than understood. In some respects race is similar to certain other four-letter words in English. It throws a hard emotional punch, and its use is studiously avoided in polite and academic circles. For all its semantic sloppiness, however, race exerts a profound influence over men's minds. As Edgar T. Thompson

---

4. E. K. Francis, "The Nature of the Ethnic Group," *American Journal of Sociology,* March, 1947, p. 396.

5. William Graham Sumner, *Folkways,* Ginn & Co., Boston, 1906, p. 12.

6. *The Decline of the West,* trans. C. F. Atkinson, Knopf, New York, 1957, Vol. II, p. 165.

stated, "The absence among the people of a clearly formulated definition of race, far from weakening it, actually adds to the potency of the race idea." [7]

Man is the amalgam of his physiological inheritance and his sociological acquisitions. He can shed the latter, but not the former. He can give up his religion, his country, and his culture. He cannot give up his race. Or, more precisely, he cannot give up the physical side of his race, which, apart from superficial alterations by plastic surgeons or beauticians, is inexorably determined by the laws of genetics.[8]

---

7. "Race in the Modern World," *Journal of Negro Education*, Summer, 1944, p. 272.

8. Even the rare phenomenon of *passing* is primarily involved with nonphysical aspects of race. Essentially the man who passes is trading the cultural trappings of one community for those of another. Biologically speaking, the alleged Negro who "looks" so white that he is accepted as a white by the white world could hardly be described as a Negro in the first place.

CHAPTER 2

Racism

As the idea is to ideology, so the concept of race is to racism.[1] This leads to the definition of racism—the British call it racialism—as a belief in the race idea. But belief implies some measure of assent, some inward or outward activation of the belief. Racism, accordingly, can be described as the overt or covert expression of the concept of race at one or more levels of human activity— in politics, art, religion, business, community life, and in the privacy of the home.

Racism, which presupposes a common ancestry, is not the same as nationalism, which presupposes a common citizenship. It is usually, but not invariably, associated with such an exalted form of nationalism as patriotism, such extreme forms of nationalism as chauvinism and jingoism, such localized forms as sectionalism, regionalism, and provincialism. Racism is present both in the foundation and in the dissolution of empires. It may reinforce nationalism in homogeneous societies and oppose it in multiracial states. In proletarian revolutions and fascist counterrevolutions, it may play a far more important role than class.[2]

---

1. "An ideology is a complex of ideas or notions which represents itself to the thinker as an absolute truth for the interpretation of the world and his situation within it; it leads the thinker to accomplish an act of self-deception for the purpose of justification, obfuscation, evasion, in some sense or other to his advantage." Karl Jaspers, *The Origin and Goal of History*, trans. Michael Bullock, Yale University Press, New Haven, 1968, p. 132. "Roughly defined, an ideologist is a thinker convinced he has discovered clear solutions to certain human problems or predicaments—solutions capable of expression in general theoretical terms." *Times Literary Supplement* (London), Jan. 29, 1970, p. 1.

2. See Chapter 25.

When races are geographically separated or isolated, racism is likely to be directed externally, across and beyond the boundaries of one province, region, or state to another province, region, or state. Where races live side by side, in the same neighborhood or in the same school district, racism is apt to be directed internally to the city block and the classroom. Racism of both types is present in most large nations. But while Russia, for example, with its autonomous and somewhat homogeneous republics has more of the externalized variety, racism in the United States with its more numerous, more varied, and more dissimilar racial elements— often living cheek by jowl in the large metropolises—is more implosive than explosive.

As far as can be ascertained, practically every society, people, or nation has passed through one or more racist cycles. In spite of their endless internecine wars and political and economic rivalry, the ancient Greeks, according to H. A. L. Fisher, "believed themselves to be one in race, language and institutions," designating all foreigners as barbarians and generally treating them as such.[3] The mass of Romans considered the Greeks corrupt weaklings. Many Jews have clung to the idea of the Chosen People even to this day. Prototypal racist attitudes were exhibited by the Spanish conqueror and the American settler towards the Indians and the Negroes. The traditionally hostile sentiments of the Chinese toward the non-Chinese need no elaboration, nor does the white supremacy once practiced by the French and British in their all but defunct empires.[4]

Like national defense or the balance of payments, racism is frequently regulated by outside events and influences. A homogeneous or even a heterogeneous society may display few signs of racism in peacetime. But once a neighboring state becomes aggressive, once a few thousand fellow nationals or racial cousins abroad become the victims of oppression, the dormant racism of the society or of one or more population groups within the society may be quickly aroused and assume a dynamic instead of a static character.

Racism, it should also be mentioned, operates in different orbits

3. As quoted by T. J. Haarhoff, *The Stranger at the Gate*, Longmans Green, London, 1938, p. viii.

4. For a more detailed summary of racist manifestations among the peoples of the world, see Sumner, *Folkways*, p. 29.

in different locations. Consider two American soldiers, one of Scandinavian, the other of South Italian origin, guarding a lonely outpost facing the North Koreans or North Vietnamese. At home the first might have called the second a Latin or an Italian when he was trying to be polite, a "Wop" or a "Greaser" when he wasn't. Now he feels himself in the presence of a fellow white.

Perhaps the first law of racism is that racism begets racism. Paradoxically, so does antiracism, which focuses so much attention on race and implants it so deeply in the public consciousness that the net amount of racism is greatly increased. Antiracism, moreover, permits many people to practice racism vicariously by adopting the cause of every race but their own.

In one respect racism is a form of group morale. It provides a protective psychic shell for the most defenseless and defensive peoples. It is also largely responsible for the high *aggression quotient* of dynamic peoples. Promoting tribalism both in the most retarded and most advanced nations, racism makes the modern tribal state with its sophisticated technology a fearsome opponent. Everything else being equal—manpower, industrial plant, scientific proficiency, and natural resources—a racist state can muster a deadlier military machine than a nonracist state.[5] In the matter of fighting spirit, the tribe or race may be regarded as the extension of the family, and death comes easier to those who believe they are dying for their people as well as for their country. The soldier with only a modicum of race consciousness has more difficulty being brave. Conscientious objectors, pacifists, and draft evaders are in short supply in racially oriented societies.

So much of racism remains below the surface in any given historical setting that students of the past seldom give it proper emphasis. Quite possibly it is the most compelling force in the record of human achievement—and human failure. Who can prove the contrary? Who can prove that racism is not a better clue to the rise and fall of civilizations than economics, religion, organic growth and decay, weather, great men, or even fate?[6]

Take the United States with the unusually homogeneous genetic

---

5. See Chapter 33.

6. "The application of this principle [racism] has governed the evolution of all advancing societies since soon after the beginning of agriculture." C. D. Darlington, *The Evolution of Man and Society,* Allen and Unwin, London, 1969, p. 607.

substrate of the Founding Fathers, the racial struggle with the Indians, the racial overtones of the Civil War, the racial differences of the Old and New Immigration, the racial mechanics of big-city and Southern politics, the mounting tempo of minority demands and agitation. Take the United Nations, now coalescing into a conglomeration of racial blocs. Take the twentieth-century revolt of the colored peoples of Asia and Africa against white colonialism. Weigh all this evidence, and then wonder at the liberal and conservative historians who grind out their thickly annotated histories which either avoid racism altogether or treat it as a disease rather than as a basic element of human nature.

At present, worldwide movements are afoot to abolish racism. But as indicated by events in the United States and abroad, far from being abolished anywhere, it is becoming intensified everywhere. All that is happening is that one form of racism is being replaced by another or by several others.

Instead of attempting to destroy the indestructible, it might be wiser to learn more about man's racial reflexes. A greater knowledge of the sources of racism might produce effective ways of civilizing and controlling it and directing it into more creative and constructive channels. Such knowledge might also aid in distinguishing between the racial behavior that helps to build nations and the racial behavior that tears them down.

CHAPTER 3

Racial Metaphysics

THE CONCEPT OF RACE and the racial ideologies which flow from
it permeated the great civilizations of antiquity. The Bible
divided the races of mankind into the sons of Shem (Semites),
Ham (non-Semitic Mediterraneans),[1] and Japheth (Northern peoples). Among the sons of Shem were the Jews, who were warned
by Jehovah to preserve their racial identity, as they were "a special
people unto himself, above all the people that are upon the face
of the earth." [2]

The Aryans who invaded India were so concerned with race
that they set up a complex caste system by means of which the
priestly Brahmans partially succeeded in preserving their original
physical type more than 2,500 years, although their once fair complexions, through mutations and some miscegenation, are now
better adapted to the blasting Indian sun.[3] The wall paintings
of the Egyptians depicted a simpler and less sophisticated form
of racism. The gods and pharaohs were always larger than life,
while Negroes and sundry other outlanders were posed in cringing
obeisance.[4]

---

1. Christian theologians later gratuitously added Negroes to this category.

2. Deut. 7:6. Strictures against exogamy are found in 7:3.

3. "The first caste division . . . was not by status but by color; it divided
long noses from broad noses, Aryans from Nagas and Dravidians . . . . The
caste system had the eugenic value of keeping the presumably finer strains from
dilution. . . ." Will Durant, *Our Oriental Heritage,* Simon and Schuster, New York,
1954, pp. 398, 487.

4. References to Negroes in the English captions of these wall paintings on
view at the British Museum in 1968 had been partially erased. Apparently some

11

As might be expected, the Greeks were the first to look for natural causes of racial differences and to philosophize about racial matters. Hippocrates' essay, *On Airs, Waters, and Places,* gave climate and geography as possible reasons for variations in human physiology and temperament.[5] Plato thought it would be good to inculcate an idea of racial purity in the youth destined for the future leadership of the commonwealth. Such an idea, which he described as a "noble lie," would develop a greater measure of pride and responsibility in the young elite—qualities which presumably made for better statesmanship.[6] Aristotle helped institutionalize slavery with his hypothesis of the "natural-born" slave.[7]

Full-blown "scientific" racial theories, however, did not take form for another two thousand years. It was not until the late eighteenth and the first half of the nineteenth century that enough data had been collected to permit a few intrepid anthropologists and systematizers to categorize mankind according to race. Along with the classifications came the value judgments. Since whites had now conquered or settled much of the earth and were remaking it in their image, an innately superior bloodline was proposed for the conquerors, who, after the decline of Spain and Portugal, were variously described as Anglo-Saxons, Nordics, or Teutons.

The theory of Northern European racial supremacy was assisted and expanded by the discovery of a surprising linguistic relationship between the Aryans, Hittites, Kassites, Persians, Greeks, and Romans of the ancient world, and the French, English, Germans, Slavs, and other peoples of modern Europe. Although a common language does not necessarily presuppose a common race, the Indo-European languages,[8] as they came to be called, and the

---

modern descendants of the victims of ancient Egyptian racism had not wanted to be reminded of past indignities.

5. Hippocrates, *On Airs, Waters, and Places,* trans. Francis Adams, Great Books of the Western World, Chicago, Vol. 10, p. 18.

6. *Republic,* III, 414–15, trans. Paul Shorey, *The Collected Dialogues of Plato,* Bollingen Series, LXXI, Princeton University Press, Princeton, New Jersey, 1969.

7. Ernest Barker, *The Politics of Aristotle,* Clarendon Press, Oxford, 1950, pp. 13–14.

8. One Indo-European root word: name (English), *nama* (Old Persian), *nama* (Sanskrit), *onoma* (Greek), *nomen* (Latin), *nome* (Italian), *nombre* (Spanish), *nom* (French), *Name* (German), *eemya* (Russian).

Indo-European speakers gave birth to a racial hypothesis in which a blond, light-complexioned people with rare creative gifts continually refertilizes dying and decadent civilizations.[9]

Among the chief advocates of this hypothesis, often designated as the Aryan theory, were Arthur de Gobineau (1816–1882), a French count and Germanophile who wrote the first coherent, though highly fanciful, racial interpretation of history;[10] Houston Stewart Chamberlain (1855–1927), an Englishman who became a naturalized German and whose grandiose *Weltanschauung* detected Teutonic genes in almost all the great men of the past, including Jesus Christ; Madison Grant (1865–1937), American lawyer and naturalist who expounded on the decline of the great culture-bearing, culture-creating Nordic peoples and whose arguments were helpful in securing the passage of restrictive United States immigration laws in the early 1920s; Lothrop Stoddard (1883–1950), American political philosopher, also active in the immigration issue, who warned that whites would soon be overwhelmed by the fecundity of the colored races.[11]

Although his Spanish ancestry and his Puritan associations in New England precluded any special affection for the Teuton, the philosopher Santayana was one of the most vigorous subscribers to the idea of racial hierarchies, as the following paragraph demonstrates:

> Some races are obviously superior to others. A more thorough adjustment to the conditions of existence has given them spirit, vitality, scope and a relative stability. . . . It is therefore of the greatest importance not to obscure this superiority by intermarriage with inferior stock, and thus nullify the progress made by a painful evolution and a prolonged sifting of souls. Reason protests as much as instinct against any fusion, for instance, of white and black peo-

---

9. Some examples of such refertilization: Aryan invasion of India; Dorian invasion of Greece; Italic invasion of Italy; Germanic overrunning of the Western Roman Empire; Norman conquest of Normandy and Sicily. For more on the Indo-European peoples, see Chapter 9.

10. "Là où l'élément germanique n'a jamais pénétré," de Gobineau declared, "il n'y a pas de civilization à notre manière." *Essai sur l'inégalité des races humaines,* Librarie de Firmin-Didot, Paris, 1884, Vol. I, p. 93.

11. Chamberlain's principal work was *Die Grundlagen des neunzehnten Jahrhunderts;* Grant's, *The Passing of the Great Race;* Stoddard's, *The Rising Tide of Color.*

ples. . . . The Jews, the Greeks, the Romans, the English were
never so great as when they confronted other nations . . . but
this greatness falls whenever contact leads to amalgamation.[12]

In the 1930s, probably for the first time in history, theories
of racial superiority became state doctrine when the National Socialist German Workers party took command in Germany.[13] But
after the inventory of Hitler's racial policies was published at the
close of World War II, all arguments for racial supremacy were
placed beyond the pale of permissible thought by the Western
intellectual community.

Race being so deeply personal a subject, it comes as no surprise
that advocates of racial superiority usually belong to, or think
they belong to, the race they consider superior. It is equally no
surprise that in America the opposition to theories of Nordic or
Northern European superiority was led by anthropologists, scientists and social scientists who were in most cases members of
minority groups. Perhaps in the belief that one good myth deserves another, Franz Boas (1858–1942), a scholar of German-
Jewish origin and a professor of anthropology at Columbia University, put forward the first comprehensively developed theory of
racial equality. In the same vein as nineteenth-century British historian Henry Buckle, who singled out environment as the determining factor of history, Boas hypothesized that nurture, not
nature, was the chief determinant of important racial differences.
He went so far as to assert that even such a persistent genetic
trait as head shape (cephalic index) [14] could be altered by an envi-

---

12. *The Life of Reason,* Scribner's, New York, 1922, Vol. II, pp. 166–67.

13. Or was it the second time? Alexander Stephens, vice-president of the
Confederacy, once declaimed: "This our new government is the first in the
history of the World based upon this great physical, philosophical, and moral
truth . . . that the Negro is not equal to the white man, that slavery—subordina-
tion to the superior race—is his natural and normal condition." Charles and
Mary Beard, *The Rise of American Civilization,* Macmillan, New York, 1930, Vol.
2, p. 68.

14. Cephalic index is maximum head breadth divided by maximum head
length times 100. The lower the index, the longer the head. Like physical scientists, anthropologists have a fondness for using complicated Greek derivatives
for simple and precise English expressions. Dolichocephalic is long-headed and
brachycephalic is round-headed.

ronmental change in one or two generations.[15] Ashley Montagu, a physical anthropologist of Anglo-Jewish origin, became the great vulgarizer of racial equalitarianism with a seemingly endless stream of best-selling books, television appearances and speeches before learned and unlearned societies.[16] Other leading members of the equalitarian school, not all of them anthropologists, were Otto Klineberg, Melville Herskovits, Alexander Goldenweiser, Isador Chein, Theodosius Dobzhansky, Gene Weltfish, Kenneth Clark, the black social scientist, and two vociferous Anglo-Saxon females, Ruth Benedict and Margaret Mead. Gene Weltfish achieved some notoriety by asserting the American army had resorted to germ warfare in the Korean War. Kenneth Clark took a leading part in convincing the Supreme Court to order school desegregation in *Brown* v. *Board of Education* (1954). In his scholarly monographs, Dobzhansky, a graduate of the University of Kiev, tactfully admitted there were some differences in racial capabilities, but practically denied them in his writings for public consumption. Leslie White's evolutionist school of anthropology and W. H. Sheldon's attempts to associate temperament with body type (endomorph, mesomorph, ectomorph) have received scant recognition because of their anti-Boas stance.

The theory of racial equality received the official sanction of the United Nations upon the publication of the 1950 and 1962 UNESCO statements on race. Sounding more like declarations of faith than reasoned scientific documents, the UNESCO papers produced the following axioms:

> The scientific evidence indicates that the range of mental capabilities in all ethnic groups is much the same. . . . As for personality and character, these may be considered raceless. . . . [G]iven similar degrees of cultural opportunity to realize their potentialities,

---

15. Franz Boas, "Changes in Bodily Form of Descendants of Immigrants," *American Anthropologist*, New Series, 14:530–62. Boas's quasi-Lamarckian hypothesis was refuted by Henry Pratt Fairchild, a prominent social scientist, in *Race and Nationality*, Ronald Press, New York, 1947, p. 105.

16. As one of the sponsors, together with the late Bishop James Pike and British-born Zen Buddhist Alan Watts, of a computer dating service, Montagu may have been able to put his theories to the ultimate test. *San Francisco Sunday Examiner & Chronicle, Date Book,* Jan. 19, 1969, p. 24.

the average achievement of the members of each ethnic group is about the same.

Although really intending to describe the credo of the behaviorist school of psychology, which worked hand in glove with the equalitarian anthropologists by stressing human malleability, sociologist Horace Kallen aptly summed up the UNESCO statements in words which deserve to be carved on Boas and Montagu's tombstones: "At birth human infants, regardless of their heredity, are as equal as Fords." [17] Many years earlier, J. B. Watson (1878–1958), the founder-expounder of behaviorism, had provided a psychological basis for equalitarianism by stating, "There is no such thing as an inheritance of capacity, talent, temperament, mental constitution and characteristics." [18] His most famous disciple, B. F. Skinner, later conditioned rats so successfully that it was assumed he could perform equal wonders with humans. In fact, Skinner designed a Utopia around his reinforcement techniques in a book, *Walden II*, which was used as a combination Bible and Constitution for a live commune which never fared too successfully. It should be stated, however, that the inventor of the Skinner Box never denied the importance of genetic factors in human behavior.

By the early 1960s the idea of innate racial equality had become so firmly established in modern education and in the communications media that no one could question it and still maintain his academic or professional respectability. Nevertheless a largely unpublicized but persistent reaction set in, stimulated by school desegregation and the violence which accompanied increasing Negro demands for a place in the American sun.

Carleton Putnam, American air transport pioneer and historian, declared that the Boas school of anthropology based its conclusions concerning racial equality on a misconceived self-interest. He advocated a realistic acceptance of the differential in Negro thought patterns and learning capacity, arguing that Negro integration on all but the economic level leads to a steady, relentless deterioration of American education, social life, and national

17. See Kallen's article, "Behaviorism," *Encyclopedia of Social Sciences*, Macmillan, New York, 1963, Vols. 1–2, p. 498.
18. *Behaviorism*, W. W. Norton, New York, 1930, p. 94.

power, as well as to the deterioration of the Negro himself.[19] Putnam maintained that Boas and his followers have "given the Negro the idea that he has a grudge against the White man and the White man the notion he should feel guilty about the Negro. . . . The grudge incites the Negro to riots and crime, and the guilt leads the White man to a policy of perpetual permissiveness and appeasement." [20] Elsewhere Putnam stated, "The core of the deceit has been in teaching that the greater part of the differences in status of individuals and groups among us is due to social injustice, whereas the scientific fact remains that, frequent as injustice is, these differences are primarily attributable to innate differences in capacity." [21]

Henry E. Garrett, chairman of the Department of Psychology, Columbia University, went further than Putnam by calling the equalitarian dogma "the scientific hoax of the century." Garrett accused social scientists of relying on moral denunciation when their real evidence regarding Negro mental abilities became feeble. He also blamed church leaders for falsifying science to bolster their ethical arguments for racial equality.[22]

William Shockley, who won the Nobel prize in physics for co-inventing the transistor, joined the controversy when he suggested that all contemporary programs for Negro betterment were based on false premises. "The major deficit in Negro intellectual performance," Shockley asserted, "must be primarily of hereditary origin and thus irremediable by practical improvements in environment." [23] He also stressed that the high birthrate of the poorest and most disadvantaged blacks was a "dysgenic tragedy."

Other believers in disparities in racial intelligence included Sir Cyril Burt [24] and H. J. Eysenck in Britain, and Wesley C. George,

19. See Putnam's *Race and Reason* (1961) and *Race and Reality* (1967), both volumes published by Public Affairs Press, Washington, D.C., and reprinted by Howard Allen, Cape Canaveral, Florida.

20. Paper on "General Race Differences," Feb. 5, 1969.

21. *Congressional Record*, Nov. 13, 1969, pp. E9630–32.

22. See Garrett's article, "The Equalitarian Dogma," in *Perspectives in Biology and Medicine*, Summer, 1961.

23. Speech before National Academy of Sciences, April 24, 1968.

24. Burt's studies of identical twins reared apart were important props of the hereditarian argument. In 1977 Leon Kamin, a Marxist professor of psychology at Princeton, launched a posthumous ad hominem attack on Burt, asserting

R. Ruggles Gates, Audrey Shuey, and Arthur Jensen in the United States. Jensen created a sensation by refusing to attribute the 15-point shortfall in Negro I.Q. scores to environmental causes or to tests that were "culturally biased." With scant regard for consistency, Julian Huxley, the noted British biologist who helped prepare the UNESCO statements on race, went on record as stating that it was probably "true Negroes have a slightly lower average intelligence than the whites or the yellows."

A few leading twentieth-century anthropologists and sociologists attempted to stand above or straddle the question of racial differences, among them A. L. Kroeber, Aleš Hrdlička,[25] and Pitirim Sorokin.[26] Hrdlička warned of the danger of a mass inflow of Negro genes into the American population but refused to say why it was a danger. Sorokin admitted the evidence of mental differences among races, but underplayed the function of heredity. Some of this reticence was doubtless due to fear, some to the natural reluctance of bona fide scientists to generalize on what they considered to be insufficient data. One of the great modern anthropologists, Professor Carleton Coon of Harvard, wrote, "The subject of racial intelligence . . . has not progressed far enough to merit inclusion in a general work of racial history." [27]

Nevertheless, Coon provided powerful ammunition for the anti-equalitarian or hereditarian school with a startling and illuminating theory on the origin of races. For thousands of years it had been taken for granted that the races of man had descended or branched out from a single species. In direct and iconoclastic contradiction to this traditional doctrine, Coon stated that the five living races of mankind, which he named Caucasoid, Mongoloid, Australoid, Capoid, and Congoid, had evolved separately into *Homo sapiens* following different timetables. If Coon was right about the parallel genesis of races, there now existed an evolutionary basis for racial differences, and the case against the equalitari-

---

he had falsified his research. Whether or not this was true, the conclusions drawn from Burt's studies have been verified time and again by the later research of other competent scientists.

25. *Proceedings of the Third Race Betterment Conference,* Jan., 1928, pp. 84–85.

26. *Contemporary Sociological Theories,* Harper & Bros., N.Y., 1928, pp. 291–93.

27. *The Races of Europe,* Macmillan, N.Y., 1954, p. vii. Coon died in 1981. His last work, *Racial Aptitudes,* so far unpublished, does deal with this subject.

ans was strengthened. Even more damaging to the equalitarian viewpoint was Coon's assertion that the Negro race, which he assigned to the Congoid group, was the last of the world's races to evolve. The blacks, according to Coon, had been in a *sapiens* state for a shorter time than the white and yellow races (40,000 versus 210,000 years).[28] This led inexorably to the conclusion that Negroes were the least developed and least articulated of mankind's principal racial divisions.

The violent and vituperative reaction which greeted Coon's theories vividly demonstrated the metaphysical nature of the race question. Ashley Montagu, who previous to the publication of Coon's work had said that the multiracial origin of man was "inadmissible," declared that Coon's facts were fraudulent and compared the former president of the American Association of Physical Anthropologists to "the racial anthropologists [of] a hundred years ago." [29] Marvin K. Opler, another anthropologist of the Boas persuasion, was equally vehement, stating, "it is easy to see why Coon's theory should make him the darling of segregationist committees and racists everywhere . . . he cannot convincingly write human history, even racial history. He will have to acquire more knowledge, more compassion and more humility for that." [30]

Instead of invective, which is often self-defeating because it publicizes the target, the silent treatment was given to another great modern anthropologist, Sir Arthur Keith (1866–1955). It was Keith's view that the greatest outburst of man's biological progress occurred in the hunting band, when a combination of geographical isolation and group cohesion produced the balanced gene pool necessary for the efficient functioning of the evolutionary process. Keith was afraid that the total racial integration demanded by the more dedicated equalitarians might have a dysgenic effect on man by swamping beneficial mutations before they have a chance to take hold. The British anthropologist also pointed out that prejudice, discrimination, xenophobia, and cer-

---

28. Coon, *The Origin of Races*, Knopf, New York, 1962, pp. 3, 4, 85, 655–59 and *The Story of Man*, Knopf, New York, 1962, 2nd Edition, pp. 35–38.

29. *Man in Process*, New American Library, New York, 1961, p. 103, and *Man's Most Dangerous Myth*, World, Cleveland, 1964, p. 86.

30. *New York Herald-Tribune*, Book Section, Dec. 9, 1962, p. 7.

tain other human characteristics now considered sinful may actually serve an important evolutionary purpose. They may be nature's chief tools for race-building and for creating favorable growth conditions for the variegated cultures and peoples which have made the mosaic of man so rich and colorful.[31]

If professional anthropologists can descend to the lowest levels of polemics, vindictiveness, and thought control, how, it may be asked, can the layman acquire enlightened ideas about race? The answer is that at least a ray of enlightenment is provided by the historical evidence, which points inescapably to the fact that certain races or peoples have accomplished far more than others in the fields of technology, material comfort and popular government. If these accomplishments are due to genetic causes, the low-achieving races in Western-dominated cultures will always be saddled, as they have been in the past, with the stigma of underperformance, even though they may be perfectly capable of overperformance in their ancestral societies, many of which are still extant.

Much of the bitterness of the present-day racial debate stems from some races being forced to compete, or choosing to compete, in a world they never made. The all-important question of whether heredity or environment has the upper hand in the shaping of human destiny hardly enters into the argument, which has degenerated into a quasi-theological dispute involving such crucial psychological ingredients as pride and face-saving. One side appeals to heredity to explain past successes and the other to environment and "historical accidents" to excuse past failures.

If heredity were proved beyond a shadow of a doubt to be the central factor in human achievement, the proof would almost certainly be rejected in the present climate of modern thought. Environmentalists have too much at stake, both physically and spiritually, to abandon their cause for any reason, least of all a negative scientific verdict on the validity of their ideas and programs. They are only too well aware that the acceptance or acknowledgment of important genetic diversities in man would seriously undermine the entire foundation of prevailing political

---

31. See Keith's *A New Theory of Human Evolution*, Watts, London, 1950; *Essays on Human Evolution*, Watts, 1948.

and social dogma, the fountainhead of the miraculous changes which have been wrought in the status of privileged and under-privileged minorities.

Nonetheless, time seems to be working unflaggingly in the service of the hereditarian party. Although investigations into racial intelligence are still largely taboo, research teams keep approaching the subject tangentially with significant new discoveries relating to racial divergence in brain structure, resistance to disease, blood group distribution, glandular function, hormone activity, and gene recombination.

By the late 1960s the investigations of Nikolaas Tinbergen, a Hollander, and Konrad Lorenz, a German, into the heritability of aggressive and territorial instincts had been widely published, both under their own names and by popularizer Robert Ardrey, whose profuse digressions often reached high levels of political and social commentary. If man had been a hunter for millions of years, a farmer for 10,000, and a factory worker for 150, Ardrey wanted to know how his deeper instincts—his reptilian and mammalian brains—could be changed by a few years of inferior education. The author advised those who wished to improve man to understand, not ignore, his instinctual nature.

Another blow was struck against the environmentalist hegemony with the publication in 1974 of *Race* by John R. Baker, an internationally renowned Oxford biologist and a Fellow of the Royal Society.[32] Dr. Baker minced no words and ducked no issues in what one respected scientific journal called "perhaps the best documented book on human races ever published." In contrast to the Boasites, Baker found significant mental, as well as physical, differences, among the races which he classified, analyzed, and evaluated with such professional skill that hardly anyone rose to challenge him. In the United States the book was ignored by the mass media, except for the *Washington Post,* which ran a splenetic review by a sociologist and former Israeli commando named Amitai Etzioni.

A year later Edward O. Wilson, a Harvard entomologist, opened

---

32. Originally published by Oxford University Press, *Race* was reprinted in 1981 by the Foundation for Human Understanding, Athens, Georgia.

up new vistas for genetic determinists when he practically invented the new science of sociobiology.[33] Genes, according to Wilson, not only govern individual behavior but social behavior as well. Death on the battlefield, for example, is a supreme act of altruism in which one sacrifices one's own genes so that the closely related genes of one's family or one's group will survive. Xenophobia is simply an inherited response to threats of gene pool contamination by outsiders.

Wilson's ideas, together with the fascinating speculations of theoretical biologists R. L. Trivers, W. D. Hamilton, J. Maynard Smith, and Richard Dawkins stirred up a vortex of controversy.[34] Two minority scientists, Richard Lewontin and Stephen J. Gould, reacted by insinuating that sociobiology was racist. Other scientists, such as George Wald, a highly politicized Nobel laureate, lashed out at Wilson and the biological determinist school by calling for an end to amniocentesis, the screening of fetuses for genetic defects. Walter Bodmer and Liebe Cavalli-Sforza wanted to outlaw investigations into Negro-white I.Q. differences. Still others demanded a government ban on any research that might substantiate racial theories or lead to any form of genetic engineering. When in regard to this latter stricture they were supported by Pope John Paul II,[34] there developed a strange inquisitional alliance between the ultrareligious and the ultraleft.

That so many anti-Wilsonians were minority members of the Marxist persuasion was probably the effect rather than the cause of their seemingly innate abhorrence of even a hint of biological determinism. Although Marx had once tried to dedicate Das Kapital to Darwin, who believed in inherited racial differences, his followers have always nourished a secret fondness for Lamarck, who believed in the inheritance of acquired characteristics. In his desperate attempt to force science to yield to ideology, Stalin elevated the charlatan Lysenko to the higher reaches of Soviet science, while allowing a brilliant geneticist like Nikolai Vavilov to perish in a Gulag. Even if biology says no, most Marxists still want man to be 100 percent moldable. Moldable men can be made into

---

33. Edward O. Wilson, *Sociobiology: The New Synthesis,* Harvard University Press, Cambridge, Mass., 1975.

34. Speech to UNESCO representatives in Paris, June 2, 1980.

good Marxists, whereas genes have no ears to hear the siren call of Lenin. Indeed the attachment for Lamarck is so persistent that, though his theory has been totally discredited, it keeps cropping up, not only in the pamphlets of extraterritorial Marxists (the Soviet Union has now rehabilitated Mendelian genetics), but in the books and sermons of many Christian fundamentalists.

The war against Wilson in particular and against all scientific manifestations of anti-equalitarianism in general all too frequently descended from words to acts—rather sordid acts. Wilson himself was physically threatened and doused with water during a conference. William Shockley had many of his college addresses disrupted by the violence of black and white radicals. H. J. Eysenck was assaulted during a lecture in London, and his eyeglasses smashed. Richard Herrnstein, who never mentioned race, was continuously harassed for proposing that a meritocracy might derive from high I.Q. matings. Edward Banfield, an urbanologist who said some unkind things about ghettos, had to sit silently on a lecture platform, while being threatened by radical students with brass knuckles. The trials and tribulations of Arthur Jensen will be recounted in Chapter 20. The only allegations of racial differences which do not provoke a bitter reaction from the intellectual establishment are those proposing the superiority of Jews (see Chapter 15).

As man's environment becomes increasingly man-made, its effect on creating and perpetuating racial differences is bound to shrink. Human surroundings are growing increasingly similar, particularly in highly civilized areas where a common technology, a common educational system, a common communications network, and common occupations are prescribing a common way of life. According to equalitarian theory, the performance and achievement levels of different races will converge as their environments converge. Consequently the supreme test of environmentalism may come in the not too distant future.

Meanwhile, as the issues raised by the hereditarians become more relevant each day, it is hard to believe that the scientific curiosity of the world's most scientifically curious society can be prevented much longer from cracking one of the most challenging and most exciting frontiers of knowledge. But the metaphysics of racial equality, although so far having failed to provide any workable solutions for modern man's most insoluble problem, still fires the hearts of tens of millions—tens of millions who can be forgiven for refusing to accept the harsh possibility that nature practices a form of racial Calvinism.

Because the faithful are certain not to let go of their cherished equalitarian dream without a fight, there is likely to be a Galileo of genetics before there is a Newton.

CHAPTER 4

The Physiological Stratum
of Race

I T HAS BEEN REMARKED that race begins with the physical. To
provide a clearer picture of the physiology of race, a few of
the better-known systems of racial classification will be briefly
summarized in the first part of this chapter. The second part
will be concerned with the race-sorting methods of the man in
the street, whose amateurish yet appraising eye is sometimes more
perspicacious in such matters than the cold professional scrutiny
of the physical anthropologist.

According to zoologists there are well over one million living
species of animals. Man, *Homo sapiens,* is one of them. The derivation goes like this: Animal Kingdom; Phylum Chordata; Subphy-
lum Vertebrata; Class Mammalia; Order Primates; Family
Hominidae; Genus *Homo;* Species *sapiens.*[1] Here zoology stops and
anthropology takes over. After the species comes the race.

Serious attempts at racial classification began almost two centuries ago. Most have been based on skin color with primary emphasis on the three most common and most noticeable shades of
pigmentation: White (Caucasoid), Yellow (Mongoloid), Black
(Negroid). J. F. Blumenbach, the father of physical anthropology,
decided that the Brown (Malayan) and Red (Amerindian) races
should be included in the color spectrum.[2] Using such criteria
as nose form, stature and head shape as well as skin color, Joseph

---

1. R. W. Hegner and K. A. Stiles, *College Zoology,* Macmillan, New York, 1959,
pp. 2, 8.

2. J. F. Blumenbach, *The Anthropological Treatises,* trans. Thomas Bendyshe,
Longmans, London, 1865.

Deniker devised a sophisticated catalog of eighteen races.[3] A. L. Kroeber, professor of anthropology at the University of California, added four races to the basic three: Australoid, Veddoid, Polynesian, Ainu.[4] Carleton Coon's classification has already been given. One or two anthropologists have classified races according to hair form: straight, woolly, and curly.[5] Relying on such identifiable genetic traits as blood groups, W. C. Boyd divided man into thirteen races.[6]

In regard to a racial classification of whites, the most popular, if not the most accurate, is that of William Z. Ripley, an influential American anthropologist whose three categories deserve some attention because of their effect on racial theories in the early part of the century. Ripley's white races, together with their "racial markers" and Old World homelands are listed below: [7]

NORDIC.[8] *Physical characteristics:* long head, narrow or elliptic face, fair complexion, light brown or blond hair, light colored eyes, narrow nose, regular features, tall and slender physique. *Old World habitat:* Scandinavia, Northern Germany, Netherlands, Scotland, England. There are also scattered Nordic populations in Ireland, Belgium, Northern France, Central and Southern Germany, Switzerland, Austria, Poland, Northwest Russia (including the Baltic states).

---

3. Coon, *The Races of Europe*, pp. 281–82.

4. A. L. Kroeber, *Anthropology*, Harcourt Brace, New York, 1948, p. 132.

5. *Encyclopaedia Britannica*, Vol. 18, pp. 864–65. For reasons of its own, the *Britannica* concealed for years references to its 14th edition. The copyright date, 1963, is the only means of identifying the volumes cited throughout this study. In 1974 the publication of the 15th edition was announced with great fanfare by philosopher Mortimer Adler in his capacity as chairman of the board of editors.

6. Coon, *The Living Races of Man*, pp. 18–19.

7. W. Z. Ripley, *The Races of Europe*, Appleton, New York, 1910, Chapter 6.

8. Most contemporary anthropologists are leery of such racial designations. When they do use them, they make it plain they are referring to frequencies and averages, mindful of the extensive racial overlapping that makes classification of the white races so difficult and so frustrating. A Nordic in current anthropological language merely means an individual who possesses more Nordic traits than Alpine or Mediterranean. After millennia of racial mixing, pure races are hard to come by, although there are still many individuals who closely approximate idealized racial models.

ALPINE. *Physical characteristics:* round head, broad face, brown hair and eyes, ruddy complexion, stocky, average height. *Old World habitat:* Ireland, Belgium, France, Germany, Switzerland, Northern Italy, Central Europe, the Slavic-speaking countries.

MEDITERRANEAN. *Physical characteristics:* long head, thin face, dark brown hair and eyes, olive complexion, regular features, small to medium height. *Old World habitat:* Portugal, Spain, Southern France, Southern Italy, Greece, the Middle East, North Africa, the Mediterranean islands.

Many anthropologists, both before and after Ripley, developed more complicated, more subtle, and often contradictory classifications for the white portion of mankind. Carleton Coon, who added seven more white races to Ripley's original three, made a special point about the Alpines, stressing not only their physical dissimilarities, but their different origin in time and place. According to Coon and a school of European anthropologists, Alpines are descended from Upper Palaeolithic races which retreated to the remote areas and mountain fastnesses of Europe upon the arrival of Neolithic (Nordic and Mediterranean) invaders. In Coon's view, the Alpine represents the reemergence of the ancient European, a racial reincarnation increasing in frequency and seemingly favored by urbanization.[9]

Of special interest to Americans is the ethnological research of E. A. Hooton, who proposed nine separate racial divisions for the white population of the United States. In the list below only the races, their physical traits and their European points of origin are given.[10] Their quantitative distribution will be found in Chapter 8.

NORDIC-MEDITERRANEAN. Long-headed with light eyes, dark hair, or dark eyes, fair hair. *Old World habitat:* British Isles.

NORDIC-ALPINE. Round-headed with high concentration of blondism or Nordic features and physical build. *Old World habitat:* Slavic lands, Germany, France.

---

9. Coon, *The Races of Europe,* pp. 220, 289–93, 510, 560.

10. E. A. Hooton, *Twilight of Man,* G. P. Putnam, New York, 1939, pp. 203–210. The above classification was based on the physical studies of some 29,000 adult American males by the Harvard Anthropological Museum.

PREDOMINANTLY NORDIC. Not quite the pure Nordic. *Old World habitat:* Britain, Scandinavia.

DINARIC. Round-headed, narrow nose, with great range of pigmentation. *Old World habitat:* Scotland, France, Germany, Poland, Near East.

KELTIC.[11] Long-headed, red or reddish hair with blue eyes, or dark hair with blue eyes. *Old World habitat:* Southern Ireland.

PURE MEDITERRANEAN. Long-headed, dark eyes, dark hair. *Old World habitat:* Portugal, Spain, Italy.

EAST BALTIC. Pure blond round-heads with short, broad noses. *Old World habitat:* Germany, Poland, Russia.

PURE ALPINE.[12] Dark-haired, dark-eyed round-heads with broad noses. *Old World habitat:* France, Spain, Portugal, Poland, Balkans, Near East.

PURE NORDIC. Long-headed, ash blond or golden hair, pure blue or pure gray eyes. *Old World habitat:* Britain, Scandinavia.

The formal terminology of Hooton's racial table has by no means penetrated the popular idiom. While the average layman may agree in principle with some of the broad racial categories of the professional anthropologist, he uses a shorter and more pungent nomenclature. To the ordinary American, Mediterranean is the name of a sea between Europe and Africa and has no racial significance. The popular synonym for Mediterranean, in its anthropological sense, is "Latin." "Foreign-looking," an even more ambivalent term, also describes the American who has darker than average skin, hair and eye coloration. But not too dark a coloration! The American Negro, for instance, is not "foreign-looking."

Popular anthropology is not afraid to subdivide the "Latin race." When someone is called "Italian-looking" or "Spanish-looking" or "Greek-looking," it means that persons of Italian, Spanish or Greek descent can presumably be recognized on sight. Other popular attempts at identifying Mediterraneans, by nation-

---

11. Some anthropologists prefer the term *Atlantic* for this category.

12. Hooton, unlike many of his colleagues, does not subdivide his Alpine category to include *Armenoid,* the dark, round-headed Alpine-Mediterranean hybrid of East-Southeast Europe and the Middle East.

ality group as well as by race, are represented by such slur words as "Wop" (Italian), "Dago" (Spaniard or Italian), and "Spic" or "Greaser" (applied to all Latins and to the part-Mediterranean, Mexican-American mestizo). Occasionally, even American Indians are categorized as Latins by urbanites who have never been near a reservation.

Alpine is another racial term never used by the general public. The stocky, round-headed assembly line worker from Central and Eastern Europe, the barrel-necked bartender from Ireland [13] and the mill hand from French Canada are too blurred a racial type to have earned separate racial status from the people at large. They may still bear the peasant look of their Old World ancestors, but they no longer have a peasant's occupation. In general, the popular classification of Alpines in the United States has been limited to localized slang expressions ("Bohunks," "Canucks," etc.) based largely on national and geographic origins.

Nordic is the only white racial designation of the professional anthropologists to have found a place in the vernacular of popular anthropology. Although the term is most frequently applied to Scandinavians, many Americans, particularly the more willowy and blonder film stars, are described as "Nordic-looking." But because of its association with old theories of racial supremacy and Hitler's master race, Nordic is used rather sparingly. An unflattering and imprecise substitute is the acronym WASP (White Anglo-Saxon Protestant), now a common tag for Americans with a preponderance of Northern European physical traits, although millions of fair-complexioned Americans are neither Protestant nor Anglo-Saxon. Since, racially speaking, there is no such thing as a non-white Anglo-Saxon, a less redundant and equally stinging acronym would be ASP.

Majority is another term of increasing importance in the American racial dictionary. Completely ignored by professional anthropologists, the American Majority comprises the Nordic, Alpine, Nordic-Alpine and Nordic-Mediterranean elements of the population, as distinguished from the darker Mediterranean and colored elements. It is far from being a tightly structured race, but

---

13. An Alpine racial specimen. The red-headed, freckle-faced Irish American and the blue-eyed colleen are Keltic in origin.

it does contain demonstrable traces of an "American" physical norm. When traveling abroad, Majority members will "look like Americans" to the local populace, to whom U.S. citizens of Mediterranean, Oriental or Negro extraction will not look "American." Even on the home front—among the towheaded school children of the Midwest farm belt, among air force officers, airline pilots and astronauts, among the members of ski and polo teams and of yacht clubs—there are those who appear more "American" than others, meaning that the former are within the racial parameters of the Majority physical model. If there is an American racial type in the making, it will almost certainly emerge from the Majority gene pool.[14]

Professional anthropology is as reluctant to extend racial recognition to the American Majority as it is to bestow racial status on American Jewry. Not one physical anthroplogist in a hundred will admit that there is a Jewish race, although Carleton Coon has found some uniformity of cephalic index, facial structure and coloration among Russian and Polish Jews, who account for 80 percent of the American Jewish population.[15] Some ethnologists have detected a certain "nostrility" in Jews, but deny there is a unique set of Jewish facial expressions and gestures.[16] "Although Jews in Europe," writes C. D. Darlington, "always have different frequencies of blood groups from the Christian populations around them, they depart from the average Jewish frequencies in the direction of these populations." [17]

Historically, Jews were Semites and belonged to the Near Eastern branch of the Mediterranean race. Many Sephardic Jews still retain Near Eastern physical traits, often characterized as Jewish in the United States because there are so few Arabs. Many Northern and Central European Jews, including some Sephardim who went to Holland after their expulsion from Spain in 1492, possess a few Nordic traits and a measure of blondism. Eastern European Jews, who also exhibit occasional signs of light coloration, are

---

14. For Wyndham Lewis's discovery of a "Super-European" American physical type, see p. 120.

15. *The Races of Europe*, pp. 643–44.

16. George Eaton Simpson and J. Milton Yinger, *Racial and Cultural Minorities*, Harper, New York, Revised Edition, 1958, pp. 57–59.

17. Darlington, *The Evolution of Man and Society*, pp. 467–68.

racially distant from the olive-skinned, long-headed Sephardim of the Mediterranean area. Their round-headedness probably comes from intermarriage with Armenoids and Alpine Slavs.

One of the oldest of racial old wives' tales attributes the origin of the Ashkenazim (Eastern European Jews) to the conversion of the Turkish tribe of Khazars to Judaism in the eighth century. Arthur Koestler, a novelist and essayist who in his lifetime has traversed the entire ideological spectrum from Communist party activist to vitalism, wrote a whole book on the subject.[18] Intrigued by the legend, A. E. Mourant, who specializes in blood group analysis, tested thousands of Jews in Europe, North Africa, and the Middle East and came to the conclusion that a strain of genetic homogeneity does run through Jewry, but not a Khazar strain. Even in Russia, Mourant found very little evidence of Khazar additions to the Jewish—or non-Jewish—gene pool. What Mourant and two associates did find was that Jews as a whole exhibit an admixture of 5–10 percent Negro genes, which they may have picked up in their stay in ancient Egypt and through subsequent miscegenation with North African peoples.[19] Another argument for a common Jewish biology is a number of specifically Jewish genetic diseases: Tay-Sachs, Niemann-Pick, and Gaucher's.

Whatever the biological verdict may be, a sizable part of the American public, as well as many Jews themselves, continue to think of Jews as a separate and distinct race. They base their judgment on Biblical references to a common Jewish historical origin and on various sets of physical traits which have a higher incidence among Jews than among members of any other American population group. The concentration of Jews in the more visible occupations and their irrepressible group solidarity does much to nourish the popular idea of Jewish racehood.

In classifying the Mongoloid population groups in the United States, amateur and professional anthropology again part company. The general public considers American Indians a race apart,

---

18. Arthur Koestler, *The Thirteenth Tribe,* Random House, New York, 1976.

19. A. E. Mourant, *The Genetics of Jews,* Clarendon Press, Oxford, 1978. If Mourant is correct, the anti-Zionists who claim Zionists have no biological ties to Palestine are wrong. The argument that Ben Gurion, Golda Meir, and Menachem Begin are the descendants of non-Jewish Khazars must then be abandoned.

in line with traditional white attitudes toward the "Red Man," but physical anthropologists put them in the broader Mongoloid racial category.[20] To the man in the street, the Mongoloid race is the yellow race and is composed entirely of Orientals—Chinese, Japanese and other Eastern Asiatics—who "all look alike," presumably because popular techniques of identifying Mongoloids do not proceed much beyond the slanted eye (epicanthic fold).[21] Professional anthropologists also place Eskimos, Mexicans, and Polynesians generally in the Mongoloid racial niche, recognizing the Mediterranean factor in the Mexican population and the Australoid presence in the Polynesian racial background.[22] Nonprofessionals often consider Eskimos, Hawaiians, and Mexicans as comprising separate races.

In the darkest area of the racial palette, professional and popular anthropologists are in some agreement. When they talk about the Negro race, they both mean approximately the same thing. Many professionals, however, estimate that the white contribution to the genetic composition of American Negroes ranges from a low of four percent in some Southern areas to a high of twenty-six percent in Detroit.[23] The public has adopted a less sophisticated approach. It simply designates as a Negro anyone with telltale traces of Negro features, hair form, and pigmentation. Except in a few large cities where they have been given a distinct racial status of their own, the darker breeds of Puerto Ricans are generally labeled Negroes, even though they may often have a much greater proportion of Mediterranean than Negro genes. In general, sensitivity to Negro coloration is so great that many Americans would call a high-caste Hindu with narrow face, long nose, and other aristocratic features a Negro because of his dark skin.

---

20. In the frontier days, because of their war paint and the sun's reflection on their highly toned skin, Indians were called Red Men. From this came the concept of a red race, an ethnological oversimplification that was later abandoned. Actually, Indian skin color varies from light yellow to mahogany. Coon, *The Living Races of Man,* p. 153.

21. Americans who have had firsthand experience in the Far East or who have lived in Hawaii or San Francisco have learned to detect certain racial differences among Mongoloids, particularly the darker coloration of Southeastern Asians.

22. Coon, op. cit., pp. 138, 184, 294.

23. Baker, *Race,* pp. 228–31.

The main variances in the popular and professional racial classification of the U.S. population are summed up in the following
Pigmentation Spectrum, designed and constructed to reemphasize
the overriding importance some anthropologists and almost all
laymen attach to skin color.

PIGMENTATION SPECTRUM

SKIN COLOR	Light White	White	Dark White	Yellow to Mahogany	Light Tan to Black
PHYSICAL ANTHRO-POLOGY	*Nordic* Nordic-Alpine Keltic Nordic-Medi- terranean	*Alpine* East Baltic, Dinaric	*Mediterranean* Armenoid	*Mongoloid*	*Negro* Mulatto
POPULAR ANTHRO-POLOGY	White Wasp Anglo		Latin	Mexican Chicano Latino Oriental Indian	Colored Negro Black

The designation Hispanic, which has been adopted by many federal agencies, is an umbrella term for various Mediterranean, Mongoloid, and Negro mixtures of Spanish- and
Portuguese-speaking peoples in the Western Hemisphere.

Broadly approximate and far from rigorous in its presentation
of the American racial amalgam, the Pigmentation Spectrum, in
addition to illustrating the spectroscopic method of racial identification, does serve to clarify in graphic fashion what seem to be
the four cardinal rules of American race relations and racial eti-
quette:

a) The farther apart races are in the Spectrum, the more race-conscious will be the behavior of their members toward each other, and
the more they will treat each other as stereotypes rather than as individuals.

b) The closer together races are in the White area of the Spectrum,
the more easily their members may submerge or ignore their racial
differences, even to the point of claiming the same racial affiliation.

c) The farther a race is to the right of the Spectrum the more it
will vary from the American physical norm as defined by Majority
racial parameters. In this respect, the Spectrum serves as an "as-

similation meter." With one important exception, the Jews,[24] the more races differ from the Majority in skin color, the less chance their members have of assimilation.

   d) The farther apart races are in the Spectrum the more the members of one race will accentuate the color differences of the other. Whites will find Latins darker, Orientals yellower, and Negroes blacker than they really are. Conversely, members of colored races will think whites much paler than their pigmentation merits.

Rule (a) above refers to the extensive use which the ordinary citizen makes of stereotypes in racial classification. The bane of professional anthropology, stereotypes often come in pairs: the idealized version of one's own race and the caricature of the other person's. The degree of caricature may depend on the degree of tension between any two races at any particular moment.

In the Philadelphia suburbs, for example, the Main Line family of old American lineage may identify with the Nordic stereotype of the tall, handsome blond with regular features, light eyes, high brow, and long head. In Philadelphia proper, Negroes may have a different image of their Main Line neighbors. The neck is thicker, the head rounder, the build shorter and stockier. Cruel lips, cold eyes, and a frigid expression add up to an almost brutish appearance. The blond beast instead of Prince Charming.

Alpine stereotypes, many imported from the Old World, range (depending on who is doing the stereotyping) from the bloated Milwaukee burgher to Santa Claus, from the thick-jointed, flat-faced trucker to the nutbrown maid. Latin stereotypes are divided between grimacing gangsters and soulful Valentinos, Carmens and Carmelites. To many non-Jews, the Jew is often a squat, plutocratic vulgarian or a bespectacled, hothouse egghead. The Jew himself clings to the stereotype of an aristocratic, white-maned Moses or a swashbuckling Israeli sabra. Negroes like to identify with towering black athletes, charismatic preachers, Emperor Joneses, and rifle-toting Black Panthers. Many whites, on the other hand, cannot dissociate the Negro image from Uncle Tom, Aunt Jemima, Stepin Fetchit, urban muggers, or head-hunting cannibal chiefs with bones through their noses.

The physiological stratum of race also includes character and

---

24. See pp. 30–31, 192–93.

intelligence, insofar as such traits have a genetic origin. Plato, who equated the beautiful with the good, posited a direct relationship between physical appearance and moral conduct.[25] Hippocrates found that people with blond complexions were "in disposition and passions haughty and self-willed."[26] Hansen's famous study of the temperamental and character differences of the fair and dark populations of Norway was cited by Havelock Ellis in his comparison of skin color with performance.[27] Dr. Morgan Worthy, a Georgia psychologist, has shown that light-eyed persons are more self-pacing, more inhibited, and less reactive to their environment than the dark-eyed.[28]

The low forehead and the pointed head have long been accepted as signs of stupidity and imbecility. In Elizabethan England there was a proverb: "Very round head, forgetful and stupid. Long head, clever and attentive."[29] In Shakespeare's *Antony and Cleopatra* (act 3, scene 3), his heroine asks: "Bears't thou her face in mind? is't long or round?" The messenger: "Round even to faultiness." Cleopatra: "For the most part, too, they are foolish that are so." The Englishman's poor opinion of brachycephalism may be explained by the fact that the English have a lower incidence of round-headedness than any other Northern European population.[30] Cromwell's Roundheads were so called, not because of their head shape, but because of their bowl-shaped haircuts, which contrasted sharply with the long flowing hair of the Cavaliers.

No matter how controversial and unpleasant, racial stereotypes which go beyond surface physical characteristics cannot be ignored if they provide meaningful clues to popular conceptions of racial differences. A case in point is the average white American of Northern European extraction who indulges in character and intelligence stereotypes by considering himself and "his kind" to be wise, hard-working, brave, dedicated, honest and God-fear-

---

25. *Lysis*, 216d, trans. J. Wright, *The Collected Dialogues of Plato.*

26. *On Airs, Waters, and Places*, trans. Francis Adams, Great Books, Vol. 10, p. 18.

27. *A Study of British Genius*, Houghton Mifflin, Boston, 1926, pp. 306–7.

28. Morgan Worthy, *Eye Color, Sex and Race*, Droke House/Hallux, Anderson, South Carolina, 1974.

29. Thomas Hill, *Pleasant History*, London, 1613.

30. Coon, *The Living Races of Man*, p. 399.

ing—on the whole a slightly deflated combination of Puritan divine, Virginia planter and Western pioneer. On the intelligence scale he rates the Orientals and Jews rather high, but finds more craftiness than wisdom. He views Latins as frivolous, sexually volatile, superficial and prone to organized crime and treachery. He considers Indians, Mexicans and Negroes as stupid, shiftless, unclean, and overfond of alcohol or narcotics.[31]

In return, the more sophisticated Latins and Jews classify the average Majority member as a plodding, credulous, loutish Philistine, while viewing themselves as the inheritors of a superior religion and culture. To the non-Jew, Jews are often as avaricious as Shylock. Jews, as might be surmised, consider themselves extremely charitable. Both Indians and Negroes are likely to typecast whites as unbridled horse traders, paragons of insensitivity, specialists in genocide, and sexually repressed Horatio Algers and Simon Legrees.

Many such stereotypes dissolve and many new ones emerge as the political, economic, and social status of Americans alters. A change in status, however, usually occurs long before a change in stereotype, and it may take some time for the public stereotype to catch up with the publicized stereotype. In less than a century, the Jewish pawnbroker has yielded to the affectionate Jewish supermother; the shuffling and obsequious Negro to the champion prizefighter; the drunken Irish brawler to the kindly priest; the opium-smoking, pig-tailed coolie to Charlie Chan. The repulsive traits, both physical and psychological, now heaped upon Nazis, Russians, and Arabs were once reserved for the "unspeakable" Turks. In many a television and stage drama the blond hero has become the blond villain.

In recent times, racial stereotypes have come under as sharp an attack as racism itself. But those most opposed to stereotypes usually have their own, and in the end all that is accomplished is the substitution of one set of stereotypes for another. Rather than concentrate on the abolition of stereotypes—as impossible a task as abolishing the human tendency to generalize—social

---

31. Medill McCormick's statement that Theodore Roosevelt understood the "psychology of the mutt" reveals another common attitude of oldline Americans toward all other Americans, white or colored. Richard Hofstadter, *The American Political Tradition*, Knopf, New York, 1949, p. 230.

scientists might welcome them as instructive signposts in the study of intergroup behavior. They have an impressive pedigree, deriving not only from gossip, hearsay and the lower depths of human depravity, but from folklore, myth, religion, literature, art, and music. Some of the most sublime expressions of human creativity have made liberal use of racial stereotypes.

Carleton Coon is one of the very few modern anthropologists who is not too disturbed about stereotypes: "Popular, subjective labels in the designation of races, used among persons ignorant of the existence of physical anthropology, are often truer than the hesitant results of erudite wanderings in the labyrinth of numbers." [32]

It is now time to enter "the labyrinth of numbers." To arrive at a broader understanding of American racial dynamics, the emphasis now shifts from the qualitative to the quantitative aspects of race.

---

32. *The Races of Europe*, p. 335.

PART II

Racial Composition of the United States

CHAPTER 5

White Immigration

IT IS TRUE that all Americans—Indians included—are either immigrants or the descendants of immigrants. It is equally true that radically different kinds of immigrants came to America for radically different reasons. One thinks of the Indian inching his way over the Aleutian land bridge in search of food . . . the Pilgrim building his city of God in the New England wilderness . . . the Negro chained to the hold of a slave ship.

From the earliest colonial times to almost the middle of the nineteenth century, white immigrants were motivated by love of fame and adventure, by land hunger, by fortune hunting, by the hope of retaining and expanding their religious identity,[1] by misgivings about the governments of their homelands and their governments' misgivings about them, by a concern for liberty,[2] and by the nagging and endemic Northern European wanderlust. The immigration was made up of farmers, artisans, tradesmen, and soldiers of fortune, with a light froth of dissident aristocrats and a thin sediment of jailbirds. Though it is often forgotten, many

---

1. The religious motivation must not be overrated. Only a small percentage of the early colonists were church members (see pp. 266–67). One reason for the Pilgrims' transatlantic passage was the fear that their sons and daughters would "wed out in the world" if they extended their period of refuge in the "swinging" Netherlands.

2. D. H. Lawrence asserts the Puritans were running away from liberty, and that they simply could not stand the ever increasing personal freedom and humanity of post-Renaissance England, that there was far more religious freedom in the England they left than in the New England they founded. *Studies in Classical American Literature*, Viking Press, New York, 1964, pp. 3, 5.

of the early white immigrants had already enjoyed a fair measure of prosperity in their native lands.[3] Where it existed the economic drive was important, but it was directed more toward economic gain than economic security.

Natural selection was extremely hard on the pioneering vanguard. Half the *Mayflower's* passengers died either on the sea voyage or during their first year in Massachusetts.[4] In Jamestown, the first permanent English colony in America, there were more than five hundred colonists in 1609. No more than sixty were alive a year later.[5] On the morning of March 22, 1622, an Indian war party fell upon colonial settlements in the upper reaches of Virginia's James River. In a few hours, 347 whites were killed without respect to age or sex.[6] Elsewhere famine, disease, Indian raids, and the rigors of the frontier carried on a relentless winnowing, culling and sifting of a people whose principal elements, from the outset, had never been a cross section of the English or of any other Old World population.[7]

In 1689 the number of whites in the thirteen colonies was approximately 200,000. By 1754 it had grown to a million—300,000 in New England, 300,000 in the Middle Colonies, 400,000 in the South. In 1790, the year of the first Federal Census, the national origins of American whites and their percentage of the total white population were estimated as follows: British (77), German (7.4), Irish (4.4), Netherlands (3.3), French (1.9), Canadian (1.6), Belgian (1.5), Swiss (0.9), Scandinavian (0.9), other (1.1).[8]

The profoundly Protestant character of white immigration persisted until the 1840s, when the Irish, driven out by a potato

---

3. Alexis de Tocqueville, *De la démocratie en Amérique*, Gallimard, Paris, 1961, Tome 1, p. 31.

4. Ellsworth Huntington, *The Character of Races*, Scribner's, New York, 1925, p. 304.

5. William W. Sweet, *The Story of Religion in America*, Harper, New York, 1939, pp. 42, 51.

6. Ibid., p. 34.

7. The Puritans came largely from East Anglia, one of the blondest regions of England. Ellis, *A Study of British Genius*, footnote, p. 39. Selective processes were apparently going on during all phases of immigration. Polish immigrants, for example, were taller and thinner than the Poles who remained at home. Coon, *The Races of Europe*, p. 565.

8. See Appendix A.

blight, began crossing the Atlantic by the hundreds of thousands, together with large contingents of Central Europeans, including political refugees from the abortive 1848 revolutions.[9] Although its religious balance may have shifted a little over the next three or four decades—three million Irish arrived, plus millions of continental Catholics—the United States still remained overwhelmingly Northern European in racial background. The Alpine, Keltic, and Dinaric genes which had been injected into the American bloodstream were of the light-complexioned variety, and the few Irish and Central European racial traits that were at odds with Northern European physical norms did not clash in the critical area of skin color. Even so, the *old* Old Immigrants mounted a large-scale, crypto-racial attack against the *new* Old Immigrants, chiefly the Irish, who in a revival of classic Reformation polemics were charged with "Popery." [10]

Long before the Old Immigration came to an end, descendants of the original settlers began a new mass migration which took them to western New York and the Midwest—eventually to Texas and the Far West—and denuded New England of half its Anglo-Saxon population. It was this migration, as historically important as the one from England to New England, which fixed the present racial character of much of the trans-Appalachian United States.[11]

The 1880s marked the start of the New Immigration, which brought in millions of Jews, Slavs, Italians and other Eastern and Southern Europeans. This time the character of white immigration, which had been changing very slowly for almost half a century, underwent a rapid and deep transformation. Most New Immigrants were brunet, olive-hued Mediterraneans or belonged

9. The Catholic Irish are to be distinguished from the Protestant Scotch-Irish, most of whom originated in the lowlands of Scotland and later moved to Northern Ireland. 200,000 Scotch-Irish arrived in the fifty years preceding American independence. Maurice Davie, *World Immigration*, Macmillan, New York, 1949, pp. 21–24.

10. The American party, whose members were called Know Nothings by the political opposition, claimed 43 representatives, 5 senators and 7 state governors shortly before the outbreak of the Civil War. The increasing urgency of the slavery issue, however, played havoc with a political party which, in addition to its Protestant bias, was drawing subtle racial distinctions among whites. Davie, op. cit., p. 88.

11. Stewart Holbrook, *The Yankee Exodus*, Macmillan, New York, 1950, p. 4.

to the darker-complexioned divisions of the Alpine race. Most came to escape starvation, not to risk it—to crowd the cities, not to clear the land. Old Immigrants had been more than willing to trade security for insecurity. The new arrivals had reverse priorities. Both groups were overloaded with dreams, but those of the New Immigrants were more mundane. Whether the fault of genetics or environment or both, the mental traits of the Old and New Immigrant types were often in sharper contrast than their physical characteristics.

The last organized nationwide manifestation of what might be called Old Immigrant solidarity was an attempt to dam the flood of the New Immigration, and culminated in the 1924 Immigration Act. Total immigration from Europe was limited to approximately 150,000 annually, as compared to the all-time high of 1,285,000 in 1907.[12] Furthermore the legislation was racially selective in that European countries were given quotas according to their relative contribution to the American population as of 1920.[13] As Congress planned it, whatever small amount of immigration still trickled in was to be weighted in favor of the Northern European racial matrix.

But events took a different course. Many Northern European countries left their quotas partly unfilled or filled them with persons in transit from other parts of Europe. Congressional and presidential dispensations were given to anti-Nazi and anti-Communist refugees, World War II displaced persons, and 120,432 "war brides," many of whom were Asiatics.[14] Some 290,000 European Jews, many of them survivors of concentration camps, came to the United States between 1933 and 1954.[15] By 1981 they had been joined by 100,000 Soviet Jews. Approximately 50,000 Hungarians arrived after their attempt to shake off Soviet rule in 1956. There were no quota restrictions on the hundreds of thousands of Cubans who fled Castro, on Puerto Ricans (American citizens), on Mexicans, or on other inhabitants of the Western

---

12. Total immigration from Southern and Eastern Europe for the period 1820–1930 was 13,944,454.

13. Davie, op. cit., p. 377.

14. *Ency. Brit.*, Vol. 15, pp. 467–68.

15. James Yaffe, *The American Jews*, Random House, New York, 1968, p. 8.

Hemisphere.[16] As of 1965 nearly 10 million legal immigrants had arrived in the United States under the quota system.[17]

Both in regard to type and number, the immigrants who came to the United States under the quota system violated the letter and the intent of the Immigration Acts of 1921 and 1924 and the McCarran Act of 1952. The primary aim of all this legislation had been to preserve the racial profile of the United States as it had been defined and defended by the Founding Fathers [18] and had become "fixed" in the late nineteenth century. It was much too late for laws that would permit a privileged caste of fair-haired Nordics to lord it over a bottom layer of black slaves and white serfs. But it was not too late for Congress to prevent the Northern European racial nucleus from being physically and culturally submerged by continuing mass migrations of Southern and Eastern Europeans.

Quotas both succeeded and failed in the accomplishment of the grand Congressional design. The Northern European preponderance was safeguarded in the quantitative sense. But immigration continued at more than a trickle, and most of it was composed of the very racial elements which Congress had sought to bar.

It goes without saying that the quota system had always been an open sore to liberal and minority organizations. It was an outrage to those who sincerely believed in racial equality, and a stum-

---

16. Puerto Rican, Mexican, and many Cuban immigrants more properly belong to the nonwhite immigration, the subject of the following chapter. For an estimate of the present size of these minorities, see the appropriate sections of Chapters 14 and 16.

17. *Statistical Abstract of the U.S.*, 1969, p. 91.

18. Washington was opposed to unrestricted immigration because he wanted to protect the "American character." Jefferson feared that, since the bulk of European immigration would eventually have to come from Central, Southern and Eastern Europe, the newcomers would import with them the ideas and principles of absolute government under which they and their ancestors had lived for so many centuries. Charles Beard, *The Republic*, Viking Press, New York, 1962, pp. 10–11. Another argument against immigration was that it limited the natural increase of the native population. According to "Walker's Law," which assumes that the fecundity of indigenous groups is cut down by immigrant competition, the 3,500,000 American whites of 1790 would have increased to a number equivalent to the present-day population if the Constitution had forbidden all immigration. Madison Grant, *The Conquest of a Continent*, Scribner's, New York, 1933, p. 276.

bling block to those who were beginning to promote other than Northern European brands of racism. In 1965, bowing to an unprecedented lobbying effort that had been gathering momentum for more than half a century, President Johnson signed a new immigration act which kept the quota system, but radically changed the nature of the quotas. The national origins provisions, so hateful to the liberal-minority forces, were abolished and immigration limited to: relatives of American citizens and permanent residents (74 percent); members of professions and others of "exceptional ability" (10 percent); skilled and unskilled workers certified by the secretary of labor (10 percent); refugees from political persecution or national calamities (6 percent). The first category, which crowded out all others, was immediately dominated by the spouses and unmarried children of immigrants of Greece, Italy and the Philippines.[19] With respect to numbers, an annual ceiling of 170,000 and 120,000 was placed on immigrants from the Eastern and Western Hemispheres, respectively, thereby imposing a quota for the first time on Canadians and Latin Americans.[20]

When the Johnson immigration bill came before the Senate, only eighteen votes were cast against it, all from Southern senators whose constituencies contained the nation's largest concentrations of old-fashioned white supremacists.[21] The great immigration debate, which had become the great racial debate, was over, at least for the foreseeable future. At the urging of a British-descended, Southern-minded, Texas-born president, Congress had decided that the British or Northern European preponderance, which had both created and given unity and direction to American civilization, no longer deserved legislative sanction.[22]

White immigrants still come to America. Some European countries continue to complain about a brain drain. A considerable

---

19. *New York Times*, Aug. 31, 1970, pp. 1, 37.

20. A 1976 amendment to the Immigration Act extended the limit of no more than 20,000 immigrants per Old World country to New World countries.

21. *Time*, Oct. 1, 1965, p. 27.

22. Representative Emanuel Celler of New York was one of the strongest opponents of the 1924 Immigration Act, often called the Johnson Act, after Albert Johnson, chairman of the House Committee on Immigration. Celler lived long enough to be the House sponsor of the 1965 bill, usually called the Kennedy-Johnson Act.

number of Cubans, at least in the earlier flights from Castro, were white. As already mentioned, 100,000 Jewish dissidents have come from the Soviet Union. Some 400,000 Israelis have left their new homeland and moved to the United States.[23]

Nevertheless, as we shall see in the next chapter, white immigration in recent decades amounted to little more than a trickle in the genetic torrent of nonwhite immigration, both legal and illegal. It is a seemingly unstoppable torrent because immigration, as government leaders now freely and supinely admit, is presently out of control.

---

23. *Time,* June 30, 1980, p. 32.

CHAPTER 6

Nonwhite Immigration

IF THE ENGLISH began the Old Immigration, the Indians, who arrived some twenty thousand years earlier, initiated what could be described as the Prehistoric Immigration. In the year 1500, there were supposedly 850,000 Indians within the geographic limits of the present-day continental United States and Canada.[1] By 1770 the Indian inhabitants of the areas occupied by the thirteen colonies had been for the most part exterminated or evicted. During and after the winning of the West, Indians were placed on reservations and at one time their total number in this country was reduced to less than 250,000.[2]

The Mongoloid migration to North America—American Indians are classified as Mongoloids—was revived after more than a score of centuries with the arrival of the Chinese coolie in California. The Chinese, who first worked in the gold mines and then helped build the western end of the transcontinental railroads, provoked a hostile reaction from whites. From time to time, western state legislatures and Congress passed acts of exclusion against the Chinese, whose number reached 107,000 in 1890.

The Japanese immigration did not begin until after the Civil War and never quite reached the proportions of the Chinese. In 1907 it was brought to a halt by the "Gentleman's Agreement" worked out with Japan by President Theodore Roosevelt. After World War I, Asiatic immigration was such a rarity that the annual

---

1. *Our American Indians at a Glance,* Pacific Coast Publishers, Menlo Park, Calif., 1961, p. 6.

2. In recent times the Indian population group has made a substantial recovery. See *American Indian* section, Chapter 16.

quota of one hundred set for China and Japan by the 1924 Immigration Act actually resulted in an increase in the number of legal immigrants from these two countries.[3]

Not aliens in the terminology of the 1924 Immigration Act, Filipinos were later so designated by Congress. By 1930 some 45,000 had come to the United States. When the Philippine Islands were granted independence in 1934, Filipinos were put in the same category as other Orientals and their annual immigration quota fixed at fifty.[4]

The nonwhite immigration which has had the most lasting effect on the nation's racial composition has of course been that of the Negroes. Blacks from Africa were never categorized as Old Immigrants because of their different skin color and because of the different set of circumstances which brought them to America. Negroes could not be considered New Immigrants, because most of them came long before the New Immigration started. In point of fact, some Negroes arrived in the colonies almost as soon as the first whites. Like many whites, they came as indentured servants. But while the whites were able to work off their servitude (the average term in the Southern colonies was four years), the Negroes' status hardened into one of permanent and perpetual indenture, otherwise known as slavery. By far the greater number of blacks, however, were slaves upon arrival.

In 1790, according to the first Federal Census, there were 697,623 Negro slaves and 59,538 free Negroes in the United States. Few African Negroes came after 1820, when the British outlawed the slave trade. But in 1860 there were supposedly 3,953,760 Negro slaves and 488,070 free Negroes. If true, this means that during most of the years slavery was legal in the United States the Negro population almost sextupled.[5] In the next 120 years it sextupled again.

The largest influx of immigration since World War I has originated not in the Old World, but below the Rio Grande and in the West Indies. Although they cannot be classified as 100 percent nonwhite, the millions of Mexican-Americans who live in California and the Southwest—most of them having moved there since

---

3. The immigration picture outside the continental U.S.—i.e., the Hawaiian Islands—is a very different one and will be briefly examined in Chapter 16.

4. Davie, op. cit., pp. 342–47.

5. Mooney, *Smithsonian Miscellaneous Collection*, XXX, 1928.

1924—are certainly more Indian than Caucasian. Also largely in the nonwhite category are the vast numbers of part-Negro, part-Mediterranean Puerto Ricans who migrated to the United States, principally to New York City, after 1945.[6]

The 1965 Kennedy-Johnson Act, which purportedly ended racial quotas, had the effect of favoring nonwhite over white immigration. Although the Western Hemisphere quota should theoretically reduce the genetic flow from Mexico and the Caribbean, Mexicans and colored West Indians have never paid much attention to immigration controls in the past and are not likely to change in the near future. Of the four to twelve million illegal immigrants or aliens estimated to be in the U.S. in 1975, probably eighty percent were Mexicans. As citizens, Puerto Ricans continue to have free entry, though recently there has been some reverse migration to the home island.

The Eastern Hemisphere quota, as well as the priorities given to relations of American citizens and to professional and skilled workers, has resulted in an increase of Asians but not Africans. African blacks are not noted for their occupational skills and have been separated far too long from American Negroes to have maintained any family ties. On the other hand, the number of legal and illegal Negro immigrants from the Caribbean area has risen sharply.

How the Kennedy-Johnson Act, which did not take full effect until 1968, is changing the pattern of American immigration, is best shown by listing the number of immigrants in fiscal years 1965 and 1977, from the ten principal immigration sources.[7]

IMMIGRANTS AND COUNTRY OF ORIGIN

1965		1977	
Canada	40,103	Cuba	66,100
Mexico	37,432	Mexico	44,600
Great Britain	29,747	Philippines	38,500
Germany	26,357	Korea	30,700
Cuba	20,086	West Indies	27,100
Dominican Republic	10,851	Canada	18,000
Italy	10,344	India	16,800
Colombia	9,790	United Kingdom	14,000
Poland	7,458	China	12,500
Argentina	5,629	Hong Kong	12,300

6. Simpson and Yinger, *Racial and Cultural Minorities*, p. 136.

7. *New York Times*, Aug. 31, 1970, p. 37, and *1980 World Almanac*, p. 200.

It is noteworthy that only two of the countries in the 1977 column, the United Kingdom and Canada, have populations of Northern European origin, and both are well down the list. The five countries or islands which furnished the most immigrants in 1977 are part-Negroid (Cuba), Negroid (West Indies), part-Mongoloid (Mexico), and Mongoloid (Philippines and Korea).

Since the new, "nondiscrimatory" quota system only adds up to 290,000 annually, this by itself would not cause an immediate shift in the racial makeup of the American population as a whole. But quotas are only part of the story.[8] Hundreds of thousands of relatives of U.S. citizens and permanent resident aliens are allowed in "above the quota." One to two million illegal aliens, 60 percent or more of them Mexicans, enter the United States each year to seek work in a country with double-digit inflation and an unemployment rate of 7.6 percent (as of early 1981). The influx, however, is partly balanced by the return of earlier illegals to their homelands. Some 40,000 Haitians, many infected with tuberculosis and venereal disease, have found their way to Florida. From Indochina have come more than 400,000 Vietnamese and other "boat people." In the spring of 1980, 120,000 Cubans streamed into Key West and Miami. The criminal elements among them proceeded to riot and burn down government buildings after they were taken to the Fort Chaffee, Arkansas, relocation center. Other thousands of immigrants arrive as the result of various congressional "deals." [9] All in all, federal, state, and local

---

8. George H. Brown, director of the Census Bureau in 1970, announced that immigration was expected to remain at 400,000 per year for some time to come—290,000 quota immigrants and the remainder refugees and other special cases. By 1985, he predicted, 6 million persons will probably have entered the country after 1970 and will have had some 1.5 million children. *Washington Post,* Dec. 29, 1970. Needless to say, these projections were made before the huge influx of Indochinese and the new influx of Cubans. Also, Mr. Brown's data do not include illegal aliens, whose numbers are almost impossible to estimate. A 1980 Census Bureau report guessed 5,000,000. Less conservative estimates go as high as 12,000,000.

9. In one such deal involving Mediterranean whites a congressman who introduced a special law to permit the entry of 5,000 Sicilians obtained the support of another congressman by promising to vote for the latter's bill to let in 3,000 Iraqi Jews. *Time,* Nov. 21, 1969, p. 86. Part of the bribe money given to congressmen in the 1980 Abscam scandal was an advance payment for private immigration bills for mythical Arab sheiks.

governments spent $1.7 billion in fiscal 1980 on domestic and foreign refugee assistance. This outlay, which is compounded by the $3 billion that aliens send home each year, will certainly be increased in fiscal 1981, when 217,000 additional refugees are expected.

What all this means is that the American population is in a state of relentless change. The number of legal and illegal non-white immigrants and refugees, combined with the relatively high birthrate of nonwhite citizens and the well-below-replacement birthrate of most American whites, is fostering a rapidly increasing proportion of nonwhites that is making an indelible imprint on the American racial mold.[10] Not imperceptibly, the national complexion is growing darker each decade.[11]

---

10. In 1977 illegal immigration probably contributed 47 percent, legal immigration 12 percent, and natural increase 41 percent to the nation's population growth. Special Report, The Environmental Fund, Nov. 1978.

11. An eerily insightful novel, *The Camp of the Saints* by Jean Raspail, a noted French writer, depicts an invasion of France by a vast armada of starving Indians from Calcutta. For humanitarian reasons the French government decides not to oppose the landing. In no time France is overrun, conquered and destroyed. The only military action is directed against the few Frenchmen who try to resist. Since the original version of the book was written in 1972, Raspail's uncanny foresight, when applied to what is happening *to* and *in* the present-day United States, is a memorable example of history imitating art. The English translation of *The Camp of the Saints* (Scribner's, New York) is now out of print.

CHAPTER 7

The Fusion and Mosaic Fallacies

THE GREAT AMERICAN DREAM has been a collection of dreams, one of the wilder variety being that of the Melting Pot. The Melting Pot visionary prophesied that any immigrant, no matter what his race, nationality or social background, once immersed in the giddy liquefaction of American life would be transformed into a uniquely American solute with all the Old World heritage of caste and cultural disparity dissolved away.[1]

That dream, long dying, is now dead. The Melting Pot, which worked to some extent in the time of the Old Immigration when the ingredients were more racially and culturally harmonious, refused to function when the New Immigration was added to the solution. Melting Pot advocates seemed to forget that different races thrown together in the same environment may dissolve and fuse, but they may also stratify or separate.[2] "The more two

---

1. Israel Zangwill wrote a book entitled *The Melting Pot* (Macmillan, New York, 1909), in which he defined America "as a crucible in which divers races and nationalities are being fused into a new and greater race with a superior culture." If Zangwill was the high priest of the Melting Pot, Emma Lazarus was the high priestess. Never much of a poet, Miss Lazarus was even less of a prophet. She may have invited the "teeming refuse" of Europe to American shores, but when they arrived they did not perform as predicted. In later life, she turned out to be something of a racist, with her uncharitable remarks about Russians and ancient Greeks and her glowing Semitism. See *The Poems of Emma Lazarus*, Houghton Mifflin, Boston, 1889, particularly "The Crowing of the Red Cock," "The Banner of the Jew" and "Gifts." Also see her ethnocentric communication to Rabbi Gottheil in H. E. Jacob's *The World of Emma Lazarus*, Schocken Books, New York, 1949, p. 78.

2. In 1930, 51 percent of all Detroit Negroes lived in predominantly white areas. In 1960, 15 percent lived in white areas. *Time*, Nov. 9, 1962, p. 62. Rural

different peoples grow alike in externals," Santayana pointed out, "the more conscious and jealous they become of diversity in their souls . . . ." [3]

What population mixing there has been in the United States has largely taken place among nationality, not racial, groups. As one sociologist, R. J. R. Kennedy, put it, "Irish, Italians and Poles intermarry mostly among themselves and British-Americans, Germans and Scandinavians do likewise, while Jews seldom marry Gentiles." [4] Integrationists predicted a big upswing in the black-white intermarriage rate after the 1967 Supreme Court decision overturning a miscegenation law in Virginia. Though large, it was not as large as expected.[5] Other forms of mixed-race mating are on the increase, but the numbers are still relatively insignificant.

Racial crossing in the United States began with Pocahontas, and it did not end with the marriage of former Secretary of State Dean Rusk's daughter to a Negro. It has either been highly publicized, as with the interracial marriages of screen stars and celebrities, or clandestine, as with white liaisons with Indian maids on the frontier, slave girls on the plantation, or fancy mulatto mis-

---

blacks in the South, whose shanties were scattered among white homes, have fled by the hundreds of thousands to totally segregated metropolitan ghettos. On the other hand, some middle-class Negroes have moved to the suburbs, a few of which are now thoroughly integrated. In the largest cities, recently arrived affluent immigrants of the unassimilable variety have crowded into the better residential areas.

3. *The Life of Reason,* Scribner's, New York, 1951, Vol. 2, p. 166.

4. Simpson and Yinger, *Racial and Cultural Minorities,* pp. 546–47. The last statement in the quotation needs some classification. Jews *are* marrying Gentiles in the upper reaches of "society," in the professional and show business world, and in the smaller cities, where marital opportunities within the Jewish community are limited. Some surveys claim, perhaps with deliberate exaggeration, that 40 percent of Jewish marriages now involve a non-Jewish spouse. In many such cases, however, the spouse, generally the wife, converts, and the children are brought up as Jews.

5. There are still miscegenation statutes in some states, but none has been enforced since the Supreme Court ruling. According to a Census Bureau estimate, the number of black-white married couples in 1960 was 148,000; in 1970, 310,000; in 1977, 421,000. The last figure still represents less than 1 percent of the 48 million American married couples living in 1977. UPI report, Jan. 14, 1979.

tresses in Charleston and New Orleans. It is a sign of the times, and of the lengthening shadow of the minority presence, that the male role in racial crossing is now being monopolized by minority members, except in the case of American servicemen stationed abroad.

But sexual role changes in interracial socializing do not necessarily mean maternity wards overflowing with hybrid offspring. Negro-white dating, a commonplace in certain entertainment, academic, and avant-garde circles, has not been accompanied by an exponential rise in Negro-white mating. Modern education is apodictically color-blind, yet classroom violence works for the separation rather than the integration of races. Rock concerts, the rallying points of the nation's supposedly unbigoted youth, are often as segregated as Metropolitan Opera performances.

In direct contradiction to Melting Pot theory, the children of interracial couples do not become any generalized American type or the progenitors of a new race. They remain Negroes or Indians or Orientals. Only in marriages between Americans of Northern European descent and "white ethnics" is it possible for the offspring to lose their minority status.

In the slavery era, when tremendous social and psychological barriers separated whites from Negroes, a wave of interracial breeding in the South introduced white genes into a large segment of the Negro population.[6] Today, when many of these barriers have been lowered, there is much less Negro-white mixing. Today, in spite of the hold that race leveling has on education and the news media, the races of America instead of disappearing in some theoretical solvent are actually precipitating out.

With the passing of the Melting Pot fantasy has come the anti-fantasy—the American Mosaic. The intellectual *mise-en-scène* has suddenly been rearranged to accommodate a new sociological fad, the *pluralistic society*, in which all races and nationality groups live harmoniously side by side, all maintaining and strengthening their racial and cultural identity, each making its own contribution in its own way to the total picture of American life.

Like the promoters of the Melting Pot, the salesmen of pluralism have misread history, which teaches that pluralistic societies are

6. See p. 32.

static and caste-ridden and a standing invitation to disorder and disaster. Historically disoriented, the voices of pluralism are also dramatically contradictory. They are opposed to racism in theory, but support minority racism in practice. They uphold group identity, but demand integration at the workplace, in the schoolroom, on the playing field, and occasionally even in the private club. They approve of racial quotas but are against racial discrimination. The Negro leadership is divided on these issues. One group advocates an increasing participation in white society, while the other demands partial or full withdrawal.

Meanwhile, the American social order totters along in the grip of rising racial tension, which is both a cause and effect of pluralism. The Mosaic theory has turned out to be as great a failure, as great a misfiring of the imagination, as the Melting Pot. Mosaics are bits and pieces of inorganic matter which once put in place stay in place. Races are pulsating, organic continuities altering in size and status, now dynamic, now static, as the age dictates and as they dictate to the age. The Darkening Immigrant is not evidence that America is entering an age of pluralism. He is a harbinger of changing racial hierarchies.

Census Update

Chapter 8 was written just as the first reports of the 1980 Federal Census were being released. These preliminary reports were somewhat confusing, particularly as they applied to the number of persons of Spanish origin, or Hispanics, the counting of whom the Census made a special project. After this new edition of *The Dispossessed Majority* was printed, the confusion was cleared up and the Hispanic contingent of 14,605,883 persons has now been added to the Census Bureau's five original categories. As a result, some adjustments will have to be made in the five tables in this chapter. The revised tables are furnished in this insert, together with a new footnote 1 for page 57.

TABLE 1

White	180,227,142
Negro	26,097,485
Indian, Eskimo, Aleut	1,323,476
Asian and Pacific Islanders	3,334,501
Hispanic	14,605,883
Other	916,338
Total	226,504,825

1. The Federal Census counted 14,605,883 persons of Spanish origin, but did not list them in the short-form Census summary. Instead, it allocated the Hispanics as follows: White, 8,113,648; Black, 390,793; Amerindian, 94,719; Asian and Pacific Island, 166,135; Other, 5,840,648. Table I has introduced a separate entry for Hispanics and reduced the other categories accordingly. Since Hispanics are overwhelmingly part-Indian or part-Negro, they have been designated nonwhites in this chapter and throughout the book. There are, of course, some whites among them. But there are also some nonwhites in the white category. To make the arithmetic easier, it will be assumed that these two groups cancel each other out. The 1980 Census, incidentally, attempted to count everyone, including illegal immigrants, but some demographers claim significant undercounts of Hispanics and Negroes. Several years ago *Time* (Oct. 16, 1978, p. 48) estimated there were more than 19,000,000 Hispanics in the United States, and the *Miami Herald* (Jan. 3, 1978, p. 7-A) believed the number ranged from 23,000,00 to 25,000,000.

TABLE II

Race	Number	% of White Population	% of Total Population
White			
Nordic	119,796,142	66.47	52.89
Alpine	48,628,000	26.98	21.47
Mediterranean	11,801,000	6.55	5.21
Subtotal	180,227,142	100.00	79.57
Nonwhite			
Negro	26,097,485		11.52
Indian, Eskimo, Aleut	1,323,476		.58
Asian, Pacific Islanders	3,334,501		1.47
Hispanic	14,605,883		6.45
Other	916,338		.40
Subtotal	46,227,683		20.42
Total	226,504,825		99.99

A revised Table III has not been furnished because the only changes are in the bottom line. Change the previous percentages

	65.22	27.99	6.79
to	66.47	26.98	5.21

TABLE IV

Race	Number	% White Population (Table I)	% Total Population
White	168,426,142	93.45	74.36
Mediterranean	11,801,000	6.55	5.21
Negro	26,097,485		11.52
Indian, Eskimo, Aleut, Asian and Pacific Islanders	1,323,476		.58
	3,334,501		1.47
Hispanic	14,605,883		6.45
Other	916,338		.40
Total	226,504,825	100.00	99.99

TABLE V

RACIAL COMPOSITION OF THE UNITED STATES (1980)

Designation	Assimilation Status	Number	% Total Population	Source
Majority	Assimilated	141,109,142	62.30	White entry, Table IV, less Assimilable White Minorities and Jews
White Minorities				
Irish	Assimilable	9,040,000	3.99	Irish-American section, Chap. 13
Polish	''	5,100,000	2.25	Polish section, Chap. 13
French Canadian	''	1,500,000	.66	French-Canadian section, Chap. 13
Other	''	6,474,000	2.86	Baltic, Slavic, Hungarian sections, Chap. 13
Subtotal		22,114,000	9.76	
Jewish	Unassimilable	5,781,000	2.55	Chap. 15
Southern Italian	''	7,011,000	3.10	Southern Italian section, Chap. 14
Greek	''	1,190,000	.53	Page 150.
Arab	''	1,000,000	.44	Page 150.
Other	''	2,022,000	.89	Pages 149-150.
Subtotal		17,004,000	7.51	
Nonwhite Minorities				
Negro	Unassimilable	26,097,485	11.52	Chap. 17.
Indian, Eskimo, Aleut	''	1,323,476	.58	American Indian section, Chap. 16
Asian, Pacific Islanders	''	3,334,501	1.47	Chinese, Japanese sections, Chap. 16.
Hispanic	''	14,605,883	6.45	Mexican, Puerto Rican sections, Chap. 16
Other	''	916,338	.40	Pages 207-8, 213
Subtotal		46,277,683	20.42	
RECAPITULATION	Assimilated	141,109,142	62.30	
	Assimilable	22,114,000	9.76	
	Unassimilable	63,281,683	27.94	
TOTAL		226,504,825	100.00	

References to the tables in later pages of the book necessitate these corrections:

p. 62, line 10   change 23.3   to   20.4
       line 11   change   6.8   to   6.5

p. 65, line 1   change 59.4   to   62.3

p. 202, line 21   change 20,446,531   to   14,605,883
      line 22   change 16,000,000   to   8,763,000

In Chapters 16 and 17 population group totals refer to Census figures before they were modified to account for the inclusion of a separate Hispanic entry.

CHAPTER 8

A Racial Census of the United States

A RACIAL CENSUS of the United States must begin with whatever applicable statistics are available from the Census Bureau. Here are some population counts from the 1980 Federal Census:

TABLE I

White	173,734,907
Negro	26,488,218
Indian, Eskimo, Aleut	1,418,195
Asian and Pacific Islanders	3,500,636
Hispanic	20,446,531
Other	916,338
Total	226,504,825

A quick reading of Table I might indicate that most of the work of a racial census has already been done.[1] The American population has been divided into one white and several nonwhite categories. A second look, however, discloses that only two of the main categories, White and Negro, would be considered ac-

---

1. In the 1980 Census the Hispanic figure was actually given as 14,605,883; "Other" as 6,756,986. But, said the Census Bureau, 5,840,648 "Others" were also Hispanics, who did not identify themselves as such and listed themselves in the "Other" group. So all Hispanics have been entered as one category in Table I, and the "Other" figure reduced accordingly. Also, the Census Bureau added the first, not the second group, of Hispanics to the White category, although most Hispanics are mestizos (part Indian), some are mulattoes (part Negro), and only a relatively few are white. There are probably some nonwhites in the White category—the Census Bureau accepts self-identification as a basis for its racial allocations—but, broadly speaking, they probably cancel out the whites in the Hispanic category. The 1980 Census, incidentally, attempted to count everyone, including illegal immigrants.

ceptable racial designations by professional anthropologists, who would prefer that such categories as Asian and Pacific Islanders and Hispanic be grouped under more authentic racial designations, such as Mongoloid, Polynesian, and other equally sophisticated classifications. Amateur anthropologists, with the backing of a very few professionals, might also insist on a breakdown of the White classification. They would insist in vain. The Census Bureau does not publish statistics on the various white races in the United States.

In a search for accurate racial statistics among the white population, some help is furnished by those minority groups which try to keep a fairly accurate count of their own members. Experts on minority affairs are also deeply interested in the accumulation of minority statistics. All such figures, if handled with discretion, can be of help in taking up the Census Bureau's unfinished business.

An estimate of the Mediterranean element in the American population can be obtained by the national origins method. The population groups from preponderantly Mediterranean countries (Portugal, Spain, Greece, etc.) can be summed up and the total assigned to a Mediterranean entry. The same process can be applied to population groups from preponderantly Alpine countries (the Slavic lands, Baltic states, and Hungary). The estimated size of most of these population groups is listed in the *Harvard Encyclopedia of American Ethnic Groups,* generally conceded to be the best source book on American minorities and nationality groups.[2] In cases where the European mother country has more than one significant racial component, Alpine allocations can usually be made according to the racial composition of the homeland, as estimated in Carleton Coon's *The Races of Europe* or in Carl Brigham's *A Study of American Intelligence.* All the methods used to obtain meaningful figures for the three white races are analyzed and explained in detail in Appendix A.

The number and racial affiliation of the rest of the white population can be obtained by subtracting the Mediterranean and Alpine totals from the White entry in Table I. This remainder represents

---

2. *Harvard Encyclopedia of American Ethnic Groups,* ed. Stephan Thernstrom, Harvard University Press, Cambridge, Mass., 1980. An older text is *One America,* eds. Francis J. Brown and Joseph S. Roucek, Prentice-Hall, Englewood Cliffs, N.J., 1962.

a broadly approximate count of the largest segment of Americans of Northern European descent—the very few pure and very many impure Nordics from preponderantly Nordic Britain and Scandinavia, partially Nordic Ireland, West and East Germany, Switzerland, Holland and Belgium, and fractionally Nordic France, Austria, and Eastern Europe. The indirect approach to the enumeration of the Nordic category is necessitated by the absence of reliable estimates for these population groups.[3] Those who wish to see a calculation of the Northern European element by the national origins method may consult Appendix A, which also contains a statistical interpretation of America's white racial history and tabulated racial allocations of all nationality groups.

In line with the procedures, changes and corrections proposed so far, the condensed Federal Census (Table I) has now been "reconstituted" into Table II.

TABLE II

Race	Number	% of White Population	% of Total Population
White			
Nordic	113,305,907	65.22	50.02
Alpine	48,628,000	27.99	21.47
Mediterranean	11,801,000	6.79	5.21
Subtotal	173,734,907	100.00	76.70
Nonwhite			
Negro	26,488,218		11.69
Indian, Eskimo,			
Aleut	1,418,195		.63
Asian and Pacific			
Islanders	3,500,636		1.55
Hispanic	20,446,531		9.03
Other	916,338		.40
Subtotal	52,769,918		23.30
Total	226,504,825	100.00	100.00

In Table II racial and population statistics and percentages have been introduced. The Hispanic and "Other" categories have been placed under a general Nonwhite classification, together with the

---

3. The nationality groups which comprise the Northern European racial amalgam have generally lost their separate identities and in a minority-conscious era no longer draw much attention from private or public census takers.

Negroes, the Indians, Eskimos, Aleuts, and the Asian and Pacific Islanders (Chinese, Japanese, Filipinos, Indochinese, Hawaiians, Guamanians, etc.). The White category has been subdivided into Ripley's white racial divisions.[4] Population and racial studies to support the various allocations will be found in Part IV (Chapters 13, 14, 16) and in Appendix A.

There is no point in denying that, mathematically speaking, Table II leaves much to be desired. White racial allocations have been arrived at by a combination of educated guesswork, arbitrary anthropological definitions, and wide-ranging projections. In some cases, whole population groups have been assigned to a Nordic, Alpine, or Mediterranean category on the basis of their national origin, although no European country contains such an unadulterated population.

But even if it should contain errors as great as 10–20 percent, Table II serves a purpose. It quantifies the Pigmentation Spectrum in Chapter 4 by attaching numbers to population groups of differing skin coloration, the chief criterion of popular racial classification. Table II also demonstrates, in a rough way, how many people are black, brown, red, yellow, and white; how many whites (Nordics and Alpines) are white enough to be considered assimilated or assimilable; and how many whites (Mediterraneans) are not.

As a partial confirmation of the white allocations in Table II, reference is again made to E. A. Hooton's racial classification of the white population of the United States.[5] Hooton's racial divisions, it will be recalled, were not based on national origins data or population group statistics, but on a Harvard-sponsored anthropological study of 29,000 adult American males. In addition to dividing whites into nine separate races, Hooton estimated the proportion of each race to the total white population. These percentages, previously omitted, are now given in Table III. In columns 3, 4, and 5, they are distributed among the racial categories of the Pigmentation Spectrum and the results compared to Table II percentages.

The close correlation of the percentages of Tables II and III can hardly be described as a coincidence. But as always in the

---

4. See pp. 26–27.
5. See pp. 27–28.

TABLE III

E. A. HOOTON'S RACIAL DIVISIONS (1)	HOOTON'S % OF TOTAL U.S. WHITE POPULATION (2)	PIGMENTATION SPECTRUM CATEGORIES		
		LIGHT WHITE *Nordic* Nordic-Alp. Nordic-Med. Keltic (3)	WHITE *Alpine* Dinaric E. Baltic (4)	DARK WHITE *Medit.* Armenoid (5)
Nordic-Mediterranean	25	25		
Nordic-Alpine	23	12	11	
Predominantly Nordic	17	17		
Dinaric	13.3		13.3	
Keltic	8.48	8.48		
Pure Mediterranean	4.38			4.38
East Baltic	3		3	
Pure Alpine	2.68		2.68	
Pure Nordic	2.44	2.44		
Percentage Total		64.92	29.98	4.38
Corresponding Table II Percentages		65.22	27.99	6.79

case of racial allocations, accuracy has been sacrificed on the altar of generalization. Hooton's East Baltics, in spite of their Alpine physique and circular crania, are probably blonder and fairer than many Nordic-Mediterraneans, who were assigned to the Light White column principally because they represent a common British racial type.[6]

Given greater authority and credibility by the Hooton estimates, Table III will now undergo one further revision to bring it in closer agreement with the American racial picture as seen by the roving anthropological eye of the man in the street. Since the public does not distinguish, or does not care to distinguish, between Nordics and Alpines and the various Nordic-Alpine shad-

---

6. See Hooton's description of the Nordic-Mediterranean, p. 27.

ings, these two white categories have been combined and designated White in Table IV below. Also, in keeping with the dictates of popular anthropology that Mediterraneans are only dubiously white, they have been removed from the White category of Table II and given a separate entry of their own.

TABLE IV

Race	Number	% White Population (Table I)	% Total Population
White	161,933,907	93.21	71.49
Mediterranean	11,801,000	6.79	5.21
Negro	26,488,218		11.69
Indian, Eskimo, Aleut	1,418,195		.63
Asian and Pacific Islanders	3,500,636		1.55
Hispanic	20,446,531		9.03
Other	916,338		.40
Total	226,504,825	100.00	100.00

However offensive it may be to the political sensibilities of the Census Bureau and to the professional sensibilities of physical anthropologists, Table IV presents a more realistic racial picture of the American population than Table I. It portrays the United States as a moderately heterogeneous nation, with about 23.3 percent of its population nonwhite and about 6.8 percent of its whites on the racial borderline. Looking at Table IV, an atomic physicist might compare the country's racial composition to a white nucleus with various electrons whose orbital radius increases linearly with skin color.

But Table IV, unfortunately, is still not the end of the racial numbers game. As stated earlier in this study, race has its cultural and psychological side. In the words of one controversial American ethnologist, there is a "blood-race" and a "thought-race" [7]—

---

7. Lothrop Stoddard, *The New World of Islam*, Scribner's, New York, 1921, p. 160. It is the "thought-race" which made it possible for Congressman Adam Clayton Powell, who genetically could hardly be distinguished from a Mediterranean, to call himself a Negro. It is the same "thought-race" which permits former Israeli Premier Itzhak Rabin, with his fair complexion, light eyes, and many other Northern European characteristics, to designate himself a Jew. When Stod-

that is, population groups which act as a race must be defined and treated as such even if they do not qualify as a race in the accepted anthropological, biological, and zoological meaning of the word. Just as dark coloration excluded some whites from the White racial category in Table IV, certain cultural "colorations" would exclude others.

Consequently one more table is necessary—to take into account the psychological stratum of race. To satisfy this requirement, Table V (see next page) is offered as a "culturally corrected" version of Table IV. The physical basis of race has been retained by using, where possible, the various categories and numerical totals of the previous Tables. The cultural basis has been introduced by classifying population groups according to their degree of assimilation. The several Mediterranean and nonwhite groups have become Unassimilable Minorities. Central and Eastern Europeans and French Canadians, as well as a considerable number of Irish Americans, have been designated Assimilable Minorities. Jews, most of whom qualify physically for Assimilable status, have been classified as an Unassimilable Minority because of their long history of non-assimilation everywhere.[8]

The thinking that went into the construction of Table V will be explained more fully in Part IV. Here it might be pointed out that assimilation, although the dictionary defines it as the merging of cultural rather than biological traits, has physical as well as psychological overtones and is a decisive and ever present factor in American race relations.

Finally, within the somewhat arbitrary confines of Table V, the demography of the United States is presented in a form which both identifies and numbers the principal participants in the present-day racial confrontation. The American Majority, briefly mentioned in Chapter 4, now takes its place as the protagonist of this study and of the American racial drama. A huge, unwieldy, ungainly population mass, five times larger than the largest minor-

---

dard wrote, "For his blood-race he will not stir; for his thought-race he will die," he apparently believed that in a test of strength between the physical and the psychological sides of race, the latter would prevail.

8. Only China has ever succeeded in assimilating its Jewish population. Nathaniel Peffer, *The Far East*, University of Michigan Press, Ann Arbor, 1958, p. 43.

TABLE V

RACIAL COMPOSITION OF THE UNITED STATES (1980)

Designation	Assimilation Status	Number	% Total Population	Source
Majority	Assimilated	134,616,907	59.43	White entry, Table IV, less Assimilable White Minorities and Jews.
White Minorities				
Irish	Assimilable	9,040,000	3.99	Irish-American section, Chap. 13.
Polish	"	5,100,000	2.25	Polish section, Chap. 13.
French Canadian	"	1,500,000	.66	French-Canadian section, Chap. 13.
Other	"	6,474,000	2.86	Baltic, Slavic, Hungarian sections, Chap. 13.
Subtotal		22,114,000	9.76	
Jewish	Unassimilable	5,781,000	2.55	Chap. 15.
Southern Italian	"	7,011,000	3.10	Southern Italian section, Chap. 14.
Greek	"	1,190,000	.53	Page 150.
Arab	"	1,000,000	.44	Page 150.
Other	"	2,022,000	.89	Pages 149–50.
Subtotal		17,004,000	7.51	
Nonwhite Minorities				
Negro	Unassimilable	26,488,218	11.69	Chap. 17.
Indian, Esk., Aleut.	"	1,418,195	.63	American Indian section, Chap. 16.
Asian, Pac. Isl.	"	3,500,636	1.55	Chinese, Japanese sections, Chap. 16.
Hispanic	"	20,446,531	9.03	Mexican, Puerto Rican sections, Chap. 16.
Other	"	916,338	.40	Pages 207–8, 213.
Subtotal		52,769,918	23.30	
RECAPITULATION	Assimilated	134,616,907	59.43	
	Assimilable	22,114,000	9.76	
	Unassimilable	69,773,918	30.81	
TOTAL		226,504,825		

ity and comprising 59.4 percent of all Americans, the Majority is physically defined by its Nordic and Alpine racial affiliations, the former strain being predominant. Whatever Mediterranean ancestry is present must be well diluted.

Psychologically defined, the Majority is the only fully assimilated population group. Until recently every minority, willy-nilly, has gravitated toward it and around it. The cultural definition of the Majority is given by its central position in American society, by its dominant role in the shaping of the American state and by its historic task as the New World propagator of the at first Anglo-Saxon, then Northern European,[9] now Americanized version of Western civilization.

But Table V, it should be noted, carries a 1980 dateline. The question may be reasonably asked if the Majority and minority proportion of the total population will not be substantially altered by the year 2000, when there may be 260,000,000 Americans.[10] The answer is that if Asians, Puerto Ricans, Mexicans, and Negroes maintain their presently high birthrate and high rate of immigration, America's racial mix will slowly be transformed. With the black population increasing twice as fast as the white,[11] with legal and illegal immigration overwhelmingly nonwhite, it is quite possible there may be as many as 60,000,000 nonwhites in 1990. Already nonwhites have surpassed the proportion (19 percent) of the total population that Negroes represented in 1790.

In contrast to the Unassimilable Minorities, whose growth is now due both to natural processes and immigration, the American Majority, although its birthrate is below the replacement level and though its proportion of the total population continues to

9. Northern European, although a geographical term, is perhaps the best racial description for the American Majority. It is broad enough to include the various Nordic and Alpine crosses, yet narrow enough to exclude the darker Southern Europeans and the nonwhite population groups

10. Assuming no change in the current fertility rate of 1.8 children per woman and legal and illegal immigration at 900,000 yearly, *U.S. Population Fact Sheet* (1979 edition), Zero Population Growth, Washington, D.C.

11. Blacks outnumber whites in Atlanta, Baltimore, Detroit, New Orleans, Newark, and Washington, D.C., and may soon outnumber them in Cleveland, Memphis, and St. Louis. Hispanics outnumber whites in San Antonio and El Paso. Blacks, Hispanics, and Asians outnumber whites in Chicago, Houston, San Francisco, and Los Angeles, and may soon outnumber them in New York.

decline, will receive some reinforcements. Half of all Assimilable Minority members will probably be absorbed into the Majority in a few generations. Barring nuclear war, revolution, famine, genocide, and nationwide epidemics, the racial composition of the United States at the start of the twenty-first century may be estimated as follows: Majority (50 to 55 percent); a reduced Assimilable Minority component (5 to 7 percent): a bigger ratio of unassimilable whites (8 to 10 percent); a much larger proportion of nonwhites (30 to 34 percent).[12]

But the power and durability of a race do not depend on numbers. A healthy morale, a healthy biology and a consciousness of kind are much more important factors. Its large size, at least for the time being, is one of the Majority's great handicaps. The multitude of its members, aggravated by their wide dispersal and the steady addition of less compatible genetic elements, makes the Majority extremely susceptible to various forms of deracination, particularly that form known as proletarianization (see Chapter 26).

To put it another way, American racial dynamics have now entered a phase where most of the spirit, most of the drive, most of the competitiveness, and most of the will to power are on the side of the smaller battalions, the dynamic minority battalions that have seized the racial initiative.

---

12. Leon Bouvier, a population consultant to the White House Commission on Immigration and Refugee Policy, predicts that at least half the U.S. population will be of black, Hispanic, and Asian origin in a hundred years. *Chicago Tribune,* Dec. 21, 1980, p. 14.

PART III

The Majority at Bay

CHAPTER 9

Majority Origins

AN UNMISTAKABLE SIGN of racelessness, a synonym for powerlessness in a multiracial state, is a general apathy toward the subject of racial origins. As Macaulay put it, "A people which takes no pride in the noble achievements of remote ancestors will never achieve anything worthy to be remembered by noble descendants." [1] At present the American Majority is little inclined to examine its racial history or prehistory. It is even less inclined to compose, embroider and propagate the myths which are the taproots and symbols of race consciousness.

In general, Majority members have satisfied their search for ethnic identity by tracing their ancestry to a European mother country. It was this emphasis on national origins which led to the assumption that the United States was an Anglo-Saxon nation, a term still used by many foreign and a few American journalists and historians when they refer, anachronistically, to America as an "Anglo-Saxon power." In the first century of American independence, the Anglo-Saxon component [2] of the population was numerically predominant, so the assumption was well founded. It was supported by a strong cultural link, as well as by the English origin of most of the citizenry. But today, although the language has come through without overmuch damage and although other cultural vestiges are still recognizable, the British-American

---

1. Macaulay, *History of England from the Accession of James II,* Macmillan, London, 1914, Vol. 3, p. 1526.

2. Included in this component were many Americans of Welsh, Scotch, and Scotch-Irish descent who had the right to object to an Anglo-Saxon pedigree.

plurality, the root of the Anglo-Saxon connection, no longer exists.

Taken in the broadest sense, the Anglo-Saxon element of the American white population (77 percent in 1790) is today less than 41.4 percent.[3] It may still comprise a majority of the Majority (53 percent), but otherwise it has become a minority (less than 33 percent of the population as a whole).[4] It has also become racially unidentifiable. Other population groups of Northern European origin are now so undifferentiated, so thoroughly a part of the Majority racial colloid, that Americans of Scandinavian, German, Belgian and Dutch descent, as well as the assimilated segments of the Irish, French, Italian, Central European, and Slavic immigration, can scarcely be distinguished from WASPs. Even the American aristocracy is by no means an Anglo-Saxon monopoly. Any American *Almanach de Gotha* or *Debrett's* would have to include Du Ponts, Vanderbilts, Astors, Rockefellers, and Roosevelts, as the *Social Register* currently does. The founders of these enterprising families were anything but Anglo-Saxons.[5]

To find more solid ancestral moorings, the Majority, including the English-descended portion of it, will have to delve much deeper in time and space. The dwarfed perspectives of British and other Northern European "national histories" will have to be considerably expanded. The genetic and cultural contribution of England to American civilization was undeniably much more important than that of any other single nation or group of nations. Nevertheless the English are only one offshoot of a great ethnic division to which other Majority members can claim equal kinship. Since Majority unity can never rest on national origins, which are inherently divisive, it might be well for Majority historians to stop treating the Majority past as a chronological patchwork of petty Old World rivalries, interlarded with tendentious sociological dogmas, and start treating it as a discrete genetic and cultural continuum.

---

3. See United Kingdom entry in Table A, Appendix A.

4. Apply 1920 U.K. percentage to White entry (Table I, p. 57). Divide result by Majority entry (Table V, p. 64) and by total population.

5. Rudyard Kipling once heard Theodore Roosevelt, who would have been a prince if there had been an American nobility, "thank God in a loud voice that he had not one drop of British blood in him." Kipling, *Something of Myself*, Doubleday, Garden City, N.Y., 1937, p. 131.

One of the great difficulties of this approach is not the unearth-
ing of the anthropological evidence. Enough of it is already at
hand. The principal deterrent is the formidable opposition of
the intellectuals who dictate the shape and content of contemporary historical interpretation. A single step in the direction of
establishing common Majority racial roots would be, in their eyes,
a direct challenge to one or more of the currently accepted fash-
ions in historicism—the materialistic fixations of Marx, the religious ecstasies of Toynbee, the morphological prophecies of
Spengler, the liberal platitudinizing of the American Historical
Association, and the anti-history of Karl Popper.

The curious and opportunistic double standards of the intellectual community actually encourage a certain amount of minority
dabbling in racial history. There is no outcry when American Jews,
bypassing the European countries from which most of them came
to America, claim descent from a Semitic race of Hebrews in
ancient Palestine.[6] This is a large concession considering that contemporary social science is dead set against the derivation of
bloodlines from cultural and religious similarities. Nor are there
loud objections from academicians when blacks write volumes
about the ethnic ties of American Negroes, not to the West African
tribes from which they sprang, but to *négritude* and to the "African
soul." The same historical license is freely granted to romantic
Irish and Welsh Americans who dream of the departed glories
of the Kelts (despite glaring evidence of their Nordicism),[7] and
to American Indians and Mexican Americans who speculate about
noble forebears in a pre-Columbian golden age.

But all such flights of racial fancy, all such imaginative attempts
to establish racial identity, are forbidden to the Majority. From
a minority standpoint this taboo is quite understandable. The
further back Majority racial history is pursued, the more inevitable
is its collision with the Aryan theory.[8]

---

6. Ludwig Lewisohn's *This People* (Harper, New York, 1933) is perhaps the
classic example of modern Jewish racial mysticism.

7. Coon, *The Races of Europe*, pp. 378, 397.

8. Some of the more vigorous advocates of the Aryan theory have already
been mentioned in Chapter 3, as well as the surprising similarity of certain
Indo-European root words. Hitler's espousal of the Aryan theory, it is unnecessary to add, did nothing to improve its already low standing in the eyes of the
Western intellectual community.

Assuming for the sake of argument that the Aryan theory deserves some credibility, it then follows that an Indo-European or Nordic protorace was the primary source of many of the world's principal civilizations—Aryan (India), Kassite, Hittite, Persian, Mycenaean, Greek, Roman, Keltic, Teutonic, Slavic, and the latter-day Western European. Moreover, if a racial as well as a linguistic connection is admitted between the ancient Indo-European peoples and present-day Northern Europeans and their racial cousins overseas, then Majority members can claim as their ancestors the authors of the *Vedas*, Homer, Darius the Great, Plato, Alexander, and Caesar, as well as many of the greatest figures in medieval and modern history. They can also claim an art almost as old as the Egyptian and Sumerian and a literature that antedates that of the Hebrews by more than a millennium.[9]

With somewhat more anthropological license the Aryan theory can be pushed back to the Cro-Magnons, the magnificent artists of the cave paintings in southern France and northern Spain, the best of which go back to 18,000 B.C. Cro-Magnon skeletons, a few as tall as six feet, five inches, have dolichocephalic crania (average volume 1650 cc, compared to the average 1350 cc brain of the modern European).[10] Such skeletal dimensions offer some indication of a partial Cro-Magnon ancestry for present-day Nordics. In addition there are the recent discoveries of beautifully wrought goldwork in Eastern Europe that antedates the gold jewelry of the Egyptians by 1,600 years. Moreover revised radiocarbon dating demonstrates that the splendid megalithic chamber tombs of Western Europe are 6,000 years old—1,300 years older than the Pyramids. Stonehenge, it appears, was operating as an astronomical observatory a thousand years before Homer had composed a line of poetry.[11] To all this might be appended legends

---

9. The Vedic hymns go back to 2000 B.C., the oldest parts of the Bible to 850 B.C. See p. 155.

10. *Ency. Brit.*, 14th edition, 1963, Vol. 6, p. 792.

11. Colin Renfrew, *Before Civilization*, Knopf, New York, 1973, pp. 16, 66, 123. Renfrew, professor of archaeology at the University of Southampton (England) and Marija Gimbutas of the University of California at Los Angeles have been in the forefront of the archaeological revisionists who have dealt crippling blows to the diffusion theory of civilization growth. Previously the advances in European culture were credited to Egyptian and Near Eastern influences. All

of Vikings in pre-Columbian Central and South America,[12] and seafarers of a highly developed Nordic culture in Helgoland, whose navy purportedly overcame the fleet of Ramses III in an Egyptian sea battle in the twelfth century B.C.[13]

Although it is not generally known, several highly respected historians and scholars have lent their support to the Aryan theory. V. Gordon Childe, described by the *Encyclopaedia Britannica* as "easily the greatest prehistorian in Britain of his generation, and probably in the world," [14] wrote that Aryans "appear everywhere as promoters of true progress and in Europe their expansion marked the moment when the prehistory of our continent begins to diverge from that of Africa or the Pacific." [15] A prominent French academician, Georges Dumézil, went well beyond the Indo-European language relationship and posited a common mythology and even a common *structure mentale spécifique*, which induced a distinct Indo-European world view.[16] Toynbee did the Aryan cause no harm with some flattering remarks about the historical acumen of the Aryanist, de Gobineau.[17]

More recently, Oxford Professor C. D. Darlington stated of the Aryans: "Although they are stretched across two continents

---

the light was supposed to have come from the East *(ex oriente lux)*. Radiocarbon dating now proves that many lights were first shining independently in Western Europe. A reverse diffusionist theory was put forward by Gustav Kossinna long before carbon-14 was heard of. In *Die deutsche Vorgeschichte, eine hervorragend nationale Wissenschaft* (1912), Kossinna declared European civilization was started by waves of "Indo-Germans" who carried their inventions of writings and metallurgy southward in the great "folk movements" of the third millennium B.C.

12. See various works of Jacques de Mahieu, a French anthropologist living in Argentina, particularly *Drakkars sur l'Amazone*, Copernic, Paris, 1977. The remote ancestors of these Vikings may have gone as far afield as China. In 1980 the well-preserved body of a tall, "extremely beautiful" woman with long blond hair, big eyes, high nose, and "tiny, thin lips" was found in northwest China. Radiocarbon dating put her age at 6,470 years. *Atlanta Constitution*, Feb. 19, 1981.

13. Jürgen Spanuth, *Atlantis*, Grabert, Tübingen, 1965.

14. *Ency. Brit.*, Vol. 5, p. 502.

15. As quoted by Darlington, *The Evolution of Man in Society*, p. 146.

16. Georges Dumézil, *L'idéologie tripartite des Indo-Européens*, Latomus, Brussels, 1978.

17. *A Study of History*, Vol. VI, pp. 216–17.

we attribute to them a common ancestry and a common origin,
somewhere between the Danube and the Don and at some time
before the end of the third millennium, B.C." [18]

Firmer evidence in support of the Aryan theory includes the
genetic imprint of properly dated skulls with the proper cephalic
index in areas where Indo-European languages were spoken, and
a wealth of literary and artistic allusions attributing fair coloration
and blondness to the gods and heroes of the early Indo-European
cultures.[19] The sensitivity of the Aryan invaders of India to skin
color—the basis of their caste system—might have been a genetic
rather than an acquired trait since it is still prevalent among Northern Europeans and Majority Americans.

Finally, to the dismay and extreme discomfort of orthodox racial
equalitarians, anthropologist Carleton Coon reawakened and gave
new life to the Indo-European speech-race correlation by stating
the "Indo-European languages were, at one time, associated with
a single, if composite, racial type, and that . . . racial type was
an ancestral Nordic." [20] Coon went on to say that the patricians
of the Roman Republic were mostly Nordic in race [21] and brought
the genetic connection up to date by describing North America
as the world's "greatest Nordic reservoir."

From any scholarly standpoint the Aryan theory is an oversimplification. A few oblong skulls, a few Nordic profiles on crumbling
statuary, a few literary references to blondism do not prove the
existence of a great culture-bearing Indo-European race. But neither do they disprove it. At all events, if the Majority intelligentsia
is too cautious or too intimidated to subscribe to a remote Indo-
European lineage, it can hardly ignore the Majority's more readily
traceable descent from the Indo-European-speaking Germanic
peoples, who began to play a commanding role in world history
during and after the fall of the Western Roman Empire.

In the fourth, fifth, and sixth centuries A.D., *Völkerwanderungen*

---

18. Darlington, op. cit., p. 140.

19. Coon, *The Races of Europe*, Chapters V and VI. Also see Chapter 12 of
this study.

20. Coon, op. cit., p. 221.

21. Ibid., pp. 554, 651. So perhaps were some of the early emperors. Suetonius
speaks of Augustus's hair as "inclining to golden," of Nero's "light blond hair,"
and Galba's "blue eyes." *De Vita Caesarum*, 2.79.

from the German forests released a torrent of Northern European genes over much of the continent, some even spilling over to Africa. For Majority members of English descent in particular and for American history in general, the most eventful part of this migration was the Germanizing or "Nordification" of England by the Angles and Saxons. Similar genetic influences were introduced into the British Isles over the next four or five centuries by the incursions of Danes and other Northmen.

Even as the wave of Germanic expansion was contracting and the Ostrogoths, Visigoths, and Vandals [22] were losing their kingdoms in Italy, Spain and North Africa, a new Northern European migration was in the making. In the next 600 years the Scandinavian Vikings and Normans conquered Normandy, Sicily, Southern Italy, England, and parts of Ireland, and settled Iceland, the coast of Greenland and, briefly, Newfoundland.[23] In the east, following approximately the same time sequence, bands of roving Swedish warriors and merchants known as Rus and Varangians became lords of the Russian riverways. Apart from giving the country their name, they set up one of their own leaders, Rurik, as the first Russian Czar. In 1042, Varangians sailing south through the Aegean and Normans sailing east from Sicily marked the Scandinavian encirclement of Europe by engaging each other in a Mediterranean sea battle.[24]

The racial drive of the Northmen, before it was enervated in *douce France* and in warmer, lemon-scented lands farther south, catalyzed the Crusades, an ill-fated but Herculean effort to found

---

22. Eighty thousand Vandals, according to the count of their king, Genseric, disappeared after three generations, presumably by indiscriminate mating. Darlington, op. cit., p. 317.

23. The Northmen almost, but not quite, captured London (895), Paris (885–886) and Constantinople (860). In *A Study of History* (Vol. II, pp. 438–43), Toynbee has inserted an entrancing piece of historical speculation in which he envisions what might have happened if the pagan Scandinavians had captured these European capitals, gone on from Iceland to permanently settle America and, instead of being converted to Christianity, had outlawed it.

24. For centuries the Varangians formed the personal bodyguard of the Byzantine emperors. After the battle of Hastings, they were replaced by Englishmen fleeing the Norman conquest of Britain. Eric Oxenstierna, *The Norsemen*, trans. Catherine Hutter, New York Graphic Society Publishers, Greenwich, Conn., 1965, p. 279.

a vast Teutonic fief in the Near East. The ostensible purpose of the Crusaders, under such Norman leaders as Tancred, Bohemund, and Richard I of England, was to make the Holy Land safe for Christianity.

In other crusading movements taking place in Europe in these times, the goals were more specifically racial. In the east and northeast the Teutonic Knights were pushing back the Balts and Slavs. In Spain the Visigothic aristocracy had reemerged after centuries of hiding in the mountain fastnesses of Galicia and Asturias and was mounting a counterattack to drive the Arabs from the Iberian peninsula—a military operation which culminated in the founding of the Spanish Empire and the colonization of the New World.[25] Needless to say, none of these crusades was conducted according to the teachings of the New Testament. Whatever moral restraints and humane acts were exhibited could as well be ascribed to chivalry as to Christianity.[26]

Before the Middle Ages ended,[27] the Holy Land was lost. The

---

25. The Visigoths and their identifiable progeny are all but gone from the racial map of Spain. But if they have vanished into Spain's overwhelmingly Mediterranean ethnic solvent, some racial memories still stirred in one of the finest minds of modern Spain. Ortega y Gasset in *Meditación Preliminar* has written, "¿Quién ha puesto en mi pecho estas reminiscencias sonoras, donde—como en un caracol los alientos oceánicos—perviven las voces íntimas que da el viento en los senos de las selvas germánicas?" *Obras Completas*, Madrid, 1963, Vol. 1, p. 356.

26. Chivalry is a refined mixture of stylized military courtesy, honor, and courtly love, which is still faintly recognizable in the unwritten rules of what in England and America is known as fair play. Tacitus detected one chivalric rite in pagan German society: "Tum in ipso concilio vel principum aliquis vel pater vel propinquus scuto frameaque juvenem ornant."*De Germania*, 13. 5–6. For a fairly comprehensive modern survey of chivalry, see F. W. Cornish, *Chivalry*, Swan Sonnenschein, London, 1901. A less reverent and somewhat hilarious view of the same subject is provided by Robert Briffault's *The Mothers*, Macmillan, New York, 1927, Vol. 3, pp. 382–423.

27. Will Durant has some pertinent remarks about the racial composition of Europe at the height of the Middle Ages. "The Germans, by a millennium of migrations and conquests, had made their type prevail in the upper classes of all Western Europe except central and southern Italy, and Spain. The blond type was so definitely admired in hair and eyes that St. Bernard struggled through an entire sermon to reconcile with this preference the 'I am black but beautiful' of the Song of Songs. The ideal knight was to be tall and blond and bearded;

Turks began their march to Constantinople, Budapest and the outskirts of Vienna. The popes, who were largely of Lombard (Germanic) origin,[28] placed themselves at the head of the populations of Southern Europe and humiliated the German emperors. Meanwhile, the Teutonic and Norman aristocracy, having developed national loyalties, began to marry into rich mercantile families. And in the east, the Nordic Slavs were being "Alpinized" as the Nordic aristocracy and soldiery died out in endless wars against Asiatic invaders and as the more docile Nordic remnants mixed with neighboring peoples and the Mongoloid enemy.[29]

The large-scale colonial undertakings of Spain and Portugal, beginning in the fifteenth century, could hardly be called manifestations of Northern European racial energy, although more than a few *conquistadores* displayed an unusual disproportion of non-Mediterranean traits.[30] The racial lineaments of the Reformation, however, were unmistakable. In the words of Macaulay: "The Reformation had been a national as well as a moral revolt. It had been, not only an insurrection of the laity against the clergy, but

---

the ideal woman in epic and romance was slender and graceful, with blue eyes and long blond or golden hair." *The Age of Faith,* Simon and Schuster, New York, 1950, p. 832.

28. Hildebrand, who became Gregory VII and the most temporal of all popes, was a Lombard from Tuscany. Before Germans in the papal office put their religious preferences above their racial ties, their pro-Teutonic sentiments often approached those of Hitler. See particularly Bishop Liutprand's tenth-century polemic on the "baseness and cowardice and avarice and effeminacy and mendacity" of the Romans in Toynbee's *A Study of History,* Vol. IV, pp. 522–23.

29. "The Slavs, like all the other Indo-European-speaking peoples whom we have been able to trace, were originally Nordic, and there is no suggestion in their early remains, in the regions studied, of the numerically predominant brachycephalic racial increments which today are considered typically Slavic." Coon, *The Races of Europe,* p. 220.

30. Vasco da Gama's great grandmother was a Hereford, a member of the highest echelon of English nobility. Henry Hart, *Sea Road to the Indies,* Macmillan, New York, 1950, p. 97. Columbus, a North Italian, was tall with long head, blue eyes and auburn hair. Samuel Morison, *Admiral of the Ocean Sea,* Little, Brown, Boston, 1942, p. 47. Cortés traced his lineage back to the Lombard kings of Italy and Pedro de Alvarado, his bravest lieutenant, was so blond that the Aztecs called him *Tonatiuh,* the Sun. Prescott, *Conquest of Mexico,* Modern Library, New York, pp. 128, 258. Balboa, the discoverer of the Pacific, was fair with reddish-golden hair and beard. Kathleen Romoli, *Balboa of Darien,* Doubleday, Garden City, N.Y., 1953, p. 31.

also an insurrection of all the branches of the great German race against an alien domination."[31] Macaulay might better have said Northern European instead of German, because Southern and Austrian Germans remained solidly Catholic.

Protestantism, the religious emancipation of the North, helped inspire and accelerate the greatest Northern European expansion of all time. In a succession of great, seafaring "Folkwanderings," which lasted from the seventeenth to the end of the nineteenth century, British, Germans, Scandinavians, and Irish shipped out by the millions to North America, South Africa, Australia, and New Zealand, and by the tens of thousands to the outposts of empire in black Africa, South America, Asia, and the Pacific Islands.

At the start of the twentieth century, despite the French Revolution which had all but demolished the old Teutonic ruling class in most of Latin Europe, Northern European power and influence were never greater. The British and German Empires with their invincible land and sea forces, their near monopoly of world commerce, their technical efficiency and the boundless energy of their industrious citizenry constituted a concentration of military and economic strength that no other nation or group of nations could match.

This immense power, it might be noted, rested on more than guns and butter. It was the end product of a set of unique institutions, among which was representative government, whose origins Montesquieu had detected in the behavior and practices of ancient German tribal assemblies.[32] A fondness for personal freedom, an independence of spirit, the unusually high status accorded women and a deep affection for the land were considered typical characteristics of Teutonic-speaking peoples by Tacitus in his essay, *De Germania.* Such attitudes and habits were probably the seeds of the Magna Carta and of the subsequent British emphasis on individual rights and liberties. Perhaps the greatest institutional achievement of all was the legal system—including that Scandinavian or Teutonic invention known as trial by a jury of one's peers,

31. *The History of England from the Accession of James II,* Vol. 1, p. 58.
32. *De l'esprit des lois,* 11, 6–8. Iceland had a parliament, the Althing, as early as the tenth century.

a rudimentary form of which was carried to England by the Normans.[33]

All these milestones of social evolution apparently have sprung from an almost instinctive recognition that "the basis of . . . society was the free man." [34] The highest refinement and expression of this political reflex was embodied in the activity and legislation of the British Parliament, which fostered a climate of political and economic stability unparalleled in history. The comparatively stable social environment produced by such institutions was the basic precondition for Northern European leadership in government, art, science, industry, agriculture, and almost every other sector of human endeavor.

It was only natural that these institutions were carried across the Atlantic and further refined and developed by the English and other Northern Europeans who settled in North America. If a special biological inheritance had accounted for the progress and prosperity of the Northern European states in the Old World, it would have been reasonable to expect that a New World country with an overabundance of the same genetic resources would become an even greater nation—perhaps the greatest nation of all.

It took less than two centuries of national independence and two World Wars for this prophecy to come true. The irony was that by the time the United States had become the dominant force in world affairs, the American Majority, the principal agent of American greatness, was no longer the dominant force in America.

---

33. See p. 390.

34. J. R. Green, *A Short History of the English People*, Harper, New York, 1892, Vol. 1, p. 2.

CHAPTER 10

The Decline of the Majority

THE DECLINE of the American Majority began with the political and military struggle between the North and South.

In addition to nationalistic and cultural differences, Northern Europeans in Europe were divided by geography, principally the Baltic and North Seas and the English Channel. In the United States, the great divider was weather. The mean July temperatures of Massachusetts and Pennsylvania are 73.5°F and 75.5°F, respectively. The mean July temperatures of Virginia and Mississippi, 79°F and 80°F. These few extra degrees of summer heat made it impossible for Southern plantation owners to recruit a labor force within their own ranks. In a hot climate the Northern European is worthless as a field hand. The South would never have obtained anything like its flourishing antebellum prosperity without a large supply of Negroes.

To meet the demands of their environment, Southerners created their own unique *modus vivendi*—a highly romanticized and heavily scented version of which still haunts American history. Northerners, prompted in part by what has been described as the Anglo-Saxon's "sentimental flaw" [1] and in part by extending the concern for their own individual rights to others, first tried to alleviate slavery, then to end it. Southerners reacted to Northern meddling much as both they and the Northern colonists had reacted to King George's meddling a century earlier. They seceded.

If the North had been more patient and had been willing to "wait out" slavery a little longer—it was already doomed by the

---

1. Madison Grant, *The Passing of the Great Race*, Scribner's, New York, 1916, pp. 14, 77.

mechanization of cotton growing, overplanting, foreign competition, and other causes—there might never have been a Civil War. In that event, the American Majority today would be substantially more numerous. The death toll in the war was 610,000—compared to 4,435 in the War of Independence—and almost all the dead were of Northern European descent. In spite of the greater number of Northern casualties,[2] the war's dysgenic effects fell much more heavily on the South. The North had a population of 22,000,000, nearly all white, as against 12,000,000 in the South, one-third of whom were slaves.[3] The Southern officer class, in its reckless chivalry, was decimated, while in the North the purchase of substitutes was a thriving business. Seventeen percent of the Confederate generals were killed, compared to 2.5 percent of the Union generals.[4]

After the carnage had ended, the Southern branch of the Majority became for all intents and purposes an oppressed minority. Northern carpetbaggers and Southern scalawags, using confused and unknowing Negroes as tools, made a successful, though short-lived, bid for political and economic control—historians called it Reconstruction—which exacerbated more Southern feelings than the war itself. The passage of time and surges of national unity during World Wars I and II served to cool Southern resentment, until it was rekindled in the 1950s by the North's reopening of the Negro question. The use of paratroopers and federal marshals to enforce Supreme Court rulings was hardly calculated to let sleeping animosities lie.

Second only to the tragic polarization of North and South as a cause of Majority decline was the tremendous development of the national economy. If too much money is the seedbed of corruption, it is also the hotbed of racial amnesia. The great wealth

---

2. There were 360,000 deaths on the Northern side; 250,000 on the Southern. The war costs amounted to about $5 billion, with an additional $3 billion for postwar rehabilitation. Beard, *The Rise of American Civilization,* Vol. 2, pp. 98–99.

3. John Hope Franklin, *From Slavery to Freedom,* Knopf, New York, 1967, p. 386.

4. Nathaniel Weyl, *The Creative Elite in America,* Public Affairs Press, Washington, D.C., 1966, p. 57. "The cost in blood to the Union," Weyl added, "was paid chiefly by the poorer classes and by those without much education and influence. The Confederacy, by contrast, enacted draft laws which bore on rich and poor equally. . . ."

generated before the Civil War by Majority plantation owners and shipping tycoons, and after the war by industrial and financial magnates, tended to concentrate their minds and energies on such mundane matters as money-making, profit-taking and business organization. Majority plutocrats gave little thought to the effect their demands for an ever larger labor force would have on America's racial makeup.

"As the Nordic planter of the South," Charles Beard explained, "in his passionate quest for wealth, was willing to sabotage his own kind in a flood of Negroes from the wilds of Africa, so the Nordic mill owner of New England, with his mind on dividends, took little thought about the nationality or color of those who stood patiently at his spindles and looms or huddled into the tenements of his cities." [5]

The political consequences of this indiscriminate call for manpower were not long in coming. Even before the Civil War, the Irish presence began to make itself felt in a few of the biggest cities, where the Majority first tasted defeat at the polls. The defeat became national many decades later when the white minorities in the North combined with still embittered Southerners to win presidential elections.

It was the Majority's obsessive materialism, its habit of putting the tangibles before the intangibles of civilization, which made possible and perhaps made certain the Great Depression. Rugged individualism, laissez-faire, the separation of powers and many other cherished possessions in the Majority hope chest went up in the smoke of emergency legislation to save the national economy. The New Deal, the first administration to inject significant numbers of non-Majority personnel and non-Majority ideology into the federal government, marked the coming of age of the liberal-minority coalition.

Minority participation in politics and in every other corner of American life has now increased to where it can be said that the Majority is no longer the racial establishment of the United States. [6]

---

5. Beard, op. cit., Vol. 1, p. 640.

6. This decline has been misinterpreted by liberal sociologists as an exclusively WASP phenomenon. "[There] is a White Anglo-Saxon Protestant establishment which . . . has been gradually losing its power and authority in the course of the twentieth century." E. Digby Baltzell, *The Protestant Establishment,* Random

The Majority image—that of Western man as derived from Northern European (principally Anglo-Saxon) antecedents and as modified by the frontier and other peculiarly American environmental conditions—is being effaced by other racial and cultural imprints. And as Majority power and influence continue to decline, American civilization, as is daily becoming more apparent, is losing much of its cultural glue. The old forms remain, but the content is either going or gone.

Because the forms remain, the American Majority is but vaguely aware of its dispossession. It still votes, but no longer chooses. It is still free to speak, but not to speak freely. It still patronizes the arts, but the arts have become a minority wasteland. It still has economic strength, but it no longer directs the economy. It is still a major influence in determining local policy, but only a minor influence in determining vital areas of national and foreign policy. Many Majority members still lead private lives that are the envy of the world. In public, however, they are circumspect to the point of pusillanimity.

Those inclined to deny the Majority's dispossession may well adopt the following line of questioning. How, they may ask, can the Majority be dispossessed when there are so many rich Americans of impeccable Majority lineage . . . when there are so many Majority politicians, writers, artists, lawyers, doctors, scientists and FBI agents . . . when the president, most congressmen and most of the governors still belong to the Majority . . . when the armed forces are still commanded by a largely Majority officer corps . . . when the Majority, still the largest population group, can easily swing the vote?

The answers to these and similar questions will constitute much of the remaining subject matter of this book. Here they will merely be summarized.

One of the principal proofs of the Majority's dispossession is that there is no Majority political party as such. For most of the twentieth century the dynamic force in American politics has been the Democratic party, largely financed by minorities,[7] the party

House, New York, 1964, p. ix. Some minority writers have not only described but exulted over the Majority's fall from power. See Peter Schrag, *The Decline of the Wasp,* Simon and Schuster, New York, 1972.

7. See Chapter 15.

of Franklin D. Roosevelt, who "headed a government of minorities." [8] Reconstructed and unreconstructed Southern Majority
members still support the Democratic party, though in ever diminishing numbers. Many are still white supremacists, but ironically
this white supremacy by definition now includes minority whites,
mostly in the North, who represent all that is most hostile to
Southern interests.

The Republican party is favored by Northern Majority members,
though many Majority poor still vote for the Democratic ticket.
Eastern Majority liberals are in much closer intellectual harmony
with minority liberals than Majority conservatives. The latter dilute
their political effectiveness by belonging to the two major parties
in the South and by a long history of compromise with Northern
and Eastern liberaldom. As for the greatly touted "Silent Majority," it is built on politics and decibels, not race. White or colored,
Majority or minority member, Christian or Jew, anyone who keeps
his voice down and votes Republican automatically qualifies for
membership. There are, however, some genuine racial implications in the Republican "Southern strategy"—a move to gather
into the Republican fold white Southerners who dislike the pro-
Negro stance of "New South" politicians and the increasing clout
of Negroes in Democratic politics nationwide. But the Southern
strategy stands little chance of capturing the entire South until
Northern Republican old pols stop trying to outliberal and outmi-
nority the Democratic party leadership.

Even that inner sanctum of Majority privilege, the presidency,
has come under successful attack. Al Smith lost the 1928 presidential race, but another Irish Catholic,[9] John F. Kennedy, won the
1960 election. Barry Goldwater, one-quarter Jewish, was the Republican standard-bearer in the 1964 presidential contest. Lyndon
Johnson, the winner, was an authentic Majority member who as
a senator from Texas had fought hard against civil rights

---

8. "Archbishop Spellman" by Robert I. Gannon, Look, Aug. 1962, p. 103.

9. Smith worked his way up the political ladder as a pure, unadulterated
Irish Catholic, although his paternal grandfather was almost certainly an Italian
and his paternal grandmother quite possibly a German. Matthew and Hannah
Josephson, Al Smith, Houghton Mifflin, Boston, 1969, pp. 13–15.

legislation.[10] But when president, he completely reversed himself, once solemnly intoning the minority rallying cry, "We shall overcome," on a national television broadcast.[11]

Richard Nixon, who succeeded Johnson in the White House, although regarded by some as a super-American, was Irish on both sides of his family tree.[12] His first vice-president, Spiro Agnew, had a father from Greece and a mother from Virginia. Ronald Reagan, the victor in the 1980 presidental election, announced he was "Irish" several times in the primary, since he had an Irish-Catholic father. He spoke little or not at all of his WASP mother. American politics had reached the point where a presidential candidate considered it impolitic to speak of his British origins.

When a man like Lyndon Johnson, with all the power of the presidency behind him, feels compelled to change his beliefs so radically and to proclaim his minority sympathies so publicly and shrilly, the lower-level Majority politician, in sharp contrast to the priorities of most minority politicians, can hardly be blamed for placing party above race. Obviously, if he represents an overwhelmingly Majority district, the Majority congressman will support the aims and aspirations of those who voted for him in regard to local and some of the less controversial national issues. But the moment he is compelled to take a stand on the wider questions that may crucially affect the nation as a whole, he usually bends and sways to the will and whim of lavishly financed, minority-oriented organizations and lobbies which seem dedicated to every interest but those of his constituents.

Turning to the field of foreign affairs, the emotional ties of some minorities to their old or sometimes new homelands overseas—kept in the warming oven by the mechanics of racism—have produced a totally disproportionate minority influence. The recent history of American foreign policy reveals example after

---

10. In 1948, Senator Johnson said: "The civil rights program is a farce and a sham—an effort to set up a police state in the guise of liberty." Clarke Newton, *LBJ, The Man from Johnson City,* Dodd, Mead, New York, 1964, p. 112.

11. March 15, 1965.

12. The Nixons came from County Cork; the Milhous family from County Kildare. Phillips, op. cit., pp. 174–75.

example of diplomatic, economic and military commitments which were the direct outcome of official sensitivity to minority pressure.

The unconditional surrender of Germany, which handed Eastern Europe over to Russia at the end of World War II and may have caused a million unnecessary casualties, is one such example. American support of Israel, which cost the United States the friendship and goodwill of over a hundred million Arabs and smoothed the way for Russia's entrance into the Middle East, is another. Still another is America's massive military and financial assistance to the emerging African nations, while leading newspapers and periodicals continue their harassment of white-controlled South Africa, the only stable political entity on the continent. Independent Rhodesia was forced to surrender to black Marxists partly as a result of United Nations' economic sanctions in which the United States willingly participated.

Whether minority interests coincided with Majority and national interests in these major foreign policy decisions is a matter for serious debate. What is not debatable was the racial motivations inherent in such decisions. The Majority, having no longer any motherland but the United States, tends to view foreign affairs from a purely national standpoint. Other population groups often look at the international scene from a different perspective. This schizoid approach to foreign policy was certainly a compelling reason for America's backing out of the war in Vietnam, where minority interests were inconsequential, while emphasizing and reemphasizing American commitments in the Middle East, where minority interests are paramount. In Cuba, for which the more influential minorities have little concern but where the threat to America's defenses is real, the stationing of Russian armed forces is considered a *fait accompli* by the White House.

The two principal achievements of Majority foreign policy—the Monroe Doctrine and non-entanglement in Old World power politics—have now been scrapped and been replaced by a foreign policy without a center of gravity, a jumble of diplomatic *non sequiturs* which flies off on one tangent to satisfy minority emotionalism, on another to placate the liberal's impassioned anti-fascism, on another to soothe the conservative phobia of communism.

For better or worse, Majority control of foreign affairs was the only means of developing and pursuing a coherent foreign policy.

Once American diplomacy became pluralistic, the succession of disasters which has taken place in this century was inevitable. Until the reign of Henry Kissinger there was no branch of government where the Majority had a greater per capita representation than in the State Department. Yet it was precisely in the area of foreign policy that the Majority interest was and is most studiously ignored.

The greatest objection to the thesis of the Majority's dispossession is bound to arise from the undeniable fact that many of the nation's largest fortunes and many of the leading corporations are still in Majority hands. Here it is sufficient to say, along with Harvard economist John K. Galbraith, that wealth is no longer equivalent to power,[13] and that the average Majority member is considerably less opulent than the average member of a few minorities, particularly the Jews, who have now begun to challenge the Majority's hold on the big corporations.[14] That these same corporations, the principal sources of Majority wealth, were forbidden by law to contribute money to political parties, while labor unions, many under direct minority control, were able to funnel millions of dollars to their favorite candidates through political action committees (PACs), was merely one more indication of the downward curve of Majority influence. In the late 1970s, however, a Supreme Court decision made it possible for both labor and business to sponsor PACs.

---

13. Professor Galbraith, one of the nation's leading liberals, exposed himself to a charge of caste disloyalty when he attempted to bury the old chestnut of a conspiratical Majority plutocracy tying up American politics and the American economy in its purse strings. As proof of his thesis that the power of private wealth has greatly declined, Galbraith cites the tremendous growth of the federal government, the rise of the trade unions, the drying up of the servant class, which robs the rich of their prerogatives, and the ever increasing multitude of new rich, who by spreading wealth around more evenly have greatly diminished the exclusive hunting grounds of the ultra-rich. John Galbraith, *The Affluent Society*, Houghton Mifflin, Boston, 1958, pp. 88–90.

14. Jewish wealth, a survey of which will be found in Chapter 15, is an exception to Galbraith's rule (see footnote 73, p. 176). Figures on the economic of the Armenian, Chinese and Japanese minorities are not readily available, but the indications are that, on the average, members of these minorities have a greater net worth than Majority members. The incalculable wealth of the Mafia probably raises the per capita income of the Southern Italian minority above the national mean.

Ironically, many of the largest Majority fortunes have now passed into the possession of vast trusts and foundations, which spend much of their income and capital on minority causes. Also, some of the richest Majority members, instead of using their wealth for the benefit of the Majority, seemed to make a fetish of non-involvement and invisibility. Of the three authentic Majority billionaires in recent times, one, J. Paul Getty, who occasionally wrote economic homilies for a sex magazine, died in splendid isolation in a baronial English mansion and had not been in his own country for decades. Another, Howard Hughes, led a secretive, cloistered life in foreign hotels after erecting the world's largest gambling empire in Las Vegas. The third, tanker tycoon Daniel Ludwig, spent most of his latter years building a vast industrial and agricultural complex in Brazil. The minority super-rich, it goes without saying, are far less inclined to dissociate themselves from what they consider to be their ethnic obligations.

Not surprisingly the dispossession of the Majority becomes most apparent in the field of public opinion. If Ortega y Gasset is right in saying, "Never has anyone ruled on this earth by basing his rule essentially on any other thing than public opinion," [15] then minority domination of the present-day United States is incontestable. Minority members now own, control, or operate two of the three major commercial television and radio networks, the public television and radio network, almost every large motion picture company (except the Disney studios), the nation's two most influential newspapers and one of the largest newspaper chains, at least half of the important publishing houses, and most of the leading journals of opinion.[16]

But this remarkable concentration of power does not stop here. There are aggressively censorious minority organizations, principal among them the B'nai B'rith's Anti-Defamation League, which monitor the printed and the spoken word for the most subtle anti-minority allusions. Should any be found, the owner or editor of the offending media and, if necessary, the writer, advertisers and stockholders are so advised and admonished. All such bowdlerizing plays down, omits, or twists news vital to the public

---

15. *La rebelión de las masas*, Espasa-Calpe, Madrid, 1966, p. 116.
16. Specifics on pp. 168–73.

interest.[17] The Majority, to its great loss, has no similar watchdog organizations.

Being a compound of what people read, see, feel, and think, public opinion is only partly the creation of the minority-dominated channels of information. No reporter, commentator, author, philosopher, or prophet can make a normally intelligent adult accept as true what he knows to be false. But as public opinion moves from local to national issues, it becomes less informed. A fool knows more at home than a wise man at his neighbor's, runs the Spanish proverb. Firsthand knowledge is supplanted by secondhand information and even thirdhand gossip. Finally, in the realm of foreign affairs, public opinion rests largely on "organized" opinion, the opinion of those who have a direct or indirect interest in conditioning public attitudes toward the events being reported and the policies under discussion.

As for public opinion polls, they are often more effective in influencing public opinion than measuring it, more revealing of the pollsters' state of mind than the public's. The newspapers who subscribe to the polls have an important influence on what

---

17. *New York Times* reporter Gay Talese has written, "The media manufactured dramatic events and colossal characters out of many small incidents and minor men." *The Kingdom and the Power,* World, New York, 1969, p. 194. Glaring examples of media distortion in recent decades were: the diabolization of Senator Joseph McCarthy; the apotheosis of the assassinated Kennedy brothers and Martin Luther King; the sniggering affection for the posturing white and black revolutionaries, draft dodgers, riot leaders, and murder gangs; the whitewash of Chappaquiddick. "Has one ever heard a balanced discussion of the situation in South Africa? Or a reasonable presentation of the 'hawk' view on Vietnam? Or of the actions of a police force confronted with unruly crowds?" asks Ernest van den Haag in *The Jewish Mystique,* Stein and Day, New York, 1969, p. 142. The tendentiousness of the media is most obvious in the technique of editorializing by headline. "Let me control the headlines and I shall not care who controls the editorials," said Frederick Birchall, onetime *New York Times* managing editor. Talese, op cit., p. 168. In the 1950s, when the slightest mention of Communist or communism brought forth the Pavlovian response of "McCarthyism," President Truman accused presidential candidate Eisenhower of "being willing to accept the principles that identify the so-called master race." *New York Times,* Oct. 18, 1952, p. 1. Reporters and columnists were unanimously mute at this muffled charge of Nazism. In the 1972 presidential race George McGovern, who promised to adhere to the issues, twice associated President Nixon with Hitler in public speeches.

kinds of questions are asked and the size and composition of the sample. On the occasion of national and state elections, the press has developed the habit of using polls for bandwagon electioneering, in which statistics favorable to the preferred candidate are played up, while unfavorable statistics are played down or buried.[18]

In the event the control of the news media is regained by the Majority, public opinion will not undergo any overnight transformation. News treatment shapes people's minds, but the dogma and dogmatic boundaries that define and circumscribe news treatment flow from the domain of culture, of which public opinion is often but a servile adjunct. At the lower strata of American culture—the Broadway stage, Hollywood films, and television shows—minority dominance is scarcely challenged. At the higher reaches—poetry, serious novels, literary criticism, off-Broadway theater, modern music, painting and sculpture—the minorities have also assumed a commanding position.[19]

It has often been remarked, maliciously rather than accurately, that America's only original contribution to art was a minority contribution—Negro jazz. Now, we are told, the minorities have taken over *all* American culture, and books have been written to document this theme. According to Leslie Fiedler, the basic tone of the creative intellectual life of the United States has become Jewish.[20] Nathaniel Weyl not only proclaims the supremacy of Jews in modern American culture, but gives biological reasons for this supremacy.[21] Expanding on Weyl's genetic approach, Ernest van den Haag, professor of social philosopy at New York University, asserts that "American sensibility itself has become in part Jewish." [22] Van den Haag admits the domination of the news media by "Jewish liberals," the cultural domination exercised

---

18. The Louis Harris Poll predicted Hubert Humphrey would win the 1968 presidential election. Without a single exception, every major American newspaper and periodical predicted a sweeping Labour victory in the 1970 British general election, which swept the Conservative party into office. The predictive abilities of the pollsters in Reagan's 1980 presidential sweep were ludicrous.

19. See pp. 248–51.

20. *Time*, Aug. 19, 1966, p. 80.

21. *The Creative Elite in America*, Chapter XVIII.

22. *The Jewish Mystique*, p. 98.

by the "Jewish cultural establishment" and, in a paroxysm of ethnic flattery which conveniently bypasses the Greeks, the Renaissance, and the masterworks of Western art and science, declares
that Jews "have given the essential meaning to the last two thousand years of Western history." [23]

As if blinded by their concentration on one cultural phenomenon, the learned Semitists mentioned above seem to have down-
graded the significance of artistic stirrings from another minority
quarter. Jews may have Majority culture on the run, but Negroes
have it cornered. The recent surge of Negro drama and semi-
biographical racist tracts is not merely remolding and redirecting
Majority culture, but is attempting to wound it mortally. The new
Negro literary celebrities have one-track minds and simple, recurring themes: [24] white women are fair game for rape; white males
have serious sexual deficiencies; [25] looting, arson, mayhem, murder, insurrection, and even massacre are often worthy and understandable goals. The language employed relies heavily on racial
slurs and repetitive incantations of profanity.

In spite of such artistic limitations, the Negro literary and dramatic naissance is actively promoted by leading publishers and
producers and often seen on educational television.[26] Majority
writers, of course, cannot reply in kind since any public exhibition
of Majority racism, cultural or otherwise, falls under an automatic

---

23. Ibid., pp. 14, 41, 129–33.

24. For a list of some of these works and their authors see Chapter 18.

25. This assertion seems especially inappropriate considering that the physiological state known as "feminization" is far more prevalent among Negroes
than whites. Atrophy of the testicles and gynaecomastia (enlargement of the
male breasts) are a fairly common Negro affliction. J. C. Carothers, *The African
Mind in Health and Disease*, World Health Organization, Geneva, 1953, p. 64.
The myth of white unmanliness is now being picked up and circulated by a
few white publications. The following was printed in *Playboy*, October, 1967
(p. 25): "Question—What do you call it when a prostitute services a white client?
Answer—The Naked and the Dead."

26. Perhaps the most violently racist drama ever to reach any stage was *Slave
Ship*, presented in Brooklyn in the fall of 1969. Its author was LeRoi Jones
(Imri Baraka), a Negro who married and then divorced a Jewess because she
was a living reproach "to the things in myself I cared about." *Village Voice*, Dec.
17–23, 1980. Antiwhite libels and "literary" appeals to racial violence are a
frequent theme of black television talk shows.

and all-pervasive ban.[27] As might be expected, since there is no counterattack or rebuttal, the cultural *putsch* is moving relentlessly toward establishing the thesis that whites are a race "accursed" and "the cancer of history." [28]

With respect to religion, the highest manifestation of culture, it is not so much that the Majority is losing its church as that the church, some fundamentalist denominations excepted, is losing the Majority. Majority Protestants cannot feel too enthusiastic at the spectacle of their ministers' devoting much of their time and their congregations' money to minority causes, including the sheltering and feeding of revolutionary street gangs. Majority Catholics have had the same experience, and in addition must face the problem that the American branch of their church has traditionally been a pillar of minority support.

Predictably, the Catholic and Protestant clergy has provided many of the more active minority Pied Pipers—Father Groppi (a Catholic turned Episcopalian), the Berrigan brothers, Jim Jones, Adam Clayton Powell, Martin Luther King, Jr.—all of whom learned to feed their followers a heady mixture of social Christianity and minority racism. In contrast, no great defender of the Majority has arisen from any religious body, or is likely to as long as the Reverend William S. Coffin, who preached civil disobedience at home and disengagement in the Far East, while keeping silent about the Mideast, holds an Episcopalian sinecure, while Billy Graham and other evangelists bemuse their audiences with their own special brands of religious fossilism, and while the Reverend Jerry Falwell preaches a "moral revival" that is tightly linked to *Israel über alles*.

An assault on a people's culture necessarily includes an assault on a people's history, history being both the storehouse and arse-

----

27. The selective ban on the use of racial expletives is not limited to literary endeavors and what appears in the communications media. In Washington, D.C., the police have received formal orders to avoid the following expressions: boy, wop, kike, chink, dago, polack, bohunk, limey, frog, kraut, nigger, burrhead and spic. *San Francisco Sunday Chronicle and Examiner, This World,* May 5, 1968, p. 12.

28. The latter phrase is the creation of the white minority social critic, Susan Sontag, and is quoted by Benjamin DeMott in *Supergrow,* E.*P. Dutton, New York, 1969, p. 74.

nal of culture. Minority muckrakers [29] began rewriting the Majority past many years ago, but only recently have school texts, ably assisted by television "Westerns" and documentaries, deliberately made it a point to discredit the Majority's starring role in American history. Majority children are still permitted to learn that their ancestors (always with the help of minority groups) opened up the wilderness, but they are no longer permitted to forget that these same ancestors burned witches and committed atrocities against defenseless Indians. It is still admitted, somewhat grudgingly, that Majority industrial giants built the railroads and steel mills and developed the oilfields,[30] but they have long been characterized as lawless moneygrubbers and brutal exploiters of labor. The South, it is taught, produced most of the world's cotton and a gracious civilization, but at the price of mass lynching bees, night riders, slave gangs and genocide in the hot sun. Little the Majority did was right and even less was decent.

29. One of the foremost was Gustavus Myers, who went to great lengths in his celebrated study, *The History of the Great American Fortunes,* to detail the fabulous wealth of the richest Majority families, while practically ignoring minority millionaires like August Belmont, who as the American representative of the Rothschilds probably had more hard money at his disposal than any of his native-born competitors. Nor did Myers balance his roster of Majority financial coups by calling attention to Jesse Seligman, who helped persuade Americans and others to put $400,000,000 into an abortive French venture to build a canal across Panama. No one got a cent back, but Seligman kept his $300,000 advance and the additional huge profits he made as an underwriter. Stephen Birmingham, *Our Crowd,* Dell, New York, 1967, pp. 273–75. Also, Myers failed to mention the possible minority ancestry of his principal villain, Jay Gould, who was descended from Nathan Gold of Fairfax, Connecticut, the "u" being added in 1806. Birmingham, op. cit., p. 132. Matthew Josephson presents the same dreary catalog of grandscale Majority peculations in his book, *The Robber Barons,* and almost totally omits the financial juggling of the minority tycoons. Another work of this genre is Ferdinand Lundberg's *The Rich and the Super-Rich.* Pages, sometimes even chapters, are devoted to Rockefellers, Mellons, Fords, Du Ponts, Hunts, and Vanderbilts, but only a few words are given the Rosenwalds, Blausteins, Zellerbachs, Loebs, Seligmans, and Warburgs. The index does not even mention the Guggenheims, Zemurrays, Baruchs, Schiffs, Sarnoffs, Annenbergs, Sulzbergers, and Hirshhorns.

30. Dr. Lucy Rockefeller Hamlin, daughter of Laurance Rockefeller, said: "I never studied American history because I didn't want to sit in a class and risk hearing my great-grandfather described as a robber baron." *San Francisco Examiner and Chronicle,* March 2, 1969, Section A, p. 21.

Conceding that the Majority has no effective political representation, that its part in the making of domestic and foreign policy
is less than decisive, that its economic influence is in eclipse, that
its religious leaders have abandoned or turned against it, that
its culture has been shredded, and its history demeaned—conceding all this, it may nevertheless be argued that the Majority cannot
really be dispossessed until it loses command of the ultimate
source of power, the armed forces. The answer here is that the
United States is not nineteenth-century Prussia. It has no military
tradition which permits its officer corps to exercise an irresistible
influence in politics. Due largely to the endurance of Majority
institutions, the American military is still firmly under the civilian
thumb.

If there are doubts about this, the verbal lashing accorded high-
ranking officers by the news media in the last several decades
should dispel them. President Truman's curt dismissal of General
MacArthur, General LeMay's "bad press" in the 1968 presidential
contest, the ups and downs of Major General Edwin Walker, [31]
the posthumous attacks on General George Patton, and the uproar
over General George Brown's criticism of the Israel lobby are
proof that, as always in America, the pen is mightier and sharper
than the sword.

The armed forces, moreover, are not as Majority-ridden as they
appear. The Carter administration had a Jewish secretary of defense, Harold Brown, and a Negro secretary of the army, Clifford
Alexander. President Reagan's secretary of defense is Caspar Weinberger. There are Jewish admirals in the navy, Negro generals
in the air force, and Negro revolutionary cadres in the army,[32]

---

31. Walker was a popular figure, at least in the North, when he commanded
the troops which enforced the desegregation of a Little Rock high school in
1957. Later when he resigned from the army and began to criticize the laws
he had previously been called upon to execute, he was temporarily committed
to an insane asylum, shot at by Lee Harvey Oswald and effortlessly transformed
into a crackpot by the opinion makers. Walker bounced back into the headlines
in 1976 when he was arrested on a charge of homosexual solicitation.

32. "But now there is another war being fought in Vietnam—between black
and white Americans. . . . 'Ju Ju' and 'Mau Mau' groups have been organized
. . . tanks fly black flags . . . elaborate training in guerrilla warfare has not
been lost upon them, and many officers, black and white, believe that Vietnam

in whose ranks blacks and Hispanics may soon outnumber Majority members. The liberal-minority coalition, not the Pentagon, presided over the Korean stalemate. Majority, not minority, soldiers did most of the dying in Vietnam, where an installment-plan defeat had already been set in motion, and victory, thanks to the television coverage, had been ruled out in advance.

At home, as violence and crime reach levels beyond the control of the police and National Guard; the armed forces may eventually be reduced to the status of a massive law enforcement agency, something like the Federal Bureau of Investigation, another organization with the hopeless mission of trying to force a diseased society to function as an orderly society. Rather than serving as an instrument to restore Majority influence in government, the military, as meek, permissive and acquiescent as any other branch of government, is busily engaged in carrying out the commands of the Majority's opponents.[33]

But of all the proofs of Majority decline, none was more conclusive than the anthology of liberal-minority post mortems on the moon landing. Here was the great Majority enterprise of the century, perhaps the most memorable moment of mankind, yet after it was over, after the television coverage had ended, it was generally treated with veiled hostility and even described as a deliberate trick to divert attention from the plight and needs of the minority poor.

---

may prove a training ground for the black urban commando of the future." *Time*, Sept. 19, 1969, p. 22. Young radicals and old-school Marxists look upon this army within the army as the vanguard of revolution.

33. The My Lai massacre trial, initiated by the lurid reporting of minority correspondent Seymour Hirsch, was staged in such a way as to allow the military to preside over its own hara-kiri. When minority military planner Daniel Ellsberg stole the top-secret "Pentagon Papers," he was treated more like a hero than a criminal. Later all charges against him were dropped and he was practically canonized by the media, after it was learned that White House investigators had broken into his psychiatrist's office in search of damaging information. The spy went free. The counterspies were indicted. Ellsberg was last heard of as a leading agitator against nuclear power and as a member of a Los Angeles sex club. Previously he had served on a defense committee for Abbie Hoffman, who jumped bail in 1973 after his arrest as a cocaine peddler and whose triumphant surfacing in 1980 was treated by the media as a sort of Second Coming. *Miami Herald*, Aug. 30, 1973, p. 16A.

The definitive liberal-minority line on the Apollo 11 mission was laid down in a rambling, three-part dissertation in a mass-circulation magazine by the Jewish novelist, Norman Mailer.[34] The author seemed to be saying that Neil Armstrong's epic flight was a wacky, unjustifiable, wasteful, semi-Nazi adventure insulting to the aspirations of Negroes. The Nazi taint, presumably, was due to the participation of German-born scientists in the space program. The whole affair, according to Mailer, was a lugubrious foretaste of the cold, computerized age to come, an age whose only salvation would be the drugs, drums, and dharma of a different and better breed of men than the astronauts. The choice of Mailer, whose clownish forays into politics had earned him bigger headlines than his literary affectations, to appraise an almost unappraisable Majority exploit was in itself a sign of the Majority's disestablishment.[35]

So now with the downgrading of the astronauts and the upgrading of repentant rapists like Eldridge Cleaver, inspired militants like Huey Newton and cultural throwbacks like Abbie Hoffman and Jerry Rubin, the wheel of Majority history has turned full circle. The Northern European element of the American population, dominant from earliest colonial times until after the turn of the century, has now been demoted to a secondary place in the American scheme of things. The Majority's institutions and its loyalties to these institutions, its work habits, and its physical presence still keep the country together, but with diminishing success each year.

The overall process of the Majority's dispossession is not too difficult to summarize. America's dominant population group, fragmented by the Civil War, then softened into a humanitarian mood by an era of peace and plenty and driven by an overpowering desire for cheap labor, decided to share the benefits of its laboriously developed political institutions with newcomers of different

---

34. *Life*, Aug. 29, 1969, Nov. 14, 1969, and Jan. 9, 1970. The magazine articles were later expanded into the bestseller, *Of a Fire on the Moon*, Little, Brown, Boston, 1970.

35. Mailer later called WASPs "the most Faustian, barbaric, draconian, progress-oriented and root-destroying people on earth"—a racial slur that earned him high marks with the intelligentsia. His final word on Apollo 11 was that WASP "nihilism found its perfect expression in the odyssey to the moon. . . ." *Time*, Feb. 8, 1971.

races and cultures. Since these new Americans were almost totally unpracticed and unskilled in the mysteries of self-government and in their own historical experience quite unfamiliar with such ideas as equality and individual rights, they were all the more eager to gorge themselves on this rich libertarian feast, although more for their own private and collective appetites than for the public good.

Full social equality, however, was held back by residual feelings of Majority racial superiority. To help overcome this final impediment, minority anthropologists introduced and publicized "scientific evidence" to the effect that all races were inherently equal. The theories developed from such evidence (or preceding it) were promoted relentlessly by an alliance of liberal and minority intellectuals and public opinion merchants. It was not long before racial equalitarianism became established dogma and was taken up with a vengeance by nonwhites, whose historical experience was even more alien to Majority social organization than that of New Immigration whites.

In its zeal for racial leveling, the equalitarian school lost sight of the fact that the very dynamism which spurs a race to obtain equality forces it to go beyond equality. After decades of struggle, the vested interests in racial climbing become too great to be shut off arbitrarily by resolutions of the American Civil Liberties Union or the Americans for Democratic Action. Inevitably, equality edges toward superequality and superequality laps over into superiority.

Today, in the form of affirmative action programs, minority racism, having been given the stamp of approval by the three branches of government, has been institutionalized in America. Black skin, a Hispanic background, or an epicanthic fold now provides its fortunate possessor special privileges in jobs, education, and even in the courts of justice.

Meanwhile, theories proposing the racial superiority of certain minorities are being published by leading book firms, featured in the news media and discussed seriously in the highest circles of the liberal-minority cognoscenti.[36] It should come as no surprise

---

36. Three cases for Jewish racial superiority, as well as one for Jewish inferiority, will be examined on pp. 190–93. Marshall McLuhan's allegations of Negro racial superiority will be briefly discussed on p. 229. An article in *Sepia* magazine

to those who understand the real motivations of the racial integrationists that the very same anthropologists who have been preaching equalitarianism most vigorously seem the least disturbed by this trend. In fact, minority member Ashley Montagu, for many years the leading advocate of the equalitarian school of anthropology, has actually recommended a recent literary *tour de force* that describes Jews as a master race innately equipped with an intellectual apparatus that makes them superior to all other races and peoples everywhere.[37]

And so it has transpired that the once dominant Majority has been given the status—and stigma—of inferiority, not only by the facts of American life and the racial dynamism of minorities, but by the *ex cathedra* pronouncements of influential social scientists. There is hardly a greater form of dispossession than becoming a servant in one's own house.

(May 1980) was entitled "Black Genetic Superiority." Dr. Asa Hilliard III, the black dean of the School of Education at San Francisco State, a university with some standing in academia, attempted to shore up this claim to superiority by asserting that Mozart, Haydn, and Beethoven were "Afro-Europeans." Address at the U.S. Air Force Academy, March 1980.

37. See full-page advertisement for Ernest van den Haag's *The Jewish Mystique* in *New York Times,* Jan. 5, 1970.

CHAPTER 11

The Split in the Ranks

Is it not incredible that the largest American population group, the group with the deepest roots, the most orderly and the most technically proficient group, the *nuclear* population group of American culture and of the American gene pool, should have lost its preeminence to weaker, less established, less numerous, culturally heterogeneous, and often mutually hostile minorities?

With all due allowance for minority dynamism and for the other external or historical causes discussed in earlier chapters, this miraculous shift of power could never have taken place without a Majority "split in the ranks"—without the active assistance and participation of Majority members themselves.

It has already been pointed out that race consciousness is one of the great social binding forces, from which it follows that when the racial gravitational pull slackens people tend to spin off from the group nucleus. Some drift aimlessly through life as human isolates. Others look for a substitute nucleus in an intensified religious or political life, or in an expanded class consciousness. Still others, out of idealism, romanticism, inertia, or perversity, attach themselves to another race in an attempt to find the solidarity they miss in their own.

Strictly speaking, as has been suggested previously, no one can change or trade his race. This is precluded by the physical stratum of race. But one can lose or give up his race-mindedness, his racial pride, his racism. One can acquire the cultural trappings, the language, and the religion of another race. One can marry a person of a different race and have hybrid children. By taking one or more of these steps, the Majority member withdraws for

99

all practical purposes from his own group and becomes, if not a bona fide, at least an ad hoc member of a minority.

Majority members split their ranks for a multitude of reasons, the chief one probably being ignorance—ignorance of the modern world about them and the ancient world behind them, ignorance derived from an unwillingness or inability to recognize the osmotic influence of race on matters that touch their day-to-day existence. Paradoxically this ignorance is greater among the higher levels of Majority intelligence, for the literate man who reads nothing but nonsense is more ignorant that the illiterate who reads nothing. Prosperity, which increases social mobility while diluting race consciousness, is also an important factor in dividing the Majority from within. Overconcern for the material comforts and conveniences of modern technology serves to dull both the reason and the instincts. But no matter what the circumstances, those who leave the racial fold weaken the racial fold. It is not so much that there is strength in numbers as there is weakness in defection.

Who exactly are the Majority Splitters of the Ranks? Generally speaking, they can be broken down into five categories.

1. GRACCHITES. The name is derived from the Gracchi, two brothers who, although belonging to one of the great patrician families of Rome, could not feed their ambition sufficiently within the orbit of their own aristocratic caste. Tiberius and Gaius Gracchus found that in times of stress in a relatively tolerant republic a descent of one or two steps in the social ladder is equivalent to an ascent of several steps in the political ladder. Accordingly, they became the standard bearers of revolution and agrarian revolt and were adulated by the plebeians. The Gracchi's political strategy, it might be added, was by no means limited to stirring up class against class, peasant against landlord,[1] exploited against exploiters. The patricians, the descendants of the Italic invaders, differed racially from the plebs, the offspring of earlier and later

---

1. There were traces of populism in the Gracchi's revolutionary program. But the racial dynamics of populism are unifying rather than divisive. There is a distinct difference between the reformer appealing to the farmers and yeomanry of his own race and the political extremist whose own proposals for land reform are only one item in a large package of revolutionary change and racial and class agitation.

immigrants.[2] The Gracchi's appeal, consequently, was directed to oppressed races as well as to oppressed classes.

In a multiracial state the well-born, ambitious member of a dominant race is constantly tempted to take the Gracchite route to power. It is harder for the patrician to win the respect of the patrician than to win the respect of the plebeian. It is also much easier to give money away than to earn it; to relax discipline than to enforce it; to be a hero to one's valet than to one's mirror.

History is full of Gracchites and the list includes famous popes, monarchs and princes. Philippe d'Orléans, who voted for the death of Louis XVI, his own cousin, to curry favor with the revolutionary mob, is perhaps the most notorious case. Teutonic aristocrats like Leo IX, who as pope stirred up the Italian masses against the Holy Roman Emperor, certainly fit the description. So do those kings and reigning dukes who in late feudal times established absolute rule by crushing their fellow noblemen with the help of the bourgeoisie and the urban rabble. A noted twentieth-century Gracchite was Prince Valerian Obolensky, who switched allegiance from the czar to the Bolsheviks and served as a high Soviet official until he was purged by Stalin.[3]

Gracchites have been particularly numerous in the United States since the 1930s. Franklin D. Roosevelt, Averell Harriman and Adlai Stevenson are three who come immediately to mind. All were born millionaires and the scions of well-entrenched Majority families. None was particularly successful in any realm of private endeavor.[4] In their public careers all specialized in catering to minorities and all surrounded themselves with minority advisers, assistants and ghost-writers.[5] Their natural stamping ground was

---

2. See p. 74.

3. *Ency. of Russia and the Soviet Union*, p. 403.

4. The long, ludicrous string of FDR's financial speculations in the early 1920s in New York included a $26,000 loss with Louis Howe in a scheme to fatten lobsters! Alfred B. Rollins, Jr., *Roosevelt and Howe*, Knopf, New York, 1962, pp. 196–97.

5. A Gracchite to watch is John D. Rockefeller IV, who in 1980 spent $10 million, or about $25.80 a vote, getting himself reelected governor of West Virginia. Jay, as he is called, may have chosen the Democratic party after watching Uncle Nelson's consistent failure to win the Republican presidential nomination. A Gracchite whose star is setting is John Lindsay, who ran under the Republican banner until repudiated by his party in the 1969 New York City mayoralty race,

the Democratic party, previously described as the party of the minorities.

But there are also Republicans who come very close to being Gracchites. Nelson Rockefeller could match his Democratic counterparts in birth, wealth and all the other accouterments of what passes in America for aristocracy, having based his career on a reputation for liberalism, tolerance, friendship for labor and a highly publicized concern for the downtrodden. But since the voter base of the Republican party consists of Majority rather than minority members, the comparison with Democratic Gracchites is only valid when restricted to the Republican Gracchites' state or city fiefs. In New York, for example, Governor Rockefeller operated almost exactly as President Roosevelt operated on the national level—that is, he was dutifully responsive to the will of the liberal-minority coalition.[6] In the field of foreign relations, however, Republican Gracchites are likely to give slightly more consideration to Majority interests.

The Gracchite makes considerable use of the family fortune to attack or undermine the system in which his family prospered. He capitalizes on his aristocratic mien, cultivated voice and fine manners to charm and win over the proletariat, much as the polished English actor, who is just another actor in London, "lays them out in the aisles" in the Iowa hustings. Cringing adulation from the lower depths is heady wine to the upper-level Gracchite.

All this is not to say that Gracchite politics is necessarily or always bad. There may come a time in the life span of every nation when certain issues become so critical they must be re-

which he won as an independent. In 1970, Lindsay told a gathering of University of Pennsylvania students, "The ones I have unending admiration for are the guys who say, 'I simply will not serve in the Army of the U.S. in Vietnam and I am willing to take the consequences for it.' These are the guys who are heroes." *Human Events,* May 16, 1970, p. 374. His father a British-born banker, his mother a member of one of the nation's oldest families, Lindsay gave his daughter in marriage to a Jewish graduate student. *New York Times,* June 7, 1970, p. 80. In spite of an expensive television campaign advertising his Nordic physical traits, Lindsay finished out of the running in the 1972 contest for the Democratic presidential nomination and in the 1980 New York senatorial primary.

6. Nelson Rockefeller became a middle-of-the-road mainstreamer in the 1970 New York gubernatorial contest in order to capitalize on a conservative groundswell in the ranks of the Irish and Italians.

solved even at the risk of revolution or racial conflagration. If no genuine leader can be found in a moment of crisis, as is often the case in a demoralized society, the Gracchite is sometimes a happier solution than the psychotic nihilist or head-rolling revolutionary. There usually remains at least a spark of feeling in the Gracchite heart for the people on whom he has turned his back.

It goes without saying that Gracchites are to be found in fields other than politics. Marshall Field III, the grandson of the Chicago merchant prince and subsidizer of the defunct minority racist New York daily newspaper, *PM*, was a dyed-in-the-wool Gracchite. So is Michael Straight, son of a Morgan partner and onetime editor-publisher of the *New Republic*. So is the son of another Morgan partner, Corliss Lamont, the well-known apologist and philosopher of Marxism. So is Hamilton Fish III, the publisher of the ultraleft *Nation*. There are Gracchite lawyers, doctors, and philanthropists. There are stage and screen Gracchites. There is a surprisingly large number of Gracchite diplomats. There are numerous female Gracchites, the most notable having been the late Eleanor Roosevelt. There are also matrimonial Gracchites—men and women of established Majority families who marry minority members for money, for a racial lark, or for the flattery and attention that social climbers extend to those with taller family trees.

The Gracchite usually pays a high price for his measure of glory. The adulation and fawning of the mob never quite compensate for the implacable hatred every group reserves for the defector.[7] In war the desertion of a general causes a much greater stir than the desertion of a private. In times of racial troubles the desertion of an aristocrat, the guardian of the race, raises emotions to a much higher pitch than the desertion of a commoner. Not only were both Tiberius and Gaius Gracchus assassinated, so were

---

7. It was this brand of hatred which prevented Nelson Rockefeller, potentially the strongest candidate, from securing the Republican nomination in 1964. It also gave rise to the stentorian booing of Rockefeller at the Republican convention in San Francisco by conservative activists, who for years had felt outraged by his Eastern habit of working harder for minority than for Majority votes. The memory of these boos probably induced Rockefeller to present a somewhat "deliberalized" image to the American people in 1974, when he was appointed vice-president of the United States.

two later Roman aristocrats of the Gracchite stamp, Catiline and Clodius.[8]

The Gracchite, even more than most liberals, has the peculiar habit of fomenting wars, but seldom fighting in them.[9] He loudly denounces the wealth of others, but keeps his own. He sneers at the upper classes, but cannot escape identification with them. He is publicly in favor of integrated schools, but sends his own children to segregated schools. It is probably asking too much of any man, particularly a Gracchite, to practice what he preaches. Giovanni di Bernadone, who became St. Francis after a brief, playboyish stint as the richest young man in Assisi, and Gautama Siddhartha, who evolved from princeling into Buddha, were the rarest of mortals, and certainly no Gracchites. They were humanitarians in the fullest and best sense of the word. The Gracchite's humanitarianism, however, always seems to be accompanied by an accumulation of power and by a torrential outpouring of hatred upon all and sundry who dare to challenge this power.

---

8. It is not quite accurate to call Clodius and Catiline Gracchites since they were both cut down in the middle of their conspiracies and rebellions, and historians never had a chance to plumb their real intentions. They might have been imitating Caesar, who practiced a far more sophisticated form of politics. Caesarism is the use of the mob to obtain the power to destroy the mob.

9. In World War I, Franklin Roosevelt, then in good health and of military age, was assistant secretary of the navy. Harriman and Stevenson sat out World War II as Washington bureaucrats, though both were extremely active interventionists. Thomas Jefferson, who lived at a time when being a Gracchite was almost unthinkable, nevertheless had some noticeable Gracchite tendencies. His father was a self-made man of uncertain lineage, but his mother was a Randolph. No one was more responsible for the War of Independence than Jefferson, yet he never once heard a gun go off in anger. His single military exploit was an ignoble and hasty retreat into the Virginia mountains when the British made a sudden descent on Monticello. "Where is Jefferson?" wrote Washington bitterly while at Valley Forge. It was this same Jefferson, so heedful of his own life, who was inspired by Shay's Rebellion to write: "God forbid! we should ever be 20 years without such a rebellion. . . . What country can preserve its liberties if their rulers are not warned from time to time that their people preserve the spirit of resistance? Let them take arms! . . . What signify a few lives lost in a century or two? The tree of liberty must be refreshed from time to time with the blood of patriots and tyrants. It is its natural manure. . . ." See Jefferson's letter to Smith, Nov. 13, 1787. Also see Nathan Schachner, *Thomas Jefferson*, Thomas Yoseloff, New York, 1957, p. 216, and Albert Beveridge, *The Life of John Marshall*, Houghton Mifflin, Boston, 1916, Vol. 1, pp. 126, 303.

What precisely are the Gracchite's true motives? Is he merely a man whose ambition outweighs his character—a man who, in spite of the immense advantages of his birthright, fails to make the first team, and consequently decides to abandon his team-mates, go over to the opposing side, change the rules of the game, and try to win anyway? Could it be that fear of competition with his peers is always his greatest concern? Is he not, in the long run, taking out his own failings on his own kind?

2. TRUCKLERS. These are the Majority members who are not born rich like the Gracchites and do not exude any of the aristo-cratic aroma that delights the olfactory organs of *hoi polloi*. They come from the middle and lower layers of the Majority. If they are men of wealth—and many are—they made their money them-selves, either in business, the professions or, in the not unusual case of Lyndon Johnson, in politics.

Trucklers play an active role in public life and in the formation of public opinion, while at the same time almost formally abjuring their own racial niche in society. The only racism they will abide is minority racism, which they help to cultivate by their zealous interest and meddling in minority matters. But their reasons for playing the minority game are more opportunistic than idealistic. They know from long experience it will gain them prestige and respectability, give them a favorable image in the press, and if they are politicians bring them more financial backing and more votes. They are also well aware of what would happen if they ever associated themselves in the slightest way with Majority rac-ism.

A typical Truckler is the young, naive Majority journalist who, after writing his first important newspaper or magazine story about some international or domestic event from a purely Majority view-point, is suddenly called into the front office and handed a sheaf of indignant and even threatening letters with fancy letterheads and illustrious signatures. At that moment he can: (1) refuse to be pressured and be discharged on the spot, (2) resign before he is discharged, (3) promise to be more "objective" in the future and keep his job. Having spent a great deal of time and money on becoming a journalist and not wanting to abandon his career at the outset, he inevitably chooses course (3). He then acquires more "objectivity" by tailoring his reporting in such a way as to eliminate further letters. Another Truckler is born.[10]

A second type of Truckler is the young Majority politician or bureaucrat who, during his first stay in Washington or in a state capital, inadvertently makes an off-the-cuff remark critical of some outlandish exhibition of minority racism. Immediately he finds himself pilloried and in danger of becoming a social outcast. He apologizes and never makes the same mistake again. Now he understands the score. Now he may engage the services of a minority adviser to keep him on his toes on minority issues and a minority ghostwriter to prepare his speeches. He will thereby avoid the possibility of any further embarrassing remarks, while at the same time improving his oratory. The dynamic language of minority racism shows up very well in audience reaction, in contrast to the listless, canned phrases of Majority speech writers.[11]

One of the most curious aspects of political truckling is its dependence on geography. Harry Truman, a chipper haberdasher who fell on hard times and flirted with the Ku Klux Klan, made his debut in politics as a member of the corrupt Pendergast politi-

---

10. The *ne plus ultra* Truckler in the newspaper field was Turner Catledge, a native Mississippian and long-time managing editor of the *New York Times*. As another Timesman wrote, Catledge's "home state had been denigrated regularly in the press for a decade . . ." Talese, *The Kingdom and the Power*, p. 143. The *Times*, of course, had been the principal denigrator. Other noted journalistic Trucklers are Benjamin Bradlee, longtime editor of the *Washington Post*, and Osborne Elliott, longtime editor of *Newsweek*. Television anchormen also fall into this category, though usually they simply read what is handed to them.

11. Judge Sam Rosenman, later chairman of the board of Twentieth Century-Fox, wrote many of the Roosevelt and Truman speeches. Many famous Kennedy and Johnson addresses were ghosted by minority writers, Theodore Chaikin Sorensen and Richard Naradoff Goodwin. The chief speech writer for Carter in his unsuccessful 1980 reelection campaign was Hendrik Hertzberg, who welcomed the Communist victory in Vietnam. The dull and turgid Eisenhower speeches were generally written by Majority professorial types. As for phrase-making, FDR's "Happy Warrior" epithet for Al Smith was dreamed up by Justice Joseph Proskauer and Kennedy's "New Frontier" was the simultaneous brain-child of Walt Rostow and Max Freedman. Ernest K. Lindley, *Franklin D. Roosevelt*, Bobbs-Merrill, New York, 1931, p. 223, and *San Francisco Chronicle, This World*. Aug. 17, 1965. Ken Khachigan is the man in charge of preparing President Reagan's speeches.

cal machine.[12] By the time he moved into the White House he was a champion of civil rights. Finally, having retired from Washington and safely back in the Majority-dominated Kansas City suburbs, he heaped vitriolic remarks on the civil rights movement and its leader, the Reverend Martin Luther King, Jr.[13] While attorney general of California, Earl Warren urged and found legal justification for the 1942 roundup and transportation to "relocation" camps of more than 110,000 West Coast Japanese, 64 percent of them American citizens—the greatest mass violation of the Bill of Rights in American history.[14] In Washington, Chief Justice Warren transformed himself into the guardian angel of the Bill of Rights.

Trucklers are not only found in the executive, judiciary and legislative branches of the government. They abound in every bright and dark corner of American life. There is the novelist who is careful to make his minority characters "inoffensive"; the playwright or scenarist who methodically gives the villain a Majority pedigree and Majority physical traits; the businessman who lends his company's name to any number of minority lobbies; the clergyman who preaches the righteousness of minority causes and is not averse to making his point by leading violent street demonstrations and sit-ins.

Aware of the immense rewards passed out to the faithful, many Trucklers become full-time minority enthusiasts, for which they not only receive numerous academic kudos and a prefabricated market for their books and articles, but also ready cash. Minority fund-raising events pay up to $1,000 a night for prominent Majority speakers. Hubert Humphrey, Senators Henry Jackson and Frank Church, and a host of lesser Majority notables made sizable grubstakes as the star attractions of Bonds for Israel dinners.

Trucklers frequently render greater service to minority projects

---

12. Truman paid $10 for his initiation fee into the Missouri Ku Klux Klan in 1922. He got his $10 back when he opposed the Klan's anti-Catholic policies—certainly the decent and loyal thing to do in view of Boss Pendergast's religion. Alfred Steinberg, *The Man from Missouri*, Putnam, New York, 1962, p. 64.

13. President Johnson's chameleon attitude toward civil rights has been mentioned in a previous chapter. For an example of Truman's post-presidential attacks on civil rights, see *New York Times*, April 13, 1965, p. 24.

14. *Harvard Encyclopedia of American Ethnic Groups*, p. 566.

than minority leaders themselves. Many legislative Trucklers have been so well trained in racial matters they are often more sensitive to minority interests than to those of their own constituents. In regard to voter appeal, a handsome, imposing Majority member is sometimes more of a political and social asset to minorities, providing he is properly "minority-broken," than a minority candidate. The latter may lack the clean-cut appearance so handy in attracting widespread support for minority-slanted legislation.

No Majority member is born a Truckler. Truckling is the result of an educational process—sometimes years in the making, sometimes an overnight conversion—in which the young Majority member has drilled into him the modern catechism of success. He learns he must be tactful rather than truthful, may question the non-controversial but not the controversial, must sail before the winds of "public opinion" but not head into them. He is taught to fear the taboos of present-day American society as thoroughly as primeval man was taught to fear the taboos of his day. He is quick to rationalize his truckling on moral and humanitarian grounds, although it has never been known to retard the advancement of his career.

One can admire a person who by changing his ideas and principles risks death, disgrace, or severe financial loss. One reserves the right to adopt a certain skepticism toward those whose ideological skin-shedding, often conveniently and beautifully timed, makes them rich, powerful, and celebrated. Perhaps Truckler is too strong a word for those political and moral trimmers who, at least superficially, are performing the age-old trick of sacrificing integrity to ambition. But the Truckler, as here defined, oversteps this common vice. He goes further than making a fetish of self-interest. In a paradoxical mixture of public altruism and private egotism, he puts the interest of other ethnic groups above the interests of his own.

3. PUSSYFOOTERS. Many Majority members take no positive action against their own group but seldom, if ever, defend it. They comprise the second and third echelons of Majority leadership—lawyers, doctors, scientists, small-time newspaper editors, professors, teachers, preachers, big and small businessmen, local, state, and federal officials.

In contrast to Gracchites and Trucklers, who betray and violate Majority interests, Pussyfooters soft-pedal and subordinate them. Immersed in their own day-to-day problems, obsessed with the material aspects of existence, often isolated in areas where the Majority is overwhelmingly predominant, Pussyfooters have less direct contact with the minority challenge and consequently are less concerned about it. When and where they come face to face with minority dynamism, in social gatherings or in community affairs, instead of standing up for the Majority viewpoint, they simply keep quiet.

Pussyfooters know that something is wrong, but they don't know what, and they do not have the time, the inclination, the courage or the intellectual initiative to find out. Some Pussyfooters tread softly because they dislike argument, while others are fearful for their livelihood. Some are just temperamentally unsuited for the verbal screaming matches and hysterical logic-chopping in which their liberal and minority neighbors like to engage them.

As long as things go relatively well for them economically, as long as their stomachs are full, Pussyfooters may be expected to go on pussyfooting. Only a solar plexus variety of racism is ever likely to rouse them from their racelessness.

But every day countless little economic and social clashes, countless little unattractive slices of American life eat away at Pussyfooter noninvolvement. Every day the Majority assistant manager at the expensive resort hotel welcomes a greater and greater influx of noisy minority millionaires. Every day the Majority artist, poet, playwright, and novelist must cope with an even tighter minority monopoly of art, literature, and drama. Every day Majority jobseekers and Majority jobholders see their employment opportunities, promotions, or seniority endangered by larger racial quotas for blacks, Hispanics, and Asians and by the extra points given nonwhites in job qualification tests. With crime, rioting, reverse discrimination, and immigration on the rise at home, with billions of dollars still being poured into the Middle East each year, minority racism is becoming so shrill even the deaf are beginning to hear.

Hearing, however, is a long way from understanding. Unlike members of the dynamic minorities who seethe and quiver as a single organism at the faintest hint of reducing welfare programs or restoring an America First foreign policy, Pussyfooters continue to drift supinely on the edge of the great social vortex, whirling clockwise or counterclockwise as public opinion dictates.

4. OLD BELIEVERS. The American political tradition is a rare and delicate blend of English Whiggery, French egalitarianism, classic Stoicism and social Christianity. This complex doctrinal amalgam was once the exclusive ideology of the American Majority. Today, considerably altered in substance and given the name of liberalism, it has been eagerly adopted, if not taken over, by the minorities.[15] Nevertheless, a great many Majority members still call themselves liberals. Those who honestly subscribe to liberalism, not in its perverted modern form, but in its original Lockean, Jeffersonian and Lincolnian version, are here designated as Old Believers. Gracchites and Trucklers are pseudo, hypocritical, opportunistic, or fearful liberals. Pussyfooters are reluctant or fitful liberals. Old Believers belong to the disappearing breed of honest liberals.

Old Believers seldom become particularly prominent or successful in present-day America. On the rare occasions they do, it is not for long. The plain truth is that the liberal establishment cannot stand liberalism in its pure, undiluted form. Old Believers, for example, not only pretend to believe in but *do* believe in the freedom of the printed and spoken word, an intolerable superstition to minority organizations who have drawn up certain critical boundaries for American thought, and equally intolerable to the politicans and opinion molders whose careers are built on a one-dimensional, one-sided, simplistic view of modern society.

Increasingly out of fashion, Old Believers are now mostly found in small universities, in libertarian circles, or among the non-fundamentalist, non-violent, non-permissive clergy. The most vocal are often the descendants of families with roots in the New England town meeting or Populist tradition. In general, they are trying to transplant a faded, withered liberalism which functioned adequately under a special set of historical and genetic conditions to a different age and an often hostile and alien environment— a transplant that is being continuously rejected by the American

---

15. The metamorphosis of liberalism is the subject of Chapter 23.

body politic. All modern teaching to the contrary, liberalism is not independent of time and race.

Two of the most prominent Old Believers in recent times were Dorothy Thompson, the columnist, and Charles Beard, the historian. Dorothy Thompson won nationwide acclaim when she was condemning Nazi persecution of the Jews with Old Testament vehemence. But when, after World War II, she used the same principles and arguments to denounce Jewish dispossession of the Palestinian Arabs, she lost her most important newspaper outlets and died in Portugal in relative obscurity. Charles Beard, in early New Deal days considered America's greatest living historian and an exemplar of liberalism, was cast out of the American intellectual community after he had accused President Roosevelt of unconstitutional acts in the handling of American diplomacy and foreign policy prior to Pearl Harbor.[16]

Old Believers also come in groups, one of the more influential being the Society of Friends or Quakers. Practicing almost total religious, political, and social tolerance and driven by a compulsion for "good works," the Friends pour their efforts and money (of which they have considerable) into projects which actively promote minority racism, although Quaker doctrine bristles at the very concept of race. The Quakers' uncritical acceptance of old-time Anglo-Saxon liberalism as applicable to a modern, racially heterogeneous society has given birth to some strange ideological hybrids within the Quaker community. Drew Pearson, the most vituperative of columnists, Alger Hiss, the most subtle of Communist conspirators, Klaus Fuchs, the most dedicated of atomic spies, as well as a few of the more notorious Majority members of Marxist terror gangs, had Quaker backgrounds.[17] As huge newspaper headlines have constantly reminded us, the distance between the Old Believer and the True Believer is often but a short step.

Quakers and other Old Believers are to be commended for

---

16. Charles Beard, *President Roosevelt and the Coming of the War, 1941*, Yale University Press, New Haven, 1948. The same treatment was extended to the distinguished historian Harry Elmer Barnes, who committed the unforgivable crime of questioning the Holocaust and accusing Roosevelt of having engineered Pearl Harbor. See Barnes's *Revisionism: A Key to Peace and Other Essays*, Cato Institute, San Francisco, Calif., 1980.

17. Pearson's mother, however, was the daughter of a Jewish dentist.

their unshakable faith in human nature. But they must be sharply criticized for their meddlesome, misdirected charity and the warped compassion which have earned them the name of Bleeding Hearts. In some respects, the Old Believer may be compared to the captain of a ship in distress. In another century and with another crew his stubborn courage might have piloted his vessel safely into port. But now, the prisoner of his own outdated seamanship, he steers blindly from reef to reef.

5. PRODITORS.[18] The fifth and final category of those who have brought about the split in the Majority ranks is unique in that its members are tainted with outright disloyalty—not only to the Majority, their population group, but to the United States, their nation. The Gracchite or Truckler, while often going against the best interests of the American people, will not knowingly stray into the ignominious realm of high treason. Franklin D. Roosevelt would compromise with Communists, promote them to high office, give them far more than he received at Teheran and Yalta but would never join them. Lesser politicos and public figures pampered them for years but finally denounced them. The Proditor, on the other hand, seems to take a savage delight in severing all his previous ties, deliberately seeking out his country's enemies, foreign and domestic, and joining enthusiastically in the upending and destruction of everyone and everything once closest to his heart and mind.

The Proditor, in short, takes up permanent residence in that far country where the Gracchite and Truckler dare not penetrate. Though he may fancy himself a Robin Hood, though he may manufacture the most plausible and idealistic excuses for his great and small treacheries, the Proditor—there is no point in being euphemistic—is a common or, more accurately, an uncommon criminal.

The circumstances which produce the Proditor do not defy analysis. As with the Gracchite, there is often the preliminary personal

---

18. The word, which means a particularly nasty form of traitor, is used here in the Shakespearean sense: "thou most usurping proditor, and not protector, of the king or realm." *1 Henry VI*, act 1, sc. 3.

failure. The accompanying drift into exotic political philosophies is more of an indicator than a cause of the treason to come.

Thomas Paine deserted his wife and then filed for bankruptcy. Next he deserted his country, England, went to America, then returned to Europe, where he helped stir up the revolutionary terror in France. In 1796 Paine accused Washington of treachery,[19] a libel which in no way has shaken Paine from his lofty pedestal in the modern liberal pantheon, though recent charges of treason against high officials by non-liberals have not been received so warmly.[20]

John Brown also went through bankruptcy before he found his true vocation: helping to ignite the Civil War. He first tasted blood during the Kansas land settlement disputes, when he and his four sons attacked five sleeping men and hacked them to death with sabers.[21] At Harper's Ferry he seemed as eager to incite the slaves to revolution as he was to free them.

It is inherent in the renegade profession that betrayal is easier the second time around. With scarcely a qualm the defector becomes the redefector and the agent the double agent. Almost ritualistically the Proditor makes a new career out of confessing his previous sins and informing against his previous co-workers and accomplices.

Whittaker Chambers was perhaps the prime example of the redefector. A sad piece of flotsam as a young man, yet gifted with a certain tasteless intellectuality, he became in succession: drifter, Marxist, Communist party courier, senior editor of *Time*, star witness against Alger Hiss, and, in the autumn of his years, author of an agonizing, best-selling confessional. If the theme of *Witness* had not been so banal, Chambers, a late-blooming

---

19. Perhaps in retaliation, Theodore Roosevelt called Paine "a dirty little atheist." Alfred Aldridge, *Man of Reason, The Life of Thomas Paine*, Lippincott, Philadelphia, 1959, pp. 244–45, and Beard, *The Rise of American Civilization*, Vol. 1, p. 270.

20. Namely, Senator Joseph McCarthy's charges against General Marshall and Robert Welch's against Eisenhower.

21. *Dictionary of American Biography*, Scribner's, New York, 1929, Vol. III, p. 132. In all there were eight members of Brown's homicide team. One of them, Theodore Weiner, was an Austrian Jew.

Quaker, might have reached the autobiographical heights of St. Augustine and Rousseau. With tortured introspection and in soap opera detail, he recounted how he first betrayed himself, then his people, then his country, then his adopted country (the Soviet Union), and finally his friends.

Oregon-born John Reed, another noteworthy Proditor, actually became a member of the Communist Party Executive Committee in Moscow. He died, aged thirty-three, at the peak of the Bolshevik ferment and lies in a grave by the Kremlin wall—eight thousand miles from home, but only a stone's throw from the bones of Stalin.

More recent Proditors are: Jane Fonda and Ramsey Clark, both of whom openly trafficked with the enemy during the war in Vietnam; the Majority men and women who belonged to the mixed-race Symbionese Liberation Army that engaged in murder, mayhem, and kidnapping; the Majority students who belonged to the Students for a Democratic Society, another organization dedicated primarily, not to class war, but to a minority racial ascendancy.

Alger Hiss, who almost deserves a special category of his own, dwarfs all other Majority traitors, past and present, both in the essence and extent of his treason. Benedict Arnold, whose forebears were English, who married a Loyalist, and who betrayed a country that was only a few years old, could not be accused of the higher treason of betraying his racial and cultural antecedents. Aaron Burr's treason was not total, since it might possibly have resulted in the establishment of an American empire in Mexico.

Alger Hiss, on the other hand, directly served a revolutionary totalitarian power whose political, social, and economic philosophy and military strategy, were unalterably anti-American. Although he moved in the highest circles and had received many of the more important rewards and honors his country was able to bestow, he put his wide-ranging talents and valuable connections at the disposal of an international complot, whose aim was the destruction or mutation of everything that had made his own success possible. Hiss is the supreme case of the brilliant mind, cut loose from all racial moorings, turning against itself. In his *Divine Comedy,* Dante reserved the greatest torments for Judas, Cassius, and Brutus, the betrayers of their benefactors. He might have been hard put to conceive of a circle of hell adequate for the likes of Alger Hiss.[22]

All Splitters of the Ranks—Gracchites, Trucklers, Pussyfooters, Old Believers, and Proditors—damage the Majority not so much by their activity or passivity, their secret complicity or open collaboration with the opposition, as they do by the confusion with which they surround the Majority-minority confrontation. The mere presence of a Majority member in minority gatherings or street demonstrations, the mere appearance of a Majority name on the executive roster of minority lobbies or fund-raising organizations helps disguise their essentially racial character. Also, by appealing to carefully selected principles of liberalism and conservatism and carefully chosen tenets of religion and ethics, Majority Splitters of the Ranks pose as the only legitimate heirs of a great Western humanitarian tradition. In this guise they can more easily lend the gloss of moral respectability and a sense of Christian urgency to minority *Realpolitik.*

The number and influence of Splitters of the Ranks will not substantially decrease until the Majority member who encourages, defends, or excuses minority-oriented liberalism and minority racism can no longer make a successful career out of depreciating the Majority stake in American civilization. Until such time, the lower ranks of the Majority will have to carry the main burden of the Majority defense, relying chiefly on their instincts, their unbrainwashed common sense, and their inexpungible consciousness of kind—in other words, on their genetic resources.

---

22. The treason of atomic spies Julius and Ethel Rosenberg, Harry Gold, Morton Sobell, and David Greenglass, even though it may have a deadlier impact on the American future (see Chapter 38), lacked the racial and cultural depravity and the self-abasement of the Majority traitors. The Rosenbergs et al. were members of an Unassimilable Minority. Since they started out with fewer real and sentimental attachments to their country of residence, the Gordian knot they had to cut was tied more loosely and made of weaker rope.

CHAPTER 12

The Aesthetic Prop

O NE SUCH GENETIC resource might be defined as the Aesthetic Prop.

Even the most committed racial equalitarian can hardly deny that the physical traits of the idealized Nordic stereotype are considered desirable by most whites and many nonwhites.[1] The current sociological line, partly derived from Marxism, is that these traits are not favored because of any inborn or universal aesthetic preference, but because they are typical of the dominant group and ipso facto bestow higher social status upon their possessors.

It is not difficult to disprove this materialistic conception of aesthetics. The first documented evidence of blondism is an Egyptian wall painting of a daughter of Cheops, Queen Hetep Heres II.[2] If one of the earliest and greatest Egyptian pharaohs had a blond daughter, both he and his wife must have had some blond genes.[3] Blondness, consequently, must have been attractive or prestigious as far back as 3075 B.C. in a highly civilized land populated almost entirely by brunet Mediterraneans.

In classical times there were constant references to the blondism of Greek and Roman gods and demigods.[4] The conventions of

---

1. The stereotype has been described on p. 26.

2. Coon, *The Races of Europe,* p. 98.

3. Blondism is a recessive trait which must be present in both parents. It may be indicated by light brown as well as by blond hair, which even in the purest Nordic is likely to darken with advancing age.

4. The Latin word *flavens,* meaning yellow, golden or auburn, was "the color universally ascribed to the hair of heroic persons by the ancients." J. B. Greenough, *Virgil and the Other Latin Poets,* Ginn & Co., Boston, 1930, p. 133, note 590.

the Greek theater called for a black-wigged and black-haired tyrant, red hair for the dishonest slave, and fair curls for the youthful hero.[5] Ovid and Martial declared that light hair was preferred by Roman matrons for wigs, a preference which spread to America 1,900 years later.[6] Pope Gregory the Great called Anglo-Saxon captives he happened to see in Rome not Angles but "angels" because they were "bright-beautied" and of "gracious outward sheen." [7]

The *Rigsthula,* a cultural poem of the Vikings, describes early Scandinavian society as consisting of a black-haired, wrinkled-skinned lower class, a yeoman class with sturdy bodies and ruddy faces and a nobility with blond hair and skin whiter than driven snow.[8] Of the medieval Caliphate of Cordova it has been written, "Most of the Caliphs were fair or ginger-haired with blue eyes." [9] Perhaps this light coloration was due to intermarriage with the earlier Visigothic nobility. The most noble families in Christian Spain, who claimed direct descent from the Visigoths, had skin so white that the blue network of their veins was highly visible. For this reason *sangre azul* (blue blood) became a synonym for aristocrat. The veins of more plebeian Spaniards were obscured by their darker Mediterranean skin.[10]

More tenuous evidence of the aesthetic appeal of light coloration is offered by the legend of Quetzalcóatl, the Aztec god of the air, who allegedly instructed the copper-skinned Mexicans in the use of metals and in the arts of government. He was said to have a white skin and a beard, the latter being practically un-

---

5. A. E. Haigh, *Attic Theater,* Clarendon Press, Oxford, 1907, pp. 221, 239.

6. "We're paying $10 a pound for Oriental hair and as much as $350 a pound for the best blond European hair," said Adolph Jacoby, an officer in a New York wig firm. *Wall Street Journal,* Oct. 17, 1962, p. 1.

7. Will Durant, *The Age of Faith,* p. 522.

8. Coon, *The Races of Europe,* p. 321.

9. Enrique Sordo, *Moorish Spain,* Crown, New York, 1962, p. 24. Also see *Cities of Destiny,* ed. Arnold Toynbee, McGraw-Hill, New York, 1967. Although it is not generally known, Arabs have always drawn a very distinct color line. In present-day Iraq a citizen can obtain a legal judgment against a person falsely accusing him of Negro ancestry. Carleton Coon, *Caravan,* Henry Holt, New York, 1951, p. 161.

10. Don Quixote says of the fictitious, not the real, Dulcinea, "Cabellos son oro . . . su blancura nieve." Cervantes, *Don Quijote,* E. Castilla, Madrid, 1966, p. 98.

known to the almost beardless natives. When he had incurred the wrath of another divinity he left Mexico and sailed east across the Great Ocean, saying he would return. In Peru, a somewhat similar myth has white, bearded men conquering the pre-Incan inhabitants and imparting to them the blessings of civilization.[11]

Today the Aesthetic Prop still persists in Latin America, including those areas where Negroes and Indians predominate. As remote a town as Ita on the upper Amazon has a simple rule of thumb for status: the lighter the skin, the higher the class, and a light complexion is acknowledged as the hallmark of beauty.[12] Even in Japan pale complexions are favored. The Japanese expression for well-born is "deep window," which refers to the lighter pigmentation of people shielded from the sun by thick-walled houses.[13]

The purely aesthetic appeal of Nordicism is undeniable throughout the contemporary United States. Light-haired, long-headed, narrow-faced males still appear in most men's fashion ads, while in the so-called counterculture, supposedly a complete rejection of present-day tastes and styles, the girl with the blond hair, whether long and straight or curled, frizzled, or cornrowed, still remains the symbol of femininity. Each year millions of American women spend tens of millions of dollars on hair bleaches. Everywhere it is proclaimed that "blondes have more fun," and the phrase "gentlemen prefer blondes" has become a twentieth-century proverb.[14]

11. William H. Prescott, *The History of the Conquest of Mexico and the History of the Conquest of Peru,* Modern Library, New York, pp. 39, 736. Other investigators of Mexico's prehistory deny that Quetzalcóatl had white physical traits. César A. Sáenz, *Quetzalcóatl,* Instituto Nacional de Antropología e Historia, Mexico, 1962. For a series of lively asides on the Mexican god, see D. H. Lawrence, *The Plumed Serpent.* Those inclined to wring history from myth can hardly escape feeling that Quetzalcoatl was a shipwrecked, homesick Viking.

12. Charles Wagley, *Amazon Town,* Macmillan, New York, 1953, pp. 128–40.

13. *Life,* Sept. 5, 1969, p. 42.

14. *Gentlemen Prefer Blondes* was the title of a novel by a brunette Hollywood film writer, Anita Loos, whose father was of French descent. Miss Loos later explained why she had written the book: "The satisfaction of getting even with Mae Davis for seducing the man I loved [H. L. Mencken] more than paid for the pains [of writing it]." She continued her vendetta against blondes in another novel, *But Gentlemen Marry Brunettes.* In spite of the author's best intentions, however, the "dumb" gold-digging Lorelei has entered American folklore as

The avalanche of artificial blondes unloosed by such publicity, accompanied by the incongruous and ugly contrast of platinum hair with dark eyes, dark eyebrows, and olive skin, should have been enough to destroy the blond ideal forever. That it did not verified an enduring, deeply ingrained aesthetic preference on the part of most Americans.[15] Many other ways of tampering with nature—nose straightening and nose bobbing, electrolysis to raise the hair line and heighten the brow and forehead, elevator shoes to increase stature—have been adopted or tried by minority members striving to give themselves a "Majority look." [16]

The power of the Aesthetic Prop is also apparent in present-day American mating and dating habits. Although the Majority is in the descendant, the most dynamic and successful minority males often marry or at least seek out the company of Majority females. For proof one has only to look at the couples who throng the most expensive nightclubs, restaurants and resort hotels. Moreover, the Nordic physical ideal has not only been the marriage ideal of the minority "New Rich" in America, but of European social climbers for at least a thousand years.

The relatively small number of Nordics in the world—an estimated 300,000,000 in 1980 and fast declining—has doubtlessly enhanced their aesthetic appeal. Rarity per se exercises a special attraction, and what is beautiful generally contains an element of the uncommon and esoteric. Just as the pure Nordic is a rarity among the part-Nordics who make up most of the American Majority, so the American Majority represents a rare racial type to the world's population as a whole. To whites and nonwhites alike,

---

the knowing young blonde who usually gets her way. Anita Loos, *A Girl Like I*, Viking Press, New York, 1966, p. 274.

15. Blondism is most appealing when accompanied by other Nordic physical characteristics. If it were not for the color sensitivity of most Americans, Nordic pigmentation and skin shade might be less important than other Nordic traits as criteria of male handsomeness and female beauty. Certainly "tall, dark and handsome" Nordic-Mediterraneans are more attractive physical specimens than shorter, squatter, though blonder, types.

16. Suntan mania does not contradict the logic of the Aesthetic Prop. The ultraviolet rays of the sun may darken the skin, but they also lighten the hair and provide a pleasing contrast to light eyes and other manifestations of light coloration. Basically, a suntan is a sign of health and wealth—both a temporary camouflage and an exotic masquerade.

Nordics are the personification of the white race because they are the "whitest" whites.

Perhaps the best description of the physical attractiveness of the Majority has been given by Wyndham Lewis:

> It is a common experience in talking to Americans to hear some magnificent human specimen (who is obviously the issue of say a first-class Swede and a magnificent Swissess, with a little Irish and a touch of Basque) refer to himself as a "mongrel." It is inconceivable yet indeed that is how a "mixed" product is apt to look upon this superb marriage of Scandinavian, Goth, and Celt—all stocks as closely related in blood . . . as the Brahmanic caste in India. . . . All you have to do is look at this sterling type of "mixed" American to admire the purity of line and fine adjustment achieved by the conjunction of these sister stocks. Far from being a "mongrel," of course, he is a sort of super-European; the best of several closely allied stocks have met in him, in exactly the same way as was constantly happening in the noble European families—where the issue of marriage between nobles, whether from England and Italy, or Spain and Russia, did not constitute a "half-breed," but rather a more exalted feudal product. . . .[17]

The possibility that the Aesthetic Prop goes beneath the skin, that there is a relationship between what Herbert Spencer called "beauty of character and beauty of aspect," raises problems which are beyond the scope of this study.[18] However, without becoming too entangled in psychobiological complexities, one must agree with Spencer's suggestion that beauty is "idealization away from the ape." Three principal sources of ugliness, according to Spencer, are recession of the forehead, jaw protuberances, and large cheekbones. Consequently only those human beings are handsome whose jaws and cheekbones have been pulled back and nasal depressions filled in. Other qualifications are the absence of any forward opening of the nostrils and a small mouth.[19]

---

17. Wyndham Lewis, *Pale Face,* Chatto and Windus, London, 1929, p. 278.

18. Herbert Spencer, *Essays,* Appleton, New York, 1910, Vol. II, p. 387. Schopenhauer was another philosopher who believed in a connection between outward appearance and inner being. The mouth, he said, expresses the thought of man, while the face expresses the thought of nature and the thought of the species. "Vielmehr ist jedes Menschengesicht eine Hieroglyphe," is how Schopenhauer summed up his opinion of the matter. *Parerga und Paralipomena,* F. A. Brockhaus, Leipzig, 1877, pp. 670–71.

19. Spencer, op. cit., pp. 390–92.

Since the idealized Nordic meets these requirements more closely than other racial stereotypes, it follows that Nordics are the least "apelike" of mortals and so most deserving of first prize in the ethnic beauty contest.[20]

The Aesthetic Prop, moreover, has often been carried over into the realm of ethics and even politics. Plato was neither the first nor the last to equate beauty with the good. All else being equal, the handsome (i.e., Nordic-looking) politician or statesman has usually been able to evoke more deference and dedication than his less handsome (i.e., less Nordic-looking) rival, whose unprepossessing appearance may be a severe handicap in winning and keeping a following. Realizing the force these aesthetic standards still exert in Western society, a perceptive intellectual like Marxist philosopher George Lukács, who stands well outside the Northern European genetic and cultural locus, has reacted by having a "liberal fear of beauty, with [an] obsessive suspicion that beauty and, by inference, a good deal of art is a mask preventing a clear view of human evil and suffering." [21]

It was the Aesthetic Prop which prolonged the survival of the decadent Teutonic aristocracy in Central and Southern Europe centuries after it had been stripped of its preeminence. It is the same Aesthetic Prop which helps the American Majority to hold on to the trappings, but not the substance, of its former power.[22]

---

20. In a work that falls distressingly short of *Moby Dick* and *Billy Budd,* Melville carried this physical argument into the spiritual plane when he attempted to equate blondism with goodness. In *Pierre,* Melville has Isabel complain: "Oh, God! that I had been born with blue eyes, and fair hair! These make the livery of heaven! Heard ye ever yet of a good angel with dark eyes, Pierre?—no, no, no—all blue, blue, blue—heaven's own blue. . . ." *Pierre,* Hendrick's House, New York, 1957, p. 370. In contrast, Melville's novella, *Benito Cereno,* which has only been matched by Joseph Conrad's *Heart of Darkness* in plumbing the dark side of Negro mentality, seemed to propose a correlation between blackness and evil. Montesquieu and Mozart were also charter members of the "Black is not Beautiful" club. In the latter's opera, *Die Zauberflöte,* his black villain, Monostatos, sings, "Weiss ist schön, weil ein Schwarzer hässlich ist."

21. *Times Literary Supplement,* June 18, 1970, p. 660.

22. After trying to persuade Negro girls to go back to natural, woolly hairdos and give up bleaching creams and Western dress styles, Negro militants themselves still search out white girls, preferring, when they have enough money for vacations abroad, Scandinavia to Africa. Fletcher Knebel, "The Black Woman's Burden," *Look,* Sept. 23, 1969, pp. 77–79.

Only in the sector of aesthetics, through the pervasiveness of the idealized Nordic biological type and its continued acceptance as the national template of physical charm and attractiveness, has the Majority been able to mount a small but successful holding action in the present racial melee.

PART IV

The Minority Challenge

CHAPTER 13

Assimilable White Minorities

IT HAS BEEN SHOWN that 22,114,000 Americans—9.8 percent of the population—belong to what have been described as Assimilable White Minorities.[1] In the terminology of physical anthropology, these minorities are predominantly Alpine, a designation which in this study also encompasses the Dinaric and East Baltic races. Geographically speaking, their countries of origin have been Ireland, France (in the case of the French Canadians and the Louisiana French), Russia and the Slavic lands, and various Central European and Balkan states. Mostly descended from those who arrived in the New Immigration, Assimilable Minority members, owing to their not too remote racial and cultural affinity to the Majority, have the capability of being absorbed into the Majority population matrix. Since hundreds of thousands are doing so each year, they might be more properly defined as assimilating rather than assimilable.

In the following sections which list and briefly examine the Assimilable Minorities, no Northern European population group, except the Irish and the Finns, will be found. This may seem strange, since many of the Germans, Dutch, Belgians, and more than a few of the Scandinavians and British who came to America were Alpines and part of the New Immigration. But Alpinism by itself is no serious impediment to the assimilation process. Neither is late arrival. What does retard or hinder the assimilation of Assimilable Minorities is a combination or, more precisely, a manifold of Alpinism, late arrival, religious and linguistic differ-

---

1. Table V, p. 64.

125

ences, a tradition of political absolutism and peonage and, in the case of the Slavic groups, an Eastern European rather than a Western cultural heritage.

Because Alpines of Northern European descent have not had this multiplicity of obstacles blocking their assimilation, most have been given Majority status and considered assimilated. The same dispensation has been extended to Alpines of Swiss, Austrian, and Northern French origin. But this is not to say that *all* Americans of Northern European descent, Nordic or Alpine, are Majority members in good standing. A substantial quota of Irish Americans have so far successfully resisted full assimilation. Other Americans of equally authentic Northern European lineage and with family trees going back to the Old Immigration still retain such minority habits as clannishness and bloc-voting [2] and cling to the customs and speech of their Old World points of origin. A rapidly diminishing number of Pennsylvania Dutch and German Catholics in the Ohio Valley are two examples. Some Welsh and Scots, minorities in their own homelands, brought along a persistent minority consciousness that has only been partly eradicated. Certain religious sects teach their members the necessity of moral or physical secession from society at large. All these groups, except the Irish, are small in number, isolated geographically and exercise very little influence on the national or even on the regional scene. Because of their separateness it is probably more accurate to classify them as clans or cults than as bona fide minorities.

Another type of Northern European who cannot be described as fully assimilated is the first-generation and, occasionally, the second-generation American from Britain, Germany, Holland, Scandinavia, or Canada. No matter how closely he approximates the Majority racial and cultural norm, the newcomer, as opposed to the latecomer, almost always retains some traces of minority consciousness—a consciousness which he often manages to pass

---

2. A nationwide but indecisive German vote was noted as late as World War II, when some German Americans turned against President Roosevelt because of his interventionist policies. Both German Protestants and German Catholics voted in large numbers for Eisenhower, but many of the latter switched back to the Democratic party when Catholic John Kennedy ran for the presidency. Kevin Phillips, *The Emerging Republican Majority,* Arlington House, New Rochelle, N.Y., 1969, pp. 296, 314, 339.

on to his children and sometimes, depending on its intensity, to his grandchildren. The foreign birth of such contemporary left-leaning public figures as Cyrus Eaton, John Galbraith, and James Reston has probably had more influence than they would admit on their political and social attitudes. If Earl Warren's father had been born in America instead of Norway and if he had not been such an intransigent socialist, it is possible that his son, when Chief Justice of the Supreme Court, would have been more concerned with Majority than minority interests.[3]

Since it is only a question of time until the progeny of most Northern European holdouts will be part and parcel of the Majority, attention will now be focused on the Assimilable Minorities proper. These are the population groups who pride themselves on their differences and are reticent about assimilation—a process they still regard as a cultural leap into the unknown and a form of ethnic surrender. It is exactly these differences, both real and imagined, which encourage their physical and occupational segregation, which in turn reinforces their separateness. As they pass in review, the diversity of these minorities will become obvious. So will their on-again, off-again participation in the war being waged against the Majority. Although Unassimilable Minorities have taken the lead in this conflict, the Assimilable Minorities, as if unaware they are being phased out by their accelerating rate of assimilation, still lend considerable conscious or unconscious support to the minority cause.

IRISH:[4] One of the major ironies of American history is that the minority which has wielded the most political power in the United States in the first half of the twentieth-century had until its arrival in the New World a very limited experience with the democratic process.[5] Although it was not necessarily a personal

---

3. Reston was born in Scotland. Eaton and Galbraith in Canada. Like Warren, Senator Henry Jackson and 1980 presidential candidate John Anderson had Scandinavian immigrant fathers.

4. For the distinction between the Catholic Irish and the Protestant Scotch-Irish from Ulster, see footnote 9, p. 43.

5. "The importance of immigrant groups in the history of American politics can hardly be overestimated and in this history the Irish have played the principal role." *One America*, p. 61.

failing or an innate antipathy to democracy—their British masters handed out freedom sparingly—the Irish were never able to establish a permanent representative government in Ireland until comparatively recently. Only in 1948, when the great Irish overseas migrations to America had long since ended, did Ireland after a few decades of commonwealth status achieve complete independence. Ireland or Eire may be a republic now, but the ancestors of present-day Irish Americans had for the most part never passed through the long, exasperating, but richly instructive cycle of political apprenticeship which led from feudal aristocracy through absolute monarchy to representative democracy.

In the detailed racial study of ten thousand Irish males in Ireland by E. A. Hooton, 28.9 percent were classified as Nordic-Mediterranean, 25.3 as Keltic, 18.6 Dinaric, 18.4 Nordic-Alpine, 6.8 predominantly Nordic, 1.1 East Baltic, 0.6 Pure Nordic, 0.3 Pure Mediterranean.[6] Carleton Coon, whose racial terminology often differs from Dr. Hooton's, speaks of a relatively large Upper Palaeolithic streak in the Irish racial makeup.[7] Irish physical types consequently range from a Nordic-flavored racial mix, scarcely distinguishable from most other Northern Europeans,[8] to the heavy-boned, heavy-set, broad-faced, large-framed Upper Palaeolithic, supposedly the genetic remains of an older European race which fled to the outermost regions of Western Europe to escape the Kelts and other invaders. One distinctive breed is the "Black Irish," the inhabitants of the Emerald Isle with the most pronounced Mediterranean cast, the reputed descendants of prehistoric Atlantic-Mediterraneans who cruised up the Atlantic coast from Gibraltar and Portugal. Some Black Irish may be the distant offspring of sailors from the ship-wrecked Spanish Armada.

The racial balance of Ireland has been reproduced fairly closely by the rank and file of Irish Americans, though possibly with less accent on the Nordic element. The Irish exodus was composed

---

6. E. A. Hooton and C. W. Dupertuis, *The Physical Anthropology of Ireland,* Papers of the Peabody Museum of Archaeology and Ethnology, Harvard University, Vol. XXX, Nos. 1–2, p. 143.

7. Coon, *The Races of Europe,* pp. 376–84.

8. Wyndham Lewis, describing a mixed Anglo-Irish demonstration in London, wrote, "I was never able to discover which were Irish and which were English . . . they looked to me exactly the same." *Pale Face,* pp. 284–85.

chiefly of the poorer segments of the population—the tenant farmers and the bog-dwelling Western Irish, who were most removed in time and place from the more Nordic Irish in the east, where Vikings, Normans, and English had been settled for centuries. One set of physical traits—pug nose, freckles, red hair and the "world's bluest eyes"—although not exclusively Irish, has come to be accepted, at least in America, as the basic ingredients of a common Irish stereotype.[9]

The racial composition of the Irish in Ireland provides a clue to one of the greatest difficulties in the compilation of an accurate census of American minorities, the difficulty of determining how many of the sixteen million Irish-American Catholics [10] belong to the Assimilable category, and how many are already assimilated and are full-fledged members of the Majority.

One way of attacking the problem is to take the blonder elements among Catholics of Irish descent, the elements which more closely approximate the median Northern European physical type, and to consider them assimilated rather than assimilable. E. A. Hooton's racial studies of Ireland can be used as a guide. According to Hooton, the Nordic Alpines, the Predominantly Nordics and the Pure Nordics account for 25.8 percent of the Irish of Ireland. This might be reduced to 20 percent for the Irish immigration to allow for the allegedly smaller proportion of Nordic elements. If these horseback estimates are not unacceptable, then 3,200,000 Irish Americans (20 percent of 16,000,000) are assimilated and 12,800,000 (80 percent) can be classified as assimilable.

---

9. Coon, op. cit., pp. 371, 381, 383. Bushy eyebrows, large heads, prominent chins, long and convex upper lips, and great malar breadth are other fairly common Irish traits.

10. According to *Life* (March 17, 1961, p. 114), 29,000,000 living Americans claim some Irish descent. The subject here, however, is not those Americans who have one or two remote Irish ancestors. It is those Irish Americans who still remain firm Catholics, are usually Irish on both sides and are quite aware of their origins. These are the Irish Americans Andrew Rolle and Paul Blanshard probably had in mind when they estimated their number at 15 million and 15–16 million, respectively. Rolle, *The Immigrants Upraised,* University of Oklahoma Press, 1968, p. 304, and Blanshard, *American Freedom and Catholic Power,* Beacon Press, Boston, 1949, p. 263. Blanshard's higher figure has been taken to compensate for the birthrate of a population group whose Church still forbids contraception.

The Irish voting record can also be of assistance in discovering the proportion of assimilated and assimilable Irish. In the 1952 presidential race, it was estimated that 38 percent of the Catholic vote went to Eisenhower, and that an even higher ratio of Catholics voted Republican in the 1956 election.[11] In 1960, however, a Gallup Poll stated that three out of five Catholics who voted for Eisenhower switched to Kennedy.[12] Applying these percentages to the Irish segment of the Catholic population and to the Irish-American population as a whole, as well as to Irish voters, this means that 6,080,000 Irish (38 percent) were in the Republican ranks in 1952 and perhaps as many as 7,000,000 in 1956. Then in 1960, 60 percent of these temporary Republicans and their families returned to the Democratic fold to support Kennedy. This left 2,800,000 Irish Republicans for Nixon, the non-Catholic loser—certainly an acid test of assimilation for Irish Americans.[13] Subtracting 2,800,000 from the total number of Catholics of Irish descent leaves 13,200,000 who can be counted as assimilable.

The 13,200,000 figure obtained by the Irish vote analysis is very close to the 12,800,000 obtained by racial estimates and projections. Averaging the two yields 13,000,000 as a fair estimate of the size of the Irish-American Assimilable Minority. In general these are the Irish Americans who still congregate in the big cities, who faithfully back Irish-American political machines, and who vote for Senator Edward Kennedy despite Chappaquiddick, and for House Speaker Thomas O'Neill despite his support of forced busing. These are the Irish Americans whom Carl Wittke had in mind when he described their character as a

> mixture of flaming ego, hot temper, stubbornness, great personal charm and warmth and a wit that shines through adversity. An

---

11. William Shannon, *The American Irish*, Macmillan, New York, 1963, pp. 410–11.

12. Ibid.

13. During the 1960 election Nixon, playing for the Majority vote, never talked about his Irish ancestry, while Kennedy with his unmistakable Keltic looks played his racial and religious background to the hilt in Northern urban areas. In the 1970 congressional election campaign, however, Nixon took a trip to Ireland where much was made of his Irish forebears. As part of their "blue-collar" and "law-and-order" strategy, the Republicans had decided to make an open bid for the Irish vote. As mentioned earlier in this study, Ronald Reagan was not at all reluctant to advertise his Irish father in the 1980 presidential contest.

irrepressible buoyancy, a vivacious spirit, a kindliness and tolerance of the common frailties of men . . . quick to anger and quick to forgive, frequently duped . . . generous, hospitable and loyal.

Wittke also asserted that the Irish, although demonstrating a talent for art and literature, have never been particularly outstanding in the fields of science and invention.[14]

It was the great potato famine of the 1840s that first brought the Irish to the United States in large numbers. They carried with them bitter memories of starvation and centuries of humiliation and suppression under the heel of the English. Once they had finished their pick and shovel apprenticeship on the Erie Canal and on the railroads, they gathered together in large cities and often renewed their feud with the British Empire by extending it to Americans of English extraction.

As Irish Americans began to control the Democratic political machine in the northern cities, they often used them as weapons of defense and revenge against the Republican party, which in many Irish-American eyes represented the interests of the English-descended establishment. Chicago Mayor "Big Bill" Thompson's well-publicized promise in 1927 to "make the King of England keep his snoot out of America" was a typical appeal to Gaelic Anglophobia.[15] A later flare-up of this century-old hostility took place in the 1966 New York City subway strike when Michael Quill, head of the Transport Workers Union and a former member of the Irish Republican Army, attempted to turn the walkout into a personal vendetta against Mayor John Lindsay, who in spite of his Gracchite ultraliberalism was deemed to be, if not as bad as an Orangeman, at least as bad as a WASP.[16]

It is almost impossible to write about the Irish in the United States without bringing in the Roman Catholic Church. Irish Catholicism, in which both men and women participate, is vastly different from Catholicism in Spain, France and Italy, where the congregations consist almost entirely of women and where anticlericalism is a traditional male prerogative. The cherished place

14. *The Irish in America*, Louisiana State University Press, Baton Rouge, 1956, p. 233.

15. *Literary Digest*, Nov. 5, 1927, p. 5.

16. *New York Times*, Jan. 2, 1966, p. 1, and Jan. 4, 1966, pp. 14, 17. The whole atmosphere surrounding the strike talks, according to one *Times* reporter was, "Down the English Protestant! Up the Irish!"

in their hearts that Irishmen everywhere reserve for the Church is largely due to its participation in the long struggle for Irish independence. Irish priests often had as high a price put on their heads as lay patriots, and the Church used all its resources to keep Irish morale from sagging in the darkest hours of the Protestant occupation. Consequently, there is a secular as well as a religious link between the Catholic Church and most Irish Americans, a stronger link than that between the Church and the people in Latin countries, where during much of medieval and modern history Catholic prelates allied themselves with aristocrats, monarchs and plutocrats.

Having helped keep Ireland alive for so many centuries, the Catholic Church has fought a dogged, rearguard action to insulate its Irish-American flock against the allurements and pressures of assimilation. The Church has always feared that joining the predominantly non-Irish, non-Catholic Majority might be the first step in abandoning the faith, a faith that fills pews and collection boxes to overflowing. Although the Irish account for less than half of all American Catholics, they remain the dominant Catholic congregaton and furnish most of the money and most of the hierarchy. Apart from the financial implications, a decline in Irish ethnocentrism and an accompanying decline in Irish religious fervor might expose the Church to a takeover by Poles, Italians, or even Hispanics.

To preclude such a development, the Church has endeavored to keep the fires of Irish racism burning by a network of parochial schools, opposition to birth control, restrictions against marrying non-Catholics, and the subsidizing and promotion of a multitude of Irish political and social activities. Unquestionably Catholicism must bear a great deal of the responsibility for the lingering, hyphenated status of many fifth- and sixth-generation Irish Americans. But despite priestly qualms, most of the Irish who attached themselves to the Majority managed to take their religion along with them.

For obvious reasons the Catholic Church is officially opposed to Marxism and communism, particularly their atheistic facets. But it does not follow that all Irish Americans are. Inspired as much by timeworn national and racial antipathies as by class antagonisms, Irish leaders have been in and out of the American Socialist and Communist movements since their beginnings. William Z. Foster, whose father was an "English-hating Irish immigrant," was the Grand Old Man of American communism and Elizabeth Gurley Flynn was the Grand Old Lady.[17] Jim Larkin was a prominent Communist rabble-rouser in the 1920s and served a term in Sing Sing before being pardoned by Al Smith, the Catholic governor of New York. Vincent Sheean, who later became a devotee of Mahatma Gandhi, wrote a book, *Personal History,* which probably attracted more Americans to the Communist cause than anything written by Engels, Marx or Lenin.

As might be expected of an extremely verbal, hard-fisted, hard-working immigrant group, the Irish have been deeply involved in American unionism, ranging from the most radical labor organizations [18] to the most conservative. John Mitchell was a founder of the United Mine Workers and P. J. McGuire one of the organizers of the American Federation of Labor. Other noted Irish-American labor leaders were Joseph Curran of the National Maritime Union, P. H. Morrissey of the Brotherhood of Railway Firemen, Teddy Gleason of the International Longshoremen's Association, James O'Connell of the International Association of Machinists, Michael Quill of the Transport Workers Union and, neither last nor least, George Meany, who headed the AFL-CIO for a quarter of a century.

Irish brawn helped build industrial America and Irish blood helped defend it. There have been great Americans of Irish descent in every era of America history and every sector of American activity. The size of the Irish contribution is impossible to determine. Historian Samuel Eliot Morison says that it has been less than the German.[19] In any case it has been considerable, and America would not be the same without it.

---

17. Flynn once wrote, "The awareness of being Irish came to us as small children, through plaintive song and heroic story . . . we drew in a burning hatred of British rule with our mother's milk." Shannon, *The American Irish,* pp. 166–67. A more modern Irish-American lady radical is Kate Millett, married to a Japanese and a "philosopher" of the Women's Liberation Movement. *New York Times,* Aug. 27, 1970, p. 30.

18. For the most radical of all, the Molly Maguires, see footnote, p. 368.

19. Samuel Morison, *The Oxford History of the American People,* Oxford University Press, New York, 1965, pp. 480–81.

While Irish-American political passions have been high, Irish political standards have frequently been low. The scandals of such mayors as Jimmy Walker and William O'Dwyer of New York, James Curley of Boston, and John Houlihan of Oakland, California, attest to the success of the Irish in securing public office and their failure to dignify it. For many years Boston, New York, Chicago, San Francisco, and several other large American cities were little more than Irish political fiefs, where the party bosses turned out huge pluralities for the candidates of their choice regardless of the issues. Recently, however, the Irish have been forced to share their urban bailiwicks with other minorities and in some cities their once undisputed political control has ended.

Generally voting the straight Democratic ticket *en bloc*, Irish Catholics, as previously noted, left their party in large numbers in 1952, when they helped swing the election to Dwight Eisenhower. The Democratic allegiance of the party bosses remained unshaken, but the ivory-towered liberalism of presidential candidate Adlai Stevenson, veering more and more toward appeasement of the Soviet Union, was too much for many of the faithful, who for the first time had achieved a certain middle-class respectability and affluence in the postwar economic boom. It is this same respectability and affluence, when spread among other Assimilable Minorities, which so often gives birth to Republican voting habits.

But most of the Irish closed ranks again in the 1960 presidential election, when they had a chance to vote for one of their own, and a war hero at that. John F. Kennedy, with the aid of his father's great wealth and his proliferating relatives, gave new life to Irish-American politics. The emergence of the Kennedy dynasty, despite the assassination of its two leading members within a six-year period, will probably provide a rallying point—and a mystique—for old-fashioned Irish bossism for many years to come. The nomination of George McGovern as the 1972 Democratic standard bearer, however, provoked another mass defection to the Republican ticket. When and if Senator Edward Kennedy becomes the Democratic presidential nominee, the pendulum may be expected to swing back again.

More pragmatic than ideological, the typical Irish machine politician wants the people's votes, not the people's minds. Although liberalism is the accepted theology of the Democratic party, Irish bosses treat it largely as a vote-getting device and in the privacy of their homes their own political beliefs are likely to have a markedly antiliberal tone. When foreign policy is involved, these beliefs are often brought into the open. Consequently the Irish have exercised a steadying and conservative influence over American international relations in recent decades, first by helping to preserve American neutrality during the Spanish Civil War,[20] second by supporting Catholic anti-Communist parties in Western Europe after World War II. Without this support a much larger portion of Europe might now be Sovietized.

At home, fear and hatred of communism inspired some Irish-American mavericks to cross party lines and attack Marxism and Marxist apologists with the demagogic innuendo that had hitherto been the monopoly of Communists and vitriolic liberals. Two such individuals were Father Coughlin, the radio priest of the New Deal era, and Senator Joseph McCarthy, not to be confused with Eugene McCarthy, the eccentric Irish-Scandinavian senator from Minnesota. A loftier intellectual tone was provided by William F. Buckley, Jr.—like President Kennedy the son of an Irish multimillionaire—whose acerbic wit and recondite posing recalled such European conservatives as Léon Daudet and Charles Maurras of the *Action Française*.[21] True to the equalitarian philosophy of their Church, many of the leading Irish-American conservatives have staunchly supported racial integration. In speaking of the Irish component of conservatism, it must not be forgotten that President Nixon "was elected to the presidency in a campaign substantially planned by New York Irish conservatives." [22]

20. Joseph Kennedy, while ambassador to Britain, took the lead in defending the Embargo Act, which forbade the shipment of war materials to both the Franco and Republican forces, at a time most American officials were ready to lift it. Hugh Thomas, *The Spanish Civil War*, Harper & Row, New York, 1961, pp. 536, 614.

21. James Buckley, William's brother, who served a term as senator from New York and ran unsuccessfully in 1980 for senator from Connecticut, and Congressman Philip Crane represent an Irish conservative clique within the Republican party that counterbalances the so-called Irish Mafia that surrounds the Kennedy faction in the Democratic party.

22. Phillips, op. cit., pp. 174–75. Nixon's campaign manager in 1968 was John N. Mitchell, later attorney general, ultimately a chief villain of Watergate. Mitchell is a Presbyterian with an Irish mother. Mitchell's deputy was banker Peter Marcus Flanigan. Many former Nixon idea men, notably Patrick Buchanan, are also of Irish descent.

Because of their Northern European racial and cultural affinities, because they have become in so many ways so typically and so generically American, it is difficult to claim Irish Americans still belong to a minority, even an assimilable one. On the surface, the American of Irish descent is a made-to-order Majority prototype. He is patriotic. He is willing to live and let live. He is not as obtrusive, acquisitive, or aggressive as members of some other minorities. He does not crowd the professions. His economic worth is not above average. It is only when matters of faith, pride, machine politics, and Ireland come into play—matters about which they are still supremely sensitive—that many Irish Americans defiantly display their minority colors. And when they do, when they continue to play minority politics, when they are willing to join their own worst enemies against the Majority, then this Irish hard-core of 13,000,000 must be classified as assimilable rather than assimilated.

But there is little doubt that this number will continue to diminish. Many of the once-compelling reasons for Irish-American separateness have now evaporated. Time, distance, and the decline and fall of the British Empire have mellowed the ancient grudge against England. (Only Ulster remains a running sore and daily reminder of the ancient feud.) The American Majority, in which the Irish used to find so many distasteful English characteristics and customs, is no longer uniquely Anglo-Saxon and has acquired a more evenly distributed Northern European (including Irish) population base. As for religious differences, the hard-line Protestantism of the frontier, resonant with the anti-Catholic and anti-papal overtones of the Reformation, has dissolved into a sweetness-and-light deism whose main concerns are tolerance and social justice. Liberalizing directives from Rome, questions about papal infallibility, demands to end the celibacy of the priesthood, the increasing number of radical priests, the de-Latinized mass, controversy over birth control and abortion—all these bits and pieces of the ecumenical movement are undermining the age-old monolithic structure of Catholicism [23] and in the process lowering the

---

23. The link between the Irish and Roman Catholicism is not congenital or unbreakable. Many of the greatest Irishmen, perhaps the very greatest, were Protestants or non-believers. The list includes Parnell, the dedicated nineteenth-century Irish freedom fighter, Douglas Hyde, Ireland's first president, Swift,

Church's prestige in the eyes and ears of those who prefer to take their religion with a large seasoning of dogma, dramaturgy and ritual.

Before the Romans came to the British Isles, the Kelts (early Nordics) of Ireland and Britain were similar in culture, civilization and race. After the departure of the Romans and the arrival of the Christian missionaries, Ireland and England shared the same religion for more than a thousand years, although for half of this period Irish Catholicism was more Keltic than Roman. If the two peoples cannot capitalize on their similarities in order to smooth over their differences in the Old World, perhaps their descendants will in the New, as so many already have. At all events it would not seem logical for *any* Irish Americans to tie their future to the coattails of irresponsible ethnic dynasts, whose principal function is to serve as political stalking-horses for liberals and Unassimilable Minorities. But taking a perverse pleasure in doing the illogical is something for which the Irish have long been famous.

Assimilable Irish Americans comprise the largest white minority and the second largest of all minorities. When and how they choose sides in the growing racial confrontation will have a crucial effect on the final pattern of American society. It goes without saying that it is in their deepest interests to see that the Majority restores the traditional American racial and cultural mold. If the mold is permanently broken, the assimilable Irish American stands to lose as much as his already assimilated brother and every other American of Northern Europe descent.

FINNISH AND BALTIC MINORITIES: Some Finns were associated with the original Swedish immigration which took place when Americans were still British colonials. But appreciable numbers did not arrive in the United States until 1864. Many went to Michigan to become miners and others started farms in Minnesota. Russian political repression in the late nineteenth century drove

---

Goldsmith, Sheridan, Wilde, Shaw, Yeats, Joyce, Synge, and O'Casey. Paul Carroll, the modern Irish playwright, echoes in his *White Steed* the feelings of many of his countrymen when his heroine inveighs against the priests and the "little men" for depriving Irishmen of their primeval pride and virility.

more Finns to America. According to one authoritative estimate, there are now 400,000 Americans of Finnish descent.[24]

In spite of their difficult, agglutinative language and their supposed Eurasian origin, most Finnish Americans are hardly to be distinguished from their Old World neighbors, the Swedes. They are nearly as Nordic and equally as Protestant (Lutheran). Only their late arrival in the United States and the nationalistic feelings still engendered by Russian bullying and aggression have delayed their complete assimilation. After World War I, Finnish Americans were accorded a sort of honorary membership in the Majority when Finland was saluted as the only European nation to pay its war debt in full. The Protestant Ethic may have died in Boston, but it lived on in Helsinki.

Like the Finns, members of the Estonian, Latvian, and Lithuanian minorities—presently numbering about 200,000, 86,000 and 331,000, respectively—came from countries situated on the shores of the Baltic. Unlike Finland, these countries no longer exist. The irredentist feelings kindled by Soviet imperialism have tended to accent the group solidarity of the Baltic minorities and decelerate assimilation. From the racial standpoint, Estonians, Latvians, and Letts (Lithuanians) have the proper physical traits for membership in the Majority. But as Eastern Europeans and as members of the New Immigration, most of them still remain in the Assimilable category. Of the three Baltic minorities, the Lithuanian Americans, who are darker than the Latvians and Estonians, and are Catholic instead of Protestant, will probably be the last to be assimilated.

SLAVIC MINORITIES: The Russians were the only whites to migrate to America by an eastward route, arriving first in Alaska and then proceeding down the Washington, Oregon and California coastline. By the time of Seward's Folly in 1867, however, the Czarist-sponsored expansion into North America had lost almost all its momentum and was recoiling to Siberia. Large-scale Russian migration, this time by the conventional westward pas-

24. *One America*, p. 206. Unless otherwise noted all subsequent minority group numberings in this study have been taken from *One America* or the *Harvard Encyclopedia of American Ethnic Groups*.

sage, did not begin until the highwater mark of the New Immigration. After World Wars I and II, tens of thousands of Russian anti-Communists sought entry into the United States, many of them unsuccessfully.

Because millions of non-Slavic immigrants listed Russia as their homeland, it is extremely difficult to arrive at an accurate figure for Americans of bona fide Russian descent. One fairly reliable estimate puts the number at 350,000. Most Russian Americans are farmers and industrial workers, though there were a few highly proficient artists and scientists among the escapees from the 1917 revolution.

Ukrainian sectional feelings, intensified by a thousand years of Russian domination or attempts at domination, are often as ardent in America as they are—or were—in the Soviet Union. Even so, what has been said about the Russian minority in America applies generally to the Ukrainian, except that the latter with some 488,000 members is more numerous. With a strong national tradition, reinforced by centuries of minority status in the Old World, Ukrainian Americans comprise a more tightly knit population group than Russian Americans and are accordingly less assimilated.

The Poles came earlier and took a more active part in American history than other Slavic minorities. Some 10,000 Polish political dissenters arrived in the United States from colonial times up to the Civil War. Two Polish officers, Thaddeus Kosciusko and Count Casimir Pulaski, fought bravely under Washington. The great Polish migration to America, however, did not take place until the first thirteen years of this century, when 1,500,000 Poles passed through Ellis Island. Today there are an estimated 5,100,000 Americans of Polish descent, a figure which does not include Polish Jews. This makes the Polish minority the largest and most powerful Slavic minority in the United States.

Like Ukrainians, Poles are anti-Russian by habit and instinct. Unlike Ukrainians [25] and Russians, they are Roman Catholics. As it does in Poland, the Catholic Church helps keep Polish ethnic

---

25. Western Ukrainians in the U.S.S.R. were mostly Uniats (Greek Catholics with ties to Rome), who were forcibly converted to the Eastern Orthodox Church in 1945–46.

feelings alive and officially encourages the preservation of the Polish language, the "tongue of the soul." Although a small percentage are farmers, most Poles reside in large cities and are spread rather evenly through industry, commerce, and the professions. Fifty years ago the Polish minority voted the straight Democratic ticket. But recently many Poles, some influenced by America's soft Russian policy, others by Negro rioting, are turning toward the Republican party, though Gerald Ford's incredible remark in the 1976 presidential race that Poland was an independent nation did not win him many votes among Eastern European population groups.

Some Czechs, notably members of the Moravian Brotherhood, landed in America in colonial days. But the great rush of Czech and Slovak immigration did not get under way until the early 1900s, when nationalist ferment in the Austro-Hungarian Empire was at its strongest. Now numbering about 1,750,000, the Czech and Slovak minorities, who mix as little in the New World as they did in Czechoslovakia, are heavily concentrated in the big cities of the Midwest. On average, Czechs and Slovaks, most of whom are Roman Catholics, have a darker coloration than Poles and Russians.

The Southern Slavs consist chiefly of Serbs, Croats and Slovenes, collectively known as Yugoslavs. At present there are some 1,000,000 in the United States—500,000 Croats, 300,000 Slovenes, and 200,000 Serbs. The Croats and Slovenes are Catholics. The Serbs are Eastern Orthodox. Almost all Yugoslav Americans are descendants of New Immigrants. Most of the breadwinners work in heavy industry, mines, and quarries. It is the Mediterranean element in the Yugoslav population which accounts for the occasional dark coloration.

Many Slavs exhibit Northern European physical traits, particularly those with ancestral origins in northwest Russia and northern Poland. Some Russian Americans have the blue eyes, blond hair, and long heads of the Swedish Varangians who founded Russia ten centuries ago. But in general, Slavic faces are usually broad, Slavic cheekbones high, Slavic heads round, and Slavic noses snub. Though there are occasionally some Mongolian traces, physical and mental, the Slavic minorities have found no insurmountable racial or cultural obstacles in the path of their assimilation. Even the Polish Americans, who a decade ago had thousands of literary, dramatic, singing, social, religious, and athletic societies in the United States, are becoming slowly but thoroughly Americanized.

HUNGARIANS: Americans of Hungarian origin cover a wide racial spectrum. Originating long ago in the Asiatic steppes, the proto-Hungarians are now thought to have been members of the white rather than the yellow race. Today there is no question about their whiteness and they are designated Alpines. As to the number of Hungarian Americans, the racial potpourri of the old Austro-Hungarian Empire made it extremely difficult to obtain a reliable count of arrivals from Central Europe. Including the 35,000 who fled across the Atlantic after Hungary's abortive 1956 uprising, it is estimated there are now 310,000 Americans of Hungarian origin.

FRENCH CANADIANS AND THE LOUISIANA FRENCH: The French are the most difficult of all American minorities to categorize. On the Majority side of the ledger are the Huguenots, Protestants of Calvinist persuasion who began their migration to the United States when Louis XIV revoked the Edict of Nantes in 1685.[26] Paul Revere and John Jay are the two most celebrated Huguenots of Revolutionary times. Although they composed a mere 0.5% of the original white colonial stock, there are now perhaps as many as 2,000,000 Americans of Huguenot descent. Another million descendants of Old and New Immigration Frenchmen, mostly from north or northwest France, may be assigned to the assimilated category. The most notable of the early nineteenth-century arrivals was Pierre Samuel du Pont de Nemours, the founder of the Du Pont industrial empire.

The status of the French-Canadian minority is not so clear cut. About 1,500,000 French Canadians are now in the United States, most of them concentrated in the rural and industrial areas of New England. Not an economically aggressive people and not noted for attempting to dominate the thoughts or politics of others, French Canadians cling tenaciously to their Catholic religion and somewhat less tenaciously to their French-Canadian cultural heritage and their French dialect. Their proximity to their long-established homeland in French Canada acts as a brake on the

---

26. Davie, *World Immigration*, pp. 19–20, 40.

assimilatory process. Like the Mexican Americans, they present the United States with a minority problem on the European model—i.e., a frontier population group with closer emotional and historical links to the far side than to the near side of the national border.

In 1886, in Rutland, Vermont, delegates attempted to organize a French-Canadian "nationality" with its own flag and national anthem, which was to serve as an umbrella organization for all French-speaking people, both in Canada and the United States.[27] The project never materialized, but it is symptomatic of why an American diplomat was quoted as saying that French Canadians are the "most difficult of all immigrant races to assimilate."[28] Although perhaps a shade or two darker than the American population norm, all but a diehard handful of French Canadians will probably be assimilated in the long run—despite their traditional separatist attitudes.

Of the 800,000 Louisianians of French descent, some 300,000 still speak a French patois inherited from their ancestors, the Acadian exiles from Nova Scotia memorialized by Longfellow.[29] Some of these "Cajuns" have countenances which exhibit a dark Mediterranean coloration.[30] Working small farms and fishing in remote bayous, they led until recently an isolated existence that offered little possibility of assimilation. As clannish as the French Canadians, they range from the Assimilable to the Unassimilable categories. But the rapid economic changes now taking place in Louisiana are prying them out of their solitude and severely modifying their endogamic marriage habits and provincial customs.

It is not proper to end a discussion of the Assimilable Minorities without saying that in many ways they are more definitely and

---

27. Wilfred Bovey, *Canadien,* J. M. Dent, Toronto, 1934, p. 100.

28. Ibid., p. 187.

29. Governor Edwin W. Edwards of Louisiana claims his mother had Cajun genes.

30. Alexis Carrel, the late French biologist and Nobel laureate, has stated that the Mediterranean elements of the French population are inferior to the Northern elements. He ascribes this to the fact that the acclimatization of white men to heat is accomplished at the expense of the development of the nervous system and the intellect. *L'homme, cet inconnu,* p. 300.

dynamically American than the Majority. Most Assimilable Minority members, for instance, still *believe* in America—believe with a nineteenth-century intensity that has all but faded in the hearts of many with deeper roots in the American past. These Assimilables, moreover, manage to hold on to this belief, even though as blue-collar workers, as office personnel, and as the largest component of metropolitan police forces, they live and work in the tumult of the big cities, where they have learned much faster than other Americans what is happening to their country.

Because the Assimilable Minorities have suffered much more than the Majority from school desegregation, the rise in crime and the deterioration of white urban neighborhoods, it is quite possible that the leadership of a Majority resurgence will come from Assimilable Minority ranks, from the ranks of men and women whose lives and livelihoods have been more openly threatened than those of suburban and rural Americans. Face-to-face exposure to problems often creates a greater interest in solutions.

But it is also possible, if the present torpidity of the Majority continues and the Assimilable Minorities are abandoned and left to their own devices, that in order to survive in the megalopolitan jungle they may revive rather than abandon their old ethnic loyalties, thereby delaying or perhaps postponing indefinitely their progress toward full assimilation.[31] In such an event, the Majority would lose an ally that could easily tip the scales either way in determining the irreversibility of the Majority's dispossession.

---

31. In the spring of 1972 Michael Novak, in *The Rise of the Unmeltable Ethnics* (Macmillan, New York), urged a political alliance of blacks and Assimilable Minorities. He said (p. 20) the latter group comprised 70,000,000 Americans of Irish, Italian, Slavic, Spanish, Greek, and Armenian descent. Jerome Rosow, a former assistant secretary of labor, was quoted as the source for this figure. Rosow, however, had merely said that 70,000,000 Americans were members of "lower-middle-income" families. Later, perhaps as a reward for the scholarly feat of changing an income group into an agglomerate of ethnic groups, Professor Novak surfaced as a speech writer for Sargent Shriver in the 1972 presidential campaign. Actually, there are at least 2,000,000 Negroes in the "lower-middle-income" bracket as well as tens of millions of Majority members. See Jerome Rosow, *Overcoming Middle Class Rage*, Westminster Press, Philadelphia, 1971, p. 87. After working for the Rockefeller Foundation, Novak became the editor of an ethnic newsletter and a nationally syndicated columnist whose writings and opinions have been exhibiting an increasingly conservative streak.

CHAPTER 14

Unassimilable White Minorities

IN CONTRAST TO the Assimilable Minorities, whose assimilation is only delayed, the Unassimilable Minorities are permanently excluded from Majority status. The color line, in the case of nonwhites, is in itself an insurmountable obstacle. With respect to the Unassimilable White Minorities, the causes that prevent assimilation may be either cultural or biological, or both.

This does not imply that the Unassimilable Minorities are bound together by similar racial or cultural backgrounds or by a common economic or social status. On the contrary, Unassimilable Minorities, white and nonwhite, are likely to differ more from each other than from some Assimilable Minorities or even the Majority. Among the Unassimilable Minorities are found the most affluent and the most impoverished American population groups, the most verbal and the most taciturn, the most physical and the least physical, the most religious and the most irreligious. In fact the divisions that bedevil the Unassimilable Minorities are great enough to give rise to occasional political confrontations and loud bursts of polemics. The Negro-Jewish brawling during the 1968 teachers' strike in New York City was one such case. Another was the dismissal of Andrew Young, ambassador to the United Nations, for talking to a representative of the Palestine Liberation Organization.

Despite their marked divergences, however, the Unassimilable Minorities have joined together in a political, economic, and cultural alliance which, with the active assistance of Majority Splitters of the Ranks, has steered the march of American events for the greater part of the century. In addition to combining their votes

144

for carefully selected political candidates, the more dynamic of these minorities have overcome their polar differences to forge the solid ideological front which is overthrowing one by one the most sacrosanct American institutions.

What then is the unifying force strong enough to prevail against all this diversity, the centripetal force mighty enough to turn off the racial centrifuge in which these minorities should logically be imprisoned? To paraphrase Nietzsche, it probably has to do with the will to power and the will to powerlessness—the desire for power by those Unassimilable Minorities who have little, the desire for more power by those who have much, and the desire to give away power by deracinated Majority members. Feeding these desires are such old psychological imponderables and intangibles as envy, insecurity, fear, hate, and even, perhaps, self-hate. These desires have also received considerable economic nourishment. In recent years, in the ghettos of the big cities, although one minority has been looting, robbing, and burning the assets of another, the latter continues to put a significant amount of its brainpower and money at the disposal of the former.

The only safe assumption to make about the force that unifies and galvanizes the Unassimilable Minorities is that it is most apparent and most forceful when directed against the Majority. Accordingly it may be said that the chief source of minority unity and coordination is that great, sick, floundering demographic whale, which can be attacked, slashed, bitten, and nipped at with impunity. Above all else, it is opposition to the Majority which has built the effective but uneasy alliance between the Unassimilable Minorities and Majority Gracchites, Trucklers, Pussyfooters, Old Believers, and Proditors—an alliance that still enjoys the partial and often less than enthusiastic support of the Assimilable Minorities.[1]

Before presenting the Unassimilable Minority order of battle, it might be wise to caution that there are always countless exceptions to all generalizations about masses of anything, particularly masses of human beings. Obviously, there are unassimilable mem-

---

1. This alliance, in its purely minority aspects, has been described by a prominent political analyst as consisting of "large, cohesive ethnic communities still half-rooted in Cork, Calabria and Cracow." Phillips, *The Emerging Republican Majority*, p. 438.

bers of every Assimilable Minority and assimilable members of every Unassimilable Minority. But in what follows the emphasis is on frequencies not individuals, on statistical averages not one-point curves.

SOUTHERN ITALIANS: By and large, Italy is a biracial nation. Alpines predominate in the north and center, while Mediterraneans are concentrated in the lower boot—Campania, Calabria and Sicily—from which came 80 percent of the Italian immigration.[2] There being an estimated 8,764,000 Italian Americans,[3] simple mathematics and the rules for assimilation defined previously in this study would indicate that about 7,000,000 are largely unassimilable.

Of all the New Immigrants, Italians were the most numerous. Although they were peasants in the old country, when they arrived in America they clustered in urban "Little Italies," where Italian speech, Italian cooking, Italian song, Italian custom, and Italian exuberance still project an Italian flavor strongly resistant to solution in any melting pot. The Catholic Church does its part in preserving this flavor, but Southern Italians are not Catholic in the Irish-American or French-Canadian way. One author explains, "Perhaps the average Italian [has been] too close to Rome . . . to be awed by it." [4] Many Italian Americans look askance at the Church because of its long association with Italy's landed interests.

New York City has 1,300,000 Italian Americans,[5] many of them in the needle trades. It is the third largest Italian city in the world, surpassed only by Rome and Milan. Unlike Southern Italians, who remained in the urban east, the more adventurous Northern and Central Italians went west, quite a few to California, where they became farmers and wine growers and where one of them, A. P. Giannini of Genoese descent, founded the world's largest

---

2. L. F. Pisani, *The Italian in America,* Exposition Press, New York, 1957, p. 143.

3. Bureau of the Census report, 1973. Some wild, politically inspired estimates go as high as 21,000,000.

4. Pisani, op. cit., p. 54.

5. *New York Times Magazine,* Aug. 10, 1969, p. 56.

and, as events have proved, the world's most dynamited bank.[6] Their dispersal, their gregariousness, and an Alpine instead of a Mediterranean complexion have made most Northern and Central Italians easy candidates for assimilation.

The Italian minority contains within its ranks a criminal organization, in which race is the prime requirement for membership.[7] The ordinary Italian American, however, has no connection with the 5,000 Southern Italians, mostly Sicilians, who dominate organized crime. To get this message across to the public, Italian pressure groups have succeeded in persuading television and film producers to "lighten up" their gangster characters and give them non-Italian, preferably Majority, names.[8] Even Sacco and Vanzetti, the radical villains of the 1920s, have been rehabilitated and exonerated by the media.

Historically, Italian Americans have voted the straight Democratic ticket,[9] although when a crypto-Communist like Vito Mar-

---

6. Other rich Italian Americans, mostly of the assimilated or assimilable variety: the DiGiorgio family (California fruit dynasty), Angelo Petri and the Gallo family (wine), John Cuneo (owner of one of the world's largest printing firms), Pio Crespi (Texas cotton king), Antonio Giaccione (paper), Ross Siracusa (television), Louis Pagnotti (coal), Joseph Martino (lead), Salvatore Giordano (air conditioning), Vincent Riggio (former president of the American Tobacco Co.), Lee Iacocca (Chrysler Corp.), the Pope family (newspapers), Bernard Castro (furniture), Jeno Paulucci (food processor). Michael Musmanno, *The Story of the Italians in America,* Doubleday, New York, 1965, pp. 247–49.

7. The record of the Mafia or Cosa Nostra will be reviewed in Chapter 30.

8. Italian ethnic sensitivities have also been aroused by the discovery of a "Viking" map which showed "Vinland" as a part of North America. Professional Italian Americans described the map as a fraud and a slur on the good name of Columbus. *Ency. Brit. Book of the Year,* 1967, p. 102. The map turned out to be bogus, but Vikings did land in the New World long before Columbus's three vessels dropped anchor off San Salvador.

9. Notable Italian-American politicians, in or out of office, include former governors Michael DiSalle of Ohio and Albert Rosellini of Washington, John Volpe, former secretary of transportation, former Senators John Pastore of Rhode Island and Peter Dominick of Colorado, Anthony Celebrezze, ex-secretary of HEW, Jack Valenti, president of the Motion Picture Association of America, Congressman George Miller of California, Mayors Hugh Addonizio of Newark and Joseph Alioto of San Francisco. Of the above, only Volpe and Dominick are Republicans. Italian Americans in the arts include: Gian-Carlo Menotti, composer; John Ciardi, poet; Frank Capra and Francis F. Coppola, film directors.

cantonio or a crypto-Republican like Fiorello La Guardia, appeared on the ballot, racial loyalties took precedence over politics.[10] Lately, reacting to the radicalization of other, more dynamic Unassimilable Minorities, particularly in New York City, Italian Americans have been crossing party lines in even greater numbers. Conservative Republican John Marchi won his party's nomination in the 1969 New York City mayoralty primary, thanks to a large-scale Italian defection from Democratic ranks. The shift was attributed in part to the fear of Italian Americans that Negroes were "after their women." [11] In 1970 the Italian vote usually earmarked for Democratic candidates helped bring about the surprising upset that made James Buckley, the Conservative party's nominee, the junior senator from New York for six years. An even more surprising victory was the election of Republican Alphonse D'Amato in 1980 to the senate seat long held by Jacob Javits.

In general, the Italian American exerts relatively little political and social influence, except in areas where the Mafia is concentrated. He is content to live in a kind of self-imposed ethnic quarantine and has little desire to impose his way of life, his prejudices, and his attitudes on others. He has more children than members of most other white minorities, less wealth and, like all Southern Europeans, displays a warm, emotional attachment to his country of origin.

Carleton Coon has found two readily identifiable subraces among Southern Italians in the United States. He calls one "coarse" Mediterranean, the other Armenoid.[12] The average Majority member is not aware of these racial subtleties. He only knows that Southern Italian pigmentation is darker than his own, that most Americans from Southern Italy and Sicily are "foreign-

---

10. Vito Marcantonio was sent to Congress by the American Labor party and his voting record revealed the often close alliance between communism and the racial antipathies of Unassimilable Minorities. He provided the sole opposition when the House of Representatives voted 350 to 1 for the 1941 War Department Appropriations Act to build up American defenses in a world heading for total war. La Guardia was the half-Italian, half-Jewish Republican mayor of New York City (1934–1945).

11. *New York Times Magazine*, Aug. 10, 1969, p. 62.

12. Coon, *The Races of Europe*, p. 558.

looking," that they are therefore predestined to the racial and cultural apartness reserved for the swarthy minorities of Mediterranean provenance.[13]

WHITE SPANISH-SPEAKING MINORITIES: The Spanish arrived in Florida, Louisiana, the Southwest, and California long before the Pilgrims landed in Massachusetts. But Spanish colonization was so thin that probably not more than a 100,000 Old World Spaniards or Mexicans of preponderantly Spanish origin ever settled permanently within the limits of the present-day United States. Time and interbreeding have assimilated their descendants except for those who, like the Hispanos of New Mexico, married local Indians. Needless to say, the Spaniards who came over in the New Immigration have remained largely unassimilated. There are perhaps 100,000 to 125,000 members of this latter category.

The Cuban minority in the United States has multiplied exponentially since the establishment of the Western Hemisphere's first Communist state by Fidel Castro in 1959. Although Cuba has a sizable Negro population, the first wave of refugees was white (Mediterranean) and belonged to the more affluent segments of Cuban society. The latest wave, in 1980, was noticeably darker and contained a large criminal and homosexual component. Today there are some 850,000 Cubans in the United States, most of them concentrated in South Florida, which they are turning into a little Latin America. About half of them are Negroes or mulattoes.

Another minority with remote cultural roots in Spain, but one that speaks a more ancient language than Spanish, is composed of 10,000 Basques, who are concentrated largely in Nevada, where they have become the American sheepherding caste. In 1966 they helped elect a fellow Basque, Paul Laxalt, governor. Laxalt later went to the Senate and played an important part in the election

---

13. Judge Michael Musmanno writes touchingly—and accurately—of the predicament faced by almost all Southern Italians in regard to assimilation. As a boy, Musmanno proposed marriage to a young girl recently arrived from England. He was only twelve at the time, but she did not turn him down on account of his age. She said she could never marry a "foreigner." Musmanno had been born in America. The English girl had only been in the United States seven months. Musmanno, op. cit., p. 7.

of President Reagan. Basques are on the borderline between Dark White and White. They have been designated unassimilable because they were never successfully assimilated by the Spanish. It is doubtful if Americans will have better luck.

MISCELLANEOUS MEDITERRANEAN AND BALKAN MINORITIES: The estimated 435,000 Americans of Portuguese origin—mostly fishermen, farmers, cattle ranchers, and textile workers—are typically Mediterranean in appearance and consequently too far on the brunet side of the Pigmentation Spectrum for assimilation.[14] Mediterranean racial influence is also quite evident among the 70,000 Albanians,[15] 90,000 Romanians, 70,000 Bulgars, nearly 100,000 Turks, and 1,400,000 Greeks,[16] the last-named being particularly active in the tobacco, candy, sponge, and shipping industries. Olive skin, black hair, and dark brown eyes offer little chance of assimilation to the 1,000,000 Arabs, 75,000 Iranians, and 2,500 Afghans.[17] The 400,000 Armenian Americans, who have their own Armenian Apostolic Church, derive from one of the world's oldest peoples, and their history of persecution often parallels that of the Jews.[18] Like the Jews, they must be considered largely unassimilable.

------

14. The blond or red-haired Azoreans of Gloucester, Mass., are an exception to this rule. They are descended from Flemish colonists who settled in the Portuguese-owned Azores many centuries ago.

15. There were once 100,000 Albanians in the United States, but about one-third of them returned home.

16. Spiro Agnew is half Greek, his mother having been a Virginian. Had he been a dark, small Mediterranean like Aristotle Onassis he might have wed Jacqueline Kennedy, but he never would have been the 39th vice-president of the United States. Agnew's minority side came out in his warm friendship with Frank Sinatra and his association with the minority influence peddlers who turned against him and destroyed him politically. Peter Peterson, former secretary of commerce is also a Greek American, as is Michael G. Thevis, the pornography magnate who has a $1,200,000 estate in Atlanta and is currently in jail.

17. Danny Thomas, the television showman, Ralph Nader, the consumerist gadfly of the large corporations, and Judge Robert Merhige, who issued the order integrating urban and suburban schools in Richmond, Virginia, are among the more prominent Lebanese Americans. Sirhan Sirhan is the most publicized Palestinian American.

18. Charles Garry, the Armenian-descended lawyer of the Black Panthers and Rev. Jim Jones's Peoples Temple, said he never forgot he was called a "god-

While Assimilable Minorities generally have culture working against them but race working for them in the assimilation process, the Mediterranean minorities have culture *and* race working against them. In Europe, Latin populations usually solved their differences with their Northern conquerors by intermarriage, by swallowing them up genetically. In the United States, where Northern Europeans greatly outnumber Mediterraneans, this process is not so easy. Neither is its opposite—the absorption of Mediterraneans by Northern Europeans. The color sensitivity of the latter, sharpened by the presence of Negroes, Indians, Mexicans, and other nonwhites, is much greater than that of Northern Europeans in Europe and more like that of Northern Europeans in South Africa.

It would take only one or two generations of intermarriage with Majority members for most Mediterraneans to obtain the proper physical credentials for assimilation. But Southern Italians, Spaniards, Portuguese, Greeks, and others are shut off from the American genetic drift by their own choosing as well as by Majority taboos. Under such conditions, it will be quite some time before any appreciable number of Majority members—the Nordics among them are "bleached-out" Mediterraneans according to Carleton Coon [19]—recombine with the smaller, darker, but otherwise somewhat similar race from which their ancestors supposedly split off a hundred centuries ago.

---

damned Armenian" in school. *Time*, Jan. 12, 1970, p. 30. Richest Armenian American is probably Kirk Kerkorian, a movie magnate, who admitted paying $21,300 to the Cosa Nostra. *New York Times*, Jan. 17, 1970, p. 1. The number of Armenians entering the United States is now on the increase because the U.S.S.R. is granting Soviet Armenians more exit visas.

19. "The Nordic race in the strict sense is merely a pigment phase of the Mediterranean." *Races of Europe*, p. 83.

CHAPTER 15

The Jews

BY RIGHTS THE Jewish minority should have been included in the previous chapter. It is white and unassimilable. But it is also the most influential, most organized, and most dynamic minority. As such, it deserves a chapter of its own.

Everywhere in the public eye, solidly ensconced at the apex of the American pyramid, Jews represent an astonishingly minute 2.55 percent of the total population—5,781,000 out of 226,-504,825.[1] These figures point |up|a rather extraordinary disproportion between the size of American Jewry and its influence—a disparity not new to history, not restricted to the United States and not well understood by non-Jews. Indeed many Americans, awed by the ubiquity of the Jewish presence, are convinced that Jews are considerably more numerous than they really are. A B'nai B'rith survey of 2,000 high school students in twenty-one cities, excluding New York, revealed that 82 percent overestimated the Jewish population—some students by as much as 70,000,000! [2] To account for this widespread popular delusion and for many other strange sociological phenomena associated with Jews, it is both helpful and necessary to make a brief excursion into Jewish history.

---

1. U.S. population from 1980 Census. Jewish population from 1979 *American Jewish Yearbook*. Like all statistics compiled by private groups whose methods of tabulation are not open to public scrutiny, these numbers must be accepted with some reservations, all the more so because organized Jewry has successfully opposed Census Bureau efforts to count Jews. *New York Times*, Dec. 13, 1957, p. 30.

2. *New York Post*, March 20, 1962, p. 12.

The Jews were a tribe of Semitic shepherds who coalesced into a nation in the second millennium B.C. At one time—presumably after, not before, they had settled in Canaan—many went as desert raiders, settlers, captives, or refugees to Egypt. There, as written in Exodus 1:7, "The children of Israel were fruitful, and increased abundantly, and multiplied, and waxed exceedingly mighty; and the land was filled with them." It was in Egypt that the Jews acquired Moses, who gave them their law and instructed them in monotheism. By no means a Jewish or a Mosaic invention, the belief in one god had been forced on Egypt as early as the fourteenth century B.C. by Pharaoh Ikhnaton.

It is barely possible that Moses (an Egyptian name) was one of Iknaton's high priests and a member of the royal family; that after the pharaoh's death and the reestablishment of polytheism Moses may have become a prophet without honor among his own countrymen. In the search for a new following, he may have preached Iknaton's "lost cause" to the Jews, whose status as bond servants could have made them quite susceptible to a new and revolutionary form of spiritual solace. This theory, proposed by one of the most celebrated modern Jews, Sigmund Freud, is supported by Moses' mysterious birth, his royal upbringing and his use of Aaron as an interpreter.[3]

It was during their sojourn in Egypt, we are told, that Jews experienced and survived the first of their countless persecutions, though the Egyptians seemed to have been paid back in kind. Before the Exodus got under way Jehovah destroyed the firstborn of every Egyptian family. Today, more than three millennia after the first Passover,[4] Jews in their reincarnation as Israelis have again been chastizing the Egyptians (in the 1967 and 1973 wars),

---

3. Sigmund Freud, *Moses and Monotheism*, trans. Katherine Jones, Hogarth Press, London, 1951. Concerning his Egyptification of Moses, Freud wrote (p. 11), "To deny a people the man whom it praises as the greatest of its sons is not a deed to be undertaken light-heartedly—especially by one belonging to that people."

4. Jehovah spared the Jews by "passing over" their houses, which they had marked with lamb's blood. As for the Egyptians, "there was not a house where there was not one dead." Passover is celebrated each year as a high Jewish holy day, though it is difficult to find much religious content in an act of mass filicide. Exodus 12:35 also tells how the Jews, before leaving, "borrowed of the Egyptians jewels of silver, and jewels of gold, and raiment."

but this time not with lice, boils, swarms of locusts, and other assorted plagues and afflictions, but with American-built Phantom jets.

Some centuries after they had reached and organized the Promised Land, Jews decided they were the Chosen People and history's most enduring ethnocentrism was in full flower. Although the Bible is filled with stirring battles, priestly fortitude, Solomonic glory, and Assyrian and Babylonian captivities, the Jewish imprint on the world's conscience and consciousness did not develop overnight. Herodotus, the Greek historian, who made an extended tour of the Middle East in the fifth century B.C. and described in detail almost all the nations and peoples in the area, made no mention of the Jews, whom he either could not locate or thought too insignificant to write about.

The Jewish state was overrun by the Persians under Cyrus in the sixth century B.C. and by Greeks and Macedonians under Alexander two centuries later. Alexander's successor generals and their dynastic heirs maintained their occupation of Jewish territory, in spite of sporadic Jewish revolts, until the Romans arrived under Pompey. Fierce rebellions against Roman rule flared up from time to time, culminating in the conquest of Jerusalem by Titus in A.D. 70 and the dispersal and expulsion of those Jews who remained by Hadrian sixty-five years later.[5]

By the first century B.C. Jews had given up Hebrew and were speaking Aramaic, the language of Jesus. The earliest extant version of the Old Testament, the Septuagint, is not in Hebrew, Aramaic or any Semitic tongue, but in Greek. Its translation was accomplished in Alexandria during the rule of the Ptolemies, traditionally by seventy rabbis, who were isolated in separate huts, but nonetheless came up with seventy identical versions, exactly alike even in punctuation. The religious writings of the Jews were their only lasting contribution to ancient civilization, unless one insists on adding the chauvinistic philosophy of Philo and the

---

5. It was the Jews' intransigence toward Rome, the ancient world's most successful attempt at federation, and the Jews' rejection of the Pax Romana that caused Gibbon to blame them for "their irreconcilable hatred of mankind" and to call them a "race of fanatics." *Decline and Fall of the Roman Empire*, Lippincott, Philadelphia, 1878, Vol. 2, p. 4.

allegorical histories of Josephus.[6] Almost no Jewish painting or sculpture—against which there were Biblical injunctions—and only the barest traces of Jewish music, architecture or science have survived from classical times.[7]

In the matter of the Old Testament, the first five books, the Pentateuch, are a collection of stories and legends, many of them long established in Middle Eastern folklore. The Mosaic Law, the flood, the woman-from-the-rib, the Garden of Eden, the story of David, all derive from specifically non-Jewish sources.[8] The remaining thirty-four books consist of genealogies and laws, racial history, the fulminations and transcendental wisdom of the prophets, miraculous occurrences, gross libels, and soulful poetry. When its leading character, Jehovah, is putting all his enemies to the sword, the Old Testament is literature and religion at their crudest. At other times, notably in Isaiah, Ecclesiastes, Job, and the Psalms, it resonates with the highest expressions of human genius. The Old Testament has a special appeal to the English-speaking world due to the resplendent and evocative language of the King James version.

The oldest books of the Old Testament go back no further than the ninth century B.C. and some were written less than 200 years before the birth of Christ—well after Greek literary influence had become predominant in the Eastern Mediterranean.[9] Eccle-

---

6. Philo tried unsuccessfully to prove that Greek philosophers had plagiarized Jewish prophets. Although Josephus sided with Titus against his compatriots, he later tried to make up for his betrayal by writing philo-Semitic histories.

7. In the *Ency. Brit.* (14th edition) there are separate articles on Greek Architecture, Art, Literature and Music. There are also separate articles on Roman Architecture, Roman Art and Latin Literature. The artistic activities of the Jews have been limited to one article, Hebrew Literature.

8. P. E. Cleator, *Lost Languages*, Mentor Books, New York, 1962, pp. 109–112.

9. "[L]ittle in the Old Testament is more than a century or two earlier than the Homeric poems . . . . Herodotus was contemporary with Malachi and Obadiah . . . . Theocritus was singing in Sicily while the Song of Songs was being compiled in Palestine." T. Eric Peet, *A Comparative Study of the Literature of Egypt, Palestine and Mesopotamia*, Oxford University Press, 1931, pp. 1–2. Peet states that when the first fragments of the Old Testament took their present form about 850 B.C., "the literatures of Egypt and Babylonia were . . . already hundreds, one might almost say thousands, of years old."

siastes was the object of much rabbinical animosity because of its Greek style and thought.

In classical times, as today, anti-Semitism stalked Semitism relentlessly. Long before the beginning of their official diaspora, the Jews had migrated throughout the Mediterranean and the Near East, and wherever they went, as the Book of Esther makes clear, the anti-Semite was soon a familiar figure. The first historically documented pogroms and anti-Jewish *bagarres* took place in Alexandria, the capital of Ptolemaic Egypt, where there were many more Jews than in Jerusalem.[10] In A.D. 19, perhaps because of their abiding unfriendliness toward all things Roman, Tiberius expelled them from his capital.[11] But the ban was only temporary. Less than a century later, Trajan was said to be surrounded by "unholy Jews." [12] In the second century A.D., Jews carried their traditional anti-Hellenism to the point of genocide. "In Cyrene," wrote Gibbon, "they massacred 220,000 Greeks; in Cyprus 240,000; in Egypt a very great multitude." [13]

A chief source of anti-Semitism in the classical world was the high degree of Jewish participation in the field of banking and moneylending. In Egypt, in the words of E. M. Forster, "They speculated in theology and grain. . . ." [14] Describing the economic conditions of Italy in the time of Julius Caesar, Theodor Mommsen, a specialist in this period of Roman history, wrote, "Alongside the estate husbandry unnaturally prospering over the ruin of the small farmers, private banking also assumed enormous proportions as the Italian merchants vying with the Jews spread over all the provinces and protectorates of the empire." [15]

But it was the Jews' religious practices and clannishness, rather

---

10. Anti-Semitic tracts abounded in Greek and Roman times and one work (no longer extant) by the Greek, Apion, was so well known and influential that Josephus devoted a whole book to its rebuttal.

11. "[T]hey alone of all nations avoided dealings with any other people and looked upon all men as their enemies." Diodorus of Sicily, trans. F. R. Walton, Loeb Classical Library, Harvard University Press, Cambridge, 1967, Vol. XII, p. 53.

12. *Oxyrhynchus Papyri*, X, 1242, 42.

13. Gibbon, op. cit., Vol. 2, p. 4, including footnotes.

14. E. M. Forster, *Pharos and Pharillon*, Knopf, New York, 1961, p. 17.

15. Theodor Mommsen, *The History of Rome*, edited by Saunders and Collins, Meridian, New York, 1961, p. 539.

than their financial acumen, which brought forth harsh comments from such "Old Romans" as Cicero, Seneca,[16] Juvenal, and Tacitus. The same criticism was leveled against Jews much later in the nascent Arabic civilization, where Mohammed borrowed so much from their religion, but harried them so mercilessly. In the larger *suqs* and trading centers of Arabia, however, where "Jews controlled many of the local banks," [17] the financial grounds for anti-Semitism probably outweighed all others.

The advent of Christianity was a mixed blessing for the Jews. It gave them a special importance as the "People of the Book"— the physical and spiritual forefathers of Jesus. But it also made them accessories to the crucifixion. It was Caiaphas, the high priests and the elders who stirred up the multitude to press for Christ's death and the release of Barabbas. Today, Jewish participation in the execution of Jesus is being de-emphasized and a papal encyclical has absolved the Jews from deicide. But the most solemn absolutions of the most solemn Holy Fathers are not likely to have much effect as long as Matthew 27:24–25 quotes Pilate as declaring, "I am innocent of the blood of this just person" and Jews replying, "his blood be on us, and on our children."

There was a possibility at the very beginning that Christianity and Judaism might merge, but the moment Gentiles were admitted to Christian services Jewish ethnocentrism forced a permanent cleavage of the two religions. At the time of Christ, Jews were longing for a Messiah to punish their enemies, not for a tolerant Son of Man who forgave everyone his sins and welcomed everyone, Jew and non-Jew, into a universal church. Within a century, the gulf between the two faiths was so wide that a few anti-Semitic allusions were incorporated into the Gospels. Even Jesus himself is made to say of Nathanael (John 1:47), "Behold an Israelite indeed, in whom is no guile!"

All in all, Christianity provided non-Jews with new reasons for respecting Jews and new reasons for persecuting them. Perhaps in the final balance, Jews gained more than they lost. Christianity was their passport to Western civilization, in which they periodi-

16. Seneca's feelings about the great influence of Judaism on his fellow Romans were vented in his epigram, *Victi victoribus leges dederunt.* Seneca, *Opera,* Teubner, Leipzig, 1878, Vol. III, p. 427.

17. R. V. C. Bodley, *The Messenger,* Doubleday, New York, 1946, p. 166.

cally plummeted to the lowest depths of degradation and rose to the empyrean heights of preeminence. Moreover, it was by appealing to the social and moral teachings of Jesus, principally to the democratic and liberal offshoots of the shattering message in the Sermon on the Mount, that Jews managed to break out of their European ghettos in the late eighteenth and nineteenth centuries.

Jews survived the fall of Rome as adeptly as they survived the fall of Jerusalem. In the Dark Ages they were alternately tolerated and persecuted by the invading Teutons. In Spain they obtained the highest public offices in the Moorish kingdom of Granada in the eleventh century, and dominated commerce and owned one-third of the real estate in Christian Barcelona in the twelfth century.[18] In England, Aaron of Lincoln, a medieval precursor of the Rothschilds, amassed enough wealth to finance the construction of nine Cistercian monasteries and the Abbey of St. Albans.[19] But Jewish fortunes declined when Europe was seized by the fervor—often more Gothic than Christian—which built the great cathedrals and triggered the Crusades. From the German Rhineland, where overzealous Crusaders organized a series of pogroms, a violent anti-Jewish reaction spread irresistibly over medieval and renaissance Europe.[20] England expelled its Jews in 1290, France in 1306, Austria in 1420, Spain in 1492, Florence in 1495, Portugal in 1496–97, Naples in 1541, and Milan in 1597.[21]

Taking with them a rudimentary Teutonic dialect which later evolved into Yiddish, most German and Central European Jews moved east to Poland, the great medieval haven of Jewry. Those pushing farther east may have met and mixed with Jewish contingents who for centuries had been working their way north from

---

18. Durant, *The Age of Faith*, pp. 371–73.

19. Ibid., pp. 377–78.

20. Generally in the Middle Ages, Jews supported monarchies because it was easier to deal with one king than scores of nobles. They were also partial to the papacy, which alternately protected and humiliated them. In 1215, Innocent III ordered all Jews, men and women, to wear a yellow badge. Darlington, *The Evolution of Man and Society*, p. 459. The tension between Jews and the English aristocracy was revealed by the Magna Carta, which contained specific restrictions concerning the payment of debts and interest to Jews.

21. Dates of expulsion are taken from articles on the applicable countries and cities in the *Jewish Encyclopedia*, Ktav Publishing, New York, 1904.

the Caucasus, on the way converting and intermarrying with non-Jews.

The Jews of Eastern Europe, the Ashkenazim, are to be distinguished from the Sephardim, the purer-blooded Mediterranean Jews expelled from Spain by Ferdinand and Isabella in the same year Columbus discovered America. The Sephardim found sanctuary in Holland, Leghorn, and Turkey, a few even getting as far as Brazil, from which they were later deported by the Portuguese. Twenty-four of these deportees, captured by the French on their way back to Holland, were deposited in Nieuw Amsterdam in 1654.[22]

The racial composition of the Ashkenazim and Sephardim has already been discussed, as have the important genetic changes wrought by 2,500 years of intermittent miscegenation with non-Jewish peoples.[23] Nevertheless, modern Jews of Sephardic or Ashkenazic origin, indeed Jews of French, American, Yemenite, or any other nationality, like to think they are all directly descended from the ancient Hebrews of Palestine. It is worth repeating that this belief in a common ancestry, reinforced by religious traditions handed down for thirty centuries, can overcome all manner of inherited biological differences in cementing a strong race consciousness.

In the late Middle Ages most European Jews lived completely apart in walled ghettos and intercourse with non-Jews was limited mainly to economic matters. In many European countries and free cities there was a total ban against Jews for centuries. As a result, hardly an identifiable or professing Jew was to be found in Chaucer and Shakespeare's England, Michelangelo's Florence, and Cervantes and Velázquez's Spain.

Jews were not permitted to return to England until Cromwell's time, and it was not until 1791 that the French Assembly granted French Jews full citizenship. From then on Jewish destiny brightened. Beginning with the Napoleonic wars, Joseph Wechsberg

---

22. Peter Stuyvesant, the governor, did not want to let them remain, but Jewish directors of the Dutch West India Company caused him to change his mind. Sachar, *The Course of Modern Jewish History,* World Publishing, Cleveland, 1958, p. 161. Also see Stephen Birmingham, *The Grandees,* Harper & Row, N.Y., 1971, Chap. 4.

23. See pp. 30–31.

writes, "The supremacy of the Rothschilds in international finance lasted one hundred years." [24] In 1858 Lionel Rothschild was the first British Jew to be elected to Parliament; in 1868 Disraeli became Britain's prime minister. As the liberalization and commercialization of the West continued through the latter part of the nineteenth century and into the twentieth, Jewish emancipation kept pace.

By the 1920s it could be fairly said that Jews were setting the tone for much of Western culture. One has only to mention Marx, Freud, Einstein, the philosophers Bergson and Wittgenstein, and the anthropologist Boas. After 500 years of eclipse and a resurgence that required little more than a century, Jews had achieved more power and influence than ever before in their history.

Then came Hitler. Although World War II was another desperate attempt by Germany to set up a continental empire in Europe, it was also a racial war between Germans and Jews. The number of European Jews actually killed by the Germans and their allies has never been correctly established. The accepted and widely quoted figure of 6,000,000 is apparently based on hearsay evidence by an SS officer, Wilhelm Höttl, who declared Adolf Eichmann had informed him 4,000,000 Jews had died in extermination camps and 2,000,000 elsewhere.[25] The *Encyclopaedia Britannica* (1963) is more conservative and uses the phrase "more than 5,-000,000." [26] One Jewish historian has placed the figure between

---

24. *The Merchant Bankers*, Little, Brown, Boston, 1966, p. 343. One aspect of Rothschild power was amply demonstrated during Wellington's campaign against the French in Spain. The British general was badly in need of gold, which the British Rothschilds had difficulty in transmitting because of the French land and sea blockade. The French Rothschilds solved the problem for their British relations by arranging for the transshipment of Wellington's gold through France. Nevertheless, Wechsberg praises the Rothschilds for their loyalty to the rulers of the countries in which they happened to reside. Ibid., pp. 338, 342.

25. *Trial of the Major War Criminals before the International Military Tribunal*, Nuremberg, Germany, Vol. XXI, Doc. 2738-PS, p. 85. Another SS officer, Dieter von Wisliceny, said Eichmann had informed him that 4,000,000 Jews had been killed. At other times, according to Wisliceny, Eichmann increased the total to 5,000,000. Höttl, who was expelled from the SS in 1942, worked for American counterintelligence after the war. In 1953 he was arrested in Vienna on a charge of espionage.

26. Vol. 13, p. 64.

4,200,000 and 4,600,000, one-third of whom died of disease and hunger.[27] On the other hand, Paul Rassinier, a French socialist and onetime inmate of Buchenwald, has written a series of books to the effect that there were only 1,000,000 to 1,600,000 Jewish victims of Nazism. He specifically denies the existence of gas chambers and charges that the death camp story was a deliberate hoax engineered by Zionists to secure reparations from Germans and obtain moral and military support for Israel.

Robert Faurisson, a French professor of literature at the University of Lyon II, Arthur Butz, an American professor of electrical engineering at Northwestern University, and Wilhelm Stäglich, a retired West German judge, have supported the Rassinier thesis in books, articles, and lectures.[28] For their pains, Butz's car was fire-bombed; Faurisson, forced to quit his teaching post, was haled into court; Stäglich had his pension reduced, and all unsold copies of his book were seized by the German police. Since no public debate on the subject has been permitted so far (except in France, Switzerland, and Italy) and since no "respectable" bookstores will carry revisionist studies of the Holocaust, it would appear that someone has something to hide. World War I propaganda of Huns mutilating nurses, cutting off the hands of Belgian babies, giving poison candy to children, desecrating altars, crucifying Canadian soldiers, establishing a "corpse factory" to make pig fodder out of the bodies of their own dead soldiers—all these atrocity tales, some accompanied by fake photographs, were debunked only a few years after the war ended and were laid to rest for all time in 1928 by the publication of Arthur Ponsonby's *Falsehood in Wartime.* World War II propaganda, on the other hand, is still going strong after thirty-five years, although all too much of it is based on forced confessions, torture, forged evidence, rehearsed witnesses, and verdicts handed down by kangaroo courts.

---

27. Sachar, op. cit., p. 457.

28. See Paul Rassinier, *Debunking the Genocide Myth,* trans. Adam Robbins, Noontide Press, Torrance, Calif., 1978; Arthur Butz, *The Hoax of the Twentieth Century,* Noontide Press, 1977; Wilhelm Stäglich, *Der Auschwitz Mythos,* Grabert-Verlag, Tübingen, 1979. A summary of Robert Faurisson's opinions and findings are found in Serge Thion's *Vérité historique ou vérité politique?,* La Vieille Taupe, Paris, 1980.

World War II was disastrous for Jews in Germany and in most of Europe. But by strengthening Jewish unity outside the area of Axis supremacy, Nazi anti-Semitism helped to seal Germany's defeat. The massive and wholehearted support of world Jewry and particularly of American Jewry in the war against Hitler was an all-important factor in the ultimate Allied victory.[29]

In the postwar period Jews reached new levels of prosperity in the non-Communist world. In Spain, for the first time since 1492, Jews were permitted to open a synagogue. Even in Germany, where 30,000 still lived, Jewish communities were reconstructed in many of the largest cities. The greatest triumph of modern Jewry, however, was the establishment of Israel, which provided Jews with a psychological lift they had not had since the days of Judah Maccabee and Bar Cocheba.[30] To the amazement of non-Jews and Jews alike, the historic Jewish stereotype shifted almost overnight from the cringing, sly money changer to the fearless desert fighter.[31] But the settlement and conquest of Palestine brought with it a new rash of anti-Semitism in an area which had been relatively free of it for ages.

Although Israel may be the spiritual home of Jewry, the United States remains the Jewish center of gravity. Just as no one can fully understand present-day world affairs without taking Jews into account, so no member of the American Majority can even begin to comprehend the pattern of current American events without a rudimentary knowledge of the aims, the habits, and the political, economic and social status of American Jews. In many respects the goals and attitudes of American Jewry are major clues to recent American history.

It was during the Civil War that Jews first came to the attention of the American public at large. The first American Jew to attract

29. The prominent role played by American Jews in the development of the atom bomb, in the call for Germany's unconditional surrender in World War II, and in the staging of the Nuremberg trials will be treated later.

30. The effect of Israel on American foreign policy will be covered in Chapter 35. Judah Maccabee and Bar Cocheba were Jewish heroes who led armed rebellions against Greek and Roman occupying forces.

31. The Zionist pioneers of Palestine were mostly Ashkenazim. They were a select group, as pioneers generally are, which helped account for their surprising display of martial valor. The "un-Jewish" temperament and character of many of these Zionists were accompanied by their "un-Jewish" appearance.

international attention was Judah Benjamin, the confederate secretary of state, who fled to England after Appomattox.[32] On the Northern side, while the Lincoln administration was leaning heavily on the Rothschilds for financial support,[33] General Grant created the first anti-Semitic furor by ordering his subordinate commanders to expel Jewish peddlers and commission merchants from behind the Union lines.[34] Yet it was Grant, when president, who seriously considered appointing his close friend, Joseph Seligman, secretary of the treasury. When President Garfield was shot in 1881, he was taken to Elberon, New Jersey, where Jesse Seligman, Joseph's brother, opened his house to the dying man's family. At a Seligman Saturday get-together in Elberon, "it was never

---

32. Florida's David Levy Yulee, elected in 1845, was the first Jewish senator.

33. Through August Belmont, the Rothschilds' American agent, who "was able, thanks to the hugeness of the Rothschild reservoir of capital, to start out in America operating his own Federal Reserve System." Belmont was one of the first Jews to crack the inner sanctum of American high society when he married the daughter of naval hero Commodore Perry. Birmingham, *Our Crowd*, pp. 27, 79–80, 101.

34. Ibid., p. 98. Up to the present, the story of American anti-Semitism has been unimportant, unimpressive, and inflated. There were a few notorious social incidents, such as the refusal of the Grand Union Hotel in Saratoga to take in Joseph Seligman (1877); a few Dreyfus-accented trials in which American courts were accused of wrongly convicting Jews, such as the Leo Frank rape case and lynching in Atlanta (1913–15) and the Rosenberg atom spy case after World War II; a few anti-Jewish flare-ups, such as the resurrected Ku Klux Klan and Henry Ford's *Dearborn Independent* in the 1920s, and Father Coughlin's radio oratory and *Social Justice* magazine in the late 1930s; a few antiwar movements, such as the German-American Bund, the Christian Front, and the Christian Mobilizers. Huey Long was the only American political leader of sufficient shrewdness to have carried anti-Semitism effectively into politics, but he was assassinated by Dr. Carl Weiss in 1935. The late Gerald L. K. Smith, one of Long's principal aides, published a wide range of anti-Semitic literature for several decades. In a nationwide radio address in 1941, Charles Lindbergh accused the Jews of warmongering and repeated the charge in his war memoirs published 29 years later (see footnote 14, p. 454 of this study). A few scattered organizations—the National States Rights party, some Ku Klux Klan factions, some American Nazi groups—preached anti-Semitism in the post-World War II period. Liberty Lobby, a conservative group based in Washington, D.C., and the tabloid *Spotlight* mounted a strong anti-Zionist campaign in the late 1970s. Running in the primaries of both major parties, candidates with white supremacist leanings won nominations for Congress in a few instances but were later defeated by their Republican or Democratic opponents.

a surprise to find a former U.S. President, a Supreme Court Justice, several Senators and a Congressman or two." [35]

The relatively few Sephardic Jews and the larger number of German Jews viewed with mixed feelings the mass influx of Jews which began in the 1890s and which derived in most part from the extensive realm of the anti-Semitic Russian czars—from Poland, Lithuania, and Russia proper. But though they did not open their hearts to the newcomers or accept them socially, Jewish Old Immigrants did open their purses. This seed money, swiftly compounded by the New Immigrants' financial flair, allowed most of them to escape their Lower East Side tenements within a generation. Today, while Jews of Western and Central European descent still retain a great deal of their wealth, the Eastern European Jews, in addition to being affluent in their own right, have assumed the leadership not only of American Jewry, but of world Jewry as well.

The administration of Franklin Roosevelt was the first to introduce scores of Jews into the decision-making echelons of government.[36] It is true that Theodore Roosevelt had made Oscar Straus secretary of commerce and labor, just as it is true that there had been scattered appointments of Jews in the Wilson and Hoover eras, including such notable figures as Paul Warburg, Louis Brandeis, Benjamin Cardozo and Felix Frankfurter.[37] But the roster of New Dealers contained many more, if less distinguished, Jewish names: Henry Morgenthau, Jr., Benjamin Cohen, Sol Bloom, Emanuel Celler, Herbert Lehman, David Niles, Samuel Rosenman, Isador Lubin, Mordecai Ezekiel, Anna Rosenberg, Morris Ernst, Nathan Straus, Donald Richberg, Lawrence Steinhardt and Robert Nathan. Bernard Baruch, in whose New York apartment Winston Churchill had been an overnight guest when

35. Birmingham, op. cit., pp. 126, 308–9.

36. Jews were especially conspicuous in the Securities and Exchange Commission, National Labor Relations Board, Social Security Board and the Departments of Labor and Justice. *Reader's Digest*, Sept., 1946, pp. 2–3. Three Jewish governors during the Roosevelt era were Henry Horner of Illinois, Julius Meier of Oregon, and Herbert Lehman of New York. When Roosevelt died, one rabbi compared him to Moses. Barnet Litvinoff, *A Peculiar People*, Weybright and Talley, New York, 1969, p. 41.

37. Warburg was largely responsible for devising the Federal Reserve System and was made the Federal Reserve Board's first vice-chairman.

making state visits to America in World War II, seemed to overlap all administrations, having been an adviser to five American presidents.[38] Like Baruch, bankers Alexander Sachs and Sidney Weinberg attended important policy sessions of both Republican and Democratic administrations.

After World War II, David Lilienthal and Lewis Strauss served as chairmen of the Atomic Energy Commission and helped guide the United States into the nuclear age. In the 1950s, Senator Joseph McCarthy brought the public spotlight to bear on his two young Jewish assistants, David Schine and Roy Cohn.[39]

President Truman kept many of Roosevelt's Jewish appointees on the federal payroll. But President Eisenhower, who only obtained a small fraction of the Jewish vote, let most of them go. Eisenhower, however, did appoint Douglas Dillon to a high State Department post. Meanwhile, Republican Senators Barry Goldwater and Jacob Javits, the former the party's very unsuccessful 1964 presidential candidate, achieved national and international prominence.[40]

Jews returned to Washington in force when John F. Kennedy assumed the presidency in 1961. Arthur Goldberg was appointed secretary of labor and Senator Abraham Ribicoff, secretary of health, education and welfare. When Goldberg moved up to the Supreme Court, Willard Wirtz succeeded him. Other Kennedy

---

38. Baruch made most of his millions speculating in copper stocks. When America entered World War I, Wilson named him head of the War Industries Board.

39. For Cohn's later career, see pp. 435–37.

40. Is it really accurate to say that men like Dillon and Goldwater are Jews? Both had Polish Jews as paternal grandfathers—Samuel Lapowski (Dillon's) came to Texas as a clothier and Michael Goldwasser (Goldwater's) arrived in the Southwest as a peddler. Both Dillon and Goldwater, as their fathers before them, married non-Jews. Ostensibly, both lead the life of well-to-do members of the Majority—Dillon, the banker, being much more well-to-do than Goldwater. But the residue of Jewish race consciousness runs deep. It is extremely difficult in a milieu of intense racial divisions, as in present-day America, to determine exactly when a Jew ceases to be a Jew. Even if an individual no longer wishes to consider himself a Jew, the world may force him to be one. Goldwater's racial background, for instance, might help account for his mystifying friendships with Jewish gangsters. For Dillon and Goldwater's antecedents, see *Time*, Aug. 18, 1961, p. 13 and July 24, 1964, p. 22. For Goldwater's gangster friends, see p. 420 of this study.

appointments included Newton Minow, head of the Federal Communications Commission; Mortimer Caplin, chief of the Internal
Revenue Service; and Pierre Salinger, presidential press secretary.
Dillon stayed on as Kennedy's secretary of the treasury. Three
of Kennedy's principal aides and mentors were Arthur Schlesinger, Jr., Theodore Chaikin Sorensen and Richard Goodwin.[41]

When Lyndon Johnson became president upon Kennedy's assassination, he shifted Goldberg from the Supreme Court to the
United Nations. Other Johnson appointments: Walt Rostow, chief
presidential foreign adviser; Wilbur Cohen, secretary of health,
education and welfare; and Abe Fortas, associate justice of the
Supreme Court.[42] Edwin Weisl, chairman of the executive committee of Paramount Pictures, served as Johnson's personal financial
consultant.[43]

Richard Nixon continued the practice of surrounding the presidency with Jewish cabinet members and high-level advisers. Henry
Kissinger was secretary of state and practically assistant president
in the high tide of Watergate; Caspar Weinberger, secretary of
health, education and welfare; James Schlesinger, who converted
to Lutheranism, secretary of defense; Arthur F. Burns, chairman
of the Federal Reserve Board; [44] Herbert Stein, chief economic

---

41. Goodwin, who in his capacity as Kennedy's adviser on Caribbean affairs
had much to do with the Bay of Pigs fiasco, was torn between Eugene McCarthy
and Robert Kennedy in the 1968 primary race for the Democratic presidential
nomination. "The trouble is, baby," he explained, "I don't know which one
of them to make president." He told Seymour Hirsch, McCarthy's press secretary,
"Just you and me and two typewriters, Sy, and we'll bring down the government."
San Francisco Sunday Examiner & Chronicle, Sunday Punch, July 14, 1968, p. 2.

42. Both before and after Johnson took office, Abe Fortas was "on the telephone [with Johnson] at least once a day and often as many as three or four
times." *Esquire*, June, 1965, p. 86. The phone continued ringing after Fortas
joined the Supreme Court. This close, somewhat unconstitutional relationship
between the executive and the judiciary was one of the main reasons the Senate
refused to confirm Johnson's nomination of Fortas as Chief Justice. Whether
Johnson was privy to Fortas's monetary dealings with the convicted stock embez-
zler, Louis Wolfson, which later led to Fortas's resignation, is not known. See
pp. 429–30.

43. G. William Domhoff, *Who Rules America?* Prentice-Hall, Englewood Cliffs,
N.J., 1967, p. 104.

44. "The Chairman of the Federal Reserve Board has greater influence over
the daily lives of all U.S. citizens than almost anyone except the President . . ."
Time, Oct. 24, 1969, p. 89.

adviser; Laurence Silberman, deputy attorney general; Leonard Garment, legal counsel and head of the White House civil rights department.[45]

As the first appointed president, Gerald Ford kept Kissinger, dismissed Schlesinger, brought in Edward Levi, an old Stalinist fellow traveler, as attorney general, and replaced Stein with Alan Greenspan.

As for the losers in the 1968 and 1972 presidential races, Hubert Humphrey had as his closest adviser, E. F. Berman,[46] and his eleven largest financial contributors were Jews.[47] George McGovern's 1972 presidential try was also heavily financed by Jews and his chief aide was Frank Mankiewicz.

The Carter administration, though not all at the same time, had Harold Brown as secretary of defense, James Schlesinger as secretary of energy (like Dillon he served both parties), Michael Blumenthal, secretary of the treasury, Neil Goldschmidt, secretary of transportation, Philip Klutznick, secretary of commerce, Stuart Eizenstat, chief adviser on domestic affairs, Robert Strauss, head of the 1980 Democratic presidential campaign, Robert Lipshutz, presidential counsel, and Gerald Rafshoon, media consultant. Sol Linowitz was chiefly responsible for the Panama Canal negotiations and later was put in charge of implementing the Camp David accords. At one time or another during the Carter presidency, Jews headed the Internal Revenue Service, Securities and Exchange Commission, Federal Trade Commission, Bureau of the Census, General Services Administration, Congressional Budget Office, Library of Congress, and held number two or number three positions in the Departments of State, Treasury, Agriculture, Interior, Labor, Commerce, Transportation, Housing and Urban Development, Health, Education and Welfare, as well as in many federal advisory groups. The National Security Council was noted for the number of Jews on its staff.

The results of the 1980 presidential election augured a sharp reduction in the proportion of minorities in the executive branch, although many Jews were attracted to the Republican platform, which outpromised the Democrats in respect to Israel. Only one

---

45. *Newsweek*, Nov. 18, 1968, p. 44. Consequently, all communications about minority problems had to clear through Mr. Garment's office.

46. *Time*, Sept. 27, 1968, p. 17.

47. *San Francisco Chronicle*, Nov. 23, 1968, p. 9.

person of Jewish background, Caspar Weinberger, who claimed to be an Episcopalian, was given a post (secretary of defense) in President Reagan's cabinet. Henry Kissinger, however, had now become America's elder statesman; Murray Weidenbaum was appointed chief economic adviser; and Jews continued to hold important job slots in most of the departments and agencies.

Considering that Jews claim to be only 2.55 percent of the population, their number in the inner circles of government is clearly out of proportion.[48] But where Jewish overrepresentation is overwhelming is in the opinion-forming sanctuaries of American society. Theoretically, the politician and the bureaucrat are the servants of the public, when they are not the servants of the political boss. In practice, however, the politician, bureaucrat, political boss, *and* the public are frequently the servants of the news media.

In the newspaper field, the large newspaper chains and mass circulation tabloids bear much of the responsibility for shaping the public mind. But only a very few select newspapers, the so-called "high-impact" press, shape the minds of those who govern the public. By far the most important are the *New York Times* and the *Washington Post.* These are the two newspapers which are read and taken to heart and mind by the powers that be. The news they carry and how they treat such news determine to a large extent what the leadership of America says, thinks, and does.[49]

The controlling interest in both of these two publications is held by Jews. The *New York Times,* the national newspaper of record, has been in the hands of the Ochses and the Sulzbergers for several generations, as has the *Chattanooga Times.*[50] A member of this dynasty, Mrs. Arthur Hays Sulzberger, controls two-thirds of the voting stock of the New York Times Co.[51] Most of the

---

48. The number of Jews elected to office, while increasing steadily, is not as disproportionate for the reasons given on p. 108. In 1981 there were 28 Jews in the House of Representatives; 8 in the Senate (counting Goldwater).

49. Fifty copies of the *Times* go to the White House each day. It is distributed in 11,464 American cities. Talese, *The Kingdom and the Power*, pp. 72, 346.

50. In 1970 the *Chattanooga Times* was the defendant in an antitrust suit for "unlawful attempts" to monopolize the newspaper business in Chattanooga. *New York Times*, May 8, 1970, p. 9.

51. *Fortune*, May, 1966, and Talese, op. cit., p. 318. Mrs. Sulzberger is the daughter of Adolph Ochs, the founder of the dynasty. Adolph's brother, George, partly anglicized his name to Ochs-Oakes. John Oakes, his son, presently directs

voting stock of the Washington Post Co. is owned by Katharine Graham, the daughter of Eugene Meyer, the Jewish banker. Mrs. Graham, described as very much "the boss lady" of her publishing empire, also directs *Newsweek,* the weekly newsmagazine, and a strategically situated Washington, D.C., television station.[52] The capital's evening newspaper, the *Washington Star,* shut down in 1981. It was owned by Time, Inc., and edited by Murray Gart.

Less important newspapers, in the sense that their influence is more regional than national, are: the *St. Louis Post-Dispatch,* controlled by a grandson of Joseph Pulitzer, the Hungarian-Jewish publisher who invented yellow journalism;[53] the *San Francisco Chronicle,* California's second most influential newspaper, owned and operated by the Thieriot family which is descended from Charles and Michael de Jung, the paper's Jewish founders;[54] and Pittsburgh's *Post-Gazette* and *Press* and Toledo's *Blade* and *Times* owned by the Block family. The twenty-one daily newspapers of the late Samuel Newhouse comprise a journalistic empire that is third in circulation and first in profits.[55] Exercising an influence that stretches far beyond the business community, the *Wall Street Journal* is owned by Dow Jones & Company, whose chairman, Warren Phillips, was born a Jew, but is now a Christian. Needless to say, many smaller newspapers are owned, managed or edited by Jews, not to mention newspapers in Yiddish or English directed specifically at Jewish communities. Also, some of the largest newspapers or newspaper chains not owned or controlled by Jews have Jewish executives, managers or editors. The Times-Mirror Company, for example, which publishes the *Los Angeles Times,* has a Jewish director, Simon Ramo. The editor of the *International Herald-Tribune,* published in Paris and read daily by top-level officials of European governments, is Murray Weiss.

the *Times* editorial page. When other editorial writers have "views [which] conflict with his, they are not published." Talese, op. cit., pp. 72, 79, 81.

52. The information concerning Mrs. Graham, like much other data on the news and communications media in these pages, was taken from the article, "America's Media Baronies," in *Atlantic,* July, 1969.

53. Beard, op. cit., Vol. 2, p. 461.

54. Stephen Birmingham, *The Right People,* Little, Brown, Boston, 1968, p. 24, and *San Francisco Chronicle* promotional ad.

55. *Business Week,* Jan. 26, 1976, pp. 55–62.

The list of magazines controlled or edited by Jews is voluminous. It includes *Vogue, Glamour, Mademoiselle, House and Garden* (all the preceding are part of the Newhouse chain), Walter Annenberg's *TV Guide,* with America's largest circulation (20,000,000) and largest yearly advertising revenue (nearly $200,000,000), *American Home, Consumer Reports, Family Circle,*[56] *Ladies' Home Journal, McCall's, Redbook, Seventeen, Woman's Day, American Heritage, Atlantic, Commentary, Daedalus, Dissent, Esquire, High Times, Ms., Nation, National Journal, New Republic, New York Review of Books, Newsweek, Partisan Review, The Public Interest, Rolling Stone, U.S. News & World Report.* Until 1980 the chairman of the board of Time, Inc. (*Time, Fortune, Sports Illustrated, Money, People,* the *Washington Star,* 13 TV stations, the publishing house of Little, Brown, and large holdings in Metro-Goldwyn-Mayer) was Andrew Heiskell, married to a Sulzberger. Henry Grunwald, of Austrian-Jewish extraction, is editor-in-chief and in charge of all the corporation's publications. In 1969, before his promotion and when he was managing editor of *Time,* he was perhaps "the single most influential linear journalist in the world."[57]

Whatever the measure of Jewish control, practically all important American publications vie with each other in procuring the services of Jewish reporters, pundits and assorted interpreters of past, current, and future events. Examples at the literate or semiliterate level have included Walter Lippman, David Lawrence, Max Lerner, Arthur Krock, David Broder, Anthony Lewis, Joseph Kraft, Midge Decter, Paul Goodman, Irving Howe, Paul Jacobs, Irving Kristol, Victor Navasky, William Phillips, Norman Podhoretz, Philip Rahv, Susan Sontag, William Safire, and Art Buchwald; at the peephole level, Walter Winchell, Drew Pearson, Leonard Lyons, Irv Kupcinet, and Herb Caen;[58] at the lonely hearts level,

---

56. In 1970, Cowles Communications, which published *Look,* twenty-nine trade journals and magazines, three newspapers, and owned three radio stations and three television stations, was in such sorry financial straits it had to sell many of its most profitable enterprises to the New York Times Co. Among them were *Family Circle,* third largest U.S. women's magazine, a Memphis television station, three daily newspapers in Florida and a textbook firm. *Time,* Nov. 9, 1970, p. 41.

57. *Atlantic,* July, 1969, p. 43.

58. When a West Coast newspaper carried the headline, "Killer Hurricane Nearing Texas," Caen set the all-time low for his profession by commenting, "Promises, promises." *San Francisco Chronicle,* Sept. 20, 1967, p. 25.

Ann Landers and Abigail van Buren. One of the nation's most influential—and savage—newspaper cartoonists is Herblock (Herbert Block) of the *Washington Post.* One of the most popular comic strips was Al Capp's *L'il Abner.*[59]

In book publishing, the Newhouse empire owns Random House, Knopf, Pantheon, Vintage and Ballantine Books; Columbia Broadcasting System owns Popular Library, Fawcett Publications, and Holt, Rinehart and Winston; Music Corporation of America owns G. P. Putnam's Sons; Gulf and Western owns Simon and Schuster. Grosset and Dunlap, Lyle Stuart, Viking Press, Stein and Day, Crown, Schocken Books, and Farrar, Straus and Giroux are among the other principal Jewish publishing houses, though nearly all leading publishers promote works of Jewish authors and employ Jews in executive and editorial positions. Jeremiah Kaplan, for example, is currently president of Macmillan, and Marc Jaffe, currently editor-in-chief of Bantam Books.

The two leading distributors of paperbacks, magazines and newspapers to newsstands and to drugstores are Jewish-owned: ARA Services, Inc., and Henry Garfinkle's Ancorp National Services. The latter has a near monopoly on the news distribution field in New York and he receives what the *Wall Street Journal* has described as bribes of $30,000 and $26,000 a year from the *New York Times* and *Daily News,* respectively. A close associate of Mafia figures, Henry Garfinkle has been known to boast about having "publishers in my hip pocket." [60] Another powerful force in the book distribution field is the Book-of-the-Month Club— close to 250 million books mailed out in forty years—which was founded by the late Harry Scherman, born in Montreal of Anglo-Welsh-Jewish parentage.[61] Equally influential are the wholesale book firms, two of the most important being Bookazine and Dimondstein, both Jewish-owned.[62]

---

59. By far the most amusing comic strip, *L'il Abner* was nevertheless a grinding, serialized attack on Majority folkways—an upside-down version of Aesop in which the city mouse triumphs over his country cousin. In the character of Daisy Mae, however, Capp is careful to render due obeisance to the Aesthetic Prop. In 1972 Capp entered a plea of guilty to a charge of attempted rape and was fined $500 by a Wisconsin judge. *Facts on File,* 1972, p. 335.

60. *Wall Street Journal,* July 3, 1969, pp. 1, 17.

61. Time, Inc. is now the owner of the Book-of-the-Month Club.

62. To simplify their accounting procedures, many of the biggest bookstores will only order from book wholesalers.

Perhaps the most convincing evidence of the Jewish hold over the media is furnished by the commanding positions of Jews in the television, radio and motion picture industries. Wi!liam Paley, the son of a Philadelphia cigar maker, is the controlling voice and board chairman of the Columbia Broadcasting System. For many years the Radio Corporation of America, the parent company of the National Broadcasting Company, was headed by David Sarnoff and his son, Robert, who finally quit as chairman in 1975. Martin Seretean, however, remained as RCA's largest stockholder (1,500,000 shares). Fred Silverman, the chief executive officer of NBC, resigned in 1981. The board chairman of the American Broadcasting Company, which operates the ABC television network, is Leonard Goldenson. President of the Public Broadcasting Service, the noncommercial TV network, is Lawrence Grossman. President of National Public Radio, the noncommercial radio network, is Frank Mankiewicz.

As for TV programming, Jews are responsible for most of the "specials," documentaries, docudramas and sitcoms, which depict minority members sympathetically and Majority members as liberal anti-heroes, ignorant rednecks, or right-wing fanatics.[63] How effective these nightly sermons have been in squelching the Majority's *élan vital* is unknown. To those who think the minority sensitivities of board chairmen do not filter down to the news program level, it should be pointed out they do not need to. The heads of the TV news departments have traditionally been Jewish—Richard Wald and Reuven Frank (NBC), Richard Salant (CBS), Avram Westin (ABC)—though most of the oldtimers have now retired or been moved "upstairs" to be replaced by a younger generation of the same race. The TV news anchormen have traditionally

---

63. Ben Stein, a conservative Jewish essayist who made an exhaustive study of television, points out that entertainment TV is in the hands of a few hundred bourgeois Jews, aided and abetted by a small number of Irish and Italians, all of whom are over thirty-five and practically all of whom come from New York and live on the west side of Los Angeles. Their salaries average $10,000 a week, yet they lean heavily toward socialism, love the poor, and hate small towns, the military, businessmen, and policemen. In their sitcoms and adventure stories, few minority members live on welfare and fewer commit crimes. The bad guy is almost always the white, and the blonder and more WASP-like the better. These TV producer-writers actually "believe that the world is run by a consortium of former Nazis and executives of multinational corporations." Ben Stein, *The View from Sunset Boulevard*, Basic Books, New York, 1979.

been Majority liberals, but most producers of the news programs and many reporters are Jewish: Paul Greenberg, Sanford Socolow, Mike Wallace, Edwin Newman, Elie Abel, Irving R. Levine, Daniel Schorr, Marvin Kalb, Martin Agronsky, Herbert Kaplow, Morley Safer, Carl Stern, Barbara Walters, George Herman, Bert Quint, to name a few.

The close link between television and the motion picture industry does not diminish Jewish influence in the latter. Hollywood from its inception has been overwhelmingly Jewish. One has only to mention such companies as Metro-Goldwyn-Mayer, 20th Century-Fox, Paramount Pictures, Warner Brothers, Universal, Columbia Pictures, United Artists, and such mythic personalities as Samuel Goldwyn, William Fox, Carl Laemmle, Joe Schenck, Jesse Lasky, Adolph Zukor, Irving Thalberg, Harry Cohn, Louis Mayer, David Selznick and the three Warner brothers.[64]

These movie moguls, of course, belong to an older Hollywood generation. But the new breed is also largely Jewish: Ted Ashley, Gordon Stulberg, Dan Melnick, Jennings Lang, Robert Evans and David Begelman. Among the leading producer-directors are Delbert Mann, Sidney Lumet, Woody Allen, John Frankenheimer, Arthur Penn, Stanley Kubrick, Stanley Kramer, Mike Nichols, and Steven Spielberg.

Hollywood's link to Broadway has always been close and here again there has been an almost fantastic overrepresentation of Jews.[65] A brief idea of the Jewish domination of American show

---

64. The few important non-Jewish decision makers of Hollywood also had minority backgrounds, e.g., Darryl Zanuck, of Hungarian descent, and Spyros Skouras, of Greek origin. However, the greatest Hollywood director, D. W. Griffith, was not Jewish. Nor were the two other great figures to emerge from Hollywood—Greta Garbo and Charlie Chaplin. The claim that Chaplin is part-Jewish is a freewheeling fiction of the wildest pro- and anti-Semites. His mother was three-quarters Irish and one-quarter Gypsy. His father was a descendant of French Huguenots who had been in England for centuries. Charles Chaplin, *My Autobiography,* Simon and Schuster, New York, 1964, pp. 18–19, 37, 45, 109. But Chaplin admitted he once pretended to be Jewish to advance himself in Hollywood. J. L. de Vilalengue, *Gold Gotha,* Paris, 1972.

65. Serious playwrights, Jewish and otherwise, will be discussed in Chapter 18. Writers of message plays and dramatized political and sociological tracts are not listed at all, but a quick reference to newspaper files will show that their producers and authors are almost all minority members, chiefly Jewish and Negro. As for pornographic drama, it is sufficient to say that the dirtiest plays of recent decades—*Ché, Geese,* and *Oh, Calcutta!*—were all written, directed

business, past and present, is furnished by the roster of such entertainment "giants" as producers David Belasco, Daniel Frohman, Florence Ziegfeld, Jed Harris, Billy Rose, Mike Todd, Hal Prince, David Merrick, and Joseph Papp; [66] such songsmiths as Irving Berlin, Richard Rodgers and Lorenz Hart, Oscar Hammerstein II, Ira Gershwin, Harold Arlen, Burton Lane, Burt Bacharach, E. Y. Harburg, Jerry Bock, Sheldon Harnick, Stephen Sondheim, and Lerner and Loewe; [67] such rasping show business personalities as Al Jolson, Fanny Brice, Eddie Cantor, Sophie Tucker, Ethel Merman, Sammy Davis, Jr. (a convert), and Barbra Streisand; such celebrated "stand-up" comedians as Jack Benny, Ed Wynn, George Burns, Don Rickles, Mort Sahl, Alan King, Jerry Lewis, Red Buttons, Lenny Bruce, Milton Berle, Joan Rivers, Sid Caesar, Rodney Dangerfield, and David Steinberg. Thanks to this last group of individuals Jewish jokes have become the touchstones of contemporary American humor.[68]

The publishing and entertainment industries feed on ideas as well as events, and in the realm of ideas American Jews are just as firmly embedded as elsewhere. Below is a sampling of Jews who in the latter half of the century have figured prominently in the social sciences.

PHILOSOPHERS: Mortimer Adler, Hannah Arendt, Morris Cohen, Irwin Edman, Sidney Hook, Abraham Kaplan, Herbert Marcuse, Robert Nozick, Karl Popper, Murray Rothbard, Paul Weiss.

HISTORIANS: Daniel Boorstin, Herbert Feis, Peter Gay, Eric Goldman, Louis Hacker, Oscar Handlin, Gertrude Himmelfarb, Richard Hofstadter, Bernard Lewis, Richard Morris, Gerald Nash, Arthur Schlesinger, Jr., Barbara Tuchman.

---

or produced by Jews, as were most of the pornographic and black exploitation ("hate whitey") films.

66. "American show business . . . owes most of its wit, animation and emotional frankness to the ebullience of Jewish talent," wrote the late Kenneth Tynan, Britain's highest paid drama critic and himself part-Jewish. Mr. Tynan was the producer of Oh, Calcutta! The quotation is taken from Holiday magazine (June 1961).

67. Tin Pan Alley is almost 100 percent Jewish. High Fidelity, July 1977, pp. 27–29.

68. Eighty percent of the nation's professional comics are Jewish. Time, Oct. 2, 1978, p. 76.

POLITICAL SCIENTISTS: Stanley Hoffman, Hans Kohn, Walter Laqueur, Hans Morgenthau, Sol Padover, Adam Ulam.

SOCIOLOGISTS: Daniel Bell, Peter Drucker, Amitai Etzioni, Nathan Glazer, Philip Hauser, Paul Lazarsfeld, Seymour Lipset, Robert Merton, David Riesman.

ECONOMISTS: Kenneth Arrow, Abraham Becker, Mordecai Ezekiel, Alfred Kahn, Ludwig von Mises, Arthur Okun, Paul Samuelson, Milton Friedman, Alan Greenspan.

PSYCHOLOGISTS OR PSYCHIATRISTS: Franz Alexander, Eric Berne, Bruno Bettelheim, Erik Erikson, Victor Frankl, Erich Fromm, Haim Ginott, Robert Lifton, Abraham Maslow, Thomas Szasz.

ANTHROPOLOGISTS: Franz Boas, Melville Herskovits, Oscar Lewis, Ashley Montagu, Edward Sapir, Sol Tax, Lionel Tiger.

Jews are also heavily represented in education, in the professions, and in the physical sciences, as their long string of Nobel Prizes attests.[69]

Before probing other areas of Jewish influence and power, it might be well to mention one of the many side effects of the Jewish ascendancy in the mass media. This is the favorable tide of publicity which overflows on Jews, partly because of their strategic position in the selection and distribution of news, partly because unfavorable publicity is often interpreted as anti-Semitism. The inevitable result of such image polishing is that when a Jew and a non-Jew have established a record of similar accomplishments in a similar line of work, the former is likely to receive more attention and recognition than the latter.

A case in point is Max Planck and Albert Einstein, the two men who gave modern physics its two seminal hypotheses, the Quantum theory and Relativity. Planck, a non-Jew, was scarcely known in America except in scientific circles, while Einstein, even when an uncritical supporter of Joseph Stalin, was the object of the American public's warmest esteem.[70] Another case is Sigmund

---

69. In the period 1901–62, 16 percent of the 225 scientists who won Nobel prizes were Jews. Weyl and Possony, *Geography of Intellect*, p. 143.

70. For Einstein's part in the promotion and construction of the first atom bomb, see pp. 540–41. For some unsung criticism of Einsteinian physics, see pp. 308–311.

Freud, still considered a semi-charlatan in many parts of Europe, but written up in the United States to the point where the popular mind thinks him a universal genius. On the other hand, Carl Jung, the most eminent non-Jewish psychiatrist, has received only a fraction of Freud's publicity, some of it extremely hostile.[71] The wide acclaim given a Jewish anthropologist like Ashley Montagu and the narrow recognition granted a much greater non-Jewish anthropologist like Carleton Coon is another example of the Semitic bias [72] of public information channels. This same bias is carried over into the field of international relations—most noticeably in the "good press" accorded Israel.

Jewish ownership of the pipelines of modern thought has perhaps superseded Judaism itself as the most important *secondary* cause of Jewish endurance, unity and power. The *primary* cause remains, as always, Jewish wealth. Ever since the diaspora and even before, the Jewish financier, money-maker and moneylender have been identified by non-Jews as quasi-biological types. For almost two thousand years of Jewish history, survival of the fittest has meant survival of the richest.[73]

---

71. See footnote 58, p. 280.

72. The Semitic "tilt" of present-day public relations is further illustrated by the outpouring of magazine articles and books stressing the Jewish enrichment of American culture but omitting such names as Arnold Rothstein, the Minsky brothers, Mickey Cohen, Meyer Lansky, Abe Fortas, Louis Wolfson, Fred Silverman, Serge Rubinstein, Julius and Ethel Rosenberg, Bugsy Siegel, Bernard Goldfine, and Jack Ruby. Sometimes this one-sided approach dissolves into pure literary sycophancy, as in the case of a "biography" of Albert Lasker. One of the first advertising magnates, and certainly the richest, Lasker was the hero of a book-length encomium by an internationally known reporter, although the high points of Lasker's career were organizing the first soap operas and introducing millions of women to the smoking habit ("Reach for a Lucky instead of a sweet"). John Gunther, *Taken at the Flood, The Story of Albert D. Lasker,* Harper, New York, 1960, pp. 4–5.

73. In Chapter 10, J. K. Galbraith was quoted as saying wealth was no longer equivalent to power in the U.S. Insofar as he was referring to Majority wealth, he was correct. As stated previously, most of the great Majority fortunes have been scattered, wasted or handed down to foundations which support projects that often work against Majority interests. Most Jewish wealth, on the other hand, is pooled and concentrated on specific, ethnic goals—Israel, anti-anti-Semitism, minority causes and political, economic and social campaigns to remove the last vestiges of Majority privilege. Professor Galbraith to the contrary, great wealth directed toward *group advantage* is not only equivalent to power, but to great power.

Jewish wealth is an extremely touchy issue. Not since *Fortune* somewhat half-heartedly examined the problem in February 1936 has there been a full-scale study of the subject in the United States. Even in 1936, *Fortune* found American Jews firmly established in certain economic areas. Now more than four decades later, it is time to take another look.

Some idea of present-day Jewish wealth is furnished by a national poll which attempted to correlate income with religious denomination. It found that 18.9 percent of all Americans enjoying an annual income over $10,000 were Jews. Episcopalians accounted for 14.1 percent, individuals with no religious affiliation 11.6 percent, Presbyterians 8.7 percent, Catholics 4.6 percent, and Baptists 2.1 percent.[74] Translated into racial terms, the poll indicated that Jews were the most affluent Americans, Majority members next, Assimilable and Unassimilable White Minority members next, and Negroes, traditionally Baptists, the poorest.

Similar findings were obtained by a special 1950 Federal Census report which revealed that of thirty-nine different U.S. population groups "foreign-born Russians" had the highest median income. The median income of Americans of native white parentage was 40 percent less. The Census report explained the economic success of the foreign-born Russians by saying, "the Russian group contains large refugee and Jewish components." [75]

Since Jews are 2.55 percent of the American population, an unwary statistician might be foolish enough to predict that 2.55 percent of American millionaires would be Jewish and that Jews would own 2.55 percent of the country's wealth. In 1955, however, *Look* magazine claimed that more than 20 percent of all American millionaires were Jewish and Jews accounted for 10 percent of the personal income of all Americans.[76]

Perhaps the best proof of the constant expansion of Jewish financial power in the United States is furnished by the activities of the great Jewish investment banking houses. Year by year, Gold-

74. D. J. Bogue, *The Population of the U.S.*, The Free Press of Glencoe, Illinois, 1959, p. 706.

75. Ibid., pp. 367–69, 371.

76. *Look*, Nov. 29, 1955, pp. 27–35. Also see Sachar, op. cit., p. 346. A Detroit study showed Jewish median income to be $6,000 compared to $4,800 for Protestants, $4,650 for Catholics, $3,500 for Negroes. James Yaffe, *The American Jews*, Random House, New York, 1969, p. 229.

man, Sachs & Co., Lehman Brothers Kuhn Loeb, Lazard Frères, Shearson Loeb Rhoades, Salomon Brothers, Warburg Paribas Becker, Wertheim & Co., Oppenheimer & Co., and several others are extending their financial control over larger segments of the nation's economy.[77] No one, of course, can determine the extent of this control, but some indication can be obtained by examining the roster of directors of America's leading corporations. Wherever and whenever a partner or officer of these investment firms appears as a director of a large corporation, it usually means that he represents a significant, though not necessarily controlling, financial interest. It might be added that although these "merchant bankers," as the British call them, may have several non-Jewish partners, the Jewish partners have the final say.[78]

---

77. Henry Ford, a hardshell Protestant, was averse to Wall Street, liberals, foreigners, Jews, and non-Protestants in general. One could well imagine his reaction if he returned to earth and found: (1) Joseph Cullman, a Jewish tobacco tycoon, a director of Ford Motor Co.; (2) the Ford Foundation, the world's richest sponsor of liberal and minority causes; (3) his grandson, Henry Ford II, a Catholic convert, married for the second time to an Italian jet setter, who later divorced him; (4) his two great-granddaughters, Anne and Charlotte, wed at one time to foreigners, the former to a Greek shipping magnate, the latter to a Florentine Jew who is a Wall Street stock jobber.

78. *Standard and Poor's Register of Corporations, Directors and Executives* (1980) lists Goldman, Sachs partners as directors of the following corporations: Associated Dry Goods, Capital Holding Corp., Kraft, Knight-Ridder Newspapers, Witco Chemical, TWA, Franklin Mint, Corning, Pillsbury, Brown Group, Eagle-Picher, B.F. Goodrich, Cluett Peabody, Cowles Communications, J. P. Stevens.

Lehman Brothers and Kuhn, Loeb merged in 1977. Since then, *Poor's* has carried much less information about the firm, now probably the largest investment house in the world. Consequently, the following information has been culled from the 1964 and 1968 editions, when the firms were listed separately. In the 1960s Lehman Brothers partners or Lehman Corporation directors were directors of: Pan American Airways, Goebel Brothers, Twentieth Century-Fox, United Fruit, Commercial Solvents, Chesebrough-Pond's, Paramount Pictures, Beckman Instruments, Singer Sewing Machine, Bristol-Meyers, General Cable, RCA, Federated Department Stores, Bulova Watch, Western Union, Shell Oil, General Analine and Film, Standard Oil of California, Greyhound, FMC, Jones & Laughlin Steel, Anchor-Hocking, Times-Mirror, United California Bank, Union Oil, Wells Fargo Bank, Hertz, Litton Industries, General Motors, Allied Chemical, Continental Can, United States Lines, Caterpillar Tractor, IBM, Southern Pacific, Chase Manhattan Bank, Pacific Gas and Electric, Air Reduction, Northern Pacific, Bendix, Smith-Corona-Marchant, Flintkote, Sperry-Rand, Allied Stores.

In the 1960s Kuhn, Loeb partners were directors of: Westinghouse Electric,

It should now be evident that Jews have more than a foothold in automobile manufacturing, steel, public utilities, railroads, airlines, insurance, oil, and chemicals—the same blue-chip corporations which supposedly have been most successful in resisting Jewish infiltration.[79] In some cases Jews have actually become chief executive officers of the oldest or most innovative corporations— e.g., Irving Shapiro, CEO of Du Pont, Michael Blumenthal, CEO first of Bendix, then of Burroughs. In some important corporate areas Jews exercise both managerial and financial control. The two largest distillers (Seagram and Schenley) belong to this category, as do some of the largest textile companies and shoe firms, two leading tobacco companies (P. Lorillard and Philip Morris), and one of the largest breweries (Miller). The clothing industry at the manufacturing, wholesale, and retail level is predominantly Jewish. So are most of the nation's department and furniture stores and cosmetic firms. Jewelry and precious stones are practically a Jewish monopoly, as is the pet supply business.

The anonymity which surrounds the operations of the investment banking firms is occasionally broken by effusive references to the wealth of their principal partners. Robert Lehman of Lehman Brothers, it was revealed before his death, had an art collection worth more than $150,000,000.[80] Gustave Levy, a Goldman, Sachs partner, was once described as the "biggest money man on Wall Street."[81] The late André Meyer of Lazard Frères,

---

Sears Industries, U.S. Rubber, Anglo-Israel Bank, Revlon, Benrus Watch, Tishman Realty, American Export Lines, Polaroid, C.I.T. Financial, Brush-Beryllium, Getty Oil, A & P, Kennecott Corp., Marine Midland Trust, Metromedia, Buckeye Pipe, General American Transportation.

The 1964 and 1968 *Poor's*, which carried much more information about Lazard Frères than current editions, showed the firm's partners to be directors of: Jones & Laughlin, National Fire Insurance, Olivetti-Underwood, Owens-Illinois, Manufacturers Life Insurance, Chemical Bank-New York Trust, Harcourt Brace, Harper and Row, Libby-Owens-Ford Glass, Warner Lambert Pharmaceutical, Sun Insurance, RCA, Engelhard Minerals & Chemicals Corp., ITT.

79. In 1980 Wall Street rumors had it that the European Rothschilds held substantial interests in Kaiser Aluminum, Atlas Steel, Bethlehem Steel, Anaconda, U.S. Borax, Aetna Life, Litton Industries, Standard Oil of California and Rand Corporation.

80. Joseph Wechsberg, *The Merchant Bankers*, Little, Brown, Boston, 1966, p. 333.

81. Martin Mayer, *Wall Street*, Harper, New York, 1955, p. 193.

founded more than one hundred years ago by a French-Jewish gold trader from New Orleans, did not even take up residence in the United States until 1940, yet was "the most important investment banker in the world." [82]

Meyer was a director of RCA and Allied Chemical in the United States and of Fiat and Montecatini Edison in Italy. President Kennedy appointed him to important government posts and his close friends included Robert McNamara, Henry Fowler, onetime secretary of the treasury, Eugene Black, former head of the World Bank, and Jacqueline Kennedy. Lyndon Johnson consulted him regularly, and David Rockefeller joined him in several real estate ventures. Lazard's New York branch has participated in vast financial transactions involving American Metal Climax, Minnesota Mining, and Lockheed Aircraft. In 1966 it arranged the McDonnell-Douglas merger for a fee of $1,000,000. Lazard has or had a $40,000,000 interest in International Telephone and Telegraph, one of the nation's largest conglomerates, and its New York, London and Paris branches manage or advise investments totaling $3 billion.[83]

Although not to be compared to the power wielded by investment bankers like Meyer, mutual funds, pension funds, and brokerage firms, which hold huge blocks of shares in the largest corporations, also exert a great deal of influence over the higher levels of the American business community. The Jewish position in this area of the financial community is very strong. There are big Jewish-controlled money pools like the Dreyfus Fund and big Jewish brokerage firms like Salomon Brothers. Jews are directors or officers of some of the largest banks, though here it must be admitted their influence is relatively weak. Jews have been presidents or chairmen of the New York Stock Exchange and of the smaller exchanges. Jews sit on the Senate and House committees that write legislation regulating corporate finance. Equally important, Jews often dominate the Securities and Exchange Commission, which has the power to make or break any corporation it deems has violated SEC rules and regulations. The television pro-

---

82. *Fortune*, Aug. 1968, p. 101.

83. Ibid. In the same article *Fortune* stated, "The hard financial core of capitalism in the free world is composed of not more than 60 firms, partnerships and corporations owned or controlled by some 1,000 men."

gram, "Wall Street Week," presided over by Louis Rukeyser, is viewed by tens, possibly hundreds, of thousands of investors or potential investors.

In May 1978, *Town & Country* published an article, "The Wealthiest Americans," which purported to list the seventy-four individuals and families with a net worth of $200,000,000 or more. Later the author, Dan Rottenberg, revised the article for *Jewish Living* (Sept.–Oct. 1979), in which he added Jewish individuals and families worth $50,000,000 or more. Here in descending order are the nation's richest Jews:

$600 million to $1 billion
> The Pritzkers (A. N., Jack, Jay, Robert). Hyatt Hotels, Hammond organs, *McCall's* magazine, real estate.

$400 million to $600 million
> The Newhouses (Samuel Jr., Donald). Twenty-one daily newspapers, five magazines, six television stations, four radio stations, twenty cable-TV systems, and several publishing houses. Since the founding father died after this assessment of the Newhouse fortune was made, some of it must have been eaten up in taxes. Nevertheless the communications conglomerate may still remain first in profits and third in revenues (after Time Inc. and Times-Mirror Co.).
>
> The Bronfmans (Edgar, Charles, Minda de Gunzberg, Phyllis Lambert). Joseph E. Seagram & Sons (34%), largest private landowners in Canada, oil, computer services, show business.
>
> Marvin Davis. Davis Oil Company, one of the largest independent oil drillers, banking, real estate, motion pictures.
>
> The Haases (Walter Sr., Walter Jr., Peter). Levi Strauss (49%).
>
> The Crowns (Henry, Lester). General Dynamics (15%), Hilton Hotels (7%), railroads, real estate, coal.
>
> Michel Fribourg. Owner of Continental Grain, possibly the nation's largest private company.
>
> Leonard Stern. Hartz Mountain Industries (pet supplies), real estate, shopping malls.

$300 million to $400 million
> Walter Annenberg. Triangle Publications, *TV Guide, Seventeen, Daily Racing Form,* six television and nine radio stations, twenty-seven cable-TV franchises.
>
> Milton J. Petri. Women's clothing stores.
>
> Edwin C. Whitehard. Medical equipment.

The Blausteins (Morton, Henry Rosenberg, Jr.). Crown Central Petroleum, real estate. The late Jacob Blaustein sold his American Oil Company to Standard Oil of Indiana.[84]

$200 million to $300 million
S. Mark Taper. First Charter Financial Corp.
Leon Hess. Amarada Hess (oil and chemicals).
Samuel Lefrak. Real estate.
The Tisches (Laurence, Preston). Loew's Corp.

$150 million to $200 million
The Guggenheims (Robert, Roger Strauss, Peter Lawson-Johnson). Mining.
The Lauders (Estee, Joseph, Leonard). Cosmetics.
Norton Simon. Norton Simon Inc. (food products, soft drinks).
Jules Stein. MCA (records and films).
Arthur G. Cohen. Real estate.

$100 million to $150 million
The Belzbergs (Hyman, Samuel, William). Canadian financiers with extensive interests in the U.S.
The Epsteins (Raymond, Sidney). Construction and engineering.
Sol Goldman. Real estate.
Katharine Graham. Washington Post Co.
Joseph Hirshhorn. Uranium mining.
Meyer Lansky. Organized crime.
The Sulzbergers (Mrs. Arthur Hays, Arthur Ochs, Marian Heiskell, Ruth Holmberg, Judith Levinson). New York Times Co.

$75 million to $100 million
Sam Israel, Jr. Coffee importer.
The Levys (Lester, Milton, Irvin). Industrial cleaners and paints.
The Meyerhoffs (Joseph, Harvey, Jack Pearlstone, Jr.). Insurance, real estate, investments.
William S. Paley. Columbia Broadcasting System.
Victor Posner. Sharon Steel, investments.
The Rosenblooms. Heirs of the late Carroll Rosenbloom, garment manufacturer, owner of the Los Angeles Rams.
The Shapiros (Henry, Albert, Merrill Bank). Paper cups, straws, plates.

---

84. *Fortune*, May 1968. In 1948, when President Truman was wondering whether or not to seek a second term, he called in six people to advise him. Blaustein, who died in 1970, was one of them. *New York Times*, Nov. 17, 1970, p. 44.

Charles E. Smith. Real estate.
Lew Wasserman. MCA.

$50 million to $75 million

The Blocks (Leonard, James, Thomas, Adele, Susan Block Stearns, Peggy Block Danziger). Block Drug Company.

Nathan Cummings. General Dynamics, Consolidated Food Corp.

Leonard Davis. Colonial Penn Group (insurance).

Harold Farb. Furniture and real estate.

Manny Fingerhut. Mail order sales.

Max Fisher. Oil distributor.

The Gordons (Harry, Aron, Daniel, James). Jewelers.

Maurice Greenberg. American International Group (insurance).

Bud Grossman. Soft drink bottling, auto leasing, oil marketing.

Irving Harris. Toni home permanents, Pittway Corp., Standard Shares.

Irwin Jacobs. Investments.

The Kempners (Harris, Isaac, Harris, Jr.). National Bank of Galveston, Imperial Sugar Co.

Helen Regenstein. Arvey Corp., Northwest Industries.

Roy V. Titus (son of Helena Rubinstein). Cosmetics.

The Smiths (A. K., Harry K., Russell K., Jaclyn). Big Three Industries.

Ervin Wolf. Offshore drilling.

The Zales (Morris, William, Donald, Ben, Bruce Lipshy). Jewelers.

Not listed above is an older generation of Jewish wealth dissipated by taxes and multitudinous heirs and often transferred to Jewish-oriented foundations. For the record it might be appropriate to mention: the Shubert brothers, operators of a $400,000,000 theater empire; [85] Billy Rose, who owned more A. T. & T. stock than any other individual (as of May 1963); [86] the Zellerbachs of Crown Zellerbach Corporation; Lester Avnet of Avnet Electronics ($252 million annual sales); [87] Rudolf Sonnenborn of Witco Chemical; Harry Winston, the jewelry magnate; Albert List, business raider; Louis Horowitz of Thompson-Starret Construction Co.; Israel Matz of Ex-Lax; Abraham Mazer of Hudson Pulp and Paper;

85. *San Francisco Sunday Examiner, Date Book*, Dec. 15, 1968, p. 2, as quoted from *The Brothers Shubert* by Jerry Stagg. Jake and Lee Shubert, according to the author, controlled 75 percent of all American theaters.

86. *Newsweek*, May 27, 1963, p. 80, and *New York Times*, Feb. 11, 1966, p. 1.

87. *New York Times*, Jan. 4, 1970, p. 77.

Charles Revson of Revlon; Samuel Rubin of Fabergé; Samuel Zemurray of United Fruit. As if imitating MGM's Louis Mayer, who was the highest-paid American in 1943 ($949,765), Frank Rosenfelt, current MGM president, received the most money of any American executive in 1979 ($5.1 million).[88]

Always to be found in the topmost echelons of American affluence are such old established families (some members of which have become Christians) as the Seligmans, Warburgs and Kahns, and the not-so-well established Strauses, Gimbels, Kaufmanns and Magnins. The elite Jewish families of San Francisco—Hellmans (Wells Fargo Bank), Fleishhackers, Sutros, and Schwabachers— also deserve mention in any census of inherited wealth.

As America's giant industrial concerns grow unwieldy and operating costs go out of sight, as accounting, financing and labor relations take precedence over invention, production and quality control, Jews have thronged to the lucrative pastures of land speculation, subdivisions, discount chains, credit cards, energy, electronics, and other technological enterprises from microcircuits to gene splicing. Among such are Milton Shapp, former governor of Pennsylvania, Armand Hammer of Occidental Petroleum, Roy Chalk, Charles Bluhdorn, Lou Chesler,[89] the Sonnabends, the Levitts, the Bakalars, Alfred Strelsin, Louis Aronson of Ronson lighters, Alfred Bloomingdale of the Diners Club, Eugene Ferkauf of E. J. Korvette Department Stores, Harry Henshel of Bulova Watch, Stanley Marcus of Neiman-Marcus, Herbert Siegel of ChrisCraft Industries, and Irving Feist, the Newark realtor who has served several terms as president of the Boy Scouts of America. The most meteoric of these wheeler-dealers is Meshulam Ricklis, born in Istanbul, raised in Israel, naturalized an American, who in one week made $2,000,000 in the stock market.[90] Promoters

---

88. Some super-rich Majority members whose families are worth a billion dollars or more (Mellons, Gettys, Rockefellers, Du Ponts, Daniel Ludwig) may have made more than Frank Rosenfelt in 1979, but their profits were in realized or unrealized capital gains.

89. Chesler made $70,000,000 in two stock operations on the American Stock Exchange. Leslie Gould, *The Manipulators*, David McKay, New York, 1966, p. 123.

90. *San Francisco Sunday Examiner*, March 12, 1968, p. 1. Schenley Industries, the giant distiller, is a subsidiary of Ricklis's Rapid American Corp.

of a similar stripe are Max Palevsky, the computer king, Lawrence Harvey, the aluminum magnate, and Felix Rohatyn, the Viennese-born Lazard Frères partner, who now manages the financial destiny of insolvent New York City.[91]

Another important source of Jewish wealth is the seemingly congenital preference of Jews for the most highly paid occupations. For example, 35 to 40 percent of working Jewish adults are in commerce, as against 13.8 percent of non-Jews; 10 to 12 percent in the professions as against 6.8 percent of non-Jews; 73 percent in "white collar" jobs compared to 43 percent of Protestants and 33 percent of Catholics; 48 percent self-employed as against 19 percent of Protestants and 10 percent of Catholics.[92]

Foreseeing a Jewish stranglehold on the professions, many American medical and law schools established a quota system at the turn of the century. Under the battering of liberal and minority pressure, this numerus clausus has now been largely abandoned.[93] At present, medical colleges receive about 14,000 entry applications a year, 5,000 to 7,000 from Jews,[94] and in New York City already half of the 15,000 doctors are Jewish. The spiraling tuitions of the medical and legal schools have given Jews an additional advantage in the race for professional degrees. Belonging to the richest American population group, Jews can afford the costs of postgraduate education better than non-Jews.

To sum up the phenomenon of Jewish affluence, what is happening in the United States today is what has been happening throughout much of Western history. The Jews, finding themselves unrestricted and uncurbed in a land rich in resources and labor,

91. The National Economic Council has found that the chief executive officers of twenty large conglomerates (conglomerate being a euphemism for an incipient cartel) are Jewish. Letter to the *Wall Street Journal*, May 1, 1972.

92. Nathan Ruck in *Economic Trends in the American Jew*, ed. Oscar Janovsky, Harper, New York, 1942, pp. 162, 165. Negroes are not included in these percentages. Although the figures are somewhat dated, they have been more or less substantiated by a similar survey in *Newsweek*, March 1, 1971, p. 63.

93. With the rise of affirmative action, however, complications arose. Quotas once imposed against Jews were becoming government-sponsored quotas for nonwhites and therefore against whites, a category which happened to include Jews. Jewish ambivalence toward these new quotas, described by Washington functionaries as "goals," will be explored later on in this book.

94. Simpson and Yinger, op. cit., pp. 677–79.

are rapidly acquiring a wholly disproportionate share of its wealth. It is almost certainly the same historic process that took place in Visigothic, Arabic and Catholic Spain, in medieval England, France and Germany—and more recently in early twentieth-century Germany. Yet no one cares—or dares—to notice it. Those who are so concerned about labor monopolies, oil cartels, or proliferating conglomerates, about the influence of the Roman Catholic Church or the military-industrial complex, about WASP domination of the big corporations or the international Communist conspiracy seem strangely silent and utterly unconcerned about the activities of an ever more powerful, ever more dominant supranational ethnocentrism with almost unlimited financial resources at its command.

But the silence is not so strange when one reflects on what the late British political analyst R. H. S. Crossman described as "the anti-anti-Semitic veto which has successfully suppressed any candid and effective writing about the Jewish problem. . . ." [95] Any critical discussion of Jewish wealth—or for that matter any critical discussion of any aspect of Jewish power—immediately exposes the author or speaker to charges of anti-Semitism.[96] Since anti-Semitism is the great heresy of modern times, a person so accused is immediately subjected to such doses of social ostracism and economic attrition that any normal private life or successful public career will be permanently closed to him. It is consequently small wonder that the entire Western intellectual establishment has shied away from such a thankless and unprofitable task. In the present-day West, one can only be truly objective about Jews when one is a Jew. A very few anti-Zionist Jews, who believe Zionism harms Jewry by exposing bipolar Jewish loyalties, declaim against Israel. A very few Jewish thinkers and scientists, and a very few Jewish novelists who let their characters run away from them, occasionally show symptoms of the ancient Jewish neurosis

---

95. R. H. S. Crossman, *Partisan Review*, Fall, 1964, p. 565.

96. "[A]mong all other ethnic groups, his [the Jew's] expressed thinking, his expressed concerns, are the most subjective. And the Jew is usually hypersensitive . . . you can't even say 'Jew' without him accusing you of anti-Semitism. I don't care what a Jew is professionally, doctor, merchant, housewife, student, or whatever—first he, or she, thinks Jew." *Autobiography of Malcolm X*, Grove Press, New York, 1966, p. 283.

of *Selbsthass* and vent their feelings in a manner inconsistent with the all-out Jewish effort to keep anti-Semitism under impenetrable wraps.[97]

The removal of all things Jewish from the arena of rational discussion automatically relegates unfriendly opinions of Jews to the hushed whispers of office, living room and country club, to underground "hate sheets" and to the verbal musings of crackpots haunted by visions of bearded elders plotting world conquest. All this lends an aura of mysticism and romantic obscurantism to anti-Semitism, which it does not deserve and which endows it with a kind of kinetic and subterranean diabolism. The day anti-Semitism breaks out into the light again—as suppressed ideologies have the habit of doing—it cannot avoid becoming the stock-in-trade of the apocalyptic avenger who knows that emotion and dogma move more mountains than reason. The sudden release of tensions and hatreds pent up during decades of censorship and indoctrination may obviate any less explosive outcome.

Instead of submitting anti-Semitism to the free play of ideas, instead of making it a topic for debate in which all can join, Jews and their liberal supporters have managed to organize an inquisition in which all acts, writings, and even thoughts critical of Jewry are treated as a threat to the moral order of mankind. The pro-Semite has consequently made himself a mirror image of the anti-Semite. The Tartuffe of the contemporary era turns out to be the Jewish intellectual who believes passionately in the rights of free speech and peaceful assembly for all, but rejoices when permits are refused for anti-Semitic meetings and rocks crack against the skulls of anti-Semitic speakers.

Admitting the almost incredible disparity between Jewish numbers and Jewish influence in the United States—and it is growing more difficult for anyone not to admit it—how does modern scholarship explain it? The answer is that most modern scholars do

---

97. One such thinker was Simone Weil, the French-Jewish poetess-philosopher who equated the spirit of Judaism with the spirit of Nazism and complained that the worship of the "earthy, cruel and exclusive Jehovah had turned Jews into a nation of fugitive slaves." One such scientist was Dr. Karl Landsteiner, Nobel laureate, who unsuccessfully sought an injunction against *Who's Who in American Jewry* for calling him a Jew. Sachar, *The Course of Modern Jewish History*, p. 404. One such novelist is Philip Roth, author of *Portnoy's Complaint.*

not try to explain it at all, or if they do, simply deny that there is anything more to the Jewish problem than environmental coincidence. Those with a more inquisitive mind or with a special ax to grind have a few interesting theories on the subject—theories, however, which are basically apologies since they are circumscribed by the present-day caveat that any discussion of Jews must never put them in an unfavorable light.

One well-circulated theory, advanced by Jewish scholar Ludwig Lewisohn, is that Jews were primarily an agricultural people who were driven into banking and commerce by papal edicts forbidding Christians to engage in usury.[98] The implication is that Jews, against their national inclinations, were forced to become rich by being compelled to set up an hereditary plutocratic caste. This proposition, however, is untenable for the obvious reason that Jews were very active in moneylending long before Christianity— not to mention the papacy—had entered the arena of history.

The late A. L. Kroeber, eminent head of the University of California's Anthropology Department, took an unruffled approach to the Jewish question. Pointing to the "exceedingly spotty Jewish participation in the great civilizations," Kroeber defined the present Jewish ascendancy as a "transitional phenomenon." It was, he said, the "released mobility" of the Jews which had the effect of propelling them forward "more quickly than Gentiles in fields which they enter newly, and temporarily with brilliant success." [99] As the years go by, however, and the Jews' upward curve shows no signs of leveling off, Kroeber's thesis is losing much of its cogency.

A more plausible thesis has a Darwinian base. It was the richest Jew who had the best chance of surviving the pogroms and lesser persecutions which have dogged Jewish footsteps over the centuries. In most cases he could buy his way out. But the richest Jew was generally the most adroit Jew, the one best suited and

---

98. Sachar, op. cit., p. 533. Lewisohn, who taught at several American universities before becoming professor of comparative literature at Brandeis, was a Jewish supremacist who inveighed against Germans, Slavs, Negroes, and Anglo-Saxon "barbarism." One might speculate on what would happen to a Majority professor who inveighed against Jewish "barbarism."

99. A. L. Kroeber, *Configurations of Cultural Growth*, University of California Press, Berkeley, 1969, p. 749.

best adapted to the peculiar conditions and requirements of urban and ghetto life. Consequently the affluent, citified Jew of today is the end product of two thousand years of a special form of natural selection, the fortunate possessor of an inbred cosmopolitanism which is a great competitive advantage in decadent, heterogeneous, urbanized societies incapable of guarding their citizens against the racial dynamism of intruders.

Richard Swartzbaugh, assistant professor of anthropology at Eastern Illinois University, believes that a fragmented, divided, class-ridden multiracial society cannot survive without massive infusions of mediation. Since Jews have always been adept as mediators, since their status as outsiders highly qualifies them as professional go-betweens, especially in the areas of labor relations, law and politics, they have almost automatically been propelled to the top of a social order that must resolve its multiplying inner conflicts by arbitration and "deals" or dissolve into war and anarchy.[100]

Perhaps the most interesting of all theories that attempt to account for the current Jewish ascendancy is that advanced by John Murray Cuddihy, an assistant professor of sociology and a scion of a prominent Irish-American family. In Cuddihy's view, Freud, Marx, Claude Lévi-Strauss, and other prominent Diaspora Jews, who have done so much to bruise Western culture, were not impelled by their love of truth or their desire to improve mankind, but by their fear and loathing of Western civility, the repressed and controlled behavior that is incomprehensible to an irrepressible people. Since they obviously could not get away with a direct attack on Gentile conduct, they consciously or unconsciously worked out highly ramified interpretations of history, economics, politics, psychology, and anthropology to undermine it. Communism was an ideal weapon to divide and destroy the Western political and economic order. Freudianism attacked Western morality by its neurotic emphasis on sex and by lending respectability to the promptings of the baser instincts. Lévi-Strauss's anthropology compared savage and civilized societies to the disadvantage of the latter. Cuddihy even hints that Einstein's physics was moti-

---

100. Richard Swartzbaugh, *The Mediator*, Howard Allen, Cape Canaveral, Florida, 1973.

vated in part by a desire to shock and shatter rather than refine and advance Western science.[101]

It is only a short step from acknowledging that peoples or races have special aptitudes for high achievement in certain occupations to the development of theories of racial inferiority or superiority. The most ardent contemporary advocate of Jewish supremacy is Nathaniel Weyl, who alleges that Jews are inherently more intelligent than other peoples because they have been breeding for intelligence since the beginning of the Diaspora. Gentile churchmen, the cream of the non-Jewish medieval intelligentsia according to Weyl, were usually celibate and died without issue, while the less sexually inhibited rabbis and Talmudic scholars were eagerly sought after by the daughters of prominent Jewish merchants.[102] Weyl's point concerning the synergistic combination and recombination rather than the ascetic stultification of clever Jewish genes would have more validity if he did not confuse intelligence with verbalism and intellectual sheen.[103] Or if he did not forget that most of the kings, artists, writers, architects, and warriors of the Middle Ages, as well as more than a few popes, were as lusty and prolific as his rabbis and ghetto tycoons.

In *The Geography of Intellect*, which he wrote with Stefan T. Possony, Weyl supported his claims for Jewish intelligence by referring to seventeen studies, "Eleven found the Jews superior in mental test scores, four found them equal, and two found them

---

101. John Murray Cuddihy, *The Ordeal of Civility*, Dell Publishing, New York, 1976.

102. *The Creative Elite in America*, Chap. XVIII. Boccaccio and Rabelais would have smiled at Weyl's assertions regarding the celibacy and intelligence of the clergy. Part of Weyl's theme, incidentally, was taken from Sir Francis Galton, who was equally bitter about the dysgenics of religious bachelorhood. But in his own intelligence ratings Galton excluded Jews and gave first place to the Athenians, whom he placed two grades above the nineteenth-century British and four grades above African Negroes. Francis Galton, *Hereditary Genius*, Macmillan, London, 1869, especially pp. 42, 257, 342, 357.

103. "All intellectuality is in the long run shallowness; never does it allow of probing to the very roots of a matter, never of reaching down to the depths of the soul, or of the universe. Hence intellectuality makes it easy to go from one extreme to the other. That is why you find among Jews fanatical orthodoxy and unenlightened doubt side by side; they both spring from one source." Werner Sombart, *The Jews and Modern Capitalism*, trans. M. Epstein, Dutton, New York, 1914, p. 269.

inferior." [104] The authors only gave details on one study, a series of tests covering almost 2,000 Jewish and non-Jewish children in three London schools, one upper class, one poor, and the third very poor. The Jewish scores were significantly higher.[105]

Weyl failed to mention it, but he must be aware that tests seeking to compare Jewish intelligence with the intelligence of such broad-spectrum groups as whites, Gentiles, or Christians are necessarily loaded in favor of Jews. Since the Jewish population is concentrated almost entirely in or around the largest cities, tests involving large numbers of Jews have to be conducted in areas where the white population is extremely heterogeneous, with a heavy emphasis on groups of other than Northern European origin. Many of these "whites" may in fact be nonwhites because when forced to label Americans as either white or nonwhite, the Census Bureau puts many Puerto Ricans and almost all Mexicans in the former category.

To obtain an accurate measurement of Jewish intelligence, it would seem reasonable to compare Jews, a select group within the white population, with other select white population groups rather than with the white population as a whole. An intelligence test restricted to Jews and Majority members might produce entirely different results than the tests cited by Weyl. Also, since some intelligence tests reveal as much information about verbal agility, quick recall, and educational levels as they do about intelligence itself, consideration should be given to the fact that Jews, being the wealthiest and most cosmopolitan population group, have readier access than other Americans to education and to such educational byproducts as memory training and vocabulary building. Although it may sound heretical in this day and age, a college degree, a subscription to the *New York Times*, and a fondness for forensics are not conclusive proof of higher intelligence.

---

104. One of the studies that found Jews to be inferior was Carl Brigham's famous analysis of the U.S. Army's World War I intelligence tests. For more on Brigham, see Appendix A.

105. Nathaniel Weyl and Stefan Possony, *The Geography of Intellect*, Henry Regnery, Chicago, 1963, pp. 162–63. The authors also failed to mention a detailed study by Dr. Audrey Shuey, which showed that Protestant college students scored better than their Jewish counterparts in intelligence tests. See *The Journal of Social Psychology*, 1942, Vol. 15, pp. 221–43.

It was educated city Jews, not hillbillies, who furnished most of the support for Henry Wallace's Progressive party in the 1948 presidential election—the party that stood for the almost total appeasement of the Soviet Union.[106] In spite of these objections the case for Jewish intellectual superiority continues to gather momentum. Ernest van den Haag devoted the opening chapter of his bestseller, *The Jewish Mystique*, to wide-ranging generalizations about the finer-tuned cerebral apparatus of Jews.[107] Although in only one instance did he supply any documentation for his allegations [108] and although he never once referred to Weyl by name, Professor van den Haag was obviously expanding on Weyl's "breeding for intelligence" hypothesis and his writing breathed the spirit of the latter's arguments.

But the case for the genetically based superiority of Jewish brains did not receive national prominence until a 1969 press interview with the British scientist-turned-novelist C. P. Snow. Quoting from a speech he was preparing to deliver to the Hebrew Union College, Snow stated that Jews were definitely superior to all other living peoples and attributed this superiority to inbreeding.[109]

---

106. A 1947 Gallup Poll showed that blue-collar workers were far more suspicious and aware of Russian expansionism than college graduates, who were still clinging to the outworn notion that Russia would join the Western democracies in the establishment of One World. *New York Times*, March 23, 1947, IV, p. 6. It might also be noted that the educated classes could not conceive of the 1939 Russo-German Nonaggression Pact until it was signed.

107. Van den Haag's remarks about Jewish cultural domination have been quoted on pp. 87–88.

108. *The Jewish Mystique*, p. 24. The author relied on an old study by Lewis Terman, who in tests of California school children found there were twice as many gifted Jewish students as their proportion of the population warranted. Here again, the tests were conducted in the largest cities— San Francisco, Oakland and Los Angeles—where California Jews were concentrated and where the Majority was underrepresented both in quantity and quality. Other population groups produced extremely high scores, but van den Haag did not mention them. The Scots did even better than the Jews on a percentage basis. The most important lesson of the Terman study was the woefully poor performance of Negro and Mexican children. Lewis Terman, *Genetic Studies of Genius*, Stanford University Press, 1925, Vol. 1, pp. 55–56.

109. *Pittsburgh Post-Gazette*, April 1, 1969, p. 26. In the same interview Snow refused to be drawn into a discussion of Negro intelligence. By side-stepping the Negro issue, Snow proved himself less courageous than Weyl, who after

Ironically, theories of Aryan, Nordic, or Teutonic racial suprem-acy, which assigned Jews to the lowest rung of the white racial ladder, have now been completely reversed. Within twenty-five years of Adolf Hitler's death and following the imprisonment or ostracism of all Northern European racial supremacists, in and out of Germany, an internationally known writer like C. P. Snow, was given a handsome stipend and treated most generously by the American press after publicly proclaiming a theory of racial superiority. But all things considered, Snow, van den Haag, and Weyl's line of reasoning does not prove Jewish intellectual preemi-nence as much as it proves the reshuffling of America's racial power structure.

When it is a matter of appraising racial intelligence, the histori-cal record, the accumulated evidence of the entire human experi-ence would seem to be more reliable than a few scattered, often self-serving academic *obiter dicta* and I.Q. scores. If Jews are truly superior to the rest of mankind, it might be asked why, with one exception, the greatest cultural achievements of civilization took place in exactly those areas where Jews were unknown, banned, segregated, or actively persecuted.[110] If superiority is to be mea-sured in political and economic rather than cultural terms, how is it that the greatest and most enduring empires, republics and city states of Western civilization were founded without Jewish assistance and reached their zenith before the appearance of influ-ential Jewish establishments within their borders.[111] No Jews

quitting the Communist party wrote extensively on the subject of Negro intellec-tual inferiority. Professor van den Haag, who also has definite ideas about black capabilities, testified for Southern white children in legal proceedings instituted in 1963 to overturn (unsuccessfully) the Supreme Court's 1954 school desegrega-tion ruling. Putnam, *Race and Reality*, pp. 87–88.

110. The list of countries and cities forbidden to Jews in different eras was given earlier in this chapter. Here the list may be lengthened by adding that there were no Jews of any influence in Pericles's Athens and minor identifiable Jewish participation in the cultural life of the Roman Republic and Empire (in their great days). In Goethe's Germany and Dostoyevsky's Russia, Jews were just beginning to stir out of their ghetto cocoon. The single example of a great and uniquely Hebrew culture, though somewhat restricted in that Judaism specifi-cally forbade painting and sculpture, evolved in ancient Palestine, where Hebrews were a majority in their own land.

111. Zenith is not meant to signify the era of greatest territorial expansion or greatest wealth, but the moment of the cresting of national morale, purpose, and unity. In this sense the greatest days of England occurred in the sixteenth

signed the Magna Carta or the Declaration of Independence. No Jews were active in the Long Parliament, the Constitutional Convention in Philadelphia or in most of the other great deliberations which gave form and substance to man's most successful experiments with representative government.

The few historic instances, at least in recent times, where bodies of Jews have assumed outright political control—the Kurt Eisner regime in Bavaria (November 1918—February 1919), the short-lived Spartacus uprising in Berlin (December 1918—January 1919) and Bela Kun's sadistic orgy in Budapest (March–August 1919)—could hardly be classified as golden ages of statesmanship. Neither could the Russian Revolution, in which Jews took a commanding role until the Stalin purges. The Jewish autonomous region of Birobidzhan fizzled out almost before it started.[112] Israel has been in a state of war since its creation in 1948.

As for the economic advantages Jews are supposed to confer upon their host countries, there is no question that they bring with them a great deal of money and financial expertise. But an increasing flow of money is often accompanied by inflation, financial crime, and a flood of speculation. If Jews are as intrinsic to the good economic life as some economists claim, it seems odd that the Weimar Republic with its plethora of Jewish financiers was an economic miasma, while the economic miracle of West Germany took place in the one large Western nation almost free of Jewish financial domination and at the very time (1952–1962) it was paying Israel $900 million in reparations and billions more to individual Jews throughout the world. A country with an equally dynamic economy in the post-World War II era is Japan, which has no Jews at all.[113]

Another way of measuring the Jewish contribution to society is to examine the political, economic and social conditions of those areas where Jews are most heavily concentrated. The two main centers of Jewish power and population in the modern world are New York City and Israel. The former, financially as well as

---

rather than the nineteenth century. America is either well past its zenith or a long way from it.

112. For the Birobidzhan debacle, see *Encyclopedia of Russia and the Soviet Union*, McGraw-Hill, New York, 1961, p. 258.

113. Japan's vastly profitable trade with the West, however, involves many Jewish import firms.

morally bankrupt, can only be described as the greatest municipal catastrophe of the day—a scabrous pile of ugliness, tastelessness, and lawlessness—certainly not the brilliant world capital of a people with superior civilizing gifts. Although they have failed to make New York bloom, Jews have nevertheless accomplished technological wonders in the Palestinian wilderness. But the true measure of a people's genius is not determined by its ability to cultivate the land, build cities, and wage a series of successful wars, however essential these factors may be. Its ultimate place in history is determined by its statecraft, that is, by its ability to create a special, fertilizing environment in which the citizenry can develop its distinctive cultural resources to the highest possible pitch.

Modern Jews may be gifted above all other peoples. Or they may be, as Toynbee asserts, the remnants of a fossilized civilization.[114] Or they may even be, as anti-Semites claim, a parasitic social organism that survives by feeding off other social organisms. Which of these descriptions is most realistic it is too early to tell. Modern Jewry has been emancipated for less than two centuries and not enough data have been collected. But if it should turn out that Jews are superior beings, as many of them feel and as their more enthusiastic scholars and well-wishers are attempting to prove, it is time for a more conclusive demonstration of their capabilities.

It is one thing to reshape and reorder the thinking habits and living patterns of a decadent United States. It is another to give the world a greater writer than Shakespeare, a greater composer than Mozart, a greater artist than Michelangelo. It is not an easy task for Israel to exist as a minuscule military and cultural oasis in the midst of a hostile human and natural environment. But it is a much more difficult task to undertake a civilizing mission in the Middle East comparable to Spain's in Latin America, Britain's in North America and France's in North Africa. As final proof of Jewish superiority, Einstein's theories must become Einstein's laws, and the net effect on the evolutionary process of Marx, Freud, and other modern Jewish prophets and sages must be positive not negative, constructive not destructive.

---

114. For saying this, Toynbee was accused by Jewish historian Maurice Samuel of perpetuating "demonological anti-Semitism." Toynbee, *A Study of History*, Vol. V, p. 76, and Samuel, *The Professor and the Fossil*, Knopf, New York, 1956, p. 194.

Until all the evidence is in, the Jewish hegemony in the United States can be more convincingly explained by the historical tensions of race differences rather than by race differences themselves. The truth seems to be that any organized minority with a given amount of intelligence can obtain supremacy over a disorganized majority of equal intelligence. A race-conscious population group is far more effective and successful in most forms of endeavor than a race-unconscious population group. Racial spirit, like team spirit, stimulates victory in all types of competition, athletic or political, intellectual or social. If the Majority were as race-conscious as the Jewish minority and had half as many organizations working for it, Jewish predominance in America would disappear overnight.

Where Jews diverge most sharply from the Majority, aside from important personality differences,[115] is in having a higher degree of ethnocentrism, not a higher degree of intelligence. To put it in a different perspective, Jewish power may derive as much or

---

115. According to James Yaffe, Jews have more interest in sex than non-Jews, less interest in athletics, less faith in an afterlife, a lower birthrate, take many more expensive vacations, live longer, spend more time in psychoanalysis, and are much more likely to be hippies. In Hollywood, Jews get more divorces, commit more adultery, and drink less than their non-Jewish neighbors. Jews use Jewish doctors 95 percent of the time; Jewish lawyers 87 percent of the time. Although they sometimes try to force themselves into non-Jewish country clubs, they are very exclusive about their own. One of them, the Hillcrest in Southern California, has the highest initiation fee ($22,000) of any golf club in the U.S. and bans non-Jews except for a few show business figures who are admitted as "honorary Jews." Jews, continues Yaffe, are noted for their "fear, obsequiousness, isolationism and belligerence"—a psychological chasm between Jew and non-Jew that may never be bridged. Traditionally dogmatic themselves, they demand rationalism in others. For the Jew "the intellect can't be just a tool . . . it has to be a weapon too. He doesn't use it simply to discover what the world is like or to create something beautiful, or to communicate his ideas. He must use it to beat down his competitors, to prove his superiority. For him controversy is inseparable from intellectual activity. Watch him at a party; note the vicious delight with which he backs lesser intellects into a corner. He's implacable; neither social decorum nor human compassion can soften his attack. If you want to observe this trait at a safer distance, read what he writes to the letters-to-the-editor pages. In all Jewish publications, from *Commentary* down to the most obscure Yiddish weekly, these pages bathe the reader in vitriol. Like his father, the garment manufacturer, the Jewish intellectual doesn't trade easy." *The American Jews*, pp. 38, 65, 68, 234–35, 268–69, 292–93.

more from Majority weakness and disorganization as from Jewish strength.

Since the anti-Semitic taboo has made it impossible to submit the Jewish question to free discussion and open inquiry,[116] Jews have only themselves to thank for having set themselves above and outside the rules of conventional democratic conduct. Considering their history and their memories, it is only human for Jews to have done so. But it is also only human on the part of Majority members to oppose the kind of organized group behavior for which their institutions were never designed. When the occasion arises, Jews may appeal to fair play and tolerance for themselves, but when the debate centers on Jewry they seldom extend these traditional democratic prerogatives to others. Let Majority members who think differently take even the first faltering step toward a racial protective organization such as the B'nai B'rith's Anti-Defamation League.[117] They will be hounded out of public life almost overnight by the media, "private" investigators, law enforcement agencies and, if need be, congressional committees—

---

116. These conspiracies of silence also extend to schools of thought and avenues of research which might strengthen Majority unity and thereby ultimately work to the Jews' disadvantage—i.e., racial interpretation of American history, genetic arguments for segregated education, statistical studies of financial crime, and so on.

117. On its 50th anniversary in 1963, the Anti-Defamation League could point with pride to a New York headquarters, regional offices in thirty cities, a staff of 150 full-time lawyers, social scientists, educators and public relations specialists. Its budget for 1960 was $3,940,000. Thomas B. Morgan, "The Fight Against Prejudice," *Look*, June 4, 1963. Although tax-exempt, the ADL plays a highly political role and occasionally usurps the power of the police. The New Orleans regional director of the ADL put up most of the money for the informers which the FBI used to entrap an alleged bomber of synagogues in Mississippi. A young female school teacher was shot to death during the arrest, but the ADL escaped the usual investigation given any individual or group involved in homicide. *Los Angeles Times*, Feb. 13, 1970. As for the B'nai B'rith itself, which was founded in 1843 and headed by a Grand Saar, it has 205,000 male members in 1,350 lodges in forty-three countries and 130,000 female members in 600 chapters. Edward Grusd, *B'nai B'rith*, Appleton-Century, New York, 1966, pp. 283, 286. The B'nai B'rith is the only private agency to have been given official "consultation status" by the United Nations, where it acts as a strong lobby for Israel and other Jewish interests, though it has never registered as the agent of a foreign government. *New York Times*, May 28, 1970, p. 21.

all prodded into action by a nationwide avalanche of Jewish protest.

In the long run, the Jewish place in American life cannot rest on the sanctity of institutions, dated dogmas, *argumenta ad misericordiam*, or the divine right of minorities. It must rest on the cause-and-effect relationship between the rise of the Jewish establishment and the Majority's disestablishment. If Jews are chiefly responsible for the present grinding assault on the nation's racial backbone, then the Jewish minority must come under public scrutiny. America could survive forever without Jews. It could not last a day without the Majority.

Meanwhile the cyclic reckoning which has marked the rhythm of Jewish survival in the past closes in on American Jewry. Although the accumulation and preservation of Jewish wealth are only feasible in an orderly society where private property is a right, not a crime, Jews seem bent on destroying the very political, economic, and social climate that has made their success possible.[118] As if in the grip of a lemming-like frenzy, they have been in the forefront of every divisive force of the modern era, from class agitation to minority racism, from the worst capitalistic exploitation to the most brutal collectivism, from blind religious orthodoxy to atheism and psychoanalysis, from total dogmatism to total permissiveness.

Moreover, as Jewish domination has become more pronounced, so has Jewish separateness—a dangerous trend for a minority which prospers best by concealing its divergence from the racial norm. Such recent historical stimuli as Nazi anti-Semitism, the Israeli experience, Soviet anti-Zionism, and the stepped-up tempo of social disintegration have filled the Jewish stockpile of race

---

118. The final effect of collectivist or welfare-state economics on Jewry has been completely misunderstood not only by most Jews but by most anti-Semites. After the Communist regime in Russia had confiscated Jewish fortunes and outlawed finance capitalism, Russian Jews had none of the usual Jewish defenses to fall back on when Stalin decided to turn against them—no Jewish-owned press, no Jewish-oriented public opinion, no lavishly financed network of Jewish societies. Today in the Soviet Union, a Marxist state largely created by Jewish thought and Jewish revolutionary activity, Zionism is a crime and Jews, fleeing the country by the tens of thousands each year, have practically disappeared from high public office. See pp. 456–57.

consciousness to overflowing. The appearance of ever more Jews in the top strata of public life inevitably produces a greater amount of Jewish self-identification, as well as a far greater awareness of Jews on the part of non-Jews. Intensified publicity, while revealing the extreme cultivation of a few Jews, also calls more attention to such unattractive Jewish traits as intrusiveness, disputatiousness, and haggling, and to the incredible garishness which permeates the Catskills, Miami Beach, Las Vegas, and other centers of Jewish resort life.

The same racial dynamics which have sporadically elevated Jews to the top of the social heap have also cast them down into the abyss. The penduluming, rags-to-riches swing of Jewish history has led to the fairyland castles of the Rothschilds, but it has also led to the barbed wire of Buchenwald. When viewed Olympianly, the story of Jewish wanderings through time and space is both fascinating and repulsive, ennobling and degrading—in part comic, in great part tragic.

The only last word that can be said about Jews is that there is no last word. Jews are such a mass of contradictions and encompass such extremes of human behavior that they are simply beyond the reach of pat formulas, casual generalizations, or prophetic clichés. They are both the "People of the Book" and the inventors of the strip tease.[119] They were pioneers of plutocracy *and* communism. They originated and lived by the concept of the "Chosen People," yet are presently the most vociferous of antiracists. They are the most God-fearing and God-hating, the most straitlaced and most hedonistic, the most cosmopolitan and most narrow-minded, the most cultivated and most vulgar of peoples. Jewish sabras in Israel fought (until the 1973 war) like 10,000 Lawrences of Arabia. In Europe, however, with the exception of the Warsaw uprising, their brethren were herded like sheep into the pens of the concentration camps.[120] As a final paradox, it should be

---

119. *New York Times*, Feb. 25, 1937, p. 10.

120. Jewish docility in Hitler's concentration camps has aroused the ire of militant Jews, particularly Israelis. "But why," asks an article in *Commentary* (April 1962, p. 354), "was there no resistance? . . . At Auschwitz the ratio of prisoners to guards varied from 20 to 1 to 35 to 1. [Yet] the Jews meekly accepted every successive order which rendered them impotent, they queued up for the deportation trains. . . ."

pointed out that many of the greatest Jews, perhaps the very greatest, have been Jewish renegades or pseudo Jews.[121]

Through all this mountain of inconsistency there glimmers but one, thin, barely visible vein of logic. The Jewish nervous system bears the load of many passions, but always evident are traces of an implacable hostility to the peoples who at different times have sheltered or persecuted them, enriched or impoverished them, deified or satanized them. The Jewish fascination for political, economic, and social experiments may not, as often supposed, be proof of a noble, unselfish desire to save mankind by a race of professional Messiahs, but of a firmly rooted, semi-conscious, semi-coordinated vendetta—Bacon called it a "secret inbred rancour" [122]—against all things non-Jewish and, in the final countdown, possibly all things Jewish as well.

If the past is an indication, if what Lord Acton said about individuals is applicable to groups, a sharp reduction of the Jewish racial vector is in the offing. This could be achieved most easily and most painlessly by assimilation. But there are no convincing signs of this on the horizon, despite the falling Jewish birthrate and the higher incidence of Jewish outmarriages. The 3,000-year record of Jewish nonassimilation has only been broken once.[123] The alternative to assimilation is repression, of which history provides many models—Egyptian bondage, Assyrian and Babylonian captivities, mass deportations, forced baptism, quarantined ghettos, Russian pogroms, and German concentration camps.

When and if a resuscitated American Majority has the strength and the will to put a stop to the Jewish envelopment of America,

---

121. Renegades in that they embraced Christianity (Berenson, Disraeli, Heine, Husserl, Mahler, Mendelssohn, Sts. Peter and Paul) or turned openly atheist (Marx, Trotsky, and other leading dialectical materialists). The possibility that Moses was an Egyptian and the fact that Josephus was a turncoat have been previously mentioned. Spinoza, the greatest Jewish philosopher, was expelled from the Jewish community in Amsterdam in 1656 by rabbinical order. Many Orthodox Jews and anti-Semites agree—or hope—that Jesus was not Jewish because he came from "Galilee of the Gentiles." A prevailing Talmudic tradition has it that Jesus was the illegitimate offspring of Joseph Panthera, a Roman centurion, and Miriam, the wife of a carpenter. *Jüdische Enzyklopädie*, Jüdischer Verlag, Berlin, 1930, Band IV/1, pp. 772–73.

122. *New Atlantis*, Great Books, Chicago, 1952, Vol. 30, p. 209.

123. See footnote 8, p. 63.

history should not be repeated. The operation ought to be accomplished with a finesse that is a credit to both parties. The guiding purpose should be moral as well as cultural and political—to transcend, for the first time, the ancient racial infighting by facing the issue with the head and the heart, not the club and the knout.

Solutions to problems arising from massive racial confrontations within the borders of one country require every drop of reason and imagination that exists in the overflowing well of the human spirit. Separation is obviously part of the solution. But how can this most delicate of all social operations be performed successfully? How can it be brought off without unbearable dislocations in the lands of exodus and intolerable sacrifices in the lands of the ingathering?

Theoretically the answer is Israel. But Israel is the sputtering fuse of World War III.[124]

---

124. The fuse sputtered a little more than usual on the occasion of Israel's air attack on the Iraqi nuclear reactor in June 1981.

CHAPTER 16

Nonwhite Minorities

THE MEXICANS: The typical Mexican is neither Spanish nor Asian, white nor yellow.[1] Although Spanish-speaking and the heir of a laminate of Spanish culture, he does not dream of Spain and the glories of the Spanish past. He is conscious of no ties to northeast Asia, the home of his Indian ancestors. Primarily a mestizo, a Spanish-Indian hybrid, the Mexican considers himself a unique racial specimen.

Aside from the genetic distinction, where Mexicans differ most from their northern neighbors is in the art of living. With its fiestas and flowers, its ancient and modern art forms, its rich and varied resources, its rugged *mesetas* and *barrancas,* and its exuberant tropic beaches, Mexico adds grace and beauty to an increasingly drab world. After the revolutions and counterrevolutions of the early twentieth century, an intense wave of nativism swept over the country, bringing with it such cultural splendors as the mural painting of Orozco, certainly the most magnificent and the most dazzling pictorial art to come out of the New World. The sworn enemy of this art is the Madison Avenue and Hollywood *kitsch* exported to Mexico from the United States, a spurious culture which vulgarizes and degrades exporters and importers alike.

The 1980 Census found 20,446,531 Hispanics in the United States. At least 16,000,000 of these were Mexican Americans—

1. *Focus,* a publication of the National Geographic Society, states the population of Mexico is 55 percent mestizo, 29 percent Indian, 15 percent European and under 1 percent Negro and Mulatto. To the casual visitor the European estimate appears high. Unquestionably the mestizo element accounts for the overwhelming proportion of Mexican Americans.

most of them in California, Texas, Colorado, and the Southwest, though large concentrations are taking root in big northern cities.[2] The *pochos* or native-born citizens and the *cholos* or legal immigrants probably account for half this number. The illegals or "undocumented workers" probably account for the other half. Members of the second largest nonwhite minority, Mexican Americans are often as poorly educated and economically disadvantaged as Negroes. Their school dropout rate is high and their per capita income is low.[3] Even so, the living standard of most Mexican Americans is far superior to that of Mexicans in Mexico.

Forever unassimilable because of their coloration and their Mongoloid traits, Mexican Americans accentuate their minority status by holding fast to their language (vast stretches of the American Southwest are now bilingual), by voting the straight Democratic ticket,[4] and by their political agitation and unioneering. Emulating Negroes, Mexican Americans have taken to playing hardball racial politics.[5] In the California valleys and in the Los Angeles and Denver barrios there have already been a few serious confrontations with Anglos, although "The Chicano (Mexican-American) revolt against the Anglo establishment is still in the planning stage."[6] Mexican-American ethnocentrism is otherwise nourished by constant reminders of American aggression against Mexico and by a demagoguery which holds that Mexican Americans are now second-class citizens in a part of North America that once belonged to their forefathers.

There is a distinct possibility, if the legal and illegal seepage of Mexican genes across the Rio Grande and the high Mexican-American and Mexican birthrates continue at present levels, that

---

2. Having come from Mexico centuries ago, some 250,000 "Hispanos" in New Mexico look upon Mexican Americans as interlopers and are perpetuating a Spanish-speaking, assimilation-proof subculture of their own.

3. *New York Times,* April 20, 1969, p. 54.

4. A solid bloc of Mexican-American votes, some from voters long dead, won Lyndon Johnson the hotly disputed 1948 senatorial primary in Texas at a crucial moment in his political career. See pp. 428–29.

5. *San Francisco Sunday Examiner & Chronicle,* March 19, 1967, p. 6. The Ford Foundation supports two Mexican-American racial protective organizations—the Mexican-American Legal Defense and Educational Fund and the Southwest Conference of La Raza.

6. *New York Times,* April 20, 1969, p. 1.

Mexican Americans will regain their lost territories of Alta California and Texas—already being called the Sarape Belt—not by violence or minority politics but simply by exercising squatters' rights.

CHINESE: The first large contingent of Chinese immigrants (13,100) arrived in Caiifornia in 1854.[7] Of an utterly alien civilization and totally unfamiliar with the American environment, the Chinese started out under the most severe cultural and economic handicaps. They built railroad beds throughout the West, painstakingly worked placer mines, and provided much of the white settlers' household help. The pigtailed Chinaman in the backroom was an institution that endured in San Francisco for more than half a century.

Once the gold boom had subsided and the railroads were running, Congress responded to pressure from Westerners fearful of the competition of coolie labor and of the rising tide of color (123,201 Chinese arrived in California in the 1870s) by passing the Exclusion Act of 1882. It was Congress's first try at immigration legislation and preceded the establishment of white quotas by almost forty years.[8]

The 1970 Census listed 435,062 Americans of Chinese extraction, of whom 52,039 resided in the Hawaiian Islands. The 1980 Census raised the figure to 806,027, which shows that the Chinese, who almost doubled in size between 1960 and 1970, almost doubled again in the next decade—both increases undoubtedly due to the 1965 Immigration Act. If relations with mainland China continue to stabilize, Chinese Americans may again begin their vintage-year, homebound voyages across the Pacific, a *westward* migration which once managed to keep their rate of growth below that of most other minorities.

Chinese Americans are the prime example of the self-sufficient, static minority. Although once the victims of almost intolerable persecution and discrimination,[9] they have now buried their old

---

7. Davie, *World Immigration*, p. 308.

8. Ibid., p. 313.

9. The entire Chinese population of 1,000 was ruthlessly driven out of Truckee, California, in 1878. The previous year in San Francisco there was almost open warfare between the Irish and the Chinese. Davie, op. cit., pp. 311–12.

resentments instead of taking them out in racial agitation and minority lobbying.[10] Rather proud of their hyphenated status, they keep their family names, they keep many of their Far Eastern ways, and they keep to themselves. Their lives are characterized by a subdued middle-class morality and respectability. When most other nonwhite minorities move into an urban area, it usually deteriorates into a slum. Chinese enclaves, on the other hand, become centers of attraction. San Francisco's Chinatown, the largest concentration of Chinese in the New World, is one of the cleanest and best-maintained sections of the city. Once the battleground of rival tongs it boasts a relatively low incidence of violent crime and juvenile delinquency, though there was one gang slaying in 1977.

The Chinese minority, at least in the continental United States, is by any standard of race relations a model minority. It gives more than it takes. It preserves and develops its own culture without seeking to impose it on others. Above all it does not ask for special treatment. In the bright serenity of the Chinese-American future only one small note of gloom can be detected. If revolutionary or racial fervor should induce China to launch a military attack against the United States, the position of the Chinese minority might become as tenuous as that of the Japanese in World War II.

JAPANESE: Much of what has been written about Chinese Americans applies to Japanese Americans, or at least to those Japanese Americans in the continental United States. The Japanese came to America later than the Chinese, but they encountered the same hostility. Although Japan itself had banned all foreigners, except for a few Dutch, for 230 years (1638–1868) and had forbidden its citizens to go abroad on pain of death, the Japanese government objected strongly to Congress's plans to include Japanese in the ban against Chinese immigration.[11] To soothe Japanese pride

---

10. In Hawaii, where nonwhites are in the majority, the Chinese are more politically active, as demonstrated by the presence in the senate (1959–77) of liberal Republican Hiram Fong. In the continental United States, the Chinese minority, like the Japanese minority, stands apart from the liberal-minority coalition by often voting for conservative candidates and taking an aggressive stand against the busing of school children.

11. Davie, op. cit., pp. 318–21.

President Theodore Roosevelt negotiated a "Gentleman's Agreement" in 1907, by which Japan agreed to halt the Japanese exodus, provided Congress passed no restrictive immigration legislation that mentioned the Japanese by name.[12] By 1940 there were some 140,000 Japanese in the continental United States, 86 percent of them in the Far West, where many had become prosperous truck farmers.[13] In 1980, counting those in Hawaii, there were 700,747 Japanese Americans.

Shortly after Pearl Harbor, which displayed the dangers of Japanese military bravado, more than 110,000 West Coast Japanese (the majority of them U.S. citizens) were removed from their homes, farms and businesses and transported to Colorado "relocation camps," at an average loss of $10,000 per family.[14] The Japanese in Hawaii, where their proportion to the population was much larger and their potential threat to national security much greater, were left in comparative peace. In 1944 the 442nd Regimental Combat Team, composed largely of Nisei, second-generation Japanese Americans from Oahu, was sent to fight crack German troops in the Italian campaign and proceeded to rack up one of the finest records in American military annals.

Quiet and unobtrusive on the mainland, where many vote Republican, Japanese play racial politics with a vengeance in the Hawaiian Islands where, as the largest population group, they vote Democratic. Hawaii's two senators are Japanese, as are Representatives Daniel Akaka and Governor George Ariyoshi. Such bloc voting belies the claim there are no racial tensions in Hawaii. The fact is that until recently the 50th state was a territory and was ruled with a strong hand by the dominant white traders and planters and the armed forces.[15] Because the more vociferous American minorities are not found in large numbers in Hawaii, it does not follow that racism is nonexistent or that in the future there will not be a bitter power struggle among the various popula-

---

12. Ibid., p. 321.

13. Ibid., p. 324.

14. Simpson and Yinger, op. cit., pp. 132–33. After the war, claims were settled at an average rate of ten cents on the dollar. *Washington Post*, Oct. 5, 1965, p. 1.

15. National defense is Hawaii's largest industry. Tourism is second, sugar third, pineapples fourth.

tion groups. Island paradises are no exception to the laws of racial dynamics.[16]

OTHER PACIFIC OCEAN AND ASIAN MINORITIES: Census statistics demonstrate the unfolding of a racial tragedy in Hawaii, the only state where nonwhites outnumber whites.[17] One of America's most colorful and romantic minorities, the Polynesian, is rapidly becoming extinct. Out of the 167,253 "official" Hawaiians counted by the 1980 Census, perhaps only 12,000 pure Hawaiians remain. A concerted effort is being made to save them by maintaining a subsidized refuge on the island of Niihau, where they live in voluntary quarantine, speak the old Hawaiian tongue, and are without benefit of television, automobiles, and liquor stores.

Another nonwhite minority with large numbers in Hawaii is the Filipino. In 1980 there were 774,680 Filipino Americans—a jump of 570,000 in ten years. Filipinos had easy access to America when their country was a U.S. possession, but they were under a quota when given independence in 1946. For all practical purposes the 1965 Immigration Act lifted the quota.

In the 1970s, in the aftermath of the Vietnam War and the conquest of large parts of Indochina by the Communist government of North Vietnam, the world was suddenly confronted with the "boat people," hundreds of thousands of Vietnamese (many of Chinese origin) fleeing South Vietnam by sea. They were later joined by smaller numbers of Cambodians whose once placid nation was torn apart by a native Communist revolution and a foreign Communist invasion. By 1980 more than 400,000 Indochinese refugees had arrived in the United States, and several hundred thousand more are expected in the years to come. Millions of Southeast Asians would like to follow in the footsteps of those

---

16. Racially motivated crime against white residents and tourists began to figure in the news in 1979. Many white students stay away from class on the last day of the school year, which is observed by many Hawaiians with such threats and intimidations—so far limited to words not deeds—as "kill a haole a day."

17. The 1970 Census showed 768,561 people in the Hawaiian Islands divided as follows: White, 298,160; Japanese, 217,307; Hawaiian and part-Hawaiian, 98,441; Filipino, 93,915; Chinese, 52,039; Negroes, 7,573; Other, 1,126. Many of the whites belong to transient military families.

who have already found refuge in this country. How many more will be permitted to settle here will depend on the policies of the various Indochinese governments and on the refugee policy, or lack of it, of the United States.

Other Asiatic or Mongoloid minorities include 354,529 Koreans,[18] 42,050 Samoans, 32,132 Guanamians, 361,544 Asian Indians from the Indian subcontinent (recent Asian immigrants), and 42,149 Eskimos and 14,177 Aleuts [19] (ancient Asian immigrants). Questions concerning the assimilation probability of these groups are best answered by Kipling's poetic cliché.

AMERICAN INDIANS: There are several theories concerning the racial origin of the American Indians, the most common being that they are descendants of fur-wearing, spear-carrying, mammoth-eating Mongolian tribesmen who island-hopped or perhaps walked across the Bering Sea some 20,000 years ago, when part of it was a grassy plain. A few dissident anthropologists point to the possibility of a partial descent from Polynesians and Melanesians who may have reached the New World from Easter Island. There are also legends of refugees from Atlantis and the lost continent of Mu, and of shipwrecked sailors from Chinese junks washing ashore in Central and South America.[20] The pockets of puzzling A_1 blood group may be accounted for by Australoid elements, and there is even the possibility of far-off kinship with the segregated Ainus of Japan.

In the year 1500, North America (above the Rio Grande) contained an estimated 850,000 Indians.[21] By 1900 the Indian popula-

---

18. The "Koreagate" scandal in 1975 revealed that prominent senators and representatives, including House Speaker Thomas O'Neill, were not averse to accepting favors from the agent of a foreign government.

19. The Aleuts were members of the early migration from Siberia, but they never went further than the Aleutian Islands. There, 150 years ago, Russian fur traders found 25,000 of their descendants. When the Russians departed, there were only 2,950 Aleuts left. If the 1980 Census is correct, they seem to be making a comeback. *Ency. Brit.*, Vol. 1, p. 565.

20. *The American Heritage Book of Indians*, American Heritage Publishing Co., New York, 1961, pp. 9, 25.

21. *Our American Indians at a Glance*, Pacific Coast Publications, Menlo Park, California, 1961, p. 6.

tion of the United States had decreased to 237,196,[22] a decline which seemed to bear out the theory of the Vanishing American and historian Arnold Toynbee's half-truth that the English-speaking peoples colonized by dispossession and genocide.[23] But today there are 1,361,869 Indians, and their number is increasing each year. Approximately 70 percent of the Indians live in 399 government reservations.[24]

The Indians of North America never became a mestizo population as did so many Indians of Latin America. The English settler, who often brought his family with him, was not as prone to miscegenation as the lonely Spanish soldier. Moreover, North American Indians were hunters, nomads, and isolated farmer and fisher folk—less adept at socializing than Mongoloids in the more urban agglomerates of the Aztec and Incan empires. This is not to suggest, however, that there was no interbreeding of Indians with trappers, traders, and other white "squaw men" in the West, and with Negro runaways in Southern states.[25] In Latin America, Southern European miscegenation diluted the white stock. In North America, Northern European miscegenation diluted the Indian stock.

Indian history furnishes an excellent confirmation of the axiom that racial tension diminishes as the physical distance between races lengthens. In frontier days, despite Rousseau's well-publicized notion of the "noble savage" and Cooper's Plutarchan Mohicans, Indians were regarded as the lowest and most debased of

---

22. *Harvard Encyclopedia of American Ethnic Groups*, pp. 58–59. Today the most numerous Indian tribe is the Navajo, with a population of 160,000. In the 17th century the Navajos numbered 9,000.

23. *A Study of History*, Vol. V, p. 46. In the same exaggerated vein Toynbee could have described the eternal warfare between nomadic Indian tribes as equally genocidal.

24. *Time*, Sept. 3, 1965, p. 72. An Indian author, Vine Deloria, Jr., disagrees with these figures. He estimates that half of all the Indians in the United States live in Eastern cities and that another 100,000 are scattered throughout Eastern rural areas. *New York Times Magazine*, Dec. 7, 1969.

25. At least 200 communities in the eastern U.S. consist largely of triracial hybrids of mixed Indian, Negro, and white ancestry. Coon, op. cit., p. 307. Madison Grant believed that half the American Indian population has some white blood.

humanoids.[26] Now that there is little or no contact with them, they are flattered and cozened by new friends, the modern generation of eleemosynary ideologues, and forgotten by erstwhile foes. Indeed, it has become a commonplace—and a measure of their depreciating race consciousness—for some whites to boast of their "Indian blood." Not too much, of course, but enough to conjure up visions of wide open spaces and Remington scouts. *Half-breed,* at one time the most contemptuous expression in American English, has been watered down to so anemic a pejorative that it hardly raises an eyebrow.

If present minority vociferousness were proportionate to past suffering, Indians would be quite justified in being the most clamorous of all American population groups. Once the sole and undisputed ruler of all he surveyed, the Indian has both fallen and been lowered to the bottom of the American social scale, where he remains. He was herded onto reservations, dosed with alcohol, decimated by smallpox, and only given full citizenship rights in 1924—rights which he has trouble exercising. In 1966 the average Indian had the lowest income of any American and an unemployment rate of nearly 40 percent. Ninety percent of his housing was below accepted standards and his life expectancy twenty-one years less than that of the general population.[27] Reservation Indians are still the wards of the Bureau of Indian Affairs, an organization of 16,000 government functionaries distinguished by a long record of administrative ineptitude.[28]

Taking their cue from the more dynamic minorities, Indians have recently made some efforts to close ranks, a somewhat formidable task in that they still speak more than a hundred different languages and belong to more than 250 tribes. As they were seldom able to unite when the white man was evicting them from

---

26. In 1866, three years after Lincoln had freed the slaves, an Arizona county was still offering $250 for an Apache scalp. *American Heritage Book of Indians*, p. 384. Francis Parkman's detailed description of Indian cannibalism and Indian habits of torturing white prisoners of both sexes makes the fierce reactions of white frontiersmen more understandable. *The Works of Francis Parkman*, Little Brown, Boston, 1892, Vol. III, especially Chapter XVIII.

27. *Time*, March 15, 1968, p. 20.

28. *San Francisco Examiner, This World*, April 14, 1968, p. 19.

their fields and hunting grounds, their endemic tribalism will surely continue to hamper the organization of any effective national lobby. The last major attempt at an Indian revival was the Ghost Dance religion (1889–90), when Wovoka, a Paiute medicine man, promised the return of the Golden Age. Million-footed herds of bison would repopulate the prairies. The dead chief's braves, Wovoka prophesied, would rise up and go on one final warpath. The paleface would be rooted out of the land. The movement was easily put down by the Seventh Cavalry.[29] Latter-day Indian stirrings, such as the sacking of the Indian Bureau office in Washington and the 1973 "uprising" at Wounded Knee, while proving Indian racism was on the uptake, are more accurately described as media events rather than serious attempts at independence.

Noblesse oblige demands that a certain respect, even if their present acts and behavior do not deserve it, should be accorded the oldest Americans, the majority that has become a minority, the sole American population group with a nonderivative culture. The Indian, although he has seldom measured up to his role, is the tragic hero of the American epic. He was the enemy for more than 250 years.[30] It is only fitting that the honors of defeat should provide both for his physical survival and his spiritual continuity.

PUERTO RICANS: The original Puerto Ricans, 20,000 to 50,000 Arawak Indians, died off in the sixteenth century after a few unsuccessful revolts against the Spaniards, who had been overworking them in the gold mines. The void in the labor supply was filled by Negro slaves from Africa. In consequence many Puerto Ricans have Negro branches in their family trees. Since those who have migrated to the United States derive largely from the poorer elements of the population—in direct contrast to the first waves of the Cuban immigration—their dark coloration and frequency of

---

29. *American Heritage Book of Indians*, p. 371.

30. The Indian wars came to an end in 1891 with the final pacification of the Sioux. Ibid., p. 400. Compared to the struggle with the Indians, American wars against France and Britain in the colonial period and against Britain, Mexico, Spain, Germany, Japan, North Korea, and North Vietnam in the nineteenth and twentieth centuries were relatively brief.

Negroid traits not only render them unassimilable, but make it difficult not to confuse them with blacks.[31]

As American citizens, Puerto Ricans come under no immigration quota. With few legal complications impeding their entry and with an extremely high birthrate, Americans of Puerto Rican descent, according to the 1970 Census, total 1,454,000, many of whom live in New York's Spanish Harlem. Like the Mexicans, Puerto Ricans have brought with them a skin-deep Spanish culture which has little in common with the original except the language. Also like the Mexicans, Puerto Ricans have placed their political fortunes in the hands of the Democratic party. To lose no time in garnering these votes, New York politicians have changed the literacy test for voters by permitting it to be taken in Spanish. As a result Puerto Ricans can arrive in New York City without speaking or reading a word of English, go on relief, and with minimum delay cast their ballots in local and national elections.

Coming from one of the world's most beautiful islands and friendliest climates, Puerto Ricans somehow manage to adapt to one of the world's ugliest slum areas and cruelest weather zones. Their economic status approaches that of the Negro, whom they look down upon in spite of their own part-African ancestry. Those who break the language barrier, however, soon surpass blacks in most levels of achievement.

Puerto Ricans in Puerto Rico, now a Commonwealth of the United States, have so far proved to be too proud for statehood, but not proud enough for independence or self-sufficiency (half the island is on food stamps). A streak of fervent nationalism which runs through some segments of the population motivated one band of Puerto Rican "patriots" to attempt to assassinate President Truman in 1950, another to shoot five congressmen in 1954, and still another to launch terroristic bomb attacks in various cities in the 1970s. Whether the separatist feelings of Puerto Ricans both in their native and adopted lands will subside and result in the birth of the fifty-first state or whether Puerto Ricans like the Filipinos will opt for independence cannot be forecast at this time. What can be predicted is that most of them

---

31. The 1950 Federal Census found 1,762,411 whites and 446,948 Negroes in Puerto Rico.

stand no more chance of being assimilated than their dark white or black racial cousins.

MISCELLANEOUS NEW WORLD MINORITIES: The Cubans are not the only West Indians who have been fleeing from poverty and the tyranny of local dictators. Some 40,000 Haitians, who speak a degraded French patois, have set sail from their island in recent years in homemade hulks that have barely made it to the Florida coast. The semantics of whether they are economic or political refugees is unimportant. What is important is that they have been allowed to land and take up residence. Hundreds of thousands of other black West Indians want to follow in their wake.

Neither are Mexicans the only Hispanics who enter the United States illegally. The Census Bureau tells us at least 597,000 Hispanics have come to the United States from Central and South America. Many take the same route as the Mexican illegals. The more affluent pay "tour directors" who move them from their homes to the American border in buses. The lengthening shadow of Castro over Central America is fueling this type of "Latin" immigration.

Since there is little possibility of electing a president with enough determination and courage to enforce present-day immigration laws, more and more arrivals may be expected, not only from Latin America but from all the impoverished, overpopulated areas in the world. Only when the immigrant finds he will receive less food and less money here than he does at home will he decamp and leave Majority Americans to sort out the chaos engendered by uncontrolled immigration. For this reason, those who wish to preserve Western civilization in the United States must be forgiven for occasionally praying for an economic collapse.

CHAPTER 17

The Negroes

THE NEGRO MINORITY, the largest and most violent minority, merits a special chapter because it presents the United States with a problem which seems beyond solution. Fanned and overheated by both black and white agitators for often different ideological purposes, Negro racism has now reached the point where it has literally grounded the once soaring American *Zeitgeist* and is threatening to mutilate it beyond recognition. For the first time since the pacification of the Indians, who themselves are resorting to frequent fits of localized violence, self-anointed leaders of an American minority are seriously talking about taking up arms against the authority of the state. Simultaneously, there is multiplying within the Negro community a large criminal caste and an even larger caste of welfare recipients and dehumanized drug addicts. A Negro middle class has taken shape, but so has a ghetto population of fatherless families whose legitimate and illegitimate children now outnumber the children of two-parent families.

The first Negroes to arrive in the British possessions in North America were twenty indentured servants who disembarked from a Dutch ship in Jamestown, Virginia, in 1619.[1] Blacks, it is evident, have been in America as long as the Majority and longer than all other minorities except the Indian. Overwhelmed by the white culture, Negroes quickly traded their tribal dialects for English, their tribal gods for Christianity, and their tribal names for those of their white masters. But they could not trade their skin.

---

1. Brewton Berry, *Race and Ethnic Relations*, Houghton, Mifflin, Boston, 1958, p. 104.

Negro slavery, one of the oldest and most enduring of human institutions, was introduced into the New World at the behest of the pious Christian bishop, Bartolomé de las Casas, who urged that only Negroes could survive the yoke of peonage the Spaniards and Portuguese had fastened on the Indians.[2] Slavery, although the "peculiar institution" was firmly established in the Southern colonies by the end of the seventeenth century, did not become big business until the stirrings of the Industrial Revolution. When cotton became king and Blake's "dark Satanic mills" began to scar the landscapes of New and Old England, only Negroes were willing, able, or available to endure the rigors of field work on Southern plantations.

Contrary to conspiratorial theories of Negro history, which blame black misfortunes entirely on whites, African tribal chiefs played a key role in the slave trade. They were the procurement agents who rounded up neighboring tribesmen, as well as many of their own subjects, and marched them off to white-owned slave ships.[3] Rum was the staple of this dubious commerce and passed for currency on the African West Coast. There, according to Charles Beard, "to slake their fierce appetite, [Negroes] would sell their enemies, their friends, their mothers, fathers, wives, daughters, and sons for New England's scalding potion."[4]

Slavery was the inhumanity of the white man to the black man. But it was also the inhumanity of the black man to his own kind. For many Negroes transportation to America was simply giving up one form of servitude for another. Often it was a fortuitous escape from starvation, disease, human sacrifice, and cannibalism. Whites who feel most guilt-ridden about slavery should also take into account that, although it has been proscribed for more than

---

2. Davie, op. cit., p. 587. De las Casas's proposal was adopted too late. Almost all the natives of the large West Indian islands were wiped out before the arrival of their replacements.

3. Negro historian John Hope Franklin points out, "Slavery was an important function of African social and economic life." *From Slavery to Freedom*, Knopf, New York, 1967, p. 31. One of the favorite roundup methods was to set fire to a village by night and capture the fleeing inhabitants. *Ency. Brit.*, Vol. 20, p. 780.

4. *Rise of American Civilization*, Vol. 1., pp. 93–94. The slaves were transported in ships from which the hogsheads had been temporarily removed.

a century in the United States, it is still prevalent in Africa. In the 1960s, $5.60 would buy a healthy, half-caste baby in Somaliland and $2,200 an attractive young girl in the Sudan.[5] In 1980 the government of Mauritania passed a law abolishing slavery, as it had done several times previously—with little effect.

The slavery question began to divide Americans from the very moment of their independence. The best minds of the day—Franklin, Patrick Henry, Washington, Hamilton, Jefferson, Madison—were opposed to slavery but unwilling to come to grips with it because of the greater urgency of unifying the young republic. Opposition to slavery, it should be noted, did not necessarily signify a belief in the equality preached so eloquently in the Declaration of Independence. Thomas Jefferson, the author of most of that document, suggested that "blacks, whether originally a distinct race, or made distinct by time and circumstances, are inferior to the whites in the endowments of both body and mind." [6]

Jefferson was particularly pessimistic about Negro intellectual proficiency.

> Comparing them by their faculties of memory, reason, and imagination, it appears to me that in memory they are equal to the whites; in reason much inferior, as I think one could scarcely be found capable of tracing and comprehending the investigations of Euclid; and that in imagination they are dull, tasteless, and anomalous. . . . They astonish you with strokes of the most sublime oratory.

---

5. Sean O'Callaghan, *The Slave Trade Today,* as reviewed in *San Francisco Chronicle, This World,* May 27, 1962. In recent years in the United States, Negroes, not whites, have been arrested for committing the crime of peonage. *Miami Herald,* March 22, 1973, p. 1.

6. *The Life and Selected Writings of Thomas Jefferson,* Modern Library, New York, 1944, p. 262. Jefferson was in favor of Negro emancipation, but warned that the black, "When freed . . . is to be removed beyond the reach of mixture. . . ." Ibid. How Jefferson's ideas were edited to fit modern liberal notions of equalitarianism is shown by the inscription on the Jefferson Memorial in Washington, which reads, "Nothing is more certainly written in the book of fate than that these people are to be free." The stone mason put a period in place of the original semicolon. Jefferson's sentence continued, "nor is it less certain that the two races, equally free, cannot live under the same government." Washington, whose concern for Negroes was not as verbal as Jefferson's, but perhaps more generous, arranged for his slaves to be freed at his death. Jefferson, who at one time had as many as 212, did not.

. . . But never yet could I find that a black had uttered a thought above the level of plain narration. . . ." [7]

After the slavery issue had reached the inflammatory stage, Maryland-born Chief Justice Roger B. Taney, writing the majority opinion in the Dred Scott decision (1857), took judicial notice that Negroes were "beings of an inferior order." Abraham Lincoln, another nonbeliever in the genetic equality of Negroes, was firmly committed to the separation of the two races and a strong supporter of the Illinois law which made marriage between whites and Negroes a crime.[8]

As pointed out earlier in this study, blacks in the United States increased from about 750,000 to nearly 4,500,000 in the years (1790–1860), when almost 90 percent of Negroes were slaves.[9] Slavery was abominable to the body and spirit, but as an almost sixfold boost in the black population in seventy years demonstrated, it was hardly genocide. Since Congress had outlawed the slave trade in 1808, most of the increase could only be ascribed to Negro fecundity.

The enormous casualties of the Civil War are proof that the curse of slavery descended on whites as well as blacks. After the war had ended and slavery was abolished by the 13th Amendment, twenty Negro representatives and two Negro senators were sent to Congress, and Southern state capitals were filled with Negro officeholders and office seekers. For a time there was a distinct

---

7. Ibid., pp. 257–58.

8. Benjamin Quarles, *Lincoln and the Negro,* Oxford University Press, New York, 1962, pp. 36–37. In one of his 1858 debates with Stephen Douglas, Lincoln was quoted as saying: "What I would most desire would be the separation of the white and black races." In 1862 Lincoln called a group of free Negroes to the White House to explain the reasons behind one of his pet projects, repatriation of American Negroes to Africa. "We have between us a broader difference than exists between almost any other two races . . . this physical difference is a great disadvantage to us both. . . . Your race suffers very greatly, many of them, by living among us, while ours suffers from your presence. . . . If this is admitted, it affords a reason, at least, why we should be separated." Carl Sandburg, *Abraham Lincoln, The War Years,* Harcourt Brace, New York, 1939, Vol. 1, p. 574. For a summary of Lincoln's attitudes toward Negroes, see the statement of Ludwell H. Johnson, an associate professor at William and Mary College, in Putnam's *Race and Reality,* pp. 134–37.

9. Franklin, op. cit., pp. 186, 217.

possibility that Northern military power and vindictiveness plus Negro numbers and Southern demoralization might change the color of Southern civilization. But Southern whites went underground and formed the Ku Klux Klan, whose night-riding troops taught the occupation forces and their white and black collaborators a few things about terror tactics and guerrilla warfare.

The North, ever more immersed in financial speculation and industrial expansion, finally grew weary of trying to enforce equality where none existed. President Rutherford B. Hayes, a moderate Republican, withdrew the last federal troops in 1877, and the South was returned to the Southerners. As the Negro sank back into serfdom and sharecropping, the Supreme Court acknowledged the constitutionality of postbellum segregation in the "separate but equal" doctrine of *Plessy* v. *Ferguson* (1896).

A casual visitor to Mississippi or Alabama at the end of the century might have come to the conclusion that except for a few legal formalities slavery had been reinstituted. He would have been right, but not for long. The Industrial Revolution, now in its middle stages, was preparing to wrench Negro destiny in a new direction. America's entry into World War I was accompanied by a great shortage of industrial manpower. Tens of thousands of Negro tenant farmers and hired hands heard the call and began a mass migration to Northern cities which only stopped in the late 70s. In 1900, 90 percent of the Negro population lived below the Mason and Dixon line; in 1950, 70 percent. Today, of the 26,488,218 blacks listed in the 1980 Census, about a million more live in the South than in the North.[10]

The transformation of the Negro minority into an urban population group ended the blacks' political isolation and brought them for the first time within reach of the liberal-minority coalition, which has dominated American politics for most of this century. In the North, and later in the South, Negroes were taught the secret of bloc voting.[11] As political careers became more dependent on these votes, citadel after citadel of white resistance began

---

10. In spite of the Negro exodus, however, the South's population is still about 19 percent black, as against 12 percent for the U.S. population as a whole.

11. In the 1964 presidential election, Negroes voted 95 percent for Lyndon Johnson. *Time*, Nov. 4, 1964, p. 4. The vote is just as topheavy for Negro candidates in local, state, and congressional elections when opposing candidates are white.

to crumble. Equally effective in the success of the civil rights or Black Power movement were the huge financial contributions of the foundations, churches, and affluent white minority organizations, as well as the legal maneuvering and lobbying of Negro organizations financed and in large part directed by white liberals and Jews.[12] The Supreme Court lent a helping hand by striking down the poll tax and literacy tests, two political safeguards which the South had erected against any recurrence of the Black Power of Reconstruction days.

By the late 1950s it appeared the Civil War was going to be fought over again in miniature. Freedom marchers, federal marshals, Department of Justice attorneys, preachers, teachers, kibitzers, liberals, ultraliberals—in short a whole new generation of carpetbaggers—converged on the South both to contain and spread the violence which greeted the Supreme Court's school desegregation decision (1954). But times—and geopolitics—had

---

12. Julius Rosenwald of Sears, Roebuck was for years the biggest financial contributor to the Negro cause. The first president of the Urban League, the second largest Negro organization, was banker Edwin Seligman. For a quarter of a century, in fact until quite recently, the president of the National Association for the Advancement of Colored People (450,673 dues-paying members and $3,300,000 annual income, as of 1969) was Jewish, the last being Kivie Kaplan, fifty-eight members of whose family held $500 life memberships. Perennial head of the NAACP Legal Defense Fund is Jack Greenberg. Yaffe, *The American Jews*, p. 257, and Arnold Rose, *The Negro in America*, Beacon, Boston, 1961, p. 267. Before he was assassinated by black separatists, Negro activist Malcolm X wrote, "I gave the Jew credit for being among all other whites the most active, and the most vocal, financier, 'leader' and 'liberal' in the Negro civil rights movement." *Autobiography of Malcolm X*, p. 372. Jewish intellectual and financial support was just as generous to radical Negro organizations as it had been to the Urban League and the NAACP. Such groups as CORE and SNCC practically lived off Jewish contributions. In January 1970, Leonard Bernstein held a party in his Park Avenue apartment and raised $3,000, to which he added the fee from his next concert, for twenty-one Black Panthers arrested for plotting to kill policemen and dynamite a police station, department stores, and a railroad right-of-way. *Time*, Jan. 26, 1970, p. 14. A week later former Supreme Court Justice Goldberg helped form a special commission to investigate whether Chicago police had violated the rights of Black Panthers. Previous to this time, the press reported that the Panthers had killed five policemen and wounded forty-two more in "shoot-outs" in twenty states. *Human Events*, Feb. 7, 1970, p. 10. Jewish money was all-important in the election campaigns of Negro Mayors Carl Stokes of Cleveland and Richard Hatcher of Gary, Indiana. Phillips, *The Emerging Republican Majority*, p. 350.

changed. The squalid desolation of the Northern ghettos was a daily reminder that the Negro problem could no longer be relegated to the lower half of a neat geographical bisection.

The white liberals and minority members who in the tradition of nineteenth-century abolitionists had enthusiastically used Negro deprivation as a political and economic club with which to beat the hated South, the last stronghold of Majority racism, were not half so enthusiastic when the same problem surfaced with even greater intensity in their own Northern cities. It is more comforting to tell others how to remedy their errors than to correct one's own. Part of the liberal-minority solution for the Negroes' predicament was to inculcate them with a hatred of Southern whites. But to the Northern Negro all whites looked the same. Ironically, the scapegoat makers were becoming the scapegoats.

The wind had been sown and the whirlwind reaped when Negroes finally sensed the hypocrisy and cowardice of their white allies. From 1964 through the first half of 1968, Negro race riots,[13] most of them in large Northern cities, accounted for 215 deaths, 8,950 injured, and $285,000,000 in insurance claims.[14] Although they were not so reported in the news media, the insurrections were not always mad, irrational acts of self-immolation, but could also be regarded as a well-conceived strategy of burning out the white merchants, mostly Jewish, who in the view of ghetto residents had been gouging and overcharging them.[15] Also not gener-

13. Swedish sociologist Gunnar Myrdal, whose two-volume integrationist tract, *An American Dilemma,* ignited the intellectual fuse of Black Power, predicted (in 1944) there would be no "further riots of any significant degree of violence in the North." His co-author, Arnold Rose, said in 1962 that all formal segregation and discrimination would end in one decade and informal segregation would "decline to a shadow" in two. *New York Times Magazine,* Dec. 7, 1969, p. 152.

14. *U.S. News & World Report,* July 15, 1968, p. 31. There were smaller riots and outbursts of looting and killing in the 1970s. The Miami riot was the largest in 1980.

15. At the end of 1968, after several years of exposure to arson and looting, 39 percent of the stores in the fifteen largest ghettos were still Jewish-owned. *Wall Street Journal,* Dec. 31, 1968, pp. 1, 12. Black militants accompanied their attacks on Jewish business with occasional flare-ups of anti-Semitic propaganda. Will Maslow, then executive director of the American Jewish Congress, resigned from CORE's Executive Committee after attending a school meeting in Mt. Vernon, N.Y., in the course of which a Negro educator stated that Hitler had not killed enough Jews. But most Jews were far too committed to the Negro

ally known was the fact that the riots were not led by the poor
or disadvantaged, but by the higher-income, better-educated
Negroes.[16]

In 1969 black paramilitary cadres endeavoring to establish
themselves as the elite guard of racial revolution turned the attack
against the police, who were ambushed in ghetto streets or gunned
down at point blank range when they stopped black militants
for traffic violations. Armed Negro bands occupied the buildings
or classrooms of several colleges, held administrative officials and
professors as hostages, and were later amnestied after forcing
tremulous presidents, deans, and faculties to bow to their demands. Other Negro groups levied tribute on churches as "reparations" for mistreatment in the slavery era. The sins of the fathers
were being visited upon the children well beyond the third and
fourth generations. The same Majority liberals and minority racists
who could not abide Hitler's Nuremberg laws were being asked
to agree—and many did agree—to a moral law holding races ac-
countable for acts committed by individuals long since dead.

When not attributed to the purposeful malevolence of "white
racism," [17] black militancy is often explained as the expected and

---

movement to imitate or even approve Maslow's act. Yaffe, op. cit., p. 261. It
was not until some Negro leaders openly attacked Zionism in 1979, after Carter's
dismissal of U.N. Ambassador Andrew Young for talking to a P.L.O. representative, that the rift in the black-Jewish alliance became a topic in the television
evening news.

16. Suspects in the police lineup following the 1968 Washington riots were
found to be "amazingly respectable." Most of them had never been in trouble
with the law, had decent jobs, and had more schooling than the average Negro.
More than half were family men. *U.S. News & World Report*, April 22, 1968, p.
29.

17. White racism was specifically named as the chief villain in the plight of
the American Negro by the government-sponsored *Kerner Report* (1967), compiled by Federal Judge Otto Kerner who, with his former associate, Theodore
Isaacs, was later found guilty of bribery, fraud, and extortion. *Time*, Dec. 13,
1971, p. 15. Such official denouncements inevitably intensify hatred of whites
as a group, which rebounds by hardening white feelings toward Negroes. Malcolm X exemplified the end point of aroused racial hostility when he said of a
plane crash which killed some thirty white Americans, mostly from Atlanta, "I've
just heard some good news!" *Autobiography of Malcom X*, p. 394. Such racial
vehemence, of course, is not the sole property of Negroes. A similar strain
was noticeable in the late Ben Hecht who wrote he had a "holiday in his heart"
every time a Zionist killed a British soldier. *New York Times*, May 20, 1947, p. 1.

excusable outgrowth of the Negro's low economic state. Reference is made to government statistics that show the presence of a huge, growing black underclass.[18] Statistics for 1978, however, demonstrate black economic advances that would have been unthinkable a few decades earlier. Black employment in the technical and professional fields rose to 8.7 percent (from 6.7 percent in 1970). Median income for working black women was $8,097 compared to $8,672 for working white women. In clerical work black women were actually earning more than white women ($169 weekly to $165). Black high-school graduates were making 77 percent of the income of their white counterparts (up from 69 percent in 1967); black college graduates were earning 80 to 85 percent of the income of white graduates (up from 54 percent in 1967). Two-income black families in the North and West were making more than two-income white families ($14,995 versus $14,030 in 1974).[19] Negro militancy, it turns out, is as much a function of Negro economic progress as it is of Negro deprivation.

There is also an abundance of historical proof that Negro violence and Negro poverty have no strong causal links. No one can deny that the economic status of blacks was much worse in the slavery and sharecropping eras than today. Yet in all that time only three Negro revolts were known to have taken place, and even these were of little consequence. The biggest was led by Nat Turner in Southhampton County, Virginia, in 1831. If this rather ignoble event—white deaths totaled ten men, fourteen women, and thirty-one children—was the greatest explosion of Negro fury on the North American mainland in three centuries, it could be concluded that blacks were not roused to violence by WASP slave owners.[20] Elsewhere, of course, the Negro record

18. Nevertheless, the income of the average Negro family in the United States exceeds the income of the average British family. *Economist*, London, May 10, 1969, p. 19.

19. The *Sunday Oregonian*, Sept. 14, 1980. These gains are offset, of course, by high white—and higher black—unemployment and by the deteriorating social conditions of the ghetto Negro. By 1978, 39 percent of all black families had no father on the premises. About half the female-headed families lived below the poverty line. As for black unemployed youth, some studies indicated that if jobs were offered to them, a large percentage would either turn them down or would soon be fired for incompetence or abstenteeism.

20. Two of these three rebellions were betrayed by Negro household slaves and each was inspired by the French Revolution or by appropriate passages

is different. The French experience in Haiti, where the massacre of the white population was almost total, and the recent war between Nigeria and Biafra, in which a million blacks died, hardly indicate a Negro proneness to pacifism. What is indicated, however, is that Negroes are more likely to revolt or riot not when they are being oppressed, but when they are stirred up by visions of loot and by the writings and speeches of white radicals.

An undeniable cause of black violence has been the weakening of white resistance. Throughout American history white supremacy has been a basic premise of the country's social relationships. Even the most fiery abolitionists exuded the air of the Great White Father. In fact, white supremacy had such overwhelming acceptance and was so firmly entrenched, so thoroughly institutionalized, that Negroes would scarcely dare to criticize it, let alone take more forceful measures. Today, however, white supremacy or, to give it its modern name, Majority racism, is so debilitated that Negro militancy, especially in the North, is not only possible but profitable. That it would come to a halt once Negroes achieved equality is the purest form of wishful thinking. Who would determine the cut-off date? Black militants? And how is equality to be measured?

If Majority members would only comprehend that the whole point, the whole drive, the very essense of minority racism is not to obtain equality but superiority, most of the misunderstandings and misinterpretations of contemporary Negro behavior would be avoided. Racism simply cannot be bought off. In its dynamic stages it can only be controlled or suppressed by superior force, a force most effectively provided by an opposing or countervailing racism. What is indisputable is that the one way not to stop Negro militancy is to reward it.

There is no better indication of the decline of the American Majority than the recent and continuing successes of black racism. Negroes belong to the most backward of the world's major races and to the most backward of America's large population groups. Nevertheless in the past two decades they have managed to erect a kind of state within a state and in the name of equality have achieved a kind of superequality which has led to the establishment

from the Old and New Testaments. Franklin Frazier, *The Negro in the United States*, Macmillan, New York, 1957, pp. 87–91.

of a double standard—one for themselves, one for whites—in the judicial, educational, and economic sectors of American society. That all this has been accomplished so quickly is vivid confirmation of the power of racism. Negroes, as a few of their own leaders will admit in private, have little else working for them.

Several theories have been advanced to account for Negro backwardness. One of the most publicized was put forward by Arnold Toynbee, whose monumental *Study of History* logs twenty-one civilizations, most of them created by white men, some by yellow men, none by black men.[21] Toynbee explained the Negro's civilizing deficiency by the theory of challenge and response. Surrounded by nature's bounty in the lush African tropics, the Negro, Toynbee postulated, only had to lift his hand to gather in his subsistence. With a minimum of challenge there was a minimum of response. Being, so to speak, spoon-fed, the Negro was not sufficiently stimulated to develop his mental apparatus to its full potential.[22]

Another hypothesis, based on what the late A. L. Kroeber called cultural diffusion, asserted that the Negro, having been shunted off the main track of social progress by geography, suffered from lack of contact with other civilizations and consequently was programmed for barbarism. A neater theory, so neat that it is practically unanswerable, states that the Negro's predicament is simply due to bad luck, that the fate of all races is the result of nothing more than blind chance and historical accident, that if fortune had not been so kind to whites, they would still be living in caves. Still another viewpoint, more rationalizing than rational, alleges that the present condition of Negroes is due to a cleverly rigged white plot. White slave traders are blamed for deliberately wiping out thriving Negro civilizations in Africa, and the white empire builders who followed them are accused of transforming the surviving tribal states into sordid financial enclaves and boss-ridden plantations.

Needless to say, some or all of these conjectures have found favor with the environmentalist schools of social science—notwithstanding that most of them are loaded with non sequiturs, guess-

---

21. Vol. 1, p. 232.
22. Vol. 2, pp. 26–29.

work and racial ax-grinding. Toynbee's challenge and response hypothesis loses much of its credibility when it is recalled that many geographical zones occupied by African Negroes—such as the East African highlands—are quite untropical and similar in climate, flora and fauna to areas which produced some of Toynbee's twenty-one civilizations.[23] With respect to the cultural diffusion theory, a great number of Negroes were situated on the southern border of ancient Egypt. They were consequently the most proximate of all peoples—just a short sail down the Nile—to one of the world's earliest and greatest civilizations. Given this headstart, Negroes should be far ahead of other races in cultural attainments. As for the historical accident theory, there is little to say except that one might suppose that in six thousand years Negro luck would have changed at least once.

Those who find genetic grounds for Negro backwardness seem to have a much stronger case than the behaviorists and equalitarians. They point to Carleton Coon's thesis that the Negro race is younger in an evolutionary sense than other races.[24] They produce medical research to demonstrate that Negro infants have a faster maturation rate than white infants, just as animals have a faster maturation rate than human beings, and that, in regard to fissuration, supragranular layer thickness and number of pyramidal neurons, the frontal lobes and cortex of the brain are less developed in Negroes than in whites.[25]

Those who put more faith in genes than environment also submit a mass of documentation derived from decades of intelligence testing to show that the I.Q. score of the average Negro is from

---

23. It may have been disease, not insufficient challenge, that has made the Negro so lethargic. Half of all African blacks suffer from sickle cell anemia, an endemic malady that helps immunize them against malaria, but slows down bodily and mental functions. Sickle-cell anemia afflicts 50,000 Americans, most of whom are Negroes.

24. See p. 19.

25. For maturation rates, see Marcelle Geber, *The Lancet,* June 15, 1957, Vol. 272, No. 6981, pp. 1216–19. For frontal lobe and cortex studies, see C. J. Connolly, *External Morphology of the Primate Brain,* 1950, Springfield, Illinois, pp. 146, 203–4; C. W. M. Pynter and J. J. Keegan, "A Study of the American Negro Brain," 1915, *Journal of Comparative Neurology,* Vol. 25, pp. 183–212; Ward C. Halstead, *Brains and Intelligence,* 1947, Chicago, p. 149; F. W. Vint, "The Brain of the Kenya Native," 1934, *Journal of Anatomy,* Vol. 68, pp. 216–23.

15 to 20 points below that of the average white.[26] They refer to studies attributing consistent Negro underachievement in education to inherent learning disabilities.[27]

They compare the emancipation of Negroes in the United States with the approximately simultaneous emancipation of the Russian serfs, contrasting the social mobility of the latters' descendants to the prolonged postslavery sluggishness of American blacks.[28] They cite the success story of Chinese coolies, who on their arrival in the United States were as illiterate and penniless as postbellum Negroes and far less familiar with American ways, yet who needed less than a century to reach the median income level. They quote Hegel, Conrad, Schweitzer, and Faulkner to suggest that Negro differences are due to nature not nurture.[29]

The upholders of heredity further substantiate their case by referring to the Negro's political and cultural record. They point out that neither in the Old World nor in the New has the Negro ever produced a system of government that went one step beyond the most elementary form of absolutism; that indigenous Negro societies have left behind no literature, no inscriptions or documents, no body of law, no philosophy, no science—in short, no

---

26. Audrey M. Shuey, *The Testing of Negro Intelligence,* Social Science Press, New York, 1966. The book analyzes 380 such tests accumulated over a forty-year period.

27. The most notable of these studies are those of Dr. Arthur R. Jensen, who found that white students had a "significantly greater ability to grasp abstract concepts." See p. 294.

28. Discussing the posterity of Russian serfs, Pitirim Sorokin wrote, they "yielded a considerable number of geniuses of the first degree, not to mention the eminent people of a smaller calibre . . . the American Negroes have not up to this time produced a single genius of great calibre." *Contemporary Sociological Theories,* p. 298, footnote 162.

29. Hegel, Marx's pet philosopher, put Negroes on a par with animals. *Vorlesungen über die Philosophie der Geschichte,* Stuttgart, 1971, pp. 137–44. For Conrad's illumination of the dark crannies of the Negro psyche, see *Heart of Darkness.* Schweitzer, who spent much of his life in Africa, said the white man was the Negro's "elder brother." He considered the average Negro a child, adding that "with children nothing can be done without the use of authority." Putnam, *Race and Reason,* p. 76, and *Newsweek,* April 8, 1963, p. 21. Much as he liked and respected Negroes, Faulkner said that if antiwhite racial agitation increased he would be forced to join his native state of Mississippi against the United States and shoot Negroes in the street. *Reporter,* March 22, 1956, pp. 18–19.

history. Even in those fields of art where Negroes have displayed some creativity and originality, the ultimate effect, at least on the West, has been anticultural—the contorted ugliness of modern painting and sculpture, the jungle screeching of jazz and rock music, the grotesque shuffling and weaving of the latest dance crazes.

It would be superfluous to say that Negro intellectuals and their white partisans disagree with these biologically tilted arguments. In rebuttal, however, they are not above retouching history. The stone ruins of Zimbabwe in Southern Rhodesia are held up as proof that an ancient and sophisticated Negro civilization was in full flower when Europeans were groping their way through the Dark Ages. A little later the "kingdoms" of Ghana, Mali, and Songhai purportedly inaugurated a golden age in West Africa, where several new emerging nations have been named in their honor. That Zimbabwe was probably built by Arab traders in the eleventh century with Hottentot labor should not be permitted to spoil a good legend. In regard to Ghana, Mali, and Songhai, the fact is they were founded by Hamitic Berbers and Semitic Arabs and were not in West Africa, but located further east.[30] Actually the most articulated, all-Negro cultural complexes were in western Nigeria and need no historical buildup from those who insist on measuring black accomplishments by white standards.

In an overzealous attempt to raise Negro pride to the boiling point, one Ghanese historian has written that Moses and Buddha were Egyptian Negroes, that Christianity originated in the Sudan, and that the writings of Nietzsche, Bergson, Marx, and the Existentialists were reflections of Bantu thought. In the same vein, the "original Hebrews" and St. Paul are described as black, and Spinoza is called a "black Spanish Jew." [31] The Nubian or 25th dynasty, which appeared in the twilight of Egyptian history (730–663 B.C.), is taken as evidence that the brilliant Egyptian civilizations of the Old and Middle Kingdoms were the work of Negroes,

---

30. R. Gayre, "Negrophile Falsification of Racial History," *The Mankind Quarterly,* Jan.–March, 1967, pp. 131–43. Also see "Zimbabwe" by the same author in the April–June, 1965, issue.

31. *Autobiography of Malcolm X,* pp. 180, 190.

which they indisputably were not.[32] To television audiences Cleopatra is sometimes depicted as a Negress,[33] and a black TV program informed its viewers that a West African king sent a hundred ships to South America 200 years before Columbus.[34] As for American history, Crispus Attucks, who may have been a Negro or may have been an Indian, has become a black hero, the first patriot to give his life in the cause of American independence.[35]

Perhaps the most far-fetched example of the new Negro historicism is a revised version of Genesis by Elijah Muhammad, the prophet of the Black Muslims. He asseverates that 6,600 years ago, when all men were Negroes, a black scientist named Yacub was exiled from Mecca with 59,999 followers. Embittered toward Allah, Yacub decided to create a devil race of "bleached-out whites." Scientifically bred for blondness, Yacub's followers became, in successive 200-year stages, brown, red, yellow and finally "blond, pale-skinned, cold-blue-eyed devils—savages, nude and shameless; hairy, like animals [walking] on all fours and [living] in trees." Later these whites were rounded up by Negroes and sent to European caves where, after 2,000 years, Moses went to tame and civilize them. They then set forth to rule the earth for 6,000 years. The white interregnum was scheduled to end when a savior, Master W. D. Fard, a half-white, half-black silk salesman, brought Allah's message and divine guidance to Elijah Muhammad in 1931.[36]

The gilding of the Negro past by religious and historical enthusiasts throws little constructive light on the great debate about Negro racial differences. If the environmentalists are correct, then Negroes ought to catch up with whites as soon as they are given equal political and legal rights, and the same educational and

---

32. The Old Kingdom constructed forts to repel Nubians. The Middle Kingdom prevented the entry of all but slaves from Nubia. Darlington, *The Evolution of Man and Society,* p. 121.

33. In reality, Cleopatra was not even an Egyptian, "being by descent half-Greek and half-Macedonian." John Buchan, *Augustus,* Houghton Mifflin, Boston, 1937, p. 77.

34. From the program, *Soul,* WNET, New York, Aug. 21, 1969.

35. In the 1770 Boston massacre. *New York Times Magazine,* April 20, 1969, pp. 33, 109–110.

36. *Autobiography of Malcolm X,* pp. 164–67. Upon Elijah Muhammad's death his son, Wallace, inherited the leadership of the Black Muslims and toned down the antiwhite racism.

economic opportunities. If, as the late Marshall McLuhan contended, the Negro is actually a superior being, the time lag should be very short.[37] Yet every day the Negro problem increases in gravity. The more Negroes are helped, the more they seem to need help, and the louder they demand it. The more they progress, the more America as a nation seems to retrogress.

If, on the other hand, those who advance the genetic argument are right, then all the short-term gains Negroes have made in the last several decades will add up to a long-term disaster. Instead of trying to be the equals of whites, Negroes should try to be better Negroes. Instead of playing the white man's game with dice that heredity has loaded against them, they should develop their own special talents in their own special ways. Negro frustrations, say the hereditarians, will only vanish when American Negroes lead a black rather than a white life.

Some of the most ardent support for the belief that Negro racial differences are so distinct as to make integration all but impossible has come from American Negroes themselves. Booker T. Washington warned his people to accept segregation and to remain well apart from the main currents of white civilization.[38] Marcus Garvey, who after World War I organized the first authentic Negro mass movement, decided the solution was to return to Africa.[39] Father Divine, although Mother Divine was a Canadian blonde, insisted on moving his congregation into walled-off communities beyond the reach of white contamination.

The most recent advocates of black withdrawal are Black Mus-

---

37. McLuhan's racial theories give first place to the Indian as well as to the Negro. Although not explaining how such gifted people could have fallen so far behind, the Canadian-born social critic has written that the "Negro and Indian . . . are actually psychically and socially superior to the fragmented, alienated and disassociated man of Western civilization. . . . It has been the sad fate of the Negro and the Indian to be . . . born ahead of rather than behind their time." Julius Lester, *Search for the New Land,* Dial Press, New York, 1969, pp. 57–58.

38. "In all things purely social," Washington said, "we can be separate as the fingers, yet one as the hand in all things essential to mutual progress." Putnam, *Race and Reason,* p. 90.

39. It is significant that Garvey was a full-blooded Negro who directed his appeal to the blacker elements of the Negro population. He was an exception to the doubtful rule that the leaders of black movements must be mulattoes, whose hybrid status makes them ideal mediators between whites and Negroes.

lims and other black separatist groups, who either demand a return to Africa or the establishment of independent Negro states on American soil. But in aligning themselves with white radicals and hostile foreign regimes, black leaders are only compounding their troubles.

The great deterrent to black separatism is not the integrationist aspirations of assorted black Marxists and black social climbers but the whole superstructure of modern liberal thought. If the notion of racial equality is surrendered to separatism, which recognizes and institutionalizes racial differences, environmentalism, behaviorism, economic determinism, and even democracy itself would soon be called into question. The prevailing Western orthodoxies might then dissolve into thin air, and the occidental mind might have to set off on an entirely new path or find its way back to an old one.

Pragmatically, black separatism would be an overwhelming political loss to the liberal-minority coalition. Racial separation of any kind is not at all uncongenial to racially minded whites and it is not inconceivable that hard-pressed Majority members, especially in the Deep South, together with harder-pressed Assimilable Minority members in the nation's largest cities, would join black separatists in a nonaggression pact to free themselves from an integrationist liberal administration in Washington. Also, if Negro separatism should ever become the order of the day, other Unassimilable Minorities might take the hint, leaving liberalism an ideology in search of a party. At the other extreme, total integration would deal an equally lethal blow to the liberal-minority axis by spelling the doom of all minorities and with them modern liberalism's *raison d'être*.[40] It is only in the boundary zone between the segregated and the integrated society, between reality and utopia, that today's liberal feels truly at home.

Because there is so much more at stake than the fate of American Negroes, the liberal-minority coalition, abetted by a sizable contingent of so-called conservatives, presses forward with integration at all costs. As always, those who have the courage to air opposing

---

40. "What we arrive at is that 'integration,' socially, is no good for either side. 'Integration,' ultimately, would destroy the white race . . . and destroy the black race." *Autobiography of Malcolm X*, p. 276.

views are either ignored or subjected to instant character assassination.

But while liberalism still rules the country's thinking, it has little control over the organic processes of society. As a tribesman, the Negro was a member of the tribal family. As a slave, he had his master's family. As a sharecropper, he had his own family. As an industrial peon or hard-core unemployed, he is beginning to have no family at all, since the present welfare system provides extra financial assistance for fatherless households and for each illegitimate child. The upshot is that the urban Negro has now reached an impasse where he has little left but his color and sense of oppression. Having lost his hearth, his roots, his religion, and his way, he is rapidly losing the few social commitments he still retains.

The worst having been done, the more dynamic elements of the Negro minority are demanding redress, somewhat as undisciplined children who have lost their innocence might seek redress from parents who abandoned them. To these demands, whites have a choice of four responses—oppression, which is immoral;[41] integration without intermarriage, which is impossible; integration with intermarriage, which is inconceivable; separation, which is impractical.

Of all these untenable courses of action the last, which would involve repatriation to Africa or the establishment of independent Negro communities tangential to white communities in states with large numbers of blacks, is perhaps the most nearly tenable. Whatever betides, the American Negro will sooner or later be out of his private wilderness. He will either return to his Old World homeland or be assigned a homeland in the New, or there will be no homeland for anyone, black or white, in urban America.

---

41. It is much too late for the tactics Tacitus put in the mouth of a Roman general endeavoring to suppress a revolt of the Gauls. "Nunc hostis, quia molle servitium; cum spoliati exutique fuerint, amicos fore." *Historiarum*, IV, lvii. "Now they are our enemies because the burden of their servitude is light; when we have despoiled and stripped them they will be our friends."

PART V

The Cultural Clash

CHAPTER 18

The Dissolution of Art

THE MAJOR THEME of Parts I-IV was the decline of the Majority and the rise of the minorities. The minor theme was the Majority-minority conflict itself, including the origins, motivations, and numbers of the combatants. The remainder of this study will examine the extension of this conflict into the realms of art, religion, education, politics, economics, law, and foreign policy. This chapter, the first of three to deal with minority inroads into the nation's culture, will be concerned with the artistic phase of the struggle.[1] In the dispossession of the Majority, it is the Majority artist who so far has been the greatest casualty.

A basic assumption of contemporary Western thought is that democracy is the political form and liberalism the political ideology most generative of art. The more there is of both, it is generally agreed, the greater will be the artistic outpouring, both quantitatively and qualitatively. The corollary assumption is that once art has been liberated from the dead weight of caste, class, and religious and racial bigotry, its horizon will become limitless.

Of all modern myths, this is one of the most misleading. If

---

1. Culture is "a pursuit of our total perfection by means of getting to know . . . the best which has been thought and said in the world; and through this knowledge, turning a stream of fresh and free thought upon our stock notions and habits, which we now follow staunchly but mechanically, vainly imagining that there is a virtue in following them staunchly which makes up for the mischief of following them mechanically." Matthew Arnold, *Culture and Anarchy*, Cambridge University Press, England, 1961, p. 6.

anything, art, or at least great art,[2] seems to be contingent on
two social phenomena poles apart from democracy and liberalism:
(1) a dominant, homogeneous population group which has resided
long enough in the land to raise up from its ranks a responsible
and functioning aristocracy;[3] (2) one or more schools of writers,
painters, sculptors, architects, or composers who belong to this
population group and whose creative impulses crystallize the
tastes, tone, and manners of the aristocratic leadership into a
radiating cultural continuity.

Few will dispute that the societies of Homeric Greece, Augustan
Rome, Medieval Western Europe, Elizabethan England, seventeenth-century Spain, Louis XIV's France, Goethe's Weimar, Mozart's Vienna and nineteenth-century Russia had an aristocratic
base. Fewer will dispute that great art was produced in these
societies. But what of Athens, scene of the most magnificent artistic efflorescence of all time, and of Florence, with the highest
per capita genius of the Renaissance? Did they not as city states
lack a nobility or formal aristocracy? Is it not true that neither
Pericles nor Cosimo de' Medici was a prince?

Before any conclusions are reached, these two cities and their
two greatest statesmen should be placed in a sharper historical
focus. If Athens was the glory of Greece, the Age of Pericles—
artistically speaking—was the glory of Athens. In 431 B.C., two
years before the death of Pericles, the adult male population of
Athens consisted of 50,000 citizens, 25,000 metics or resident
aliens and 55,000 slaves.[4] Since the slaves had no rights at all,

---

2. Great art in this context is considered timeless, not dated; great artists
to be creative, not interpretative geniuses.

3. Aristocracy is here meant to designate the rule of the well-born. Its meaning
is not restricted to families of high social standing or to the products of one
or two generations of political or financial preeminence. Aristocrats of the latter
sort can be found in all states, including proletarian and plutocratic societies.
For those convinced there is an unbridgeable gap between aristocracy and freedom, Alexis de Tocqueville wrote the following words of caution: "parmi toutes
les sociétés du monde, celles qui auront toujours le plus de peine à échapper
pendant longtemps au gouvernement absolu seront précisément ces sociétés
où l'aristocratie n'est plus et ne peut plus être." *L'ancien régime et la révolution.*
Michel Lévy Frères, Paris, 1856, p. xvi.

4. Cyril Robinson, *A History of Greece,* Barnes & Noble, New York, 1957, p.
83.

since metics and women could not vote and since citizenship was limited to those with Athenian parents on both sides, one historian has described Athens as "an aristocracy of a half-leisured class." [5] This aristocracy, of which Pericles was a prominent member, traced its ancestry back to the Trojan War.[6]

In regard to Florence one should not be surprised to learn that in 1494, when the city's most liberal constitution was in force, there were not more than 3,200 citizens out of a total population of 90,000.[7] From Dante's day until the rise of the Medici, except for a few brief attempts at popular government by the merchants and guilds, Florence was largely the political plaything of two rival aristocratic factions, the Guelphs (pro-pope) and the Ghibellines (pro-emperor). As for Cosimo de' Medici, the patron of Donatello, Ghiberti, Brunelleschi, and Luca della Robbia, he could pride himself on a lineage that stretched back through ten generations of Florentine history. Although Cosimo himself shunned titles, cardinals, princes, reigning dukes, and even two popes later bore the Medici name.

If Florence and Athens are admitted to be semi-aristocracies, or at least aristocratic republics, it is evident that all the great artistic epochs of the West have taken place in aristocratic societies. There has been art in non-aristocratic societies, often good art, but never anything approaching Greek sculpture and drama, Gothic cathedrals, Renaissance painting, Shakespeare's plays, German music, or Russian novels.

The mere existence of an aristocracy, of course, does not guarantee great art. It has to be a vital aristocracy with its attitudes, manners, and ways of life firmly imprinted on the society in which it functions. It need not be, in fact it should not be, too wealthy. More important is the possession of a cultural conscience, plus the leisure and will to express this conscience in the form of art. To the artist an aristocracy is of immense practical value because it provides a cultivated and discriminating audience to keep him on the creative *qui vive*, as well as a sense of refinement and

---

5. Ibid., p. 82.

6. The mother of Pericles was descended from an ancient Athenian family, the Alcmaeonidae, and his father was a victorious naval commander.

7. Pasquale Villari, *Life and Times of Machiavelli*, trans. Linda Villari, Fisher, Unwin, London, 1892, p. 4.

a set of critical standards that are both a model and an incentive for the highest quality of artistic craftsmanship.

Paradoxically, relations between artist and patron are generally more "democratic" in an aristocracy than in a democracy.[8] The aristocrat, having both by birth and upbringing acquired an easy familiarity with art, is quite at home in the company of artists and generally makes a practice of seeking them out. The self-made man, on the other hand, no matter how high he climbs in politics or business, can never quite shed his native philistinism. He may take an interest in art, often surreptitiously to avoid accusations of effeminacy, but he will always have difficulty moving freely in artistic circles.

The close alliance between art and aristocracy is also advantageous to the artist in that it facilitates personal acquaintance with many of the leading men of his day. According to Aristotle, tragedy only really succeeds when it concerns the fall of a great or noble man—a theory still uncontradicted by the most valiant efforts of liberal and Marxist dramatists. History or current events may provide names and plots but only close contact with the leading public figures of his time furnishes the playwright who tackles high tragedy with the meat and sinew of believable portrayal and characterization.

That great artists must belong to the dominant population group of a nation seems to be as unassailable as the law that great art grows best in aristocratic soil. A racial and cultural background similar to that of his patron makes it possible for the artist to avoid the usual psychological and social hurdles that often

---

8. Pericles, Augustus, and the Medici freely mixed with the great artists of their time. Virgil read Augustus his completed *Georgics* on the latter's return from Egypt in 30 B.C. The meeting was momentous because Virgil's lines may have revived Augustus's latent Italianism. Buchan, *Augustus*, p. 124. Lincoln, beyond a brief handshake at a White House reception, never met Melville. Raymond Weaver, *Herman Melville*, Pageant Books, N.Y., 1961, p. 375. Nor did Franklin D. Roosevelt ever meet Faulkner or T. S. Eliot. Kennedy may have bestowed a few minutes of friendship on Robert Frost, but this could hardly be compared to the attention Louis XIV lavished on Racine and Molière. At one time the Sun King acted as "advance man" for Racine's *Esther* and actually played a role in one of Molière's productions. Racine, *Théâtre complet*, Edition Garnier Frères, Paris, 1960, p. 598; H. C. Chatfield-Taylor, *Molière*, Duffield, New York, 1906, pp. 189–90.

slow or break down communication between members of racially and culturally differentiated human groups.

The fatal flaw which denies the minority artist a place among the artistic great is his inherent alienation. Because he does not really belong, because he is writing or painting or composing for "other people," he pushes a little too hard, raises his voice a little too high, makes his point a little too desperately. He is, inevitably, a bit *outré*—in the land, but not of the land. His art seems always encumbered by an artificial dimension—the proof of his belonging.[9]

In a non-aristocratic, heterogeneous, fragmented society which has become an arena of contending cultures or subcultures, the minority artist may concentrate on proving his "non-belonging." Instead of adopting the host culture, he now rejects it and either sinks into nihilism or returns to the cultural traditions of his own group. In the process his art becomes a weapon. Having sacrificed his talent to immediacy and robbed it of the proportion and subtlety which make art art, the minority artist not only lowers his own artistic standards, but those of society as a whole. All that remains is the crude force of his stridency and his "message."[10]

Perhaps the clearest proof of the art-building and art-nourishing qualities of aristocracy and racial homogeneity can be found in the history of those nations which have passed through both aristocratic and democratic, homogeneous and heterogeneous cycles. It was not in the First, Second, Third, or Fourth French Republics that the cathedrals of Chartres and Rheims were constructed, but in feudal France, when there was a dominant population group (the Teutonic) and the structure of society was aristocratic. The highest flights of English genius took place in the reigns of abso-

---

9. A few examples that come quickly to mind are Heine's super-romantic German lieder, Mendelssohn's thumping Christian hymns, El Greco's hyperbolized Spanish landscapes and elongated holy men, Jakob Wasserman's souped-up *Christian Wahnschaffe*, Siegfried Sassoon's synthetic *Memoirs of a Fox-Hunting Man*, and Rodgers and Hammerstein's totally counterfeit *Oklahoma*. For a better understanding of the difference between the authentic and the inauthentic in art, compare Goethe's *Faust* with Heine's *Doktor Faust*.

10. Examples of contemporary minority stridency are the music of Darius Milhaud, the sculpture of Jacques Lipchitz, the poetry of Allen Ginsberg, and the plays of LeRoi Jones.

lute, not constitutional, monarchs and before the English were absorbed in the enlarged and more heterogeneous citizenry of Great Britain and the United Kingdom. The Rome of Augustus, who favored and protected the patricians and heaped restrictions upon plebeians, non-Romans, and slaves, produced the Golden Age of Latin literature. The Rome of Caracalla, who in A.D. 211 extended citizenship to all the free inhabitants of the Roman Empire, left little of artistic consequence. The Spain of Philip II, III, and IV, with all its religious bigotry and inquisitional zeal, was the era of Cervantes and Calderón, artists of a caliber that were not to be found in more liberal eras of Spanish history. Dostoyevsky and Tolstoy, the culmination of Russian literary genius, flourished under the czars, not minority commissars.

Liberal dogma to the contrary, such popular goals as universal literacy are not necessarily conducive to great literature. The England of Shakespeare, apart from a much smaller population, had a much higher illiteracy rate than present-day Britain.[11] Neither does universal suffrage seem to raise the quality of artistic output. When Bach was *Konzertmeister* in Weimar and composing a new cantata every month, no one could vote. Some 220 years later in the Weimar Republic there were tens of millions of voters, but no Bachs.

Great drama, which usually incorporates great poetry, is the rarest form of great art. Art critics and historians have been at some loss to explain why great plays have appeared so infrequently in history and then only in clusters—fifth-century (B.C.) Athens, late sixteenth- and early seventeenth-century England, seventeenth-century Spain and France. The answer may be that conditions for great drama are only ripe when artist and audience are in biological as well as linguistic rapport. Such rapport, unfortunately, is bound to be short-lived because the era of great drama is usually accompanied by large-scale economic and material advances which tend to soften national character, sharpen class divisions, and attract extraneous racial and cultural elements from

---

11. Literacy here signifies the simple ability to read and write. The rich language of Elizabethan literature and drama would indicate that if fewer Englishmen could write at that period, those who could wrote much better than those who came later. The "illiterates" of that day seemed to have a deeper appreciation and better understanding of literature than their literate successors.

abroad. To the great playwright a heterogeneous or divided audience is no audience at all.

Not only great art but all art seems to stagnate in an environment of brawling minorities, diverse religions, clashing traditions, and contrasting habits. This is probably why, in spite of their vast wealth and power, such world cities as Alexandria and Antioch in ancient times and New York City and Rio de Janeiro in modern times have produced nothing that can compare to the art of municipalities a fraction of their size. The artist needs an audience which understands him—an audience of his own people. The artist needs an audience to write up to, paint up to, and compose up to—an aristocracy of his own people. These seem to be the two *sine qua nons* of great art. Whenever they are absent great art is absent.

How else can the timeless art of the "benighted" Middle Ages and the already dated art of the "advanced" twentieth century be explained? Why is it that all the cultural resources of a *dernier cri* superpower like the United States cannot produce one single musical work that can compare with a minor composition of Mozart? Why is it that perhaps the greatest contribution to twentieth-century English literature has been made not by the English, Americans, Australians, or Canadians, but by the Irish—the most nationalistic, most tribal, most religious and most racially minded of all present-day English-speaking peoples. Modern England may have had its D. H. Lawrence and the United States its Faulkner. But only Ireland in recent times has assembled such a formidable literary array as Yeats, Synge, Shaw, Joyce, O'Casey, Elizabeth Bowen, Paul Vincent Carroll, Joyce Carey, and James Stephens. If, as modern opinion holds, liberal democracy, internationalism, and cultural pluralism enrich the soil of art, then these Irish artists bloomed in a very unlikely garden.

The historical sequence of large states seems to be race-building, nation-building, art-building, and empire-building. As the nation moves closer to imperialism, the people move farther apart. The binding forces of state are weakened by war, civil strife, and entropy, as the cultural shell is penetrated by outsiders. The aristocracy withdraws into an isolated decadence, its place taken by a plutocracy. Members of the once dominant population group mix with the newcomers and in order to compete are forced to adopt many of their attitudes and habits. Art becomes multiracial, multinational, multidirectional, and multifarious.

Much of Western art, particularly in the United States, is now in such a stage of dissolution. The surrealist painters, atonal jazz musicologists, prosaic poets, emetic novelists, crypto-pornographers, and revanchist pamphleteers say they are searching for new forms because the old forms are exhausted. Actually, they are exhuming the most ancient forms of all—simple geometric shapes, color blobs, drum beats, genitalia, four-letter words, and four-word sentences. The old forms are not exhausted. The minority artist simply has no feeling for them because they are not his forms. Since style is not a commodity that can be bought or invented, the avant-garde, having no style of its own, can only retreat to a styleless primitivism.

The dissolution of art is characterized by the emergence of the fake artist [12]—the man without talent and training who becomes an artist by self-proclamation. He thrives in a fissiparous culture because it is child's play to bemuse the artistic sensibilities of the motley *nouveaux riches,* assorted culture vultures, sexually ambivalent art critics, and minority art agents who dictate the levels of modern taste. It is not so easy to deceive those whose standards of taste were developed in the course of generations.

In a homogeneous society the artist has to contend with fewer sets of prejudices. He does not have to weigh and balance his art in order to be "fair." He need not be mortally afraid of wounding the religious and racial feelings of others. Though his instincts, opinions, and judgments often add up to bias, to the artist himself they may be the driving forces of his creativity. What really limit and devitalize art are not the artist's prejudices but his audience's prejudices, of which in a vast heterogeneous society like the United States there is an almost infinite variety. The artist has trouble enough with one censor. When he has twenty, his art becomes a day-to-day accommodation.

Aristocracies have been sharply criticized for freezing commoners into castes and classes. Yet the artist certainly stands a better chance in a state directed by a cultivated nobility than in one

---

12. The fake artist is not unrelated to the antiartist—the type of individual who blew up *The Thinker* outside the Cleveland Museum in the spring of 1970. It was one of the eleven castings made under the personal supervision of Rodin. *New York Times,* July 17, 1970.

directed by a convention of Babbitts. By no means to the manor born, Homer, Virgil, Dante, Chaucer, Michelangelo, Shakespeare, Cervantes, Molière, Mozart, Beethoven, Wagner, and Dostoyevsky managed to acquire enough social mobility in aristocratic societies to climb to the summit of artistic perfection. How many of these geniuses would have been flattened by the leveling pressures of present-day America is an open question.

Aristocracies have also been attacked for stultifying art, even though artists working in or believing in tradition-oriented societies have made many more artistic breakthroughs than *soi-disant* liberal or progressive artists. Aristophanes, who revolutionized comedy, Wagner, who revolutionized music, Dostoyevsky, who revolutionized the novel, and T. S. Eliot, who revolutionized modern poetry,[13] were certainly not liberals. The proletarian or Marxist artist, on the other hand, hardly goes beyond photographic naturalism or childish doodling—the mandatory tractor art of the Soviet Union and the op art, pop art, and spray-paint art of the "free world." [14]

No great art ever emerged from isolation and no great artists ever sprang full-blown from the forehead of Zeus. Great artists are the products of schools of art, and their works are the peaks rising above a high cultural plateau. "First families," whose attitudes and tastes have been shaped by centuries of participation in national life, are not merely content to collect old art. They keep the schools busy elaborating and improving on what has been done before—the surest approach to artistic evolution. Conversely, the present-day ragtag collection of semiliterate millionaires, who speculate in art as they would in copper futures,[15] spend their money on old masters and "name" artists whose works can

---

13. Compare the startlingly new effect of the poetry of Eliot, who declared himself a royalist and Anglo Catholic, with the almost classical verse of the best work of the French Communist poet, Louis Aragon.

14. Andy Warhol's painting of a Campbell Soup can was sold for $60,000 at a New York City auction in 1970. The late British art critic, Herbert Read, had two paintings by chimpanzees who, he said, allowed "their brushes to be guided by instinctive gestures, just like the action painters of America." *Times Literary Supplement*, Aug. 28, 1970, p. 944.

15. Regarding Joseph Hirshhorn, the uranium king, James Yaffe has written, "When he likes the painter's work, he often buys it in bulk and insists on a reduction in the price, just like any garment manufacturer buying fabrics." Yaffe, *The American Jews*, p. 233.

be resold at a handsome profit or given away at a handsome tax deduction. With no more demand for continuity in art, schools of artists disappear, to be replaced by artistic cliques.[16] The arbiter of taste is no longer the art lover, but the art dealer.[17] Art is transformed into artiness.

The historic patterns and processes of artistic growth and decline as outlined in the preceding paragraphs have already blacked out most of the creativity of the Majority artist. Today in the United States, the Jewish-American writes of the Jew and his heritage, the Negro-American of the Negro, the Italian-American of the Italian, and so on. But of whom does the American-American, the Majority writer, write? Of Nordics and Anglo-Saxons? If he did, he would be laughed out of modern literature. Consciousness of one's people, one of the great emotional reserves of mankind, one of the greatest of artistic stimulants, is denied the Majority artist at the very moment the minority artist feeds upon it so ravenously. Besides its other psychological handicaps, this one-sided, selective censorship obviously builds a high wall of frustration around the free play of the imagination.

Aware or unaware of the forces working against them, many Majority artists have fled abroad to seek the cultural kinship they miss at home. Eliot became a British citizen. Robert Frost was first discovered and published while living in England. Pound, who probably exercised more influence on modern literature than any other poet, settled down in Rapallo, and dabbled in European right-wing politics.[18] Hemingway moved to France, Italy, Spain,

---

16. Picasso, often considered the greatest twentieth-century painter, is alleged to have said this about his role in modern art, "I am only a public entertainer who has understood his times and has exhausted as best he could the imbecility, the vanity, the cupidity of his contemporaries. Mine is a bitter confession, more painful than it may appear, but it has the merit of being sincere." Whether Picasso really uttered these words has not been verified. Nevertheless, *Life*, at a time when it was America's largest-circulation magazine, attributed them to Picasso (Dec. 27, 1968, p. 134).

17. Frank Lloyd, a former oil entrepreneur from Vienna, operates a chain of art galleries in London, Rome and New York, which in the art world stands out "like U.S. Steel [in] a community of blacksmiths." A competitor said of Mr. Lloyd, who does not collect pictures himself, "he might as well be in the used car business. . . ." *Wall Street Journal*, Dec. 31, 1968, pp. 1, 10.

18. See p. 551.

Africa, Cuba, and eventually committed suicide. Thomas Wolfe and F. Scott Fitzgerald spent many of their most creative years abroad and returned to gypsy-like, coast-to-coast peregrinations and an early death that was either helped along or brought about by alcohol poisoning.[19]

Some Majority artists tried to escape the dilemma of deracination by a form of spiritual emigration. Poet Robert Lowell, of the Boston Lowells, became a Roman Catholic convert.[20] Others took more desperate measures. Hart Crane, a poet of promise, jumped off a ship and drowned in the Caribbean.[21] Ross Lockridge, Jr., wrote an excellent first novel, *Raintree County*, then shut his garage door, got in his car, and started the engine.[22] Thomas Heggen, another young author who learned the hollowness of success in an alien society, wrote *Mister Roberts* and then took an overdose of sleeping pills in a rented New York apartment.[23] F. O. Matthiesen, one of the most brilliant modern American literary critics, heard the siren wail of communism and leapt to his death from a Boston hotel room.[24] W. J. Cash, a Carolina-born essayist with a fine intelligence, lambasted his native South to the delight of liberal critics and shortly afterward was found hanging by his necktie in the bathroom of a hotel in Mexico City.[25] Other talented Majority writers retreat to the sterilities and barbar-

---

19. Cinema director D. W. Griffith was another casualty of the bottle.

20. *Time*, June 17, 1965, p. 29.

21. *New York Times*, April 28, 1932, p. 4.

22. *New York Times*, March 8, 1948, p. 1. Other majority writers who took their own lives: poets John Berryman and Sylvia Plath; Laird Goldsborough, *Time* foreign affairs writer; Parker Lloyd-Smith, genius of *Fortune*.

23. *New York Times*, May 20, 1949, p. 1.

24. *Time*, April 10, 1950, p. 43. Another who heard the same song and who perhaps symbolized better than anyone the tragic fate of the Majority artist in a minority-obsessed society was Howard Rushmore. A tenth-generation American born in South Dakota, Rushmore first wrote for the *Daily Worker*, eventually losing his job for refusing to inject Negrophile sentiments in his film reviews. He then switched to anti-Communist bombast for Hearst newspapers and finally was employed by the libelous gossip magazine, *Confidential*, for which, unbeknown to himself and to his publisher, he wrote some of the finest satire in American literature. In 1958 he shot and killed himself and his wife in the back seat of a taxicab. *Newsweek*, Jan. 13, 1958, pp. 19–20.

25. W. J. Cash, *The Mind of the South*, Knopf, New York, 1941. Also see Joseph L. Morrison, *W. J. Cash*, Knopf, New York, 1967, p. 131.

ities of college campuses where they avoid the problem of content by concentrating on form, in a hopeless attempt to separate the inseparable.

All Majority artists necessarily experience the wrenching depression that comes from enforced cultural homelessness. Less than any other person is the artist capable of working in a vacuum. Prevented from exercising his own "peoplehood," the Majority artist looks for substitutes in minority racism, in exotic religions and Oriental cults, in harebrained exploits of civil disobedience, in African and pre-Columbian art, psychoanalysis, narcotics, and homosexuality.

The ban on displays of Majority ethnocentrism in art—a ban written in stone in present-day American culture—also reaches back to the Majority cultural past. Chaucer and Shakespeare have been cut and blue-penciled and some of their work put on the minority index.[26] The motion picture of Charles Dickens's *Oliver Twist* had a hard time being released in the United States because of the recognizably Jewish traits of Fagin.[27] The masterpiece of American silent films, *The Birth of a Nation,* can no longer be shown without the presence of picket lines, while Jewish-written and Jewish-produced black "sexploitation" films like *Mandingo* (1975), replete with the crudest racial slurs against whites, are shown everywhere. Mark Twain's *Huckleberry Finn* has been blackwashed and expurgated by liberal-minority watchdog organizations.[28]

---

26. The New York Board of Rabbis protested the television showing of the *Merchant of Venice* and it has been removed from the English curriculum of New York City high schools. *Time,* June 29, 1962, p. 32. An American Broadcasting Company television presentation of *The Merchant of Venice* (Nov. 16, 1974) ended with Rachel turning away from her husband's house as a Jewish cantor sings in the background. Shakespeare, always the reconciler, had her walking into the house. A 1941 Simon and Schuster edition of Chaucer's *Canterbury Tales* appeared with a foreword by Mark Van Doren but without *The Prioresses Tale,* which recounts a heinous murder committed by Jews. The Oberammergau passion play, a fixture of European culture since 1634, has been under constant attack by the American Jewish Congress for its "notoriously anti-Semitic text." In 1980 organized tours to the play for servicemen stationed in West Germany were forbidden by the secretary of the army.

27. *Saturday Review of Literature,* Feb. 26, 1949, pp. 9–10.

28. The Philadelphia Board of Education banished *Huckleberry Finn* from the public school system and replaced it by a version in which all derogatory refer-

Henry Miller's *Tropic of Capricorn* was attacked by millionaire novelist Leon Uris as "anti-Semitic." [29] Southern high-school and college bands have been forbidden to play "Dixie" at public gatherings. Even nursery rhymes and Stephen Foster are being rewritten and bowdlerized.[30] A private school in Chicago actually changed the title of the theatrical performance of *Snow White* to *Princess of the Woods* for fear of being accused of racism. Meanwhile a tireless, clandestine literary vendetta is being waged against such towering modern writers, composers,[31] and scholars,[32] both American and European, as Eliot, Dreiser, Pound,[33] Toynbee, Ernst Jünger, D. H. Lawrence, Céline, Roy Campbell, Wyndham Lewis, Kipling, Hamsun, Franz Lehar, and Richard Strauss. Their crime has been to have let slip some chance remark, written some poem, novel or essay, joined, or at least not opposed, some politi-

---

ences to Negroes were deleted. *San Francisco Chronicle, This World,* May 27, 1962, p. 16 and April 27, 1963, p. 8.

29. *Los Angeles Times,* Feb. 16, 1962, Letter Section. Uris's attack was particularly ungracious because he is the minority racist writer *par excellence.* His bestseller, *Exodus,* about the Israeli conquest of Palestine, is fifth-rate Kipling.

30. In "My Old Kentucky Home," the state anthem of Kentucky, such expressions as *Massa, Darkies* and *Mammy* have been carefully deleted. The Virginia state anthem, "Carry Me Back to Old Virginny," has been attacked by a Negro state senator as "abhorrent to his race." One Southern congressman has predicted, not altogether facetiously, that minority lobbying will eventually bring about the renaming of the White House. *U.S. News & World Report,* Aug. 9, 1957, p. 43 and *New York Times,* March 2, 1970, p. 28.

31. Practically all the leading conductors, musicians, and operatic performers who remained in Europe during World War II were victims of Jewish boycotts after the war came to an end. The list includes: Wilhelm Furtwängler, Herbert von Karajan, Walter Gieseking, Kirsten Flagstad, and Elisabeth Schwarzkopf. Yaffe, op. cit., p. 58. Jewish racism has also been responsible for depriving American audiences of the Bolshoi Opera company, whose American tour was cancelled in 1970 after a series of Zionist attacks, including a bombing, against Soviet installations in the New York area.

32. Perhaps the most bigoted censorship was exercised by refugee academicians who for years successfully "shut out" the philosophy of Martin Heidegger, one of the most original and disturbing thinkers of the modern era, only permitting it to seep through in the thinned-down adaptations of Sartre.

33. Random House barred all works of Pound from a poetry anthology, even though Conrad Aiken, one of the editors, had specifically chosen twelve Pound poems for inclusion. Charles Norman, *Ezra Pound,* Macmillan, New York, 1960, p. 416.

cal movement offensive to one or more minorities. There is, of course, no countervendetta of Majority literary critics against artists who indulge in minority racism.

The power and sustenance that an artist derives from being part of a racially and culturally homogeneous community helps explain the success of William Faulkner, the one first-rate Majority writer who survived both as an individual and as an artist the nationwide uprooting of his cultural heritage. Faulkner was born, lived, flourished, and died in Mississippi, adjudged to be the fourth most illiterate state.[34] Because they totally ignore the communal nature of art, liberals and Marxists can only treat Faulkner as a paradox.[35] Environmentalist logic can no more explain why a supposedly backward state in the Deep South should produce America's greatest twentieth-century novelist than why the most literate nation in Europe succumbed to Hitler.

Outside the South, American art has been overwhelmed by members of minorities. To lend substance to the allegation that the basic tone of American creative intellectual life has become Jewish, one has only to unroll the almost endless roster of artists, of Jewish or part-Jewish origin.[36] The contingent of Negro and

---

34. 1960 estimate by Bureau of Census.

35. Just as they treat as a paradox the fact that a disproportionate number of all modern Majority literary lights are Southerners—James Agee, Flannery O'Connor, Katherine Anne Porter, John Crowe Ransom, Robert Penn Warren, Thomas Wolfe, Walker Percy, James Dickey, Stark Young, Carson McCullers, Eudora Welty, Allen Tate, Tom Wolfe, to name a few.

36. Among those who have been active in the middle third of the century:

Writers: Edna Ferber, Gertrude Stein, Fannie Hurst, Mary McCarthy, Nathanael West, Bruce Friedman, J. D. Salinger, Herbert Gold, Harvey Swados, Bernard Malamud, Saul Bellow, Norman Mailer, Irving Stone, Jerome Weidman, Irwin Shaw, Howard Fast, Budd Schulberg, Ben Hecht, Irving Wallace, Harold Robbins, Philip Roth, Joseph Heller, Herman Wouk, Meyer Levin, S. J. Perelman, Alexander King, E. L. Doctorow, Rona Jaffe.

Poets: Louis Untermeyer, Dorothy Parker, Delmore Schwartz, Kenneth Fearing, Babette Deutsch, Karl Shapiro, Allen Ginsberg, Joseph Auslander, Howard Nemerov, Muriel Rukeyser.

Playwrights: Elmer Rice, George S. Kaufman, Moss Hart, Lillian Hellman, Sidney Kingsley, Clifford Odets, Sam and Bella Spewack, Arthur Miller, J. Howard Lawson, Neil Simon, Jack Gerber, Arthur Kopit, Paddy Chayevsky, Abe Burrows, Murray Schisgal, S. N. Behrman.

other minority artists, writers, and composers, though it cannot compare to the Jewish aggregate, is also substantial.[37]

The minority domination of the contemporary art scene is complicated by the presence of another, as yet unmentioned minority, unique in that it is composed of both Majority and minority members. This is the homosexual sect. Homosexuals, as is well known, are one of the two principal props of the American theater, the second being Jews.[38] Jews own almost all the theater houses, com-

---

Critics: Charles Angoff, Clifton Fadiman, Leslie Fiedler, John Gassner, Milton Hindus, Alfred Kazin, Louis Kronenberger, Norman Podhoretz, George Steiner, Diana Trilling, Lionel Trilling, Irving Kristol, William Goldman, Paul Goodman, Paul Jacobs, William Phillips, Irving Howe, Joseph Wechsberg, Midge Decter.

Painters and Sculptors: George Gross, Saul Steinberg, Moses and Raphael Soyer, Leon Kroll, Saul Raskin, Jacques Lipchitz, Jacob Epstein, Larry Rivers, Chaim Gross, Helen Frankenthaler, Mark Rothko.

Composers: Aaron Copland, Ernest Bloch, Darius Milhaud, George Gershwin, Leonard Bernstein, Jerome Kern, Sigmund Romberg, André Previn, Marc Blitzstein.

Orchestra Conductors, Virtuosos, and Singers: Bruno Walter, Serge Koussevitsky, Monteux, Erich Leinsdorf, Eugene Ormandy, George Szell, Mischa Elman, Jascha Heifetz, Yehudi Menuhin, Rudolf Serkin, Artur Schnabel, Alexander Kipnis, Nathan Milstein, Artur Rubinstein, Jan Peerce, George London, Robert Merrill, Vladimir Horowitz, Gregor Piatorgorsky, Arthur Fiedler, George Solti, Richard Tucker, Michael Tilson Thomas, James Levine, Antal Dorati, Otto Klemperer, Roberta Peters, Regina Resnik, Beverly Sills, Wanda Landowska, Emil Gilels, Dame Myra Hess, Isaac Stern, Joseph Szigeti.

37. Negro writers include: Ralph Ellison, Frank Yerby, Langston Hughes, Countee Cullen, Claude McKay, Richard Wright, James Baldwin, Lorraine Hansberry, Claude Brown, James Weldon Johnson, Willard Motley. Other minority writers: Russian-born Vladimir Nabokov (considered by *Time* as America's greatest living novelist), Pietro di Donato and Lawrence Ferlinghetti (Italian Americans), William Saroyan (Armenian American) and Jack Kerouac, of French-Canadian descent, the progenitor of the beat generation. Isami Noguchi, it might be noted, has been called by *Time* (Mar. 17, 1980, p. 84) "the pre-eminent American sculptor."

38. "Without either one of [these minority groups] Broadway would be desperately enfeebled; without both, it would be a clear case of evisceration." William Goldman, *The Season*, Harcourt, Brace & World, New York, 1969, p. 12. In his statistical analysis of the fifty-eight plays of the 1967–68 Broadway season, Goldman stated that homosexuals produced eighteen and directed twenty-two. Ibid., p. 237. The Jewish share of Broadway was indicated by the fact that of the thirty members of the Dramatist's Guild Council at least two-thirds were Jews. Ibid., p. 148. Regarding David Merrick and Hal Prince, the Jewish producers

prise most of the producers and almost half the directors, and furnish half of the audience and playwrights. The other playwrights are mostly well-known Majority homosexuals.[39] Combine these two ingredients, add the payroll padding, kickbacks, ticket scalping, and union featherbedding which plague all Broadway producers, and it is readily understandable why in New York, still the radiating nucleus of the American theater, the greatest of all art forms has degenerated into homosexual or heterosexual pornography,[40] leftist and Marxist message plays, foreign imports, and blaring, clockwork musical comedies.[41] It is doubtful if a new Aeschylus, Shakespeare, or Pirandello could survive for one minute on the Broadway of today.

The minority penetration of the communications media shores up minority cultural domination because the press, magazines, and TV are the transmission belts of art and, as such, its supreme arbiter. By praising, condemning, featuring, underplaying, or ignoring books,[42] paintings, sculpture, music, and other artistic works the media decide, in effect, what will be distributed (and become known) and what will not be distributed (and remain unknown). A book not reviewed favorably or not reviewed at all

---

who raked in 40 percent of the season's gross, Goldman wrote, "The point is this: neither of them has the least interest, time, taste, skill or knowledge to produce an original American play." Ibid., p. 111.

39. The chief dramatic contribution of the homosexual playwright has been the sensitive heroine in an insensitive society and the bitchy heroine in a depraved society, the former representing how the author feels, the latter how he acts. Homosexuals devise most of the flashy sets and fancy dance routines of the musical extravaganzas.

40. *Che*, by minority playwright Lennox Raphael, was the first American play to present the act of copulation on stage.

41. "The American musical comedy . . . sometimes seems to be largely the invention of Jews." Yaffe, op. cit., p. 225. Owen Wister, describing the Boston musical offerings of the late 1870s and contrasting them with those of New York fifty years later, wrote, "Pinafore had recently blazed its trail of tune and laughter all over our map, pretty and witty comic operas from Paris and Vienna drew crowded houses, not a musical show had yet been concocted by the Broadway Jew for the American moron. . . ." Owen Wister, *Roosevelt, The Story of a Friendship*, Macmillan. New York, 1930, pp. 17–18.

42. In speaking of books, it should be remembered that just under 50 percent of the major American publishing houses are Jewish. Yaffe, op. cit., p. 225.

in the influential, opinion-shaping columns of the *New York Times,* the *New York Times Book Review, Time,* and a few "higher-brow" weeklies and monthlies [43] has little or no chance of getting into libraries or the better bookstores.

This effective winnowing process also extends to advertising. Books promoting minority racism are acceptable for advertising in most newspapers and magazines. Books promoting Majority racism are not. Not only would no major newspaper or magazine review *The Dispossessed Majority,* no weekly newsmagazine would run paid advertising for it.[44] Press-agentry in the form of praise from columnists and television personalities is another tested means of lending a helping hand to minority artists or Majority artists who specialize in minority themes. Perhaps the most banal example of minority mutual admiration in the arts is the practice adopted by the *New York Times Book Review* of permitting books espousing Negro racism to be reviewed by Negro racists. For example, *Die Nigger Die!* by H. Rap Brown, a fugitive from justice rearrested after holding up a New York saloon, received a generally favorable review, although Brown wrote that he "saw no sense in reading Shakespeare," who was a "racist" and a "faggot." [45]

Throughout his life and career the minority-conscious artist identifies with one group of Americans—his group. In so doing he inevitably attacks the Majority and Northern European cultural tradition because Majority America is not his America. The Puritans are reduced to witch-hunters, reactionary pietists, and holier-than-thou bigots. The antebellum and postbellum South is turned into a vast concentration camp. The giants of industry are de-

---

43. "American literary and political 'highbrow' magazines offer the clearest example we have of this [Jewish] predominance. Here a bias, oddly enough quite unconscious, selects the subject matter, the treatment, and the authors most appealing to the Jewish sensibility (or which can best be fitted into it). It can be fairly said that these magazines are dominated by what may be called the Jewish cultural establishment." Van den Haag, *The Jewish Mystique,* p. 129.

44. See Wilmot Robertson's *Ventilations,* Howard Allen, Cape Canaveral, Fl., 1974, Chapter 3.

45. *New York Times Book Review,* June 15, 1969, pp. 6, 38. Brown, the reviewer seemed happy to report, stole a few articles from the White House during a meeting with President Johnson. He wanted to steal a painting, but was unable to think of a way of concealing it under his coat.

scribed as robber barons. The earliest pioneers and settlers are typecast as specialists in genocide. The police are "pigs." Majority members are "goys, rednecks, honkies," or just plain "beasts."

To accommodate the minority *Kulturkampf,* a Broadway play transforms Indians into a race of virtuous higher beings, while whites are portrayed as ignoble savages, and the quondam heroic figure of Custer struts about the stage as a second-rate gangster.[46] A Hollywood film shows U.S. cavalrymen raping and mutilating Indian maidens.[47] A television play set in the depression years of the 1930s puts the blame for America's ills squarely on the Majority and ends with a specific tirade against "Anglo-Saxons." [48]

But it goes far beyond this. A principal theme of modern Negro writing is the rape or violation of Majority women. In his bestselling *Soul on Ice,* which is required reading in the English curriculum of hundreds of colleges, Negro militant Eldridge Cleaver, a bail-jumping black leader who after a stay in Cuba and Algiers returned home and instead of going to jail started working the born-again Christian circuit, tells how he feels about "consciously, deliberately, willfully, methodically" despoiling white women. "It delighted me that I was defying and trampling upon the white man's law . . . that I was defiling his women. . . . I felt I was getting revenge. . . . I wanted to send waves of consternation throughout the white race." [49]

On the same page Cleaver quotes approvingly some lines from a poem by Negro writer LeRoi Jones: "Rape the white girls. Rape their fathers. Cut their mothers' throats." Intercourse with Majority females, although on a more sedate and controlled scale, is a theme that also appears frequently in the so-called Jewish literary renaissance. The heroes of Jewish fiction often seek out Gentile girls because "there is less need for respect, and thus more possibility . . . to do things that could not be done with a person one has to respect." [50]

---

46. Arthur Kopit's *Indians.*
47. *Soldier Blue.*
48. Millard Lampell's *Hard Travelin',* WNET, New York, Oct. 16, 1969.
49. Eldridge Cleaver, *Soul on Ice,* McGraw-Hill, New York, 1968, p. 14.
50. Van den Haag, op cit., p. 217. The author refers in particular to Philip Roth's novel *Portnoy's Complaint* (Random House, New York, 1969), in which this passage appears (pp. 143–44): "But the *shikses* ah, the *shikses* are something

Contemporary white artistic efforts are dismissed as "pimp art" by LeRoi Jones on the front page (second section) of the Sunday *New York Times*.[51] One Jewish author states, "The family is American fascism." A Jewish literary critic calls the late Thomas Wolfe, who had twice the talent of any minority novelist yet to appear in American literature, a "professional hillbilly." A leading Negro writer labels America, "the Fourth Reich." As mentioned previously, a literary Jewess describes the white race as "the cancer of history." [52]

But the ultimate objective is not limited to the destruction or upending of Majority institutions. There is an increasing frequency in minority writing of subtle and not so subtle appeals for the physical molestation and even the outright massacre of whites. Such was the message of LeRoi Jones's play, *Slave Ship*.[53] With the same vitriolic splash, Eldridge Cleaver writes of "young blacks out there right now who are slitting white throats." [54] A black poetess, Nikki Giovanni, has a poem in a popular black anthology which contains these lines: Can you kill/Can you run a Protestant down with your/'68 El Dorado/. . . . Can you [obscenity] on a blond head/Can you cut it off." [55] Julius Lester, another much applauded Negro writer, may have identified the minority artist's real grudge, the radiant Western artistry that seems forever beyond his reach. Ranging as far afield as Paris, he called for the destruction of Notre Dame "because it separated man from himself." [56]

The communications media and principal academic forums be-

---

else again. . . . the sight of their fresh cold blond hair spilling out of their kerchiefs and caps. . . . How do they get so gorgeous, so healthy, so blond! My contempt for what they believe in is more than neutralized by my admiration of the way they look. . . ."

51. *New York Times*, Nov. 16, 1969, Sec. 2, p. 1.

52. Originators of these quotations are in order: Paul Goodman, Alfred Kazin, James Baldwin, and Susan Sontag. See Benjamin De Mott, *Supergrow*, pp. 74–75. James Agee, a Truckler of some talent, preferred Chinese and Negroes to his own people, despised Irishmen and Germans, and married a Jewess, *Letters of James Agee to Father Flye*, G. Braziller, New York, 1962, p. 151.

53. See footnote 26, p. 91.

54. Cleaver, op. cit., p. 15.

55. *The Black Poets*, Bantam Books, New York, 1971, pp. 318–19.

56. Lester, *Search for a New Land*, p. 144.

ing closed to him, the Majority artist has no adequate defense against the blistering minority assault on his culture. He must avoid praising his own people *as a people*—and he also must avoid castigating other peoples, particularly the more dynamic minorities. The minority artist, on the other hand, wears no such straitjacket. He freely praises whom he likes and freely damns whom he dislikes, both as individuals and as groups. The Majority artist, with a narrower choice of heroes and villains, has a narrower choice of theme. Lacking the drive and brute force of minority racism, Majority art tends to become bland, innocuous, emotionless, sterile, and boring.[57] Forbidden to explore the text and context of his collective consciousness, the Majority artist retreats to surrealism, science fiction, murder mysteries, fantasy, travel guides, and pornography.[58] In the process he becomes the punch-

---

57. An art historian of the future, having only at his disposal lists of bestsellers, art expositions, and musical recitals for the period 1950–80, might conclude that the American Majority had ceased to exist. As reported by *Time* (May 19, 1969, p. 12), the nation's five leading fiction bestsellers were: #1, *Portnoy's Complaint,* which has a Jewish hero or antihero; #2, *The Godfather,* an Italian-American novel about Italian Americans and the Mafia; #3, *The Salzburg Connection,* a spy tale with stock Nazi villains by an Englishwoman; #4, *Slaughterhouse Five,* a World War II novel by a Majority Truckler; #5, *Sunday the Rabbi Came Home.* The three top fiction bestsellers as reported by the *New York Times* (Sept. 5, 1976) were: #1, *Trinity* by Leon Uris; #2, *Dolores* by Jacqueline Susann; #3, *My Lonely Lady* by Harold Robbins. All three authors are Jewish. When it is known that only 17 percent of American adults read one book a year, that 50 percent of American college graduates do not read one book a year, that 50 percent of Americans have never read one book through, American reading habits are even more of a tragedy than indicated by bestseller lists. See Nancy Polette and Marjorie Hamlin, *Reading Guidance in a Media Age,* Scarecrow Press, Metuchen, New Jersey, 1976.

58. Pornography assumes an ever greater place in eras of cultural breakdown, not, as some apostles of permissiveness like to pretend, because it expands artistic horizons but because it shrinks them. As bad money drives out good, the art of the private parts drives out the art of the heart and mind. Of all man's artistic activities pornography, if it can be called an art, requires the least amount of mental effort. Perhaps nothing has done more harm to the torn fabric of American civilization than the Supreme Court's 1957 ruling in *Roth* v. *U.S.,* which defined obscenity as something "utterly without redeeming social importance." Since a sharp lawyer can find at least a trace of "social importance" in any kind of trash, Pandora's box was opened, and the minority

ing bag of the minority activist, who sees "man's essential struggle as social, against other men, rather than the moral one against himself." [59]

Many potential Majority artists [60] probably sense well in advance the roadblocks in the way of a successful artistic career and turn to science, where their creativity is less hampered. Similar situations in the past may illustrate why in the life span of nations the artistic efflorescence has generally preceded the scientific—why Sophocles came before Archimedes, Dante before Galileo, Shakespeare before Newton and Faraday, Goethe before Planck. Mathematics, physics, and chemistry, but not the life sciences, are less controversial than art [61] and in a divided, pluralistic society may be the last refuge of free expression and free inquiry. It has been said by Ortega y Gasset that "people read to pronounce judgment." The aphorism might be extended by saying that as nations become older and more divergent in politics, religion,

---

tycoons of Hollywood, Broadway, and Publishers' Row were quick to seize the opportunity—and the profits.

59. John Leggett, "The Wasp Novel," *New York Times Book Review*, Nov. 30, 1969, p. 2.

60. The genius bathed in what Matthew Arnold has called "the national glow" has a less difficult row to hoe than the genius in a fragmenting culture, which forces partisanship of one kind or another on everyone. As Goethe put it, "Bedauert doch den ausserordentlichen Menschen, dass er in einer so erbärmlichen Zeit leben, dass er immerfort polemisch wirken musste." Eckermann, *Gespräche mit Goethe* (Feb. 7, 1827).

61. The least controversial art is music and consequently the last to be devitalized by censorship. Properly speaking, the only art that still remains in Majority hands is "country music," and even this is falling under the triple assault of Negro jazz, the drug traffic, and cynical show business promoters. Critic Richard Goldstein, writing for the young female readership of *Mademoiselle* (June 1973), charged that country music was "threatening" to Jewish sensibilities and in its stead recommended the lubricious lilt of Negro rhythms. The rock festivals, which have drawn such gigantic audiences and such gigantic attention from the media, are in part a confused attempt to rescue popular music from Tin Pan Alley. But they are by no means as impromptu as the press makes them appear. The Woodstock Festival had an advance ticket sale of $1,400,000, generated by the $200,000 its two Jewish producers, John Roberts and Mike Lang, spent in radio and newspaper advertising. *New York Times Magazine*, Sept. 7, 1969, pp. 122, 124.

class, and race, people read to soothe or excite their prejudices.

The glimmering of a great artistic era appeared in the United States in the first half of the nineteenth century. In New England, New York, Philadelphia, and the South, a native American aristocracy was evolving out of generations of landowners, shipping magnates, army and navy officers, and government, church, and educational leaders. At the same time, schools of Majority artists were emerging, their growth rate synchronized with that of the budding aristocracy. It was perhaps no coincidence that the Hudson River Valley, the stamping ground of the first American aristocrats, produced the first great American writer, Washington Irving, the greatest American writer, Herman Melville, and the first American school of painting. The Dutch patroons of New Amsterdam had carved out their riverine estates decades before the founding of the Virginia plantations and while Boston was still a log-cabin theocracy.[62]

The traumatic experience of the Civil War was not entirely responsible for putting an end to America's great artistic promise. There was the overbrimming social fluidity which followed the war and made possible the settlement of the West. There were fortunes to be made—in commerce, in industry, in mining, in land—and as plutocracy waxed, art waned.[63] There was also the New Immigration, which played havoc with the normal, organic processes of artistic evolution.

In the last moment of the Republic, when Roman culture was displaying signs of rigor mortis, Augustus stopped the dissolution of Roman art by halting the dispossession of the Roman Majority. The outcome was the Golden Age of Latin literature. It was not until Rome's decline properly began—according to Gibbon, with

---

62. Significantly, Melville's mother, Maria Gansevoort, a descendant of one of the oldest Dutch families, was a "cold, proud woman, arrogant in the sense of her name, her blood and the affluence of her forebears." Raymond M. Weaver, *Herman Melville*, p. 34. Also see Morison, *Oxford History of the American People*, pp. 177, 487 for a chronological comparison of the New York and New England aristocracies.

63. "The real revolution [in the U.S.] was not what is called the Revolution in history books, but is a consequence of the Civil War; after which arose a plutocratic elite." T. S. Eliot, *Notes towards the Definition of Culture*, Harcourt Brace, New York, 1949, p. 44.

the accession of Commodus in A.D. 180—that the demise of Roman art and the Roman Majority could be considered official.

For the sake of the American Majority and of American art, it is to be hoped that the United States is now in its pre-Augustan, not its pre-Commodian era.[64]

---

64. The ways and means adopted by Augustus in his rehabilitation of the "Old Romans" and Roman art should provide those interested in reversing the dispossession of the Majority with ample food for thought and with a fairly comprehensive blueprint for solving problems similar in many respects to those facing present-day Americans. Augustus's point of departure was "that the Italian race was immeasurably the superior of any other, and he did not wish to see it lost in a polyglot welter." Buchan, *Augustus,* pp. 16, 20, 124, 128, 130, 170–71, 206–9, 235, 244. "Considering it also of great importance to keep the people pure and unsullied by any taint of foreign or servile blood, he was most chary of conferring Roman citizenship and set a limit to manumission." Suetonius, *Divus Augustus,* trans. J. C. Rolfe, XL, 3.

CHAPTER 19

The Secularization of Religion

A RT IS ONE OF the battlegrounds of the cultural clash now taking place in the United States. Religion is another. The intention of this chapter, however, is not to indulge in theological speculations or question the truth or error of any particular faith. It is to examine the purely social and pragmatic side of religion and its relationship to the present tides of political, economic, and social change.

God may be dead, as it was once announced that great Pan was dead and as many twentieth-century churchmen, echoing the wishful thinking of Nietzsche, presently proclaim. But the religious instinct is very much alive. Though science is a long way from confirming it, it almost seems that men are born with a religious gene. There may have been an alarming decrease in the spiritual magnetism and uplift of formal religion in recent times, but men have made up for it by shifting their innate religiosity to more mundane creeds—democracy, liberalism, capitalism, nationalism, fascism, socialism, and communism. If an abundance of saints, devils, martyrs, and prophets is a sign of religious zeal, the twentieth century ought to rank as the most religious of all centuries. Never since the days of Rome have so many heads of state, both living and dead, been deified or diabolized on such a grand scale. Belief in the old gods may be flickering, but belief in the more worldly deities of the present is laser bright.

A review of organized religion in America must concentrate on a discussion of Christianity. Until quite recently, the United States was called a Christian nation and statistically about 60 per-

258

cent of all Americans still belong to a Christian church.[1] But what exactly is a Christian? The definition seems to depend on the religious denomination of the definer. In Roman Catholic eyes, St. Francis, one of the few who ever took Christ literally, and Boniface VIII, more Caesar than pope, were both Christians. In Protestant eyes, so was Captain (later Reverend) John Newton, who composed the ever popular hymn, "How Sweet the Name of Jesus Sounds," while the vessel he commanded waited off the Guinea coast to pick up a new shipment of slaves from the interior.[2] Other Christians have included Syrian column-sitters, sword-wielding Norsemen, cannibalistic blacks, lust-ridden empresses, and piety-stricken nuns.

The difficulty of defining a Christian stems in part from the massive polarizations and cyclic sweeps of Christianity in the first nineteen centuries of its existence. No religion has been so many things to so many believers and so many theologians. None has provoked so many heresies and schisms, so much war and so much peace, so much animosity and so much love. Perhaps the only time that Christianity was truly unified and truly one religion was in its very beginnings, when it was a simple offshoot of Judaism—one of the many sects that flourished in the spiritual ferment stirred up by Roman encroachments on Jewish statehood.

The first great problem of Christianity was a purely racial one. Would it be a religion for Jews or for Gentiles? Jesus himself

---

1. The *1980 World Almanac* lists 169 religious denominations in the United States with a total membership of 170,185,693 or 78% of the population. Of these, 49,836,176 are Roman Catholics, 3,970,735 Eastern Orthodox, 1,850,000 Jews, 2,000,000 Moslems, 21,000 Buddhists, etc. Of the remaining 112,507,782 most are Protestants, quasi-Protestants, and members of unaffiliated Christian sects. The number of Roman Catholics is quite misleading because the Catholic Church counts as members all who are baptized. The Jewish figure was inexplicably increased to 3,985,000 in the *1981 World Almanac*, though Jews are known to be the most irreligious American population group (see p. 269). Many of the larger Protestant churches, on the other hand, only count practicing churchgoers and communicants. The breakdown of the larger Protestant denominations is as follows: 15,862,749 Baptists, 12,486,912 Methodists, 10,331,405 Lutherans, 3,745,526 Presbyterians, 2,818,130 Episcopalians, 2,237,721 Pentecostals.

2. *Times Literary Supplement*, Jan. 9, 1964, p. 25.

was a Galilean from "Galilee of the Gentiles." [3] There is no definite proof that he was a Jew, but it is almost certain he was brought
up in a Jewish cultural ambiance. At first many Jews looked upon
him as a possible Messiah come to satisfy their craving for a return
to the temporal glories of Solomon. Later, when the ministry of
Jesus began to include outsiders and when he demonstrated more
interest in an otherworldly than in a worldly kingdom, the Jews
quickly closed their hearts and their purses.[4] In the words of Toynbee, "this inspired Jewish scion of forcibly converted Galilean
Gentiles was then rejected and done to death by the Judaean
leaders of the Jewry of his age." [5]

The next problem facing Christianity, once it moved away from
the Jews, was how much of its original Jewish background and
tradition would or should be preserved. One faction, the Marcionites, attempted to purge the early church of all Jewish influence
and went so far as to brand the Old Testament the work of the
devil. The Petrine Church, on the other hand, accepted the Jewish
Bible, a great deal of Jewish theology and law, and the special
position of the Jews as midwives of Christianity—indeed almost
everything Jewish except the Jews themselves. Eventually the Ju-
daizing party won, though remnants of Marcionite influence persisted until the Cathars of Southern France were liquidated by
papal auxiliaries in the twelfth century.[6] If the Marcionites had

---

3. "Galilee of the Gentiles" is found in Matthew 4:15. At the time of Jesus'
birth, Galilee, a Roman province in northern Palestine, had a mixed Jewish-
Assyrian population and had been considered Jewish for less than a century.
Toynbee, *Study of History,* Vol. II, pp. 73–74, and *Ency. Brit.,* Vol. 9, p. 978.
Both ultra- and anti-Semites have occasionally tried to make Jesus something
other than a Jew. The Talmudic tradition of a part-Roman ancestry has been
noted in footnote 121, p. 200. One Aryanizer of Jesus points to a descent from
"Proto-Nordics" who once lived in and about Galilee. C. G. Campbell, *Race
and Religion,* Peter Nevill, London, 1973, p. 151. Houston Stewart Chamberlain in his *Foundations of the Nineteenth Century* also claimed Jesus was not a
Jew.

4. The Spanish philosopher Miguel de Unamuno gave another reason why
Jews turned their backs on Jesus. He preached immortality, in which Jews have
scant interest. Unamuno, *Del Sentimiento Trágico de la Vida,* Las Americas Publishing, New York, 1966, Chapter III.

5. *A Study of History,* Vol. V, p. 658.

6. *Ency. Brit.,* Vol. 5, p. 72, and Vol. 14, p. 868.

prevailed, there would have been very little Judaeo in the Judaeo-Christian heritage of Western civilization.[7]

One of the principal themes of Gibbons's magnificent obituary of the Roman Empire was the important role of Christianity in its decay and dissolution.[8] If the great historian had explored the workings of the early church more penetratingly, he might have found the real culprit was not the Christian religion as such, but those who played up the equalitarian and insurrectionary elements of Christianity at the expense of the more fundamental Christian concept of otherworldliness. On the one side, the power and privilege of the dwindling Roman elite were undermined by the New Testament's accent on brotherhood and renunciation.

---

7. Certain racial manifestations can be detected in this divided inheritance. Marcion, a native of northern Asia Minor, was born outside the Semitic ecumene. Saints Peter and Paul and many other leaders of the Petrine Church were converted Jews. An important Jewish legacy to Christianity was the doctrine of original sin, strongly supported by St. Augustine, a North African, and strongly opposed by Pelagius, a native of the British Isles, during one of Christianity's most serious theological feuds. Alien to Hebrew thought and tradition, but too well established to be purged by the more fanatic Judaizers, were the New Testament's three wise men, the temptation on the mountain, baptism, paradise, and the resurrection. This non-Jewish side of Christianity, according to one view, was originated by the Persian prophet, Zoroaster, whose teachings had become familiar to Jesus as a result of his association with and perhaps blood relationship to the Amorites, who had close contacts with the Persians. C. G. Campbell, op. cit., Chapter II. T. E. Lawrence had this to say in regard to the seemingly congenital differences in the religious sensibilities of Semites and non-Semites: "I had believed Semites unable to use love as a link between themselves and God. . . . Christianity had seemed to me the first creed to proclaim love in this upper world, from which the desert and the Semite (from Moses to Zeno) had shut it out. . . . Its birth in Galilee had saved it from being just one more of the innumerable revelations of the Semite. Galilee was Syria's non-Semitic province, contact with which was almost uncleanness for the perfect Jew. . . . Christ by choice passed his ministry in its intellectual freedom. . . ." T. E. Lawrence, *Seven Pillars of Wisdom,* Doubleday, Doran, Garden City, N.Y., 1935, p. 356. There might also have been a racial repulsion on the part of Gentiles for some Jewish religious practices, in particular that aspect of the circumcision ritual in which a "venerable and honored guest is asked to apply his mouth to the penis, and suck up the first drop of blood." Van den Haag, *The Jewish Mystique,* p. 160.

8. *Decline and Fall of the Roman Empire,* Chapters 15 and 16.

On the other, the subject races were aroused to violence by the inflammatory sermons of the Early Fathers, whose strictures against Roman paganism demanded the destruction of everyone and everything connected with the old religion. In A.D. 310 there was one last flare-up of pagan repression when the Emperor Galerius poured molten lead down Christian throats and fed the lions a final meal of martyrs in the Coliseum. Two years later, Constantine saw the blazing cross and Rome soon had a Christian Emperor.

When Christianity became a state religion the bishops changed their tune. Instead of opposing the government the Church became its guardian. Instead of attacking military service it advocated it. Once the oppressed, Christians were now the oppressors and the flames of Greek and Roman temples lit the night sky of dying Rome. Although it was too late to prevent the Empire's collapse, the bishops did manage to convert, in a fashion, the conquering Teutons, who later saved Western Christianity from the Huns, Arabs, Turks, and other heathen marauders.

By the time of the Crusades, Christianity had divided into the Roman Catholic and Greek Orthodox churches. It divided again when Northern Europe, incited by princes with a covetous eye on the heavy gold exports to the Holy See, broke away from the spiritual absolutism and temporal *Realpolitik* of the Latinized Popes. The Reformation drew the religious frontiers which today separate Protestant from Catholic Europe and the racial frontiers which in many areas separate Nordic from Alpine Europe.

Professor Guignebert of the University of Paris, perhaps the most informed modern biblical scholar, has provided an interesting sidelight on the development of Christianity by noting the changing "appearance" of Jesus through the ages.[9] The first depictions of Jesus made him hairy, ugly, and abject. Later in Gothic rose windows and statuary and in Renaissance paintings and frescoes, Christ was endowed with Nordic features and at times looked more like Siegfried than the son of a Mediterranean carpenter. Many paintings of the Holy Family portrayed the Virgin and the

---

9. Charles Guignebert, *Jésus*, Le Renaissance du Livre, Paris, 1933, pp. 189–96. In *The Everlasting Gospel*, Blake expatiated on two different faces of Jesus: "The Vision of Christ that thou dost see/ Is my vision's greatest enemy./ Thine has a great hooked nose like thine;/ Mine has a snub nose like to mine."

Christ Child with blond hair and blue eyes. The Aesthetic Prop was everywhere visible in the greatest masterpieces of Church-sponsored art.

Christianity was brought to the United States by members of practically every Christian denomination—Anglicans and Anabaptists, Catholics and Mennonites, Lutherans, Quakers and Shakers, Greek Orthodox and Doukhobors. The Episcopal Church—two-thirds of the signers of the Declaration of Independence were Episcopalians [10]—and the Calvinist churches (principally the Congregational and the Presbyterian) remained dominant until the rise of the revivalist and evangelical sects in the early nineteenth century. The slavery issue dissolved whatever Christian unity existed between North and South, turning many Yankees from the eye-for-an-eye morality and ironbound predestination of Calvinism [11] to Unitarianism and other less rigorous and less selective creeds. In the same years Southern churches fastened a stratified, black-and-white Christianity on the slave states, justifying their actions by murky biblical passages on human bondage.[12]

Shortly before the Civil War, Roman Catholicism began to assume some prominence in national affairs. In addition to its religious function the Church served as an immense social service organization for the mass influx of hungry, homesick Irish immigrants. Decades later, it became the spiritual and, on occasion, the political shepherd for the millions of Central and Southern European Catholics who furnished the bulk of the New Immigration. By the early 1930s the Catholic Church was the largest and most powerful religious body in the United States. In 1928 Alfred E. Smith lost the presidential election partly because he was a Catholic. In 1960 John F. Kennedy won the presidency partly

---

10. *Ency. Brit.*, Vol. 18, p. 612.

11. The earlier New England Calvinist was typified by Samuel Adams, who "was no revolutionist, but a racist, anti-Catholic—with no favor for minorities." Morison, *Oxford History of the American People*, p. 211.

12. The most quoted was Genesis 9:22–27. Ham, considered by some theologians to be the progenitor of the Negro race, sees his father, Noah, naked in his drunkenness. When Noah hears about it, he lays a curse on Canaan, the son of Ham, destining him to be a "servant of servants." Shem (the first Semite) and Japheth (the first non-Semite?), Ham's brothers, were thereafter to be served through all eternity by Canaan, according to proslavery interpreters of the Old Testament.

because he was a Catholic. In the 97th Congress (1981–82), more congressmen belonged to the Catholic Church than to any other religious denomination.

Today, Christianity in the United States has come full circle. Once again it has turned its attention from God to man and become the champion of the minorities. Many Protestant ministers take the money from their collection plates and spend it on projects for blacks and Hispanics, projects which are often more political than charitable. Churches are transformed into meeting places for black gangs.[13] Clergymen record their "deep appreciation" to the black militant who stormed into Manhattan's Riverside Church and demanded $500 million in "reparations."[14] Long tolant of communism in its various Stalinist, Titoist, and Maoist guises,[15] many churchmen now openly endorse certain forms of revolution,[16] support civil disobedience, are jailed for unlawful picketing,[17] raise $100,000 bail for Black Panthers,[18] and conspire

---

13. All in vain, as Nietzsche predicted a century ago: "There is nothing more terrible than a barbaric slave class, who have learned to regard their existence as an injustice, and now prepare to avenge, not only themselves, but all future generations. In the face of such threatening storms, who dares to appeal with any confidence to our pale and exhausted religions. . . ." *The Birth of Tragedy* from *The Philosophy of Nietzsche,* trans. Clifton Fadiman, Modern Library, New York, p. 1048.

14. *Time,* May 16, 1969, p. 94.

15. According to congressional investigator J. B. Matthews, 7,000 clergymen once espoused the Communist party line. As the Soviet Union became more grasping and bellicose, many of them adopted safer and more acceptable brands of Marxism. For Matthews's estimate, see Walter Goodman, *The Committee,* Farrar Straus, New York, 1968, p. 335.

16. A London conference organized by the World Council of Churches (Protestant) produced a report which stated that "guerrilla fighters struggling against racist regimes must be given the support of the church if all else has been seen to fail." It also stated that in certain circumstances, "The church must support resistance movements, including revolutions, which are aimed at the elimination of political or economic tyranny that makes racism possible." The conference was under the chairmanship of Senator George McGovern, a Methodist lay delegate. *Time,* June 6, 1969, p. 88. Over the years the World Council, to which most American Protestant denominations belong, has continued to support black terrorist groups in Africa with sermons and cash.

17. *Time,* Dec. 10, 1965, p. 96.

18. *New York Times,* Jan. 31, 1970, p. 9. In September 1970, black militant Angela Davis, while on the FBI's list of the ten most wanted criminals for owning the guns which killed a California judge, was honored by having her portrait

against a future draft as they conspired against the American war effort in Vietnam.[19] Some Catholic priests have been active in inciting Mexican-American strikes against California farmers.[20] Others, notably the Berrigan brothers, have broken into Selective Service offices and destroyed draft records.[21] Still others have taken to the streets and led mass sit-ins in defiance of state and local laws. In only a very few cases were such activities censured or forbidden by the Catholic hierarchy.

Altogether the present liberal-minority stance of Christianity in America lacks credibility and smacks of dilettantism. Jesus *was* an underdog and his poverty and minority status stimulated an honest concern for the oppressed and downtrodden. The well-fed, well-funded clergyman who walks a mile or two in a "freedom march" and drops in from time to time to see how his Negro friends are doing in the slums seems a little counterfeit. So does the "social conscience" of the Vatican ($80 billion in assets, including a $5.6 billion stock portfolio) [22] and of the United States religious establishment (property alone valued at $102 billion).[23] Such a vast hoard of wealth, which is nothing new in church history,

prominently displayed in the annual Liberation Sunday of St. Stephen's Episcopal Church in St. Louis. *Miami Herald,* Sept. 27, 1970, p. 30A. Miss Davis was later exonerated by an all-white jury.

19. Yale University Chaplain William Sloane Coffin, Jr., once married to the ballerina daughter of Artur Rubinstein, was sentenced to two years in prison in 1968 for conspiring to counsel young Americans to evade the draft. The jury's verdict was later thrown out by a higher court. *1970 World Almanac,* p. 922.

20. *Time,* Dec. 10, 1965, p. 96.

21. *New York Times,* Aug. 9, 1970, Sec. 4, p. 7. In January 1971, the Berrigans were charged with plotting to blow up the heating systems of five government buildings in Washington and kidnap Henry Kissinger. According to *Time,* the two brothers were "cradle rebels." Their father, Tom Berrigan, was a trade union organizer and the son of Irish immigrants who had fled to the U.S. to escape the poverty of Tipperary. *Time,* Jan. 25, 1971, pp. 14–15.

22. Nino Lo Bello, *The Vatican Empire,* Fireside, Simon and Schuster, New York, 1970, pp. 23, 135. The Holy See has formally denied these estimates, though admitting it is so enmeshed in high finance it has established close relations with the Rothschilds. *New York Times,* July 22, 1970, p. 8. Pope John Paul II revealed the Church had a $20 million deficit in 1979. UPI report, Nov. 10, 1979.

23. *Time,* May 18, 1970, p. 44. Of the $17.6 billion that American individuals or organizations contributed to charity in 1969, $7.9 billion was earmarked for religious purposes. *U.S. News & World Report,* July 13, 1970, p. 65.

has always made Christianity suspect in the eyes of left-leaning radicals. It helps explain why, despite all that Christian liberals did to prepare the way, in the three great revolutions of modern history—French, Russian, and Chinese—Christianity was officially or unofficially proscribed.

Although Christians are almost a billion strong, their faith is cooling.[24] Popes no longer command armies, excommunicate kings, and organize crusades. There are no more Sainte Chapelles abuilding and no artists with one iota of the religious intensity found in a Fra Angelico painting. The pens of Luther and Milton are still, and the rousing Protestant hymns of yesteryear have lost their Sunday punch and are increasingly unsung. Revival meetings in tents and on television continue to draw large audiences, but more lips are converted than hearts. The old-time religion is still alive and well in some areas, but it has more relevance to the ambitions of prominent evangelists than to God. Catholic and Protestant clerics may get reams of favorable publicity in the press when they abandon their flocks to spread their "good works" among the minorities, but it gains them few points with their hometown congregations. The leaders of the so-called Moral Majority have won a certain amount of acclaim, not, however, for spreading the gospel but for attacking the pandemic corruption and immorality of the times.

The deformation of religion in America, the shift from the Old Testament stamp of the original white settlers to the permissive social Christianity of the present, brings up the age-old question of how effectively religion shapes a people's character and how effectively a people's character shapes religion. According to modern standards the colonial American, his rifle in one hand and his Bible in the other, was a caricature of a Christian. He may have read the Good Book to his family once a week, but he seldom went to church. The Pilgrims, it is known, had no pastor for nine

---

24. According to the *1980 World Almanac*, there are 968,184,100 Christians, as compared to 546,025,000 Moslems, 470,998,150 Hindus, 256,029,050 Buddhists, 168,158,700 worshippers of Confucius, 56,152,000 Shintoists, 31,233,650 Taoists, 14,383,100 Jews, and 254,000 Zoroastrians. Despite the huge number of Christians, Rabbi Arthur Hertzberg, president of the American Jewish League, is known to have said, "I think Christianity is dead." *New York Daily News*, May 13, 1975, p. 44.

years after their arrival. In Virginia fewer than one out of nineteen were church members. Among Massachusetts Bay colonists only one-fifth were even professing Christians.[25] Joshua, though perhaps not the late Bishop Pike,[26] would have been proud of the Pilgrims. When they did go to Plymouth Church, they marched in three abreast with their muskets and firelocks at the ready, while other members of the congregation manned six cannon on the roof, each capable of shooting iron balls of four to five

---

25. William W. Sweet, *The Story of Religion in America*, Harper, New York, 1950, pp. 5, 45, 48.

26. The public immorality of many modern church leaders is the best proof of the profound change that has taken place in American religion. Bishop Pike, for example, was almost the antithesis of the seventeenth-century Puritan divine. Born a Roman Catholic in Hollywood, Calif., Pike attended a Jesuit school and became a lawyer before being ordained an Episcopal priest. An alcoholic when promoted to bishop, Pike was thrice married and twice divorced. His son and a favorite secretary committed suicide, and his daughter attempted suicide. Before he died in Israel, he resigned his bishopric under fire and devoted himself to spiritualism. *Time*, Nov. 11, 1966, p. 56, and *New York Times*, Sept. 8, 1969, p. 1. Two prominent black churchmen set equally poor examples. Adam Clayton Powell, with his padded payrolls and expense-account shenanigans, and Martin Luther King, Jr., with his attempts to direct the course of American foreign and domestic policy, behaved more like Renaissance cardinals than Baptist ministers. *New York Times*, Jan. 4, 1969, p. 1, and *Time*, Aug. 17, 1970, p. 13. Even the "prophet" of the Black Muslims, Elijah Muhammad, who served a three-year prison term for draft dodging, scandalized his principal lieutenant by his dalliance with the office help. *Autobiography of Malcolm X*, pp. 209–10, 299. Dean Moorehouse, a former Methodist minister, went to jail for giving LSD to minors. He was the friend of Charles Manson, leader of a West Coast cult that committed more than nine murders. Moorehouse remained Manson's friend, even after the latter "adopted" Moorehouse's fifteen-year-old daughter into his homicidal band. *New York Times Magazine*, Jan. 4, 1970, p. 32. When Episcopal Bishop Robert Hatch was informed that his daughter was appearing nude in a San Francisco theater, he said, "I am glad she has a chance to express herself." *Time*, June 8, 1970, p. 40. The Reverend Ted McIlvenna, a Methodist minister in San Francisco, made sixty-four explicit sex films and sold them for $150 to $250 each to 8,000 customers "one of our largest being the federal government." He used a cast of ten unpaid volunteer couples. *New York Times*, May 18, 1980. A few years earlier, ninety leading Episcopal priests agreed homosexual acts between consenting adults are "morally neutral" and might even be a good thing. *New York Times*, Nov. 29, 1967, p. 1. Perhaps the low point in religion in America was reached in Jonestown, Guyana, where the genuinely diabolical Reverend Jim Jones ordered the mass suicide of his largely black flock in 1978.

pounds.[27] Was this a different kind of Christianity? Or was it a different kind of Christian?

Many other aspects of early American Christianity are equally abhorrent to modern church leaders. John Winthrop, the first governor of the Massachusetts Bay Colony, probably spoke for all the Puritan elders when he said that democracy "has always been counted the meanest and worst of all forms of government." [28] In Connecticut and Massachusetts the right to vote was restricted to church members, upsetting as this may be to those who believe that the American political tradition is unalterably bound to the separation of church and state.[29] Equally upsetting is that the New England church thrived on the slave and rum trade, and that many well-known Congregational ministers owned slaves.[30]

The Protestant religion has passed through its Old Testament pioneering phase and, despite some noisy fundamentalists, its New Testament evangelical phase. It is now well into its liberal phase. The Catholic religion is on a somewhat similar, but later-starting, timetable.[31] The burning faith brought over by immigrants from Ireland and Central and Southern Europe has gradually cooled. Many of their descendants now obey a less rigid and more tolerant code, which permits them to defy their Church's ban on contraceptives and divorce, skip mass for golf, and escape or think about escaping from the warm protection of their religious cocoon into the uncharted spaces of agnosticism.

Priests and even nuns are marrying, not always within the Church.[32] Parochial schools are shut down for lack of funds. Members of the hierarchy are challenging papal infallibility. As the possibility of another great schism looms, the Church in America will have an increasingly difficult time keeping its decreasingly

---

27. Sweet, op. cit., pp. 46–47.　　　28. Ibid., p. 51.　　　29. Ibid. p. 53.

30. Ibid., pp. 285–86. There were 6,000 slaves in Massachusetts in 1776.

31. The "Catholic" colony of Maryland was largely a fiction. During most of its existence Catholic immigrants were forbidden and Catholic worship prohibited. Beard, *The Rise of American Civilization*, Vol. 1, p. 65.

32. Sister Jacqueline Grennan married Paul Wexler, a Jewish widower. Mrs. Wexler is now president of Hunter College. Philip Berrigan, the radicalized ex-priest, married a nun who was later arrested for shoplifting. *Time*, Sept. 18, 1973, p. 46.

devout communicants under one roof. If it moves to the left to appease its growing Hispanic contingent, it must alienate its Irish and white ethnics. As racial divisions within its ranks sharpen, as the old external battle against the Protestants turns into an internal struggle for power, Catholic unity, once such a strong political force in the United States, may soon decline to the point where Catholics will no longer vote according to their religion but according to their race.[33]

Judaism in America has followed the same hylotheistic route as Protestantism and Catholicism. The orthodox zealotry of the Sephardim of pre-Revolutionary and Revolutionary days compares to the more rational religious approach of contemporary Reform and Conservative Judaism as an acetylene torch to a candle. At present no more than 10 percent of American Jewry observes dietary laws and surveys show that Jewish college students are considerably less religious than non-Jewish students.[34] There are some 4,000 Jewish congregations in the United States, comprising approximately 70 percent of all Jewish families, but most Jews affiliated with synagogues can hardly be described as pious. Only 19 percent of American Jews visit a temple once a week.[35]

The establishment of Israel has reversed or at least slowed this secular trend and drawn some Jews back into the religious fold by renewing their interest in Jewish history.[36] Judaism also contin-

---

33. This is not to say that American Catholics are decreasing numerically. According to the anti-Catholic historian Paul Blanshard, Catholics in America will outnumber Protestants by the year 2125. *American Freedom and Catholic Power*, Beacon, Boston, 1958, p. 298.

34. Albert L. Gordon, *Intermarriage*, Beacon, Boston, 1964, pp. 42, 47–8, 50, 97.

35. Gallup Poll, Jan. 13, 1974.

36. Nevertheless, in respect to numbers, religious Jewry is barely holding its own. At best there are only 3,000 conversions a year—mostly Gentile women preparing to marry traditionally oriented Jewish males. Not many of them, however, convert to the Orthodox branch of Judaism, a process which includes sitting in a tub of water up to the neck while two learned elders discourse on the major and minor commandments. Litvinoff, *A Peculiar People*, p. 26, and Yaffe, op. cit., pp. 46, 100, 102. The declining number of Jews has caused Rabbi Alexander Schindler, president of the Union of American Hebrew Congregations, to propose a radical remedy. Normally, Jewish law regards only the child of a Jewish mother as a Jew. In consideration of the growing rate of mixed

ues to be attractive to many Jews for a reason that has nothing to do with religion and much to do with practical politics. As one prominent American Jew explained, "In fighting the cause of Jewish rights abroad, the religious approach is usually the one that Jewish leadership finds it most advisable to take." [37] He might have added that Judaism also serves as a useful camouflage for Jewish activity in domestic affairs. In the meantime their old religious animus against Christianity has been mollified as Jews discover the advantages to be gained from the present Christian emphasis on selective tolerance.

The ecumenical movement, though successful in bringing Protestants and Catholics closer together than at any time since the Reformation, has been powerless to prevent the various Christian denominations from abandoning their moral ascendancy over American life. If secularization continues at its present pace, Christianity may soon have no deeper significance in the American scheme of things than sports. Protestantism, in fact, has become so lukewarm that even the issue of federal aid to education no longer secretes undue amounts of adrenaline in Baptist or Methodist glands. Without regard to small, scattered voices of protest, national, state, and local governments often subsidize parochial schools with free lunches and transportation and aid parochial institutions of higher learning with five- and six-figure monetary grants for the physical and social sciences. There is even less public outcry when the flaming liberal Jesuit priest, Robert Drinan, his white collar resplendent in television floodlights, runs for public office.[38]

In recent years the most sensitive area of church-state relationship has not been the mixing of religion and politics, but the public observance of religion. Supreme Court rulings against pray-

---

marriages, Rabbi Schindler suggested that the child of a Jewish father and a Gentile mother be recognized as a Jew. Conservatives and Reform Jews did not seem to bridle at the suggestion. Orthodox Jews were outraged. Chicago *Sentinel,* Dec. 20, 1979, p. 6.

37. Dr. Israel Goldstein, *The American Jewish Community,* Block Publishing, New York, 1960.

38. But there is a public, or rather a media, outcry when fundamentalist preachers give political sermons. Father Drinan relinquished his seat in Congress by command of Pope John Paul II in 1980.

ers in public schools[39] and the display of religious symbols in public places,[40] minority attacks on Christmas pageantry in the classroom,[41] minority complaints about Christmas stamps with religious themes [42]—all these are the outgrowths of what is essentially a mounting racial controversy.

Formerly, separation of church and state meant that churches were to stand alone without financial, legal, or any other kind of assistance from government. Now it is beginning to mean that religion must be isolated and even quarantined from public contact. This could be construed as more of a constriction than an extension of religious liberty. The free exercise of religion is hardly possible without freedom of religious expression.

The campaign against public celebrations of the nation's religion,[43] in addition to its built-in iconoclasm, cannot avoid becom-

---

39. In 1962, the Court decided that the recitation of the Lord's Prayer or Bible verses in public schools was unconstitutional, thereby, according to Senator Ervin of North Carolina, making God Himself unconstitutional. L. A. Huston, *Pathway to Judgment*, Chilton Press, Philadelphia, 1966, p. 4. The prayer on which the Court ruled said simply, "Almighty God, we acknowledge our dependence upon Thee and we beg Thy blessings upon us, our parents, our teachers and our country."

40. The Court ruled five to two in forbidding the erection of a cross in a city park in Eugene, Oregon, *New York Times*, Oct. 5, 1969, p. 68.

41. In 1969 the superintendent of the Marblehead, Massachusetts, public school system banned all mention of Christmas in 1969, but finally reversed himself after a series of demonstrations by Majority children. *Washington Evening Star*, Dec. 1, 1969, p. 4.

42. The U.S. Post Office was bitterly condemned by the American Jewish Congress for issuing a stamp which contained a reproduction of Hans Memling's great Renaissance painting, *Madonna and Child*. *New York Times*, July 17, 1966. In deference to Negro pressure, black Santa Clauses and "integrated angels" are now showing up on television.

43. Christianity is designated the national religion of the U.S. in the sense that at most only 4 percent of the population belongs to non-Christian churches and that the remaining 96 percent either by religious affiliation, church attendance, birth, baptism, tradition or inclination exhibits some degree of attachment to Christianity. It is true that a 1968 Gallup Poll reported only 50,000,000 Americans attend church regularly. Nevertheless most Americans who do not go to church still consider themselves Christians. *San Francisco Sunday Examiner & Chronicle, This World*, Dec. 29, 1968, p. 10. A 1974 Gallup poll indicated that 55 percent of Catholics, 37 percent of Protestants, and 19 percent of Jews attend church every week.

ing a campaign against the nation's culture. Quite apart from its religious significance, Christmas—decorative tree, yule log, Santa Claus, elves, reindeer, and sky-riding sleigh—is an exuberant manifestation, perhaps the most exuberant manifestation, of Majority folkways.

Already Majority members have permitted their biggest holiday to be transformed into an overcommercialized Oriental bazaar by the great department store chains, many of which are owned by non-Christians. Any further censorship or perversion of Christmas would be a further abridgement, not just of the Majority's religious freedom, but of its cultural freedom. Justice Potter Stewart, the lone dissenter in the Supreme Court's school prayer rulings, made this point clear when he said that the Court, instead of being neutral toward religion, was actually showing signs of hostility by denying students "the opportunity of sharing in the spiritual heritage of the nation." [44]

In *Notes towards the Definition of Culture,* T. S. Eliot writes, "the culture of a people [is] an incarnation of its religion," and "no culture has appeared or developed except together with a religion. . . ." [45] This is tantamount to saying that religion and culture are indivisible, that one cannot be isolated from the other without severe damage to both. In Eliot's view, it was no coincidence that mankind's greatest artistic achievements occurred when church and state were working together, not apart.

Nine of the thirteen colonies had established churches, as did England and the Scandinavian countries throughout most of their history. Church disestablishment in America came about during the War of Independence, which disrupted colonial ties to the Church of England. It was made official by the First Amendment, which was chiefly the work of Franklin, Jefferson, and Madison, many of whose religious (or irreligious) ideas had been taken from the French Enlightenment.

If the Greeks had been disestablishmentarians, there would have

44. *New York Times,* June 26, 1962, p. 16, and June 18, 1963, p. 28. In Boston the *Jewish Advocate,* in an editorial agreeing with the prayer decision, suggested it might logically be extended to bar the traditional display at Christmas of the Nativity scene and other religious symbols at any public gathering or party. *Wall Street Journal,* July 6, 1962, p. 1.

45. *Notes towards the Definition of Culture,* pp. 32, 13.

been no Parthenon, which was built with government funds, and none of the great plays of Aeschylus, Sophocles, Euripides, and Aristophanes, which were staged in a government amphitheater, subsidized in part by the state treasury and offered to the public during state-sponsored religious festivities. If church and state had been separated in the Middle Ages and Renaissance, there would have been no abbey of Cluny, no Gothic cathedrals, no Florentine Baptistery, no Sistine Chapel, no *Last Supper*. Bach, it should be added, spent much of his musical life in state-supported churches. Finally, since the most ardent advocates of church-state separation are frequently those who consider every word of the Bible divine revelation, it might be recalled that the Old Testament was the book of the ancient Hebrews, who more than any other people believed that church and state were one.

It is ironic that the Supreme Court, presently the most powerful opponent of church-state unity, sits in an imitation Greek temple, the originals of which would never have been built without the subsidies of established churches.[46] Could it be that the poverty and unoriginality of Washington's architecture—with its highest monument copied from an Egyptian obelisk and its most famous landmarks slavishly duplicating Greek, Hellenistic, and Roman building styles—have something to do with the fact that Washington is the capital of the only large nation where church and state have been separated for more than a hundred years?

The greatest attraction of religion, according to Miguel de Unamuno, is the promise of immortality.[47] Equally as attractive, if

---

46. The anachronism of imitating ancient architectural styles in an age of magnificent new construction materials was made plain to all when the Corinthian columns of the Supreme Court building were installed after the roof was in place.

47. *Del Sentimiento Trágico de la Vida*, p. 42. In addition to its purely religious impact, the concept of an afterlife obviously has enormous social utility. It is easier for individuals and races to put up with the inequalities of earthly existence if they believe, or can be persuaded to believe, they will have another—and better—chance in the Great Beyond. In this context, the promise of immortality cannot help but exercise a calming and stabilizing effect on society. On the other hand, the effect may be too calming and too stabilizing, perhaps to the point of social stagnation. In the view of Martin Heidegger, whose teachings have been twisted beyond all comprehension by the so-called existentialist school of philosophy, immortality tends to devalue life. According to Heidegger, it is

endurance and survival are signs of attractiveness, are religious ceremonies, rites, sacraments, liturgies, and feast days—the intersecting points between religion and folkways, between faith and art. The Northern gods have gone to Valhalla, but the yule log still blazes. In Russia the Eastern Orthodox Church has been stripped of its primacy and its privileges, but the spectacular Russian Easter services continue to enthrall believers and nonbelievers alike. In Mexico, priests are not supposed to wear cassocks in the streets, yet each year hundreds of thousands of Mexicans go on pilgrimages, some even bloodying their heads with crowns of thorns in gruesome reenactments of the stations of the cross.

Unamuno to the contrary, most people want to live in the present as well as in the hereafter. The immediately understandable and enjoyable emanations of religion—its dramaturgy—seem as necessary to Western man and to Western aesthetics as its theology. As if sensing this, the liberal-minority coalition now attacks the manifestations of Christianity rather than Christianity itself. Those in the vanguard of the attack, however, are already finding it simpler to remove prayers from public schools than Christmas carols.

Many devout Christians, having taken note of the intelligentsia's open season on religion and religious observance, have concluded they are living in a profane age. They are right to the extent that the times are inauspicious for organized religion. But, as pointed out earlier, the reservoir of human faith is always full.

---

the awareness of death and its finality that intensifies human existence and gives it its deepest meaning. Just as the drama without a final curtain is hardly a drama, so endless, immeasurable time is not time at all. Heidegger's philosophy increases man's individuality to where it becomes almost godlike—and almost unbearable. It goes well, however, with the new anti-Copernican view. Man, sharply reduced in size when the earth was demoted from the center of the universe to galactic speck, has now grown large again, perhaps larger than before. Just possibly, man is the only intelligent being in all space—the exalted status accorded him until the Renaissance. If there are higher life forms in the cosmos, it is almost mathematically certain that some would be far enough ahead of man in the evolutionary process to send him simple signals that could be picked up on radio telescopes and other sophisticated electronic listening devices. But, at least for the moment, outer space is very still. For the almost impossible odds against intelligent extraterrestrial life, see *Science News*, Feb. 24, 1979, and *Natural History* magazine, May 1979.

It is not the amount of faith that changes, it is the direction. Religious ages do not yield to ages of skepticism, as some historians pretend. Old established faiths simply give way to new inchoate faiths. Much of the religious feeling loose in the world is in the hearts of those who most object to being called religious.

The usual sequel to the decline of formal religion is the reappearance of the shaman or witchdoctor, whose bag of magic potions and cure-alls is as old as humanity itself. In times of established churches, the shaman must work in the shadows. But in eras of religious "freedom" he is everywhere at once, gathering followers here, collecting donations there, and spreading the tidings of his own peculiar metaphysics up and down the land. Sometimes the shaman operates on the outer fringes of a universal religion. Sometimes he leads his flock out of one universal religion into another, as did Elijah Muhammad of the Black Muslims. Frequently, he dissociates himself from all contemporary religious manifestations and goes back to the primeval bedrock of religion— to animism and anthropomorphism.

The phenomenal resurgence of astrology and soothsaying is one example of this trend.[48] But the most striking evidence of the descent of religion from the sublime to the subliminal is provided by that special and somewhat illegitimate branch of psychology known as psychoanalysis. Here in one beguiling gift-wrapped box is almost all the religious stock-in-trade of ancient man— interpretations of dreams, casting out of devils, incest myths, obsessive sexual teleologies, and confessionals. And the jack-in-the-box is none other than the grand old shaman himself, Sigmund Freud.

As a scientific method for the investigation of the inner man or as a therapeutic tool for mental illness, psychoanalysis can hardly be taken seriously by any rational person. Yet this masterwork of spiritual primitivism has been raised to such psychological, philosophical, and even religious heights that it has exercised and continues to exercise a deeply corrosive effect on Western manners and morals. In the realm of art and aesthetics, where it has probably done the most harm, psychoanalysis has taken

---

48. So phenomenal it rated a cover story in *Time*, March 21, 1969.

man, once thought to be a little lower than the angels, and deescalated him to the level of the brute.

To learn about the workings of the human brain it would have seemed wiser to investigate the neuron, a physiological fact, than the id, ego, or superego, which are hardly more than psychological or, more accurately, *psychomantic* fancies. That Freud did not take the more difficult approach is one of the secrets of his popularity. Intuition and revelation, the scientific euphemism for which is synthesis, pack in a much bigger audience than long hours of controlled laboratory experiments.[49] To establish and preserve his professional status, Freud coated his teachings with just enough psychological lore to convince the unwary, unstable, and untutored that he was not a humbug. His scientific pretensions notwithstanding, he operated more in the tradition of Joseph and Daniel, his remote forebears, than in the footsteps of those who performed the plodding, painful research responsible for the real advances in the study of human behavior.[50]

After reading Freud one has difficulty in imagining how the world managed to get along until the advent of psychoanalysis. Either the pre-Freudian victims of neurosis never knew what they were suffering from, or the affliction was no older than the diagnosis. Though only the rich can afford psychoanalysis—at rates presently ranging from $50 to $200 an hour—the man-in-the-street undergoes it daily at bargain prices through the massive Freudian backwash in the arts. The greatest writers in modern English literature—Eliot, Yeats, and D. H. Lawrence, to name three—abhorred Freud, and Lawrence even went to the trouble of writing two anti-Freudian tracts, *Fantasia of the Unconscious* and *Psychoanalysis*

---

49. The tendency of Jewish scientists to rely on mathematical instead of physical laws, on inductive leaps instead of the laborious accumulation of evidence, is so pronounced that it can almost be described as a racial trait. Einstein is the most celebrated case. Spengler wrote that Hertz, who was half-Jewish, was the only important modern scientist to attempt to eliminate the concept of force from his physics. *The Decline of the West,* Vol. 1, p. 414.

50. While Freud was postulating about neuroses and psychoses, John Houghlings Jackson (1835–1911), the noted British neurologist, spent his life studying the function and development of the nervous system. Jackson's evolutionary theory of brain development is fundamental to the study of the function or malfunction of the human intellect. But how many have heard of John Houghlings Jackson?

and the Unconscious. But second-rate writers made Freudian theories and characters a central part of their work. James Joyce and Thomas Mann were two of the better novelists who borrowed from Freud, although the latter warned that there is an aspect of psychoanalysis which "maims life at its roots." [51]

Liberalism raised the environment to godhood. Freud preached the unconscious, the id, that seething mass of sex-ridden instincts and drives, that interior devil that can only be effectively exorcised by Freudian priests. Theoretically modern liberalism and psychoanalysis should have not one square inch of common ground. The former appeals to the rational in man; the latter to the irrational. Nevertheless there are subterranean links that establish a very strange symbiosis. Himself an authoritarian, Freud never let his writings stray beyond equalitarianism into the political area of race. A liberal in politics, a minority member, and an enemy of Nazism, he probably did more than anyone to change the face of Western civilization, at least in the United States, where he was forgiven for his illiberal view of history and his sickening stress on the reptilian and mammalian aspects of human behavior, and welcomed into the club.

Freud sharpened his attack on the freedom of the will by classifying several important manifestations of individuality as repressions, which he defined as harbingers of neuroses, psychoses, or worse. One such repression was guilt, Freud's favorite bogeyman, the elimination of which he set as one of the principal goals of psychotherapy.[52] But by getting rid of guilt, one also gets rid of a bulwark of social stability—the most practical, or at least the most inexpensive, of all crime deterrents. If it had the choice, which would society prefer, murderers who feel guilty or those who don't?

Freud's advocacy of compliant adjustment to one's surroundings is not unrelated to the widespread intellectual conformity which has descended on America. His cloacal approach to the

---

51. *The Magic Mountain,* trans. H. T. Lowe-Porter, Knopf, New York, 1961, p. 222.

52. When it is a question of the guilt of Majority members toward Negroes and other minorities or of Germans toward Jews, most faithful Freudians have convenient dogmatic lapses and turn from the teachings of psychoanalysis to the Old Testament.

roots of human thought and action has opened up a whole new dimension of vulgarity and tastelessness and helped smooth the way for the present Age of Pornography. The Freudian antidote for the mental imbalance caused by technology, deracination, and the contemporary social centrifuge is to rummage around the events of one's childhood for sexual ghosts. Freud's seething concern for the bizarre, the banal, and the perverse [53] has attracted so many neurotic personalities to his camp it is often difficult to distinguish between patient and analyst.

A case in point is Dr. Douglas Kelley, one of the court-appointed psychiatrists of the Nuremberg trials, who wrote a bestseller on the neurotic tendencies of the incarcerated Nazi leaders, much of the space being devoted to an analysis of Hermann Goering. Later Kelley, like Goering, committed suicide by swallowing cyanide.[54] Another Freudian doctor, Wilhelm Reich, who died in Lewisburg Federal Penitentiary in 1957 while serving a sentence for mail fraud, founded and directed a schismatic psychoanalytic cult dedicated to the knowledge, function, and psychological ramifications of the orgasm.[55]

---

53. Only a specialist in perversity could have taken such liberties with the beautiful Greek legends of the phoenix and Prometheus. Of the former, Freud wrote, "Probably the earliest significance of the phoenix was that of the revivified penis after its state of flaccidity, rather than that of the sun setting in the evening glow and rising again." Freud dismissed Prometheus as a "penis-symbol" and gave his own version of the discovery of fire. "Now I conjecture that, in order to possess himself of fire, it was necessary for man to renounce the homosexually-tinged desire to extinguish it by a stream of urine . . . to primeval man the attempt to extinguish fire by means of his own water signified a pleasurable struggle with another phallus." It was for these reasons, according to Freud, that primitive societies put women in charge of fire because their anatomy precluded yielding to the temptation faced by males. Freud, *Collected Papers*, Hogarth Press, London, 1950, Vol. 5, pp. 288, 291–92, and *Civilization and its Discontents*, trans. Joan Riviere, Jonathan Cape and Harrison Smith, New York, 1930, p. 50, footnote 1.

54. *New York Times*, Jan. 2, 1958, and Douglas Kelley, *22 Cells in Nuremberg*, Greenberg, New York, 1947, pp. 76–77. Kelley described Goering, whose suicide was never satisfactorily explained, in unusually moderate terms. Could the author himself have slipped the Reich Marshal the pill?

55. Wilhelm Reich, *Selected Writings*, Noonday Press, New York, 1956. Reich established a thriving business selling "orgone boxes" to his band of true believers.

In its aberrant attempts to cure or control mental disorders, psychoanalysis has been able to obscure but not bury certain axiomatic truths. The mind breaks down permanently or temporarily from overwork or overleisure. Some minds are born with organic defects. Some develop them. If the mind lives alone, if the mind tries to survive on its own waste, it becomes disordered. Sanity is a function of purpose. Remove the spiritual props, the cultural reinforcements, the time-tested morale builders, the four-dimensional insurance of family, race, nation, and church, and the delicate balance of the human mentality can easily crack. Even a brain as powerful as Nietzsche's could not stand the strain of continuous isolation.

Psychoanalysis recognizes rootlessness as a cause of mental disorder, but it avoids the subject of racelessness, the extreme case of rootlessness. It stresses the importance to mental health of the feeling of belonging, but it ignores race consciousness, one of the most intensive expressions of the feeling of belonging. For such reasons psychoanalysis totally misses the point when it tries to explain the origins of the most pernicious mental affliction of all—the state of mind which leads to suicide.

Suicide is the tenth cause of death in the United States among the general population, the third cause among the 15–19 age group and the second cause among college students.[56] Some of the lowest suicide rates are found in Mississippi and South Carolina; some of the highest in the Pacific states. One study revealed that the suicide rate of American whites was more than twice as great as that of American nonwhites.[57] In 1950–77 the annual suicide rate for young white males rose from 3.5 per 100,000 to 15.3 per 100,000, an increase of 437 percent. In 1977, 1,871 Americans in the 15–19 year age bracket killed themselves.

The racial patterns that emerge from these statistics seem to be almost totally lost on psychoanalysts, who continue to explain suicide in terms of death wishes, depressive states, the frustration of high expectations (the poor don't have such expectations), and

---

56. *Time*, Nov. 25, 1966, p. 48.

57. The low nonwhite suicide rate was almost entirely due to Negroes, since the rate for American Indians was 11.5, for Japanese Americans, 6.9, and for Chinese Americans, 13.1. Louis Dublin, *Suicide*, Ronald Press, New York, 1963, pp. 33–35.

the implosion of aggressive instincts. The statistics also stand in sharp contradiction to Marxist and environmentalist theories which would predict that the rich with their greater material blessings would be less apt to commit suicide than the poor.

It is, of course, the opposite that takes place. The greatest number of suicides occur not in the world's backward areas, but in the more advanced. It is among the rich and "successful" that the highest suicide rates are usually found, not among the poor. Where there is more racism, there is likely to be less suicide. Urbanism, loss of religion, career setbacks, and intellectual exhaustion are contributing factors to suicide, but an all-important correlation remains the "racial morale" of a given population group at a given time.

Almost everyone who has studied the origins of psychoanalysis is aware that it is the product of the minority mind. Not only was Freud Jewish, but so were almost all his associates.[58] Few, however, are aware that psychoanalysis is also the product of minority animus. According to Howard Sachar, a chief motivation of the pioneer Freudians was

> the unconscious desire of Jews to unmask the respectability of the European society which closed them out. There was no more effec-

---

58. Sachar, *The Course of Modern Jewish History*, p. 400. The original Freudian circle included Kahane, Reitler, Heller, Graf, Sadger, Steiner, Sachs, and Silberer. Among Sigmund Freud's principal followers, though some strayed well beyond the doctrinal frontiers of the founder, were Adler, Rank, Abraham, Stekel, Federn, Klein, Reich, Horney, and Fromm. Ruth L. Monroe, *Schools of Psychoanalytic Thought*, Dryden Press, New York, 1955, p. 14. The three most prominent non-Jewish psychoanalysts were Ernest Jones, the glib and gifted Welshman known as "Freud's apostle to the Anglo-Saxons," who had a Jewish wife. Harry Stack Sullivan, of Irish extraction, the one top-ranking American psychoanalyst; and Carl Jung, a Swiss. Freud was so interested in preventing psychoanalysis from being known as a "Jewish science" that he tolerated Jung as head of the International Psychoanalytic Society despite the latter's basic disagreement with Freudian dogma. Jung eventually became interested in the collective rather than the individual unconscious and flirted with problems of racial memory and racial archetypes. For this and for making a few not too unfriendly remarks about National Socialist Germany, he was branded a fascist. Weyl, *The Creative Elite in America*, p. 95, and the *Saturday Review of Literature*, Sept. 6, 1947, p. 21, and June 11, 1949, p. 10. Although he never quite escaped the Freudian taint, Jung's most important work may eventually prove to have been in the fields of mythology and culture history rather than in the plumbing of the psyche.

tive way of doing this than by dredging up from the human psyche the sordid and infantile sexual aberrations. . . . Even Jews who were not psychiatrists must have taken pleasure in the feat of social equalization performed by Freud's "new thinking." The B'nai B'rith Lodge of Vienna, for example, delighted in listening to Freud air his theories. . . .[59]

Freud can also count a large number of prominent social scientists among his following. Claude Lévi-Strauss, the "structural anthropologist," has injected the Freudian schematic into modern anthropology, writing in typical psychoanalytical jargon, "In the language . . . of myth vomit is the correlative and inverse term of coitus and defecation is the correlative and inverse term to auditory communication." [60]

Herbert Marcuse, the late mentor of the New Left, constructed a synthesis of Marx and Freud, modifying and rearranging the Oedipus Complex in such a way that the father stands for capitalism and the parricidal son, the proletariat.[61] Such fanciful nonsense would make interesting footnotes in a history of scholarly tomfoolery, if it were not taken seriously by so many liberal intellectuals.

It is to Freudianism and its basically hostile practitioners that the Majority member often comes when seeking relief from real or imagined mental illness. He is at once subjected to a sordid, demeaning, demoralizing, and deracinating interrogatory that extinguishes whatever sparks of self-respect he has left.[62] The crux of his problem is not touched, and the problem itself is exacerbated. For the Majority patient, as he or, more usually, she may not discover in time, the psychoanalyst's couch is the

---

59. Sachar, op. cit., pp. 400–401.

60. Edmund Leach, *Lévi-Strauss*, Fontana/Collins, London, 1970, p. 81.

61. Alasdair MacIntyre, *Marcuse*, Fontana/Collins, London, 1970, pp. 41–54 and *New York Times Book Review*, Oct. 26, 1969, p. 66.

62. Jewish patients fare little better, even though their high racial quotient offers more resistance to deracination. As they turn from Judaism, Jews take to analysis in ever greater numbers because "such concepts as equality, brotherhood and internationalism, have been differentially attractive to Jews." It was especially "attractive to Jews of East European origin . . . steeped in Talmudic traditions, because it involved a highly abstract manipulation of abstruse concepts and a minimum of scientific experimentation." Weyl, op. cit., p. 96.

bed of Procrustes. In no area of the cultural clash has the toll of Majority psyches been so heavy.[63]

Religiosity can be a great catalyst of human energy. But a pseudo religion like Freudianism, when ministered by a minority priesthood to a Majority congregation, can only induce a lethargic hedonism that brings out the worst in everyone concerned. What genuine religion can possibly be provided by what Jung has called those "frightful gods [who] have only changed their names and now . . . rhyme with 'ism.' "[64]

Dr. Percival Bailey, director of research of the Illinois Psychiatric Institute, in perhaps the most devastating attack ever written on Freud and his works, has predicted that psychoanalysis in the long run will probably be remembered as something akin to animal magnetism.[65] As a means of avoiding the Freudian cul-de-sac

---

63. "Thus it is a quite unpardonable mistake," Carl Jung has written, "to accept the conclusions of a Jewish psychology as generally valid. Nobody would dream of taking Chinese or Indian psychology as binding upon ourselves. The cheap accusation of anti-Semitism that has been levelled at me on the ground of this criticism is about as intelligent as accusing me of an anti-Chinese prejudice. No doubt, on an earlier and deeper level of psychic development, where it is still impossible to distinguish between an Aryan, Semitic, Hamitic, or Mongolian mentality, all human races have a common collective psyche. But with the beginning of racial differentiation, essential differences are developed in the collective psyche as well. For this reason we cannot transplant the spirit of a foreign race *in globo* into our own mentality without sensible injury to the latter, a fact which does not, however, deter sundry natures of feeble instinct from affecting Indian philosophy and the like." *Collected Works,* trans. R. F. C. Hull, Pantheon Books, New York, 1953, Vol. 7, p. 149, footnote 8.

64. *Psychological Reflections,* Harper & Row, New York, 1961, p. 134.

65. Percival Bailey, "A Rigged Radio Interview—with Illustrations of Various Ego-Ideals," *Perspectives in Biology and Medicine,* The University of Chicago Press, Winter, 1961, pp. 199–265. Another prominent anti-Freudian is Dr. Thomas Szasz, who considers mental illness not so much a disease as a form of role playing where the patient deliberately acts irrationally in order to get his own way. Thomas Szasz, *The Myth of Mental Illness,* Hoeber-Harper, New York, 1961, Chapter 13. Ronald Laing, a psychiatrist very much in the news, asserts that every psychosis carries the seed of its own cure, and that some forms of madness are a vastly enriching human experience if allowed to run their course. For more on Laing's theories see *Time,* Feb. 7, 1969, p. 63. Philosopher Alfred North Whitehead found more fault with Freudians than with Freud himself. "The ideas of Freud were popularized by people who only imperfectly understood them, who were incapable of the great effort required to grasp them in

which he asserts has never kept a psychiatric patient out of an asylum,[66] as well as providing a cautionary guideline for the Majority member in search of a religion, Dr. Bailey invokes some memorable words of D. H. Lawrence:

> The soul is not to pile up defenses around herself. She is not to withdraw and seek out her heavens inwardly, in mystical ecstasies. She is not to cry to some God beyond, for salvation. She is to go down the open road, as the road opens, into the unknown, keeping company with those whose soul draws them near to her, accomplishing nothing save the journey, and the works incident to the journey, in the long life-travel into the unknown, the soul, in her subtle sympathies accomplishing herself by the way.[67]

---

their relationship to larger truths, and who therefore assigned to them a prominence out of all proportion to their true importance." *Dialogues of Alfred N. Whitehead*, Little, Brown, Boston, 1954, p. 211. Henri Ellenberger, author of *The Discovery of the Unconscious* (Basic Books, New York, 1970), has shown that many of these "ideas of Freud" were borrowed and that Freud received the credit for them because of his genius for self-popularization. Certainly the media have treated Freud most kindly. It was not until the late 1970s that the general public learned that the founder of psychoanalysis had been a cocaine addict and in 1885 had actually "published an essay on the glories of cocaine. . . ." Martin Gross, *The Psychological Society*, Random House, New York, 1978, p. 235.

66. One prominent psychologist, Franz Winkler, has vaguely implied that Freudian psychoanalysis has never effected any cures at all. "Almost invariably an increasing indifference to other people's needs, a shifting of symptoms with serious psychosomatic ailments, and a deep-seated unhappiness replaced the emotional conflicts and struggles which had been 'cured.'" *Man: The Bridge Between Two Worlds*, Harper, New York, 1960, p. 2.

67. D. H. Lawrence, *Studies in Classical American Literature*, Viking Press, New York, 1964, p. 173.

CHAPTER 20

The Atrophy of Education

EDUCATION, THE THIRD of the three principal combat zones in the cultural clash, is the process whereby man's most priceless possession, his culture, is passed on to posterity. If the process is tampered with, if the cultural testament of a people or race is altered, so to speak, while still in probate, the inheritance itself may waste away. It is the creeping atrophy of the traditional mechanics of cultural flow from one generation to another which characterizes the present state of American education.

In the terminal chapter of the *Decline and Fall of the Roman Empire,* Edward Gibbon said he had described the triumph of barbarism and religion. A future historian completing a survey of the deterioration of American education might say with equal oversimplification that he had described the triumph of John Dewey and Benjamin Spock. Dr. Spock has been singled out because his *Common Sense Book of Baby and Child Care* has sold more than 19,000,000 copies and, except for the Bible, *World Almanac,* and *The McGuffey Reader,* may be America's all-time best seller.[1] It has been estimated that one out of every four American children since World War II has been brought up according to Spockian precepts.[2] Since the home phase of education is as important as any of the later stages, Spock has probably wielded more influence than any other person, living or dead, on American education.

---

1. Alice Hackett, *70 Years of Best Sellers,* Bowker, New York, 1967, p. 12, and the *Guinness Book of World Records, 1981,* p. 212.

2. *Current Biography,* 1956, pp. 599–601. The percentage since 1956 has tapered off but is still significant.

As for the merits or demerits of such influence, one point should be made clear: Dr. Spock is not only a pediatrician, but a psychiatrist, and a Freudian psychiatrist to boot. Consequently his theories are grounded in such banal Freudiana as birth trauma, infantile sexuality, oral and anal stages, and penis envy.[3] Spock, moreover, centered the child's preschool education on the child himself instead of on parent and child as a unit—on the link rather than the chain of human continuum. Self-expression, in Spock's *Weltblick,* is more important than discipline, and affection more important than guidance. Most important, although he never mentions it as such, is what might be called the economy of parental worry. Almost nothing will go wrong, according to Spock, if things are allowed to run their course. In this respect Spock's wildlife approach to pediatrics reduces to a gigantic nostrum for the relief of parental anxiety. In appreciation for lightening their traditional burden of responsibility and pushing a great deal of it off on the child, millions of American mothers have made Spock a multimillionaire.[4]

It was obvious from the start that parents who followed Spock's teachings would pamper and spoil their children for fear of wounding their egos and implanting neuroses they might carry about with them for the rest of their lives. The fruits of such permissiveness were to be seen in the activities of the "flower children," hippie cultists, and student insurrectionaries, all of whom belonged to the first Spock-trained generation of Americans.[5] The

---

3. Spock began his career as a psychiatrist and only later became a pediatrician. Even after *Baby and Child Care* was first published in 1946, he served as associate professor of psychiatry at the University of Minnesota and then as a member of the Psychiatry Department of Western Reserve University, a post he held for almost two decades. Freud's daughter, Anna, who specializes in applying psychoanalysis to childhood disorders, has had almost as much influence on Spock as Freud himself.

4. Spock's popularity may be attributed in part to what Alexis Carrel has described as "la trahison des femmes." Carrel accused modern women of putting careers, sexual pleasures, bridge-playing, and movie-going above child-rearing. He urged women "non seulement de faire des enfants, mais de les élever." *L'homme, cet inconnu,* pp. 372, 431.

5. One wonders how much of the speech of Jerry Rubin, one of the "Chicago 7" hooligans, to a gathering of Ohio college students could be traced to Spock. Rubin's remarks included: "The first part of the Yippie program, you know, is

results are also to be found in Spock's oldest son, Michael, a problem child and three-time college dropout who spent nine years in deep analysis.[6]

Too late and too half-heartedly, Spock came to see, at least dimly, the error of his ways. Admitting he had been "over-permissive," Spock recanted to the extent of drawing in some of the latitudinous boundaries he had placed on self-expression and in later editions of his book the word discipline is seen more frequently. In 1968, after shifting his sphere of interest from pediatrics to the war in Vietnam, Spock was sentenced to jail for conspiracy to counsel draft evasion. He had finally become a martyr, albeit a short-lived one because the verdict was later reversed.[7]

When Spock began to devote most of his time to protest movements and legal maneuvers to escape imprisonment, his place was filled in part by the Israeli-born Dr. Haim Ginott, described as the "Dr. Spock of the emotions." Ginott's principal thesis is that parents should become amateur psychologists in order to "decode" their children's behavior. Misbehavior may be tolerated but not sanctioned, and a balance between strictness and indulgence is best achieved by a strategy of sympathy.[8]

The minority grip on the upbringing of Majority children has been further tightened by newspaper and magazine pundits whose readers can be counted by the millions. The columnists who hold the most authoritative sway over parental and teenage attitudes are those who deal with personal problems in the form of replies

---

kill your parents. And I mean that quite seriously, because unless you are prepared to kill your parents, you're not really prepared to change the country. . . ." *Human Events,* May 16, 1970, p. 31.

6. Michael Spock, "My Father," *Ladies Home Journal,* May, 1968, p. 72. Michael also revealed—rather surprisingly considering the emphasis his father put on parental love—that his father had never kissed him.

7. It should be pointed out that Spock is a selective pacifist. He has admitted, "If another Hitler came along, I would just as soon go to war and take the chance of being killed." But when he had the chance to do just that in World War II, he spent most of his time serving in a San Francisco Naval Medical Facility, writing his book in the evening. Jessica Mitford, *The Trial of Dr. Spock,* Knopf, New York, 1969, pp. 8, 10–12.

8. *Time,* May 30, 1969, pp. 62–63. Ginott adamantly refused to say whether he himself had any children. His book, *Between Parent and Child* (Macmillan, New York, 1965), has been translated into thirteen languages.

to letters, some of which are bona fide, some obviously planted. The two most widely read "sob sisters" are Abigail van Buren ("Dear Abby") and Ann Landers, who are Jewish identical twins.[9] The creator of "Sesame Street," the network television program that teaches integration to children at the preschool level, is Joan Ganz Cooney, also of Jewish extraction.

Once the child leaves home for school, the dogmatic lures of child psychiatrists, amateur and professional, are traded for those of formal educationists. Here, even in the first grade, children will fall under the long, quixotic shadow of the late John Dewey, the driving force of what has become known as progressive education. To Spock the child was the senior partner of the parent. To Dewey the student was the senior partner of the teacher.

The subject matter of education, in Dewey's view, was not as important as the method. Character forming and moral training yielded to problem solving and learning by doing. The use of religious and historical example to instill courage, loyalty, pride, and good citizenship was discouraged. The true goal of education was determined to be the search for a better social order. The study of the classics and of Latin and Greek was dropped and replaced by the social sciences. Classroom discipline was relaxed in favor of teacher-student dialogues. The instructor himself became more concerned with the *how* of learning than the *what.*

Predictably, progressive education soon progressed into a state of educational anarchy. It was a noble attempt, as so many of the great ideals of liberalism and democracy are noble in theory before their indiscrimate application makes them ignoble in practice. Unhappily man, who belongs to *Homo sapiens,* not to a race of gods, is neither mentally, morally, nor physically self-sufficient. The most intelligent, the most advanced, and the most responsible society in history could hardly have profited from such uncontrolled and uncoordinated experimental stabs at the learning process. Yet they were thrust upon increasing hordes of slum-dwelling, uprooted children, whose upbringing, surroundings, and educational capacity were hardly above the Neanderthal level.

---

9. Born on July 4, 1918, to Mr. and Mrs. Abraham Friedman of Sioux City, Iowa. *Current Biography,* 1957, p. 315. In her column in the *Miami Herald* (Jan. 28, 1974, p. 3D), Ann Landers subscribed to the theory of Jewish racial superiority.

In no time, all the high hopes and good intentions were reduced to shibboleths of racial and class agitators, while in large urban areas the lack of ethical indoctrination and the incessant depreciation of tested societal values turned out a whole generation of mentally anesthetized, morally disoriented nihilists.

Even Dewey began to see the light in his latter days. Like Spock, he shortened his sails by advocating the reestablishment of a measure of educational discipline.[10] But it was much too little and far too late. The blackboard jungle, student assaults on teachers, campus violence and sit-ins, the senseless destruction of laboratories and libraries—all signaled the death agonies of a once great educational system. If Dewey had lived, he would have been forced, as an Old Believer and an honest pragmatist who knew the proof of the theory was in the testing, to have abandoned almost all his educational ideas.[11] *Si monumentum requiris, circumspice.*

One extreme example of education failing completely to equip young Americans to meet the trials and tribulations of modern life was the mass murder of eight nurses in Chicago in 1966. A ninth nurse, a Filipino girl, was the only one to escape. It was no coincidence that she happened to be the one who had been least exposed to contemporary educational techniques. She hid under the bed while the others were led off one by one to be knifed to death. The other nurses did not resist because they felt they could reason with the murderer. They thought they could calm him with procedures they had learned in class. According to newspaper reports, they "all had psych and they were pretty sharp." [12]

Although American education is *in extremis*, there have been

---

10. *Ency. Brit.*, Vol. 7, p. 347.

11. It is unfortunate that the brilliant minds who so frequently attempt to propel society up new educational byways have the habit of warning their social guinea pigs of the obvious pitfalls *after* rather than *before* the event. With all due allowance for Dewey's epistemological flair and contributions to modern philosophy, there is simply no excuse for his avoidance of the racial factor in education and for stating, as he did, that any learning activity "done under external constraint or dictation . . . has no significance for the mind of him who performs it." *Intelligence in the Modern World, John Dewey's Philosophy,* Modern Library, New York, 1939, pp. 607–8. How much of the chaos of modern education flows from such a premise?

12. *San Francisco Chronicle,* July 23, 1966, p. 7.

few attempts to save it. One proposal has been to bring back the "great books" and let them stand as permanent guideposts for learning.[13] But the problems of American education are much too complex to be solved by the simple substitution of the very old for the very new. Another proposal has been put forward by the "essentialist" pedagogues who describe a common core of learning to be absorbed by everyone, regardless of ability or personal aims.[14] A few educators are turning back to Plato, who believed that education was the drawing out of innate ideas and who could not insist enough on the moral aspects of teaching.

> [I]f the question is univerally what considerable advantage the city derives from the education of the educated, the answer is easy. Education is the way to produce good men, and, once produced, such men will live nobly. . . .[15]

Aristotle, once considered the greatest of all authorities on education, has been largely abandoned by Western educationists. It is not hard to understand why. Aristotle asserted that the chief purpose of education was the molding of citizens to fit the form of government under which they lived, to develop in them a sense of affection for the state, and to encourage the growth and unfolding of human intelligence.[16] Still widely prevalent, on the other hand, are the educational theories of Locke, who stressed the teaching of tolerance and civil liberty. Even more popular are the ideas of Rousseau, who abandoned his own five offspring, but whose *Émile* had more influence on child upbringing than any other work until Dr. Spock's *magnum opus*. Although Rousseau declared that Negroes were intellectually inferior to Europeans,[17]

---

13. S. E. Frost, Jr., *Introduction to American Education*, Doubleday, Garden City, N.Y., 1962, p. 42.

14. Ibid., pp. 26–27.

15. *Laws*, trans. A. E. Taylor. I, 641c.

16. Plato was more favorable than Aristotle to the Spartan educational system, which removed all male children from home at the age of seven and put them in state institutions, where they received an eleven-year indoctrination course in such soldierly qualities as bravery and courage. Because ROTC began so early in Sparta, Spartans have been considered educationally backward, even though they were the only Greeks who provided for the education of women. For Aristotle's thoughts on education, see *Politics*, VIII, 1, and *Ency. Brit.*, Vol. 7, pp. 983–84.

17. *Émile*, Editions Garnier Frères, Paris, 1964, p. 27.

he is a favorite theorist of those who press hardest for school desegregation. Whereas Plato suggested that goodness be implanted in the student by education, Rousseau decided that goodness was already there and that the teacher's job was to coax it to the surface.

In colonial times and in the early days of independence, American education was primarily a religious undertaking. It did not become public, secular, compulsory, and "universal" until the last half of the nineteenth century. At present, religious control and sponsorship of education are limited to parochial schools, of which the Roman Catholic church has by far the largest number. Today about one-half of the 11,000,000 American Catholics of school age are in parochial schools, a ratio that is expected to fall to one-third in the next generation. Catholic education is assisted by the fact that tens of thousands of members of religious orders are willing to teach for next to nothing in salary. Needless to say, the steady increase in living costs and the steady decrease in faith seriously threaten the future of the Catholic teaching profession.

From 1965 to 1976 the number of nonpublic schools declined from 19,946 to 17,950 and nonpublic enrollment from 6.3 to 4.8 million. Most of this loss occurred in Catholic parochial schools, even though the number of minority students in these schools increased by 67,000. The number and enrollment of other private schools, especially Christian academies in the South, have shown a marked increase in this period, as white families move their children from desegregated public schools. Jewish school enrollment, on the other hand, declined to 360,000 (from 600,000 in 1963).[18]

As suggested previously, a decline in formal religion does not necessarily result in a nation of atheists. The religious instinct does not mortify. It flows into different channels in the search for different divinities. In the school system, as in so many other American institutions, Christianity is simply being phased out by the modern religious syncretism of democracy, equality, and minority racism. Anyone familiar with contemporary school and college curricula can hardly fail to detect a theological tone in much

---

18. *Standard Education Almanac (1979–80)*, p. 225, and *Christian Science Monitor*, March 17, 1978, p. 18.

of the subject matter. Whatever else they may be, political science lectures are becoming increasingly difficult to distinguish from sermons.

No attack on American education—not even the bombings or the armed incursions of black students—has been as shattering as school desegregation. The 1954 Supreme Court ruling in *Brown* v. *Board of Education of Topeka* may some day be ranked as the Fort Sumter of the Second American Civil War. Although the Constitution says nothing about education, the Court ordered the desegregation of all public schools on the ground that segregation denies equal opportunities to minorities. Even if school facilities were equal—as some were, but most were not—the very fact of separation, in the Court's view, was generating in children "a feeling of inferiority as to their status in the community that may affect their hearts and minds in ways unlikely ever to be undone." The Court built its case on the equal protection clause of the 14th Amendment.[19]

In reaching its decision the Court took judicial notice of sociological evidence that had not been heard in the lower courts and that was introduced during the hearings by a legal technicality known as the "Brandeis brief." Normally, appeals courts do not permit the injection of new facts or new evidence. But Brandeis, when a Supreme Court Justice, broke this longtime precedent by encouraging the admission of briefs containing materials which he considered unquestionable and not openly prejudiced against either side of the dispute. As it turned out, the "Brandeis brief" heard by the Supreme Court in *Brown* was simply the repetition and elaboration of the liberal-minority thesis of racial equalitarianism. The genetic side of the argument and the effect of integration on the education of white children were totally ignored.[20] The defense was permitted no rebuttal.[21]

---

19. Frost, op. cit., pp. 305–6.

20. In its opinion the Supreme Court mentioned the Swedish sociologist, Gunnar Myrdal, by name. Myrdal's tract, *An American Dilemma,* bears somewhat the same relationship to the contemporary black revolution in America as Diderot's *Encyclopédie* bore to the French Revolution. The author's significant misconception of current social trends in the U.S. is the subject of footnote 13, p. 220.

21. An attempt to overturn *Brown* by introducing such evidence in another desegregation case, *Stell* v. *Savannah Board of Education,* failed when the Supreme

Because desegregation led to social mixing of whites and Negroes, resistance to the Supreme Court's ruling flared up immediately in the South.[22] It took longer to develop in the North, where *de facto* segregation in the ghetto areas gave authorities the chance to look the other way. In both the North and South, however, integration meant abandoning the concept of the neighborhood school, since it could only be accomplished by the educational gerrymandering of entire school districts and by forced busing.[23] Once such steps were undertaken or considered seriously by local school boards, the North often became more uncooperative and hostile than the South.

School desegregation, slowed by massive white noncompliance, has provoked a white exodus to the suburbs. In the birthplace of integration, Washington, D.C., the public school system is now almost entirely black. Although it might be expected that the government sponsors of desegregation would at least make a pretense of doing what they are trying to force others to do, there are only a very few authenticated cases of highly placed white members of the executive, legislative, or judicial branches sending their own children to desegregated public schools.

Preliminary to the Supreme Court's ruling in the *Bakke* case, it was shown that less qualified black and Hispanic applicants to the Medical School of the University of California at Davis had been accepted and much more highly qualified white applicants had been rejected. The learned justices admitted this was wrong but did agree that race should be taken into consideration by the admissions boards of institutions of higher education. As a result, these boards pursue the same racial admissions policy as before, although they are now careful not to rely on fixed quotas,

---

Court refused to act on an appeal from the Fifth Circuit Court of Appeals. For a detailed description of the *Stell* trial, as well as an analysis of certain factual errors in the testimony presented in *Brown*, see Putnam, *Race and Reality*, Chapter IV.

22. The *Brown* ruling "crowned a generation's work by the American Jewish Congress in domestic affairs, consummating the alliance between the two minorities but incurring deep resentment among white conservatives." Litvinoff, *A Peculiar People*, p. 51.

23. The Nixon, Ford, and Carter administrations continued to implement forced busing, although one Gallup poll showed that Americans opposed it by an eight-to-one margin. *New York Times*, April 5, 1970.

preferring to call them goals. Flying directly in the face of the Constitution, the Supreme Court had made race a factor in college admissions.

In the once all-white schools where about half of the nation's Negro pupils are now enrolled, the results have been far from gratifying.[24] Students of each race have tended to adopt the worst customs, habits, morals, and speech of the other. Bright pupils, black and white, have either left or attempted to leave, and in many schools all social activities have had to be abandoned.[25] Classroom violence and vandalism have reduced the quality of education as much as they have raised its costs (about $181 billion in 1980–81).[26]

The steady decline of national averages of the Scholastic Aptitude Tests taken by millions of college applicants is a dramatic example of what has happened. In 1962 the national average for the SAT verbal was 478; in 1979–80, 424. The national average for the SAT math test dipped from 502 to 466 in the same period. Anyone with the faintest understanding of racial differences in intelligence could have predicted these results, but the experts came up with every reason except the true one. The decrease in these examination scores over half a century were almost exactly proportional to the decrease in the percentage of Majority members taking the test.[27]

The mixing of white children with blacks two to three years

---

24. Twenty-five years after *Brown*, 60 percent of black students attended schools that were at least half black. Rather than send their children to desegregated city schools, millions upon millions of white Americans lost hundreds of millions of dollars moving to the suburbs. When middle-class blacks followed them, many white families moved again. To the dismay of its avid supporters, *Brown* has turned out to be the most effective social tool ever devised for the residential separation of races.

25. *Los Angeles Herald-Examiner*, Oct. 10, 1980, p. 19.

26. A Senate study of 757 public school districts indicated that in three years school vandalism cost American taxpayers $500 million; that there were 70,000 assaults on administrators and teachers, and several hundred thousand on students; that over a hundred students had been murdered. *Christian Science Monitor*, April 10, 1975, p. 5.

27. A more devastating comment on the present state of American education was furnished by the National Center for Health Statistics which stated in a 1974 report that a million Americans in the twelve- to seventeen-year-old age bracket were illiterate.

behind them in educational level and fifteen to twenty points lower in I.Q. scores has not only substantially slowed the progress of students as a whole, but increased the number of dropouts by pressuring Negro students to perform beyond their ability. The celebrated Jensen study, which claims that heredity accounts for about 80 percent of individual I.Q. variations, concluded that Negro pupils, while as adept as whites in rote learning, are much less adept in cognitive learning.[28] Although these findings clearly call for different curricula for black students, the drive for nation-wide educational conformity goes forward unabated.

To help them "catch up," Negro students are frequently promoted on the basis of age, not achievement, with the result that some students with a third-grade reading level are found in the ninth and tenth grades.[29] As for higher learning, only about one-half of black high-school graduates are fully capable of handling

---

28. Dr. Arthur R. Jensen is director of the Insitute of Human Learning at the University of California and vice-president of the American Educational Research Association. The *Harvard Educational Review* (Winter, 1969) was largely devoted to Jensen's statistics-studded examination of the inability of education to correct genetic differences in Negro and white intelligence. After publication, Jensen received an unprecedented amount of hate mail, including a few death threats. In Berkeley, the Students for a Democratic Society engaged a sound truck to demand Jensen's dismissal, later invading his classroom and forcing him to hold his classes in secret. He finally had to call on the police to protect his files and had to keep the lights on in his office all night to discourage looters. A number of his liberal colleagues brought him before a specially organized investigatory board with all the trappings of a medieval witch trial—the first time in American academic history that a professor has had to defend a scholarly paper before an inquisitional proceeding that included videotape cameras. *New York Times Magazine*, Aug. 31, 1969, p. 11. In 1970 a group of Harvard students called on the *Harvard Educational Review* to turn over to the Black Panther legal fund all revenues from the sale or distribution of the Jensen article. They further demanded that all copies and reprints in circulation be destroyed and no further reproduction and distribution be permitted. In addition to the heresy of racism, the fundamental charge against Jensen was that I.Q. tests were culturally biased against nonwhites, although Orientals sometimes obtained higher scores than "whites" (a category that often included Hispanics) and American Indians did better than blacks. Jensen demolished these allegations in his book, *Bias in Mental Testing*, The Free Press, New York, 1980. In the meantime a federal court judge in San Francisco ruled that I.Q. tests *were* biased, and another federal judge in Chicago ruled they *were not*.

29. *San Francisco Sunday Examiner*, May 20, 1967, p. 2.

a college curriculum.[30] Once they get to college, Negroes may be given two grades higher than whites for the same work.[31] One professor has been known to pass everyone in his class because he will not fail a Negro student.[32] This same two-tier grading system is applied by other teachers to forestall accusations of racial prejudice.[33] The envy, frustration, distrust, and cynicism aroused by such practices, including widespread cheating, are more noticeable in those universities and colleges which, in their race to enroll Negroes, have dropped their traditional entrance requirements.[34] Minorities are now insisting this practice become universal and actually closed down City College of New York to enforce their demands. Mayor John Lindsay and his Board of Education surrendered, and an open enrollment policy for City College was begun in 1970. Any New Yorker who finished high school, no matter what his grades, was qualified to enter. In 1978, after City College had become an academic monstrosity, the door was partially closed on open enrollment. High-school graduates with mathematics and reading skills below the eighth-grade level were excluded! [35]

Admission to college without proper academic credits is a new idea in American education. If pursued, it could lead to certain complications, particularly in the area of scientific studies. If students can enter college with insufficient preparation, will they then be given degrees even though failing most of their courses? And if given such degrees, can they then use them to obtain employment designing skyscrapers, bridges, and aircraft? [36] The answers have a direct bearing on national security, since Soviet

---

30. According to Fred Crossland, a Ford Foundation education expert. Other estimates are much lower.

31. One such case, in New York University, was reported by James Burnham in his *Suicide of the West,* John Day, New York, 1964, p. 197.

32. *New York Times Magazine,* July 28, 1969, p. 49.

33. Ibid.

34. In 1964 there were 234,000 Negroes in college; in 1980, 1,100,000.

35. *Time,* May 16, 1969, p. 59, and *New York Times,* Feb. 8, 1970, p. 25. In 1971 half of the City College students were on drugs. *New York Daily News,* Feb. 24, 1971, p. 4. Also see *Chicago Tribune,* April 29, 1979, Sect. D.

36. One way to reverse this trend might be to force the professors and college administrators who hand out such degrees to live in the buildings, drive across the bridges, and fly in the airplanes designed and built by these ersatz engineers.

engineers are still awarded degrees on the basis of their grades, not their race.

The Negro invasion of American education has brought with it Black Studies programs, which teach minority racism in classrooms where Majority racism is forbidden. But the injection of minority racism into college and high-school curricula is not exclusively the work of Negro groups. Jewish and Hispanic organizations are also on the lookout for "racial slights" in courses and textbooks which do not elaborate fully on minority contributions to American history or on the persecution of minorities abroad.[37] At their insistence, which often borders on outright coercion, many such textbooks have been rewritten, and more have been replaced.[38] Concurrently, public educational facilities have been put at the disposal of minority groups for research projects highly critical of Majority institutions.[39]

Although minorities generally supported the British or were neutral in the War of Independence,[40] a reading of recently published school and college texts would indicate that without minority assistance Americans might now be swearing allegiance to Queen Elizabeth II. Crispus Attucks has become such an important figure in American history that an illustrated child's history of colonial times gives him more space than George Washington.[41] Haym Salomon, a Polish-born commission merchant, is another recently discovered minority "hero" of American independence and has been awarded an article under his own name in the *Encyclo-*

---

37. In October 1960, the New York City Board of Education sent a letter to 100 textbook publishers asking for "substantial revisions" in history books to place a much sharper emphasis on German atrocities against minorities in World War II. *Overview*, October, 1961, p. 53. In many colleges "Holocaust Studies" are becoming a supplement to Black Studies.

38. In California, minority lobbies forced a resolution through the Oakland Board of Education to purchase textbooks which "accurately portray the contribution of minority groups in America." *San Francisco Chronicle*, Jan. 23, 1963, p. 30.

39. The B'nai B'rith Anti-Defamation League gave $500,000 to the University of California, a state university, to investigate the role Christian churches play in fostering anti-Semitism. *Look*, June 4, 1963, p. 78.

40. William H. Nelson, *The American Tory*, Beacon Press, Boston, 1968. p. 89.

41. Review of *An Album of Colonial America* in the *New York Times Book Review*, July 6, 1969, p. 16.

paedia Britannica, although he was more than once welcomed be-hind the British lines.[42] On the other hand, those Negroes in the War of Independence who supplied British warships off the Southern coast and who remained on board as volunteers are seldom featured in the "new history." [43]

Whatever may be said about American education, its present state is a far cry from the 1660s when the entire student body and faculty of Harvard conversed freely in Latin.[44] It is an even further cry from the onetime disciplined earnestness of Western education as summed up by the Latin hexameter with which Winchester School in the Middle Ages greeted its new pupils, *Aut disce aut discede; manet sors tertia caedi.*[45] There was an air of Melville's *Benito Cereno*[46] about the armed band of black militants who occupied Cornell University's student union center for thirty-four hours and then marched out, guns at the ready, to receive a general amnesty from administration and faculty.[47] There was an air of surrealism about Princeton making Brent Henry a trustee after the twenty-one-year-old Negro senior distinguished himself in the seizure of a campus building.[48]

If the purpose of education is the transmission of culture, as the greatest modern poet has opined,[49] then the duty of educators

---

42. *Ency. Brit.,* Vol. 19, p. 890.

43. Nelson, op. cit., p. 111.

44. *Ency. Brit.,* Vol. 5, p. 876.

45. "Learn or depart; a third alternative is to be flogged."

46. The character of Benito Cereno, a Spanish sea captain made prisoner on his own ship by blacks, is most nearly duplicated in the modern educational scene by Kingman Brewster, former president of Yale University. Brewster banned George Wallace from the Yale campus in 1963, yet opened it wide to a 1970 May Day meeting of Black Panthers. *New York Times,* April 30, 1970, p. 38. Brewster, who claimed that blacks could not get a fair trial in the United States, took a large part in the nationwide mourning for the "Kent State 4," who were presented by the press as typical American students, although three of them were Jewish and the girl kneeling beside the dead student in the widely distributed photograph was a fifteen-year-old runaway from Florida, who was later arrested for prostitution. But Brewster and his New Left constituency made no outcry when a student was murdered and other students wounded in the left-wing bombing of a University of Wisconsin physics and mathematics center. *Time,* Sept. 7, 1970, p. 9.

47. *Time,* May 2, 1969, pp. 37–38.

48. *New York Times,* June 8, 1969, p. 1.

49. Eliot, *Notes towards the Definition of Culture,* p. 98.

is the safeguarding of culture. Here the failure of American education is most glaring. One of the many instances of this failure is the career of Dr. Hsue Shen-tsien. With the help of scholarships paid for in part by the American government, Dr. Hsue received his master's degree from the Massachusetts Institute of Technology and his Ph.D. from the California Institute of Technology. He then returned to his homeland where he was put in charge of the design and production of rocket systems for Red China's new H-bombs.[50]

The concept of American education as a denationalized data bank whose deposits belong to everyone and should be passed on by everyone to everyone is not very realistic—especially in a world where most nations have a totally different idea of the learning process. The Communist countries hold to the old-fashioned view that the job of education is to strengthen the state and that all instruction, a Marxist synonym for indoctrination, should ultimately be directed toward that end. This attitude is essentially Aristotelian (*Politics,* 1337), in spite of what the heirs of Lenin may say, and is shared by those members of American minorities whose cry for special educational opportunities is really a demand for power, not learning for learning's sake.

The Soviet Union coddles its minorities or non-Russian nationality groups by giving them their own schools and universities where they may pursue the study of their history and literature in their native languages.[51] No matter what his origin, however, every student must take the same required basic courses in Marxism-Leninism, in line with the dictum of the Eighth Party Congress (1919) that Russian schools be transformed into a "weapon of the Communist rebirth of society."[52] Aside from this political

---

50. *Life,* May 28, 1965, pp. 92, 94.

51. Nicholas Hans, *Comparative Education,* Routledge, London, 1949, pp. 28–31, 58.

52. *Encyclopedia of Russia and the Soviet Union,* p. 150. It is noteworthy that the Russians developed a special educational system for their *bezprizorny,* the great numbers of homeless children who lived by their wits and by crime during the tumult and chaos of the Revolution. For equally large numbers of homeless ghetto children, who are displaying similar criminal symptoms, American educators, rather than put them in remedial schools, are trying to solve the problem by placing them in the same classroom with normal children.

indoctrination, applied sciences and vocational training are given preference over academic subjects in the Soviet educational system. One consequence has been that the U.S.S.R. claims to have many more scientists and engineers than the United States.[53] The teachings of Freud, which have assumed such importance in the American educational process, are hardly known in Russia.

There are some who ascribe the crisis in American education to the generation gap, a social phenomenon which has always existed to some extent in fragmenting societies. But in contemporary America the gap is more publicized than real. Those who do fit the description of belonging to an alienated younger generation have not so much turned, *as been turned,* against their parents— often by minority intellectuals old enough to be their grandfathers. It was the septuagenarian German refugee philosopher, Herbert Marcuse, who gave most of the ideological impetus to that segment of the teaching profession which seeks not only to set Majority students against their families, but against their history, their institutions, their race, and even against themselves. Having decided that revolution is no longer possible according to the old Marxist formula of class war, Marcuse proposed building a new revolutionary base on an alliance of students and blacks.[54] He further proposed withdrawing the Constitutional right of free speech from those advocating war, racism, exploitation, and brutality.[55] Marcuse died in 1979. Another equally venerable, equally professional, and equally Jewish leader of "revolutionary youth" is George Wald of Harvard, born in 1906.

In spite of intensive brainwashing by their Marcusian-minded social science departments, 22 percent of American college students were not afraid to identify themselves in 1970 as "right

---

53. In 1975 there were 9,477,000 Soviet scientists and engineers, as compared to a 1976 count of 1,647,000 American scientists and engineers. *United Nations Statistical Yearbook (1978),* United Nations, New York, pp. 933–37. These ostensibly hyperbolic numbers were partially tempered by statistics indicating that in 1977 there were between 1,147,800 and 1,299,100 Soviet scientists and engineers in research and development, as compared to 571,000 in the same category in the United States. *National Science Foundation Abstracts,* 1979, p. 143, and *Science Indicators 1978,* National Science Foundation, Washington, D.C., 1979.

54. MacIntyre, *Marcuse,* p. 88.

55. UPI report, May 18, 1964.

of center." [56] It was obviously not this group that provoked the campus violence that descended on the country. Nor was it always the radical students. Students did not seize a New York University computer and threaten to destroy it unless $100,000 was given to the Black Panthers. It was, according to the New York District Attorney, the act of two minority professors, Robert Wolfe and Nicholas Unger.[57] A student shotgun did not shoot down a judge in San Rafael, California, in an abortive courtroom kidnapping. It had been bought two days previously by black philosophy instructor, Angela Davis, whom Marcuse had described as his "best" pupil.[58] It was not the student body as a whole which turned the University of California at Berkeley, once the pride of American public education, into an intellectual skid row. It was a mindless clique of nonstudents, minority students, dropouts, radicalized faculty members, and spineless administrators.

It is not difficult to find a better explanation than the generation gap for the change that has come over American education. In the year preceding the student deaths at Kent State, minority enrollment in Midwest colleges jumped 25 percent.[59] The faculty at Harvard, one of the greatest centers of unrest and agitation, is now "dominated by Jews" and 15 to 25 percent of the faculty of other leading universities are Jewish.[60] Jews now comprise 25 percent of the undergraduates at Harvard, 18 percent at Yale, 15 percent at Princeton, and 40 percent at Columbia.[61]

By way of summarizing the present state of American learning, one point should be stressed. Like established institutions every-

---

56. Gallup Poll, *Baltimore Evening Sun*, May 26, 1975. Predictably, the longer students stayed in college the more they moved to the left. Only 40 percent of freshmen identified themselves as "left of center" or "far left." Fifty-three percent of the seniors so identified themselves.

57. *New York Times*, July 30, 1970, p. 54.

58. *Life*, Sept. 11, 1970, pp. 26–27.

59. *New York Times*, May 20, 1970, p. 1.

60. Yaffe, op. cit., p. 51. The percentages are probably higher in the social science departments, in which Jewish educators congregate. It is this high concentration of Jews in the more sensitive areas of the educational process that lends support to van den Haag's comment, "The literate American mind has come in some measure to think Jewish, to respond Jewishly. It has been taught to, and it was ready to." *The Jewish Mystique*, p. 98.

61. Yaffe, op. cit., p. 52.

where, the American system of education was the outgrowth of a specific concrescence of people, environment, and history. To suppose this system would function efficiently, or at all, under different conditions and for different ethnic groups is asking man to construct timeless macrocosms out of ephemeral microcosms. A multiracial state, especially one which both permits and advocates cultural pluralism, would seem to require a multiracial educational program, not only because population groups differ in learning capacities but because they differ in learning goals. To force-feed minority and Majority students alike on a thin, curricular soup of one part liberal dogma, one part Majority belittlement, and one part minority mythology is to provide little educational nourishment for anyone.

Some Negro separatists, to the confusion and dismay of black and white desegregationists, call for more, not less, educational segregation so they can more fully develop their racial and cultural identity. Acceding to this proposal could lead to the establishment of separate schools and colleges for all Unassimilable Minorities, who by definition can never be assimilated by education or by any other means. This would formalize the apartness of all such minorities and at the same time penetrate the assimilationist disguise of some. In any event, such a measure could not help but give Majority education a new lift by removing it from the control of its detractors and despoilers.

All in all, the great failure of a heterogeneous school system remains its inability to stress effectively the morale-building aspects of education. There is no higher incentive for learning than the self-esteem that flows spontaneously from the awareness of a great past—an awareness that does not come from guidelines published by the Department of Education or from sterilized textbooks designed to please everyone and educate no one.

The kind of learning that prepares a people to prevail and endure must be primed by centuries of common history and millennia of common ancestry. Desegregation kills it by destroying its binding force—the homogeneity of teacher and pupil. The disappearance of this vital bond from the American classroom may prove to be the greatest educational tragedy of all.

PART VI

The Political Clash

CHAPTER 21

The Adaptability of Dogma

IF THE CULTURAL PHASE of the Majority's dispossession may be described as the assault on the Majority soul, the political phase is the assault on the Majority mind. Political power may emanate from the barrel of a gun, as Chairman Mao once proposed.[1] But a gun is quite ineffective without the will to shoot, an ingredient supplied by that form of intellectual programming known as dogma.

The mind feeds voraciously on dogma because human beings seem to need some system of thought, some frame of reference, from which to view the world. Only a very few lonely souls have the stamina, courage, and wisdom to develop their own beliefs from independent observation. And there are fewer every day. The farther the frontiers of knowledge are pushed outward, the more elusive this knowledge becomes and the farther it moves beyond the individual's grasp. Desperate for truth, ravaged by doubt, even the best minds home in on dogma, the great enemy of doubt, which is always willing, but seldom qualified, to fill the intellectual void. Pontius Pilate received no immediate response when he posed his celebrated question.[2] When Christianity was properly organized, the Church answered him—with dogma.

Of the major components of dogma—truth, falsehood, opinion, and authority—the greatest is authority. One of the oldest human habits, a habit roundly encouraged by the brain's immeasurable

---

1. See Chapter 34 for other Nietzschean utterances by the founding father of Chinese communism.
2. John 18:38.

inertia, is to surrender one's mind to a particular dogma, simply because of the dogma's ancient pedigree. It was the authority of age which made it possible for readily detectable falsehoods in the Old Testament and Aristotelian natural philosophy to be held as truths for more than fifteen hundred years.

Those few who accept dogma halfheartedly instead of wholeheartedly do pick and choose to some extent. But the dogma they finally light upon is usually selected not for its relevancy or correspondence to the facts, but because it coincides with their own particular set of prejudices, animosities, and fears. Modern intellectuals continued to subscribe to Communist dogma long after they had recognized its contradictions, its persiflage, and its errors. Indeed they seemed to venerate it most at the very moment (the climax of the great Stalinist purges of the 1930s) they were being most deceived. They wanted to believe, so they did believe. *Credo quia absurdum.*[3]

Unfortunately for the human race, the intellectual has a near monopoly in the formulation and propagation of dogma because of his verbal training and linguistic agility. The facile tongue (or pen) and dogma seem mutually generative. It was this close, almost predestined connection between dogma and intellectuals that led Brunetière, the French literary critic, to define an intellectual as one who meddles dogmatically in matters about which he is ignorant.[4]

One would logically suppose that the more education one has the less would be one's susceptibility to dogma. It is quite the opposite. Education, apart from the physical sciences, and even these are not always exempt, has always been the most notorious example of organized indoctrination. Indeed, the well-educated person or, more precisely, the "most educated" person is often the most dogmatic. The teacher who spends his life teaching

---

3. In more ways than one Tertullian strikes a modern note. A Carthaginian lawyer and the most dogmatic of the early church fathers, he advised Christians to refuse military service under the Roman emperors and not to obey laws they deemed unjust. Will Durant, *Caesar and Christ,* p. 647. For Tertullian's exact words, see Toynbee, *Study of History,* Vol. V, p. 56.

4. *Times Literary Supplement,* June 22, 1962, p. 462. The difference between an intellectual and an intelligent man might be described as the difference between one who uses his mind and one who uses his mind wisely.

dogma has become, so to speak, dogmatically blind. He or she is quick to attack opposing dogma, but slow to condemn or even to recognize his own.

Only unsophisticated minds, whose number is legion, and great minds, *rarissimae aves,* seem to have developed some immunity to the dogma at the bottom of prevailing Western political and social ideology. The former are equipped by neither upbringing, training, nor inclination to comprehend such dogma, while the latter are reluctant to swallow it because they comprehend it all too well.

Consequently it should not come as a shock to say that the intellectual or "educated" man can be more harmful to society than the uneducated or unsophisticated man. The literate person has the ability to spread his ignorance abroad, to sell his dogma wholesale. The unlettered person can only pass on his beliefs to those in his immediate vicinity.

At times political dogma becomes so firmly rooted in the social order that merely to question it is to put oneself beyond the pale. Often the entire intellectual establishment of a culture will draw in its head, turtle-fashion, at the slightest attempt to throw an objective light on the darker recesses of the dogma it has come to live by. The merest trace of criticism will be judged as a cynical, antisocial mixture of iconoclasm and desanctification. If the critic works in secret, he eventually begins to feel like a criminal. If he comes out in the open, he is regarded as one. In the words of Charles Peirce, "let it be known that you seriously hold a tabooed belief, and you may be perfectly sure of being treated with a cruelty less brutal but more refined than hunting you like a wolf." [5]

Political dogma, as all dogma, ultimately rests on opinion and feeling rather than on fact. It can only be tested objectively by the almost impossible method of placing similar population groups in similar environments over a period of generations while subjecting each to a different political system. Even then the results of these lengthy and complicated tests would have to be measured according to such dubious criteria as economic prog-

---

5. *The Fixation of Belief, Collected Papers,* Harvard University Press, Cambridge, 1934, pp. 245–46.

ress, cultural achievement, governmental stability, and public security—all of which easily lend themselves to varying interpretations.

Not surprisingly, in view of man's incurable "dogmatitis," scientific dogma often receives the same uncritical acclaim and acceptance as political dogma, as amply demonstrated by the life and
works of Albert Einstein. The German-Jewish physicist is universally credited with being the father of relativity, although in 1904,
the year before Einstein published his paper on the Special Theory
of Relativity, Henri Poincaré, the French physicist, gave a lecture
in St. Louis on "The Principle of Relativity." [6] Moreover, the
various parts of the Special Theory that have checked out rather
well are largely based on the mathematical equations of George
FitzGerald, an Irish theoretical physicist, and Hendrik Lorentz,
a Dutch theoretical physicist (the FitzGerald-Lorentz contraction
and the Lorentz transformations).

In 1916, when Einstein introduced his General Theory of Relativity, he was still practically unknown in the world of physics.
In fact, whenever relativity was mentioned, it was likely to be
associated with the name of Lorentz.[7] Then, in 1919, came the
famous British scientific expedition to study the total eclipse of
the sun. The bending of light as it passed through the sun's gravitational field roughly approximated Einstein's predicted measure-
ments. Almost overnight the media, with the help of the well-
known British scientist, Sir Arthur Eddington, made Einstein an
international celebrity. In 1921 he made a triumphant tour of
the United States, not, however, to preach his new physics, but
to raise money for Zionism.

In the Weimar Republic the enthusiasm was more muted. Some
leading German physicists convoked an anti-relativity congress
at which Einstein was accused of leading Western science away
from the path of experiment into the wild blue yonder of mysticism, abstraction, and speculation. One hundred scientists and
intellectuals contributed to a book that denounced Einstein for
developing a physics that was no longer in touch with physical
reality.[8] When Hitler came along and the attack was expanded

---

6. *The Einstein Myth and the Ives Papers*, eds. Richard Hazelett and Dean Turner,
Devin-Adair, Old Greenwich, Conn., 1979, p. 154.

7. Ibid., p. 266.

8. *Hundert Autoren Gegen Einstein*, R. Voigtländer Verlag, Leipzig, 1931.

into a loud broadside against "Jewish physics," Einstein left for America.

Germans were not the only critics of relativity. Some prominent British and American physicists disagreed with some or all of Einstein's ideas and were not afraid to say so. Among them were luminaries like Dayton C. Miller, president of the American Physics Society, Herbert Dingle, president of Britain's Royal Astronomical Society, Herbert Ives, the brilliant American optical physicist who helped develop television, and, after World War II, Louis Essen, the British expert on atomic clocks. But as Einstein's fame grew these voices were more or less shut off. The names of FitzGerald, Lorentz, Poincaré, and other pioneers were largely forgotten as the media awarded Einstein an exclusive patent on relativity.

Special Relativity posits that nothing can move faster than the velocity of light and that mass increases with velocity and becomes infinite at 186,282 miles/sec. Just as there was a sound barrier there is now a light barrier. Who knows how long Einstein's light barrier will hold? At this writing four extragalactic radio sources have been observed to be expanding at velocities from two to twenty times that of light.[9] Relativity enthusiasts have written off these observations as illusions, the same word geocentrists applied to Galileo's discovery of the moons of Jupiter.

In contrast to the Special Theory, the General Theory of Relativity has been confirmed only rarely and tenuously. Every time there is a solar eclipse or some mysterious object is discovered in deep space, the media have the tendency to announce that Einstein has once again been proved right. If the General Theory is so solid, why must it be proved and reproved so often? The fact is there are several other plausible theories dealing with gravity. One of them, the Brans-Dicke Theory, has occasionally proved out as well as the General Theory when put to the test.[10] Despite the increasing mortality rate of the most firmly established physical laws,[11] however, General Relativity remains almost unassailable.

---

9 *Scientific American.* Aug. 1980, p. 82B.

10. *Scientific American,* Nov. 1974, pp. 25–33.

11. In 1962 a theory more firmly ensconced in the scientific decalogue than relativity was jettisoned when Professor Bartlett of the University of British Columbia made some xenon-platinum hexafluoride. Until then there had been an "immutable" law in chemistry that platinum and xenon, a noble metal and

One good reason is that, if a scientist should speak out too loudly against Einstein, he might jeopardize his career.

Einstein's political meanderings—his support of the Communist-leftist coalition in the Spanish Civil War, his utopian socialism, his association with at least eleven Communist-led organizations in the United States, the lending of his name to countless Stalinist manifestos,[12] his role as "salesman" for the atomic bomb,[13] his friendship for Communist East Germany after World War II—all this has earned him bad marks with such an eminent Westerner as Ortega y Gasset:

> Albert Einstein has assumed the right to offer an opinion on the Spanish Civil War and to take a one-sided stand on it. Albert Einstein displays a profound ignorance about what has happened in Spain today, centuries ago, and always. The spirit that inspired this insolent intervention is the same that has brought universal discredit to other intellectuals, as they set the world adrift by depriving it of *pouvoir spirituel.*[14]

H. L. Mencken was even harsher:

> [N]o Jewish scientist has ever equalled Newton, Darwin, Pasteur, or Mendel . . . such apparent exceptions as Ehrlich, Freud, and Einstein are only apparent. . . . Freud was nine-tenths quack, and there is sound reason for believing that Einstein will not hold up; in the long run his curved space may be classed with the psychosomatic bumps of Gall and Spurzheim.[15]

However history treats Einstein, however his achievements withstand the test of time, it is indisputable that he has received much more acclaim than he deserves. What "put him across" was his ability to adapt so well to the prevailing liberal-minority dogma, the humanitarianism run amuck, the rootless internationalism,

---

a noble gas, were totally resistant to chemical combination. *San Francisco Chronicle, This World,* Dec. 9, 1962, p. 25.

12. For Einstein's long-lasting flirtation with Stalinism, see *Fifth Report of the Senate Fact-Finding Committee on Un-American Activities,* California Legislature, 1949.

13. See pp. 540–41.

14. *La rebelión de las masas,* p. 189. The paragraph was translated by the author of this study.

15. *Minority Report, H. L. Mencken's Notebooks,* Knopf, New York, 1956, pp. 273–74.

the anti-Nazism, the Zionism, the tolerance of and occasional downright affection for Marx and Freud. All these ingredients were combined into a recipe that was irresistible to the media. Einstein was bathed in an ocean of favorable publicity far greater than that accorded any of his contemporaries, with the possible exception of Roosevelt and Churchill. An ingenious physical scientist who dabbled incessantly and confusingly into political science was transformed into the greatest brain of the twentieth century, if not of all centuries.

As Einstein himself would have admitted, there is one notable difference between scientific and political dogma. Although it may take centuries, the former can be put to the test under controlled laboratory conditions.[16] When validated, it becomes a law, an exalted status seldom achieved by a political dogma. When it is overturned, a wave of astonishment ripples through the scientific community, and that is that. But when a political dogma goes under—it may be whittled away by reason, but it can only be supplanted by another dogma—its demise is frequently accompanied by social chaos, revolution, and the destruction of thousands or even millions of lives.

The most powerful dogmas are those which have a timeless,

---

16. Macaulay was one of the few politicians who favored applying the scientific method to politics: "How, then, are we to arrive at just conclusions on a subject so important to the happiness of mankind? Surely by that method which, in every experimental science to which it has been applied, has signally increased the power and knowledge of our species—by that method for which our new philosophers would substitute quibbles scarcely worthy of the barbarous respondents and opponents of the Middle Ages—by the method of Induction—by observing the present state of the world—by assiduously studying the history of past ages—by sifting the evidence of facts—by carefully combining and contrasting those which are authentic—by generalizing with judgment and diffidence—by perpetually bringing the theory which we have constructed to the test of new facts—by correcting, or altogether abandoning it, according as those new facts prove to be partially or fundamentally unsound. Proceeding thus— patiently, diligently, candidly—we may hope to form a system as far inferior in pretension to that which we have been examining, and as far superior to it in real utility, as the prescriptions of a great physician, varying with every stage of every malady and with the constitution of every patient, to the pill of the advertising quack which is to cure all human beings, in all climates, of all diseases." *The Miscellaneous Works of Lord Macaulay*, "Mill on Government," Universal Library Association, Philadelphia, Vol. 1, p. 399.

universal appeal to the hearts and minds of all men. Yet it is the very universality of the great dogmas which makes them so fickle and unpredictable, which allows them to play so fast and loose with the hopes and aspirations of their expounders. Dogmatic pronouncements concerning mankind's inalienable rights have a totally different political and social effect in monoracial than in multiracial societies. The same religious dogma which helped destroy the Roman Empire helped preserve the Holy Roman Empire. The same political dogma which inspired one people to put American society together now inspires other peoples to tear it apart.

It seems reasonable to suppose that the great dogmas have not survived for centuries and even millennia on content alone. Their vitality must also have depended heavily on their adaptability, on their capacity to alleviate so many conflicting human sorrows, to satisfy so many conflicting human goals. The gift of adapting dogma to national growth and progress is surely one of the greatest a people can possess. A greater gift, however, is the ability to reject dogma when it can no longer be put to any constructive use.

From the standpoint of the American Majority, the political dogma which served it so well during most of American history has now become one of the chief agents of its decline. From the standpoint of the minorities, this same dogma has become a powerful tool for their advancement, since almost every political act, past and present, is now measured against the yardstick of minority interests and assigned to some way station on the March of Democracy. This leads to the deceptive and distorted view that the contemporary political struggle is between liberalism and conservatism, exploited and exploiters, tolerance and intolerance, equality and inequality, freedom and oppression. Since the real nature of what is happening and the real intentions of the dogmatizers are thereby concealed, intelligent Majority members must come to understand that they are living in an age and in a world where the interpretation of dogma has become as powerful a force as dogma itself.

CHAPTER 22

The Three Phases of Democracy

Sociologist William Graham Sumner once said of democracy, "It is impossible to discuss or criticize it. . . . No one treats it with complete candor and sincerity." [1] In the years since Sumner wrote these lines the climate for objectivity has not noticeably improved. Yet without some clearer understanding of democracy than exists in the popular mind there can be little comprehension of present-day American politics.

Most contemporary political scientists like to place democracy on top of the ladder of political evolution. But traces of democracy have been found in the tribal organizations of the most backward and most ancient peoples. In the opinion of Robert Marrett, Oxford don and noted anthropologist, "Where society is most primitive it is most democratic. . . ." [2]

Historically, democracy did not appear as a recognized form of government until the flowering of the Greek city states, when it acquired enough status to be included among the five political taxons of Plato. In order of precedence these were: (1) Aristocracy (rule of the best); (2) Timocracy (rule of the honorable); (3) Oligarchy (rule of the few); (4) Democracy (rule of the people); (5) Tyranny (rule of the despot or upstart).[3] Plato's classifications were five steps of a descending staircase down which most Greek city states were doomed to travel. The stairs could be climbed again, either partly or all the way, but inevitably there would be another descent, even after the creation of the perfect state, that

---

1. *Folkways*, p. 77.   2. *Ency. Brit.*, Vol. 19, p. 105.
3. *Republic*, trans. Paul Shorey, VIII, 544–45.

supreme feat of Platonic utopianism, where "either philosophers become kings . . . or those whom we now call our kings and rulers take to the pursuit of philosophy. . . ." [4]

Aristotle found a similar degenerative process at work in politics. He divided government into three good and three bad forms. The good forms were monarchy, aristocracy, and constitutional government which, he explained, were "perverted" into tyranny, oligarchy, and democracy, respectively.[5] In Aristotle's view there were five different varieties of democracy, but he had trouble delineating them. He did, however, make a sharp distinction between democracies where the law was above the people and democracies where the people were above the law.[6]

Aristotle's politics were shaped in part by his faith in the middle class, to which he happened to belong. His preferred state was a middle-class republic not too dissimilar to the limited representative government of the United States in the early years of its independence.[7] But Aristotle was also a political relativist, allowing that the best government might be the one best suited to the people, time, and circumstance. He was not a fanatic believer in the inherent superiority of any one political system.[8]

The aristocrat Plato was more hostile than Aristotle to democracy, whose end stages he described in terms which have a curiously modern ring:

> [T]hose who obey the rules . . . it reviles as willing slaves and men of nought, but it commends and honors in public and private rulers who resemble subjects and subjects who are like rulers. . . . [T]he father habitually tries to resemble the child and is afraid of his sons, and the son likens himself to the father and feels no awe or fear of his parents. . . . And the resident alien feels himself equal to the citizen and the citizen to him, and the foreigner likewise. . . . The teacher in such case fears and fawns upon the pupils, and the pupils pay no heed to the teacher or to their overseers either. And in general the young ape their elders and vie with them in speech and action, while the old, accommodating themselves to the young, are full of pleasantry and graciousness, imitating the young for fear they may be thought disagreeable and authoritative. . . . And I almost forgot to mention the spirit of

---

4. Ibid., V, 473d.   5. *Politics,* trans. Jowett, III, 7.   6. Ibid., IV, 4.
7. Ibid., IV, 11.   8. Ibid.

freedom and equal rights in the relations of men to women and
women to men. . . .[9]

It was shown in the earlier discussion of the aristocratic origins
of great art that Greek democracy had very little in common with
the kind of democracy affected by present-day democratic regimes.
In their democratic phases, almost all Greek city states clung tenaciously to the institution of slavery and refused voting rights to
women, foreigners, and metics—even disenfranchising many of
the native born by means of racial and property qualifications.
On the other hand, some cities like Athens carried democracy
to extremes by the practice of sortition, in which office holders
were selected not by vote but by lot. Sortition, a kind of democratic
bingo, is only conceivable where a small, homogeneous, highly
intelligent citizenry possesses a high degree of political sophistica-
tion.

The Roman Republic had its democratic moments. Greek experiments in democracy were well known to Roman politicians,
and with the passage of time the plebs wrung concession after
concession from the ruling families, perhaps the greatest being
the control of the tribunate. But the Senate, the most enduring
and most prestigious Roman political institution, was congenitally
authoritarian and the repository of privilege. When the dim lamp
of democracy was finally turned off by the Gracchites and dictators
who buried the Republic,[10] it did not burn again until the seventeenth century.

During this long hiatus, however, there were some feeble democratic stirrings. In A.D. 930, Iceland's *Althing* had its first session.
As this parliamentary body still sits today, Icelanders can claim

---

9. *Republic,* trans. Shorey, VIII, 562–64. One of Plato's most telling complaints against democracy was its failure to encourage the emergence of virtuous
statesmen: "[Except] in the case of transcendent natural gifts no one could
ever become a good man unless from childhood his play and all his pursuits
were concerned with things fair and good—how superbly [democracy] tramples
underfoot all such ideals, caring nothing from what practices and way of life a
man turns to politics, but honoring him if only he says that he loves the people!"
Ibid., 558b.

10. Roman imperial rule was perhaps best summed up by Tiberius, who wrote,
"it was the part of a good shepherd to shear his flock, not skin it." Suetonius
Tiberius, trans. J. C. Rolfe, Loeb Classical Library, XXXII.

to be the founders of history's most enduring representative government.[11] Other libertarian manifestations can be detected in the early days of the English Parliament, in the Swiss cantons, and in the medieval communes, "the chief parent of modern democracy." [12]

It is generally conceded that modern democracy was born during the popular reaction against the Stuart dynasty in England. Its midwife was John Locke, whose treatises on civil government contained many seminal democratic ideas. In phraseology that was later reworked and partly plagiarized by Jefferson in the Declaration of Independence, Locke asserted that men, all of whom had certain natural rights, were "free, equal and independent" and that "no one ought to harm another in his life, health, liberty or possessions." [13]

But then Locke took a dogmatic tack that alienated him forever from the oracles of modern democratic thought. The basic purpose of government, he declared, was the preservation of property.[14] He added that, if monarchs could not protect the material possessions of their subjects, people had the right to look elsewhere for protection, even if need be to themselves.[15]

In Locke's opinion the preservation of property was tantamount to the preservation of human liberty. To safeguard this liberty he called for the division of government into legislative and executive branches. Later the French philosopher Montesquieu went beyond Locke in the separation of powers by adding a third branch of government, the judiciary.[16] Jean Jacques Rousseau rounded out the basic structure of pre-Marxist democratic theory by making man inherently good, that is, capable and worthy of controlling his own destiny without outside interference or regimentation.[17]

---

11. *Ency. Brit.*, Vol. 12, p. 45.

12. Durant, *The Age of Faith*, p. 641.

13. Locke, *Of Civil Government*, First Treatise, preface, p. 3. Also *Ency. Brit.*, Vol. 16, p. 172D and Vol. 7, p. 217. It might be noted that in the constitution he was asked to draw up for Carolina, Locke included such strange democratic bedfellows as hereditary serfdom and primogeniture. Beard, *Rise of American Civilization*, Vol. 1, p. 66.

14. Locke, op. cit., Second Treatise, No. 94.

15. Ibid., Nos. 228–29.

16. *L'esprit des lois*, XI, vi.

17. At least this is the impression gathered from reading the first pages of Rousseau's *Du contrat social.* In the latter part the citizen is threatened with death

It was less of a mental strain for Rousseau, born in the relatively pure moral atmosphere of Geneva, to entertain such optimistic views than for philosophers brought up in the fleshpots of Paris or London.

English democracy, though it made important strides after the Stuarts had been sent packing a second and final time, did not lose its aristocratic flavor until the Reform Act of 1832. But across the Atlantic in some of the British colonies, more safely removed from the conservative restraint of king and lord, democracy had a freer hand. In New England, after the relaxation of Puritan theocracy, the right to intervene in government affairs, public accountability of magistrates, trial by jury of ordinary citizens, statutory guarantees of personal liberty, and taxation initiated by taxpayers—reforms that made English democrats green with envy—came to be considered the birthright of every citizen.[18]

The democratic exuberance of the New England town meeting, however, did not spill over into the nation as a whole when the colonies obtained their independence.[19] Some of the intellectuals among the Founding Fathers, notably in the South, subscribed to many of the ideas and platitudes that were giving birth to the French Revolution. But this doctrinaire brand of political and social leveling was in sharp contrast to the evolutionary and pragmatic democracy of most independence-minded American colonists. While it is true that Jefferson's clarion appeals to human liberty helped build up the colonists' inclination for war, they were mere rhetorical shadows compared to the substantial democratic achievements of Majority pioneers and settlers who had never heard of natural laws, social contracts, or "unalienable

---

if he does not believe in the articles of the religion of the state in which he happens to reside. Rousseau, parenthetically, considered a mixture of aristocracy and democracy the best form of government. He felt direct democracy was impossible and that people living in arctic or tropical zones might require absolute rule. Durant, *Rousseau and Revolution*, pp. 173–74.

18. De Tocqueville, *De la démocratie en Amérique*, Tome 1, p. 38, and Tome 2, p. 298.

19. When the United States became a sovereign nation in 1776, the American population numbered less than four million, of which only 6 percent voted. *Time*, March 22, 1963, p. 96. Since citizen participation in government was much higher in New England than elsewhere, it must have been extremely low in most other colonies.

Rights" and to whom "the pursuit of happiness" would have seemed blasphemous and downright hedonistic.

Perhaps more than any other American, Jefferson must assume the responsibility for loading American democracy with the ambiguity and cant that have pursued it down to the present day. When one of the largest slave owners in Virginia solemnly writes, "all men are created equal," either his semantics or his integrity must be called into account. What Jefferson and most of the other signers of the Declaration of Independence meant by equality was that English colonists had the same natural right to self-government as the English in the mother country.[20] But that is not what they wrote. And it is what they wrote that, carried forward to another century and used in another context, has proved to be such an effective time bomb in the hands of those who advocate projects and policies totally antithetical to Jeffersonian democracy.

To obtain a clearer picture of Jefferson's interpretation of equality, one need only read the Declaration of Independence all the way through. In the beginning the tone is equalitarian. But further on, Jefferson writes of "the merciless Indian Savages, whose known Rule of Warfare, is an undistinguished Destruction of all Ages, Sexes and Conditions." [21] Other signs of a basically anti-equalitarian disposition are provided by Jefferson's belief in "natural aristocracy" and by his insistence on the innate supremacy of the American yeoman or small farmer. In spite of his strong sympathies for the French Revolution, he wrote to Lafayette, "The yeomanry of the United States are not the *canaille* of Paris." [22]

Jefferson gave American democracy a chance of survival only so long as the country remained basically agricultural. He was convinced that members of the working class, merchants, and

20. Richard Hofstadter, *The American Political Tradition*, p. 12. Stephen Douglas said (1858): "the signers of the Declaration had no reference to the Negro whatever . . . [they were referring to] white men, men of European birth and European descent . . . that such was their understanding, is to be found in the fact . . . everyone of the thirteen colonies was a slaveholding colony, every signer of the Declaration represented a slaveholding constituency . . . if they intended to declare that the Negro was the equal of the white man . . . they were bound, as honest men, that day and hour to have put their Negroes on an equality with themselves. . . ."

21. For Jefferson's remarks on Negroes, see pp. 216–17.

22. Hofstadter, op. cit., p. 22.

speculators were corrupt; that cities were "pestilential" and city mobs "the panders of vice and the instruments by which the liberties of a country are generally overturned." [23] Paradoxically this same Jefferson is now, with Lincoln, the idol of the very sort of people he held in abomination. The paradox has been compounded by the Democratic party which, despite its power base in the big cities, has nominated itself Jefferson's political heir.

Jefferson was in France during the framing of the Constitution [24]—one good reason the word democracy appears nowhere in that document. The Founding Fathers, most of whom were of a conservative bent, determined to call the United States a republic, which in those days meant almost any government that was not a monarchy.[25] The few delegates to the Constitutional Convention who did profess democratic sentiments certainly held views closer to Greek and Roman concepts of democracy than to the leveling notions of utopian Parisian regicides. John Adams probably represented the feelings of most of his colleagues when he expostulated, "Remember, democracy never lasts long. It soon wastes, exhausts, and murders itself. There never was a democracy yet that did not commit suicide." [26]

Such prophetic gloom was in no small measure responsible for the fear of democracy inherent in many of the laws and procedures which shaped the political stance and behavior of the nation during its childhood and adolescence. Senators were chosen by the legislatures of the various states, not by direct popular vote.[27]

---

23. Ibid., pp. 31–32.

24. "The men who put 'We, the People' into the Constitution, with a few exceptions perhaps, feared the rule of the people and would have been horrified if they could have foreseen all that was to happen under their Constitution in the next 150 years." Beard, *The Republic*, p. 4. The Constitution, it might be added, was even created in an undemocratic atmosphere, since all sessions of the Convention were secret.

25. Needless to say, democratic shades of meaning have now been introduced into the word. *Webster's Third New International Dictionary* offers as an alternate definition of republic, "a community of beings . . . characterized by a general equality among members."

26. Hofstadter, op. cit., p. 13. Hamilton, who called the people a "great beast," was even more pessimistic about democracy than Adams. Beard, *The Republic*, p. 11.

27. Constitution, Art. I, Sec. 3, Par. 1.

There were property, occasionally even religious, qualifications for voting in almost all the states. A Negro, for statistical purposes, was counted as three-fifths of a white man, and slavery was acknowledged and protected by the federal government and most states.[28] There was much interest in guarding the rights of citizens, as demonstrated by the Bill of Rights, but much less interest, as evidenced by the emergence of machine politics, in encouraging citizens to participate independently in the governmental process.

Nevertheless, the democratic seed had been planted. The subsequent campaign to broaden and widen the voting base, to make everyone a citizen and every citizen a voter, is one of the most discernible threads in American history. It started rather slowly. The last of the states did not remove the last of their property requirements for voting until 1856.[29] The slaves were freed in 1863, but the Negro's right to vote was not specifically spelled out until 1870.[30] Senators were not elected directly until the 17th Amendment (1913), and women not given the ballot until the 19th Amendment (1919). The electoral process for selecting presidents is still retained, but is now almost wholly dependent on the popular vote. The poll tax was not prohibited until the 24th Amendment (1962). The "one man, one vote" Supreme Court decisions in 1962, 1964, and 1968 made it mandatory that districts electing representatives to legally constituted city, county, and town governments be substantially equal in population.[31] If the constituencies of representatives to the same legislative body differed too greatly in population, they were to be brought into line by reapportionment. Only members of the United States Senate, some of whom now represent states with ten to twenty times the population of other states, are exempt from this rule.[32]

That universal suffrage and equal representation now exist in

---

28. Art. I, Sec. 2, Par. 3; Art. IV, Sec. 2, Par. 3. Slavery was forbidden in the Northwest Territory in 1787. The last Northern state to abolish it was New Jersey, which began to phase it out in 1804.

29. *Ency. Brit.*, Vol. 7, p. 218.

30. The 15th Amendment (1870) forbade denying the right to vote to any citizen on account of "race, color or previous condition of servitude."

31. *Time*, July 6, 1969, pp. 62–63.

32. The exemption is provided by the 17th Amendment and Art. 1, Sec. 3, Par. 1 of the Constitution.

theory in the United States does not mean that everyone votes.[33] In the 1976 presidential election, for example, only 56.5 percent of the voting population went to the polls.[34] In off-year congressional elections voter participation is sometimes as low as 10 to 15 percent.[35]

One explanation for this poor showing is that candidates for public office seldom address the issues of most concern to voters. If people cannot register their feelings on the national and local problems of most interest to them, why should they bother to vote? Also to blame are the lackluster candidates who, despite belonging to different parties, often seem to speak the same political language, a bland soporific rhetoric whose sole effect is to multiply voter apathy. Add to this the hopelessness of defeating political machines whose concept of universal suffrage extends to the registration of voters who are repeaters, deceased, or fictional,[36] and the result is a general cynicism and a growing disbelief in the political system. Those who have lost their trust in democratic government can hardly be expected to participate in great numbers in the voting process, which is the fundamental mechanism of democratic government.

Belgium, Australia, and a few other nations lure voters to the polls by fining absentees. Without going to such extremes, American politicians might accomplish the same purpose by presenting their constituents with clear-cut issues they can either support or oppose. The candidates' long established habit of dividing on secondary rather than primary issues is one of the great failures of American democracy.

In the 1940 presidential election, when the overriding question was intervention or nonintervention in World War II, both major party candidates promised to keep the United States out of war,

---

33. There are still restrictions on residence, voting age, and literacy tests, where such tests do not imply racial discrimination.

34. *1980 World Almanac*, p. 280.

35. Ferdinand Lundberg, *The Treason of the People*, pp. 9–10.

36. In the 1960 presidential election 150,000 "ghost" votes were turned in by 5,199 Cook County (Chicago) precincts. In the same election Texas judges threw out an estimated 100,000 ballots on technicalities. A shift of 23,117 votes in Texas and 4,430 votes in Illinois would have given Nixon the presidency. *Reader's Digest*, July, 1969, pp. 37–43.

although both were interventionists at heart. In fact, while campaigning for his third term, President Roosevelt was already implementing a policy of military aid to Britain that made American involvement all but inevitable.[37]

The situation was similar in regard to Affirmative Action more than a quarter of a century later. All Republican and Democratic presidential candidates supported it or treated it with silence, though polls showed a majority of the voters were opposed. In the 1970s at least 75 percent of Americans were against forced busing, but it was expanded rather than curtailed. Both major parties supported huge amounts of military and financial aid to Israel before, during, and after the 1973 Arab oil embargo, which sent the price of gasoline skyrocketing. Here again voters had no effective means of approving or disapproving policies of crucial importance.

In 1964, in the very same election in which President Johnson, an ardent backer of civil rights, carried California by 1,200,000 votes, the people of California voted two to one to repeal an open-housing statute in a statewide referendum, which was then promptly ruled unconstitutional by the state's Supreme Court.[38] Proposition 13, which provided for the reduction of property taxes, was another California referendum that won the overwhelming support of the voters, though it was fought tooth and nail by the state government, the media, and the money magnates. So far, despite some agitation to do so, the courts have not overturned it. Meanwhile constitutional amendments to make forced busing illegal and to forbid racial quotas cannot get out of congressional committees, although both the Senate and House approved by the necessary two-thirds vote liberal amendments for equal rights for women (ERA) and statehood for the District of Columbia and sent them out to the state legislatures, where they have met with much less enthusiasm.

---

37. Beard, *President Roosevelt and the Coming of the War, 1941*, pp. 5, 413.

38. *Time*, Nov. 13, 1964, pp. 39, 43. That the courts can overturn a referendum—the purest expression of democracy—raises questions about how democratic the American democratic process really is. Since open housing was almost universally supported by the news media, the referendum also served to demonstrate that editorial opinion is usually much closer to minority than Majority opinion.

One of the greatest of all voter shutouts developed during the Vietnam War. In the 1968 presidential campaign, both major party candidates proposed a strategy of slow disengagement. Those Americans who wanted to win the war or who wanted immediate withdrawal simply had no vote, or no vote that counted. The only candidate who promised a harder line on both the war and the race issue was George Wallace, whose American Independent party received 9,897,141 votes or 13.53 percent of the total cast, the largest percentage obtained by any third party since Senator La Follette ran on the Progressive ticket in 1924.[39]

Wallace performed this minor miracle although the entire American political establishment and communications network were solidly arrayed against him. Even in the South not one important newspaper came to his support.[40] If Wallace had had the political machine of a major party, if even 10 percent of the press had backed him, if Republicans had not tried to steal his thunder as the campaign progressed, he might have won almost as many votes as Nixon or Humphrey.[41]

All of which goes to show that democracy, as it now operates in the United States, cannot genuinely reflect the wishes of the public. The voter is simply not given a real chance to make his opinion known. Even on the rare occasions he does have such a chance, his duly elected representatives will hedge on their most solemn campaign commitments once they feel the hot breath of the news media and the liberal-minority lobbies.

A principal cause of this powerful and pervasive antidemocratic element in modern American democracy is that elections come every two, four, or six years, while the press and pressure groups grind out their propaganda every day. It is extremely difficult for any political figure to stand up for long against the combined

---

39. *San Francisco Chronicle*, Dec. 12, 1968, p. 11.

40. *Time*, Oct. 18, 1968, p. 70.

41. Wallace performed more spectacularly in the 1972 Democratic primaries, even carrying the state of Michigan. But the Alabama governor was immobilized physically by a bullet in the spine and politically by the McGovern steamroller at the Miami Democratic convention. Again the wishes of the ordinary voter counted for little. In the 1980 election liberal Republican John Anderson, running as an independent with all the power of the media behind him, won less than 7 percent of the vote.

onslaught of the press, hundreds of radio and television stations, and scores of policy-making periodicals. To all but the hardiest politician, the partial betrayal of his constituency or even the loss of an election are preferable to the social Siberia reserved for the maverick who insists on putting the interests of society as a whole above special interests. The fate of James Forrestal and Senator Joseph McCarthy should be an unforgettable object lesson on the danger of promoting policies with a broad appeal to the people, but with a narrow appeal to the people who count.[42]

Allowing the voter a limited choice or no choice at all has had the effect of moving government toward a "corporate democracy"—Mussolini would have called it a corporate state—in which professions, religions, regional economies, classes, business and labor groups, and races supplant the individual as the basic voting unit. Every politician is extremely sensitive to the labor vote, religious vote, farm vote, and minority vote. His political reflexes, however, respond more slowly to the wishes of the individual voter who does not enjoy the bloc voter's ready access to the media. It is this corporate system of representation—the organized vote or, more accurately, the fear of the organized vote—which inspires most of the policies and decisions of present-day elected officials.

The economic blocs which spring up under the protective roof of representative government are storm signals of the second stage of the democratic cycle, the progression from political to economic democracy.[43] Leading contributors to the development of political

42. An extraordinary series of personal attacks by newspaper columnists and radio commentators helped drive the nation's first secretary of defense to suicide in 1949. One commentator, Ira Hirschman, went so far as to accuse Forrestal of preventing the bombing of an I.G. Farben chemical plant in Germany in World War II because he owned stock in the company. Another, Walter Winchell, accused Forrestal of running away while his wife was being robbed. Forrestal had incurred the wrath of the press because he was opposed to American support of the Zionist occupation of Palestine and the stirring up of the Arab world against the United States. Arnold Rogow, *Victim of Duty,* Rupert Hart-Davis, London, 1966, especially p. 24. The news media's vendetta against McCarthy, together with his almost unprecedented censure by the Senate, seemed to break him down physically as well as mentally, and certainly had much to do with his untimely death in 1957. *Time,* May 30, 1949, pp. 13–14, and *U.S. News & World Report,* June 7, 1957, p. 143.

43. The purely economic aspects of the three types of democracy will be taken up in Part VII.

democracy—Locke, the eighteenth-century British Parliamentarians, a few philosophers of the Enlightenment, and the authors of the American Constitution—generally held economic democracy in contempt and dismissed it as the fantasy of disorderly and dangerous minds. But there are many who claim—and if the equalitarian premises of democracy are granted their logic can hardly be refuted—that without an "equitable" distribution of wealth there can be no democracy at all. The one great stumbling block to this line of reasoning is usually passed over in silence. To prevent the accumulation of vast amounts of property in individual hands and to effectively flatten out the highs and lows of the national income curve requires a centralized control which is only a step removed from absolutism.

Economic democracy has haunted the halls of government almost as long as political democracy. The Levellers, founders of the first political party in modern history, were ardent supporters of Cromwell in the initial stages of the English Civil War, although their economic demands, which included the abolition of trading monopolies, finally caused Cromwell to turn against them.[44] Thereafter, both in England and on the Continent, there were few evidences of economic democracy until the French Revolution. What helped to keep it in check was the absence of any developed body of doctrine, any corpus like Locke's, to give it direction and coherence.

If Locke was the apostle of political democracy, Marx was the prophet of economic democracy. Borrowing many of his ideas and methods from the hardline, "share-the-wealth" faction of French Jacobinism, Marx drew up an impassioned, encyclopedic agenda of utopian eschatology, obsessive materialism, and crude economic leveling which clashed so violently with classical democratic theory that the latter has never fully recovered. "Passionately concerned with the achievement of economic democracy as he conceived it, [Marx] had no real interest in or comprehension of the problems of democratic politics." [45] The lack of this comprehension among his followers was made plain in the Bolshevik Revolution.

---

44. *Ency. Brit.*, Vol. 13, p. 964.
45. Frederick M. Watkins in the article, "Democracy," *Ency. Brit.*, Vol. 7, p. 222.

Economic democracy first became a permanent fixture in the American political scene with the advent of populism. Bryan may not have prevented mankind from being crucified on a cross of gold, but he and the Populist party which supported him firmly implanted an enduring awareness of economics in the American political consciousness. The trust-busting Theodore Roosevelt, Senator La Follette and his Progressive party, Woodrow Wilson and his graduated income tax and, most important, the rise of Big Labor—all these set an economic tone to democracy culminating in the New Deal, which in its early years was concerned almost exclusively with democratic solutions to economic problems. Welfare in the form of security for the aged, the minimum wage, medical and unemployment insurance, and all the other dollar-and-cents legislation of recent administrations were further examples of democracy's continuing accent on economic issues.

The third phase of democracy is the social phase. Like political and economic democracy, social democracy is not new. But it seems to come last in the cycle of democratic growth (or decay). Because it capitalizes on the deeper, instinctive undercurrents of human behavior, its historical manifestations are not always easy to recognize and do not often penetrate conventional history books. Its theoretical genesis, however, is not difficult to trace, being a composite of the religious concept of the brotherhood of man, Lockean and Jeffersonian assertions about human rights, Marxist class agitation, and the pronouncements of modern anthropologists and sociologists concerning human sameness.

Once the political and economic forms of democracy take hold in a society, the pressure for social democracy is certain to mount. This is especially true in a multiracial state. Inevitably the unwashed, the disadvantaged, and the envious will begin to ask, or will be asked to ask by ambitious politicians, "Why, if man is politically equal and getting to be economically equal, should he not be socially equal?" In the context of contemporary democratic politics, such a question has but one answer.

Social democracy is the thorniest stage of democracy, especially in a multiracial state, because it greatly expands the area of contact, the social interface, of the various demographic elements. Political democracy ordains that members of different population groups vote together, legislate together, and rule together. Economic democracy ordains that they work together. Social democracy exponentially enlarges the area of contact by forcing the most diverse elements of the population to live together. At present this social mixing is mostly restricted to neighborhoods, schools, playgrounds, and clubs.[46] But there are forces at work—last night's television program, yesterday's newspaper editorial, the latest federal regulation—to inject social democracy into the last redoubt of individualism and privacy, the home.

The internal contradictions of the three phases of both ancient and modern democracy become apparent when it is remembered that political democracy begins as a means of protecting property, whereas economic democracy seeks to distribute it, and social democracy encourages its theft. In the ironic chain of events that governs the democratic cycle, the same rights which were secured and recognized, often with great difficulty, in the political phase of democracy are frequently revoked in the economic and social phases. It is hard to believe that the right to privacy, the right to choose friends, neighbors and schoolmates, the right to join fraternal or social organizations, the right to air one's opinions in public and *the right of access to one's own culture* are not as fundamental to human liberty as any other. Yet these are precisely the rights held in lowest esteem by the most ardent advocates of social democracy.

Hindsight and a certain amount of historical streamlining make it possible to view the three phases of democracy as three stages of the Majority's dispossession. Political democracy divided the Majority into parties representing various geographical, regional, and sectional interests. Economic democracy with its accompanying inflation, welfare subsidies, and high taxation depleted the Majority's wealth. Since economic leveling, at least in its early

---

46. Jews, who proportionately have a far greater number of clubs and organizations than any other population group, have waged a ceaseless campaign under the leadership of the American Jewish Committee to force non-Jewish clubs to accept them as members on the ground that exclusion discriminates against them financially as well as socially. Many prominent politicians and other public figures have been persuaded to resign from such clubs in order to escape charges of anti-Semitism. More recently, nominees for high government posts have resigned from "all-white" clubs to prove to Senate committees they are not prejudiced against blacks.

stages, raises class consciousness, the Majority was further weakened by the sharpening of its internal class divisions.

Deprived of its political and economic power, the Majority was next subjected to an attack of a kind that most pleased its opponents. It was attacked as a race. The strategy, sometimes conscious, sometimes unconscious, always subconscious, was to raise minority racism to the boiling point while submitting Majority race consciousness to the numbing ideology of liberalism. The secondary plan was to develop a refined technique for quashing any Majority attempt at resistance. This was accomplished in two ways: (1) controlling the votes by managed news, educational indoctrination, and the nomination of carefully screened candidates; (2) going around the vote, when necessary, by Supreme Court rulings and secret foreign policy commitments. Whenever social democracy went too far, too fast, and a spark of resistance flared, it could be taken care of by character assassination, shouting down Majority activists and breaking up their meetings and demonstrations, occupying plants, government offices, and centers of learning or, if worse came to worst, resorting to entrapment. starting a riot, or releasing a new docudrama on network television.

Though the march of social democracy seemed unstoppable, there was always the nagging fear that some day the Majority might come alive and form a Majority political party. In this case the laboriously assembled liberal-minority infrastructure would collapse like a house of cards. To prevent this, the prophets of social democracy have formulated doctrinal antidotes to any possible manifestation of what they nervously refer to as the "tyranny of the majority," a phrase dredged up from John Stuart Mill. One proposal is to make minority votes count more than Majority votes by the simple expedient of permitting ethnic and economic groups to have their own representatives, in addition to representatives chosen in the traditional manner. This would permit delegates of minorities, urban conglomerations, and welfare groups to wield as much power as delegates of the people at large.[47]

---

47. *New York Times Magazine*, Aug. 3, 1969. That this proposal appeared in the form of a long article in America's most prestigious newspaper meant that it was to be taken seriously. The author was Herbert J. Gans, a prominent sociologist. In the course of his argument Gans suggested that the approval of 25 percent of a legislative body would be sufficient for the introduction of

American democracy, even in its social or "depraved" [48] phase, could hardly survive such minority gerrymandering. All things considered, the only hope of a democratic revival lies in the creation of a united Majority voting bloc. But before this is done, it must be clearly understood, as it was once so clearly understood, that democracy makes the highest demands of its participants and offers a measure of freedom only to those who can handle freedom. It is the rule of a people, not several peoples. The loftiest and most quixotic of all political ideas, it may be the natural political expression of a racial trait. If this be so, modern political scientists have been the biggest prospectors of fool's gold in the history of human thought.

---

minority-sponsored legislation while 76 percent would be necessary to prevent its passing. If the Majority took advantage of this situation to slip through legislation favorable to the Majority, the Supreme Court, leaning on a new "racial and economic Bill of Rights," would throw it out.

48. De Tocqueville used the word advisedly when he predicted that the political future of Americans "lay between two inevitable evils; that the question had ceased to be whether [it] would have an aristocracy or a democracy, and now lay between a democracy without poetry or elevation indeed, but with order and morality, and an undisciplined and depraved democracy." Letter to M. Stoffels, Alexis de Tocqueville, *Democracy in America*, trans. Phillips Bradley, Knopf, New York, 1963, Vol. I, pp. xx, xxi.

CHAPTER 23

The Metamorphosis of Liberalism

WHEN DISCUSSING democracy and liberalism in the same breath, it is hard to make a distinction between the two. One way to resolve the difficulty is to treat democracy as a political system rather than a political theology, as the expression of a dogma rather than the dogma itself. Then liberalism can be considered the democratic credo—the ideology that provides democracy's intellectual justification as well as its emotional drive.

Webster's Third New International Dictionary offers as one definition of liberalism, "a political philosophy based on belief in progress, the essential goodness of man, and the autonomy of the individual and standing for tolerance and freedom for the individual from arbitrary authority in all spheres of life. . . ." With less elaboration and bombast, and in better English, a popular dictionary describes the liberal as being "free from prejudice or bigotry." [1] If a historical reference will help nail down the elusiveness of liberalism, the first liberal, according to Walter Bagehot, was Jeroboam.[2]

In a more irreverent vein a modern liberal might be defined as one who, while professing a horror of totalitarianism, favors

---

1. *The American Everyday Dictionary*, Random House, New York, 1955.

2. Walter Bagehot, *Physics and Politics*, Knopf, New York, 1948, p. 31. Jeroboam was presumably classified as a liberal because he appointed "the lowest of the people priests of the high places" and asked King Rehoboam to "make the yoke which thy father did put upon us lighter." In reply, Rehoboam promised to chastise Jeroboam, not with whips but with scorpions. Jeroboam thereupon permanently split the Jewish state by setting up the northern kingdom of Israel, where he worshipped two golden calves. I Kings 12:4–19; 13:33.

one brand of totalitarianism over another;[3] who, professing a horror of racism, actively promotes minority racism; who, professing a horror of big business, is an enthusiastic supporter of big labor. The intolerant champion of tolerance, the modern liberal is the bigoted enemy of bigotry. It is true he is willing to forge ahead, recklessly ahead, in the search for new ways of promoting equalitarianism in politics, education, and intergroup relations. But he is not so progressive about space exploration,[4] political science (the only form of government he will hear of faces to the left), and anthropology (except for the Boas and Lévi-Strauss schools). It is unnecessary to add that he is very suspicious of genetics and keeps his mind firmly closed on the subject of eugenics.

The sharp discrepancies between liberal pretensions and liberal behavior, between liberal pose and liberal performance, are relatively recent phenomena and not typical of the liberalism that existed two centuries or even two millennia ago. Like democracy, liberalism made a brief appearance in Greece and Rome, where Cynic and Stoic philosophers occasionally threw anti-establishment epigrams at kings and dictators. There were liberal sentiments in some of the sayings of Jesus[5] and a liberal outlook in some of the writings of Spinoza.[6] But liberalism never really found its voice until the time of John Locke—a voice which swelled into a chorus when joined by the thunderous pronouncements

---

3. In August 1939, the month of the signing of the Russo-German Nonaggression Pact which set the stage for World War II, the names of 400 leading American liberals appeared on a manifesto affirming that Russia was a bulwark of peace and that Soviet citizens enjoyed as many civil liberties as Americans. *Nation,* August 26, 1939, p. 228.

4. Nobel laureate Linus Pauling, a pillar of modern American liberalism, called the Apollo project, long before it got off the ground, a "pitiful demonstration." *Science,* Nov. 1, 1963, p. 560.

5. Both liberals and conservatives can quote scripture to their advantage, but the present accent of Christianity is decidedly liberal—on the radical, antifamilial Jesus who set father against son and mother against daughter (Luke 13:53), not on the apolitical Jesus of "render unto Caesar," nor on the authoritarian Jesus who said, "But those mine enemies, which would not that I should reign over them, bring hither, and slay them before me" (Luke 19:27).

6. "The political philosophy of Spinoza is the first statement in history of the standpoint of a democratic liberalism." Lewis Feuer, *Spinoza and the Rise of Liberalism,* Beacon Press, Boston, 1966, p. 65.

of such other liberal sages as Hume, Voltaire, Rousseau, Adam Smith, and Thomas Jefferson. The word of liberalism became flesh with the eighteenth-century Whig governments in England, the founding of the United States, and the European *Aufklärung*.

But the Old Liberalism of Locke and Jefferson was an entirely different breed of ideology from the New Liberalism of today. The Old Liberalism stressed individual not collective enterprise, less government not more, states' rights not federal control, laissez-faire not welfare, liberty not security, evolution not revolution. Moreover, very few of the great liberals of the past, in spite of their ringing appeals to equality, were willing to concede the equality of races.

Today, in the hands of those who call themselves modern liberals, the grand humanistic design of eighteenth- and nineteenth-century liberalism has been reduced to a mechanical catechism of "other caring." Contemporary liberal artists care more about what others think of their work than what they themselves think. Liberal statesmen and politicians do not act. They react. The liberal guardians of national security put defense above offense and base their nuclear strategy on mass retaliation and the indiscriminate annihilation of urban populations, not on a preemptive strike against enemy ICBM installations. On the rare occasions their thoughts turn to God, liberal intellectuals prefer to blame Him for the evil in man rather than praise Him for the good.[7] Again and again the focus shifts from the heart of the matter to the periphery.

Although the liberal's obsessive extroversion leaves him little opportunity to solve his own problems, he nevertheless feels obliged to tell the rest of the population how to solve theirs. Public figures whose private lives have been a shambles and who have proved utterly incapable of raising their own children presume to write copious newspaper columns and magazine articles on family life, marital problems, and child upbringing. The mother with a delinquent daughter, instead of improving conditions in

---

7. "God made my body, and if it is dirty, then the imperfection lies with the manufacturer, not the product." The quotation is from the late Lenny Bruce, a comedian whom many liberal writers have endeavored to elevate to sainthood. *Holiday*, Nov. 1968, p. 74.

her own home, becomes a social worker and attempts to help other families with delinquent daughters.[8]

In the liberal scheme of things there is a widening gulf between the person and the act, the thought and the deed. The politician who fights for school integration sends his own children to private schools. The criminal is not really guilty. He has merely committed an unfortunate act caused by an unfavorable environment. Someone else or something else is guilty. Millionaires of the liberal persuasion are often more interested in helping poor foreigners than poor Americans, and transfer much more money overseas than to the ghettos. The liberal loves everyone of every race, but he flees to the suburbs where he prefers to live among whites, even conservative whites.

It is no secret that liberals are fonder of mankind than men. The tragic view of life—the struggle of one man, not mass man, against the irreversibility of fate—does not fit easily into liberal thought. Nor does patriotism. While the average American looks upon the United States as *his* country—no more, no less—the liberal regards it chiefly as a repository of liberal principles.

It is this habit of reification, this fear of the personal touch in human affairs, which may explain why the modern liberal pantheon only has room for heroes who have displayed a noticeably anti-heroic streak. Woodrow Wilson and Franklin Roosevelt won two important wars, but lost two equally important peaces. Winston Churchill, who as a British Conservative was roughly equivalent to a liberal Republican, beat back the Germans, but presided over the liquidation of the British Empire.[9] Charles de Gaulle,

---

8. Such a case was documented in the report, "Girls on the Run," by Jane Conant in the *San Francisco News-Call Bulletin*, Feb. 22, 1961, p. 1.

9. Churchill's phrasing and cadences may have sounded like Gibbon and Macaulay to those who like their oratory served with sonorous corn, but hero is hardly the word for a brilliant political opportunist who takes the helm of the ship of state during a storm and in spite of some gallant steersmanship leaves it a drifting hulk. In some of his most trying moments in World War II, for motives not too difficult to decipher, Churchill made much of his American ancestry. His mother, Jennie, was the daughter of Leonard Jerome, a New York City playboy promoter. But Churchill said little of the Indian blood which may have been transmitted to him through the Jerome family. Ralph Martin, *Jennie: the Life of Lady Randolph Churchill*, Prentice-Hall, Englewood Cliffs, New Jersey, 1969, Vol. 1, pp. 2, 12.

hailed as a great liberal crusader when leading the Free French against Hitler, surrendered France's richest possession, Algeria. It was the deified liberal Democrat, President John Kennedy, who permitted Cuba, once an American economic outpost, to become a Russian client state.

To recapitulate, the metamorphosis of classical liberalism—the liberalism of Locke, Jefferson, and Lincoln—into modern liberalism has been as miraculous and complete as the tadpole's transmogrification into the hoptoad. What was man-centered has become state-centered; what was dedicated to the protection of property now threatens it; what attempted to get the crushing load of absolutism off man's back now weighs him down with more regimentation every year; what was once progressive in the truest sense of the word has now become the ideological crutch of nihilists, cranks, obscurantists, and, yes, reactionaries.

How is this 180-degree shift in liberal orthodoxy to be explained? How has this sophistic, schizophrenic, new-style, illiberal liberalism managed to fob itself off as the authentic product and not been argued or ridiculed out of existence? Above all, how does it keep such a firm hold on the American mind?

One answer has to do with the tenacity of tradition. As the credo of democracy, liberalism has gone down much the same path as democracy itself. Its articles of faith nourished and inspired the popular movements that freed Europeans in the Old World and European colonists in the New from the stifling authority of decadent monarchs. Its heuristic pronouncements on the nature of man produced some of the finest hours of the British Parliament and the American Congress. In its great days classical liberalism transformed the political soul of the Western world.

But as times changed, as the proprietor of forty acres and a mule moved into a rented coldwater flat, as financial and industrial monopoly passed beyond the bounds of reason, as the population doubled and redoubled, liberals began to concentrate on economic problems. Somewhat apologetically, they explained that a decentralized government of checks and balances, the kind of government they had always upheld in the past, did not have the power to enact and enforce the economic legislation and control which the injustices and the inanities of mass unemployment, boom-and-bust business cycles, and unbridled exploitation of the environment demanded. Accused of neglecting property rights, they pointed to the blight of poverty and declared that "human rights" must now take precedence.

It was this new "programmed" liberalism, hardly to be distinguished from the milder forms of socialism, which prepared the way for the welfare state. Its continuing popularity resides in the social services made possible by deficit financing. It is lotus-eating politics, and it might last forever were it not for the inflation and pacifism which leave the nations that adopt it fair game for hardier, more frugal, and more aggressive peoples.

In its attachment to collectivism, modern liberalism has taken the same direction as socialism and communism, without going quite as far. Continually assailed and insulted by Communists for their lukewarm attitude toward revolution, liberals have turned the other cheek and gone on lending their support and respectability to a variety of Marxist causes. When the twists and turns of Kremlin policy permitted, European liberals joined Communists in Popular Front governments. During the Roosevelt and Truman administrations, it became so difficult to differentiate between ultraliberals and Communists that their opponents could be forgiven for considering them identical twins.

In recent years liberalism and the Soviet Union's version of communism have tended to drift apart, even though their hostility to laissez-faire economics coincides as closely as ever. The reason has been liberalism's recent concentration on social democracy, on race leveling rather than economic leveling, and on human rights, a topic given short shrift by the Russians. In many Third World nations, however, the liberalism of social democracy has acquired the status of a quasi-religion.

Within the last two decades in the United States, modern liberalism has become the party platform of minority racism. With just a few changes in wording—*race* for *men, security* for *liberty, minority rights* for *the people's rights*—the whole apparatus of Western liberal thought has moved bag and baggage into the minority camp. The enemy—always the most important figure in any ideology— is no longer dissolute European monarchs, Hamiltonian reactionaries, Southern slave owners, nineteenth-century robber barons, twentieth-century economic royalists, Italian and German fascists, or Japanese militarists. It is now the corporate elite, the military-industrial complex, the white power structure, white racism, WASPs—in short, the American Majority.

Modern liberalism, of course, does not admit to being racist. In fact it pretends to be antiracist. But every word it speaks, every policy it supports, every program it publicizes, every cause it underwrites, every piece of legislation it introduces is likely to have some direct or tenuous racial connotation. Classical liberalism in America, in spite of its emphasis on mankind, was principally concerned with the interests and aspirations of the Majority at a time when Negroes, Indians, and other minorities hardly counted. Modern liberalism, in spite of its bewitching ecumenical clichés, is also dedicated to one segment of the American population, this time to the Unassimilable Minorities.

Its original purpose subverted, its original ideals redirected and reinterpreted, liberalism has become a grotesque masque in which the players will not and cannot suit the action to the word and where the platitudes of the script almost totally obscure the plot, which is woven around the protagonists' thirst for power. This incessant clash of dialogue and motive lies at the root of the dramatic contradictions between modern liberal thought and modern liberal behavior, contradictions unresolved by the fustian soliloquies on humanitarianism designed to conceal the close collaboration between liberalism and minority racism in major areas of political, economic, social, and foreign policy.[10]

Modern liberalism is particularly useful to the minorities because it has the effect of dimming the Majority's racial perspective. Its ambiguous idealism and counterfeit Good Samaritanism encourages Majority members to support the minority side without realizing they are working against the interests of their own people. It also allows those Majority members who are quite aware of what they are doing to rationalize their anti-Majority behavior.

One of the notable curiosities of modern liberalism is the striking variance between the Majority and the minority liberal—a variance of intent, not content. Majority and minority liberals not only have different motivations, but they are accorded strikingly

---

10. "Liberalism is the American Jew's lay religion," writes James Yaffe, who also points out that half the membership of the Peace Corps, perhaps the most liberal agency of the U.S. government, is Jewish, Yaffe, op. cit., pp. 245–46.

different privileges. To the Majority liberal, liberalism is at best a warm faith in human goodness and human intelligence, at worst a dubious set of value judgments which it is wiser and safer to accept than reject. To the minority liberal, liberalism represents a package of solid accomplishments that has not only put money in his pocket but has armed him with an ideology to batter away at the Majority, the traditional enemy. Liberalism, consequently, is to the minority member a pragmatic program of advancement, a means of revenge, and an idealistic crusade. It wraps him in a glittering robe of shining generalities, while allowing him the privilege of being a racist. The Majority liberal is permitted no such double standard. A minority racist can be a good liberal. A Majority racist cannot be a liberal at all and is anathematized as an incipient Nazi.

The question was previously raised as to how liberalism with its monumental inconsistencies and aberrations could survive in present-day America. It can now be answered in specific instead of general terms. Liberalism has survived and even prospered because it has become directly attached to the cause of minority racism, the most dynamic movement in contemporary American life. It will continue to survive and prosper until minority racism has no further use for it, until it is no longer able to function as the "emotional cover" of Majority liberals in their role as minority fellow travelers.

But as the years progress and the racial struggle in America hardens, the Majority liberal is bound to become increasingly suspect, not only to Majority members at large, but also to minority members who, as good racists, can only have contempt for racial renegades. As the Majority liberal continues to lose face, as he finds it ever more difficult and humiliating to tout other people's racism, he will probably have no choice but to retreat to conservatism, which in its present guise, as the next chapter will show, is simply a selective and expedient rehash of classical liberalism inspired by people, many of them ex-Marxists, whose motives are far from pure.[11]

---

11. "The development of Neo-Conservatism in the last 20 years has consisted of a reaction to one major trauma—the fear of anti-Semitism." Isadore Silver, professor of constitutional law at John Jay College of Criminal Justice. *New York Times*, Dec. 4, 1977, p. 73.

In the very largest and broadest sense, the metamorphosis of
liberalism signifies the transformation of an *intra*racial struggle
for individual rights and liberty into an *inter*racial struggle for
power. The struggle is a total one. It encompasses every domain
of American endeavor, particularly the highest levels of such endeavor—the realms of art, religion, education, and philosophy.
It was not Socrates—*pace* Nietzsche—who put an end to Greek
creativity. He was a sower and a reaper of the intraracial conflict,
and the great works of Plato and Aristotle came later. What did
signal the decline of Greece and the metamorphosis of liberalism
which accompanied it was the establishment, still later, of the
Cynic, Epicurean, and Stoic schools of philosophy.[12] It should
be no surprise to those familiar with the workings of racial dynamics to learn that the founders of these schools did not come from
Greece proper, but from Asia Minor.

Diogenes, the most cynical of the Cynics and the archetypal
hippie, was a self-confessed forger from Sinope, a semi-Greek
colony far up the Black Sea coast of Asia Minor. He fancied himself
a "world citizen" and celebrated "freedom of speech" above all
other human rights. He also came out strongly for cannibalism
and incest. Menippus, another prominent Cynic, was a native of
Coele-Syria. Although starting out as a moneylender, he taught
that the rich must share their wealth with the "virtuous" poor.
Epicurus, the pivot man of the Epicurean philosophy, was born
in Samos, an island one mile off the Asia Minor shoreline. According to Will Durant, "He made no distinctions of station or race.
. . . ." Zeno, the first Stoic, came from Citium, a Phoenician city
in Cyprus. One of the richest men of his time, he may have been
the first man to say, "All men are by nature equal." Stoicism,
writes Durant, derived from "Semitic pantheism, fatalism, and
resignation. . . ." [13] Epictetus, the apostle of Stoicism to the Romans, was originally a Phrygian slave.[14]

---

12. Socrates died in 399 B.C.; Plato, 347 B.C.; Aristotle, 322 B.C. The Cynic,
Epicurean, and Stoic philosophies began to flourish after the death of Aristotle.
The Stoics proposed, "one vast society in which there would be no nations,
no classes, no rich or poor, no masters or slaves. . . ." Durant, *The Life of
Greece*, pp. 506–7, 656.

13. Ibid., pp. 644–45.

14. Biographical data from Diogenes Laertius, *The Lives and Opinions of the
Eminent Philosophers*, trans. C. D. Yonge, Bohn's Classical Library, London, 1904.

Both as to content and timing, the latter-day schools of Greek philosophy are in many ways analogous to the latter-day "Western" doctrines of Marx, Freud, and Boas. Although a strong equalitarian strain runs through all of them, the end result is never equality. It is the casting up of new class or racial hierarchies. Distributed under a universal label, they are seemingly aimed at all men. The special allure of these ancient and modern doctrines, however, is to those intent on revolutionizing the social order. It need not be added that, in the ranks of the leading proselytizers and leading proselytes, Majority members are in very short supply.

The metamorphosis of liberalism takes place when the normal defenses of society are lowered, when the euphoria and exaltation of conquest, settlement, and nation-building give way to the racelessness and mindlessness which are the bitter fruits of a job well done. Prosperity brings materialism and materialism brings what Gustave Le Bon has wisely described as the "enfeeblement of character." [15] The situation might be compared to that of an airfoil, the pressure over which decreases as the wind velocity increases. As the winds of Babbittry blow more furiously, the minorities flow into the vacuum.

---

15. "Or ce fût toujours par cet affaiblissement du caractère, et non par celui de l'intelligence, que de grands peuples disparurent de l'histoire." *Psychologie Politique*, Flammarion, Paris, 1919, p. 295.

CHAPTER 24

Conservatism Redefined

Now THAT THE INDIAN no longer fits the label, the classical conservative has become the Vanishing American. Considering his beliefs—and considering the times—it is no wonder. The classical conservative upholds the mystique of authority and rank in society. He is an aristocrat by birth, an anti-democrat by nature, and his principal concern is family, race, and continuity. To him the chain is more important than the links. He perceives the divine afflatus in man, but he also recognizes the odds against which it is working. He places the collective wisdom of the species (folkways and institutions) above the wisdom of governments and individuals (laws and politics).

The modern conservative has little in common with these views. He favors democracy up to a certain point, believes in racial equality—or says he does—and wants less government, not more. He is all for human rights, but he is all for property rights as well. He believes himself a rational, commonsensical being and takes his religion with a grain of salt. He is, in sum, a classical liberal [1] and has strayed as far from the fountainheads of classical conservatism—Plato, Dante, and Hobbes—as the modern liberal has strayed from Locke. Where modern conservatism differs from modern liberalism—in its concern for property, decentralized government, and laissez-faire—is precisely where classical liberalism parts company with modern liberalism.

---

1. "Classical liberalism, which took on its characteristic form in the eighteenth and nineteenth centuries, has with modification become the conservatism of our time." Henry Girvetz, *The Evolution of Liberalism*, Collier Books, New York, 1963.

Modern conservatism diverged from what might be described as the conservative world line under the direction of Edmund Burke at the end of the eighteenth century. Burke, an Irish Protestant who married a Roman Catholic and went to an English Quaker school, had surprising credentials for a leader of conservative thought. He belonged to the Whig party, was a conciliator and appeaser in the dispute with the American colonies, and strongly opposed the policies of King George III and British imperialism. What propelled Burke into the rarefied heights of political philosophy was the anarchism of the French Revolution. He was one of the first to realize that the Jacobin fury was deadly to the existing European social order. In his *Reflections on the Revolution in France,* Burke, like Locke before him, advocated individual responsibility, the sanctity of property, and minimal political and economic controls. Unlike Locke, he stressed religion, tradition, and *prescription,* by which he meant the totality of a people's ancient rights, moral precepts, and customs.[2]

In spite of the loss of the most aristocratic element of the American population, the 100,000 Loyalists who were expelled or retired voluntarily to Canada or elsewhere during the War of Independence, American conservatism got off to a relatively good start. President Washington, the Federalist party and its leading intellectual, Alexander Hamilton, as well as most of the judiciary, were all conservatives in the Burkean sense, while the Constitution was as conservative a document as could be expected from men who had recently established a representative government that seemed like a raging ochlocracy to horrified European autocrats. John Adams, the second president, though not as good a Christian as Burke, was a little farther to the right. Owing to his high office he was able on occasion to manifest his conservatism by executive order—something that Burke, in spite of his brilliant, oracular career in the House of Commons, was never able to do.

As the years passed, American conservatism followed the liberal drift of American history, though generally with a time lag of one or more decades. Jeffersonian and Jacksonian democracy dealt conservatism some hard blows, but the hardest blow was the Civil War, which divided Northern and Southern conservatives and cut

---

2. *Reflections on the Revolution in France,* Dolphin Books, New York, 1961, pp. 71, 167.

short Southerner John Calhoun's dream of an aristocratic, racially oriented, slave-holding republic on the Periclean model.[3]

The great industrial expansion in the latter nineteenth century, together with the winning of the West, helped conservatism indirectly by the political stability inherent in prosperity and economic growth. Conversely, the conservative cause was hurt by the tidal waves of the New Immigration, which brought in millions of liberal recruits. Despite certain liberal tendencies Theodore Roosevelt's dynamic blend of enlightened patriotism, the strenuous life, and an America First foreign policy was perhaps the last expression of an American conservatism with a high sense of national purpose. (When he was no longer in the White House and vainly seeking the presidency as a third-party candidate, Roosevelt changed his tune. His call for intervention in World War I foreshadowed the tragic and disastrous international adventurism of Wilson, Franklin Roosevelt, and all the nation's chief executives thereafter.)

The Great Depression was a setback of almost catastrophic proportions. As the champions of property, unrestricted capitalism, and an unregulated stock market, conservatives were directly blamed for the financial chaos and misery of the depression years. Modern liberals, on the other hand, since they had long ago shaken off their Lockean anchor to property, were able to profit politically from the fear and confusion and claim all the credit for imposing the urgent economic countermeasures.[4] As the New Deal wrestled boldly with the frightening problems of production and distribution in the world's most highly industrialized society, conservatives made matters worse by their destructive criticism, their reactionary financial nostrums, and their antiquated and pathetic appeals for a return to the "good old days."

---

3. In the postbellum period, after the battered South had sunk back into a hermetic nativism, such innately conservative Northerners as Herman Melville, Henry Adams, and Brooks Adams eventually turned their backs on the American dream altogether, the later Melville polarizing into a bleak pessimism *(Clarel)* and a high-pitched religious mysticism *(Billy Budd)*. Henry Adams focused his attention and imagination on the Middle Ages *(Mont-Saint-Michel and Chartres)* and the dreadful future *(The Education of Henry Adams)*, while brother Brooks threw in the sponge by predicting and even blueprinting the inevitable triumph of a cold, gutless scientific determinism *(The Law of Civilization and Decay)*.

4. The economic Achilles' Heel of conservatism will be discussed more fully in Part VII.

The rise of European fascism provided liberals with another opportunity for demeaning and demoralizing the conservative opposition. There are, of course, vague bloodlines that link certain aspects of conservatism to the Nietzschean attitudinizing of Hitler, just as there are historic ties between certain aspects of liberalism and the demoniacal politicking of Lenin.[5] Both liberals and conservatives had often taken advantage of these tenuous analogies for purposes of mutual slander. But since liberals held the reins of power from the 1930s on, they were better able to make their calumnies stick.[6] These calumnies, given further credibility by the events and alleged events of World War II, plus lingering memories of the depression, kept millions of normally conservative voters in the Democratic party. It was not until mid-century, when crucial liberal failures in foreign affairs and incredible liberal lapses in national security could no longer be concealed, that a resurgence of conservatism became noticeable. In the 1960s and 70s the conservative cause profited greatly from the white backlash generated by Negro riots, reverse discrimination, accelerating crime, and massive illegal and legal immigration.[7] Inflation, however, was probably the primary cause of the Reagan electoral victory in 1980.

But even the conservative resurgence was in part a liberal victory. By now modern liberalism was so entrenched it was able

---

5. It is also possible to argue that classical conservatism and modern liberalism in their high regard for governmental authority stand closer to each other and to Lenin and Hitler than to classical liberalism and modern conservatism.

6. ". . . to the Jewish mind, the *Gestalt* of the rightist requires anti-Semitism." Van den Haag, op. cit., p. 139.

7. Conservatism had little intellectual leadership after the takeover of the New Deal. The works of the racial historians, Madison Grant and Lothrop Stoddard, fell into disrepute and the voices of two college professors, Paul Elmer More and Irving Babbitt, who tried to rehabilitate Burke, were barely audible. After World War II the ideas of three Central European economists, Wilhelm Röpke, Ludwig von Mises, and F. A. Hayek, all of whom proposed the removal of economic controls and the reestablishment of a free market, were given some cursory attention. The monarchism and Anglo-Catholicism of expatriate T. S. Eliot had no discernible impact on American thought. Nor did the economic and racial theories of Ezra Pound. The two most influential conservative intellectuals in the third quarter of the century were William F. Buckley, Jr., and Russell Kirk, whose thinking was pure Burke and who shied desperately away from the race issue. Kirk, incidentally, attacked universal military training as adamantly as any liberal. *The Conservative Mind,* Henry Regnery, Chicago, 1960, p. 378.

to dictate the arguments and even the tactics of its critics. Before he was allowed a nationwide platform the modern conservative had to demonstrate that he was a member of the loyal opposition, that on the "sensitive" issues he was of one mind with the liberal himself. No public manifestation of classical conservatism—i.e., no forthright attack against democracy and minority racism—was to be tolerated. If the fires of minority illiberalism and minority racism could not be quenched by modest, low-decibel appeals for decorum, they were to be left raging. The only notes of dissension permitted the modern conservative were the safe ones. He could be more reverent toward big business, property, patriotism, religion, government decentralization, and law and order. He could be more realistic toward the U.S.S.R., Castro, overregulation, labor unions, and budget cutting. But the permissible differences were differences in degree, not in kind. On the larger issues, the issues behind the issues, modern liberalism and modern conservatism were in many cases becoming synonymous.[8]

Such were and continue to be the liberal rules of the road, the liberal-minority limitations on conservative political debate and inquiry. Not one prominent conservative politician in recent memory has failed to observe them.[9] The three most prominent— the late Senator Robert Taft, Senator Barry Goldwater, and Ronald Reagan—were each very careful to proclaim, throughout their criticism of the liberal establishment, their total commitment to the democratic process, to racial equality, and to liberal dogma in general.[10] As for such middle-of-the-roaders as Presidents Eisenhower and Nixon, conservatives only in a comparative sense,

---

8. As conservatives were becoming liberals, so some leading Communists in the U.S.S.R. were becoming conservatives. "Suslov is the leader of the party conservatives," wrote Stalin's daughter, Svetlana Alliluyeva. *Only One Year,* Harper & Row, New York, 1969, p. 47.

9. Even political maverick George Wallace complied with the ban on open discussion of the race problem. In his campaign speeches Wallace relied on inference rather than statement, allowing his listeners to draw their own conclusions whenever he attacked school integration. In his December years the crippled Wallace reverted to type by supporting President Carter.

10. It was not as great a mental leap as some imagined for Karl Hess, a trusted Goldwater speechwriter and idea man, to change into a "radical and philosophical anarchist" and a backer of the North Vietnamese and the Students for a Democratic Society. *New York Times,* Sept. 28, 1969, p. 62.

they both preached the fundamental tenets of modern liberalism as loudly as any Americans in public life. Plato, not to mention Locke and Jefferson, would probably have judged all these political figures as little better than wild-eyed radicals.

It is relatively simple to identify the modern conservative pundit and politician. But who are the members of the conservative rank and file? There must be a great many because a 1970 Gallup Poll claimed there were more American conservatives than liberals. Of those who agreed to give themselves either a conservative or liberal label, the former outnumbered the latter almost three to two.[11]

Occupationally, farmers, business executives, officers in the armed forces, professional people, and white-collar workers are supposed to be conservatives. Clergymen, college professors, toilers in the news media, blue-collar workers, and welfare recipients are usually categorized as liberals. Property and a stock portfolio allegedly turn a man into a conservative. Lack of property and a mass of unpaid bills make him a liberal.

Such generalizations, which have become articles of faith to many sociologists, fit some but not all of the facts. The richest population group in America—richest, that is, on a per capita basis—is solidly liberal,[12] and the blue-collar workers, many of

---

11. The breakdown was conservative, 52 percent; liberal, 34 percent; no opinion, 14 percent. Gallup Poll, *New York Times*, May 11, 1970, p. 56. In a 1977 Gallup Poll, 47 percent of the respondents described themselves as "right of center," 32 percent as "left of center," 10 percent as "middle-of-the-road."

12. "All the available evidence indicated that politically Jews remain disproportionately on the left. They vote 75–85 percent Democratic. . . . Jewish money supports much of the civil rights activity in this country. . . . Radical movements in America . . . are again disproportionately Jewish in composition." *Commentary*, July, 1961, p. 68. In the 1960 presidential election the Jewish vote was 80 percent Democratic. Yaffe, *The American Jews*, p. 240. In the 1968 election Jews voted better than 90 percent Democratic. *Time*, Nov. 10, 1968, pp. 21–22. In 1968 the voters of Scarsdale, New York, one of the richest suburbs in the U.S. and heavily Jewish, chose Humphrey over Nixon. Phillips, *The Emerging Republican Majority*, p. 179. That many Jews voted for Nixon in 1972, Ford in 1976, and Reagan in 1980 did not mean that they were abandoning liberalism, any more than their increasing affection for neo-conservatism meant they were abandoning liberalism. They simply felt these politicians were "better for Israel" and that the Republican party's accent on a strong economy and a strong military would put the United States in a better position to defend the Zionist state.

them unionized, are increasingly conservative. Whenever there is a direct political confrontation between the white and the non-white poor, the former become less liberal in their voting habits.

Geographically, big cities are marked off as liberal territory; suburbia and the rural areas as conservative country. The flight from the land to the cities, which began in World War I, was accompanied by a great increase in the number of liberals, just as the more recent flight from the cities to suburbia swelled the number of conservatives. The Midwest, the Deep South, and the so-called "Sun Belt" are said to be conservative, while the Northern industrial states, the minority megalopolises, and the Northwest are liberal.

Here again there is much truth, but more half-truth. The Deep South has its "liberal" Negroes, now casting ballots in great numbers, and the Sun Belt its "liberal" Mexican Americans, also increasingly addicted to the bloc-voting habit. The Northwest is still liberal, but more by tradition than conviction, and the old Democratic pluralities are dwindling. Because of its relatively high degree of homogeneity, the Northwest is one of the few regions in America that has remained relatively unscathed by minority violence. Without racial problems, as the Scandinavians have discovered, liberalism wears better.

The racial correlation of liberalism and conservatism is more clear-cut than geographical, economic, or other environmental correlations. The American Majority is largely conservative. The Unassimilable Minorities are liberal, though one or two Asian population groups (in the continental United States) vote Republican, and the Indians have so far exhibited few enduring political commitments of any kind. Since conservatism is, among other things, a function of assimilation, the Assimilable Minorities are moving from the liberal to the conservative side.

From the political standpoint both liberalism and conservatism have probably been more hampered than helped by the two-party system. Southern Democrats, once the most conservative Americans, have long acted as a brake on the ultra-liberalism of Northern Democrats. At the same time the liberal wing of the Republican party has consistently stunted the growth of conservatism within Republican ranks.

If parties are supposed to represent basic differences in political attitudes and political thought, the Republican should be the party of conservatism and the Democratic the party of liberalism. To some extent this desideratum has already been accomplished by liberal Northern Democrats, who in the last several decades have outmaneuvered and overshadowed the party's Southern membership. The presence of President Carter, a New South liberal, had only the smallest braking effect on this power play. By 1980 it could be fairly said that the Southern Democrats, instead of mobilizing to resist the Northern wing of the party, had split in two. The New South faction went along with the Northern liberals, partly for ideological reasons, partly to hold the Negro vote, while the Old South faction either voted for oldline conservative Democrats or for Republicans.

The Republican party, however, has a long way to go before it becomes the champion of conservatism. Its present attempt to enlarge its following in the South, the so-called Southern strategy, will have no more than limited success as long as Republican presidents enforce Supreme Court rulings on busing and reverse discrimination. As for the hard-hat strategy, the Republican beguilement of labor by siren promises of safer streets, more jobs, and less inflation may win over many Assimilable Minority voters, but it may infuriate just as many old-line Republicans, who still associate unions with Red flags and street barricades.

Even if Republican conservatives did manage to assume undisputed control of their party, even if both the Southern and hard-hat strategies paid off handsomely, even if Republicans were able to dominate American politics as long and as effectively as the Democratic reign inaugurated by Roosevelt, they would still have little to offer the American Majority. By combining the humanistic abstractions of classical liberalism with modern liberal notions of equality and social democracy, the modern conservative's net effect on Majority members is to anesthetize them into dropping their racial guard at the very moment they need it most.

That is why, of all those who consciously or unconsciously oppose the Majority cause, the modern conservative is the most dangerous. Majority and minority liberals are always somewhat suspect to the average, uncommitted Majority member. The dissimilarity in racial or religious background of the minority liberal may affect his credibility, while the fake humanitarianism and spe-

cial pleading of the professional Majority liberal may have a hollow
and unconvincing ring. The modern conservative, on the other
hand, is given a more attentive hearing. His ideas and arguments—
less minority-oriented and less apocalyptic—are presented less
abrasively and are not as likely to rub Majority instincts the wrong
way. That the modern conservative politician usually belongs to
the Majority also works to his advantage. People are more amena-
ble to following "one of their own."

The Old Believer,[13] who is the quintessential modern conservative because he is the quintessential classical liberal, is probably
the most effective of all Americans in keeping the Majority in
what might be called the deep freeze of racial apathy. The Old
Believer has come by his political views honestly and he does
not degrade them with ulterior motives. He sincerely feels that
the principles of Locke and Burke are still operative in the United
States. He still believes in the innate goodness of man and in
the power of reason. Unlike the modern liberal, he is devoted
to the advancement of all people, not just minorities, and he
still finds a place in his heart for religion, though he prefers the
social teachings of Christ to Christian theology. He does not realize that by publishing the tidings of equalitarianism and tolerance
at this particular moment in time he is disarming the Majority
in the very throes of its dispossession. Also, since he stands for
all that was best in the American experience, the Old Believer's
rationale is embellished by the appeal to tradition.

There are, of course, many less idealistic conservatives. There
are the economic conservatives, the millionaires and hectomil-
lionaires who support conservatism in the hope that it will keep
their taxes down and their profits up. There are the members
of the Ayn Rand cult who have actually gone so far as to deify
capitalism and sanctify the dollar bill. There are the religionists
of the fundamentalist or evangelistic variety, who are more interested in saving their church than their congregations. There are
the fearful conservatives, who know that modern conservatism
is not enough, but also know it is as far right as they can go
without losing their respectability or their livelihood.

There are the sunshine patriots and the professional patriots,

---

13. See pp. 110–12.

who ease their consciences and fill their pocketbooks by specializing in a reactionary conservatism aimed principally at little old ladies and big old generals. There are the obsessive anti-Communists who avoid the racial issue by discovering bearded Bolsheviks under every mattress.[14] There are the reformed liberals, ashamed of their political myopia, and the bathetic ex-Communists, avidly aware of the pecuniary rewards of informing. Finally, there are the nostalgic Southerners who wistfully believe that the day will come when a loosening of government controls and a reaffirmation of states' rights will allow the South to work out its own destiny.

It is probably unnecessary to explain that there are more than a few minority members in the above categories. After all, modern conservatism is now as safely equalitarian as modern liberalism and the presence of minority intellectuals in its higher echelons can only serve to keep it that way. Leading Jewish conservatives include: Ayn Rand, the Russian-born authoress of *Atlas Shrugged*, a wordy, hero-worshiping, capitalistic soap opera featuring a poltroonish industrial giant;[15] Marvin Stone, editor-in-chief of *U.S. News & World Report*, the mass-circulation conservative newsmagazine; Lionel and Diana Trilling (literary criticism); Herman Kahn (futurology); Alan Greenspan and Milton Friedman (economics); Nathaniel Weyl (history and social criticism); Ralph de Toledano[16] and Victor Lasky (punditry); Fred Schwarz, the Australian-born head of the Christian Crusade; Arthur Burns, longtime chairman of the Federal Reserve System; Lewis Strauss, former head of

---

14. It is easier to understand and condone conservative and Catholic hypersensitivity to the handful of American Communists if it is remembered that there were only 10,000 card-carrying Communists in Spain at the beginning of the Spanish Civil War—during which the Republican side murdered 12 bishops, 283 nuns, 5,255 priests, 2,492 monks, and 249 novices. Hugh Thomas, *The Spanish Civil War*, pp. 99, 172–74. In 1917, the year of Lenin's successful revolution, there was one Russian Bolshevik for every 2,777 Russians. In 1947 there was one American Communist for every 1,814 Americans. Goodman, *The Committee*, p. 196.

15. Poltroonish because when hounded to the breaking point by liberals and Communists, instead of fighting back, Miss Rand's hero "went on strike" and retreated to the safety of a Rocky Mountain fastness. Ayn Rand, *Atlas Shrugged*, Random House, New York, 1957, Part III.

16. The "de" was added by Toledano himself in an act of self-ennoblement.

the Atomic Energy Commission; the late Lessing Rosenwald [17] of the American Council for Judaism; such tirelessly polemicizing ideologues as Irving Kristol, Daniel Bell, Martin Diamond, Nathan Glazer, Aaron Wildavsky, Seymour Martin Lipset, Norman Podhoretz, Milton Himmelfarb, Walter Laqueur, Midge Decter, Sidney Hook, Edward Shils, Peter Berger, Daniel Boorstin, Lewis S. Feuer, Arnold Beichman, Ben J. Wattenberg, and Richard Hofstadter.[18]

Although Unassimilable Minority intellectuals and politicians have infiltrated modern conservatism, the Unassimilable Minority masses keep their distance. They are not at all fearful of conservatism in its present-day anemic form, but they are afraid of what conservatism has been in the past and what it could be in the future. They can hardly forget the aristocratic, classical conservatism that for centuries kept their forebears "in their place" in both the Old and New Worlds. They are well acquainted—and some have had firsthand experience—with National Socialist racism in Germany, which they identify with conservatism, although Nazism had many radical facets. They quite understand that the quiescent racism of the Majority could one day be reawakened and turned against certain kinds of whites as well as all kinds of nonwhites.

In spite of their savage overreaction to the slightest sign of serious conservatism on the American political horizon, most minorities are generally far more conservative (old-style) than the Majority.[19] Minority whites may be liberals in the voting booth, but they are often reactionaries in the living room. They run their inner world according to rules and regulations they publicly decry in the outside world. Their family life is authoritarian, with

17. Rosenwald, of the Sears, Roebuck Rosenwalds, led the small, almost invisible band of American Jews who felt that Zionism is detrimental to the interests of the United States—as well as to Jewish interests. At this writing, the most prominent anti-Zionist Jew is Alfred Lilienthal.

18. Peter Steinfels, *The Neoconservatives,* Simon and Schuster, N.Y., 1979, p. 5.

19. Even Negroes, whose frail links to the past are partially responsible for making them the most unconservative of all Americans, are becoming more conservative as they search for bits and pieces of their African heritage and invent what they cannot find. But this should be of small comfort to Majority conservatives. An upsurge of Negro tribalism may strengthen rather than weaken the liberal-minority coalition.

the father still the paterfamilias and the children, when home from college, still filial. It is this fireside conservatism, this basically tribal psychology, which germinates the racism that has won so many minority victories in the ethnic scramble for power.

Modern conservatism, which lacks the racial drive of modern liberalism, has been and will continue to be of little help in unifying the Majority and rousing it to the high pitch of performance necessary to reverse its present decline.[20] Stronger medicine is required for those who are trapped in a racial conflagration that is getting out of hand and who must fight fire with fire to avoid being consumed in the flames.

The only conservatism that can be useful to the Majority in its present state of siege is a conservatism stripped of the dead weight of outmoded political dogma, one that appeals to the young as well as the old, to the heart as well as the pocketbook, to the powers of imagination as well as the powers of reason—a conservatism, in short, which vitalizes tradition and builds continuity, as it concentrates on the care and feeding of the ethos.

---

20. Some of the most bitter attacks against Majority racism and some of the kindest words for minority racism have emanated from modern conservatives. It was William F. Buckley, Jr., not Senator Javits or Senator Kennedy, who proposed that Israel become the fifty-first state.

PART VII

The Economic Clash

CHAPTER 25

The Biology of Revolution

IF THERE WAS EVER a discipline that should be founded on reason, and on reason alone, it is economics. Yet, like politics, economics has now been so theorized and theologized, so supercharged with tendentiousness and unreason, as to be almost completely shrouded from the prying eye of objectivity.[1] Officiating as the priesthood of the various fiscal cults that dominate modern economic thought—many of which wander far afield from the traditional concerns of economics and meddle in practically every aspect of human behavior—is a mishmash of liberal historicists, doctrinaire materialists, bureaucratic statisticians, and tax-happy plutocrats.

Any given economic system must prove to be false or inadequate over a period of time, for the obvious reason that no one economic system can effectively adjust to the wildly fluctuating economic conditions which harry and bedevil every nation during its life span. What is good economics for a country with unlimited natural

---

1. A course in comparative economy would be an extremely enlightening addition to the college curriculum. Equally enlightening would be a compulsory test on the scientific method to be taken and passed by every writer on economic subjects *before publication*. "The scientific method," according to one interpretation, "involves skillful handling of the material being studied, careful observations, controlled experiments, if possible, close attention to detail . . . intellectual honesty . . . open-mindedness . . . cautiousness in reaching conclusions . . . willingness to repeat experiments . . . vigilance for the occurrence of possible flaws in hypotheses, theories, evidences and conclusions." Hegner and Stiles, *College Zoology*, Macmillan, New York, 1959, p. 11. Also see pp. 296–97 of this study.

resources and an industrious, expanding population can be bad economics for a nation without resources and with a declining birthrate. Also, foreign or civil wars have a habit of overturning the best-laid economic plans, and in an ever more interdependent world even a small shift in the economy of one nation may produce a chain reaction in the economies of others.

One of history's most dismal sights is that of two political factions tearing a country apart in order to force a pet economic dogma on the population at large. The best that can happen when two economic doctrines are in sharp opposition is that one of them is right, or at least better geared to serve the country at that particular moment. Often both are wrong and totally inappropriate. Nevertheless thousands, sometimes millions, of people have to die so that one side or the other can make its point. Two physicists who fought a duel to the death over the outcome of a laboratory experiment before performing it would be considered hopelessly insane. But mass duels to the death between partisans of economic systems over unproved and unprovable economic assumptions have become increasingly common.

It seems almost impossible for modern man, as it was impossible for ancient man, to understand or accept the basic relativity of economics. By reducing economics to the common denominator of the pocketbook and by capitalizing on the economic breakdowns that affect living standards and sometimes even life itself, the political agitator manages to inject irrationality, emotion, and fanaticism into a subject that requires the highest degree of rationality. Just as he attunes his politics to the fact that there are more commoners than aristocrats, he attunes his economics to the fact that there are more paupers than millionaires. Consequently, the politician who promises to take from the rich and give to the poor always has more votes or more potential votes in his pocket than his opponent. Except in those rare eras when a highly responsible and gifted people finds itself in the midst of an almost limitless expanse of fertile, undeveloped land and is too busy pioneering, exploring, or acquiring worldly goods to hear the songs of economic Loreleis, Robin Hood is always a more popular figure than Horatio Alger.

If the two great rival economic systems of the twentieth century, capitalism and socialism, are judged on the basis of production, it is found that the former (in its American version) outproduces the latter (in its Russian version) by as much as twenty to one in consumer products.[2] In spite of its lower living standards, however, throughout most of this century socialism has greatly outdistanced capitalism in gaining new converts, while capitalism itself has adopted more and more socialist controls.

Repetitious references to the successes of capitalism no longer evoke the Pollyanna responses of the past. Nor do they help to justify capitalism's cyclic recessions and depressions, creeping and galloping inflation, high unemployment, vast pockets of desolation and poverty, and the monopolistic proclivities of the large producers. But the defects of socialism are also considerable. Socialist economies have their own inflationary periods and suffer from other severe economic dislocations. They have never solved the agricultural impasse created by the collectivization of the land. Socialism also stifles individual initiative by the formation of monstrous, bumbling bureaucracies whose heartlessness and spinelessness exceed those of the capitalist variety.

The swing to socialism, which offers no real economic advantages to consumers, must be explained by other than economic factors. The most important of these is that socialist economic doctrine—though not socialist economic practice—is tailored to the spirit of the age. In a time of equalitarianism and minority racism, economic policy concentrates on the sharing, not the creation of wealth, on job security, not job betterment. It is no longer a question of *making* a decent wage, but of being *guaranteed* a decent wage—no longer a matter of accumulating savings for retirement but of being given a retirement income. In psychological terms, as capitalism moves toward socialism, proletarian feelings of envy and insecurity supersede Yankee superconfidence.

Votes are still bought with economic promises, but the promises are now made to races and population groups as well as to religions, classes, and individuals. The attack on private ownership

---

2. In 1964, after nearly half a century of Marxist-Leninist economics, the average Moscow citizen still had to work 16 minutes for a loaf of bread, 315 minutes for a two-pound chicken, 71 minutes for a quart of milk. The average New Yorker, on the other hand, worked only 8 minutes for his bread, 23 minutes for his chicken, 7 minutes for his milk. *San Francisco Chronicle,* Nov. 12, 1964, Financial Section.

grows fiercer, not because, as official socialist doctrine has it, state control of the means of production will bring about greater economic benefits, but because private property is one of the biggest stumbling blocks in the way of latter-day democracy and liberalism.[3] The liberal-minority coalition does not covet property solely to divide it more equitably among the citizenry. The affluent minorities and most Majority liberals already have enough possessions, and the poor minorities are as envious as they are needy. The prime motivation is an odd mix of compassion and resentment. The declining fortunes of those on the way down seem to provide a kind of ghoulish satisfaction to those on the way up.

Similarly, Majority members are not merely defending private property for its own sake or for the power and physical comfort it affords. They are defending an institution handed down from the Majority's great days.[4] Property, particularly property in the form of farm land, was a fixation of the Majority settlers who transformed America into the cornucopia which now feeds populations whose rulers favor collective agriculture.

The noneconomic foundations of most economic doctrine show up most clearly in times of revolution, which modern historians define as wars between classes. This assumption may have some relevance when confined to monoracial nations, but in most instances of class warfare the racial factor has probably outweighed the economic.[5] In the incessant clashes between the Roman patri-

---

3. Private property is not dead in the Soviet Union. People can still own homes, have bank accounts, and leave their possessions to heirs. But the elimination of the profit system has prevented the accumulation of great fortunes, even though the gulf between high and low wages in the U.S.S.R. makes Marxist purists shudder. See footnote 32, p. 365.

4. Max Weber has alleged that the great economic feats of nineteenth-century capitalism were inspired by the Protestant Ethic. He might have traced the inspiration back farther, to the Northern European peoples themselves, who were not only responsible for Protestantism but for capitalism and the industrial revolution which accompanied it. Weber, however, was careful to distinguish between Protestant capitalism, the "bourgeois organization of labour," and Jewish capitalism, a "speculative pariah-capitalism." Max Weber, *The Protestant Ethic and the Spirit of Capitalism,* trans. Talcott Parsons, Allen and Unwin, London, 1930, especially p. 271, footnote 58.

5. Darlington finds that the makers of revolution have few economic motives. "Most [revolutionaries] came from groups denied their opportunities in society

cians and plebeians and between the medieval peasantry and the
Teutonic nobility, the contending parties differed racially as well
as economically, and the racial differences preceded rather than
followed the establishment of class and caste.[6]

Although the French Revolution is supposed to be the prototype
of the modern class war, it might be profitable to heed what a
leading British literary journal had to say about Restif de la Bre-
tonne, whose eyewitness accounts of Paris in the heyday of the
Terror provide an almost inexhaustible storehouse of background
material for historians.

> There are hints in Restif too of a class racialism, of the fears
> felt by the bourgeois and by the artisan for the pale men with
> dark ill-kempt hair, piercing eyes and shaggy mustaches. . . . His
> canaille is always dark and glowering. . . . The respectable, the
> men of property, the virtuous craftsmen, are fair and have good
> complexions. . . . Restif dwells on Charlotte Corday's essential
> innocence, for she is blonde and Norman. In the 1780s the popula-
> tion of Paris . . . was still predominantly fair. In the 1790s Royalist
> pamphleteers make much of the fact that the terrorists tended to
> be dark and from the Mediterranean area: Marat in particular served
> their purpose in this respect. And so too Restif's massacreurs would
> almost inevitably be depicted as men of the South.[7]

Abbé Sièyes, who also happened to be from the South and
who with perfect timing turned from Catholicism to Robespierre's
Goddess of Reason and back again, revealed the racial motivations
of the revolutionists when he urged returning the French aristocracy to the "German marshes" whence they had come.[8] Sièyes's
racial line was echoed by thousands of more authentic sansculottes
who insisted on portraying themselves as Gauls fighting for liberation from the barbarous Franks.[9]

If race had something to do with the overthrow of the Bour-

---

on national, racial or religious grounds: Irish in Britain, Poles in Russia, Jews
in Germany and later in Russia, bastards (like Herzen) anywhere." *The Evolution
of Man and Society,* p. 543.

6. "Indeed class differences ultimately all derive from genetic and, usually,
racial differences . . . it is the inequalities which create advances in society
rather than advances in society which create the inequalities." Ibid., p. 547.

7. *Times Literary Supplement,* Oct. 27, 1961.

8. Ripley, *The Races of Europe,* p. 156.

9. Toynbee, *Study of History,* Vol. VI, p. 217.

bons,[10] it had much to do with the overthrow of the Romanovs. Almost to a man, the Bolshevik ruling clique was composed of members of Russian minorities.[11] Lenin was a farrago of races. "Young Vladimir's slanted eyes and high cheekbones bore witness to his father's Tartar blood." [12] Lenin's grandmother "married a well-to-do retired Jewish physician, Alexander Blank. . . . Lenin's four grandparents were . . . of four different races and religions. . . . " [13]

Once the revolution had been won and the expropriators expropriated, Marxist theory predicted there would be no more cause for internal power struggles or Machiavellian horseplay. Reactionary and internecine politics were the offshoots of such primitive economic systems as feudalism and capitalism. Racial theory, on the other hand, predicted that once the minorities had driven out the czar, the aristocracy, the Orthodox Church, and the capitalist elite they would then direct their racism against each other. And this, of course, is what happened. After Lenin's demise Stalin, a member of Russia's Georgian minority, began his tortuous rise to one-man rule, first by exiling his rival, Trotsky (whom he later

---

10. The deracination of the French nobility and the higher strata of the Catholic hierarchy represented an aristocratic split in the ranks. The Third Estate by itself would never have been strong enough to bring about the French Revolution if it had not been joined by 50 nobles, 44 bishops, and 200 parish priests in 1789. In 1792 the National Convention was composed of 782 delegates, of whom only two were workmen. Even Danton and Robespierre were so unproletarian that they originally wished to be known as d'Anton and de Robespierre. Darlington, op. cit., p. 534.

11. "[W]ith a population ratio of 1.77 percent, Jews in Lenin's Russia made up 5.2 percent of the total party membership, 25.7 percent of the party's Central Committee and from 36.8 percent to 42.9 percent of the ruling Politburo, while among Soviet diplomats and especially senior officials of the secret police the percentage of Jews was even greater." Geoffrey Bailey, *The Conspirators*, Harper, New York, 1960, p. 129, footnote.

12. *Look*, May 22, 1962, p. 36.

13. Darlington, op. cit., p. 557. Darlington also points out the minority status of two other historic equalitarians—Engels, the British capitalist and cotton magnate who was a German of French Huguenot descent, and Rousseau, the French moralist from Switzerland. Ibid., pp. 543, 545. Some students of the Russian Revolution disagree with Darlington by asserting that Alexander Blank was not a Jew but a German. Whatever he was, he was a member of a Russian minority and must have passed some minority consciousness on to his daughter, Lenin's mother.

had murdered in Mexico City), then by the sequential liquidation of Kamenev, Rykov, Zinoviev, Yagoda, and Radek, all of whom happened to be Jews.[14]

During World War II other minorities were brought to heel: 600,000 Volga Germans, as well as most members of the Tatar, Kalmyk, Karachai, Balkar, and Chechen-Ingush nationality groups were deported to Siberia.[15] At the height of the German attack, when Russia was on the verge of collapse, the Russian Majority came back into favor, since it was called upon to do most of the fighting.[16] Stalin died in 1954 and was succeeded as Communist party leader by Malenkov, a Southern Russian with a "Mongolian admixture," [17] who in turn was followed by Khrushchev, the Ukrainian, and Brezhnev, born in the Ukraine.[18] It was Malenkov who deposed and ordered the shooting of Beria, Stalin's fellow Georgian and longtime chief of the secret police, though he retained Mikoyan, the Armenian financial expert.[19] Alexei Kosygin, a Great Russian, was prime minister under Brezhnev. When Kosygin resigned in 1980, he was replaced by Nikolai Tikhonov, who met Brezhnev when they were students in the Ukraine. Today, the Soviet Union's ruling clique is once again composed almost entirely of Slavs, with a strong emphasis on Great Russians. As for Soviet Jews, they eventually became the targets of an official anti-Zionist and a quasi-official anti-Semitic campaign—a turn of events which constituted a supreme act of ingratitude toward Marx and other Jewish prime movers of Soviet communism.[20]

---

14. Only a few high Jewish officials escaped judicial murder or Siberia. Among them were Maxim Litvinov and Lazar Kaganovich. In all, thousands of Jewish members of the old Bolshevik hierarchy were purged. See article, "Jews," *Encyclopedia of Russia and the Soviet Union,* as well as Chapter 33 of this study. The highest Soviet officer purged by Stalin, it might be noted, was Marshal Tukhachevsky, who was half Italian.

15. *Ency. of Russia and the Soviet Union,* p. 230.

16. "[Stalin] abolished . . . the extensive cultural autonomy which the minorities had enjoyed in the 1920s, leaving them in the end with little more than the right to use their language . . . and to enjoy folk art. Stalin . . . felt impelled to discriminate against the minorities, not only in the matter of state and party appointments, but also in cultural affairs. This discrimination was particularly intense in [his last ten years]." Ibid., p. 380.

17. Milovan Djilas, *Conversations with Stalin,* Harcourt Brace, New York, 1962, p. 108.

18. Ibid., pp. 74–75, 274, 329.   19. Ibid., pp. 329, 355.

20. See pp. 473–75.

The commanding role played by minorities, particularly Jewish minorities, in the abortive or short-lived post-World War I revolutions in Hungary, Bavaria, and Prussia has already been noted.[21] Marshal Tito, the architect of Communist Yugoslavia, belonged to the Croatian minority in his country. The original leadership of the Polish and Czechoslovakian Communist parties was heavily Jewish and, accordingly, decimated by Stalin.[22] In China the chief advisers to the local Marxists in the 1920s were Vasili Blücher, a Russian, and Mikhail Borodin, a Russian Jew who once taught school in Chicago.[23]

In the United States, minorities dominated the Communist party from its inception. Although the number of Irish Americans in the highest Party councils was large,[24] the proportion of Jews was staggering.[25] When Jews began resigning as a result of Stalin's purges and the 1939 Russo-German Nonaggression Pact, they did not necessarily abandon their traditional radical leanings, but channeled them into other non-Soviet or anti-Soviet forms of Marxism.[26] By the close of the 1960s, American Jews composed

---

21. See Chapter 15. Typical of the revolutionaries who peregrinated about Europe in the early part of the century was Parvus-Helphand, born in Hungary of Jewish parents, student of Marxism in Switzerland, leading ideologue of the German Socialist party's left wing, friend of Lenin, German spy, booster of the Bolsheviki, and finally a millionaire land speculator. Parvus-Helphand will probably be best remembered for his deathless words on first arriving in Germany: "I am looking for a fatherland. Where can I buy one cheap?" *Ich suche ein Vaterland, wo ist ein Vaterland zu haben für billiges Geld?* Winfried Scharlan and Zbynek Zeinan, *Freibeuter der Revolution,* Verlag Wissenschaft und Politik, Cologne, 1964, especially p. 36.

22. Sachar, *The Course of Modern Jewish History,* p. 545.

23. *Ency. of Russia and the Soviet Union,* pp. 70, 72–73.

24. See pp. 132–33.

25. Even as late as 1947 it was estimated that 39.3 percent of American Communist party activists were Jewish—at least twelve times larger than the Jewish proportion of the population at that time. This figure, needless to say, did not include Jewish fellow travelers. Weyl, *The Creative Elite in America,* p. 103.

26. A few Jews became strident anti-Communists, but their anti-communism was dialectical, polemical, and frequently hysterical. Some remained in the Party in spite of the shabby treatment accorded Russian Jews. Herbert Aptheker, for example, is presently the chief theoretician of the U.S. Communist party. Other Jews combined a lingering sympathy for communism with a new sympathy for

"at least half of the active protestors among the New Left," [27] and "the nonpopulist brand of radicalism [was] noisy, intellectual, ideological, and primarily Jewish." [28]

In the mind's eye of Marx,[29] the proletarian revolution, the

---

Israel. An example of such mixed feelings, if it were not taken from the *Wall Street Journal* (July 3, 1962), would seem appropriate to the wilder pages of the *Protocols of Zion*. It concerned the Communist spy, Robert Soblen, who jumped $100,000 bail and sought refuge, not in Russia, but in Israel. Part of the bail was raised by Mrs. Benjamin Buttenwieser, the wife of a Kuhn, Loeb partner, who lent Mrs. Soblen $60,000 with the understanding that George Kirstein, publisher of the *Nation,* would reimburse half the amount in case of a loss. Soblen, a psychiatrist, later committed suicide in England while being returned to the U.S.

27. According to an estimate by Nathan Glazer, professor of sociology at the University of California. *New York Times,* May 4, 1969, p. 80. Another sociology professor phrased his estimate differently, "Out of ten radicals, five are likely to be Jewish." Van den Haag, op. cit., p. 118.

28. Yaffe, op. cit., p. 255.

29. One sign that human evolution has just begun or is already at an end is the seriousness and respect which generations of Western minds have bestowed upon the "thinking" of Marx and Engels. Like most of their contemporaries both were as knowledgeable in biology and genetics as a present-day "flat-worlder" is in celestial mechanics and astrophysics. Although they made disparaging remarks about Negroes and sneered at the "tartarized and mongolized" Slavs, the two founding fathers of communism were convinced that all evidences of racial inferiority would be quickly eradicated and all inferior beings quickly raised to the level of the advanced races once the proletariat took over the direction of human society. Weyl and Possony, *Geography of Intellect,* p. 20, and Darlington, op. cit., p. 546. Engels was particularly noted for a perverted brand of Hegelian gibberish that would be utterly ludicrous were it not now considered Holy Writ by a large segment of mankind. "Butterflies, for example, spring from the egg through a negation of the egg," wrote Engels in *Anti-Dühring,* trans. Emile Burns, International Publishers, New York, 1966, p. 149. "But if we take . . . a dahlia or an orchid: if we treat the seed and the plant which grows from it as a gardener does, we get as the result of this negation of the negation not only more seeds, but also qualitatively better seeds [and] each repeated negation of the negation increases this improvement." Ibid. Like the cavemen of the Stone Age, who saw the world as a battleground of rival supernatural powers, Engels had an equally simplistic view—a world struggle between exploiters and exploited, capitalists and workers. "All past history was the history of class struggles . . . the warring classes of society are always the product of the modes of production and exchange. . . . " Ibid., p. 33. There was, of course, no possibility of rational debate with Marx, Engels, and company since "their

ultimate extension of class war, would first occur in the highly industrialized nations, which in his time were Britain and Germany.[30] He put Russia toward the end of the revolutionary timetable and China at the very end. He paid little or no attention to the influences that racial homogeneity or heterogeneity might have in provoking or dampening the revolution. Marx's predictions might not have been so absurdly wrong if he had stopped to consider that just as some races are more prone to industrialization than others, some are more resistant to revolution than others, particularly revolution in its proletarian form.

Why have there been no successful proletarian revolutions and few attempts at any kind of revolution in Northern European na-

---

adversaries could only be either bourgeois idiots or proletarian traitors." Ludwig von Mises, *Theory and History*, Arlington House, New Rochelle, N.Y., 1969, p. 131. As time went on, Marxists "no longer based their hopes upon the power of their arguments but upon the resentment, envy, and hatred of the masses." Ibid., p. 65. In his *Address on the Civil War in France* (1871), Marx displayed his philosophical detachment by accusing Vice-President Jules Favre, of "living in concubinage with the wife of a dipsomaniac." Ibid., p. 134. "As far as the original-ity and content of the theory of Marx's materialistic conception of history is concerned . . . there seems to be no possibility to claim that Marx added any single new idea in this field or gave a new and scientifically better synthesis of the ideas which existed before him." Pitirim Sorokin, *Contemporary Sociological Theories*, p. 520, footnote 24. Sorokin added that a little known Prussian econo-mist, Georg Wilhelm von Raumer, formulated an economic theory of history almost identical to Marx's. Ibid., pp. 521–22.

30. The despised "racist," de Gobineau, was a much better prophet of Euro-pean events than Marx. In an 1866 letter the author of *The Inequality of Races* wrote that if present trends in German politics continued, "power will fall to the first corporal who, in passing, will seize it." Dostoyevsky, in his novel *The Possessed*, painted an almost exact picture of twentieth-century Russia. However, the most uncanny forecaster of the future was the French anthropologist Vacher de Lapouge, who predicted in 1899: (1) the meteoric rise and fall of the Third Reich; (2) absolute socialism in Russia; (3) a contest for world supremacy between Russia and the United States, with the latter being favored because it had 15 percent of the world's Nordic population as against Russia's 9 percent; (4) the Jewish ascendancy, which he said could only be broken by socialism. An anti-Semite himself, Lapouge was opposed to the French anti-Semitism of his day, which he characterized as being a weird compost of economic protectionism and liberal clericalism that favored France's Gallic element to the detriment of the Germanic. *L'Aryen, son rôle social*, Fontemoing, Paris, 1899, pp. 345, 371, 464, 469, 482, 510.

tions or in nations with predominantly Northern European populations? Is it unreasonable to assume that the genetic composition of the Northern European peoples has something to do with this record? Why is Japan, in spite of a defeat in World War II that involved atomic devastation, the most stable great power in Asia and the least susceptible to revolution? Is not part of the answer that Japan is the most racially homogeneous of the large Asian nations? Why is Costa Rica the most prosperous and progressive country in Central America? The fact that it is the one Central American state with a largely white population (aside from the mestizos, only 2 percent Negro, 0.4 percent Indian) may provide a clue. Why did Germany almost succumb to revolution after defeat in World War I, yet become the most affluent and most stable nation in Europe after its much worse defeat in World War II? Could it be because the dynamic minority which was present in large numbers after the First World War could hardly be said to exist after the Second? [31]

And was not this same minority, hyperactive in stirring up the revolutionary chaos that helped bring about Russia's defeat in World War I, mute, restricted, and oppressed in the Soviet Union at the end of World War II? From the latter war, although having suffered much greater destruction and casualties, Russia emerged victorious and was stronger and more united than ever before in its history.[32] How could this be? Why was there not another Russian Revolution in the worst days of World War II when the conditions for revolution were even riper?

The long interrogatory in the two preceding paragraphs is not

---

31. There were 600,000 Jews in Germany at the end of World War I—only 25,000 in West Germany at the end of World War II. Sachar, op. cit., pp. 425, 489.

32. The military situation in the Soviet Union was as hopeless in 1941–42 as it was in 1917. Moreover, the Communist hierarchy had formed a new upper class which was almost as far removed politically, socially, and economically from the mass of the people as was the old Russian aristocracy and capitalist and merchant class. By the middle 1950s the average Russian industrial worker earned 10,000 rubles a year, the average member of the intelligentsia 50,000 rubles, while the heads of the major ministries and government committees were given annual stipends of hundreds of thousands of rubles. The salaries of the highest political officials are a state secret. *Ency. of Russia and the Soviet Union*, pp. 522–23.

meant to lay the foundation for a comprehensive racial interpretation of history. It merely suggests that race may often provide a better explanation of events than class.[33] Perhaps this is why in the vernacular of modern liberalism, class has become a euphemism, if not a code word, for race. Race has an ugly ring and tends to reduce all arguments to the personal equation. Class, on the other hand, is well suited to current political and economic semantics. Intelligent minority leaders, knowing at firsthand the racial background of most class antagonism, realize that by bringing race out in the open they may awaken the race consciousness of those who have been so effectively divided and disarmed by class propaganda. Also, since in some countries a coalition of minorities is necessary for a successful revolutionary struggle, too much talk about race might set one minority against another.

If the Marxists' prayerfully awaited proletarian revolution ever breaks out in the United States, it will not be because of the hardening of class divisions or capitalist exploitation,[34] but because of the heterogeneity of the American population, the racial dynamism of minority elements within this population, and the deracination of the American Majority. The order of battle is already drawn up. On the revolutionary side of the barricades will be the fire-breathing militants of the Unassimilable Minorities,

---

33. The *reductio ad absurdum* of Marxism is the case of Marx himself. If the Marxist diagnosis of the economic motivation of human behavior is correct, then Marx's own career must be the exception that proves the rule. The middle-class son of an affluent Jewish lawyer who converted to Protestantism, Marx had aspirations toward the aristocracy, as evidenced by his marriage to Jenny von Westphalen, the daughter of a government official who was a member of the petty nobility. What class motivations could possibly have influenced Marx to take up the cause of the proletariat? As a member of a minority, however, his social climbing, his self-serving dogmatism, and his hatred of nineteenth-century European civilization become more understandable. What is more, like all professional dogmatists, Marx was loathe to practice what he preached. At the very time he was finishing his masterwork, *Das Kapital*, he invested heavily and foolishly in the London stock market and had to call on his banker uncle, Philips, whose descendants founded the giant Dutch electronics firm of the same name, to bail him out. See the German periodical, *Capital*, Hamburg, June 1970, p. 166.

34. In direct contradiction to Marxist theory and as already noted on p. 222, Negro militancy in the United States seems to be increasing in direct proportion to Negro income.

the less assimilated leaders of some Assimilable Minorities, and the more desperate and more compromised Majority liberals. On the counterrevolutionary side [35] will be the Majority core and the more assimilated members of the Assimilable Minorities. As in all revolutions, most of the population will assume, or try to assume, a very low and very neutral profile.

A proletarian revolution would obviously put the finishing touches on the dispossession of the Majority. To speed the day, the inflammatory rhetoric, the urban insurrections, and the guerrilla war the media still prefer to call a crime wave are putting so many Americans in such a revolutionary mood that a further escalation of violence will hardly be necessary. A few more decades of this softening up, this preparation for the kill, could be as damaging to the Majority as an all-out Marxist putsch.

With this in mind or, more accurately, with this not in mind, many of the richest and most influential Majority members continue to lend substance to the notion of class war by their stiff-necked subservience to nineteenth-century economic dogma. Their voting record, their reading matter, and their speeches often give the impression that they are more interested in saving an economic system than in saving their people, their country, or themselves. The Marxists, who also believe in associating economic doctrine with the destiny of nations and races, rejoice at the paranoid materialism of the Majority Old Guard.

When economics becomes a sacred cow, it also becomes a Trojan Horse. The only true measure of any given economic system is its ability to prime the environment for the maximum expansion of the people's creativity. To measure economics any other way, to allow economics to degenerate into the peevish little dogmas which presently disarm Majority resistance is to hasten the economic breakdown that the liberal-minority coalition awaits with bated breath.

---

35. The terms revolutionary and counterrevolutionary can be misleading when applied to the proponents and opponents of revolution. In the long run, a successful counterrevolution may overturn more institutions and change society more radically than the revolution which inspired it.

CHAPTER 26

The Proletarian Syndrome

A BRIEF SURVEY of American unionism will furnish additional evidence of the racial nature of the class struggle. Whatever form labor unions have taken in the United States—the paternalistic craft unions, the revolutionary Industrial Workers of the World, the dynamic industrial unions of the thirties, the huge million-membered union conglomerates of the present—almost all have had one thing in common. Their leadership has seldom been drawn from the ranks of the Majority.

It is not news to say that there is little of the medieval guild in modern unions. The religious ties of the guild, the oaths of brotherhood, the emphasis on quality instead of quantity, the personal pride in the finished work—all these are far removed from the practice and philosophy of today's giant unions. The guildsman worried about what he received for his labor. But he also cared about the product of his labor. In comparison, the typical member of the large industrial union is concerned almost exclusively with his pay and his fringe benefits.

Unions had a spotty and somewhat violent history in nineteenth-century America.[1] Often their very existence was ruled illegal, and well into the twentieth century courts were liberally handing out antistrike injunctions. Then came the economic troubles of the early 1930s, when the weight of the law shifted to the union

---

1. The most dramatic example of a nineteenth-century racial labor union was the Molly Maguires, a secret group of Irish miners who committed murder and mayhem in Pennsylvania coal-producing counties during the years 1862–76. Nineteen members of the group were hanged and many others imprisoned. *Ency. Brit.*, Vol. 15, p. 678.

side. Instead of the employee being punished for union activities, it was now the employer who was penalized for antiunion activities. The closed shop became a hallowed institution, and the yellow-dog contract (prohibiting workers from joining a union) was forbidden.

It was not until mid-century that the seemingly irresistible force acquired by Labor in the New Deal era was challenged. The Taft-Hartley Act (1947), passed over President Truman's veto, curbed certain union abuses by providing a cooling-off period in strikes affecting the national interest and by permitting states to hamstring the union shop with "right-to-work" laws. The economic determinists who automatically deny any connection between unionism and race might take note that the nineteen states which had "right-to-work" laws in 1966 were those states, with one or two exceptions, where majority political influence was strongest.[2]

The minority vise on the American labor movement was apparent from the very start. The Knights of Labor became the first important national labor organization, thanks largely to Terence Powderly, the lawyer son of immigrants from Ireland.[3] The Knights of Labor later evolved into the American Federation of Labor, whose first and foremost president was cigarmaker Samuel Gompers, born in Britain of Dutch-Jewish parentage. Eugene Debs, organizer of the first large railway union and perennial Socialist party candidate for president, was the son of French-Alsatian immigrants.[4]

The huge needle trades unions were almost solidly minority in composition from the Jewish leadership at the top to the Jewish

---

2. The states were: Alabama, Arizona, Arkansas, Florida, Georgia, Iowa, Kansas, Mississippi, Nebraska, Nevada, North Carolina, North Dakota, South Carolina, South Dakota, Tennessee, Texas, Utah, Virginia, and Wyoming.

3. For a roster of Irish-American labor leaders, see p. 133.

4. Assimilable Minority members, some of whom are themselves descended from minorities in their Old World homelands, have as labor leaders both a professional and personal stake in resisting assimilation. In a multiracial nation like the United States, since unions can hardly avoid a certain amount of pandering to the minorities, a minority background is a helpful and often necessary qualification for union leadership. The carefully cultivated "minority pose" of many union officials who belong to Assimilable Minorities cannot help but rub off on their private attitudes and feelings and strew many psychological roadblocks in the path of their assimilation.

and Italian rank and file at the bottom. Both David Dubinsky and Sidney Hillman, who headed, respectively, the International Ladies Garment Workers and the Amalgamated Clothing Workers, were born abroad of Jewish parents. Hillman played a principal part with John L. Lewis, the colorful son of a Welsh miner,[5] in the formation of the CIO (Congress of Industrial Organizations), and personified the apogee of union power in the 1944 Democratic Convention when President Roosevelt gave instructions that anyone wishing to make proposals concerning the party platform or political strategy first had to "clear it with Sidney." [6]

Other high-ranking labor leaders with minority backgrounds were or are: William Green, the second president of the American Federation of Labor, like Lewis the son of a Welsh miner; George Meany, longtime president of the AFL-CIO, an Irish American; Ike Gold of the United Rubber Workers; Sol Stetin of the Textile Workers; Caesar Petrillo of the American Federation of Musicians; Philip Murray of the United Steelworkers, born in Scotland of Irish parents; Joseph Curran of the National Maritime Union; Mike Quill of the Transport Workers; Walter Reuther of the United Auto Workers, son of a German socialist and husband of a Jewish social worker; Harry Bridges, an Australian, chief of the International Longshoremen, married to a Japanese; Albert Shanker of the American Federation of Teachers; Jerry Wurf of the American Federation of State, County and Municipal Employees; Cesar Chavez of the United Farm Workers; and James Hoffa, the murdered head of the Teamsters' Union, whose father was Pennsylvania Dutch, whose mother was Irish, and whose wife was Polish.

There are, of course, millions of Majority members in the rank and file of American unions, but they are not often found in the top echelons of union management. It is the high concentration of minority members in labor's ruling circles that has given a minority tone to unionism and explains the expenditure of vast

5. Lewis's father was a member of a British minority. His son must have allowed his inherited minority sentiments and his unionism to delay the assimilation process usually completed by a second-generation American of British descent. It is extremely doubtful if a fully assimilated American would have called a nationwide coal strike in 1944 while his country was engaged in a world war.

6. The story is related as a historic fact by Adrian A. Paradis in *Labor in Action*, Julian Messner, New York, 1963, p. 119.

amounts of union funds on minority-oriented politicking which is often opposed to the interests of the membership at large.[7] Certainly school desegregation, appeasement of black militants, sanctions against South Africa and Rhodesia, interventionist policies in the Middle East, and monetary grants to anti-American European labor organizations cannot be said to represent the wishes of the typical union member.

American labor in conjunction with American business has been responsible for the avalanche of goods and services that until very recently made the American standard of living the world's highest. But while achieving notable success in raising the income of working people and in ending some of the worst abuses of tooth-and-claw capitalism, unionism has not had a spotless record. The loss in production caused by featherbedding and strikes has been one of the greatest economic wastes in history.[8]

Unions still like to assign themselves to the progressive side of the political balance sheet, but their selfish and fearful attitude toward automation has made unionism one of the most retrogressive and reactionary forces in American life.[9] In the communications field, unions have succeeded in accomplishing what the press

---

7. Both unions and corporations are prevented by law from contributing directly to national political campaigns, though both can sponsor "Political Action Committees" to funnel money to candidates. Needless to say, the management can put pressure on employees to contribute and the union leadership can put similar "heat" on its rank and file. The result is that company employees and union members may be more or less forced to support a party, issue, or candidate to which or to whom they are opposed. Business PACs, surprisingly, are often willing to finance antibusiness, prolabor candidates. In a preliminary tabulation of the 1980 presidential campaign, 867 registered corporate PACs gave $3.8 million to Democrats, $3.6 to Republicans. In the same period labor PACs gave Democrats $4.9 million, only $400,000 to Republicans. *Wall Street Journal*, Oct. 13, 1980, pp. 1, 13. In the 1968 presidential race, unions donated $60 million to the campaign of Hubert Humphrey, although 44 percent of the labor vote went to Nixon. See Victor Riesel's newspaper column, Nov. 11, 1968. The Teamsters' Union supported Nixon in 1972 after the president had commuted James Hoffa's prison term.

8. In 1970, 66,414,000 man hours were lost in 5,716 work stoppages.

9. Labor's fear of technological progress might be described as Vespasian-like. When offered a machine that would eliminate the use of manpower in transporting heavy stone columns, Roman Emperor Vespasian refused, saying, "Let me feed my poor commons."

lords were never able to do—reduce some of the largest metropolitan areas to a diet of two daily newspapers, often owned by the same publisher. In the cultural area union influence has been catastrophic. Fantastic wage scales and the forced hiring of superfluous stagehands and musicians have transformed the theater, opera, and concert hall into a big business operation, where the art of financing has taken precedence over art itself.

The Majority has nothing to fear from American labor, union or nonunion. Most working people are either bona fide Majority members or are rapidly being assimilated into the Majority. What the Majority has to fear are the unassimilable or half-assimilated union leaders who call strikes during national emergencies, who use their stranglehold on various sectors of the economy to drive wages so high American products are priced out of the foreign market, who divert union dues to nonunion causes, and who are more concerned with what is happening abroad or in Washington than in their own unions.

In a relatively homogeneous country like Britain, unionism is the incarnation of the class struggle and not to be viewed as the outgrowth of a racial conflict, even though the minority component of the British population is almost always found on the union side. The success of the British trade union movement, which helped turn an empire into a welfare state, can be more accurately attributed to an aging process, in which the aristocracy, landed gentry, and civil service, thinned out to the point of extinction by centuries of imperial swashbuckling and two genocidal world wars, lost their grip. In other words the class war in Britain is not being won by British unionism. It is being lost by the entropy of the British ruling class. And since the institutions of a nation can survive the surrender of power to another class, but not to another race, Britain in recent years has been spared widespread violence.[10]

In a multiracial state, on the other hand, unionism cannot avoid becoming a prop of minority racism. Fortunately for the American Majority, it is a weak prop because of the racial differences which

---

10. There is a growing colored population in Britain and a very rich, though small, Jewish minority. It is just possible that these abrasive minority elements, with some substantial help from British proles, will be able to turn Britain from evolutionary socialism to revolutionary Leninism.

have opened a broad gap between union leadership and union membership. As long as labor leaders produce higher wages and greater fringe benefits for the union rank and file, all is well.[11] But when union policies clash too sharply with the social attitudes and political instincts of a considerable part of the union membership, the delicate alliance begins to crumble.

Some elements of the labor movement have actually taken a militant stand against the encroachments of social democracy— encroachments fostered and in part subsidized by the bosses of the labor movement. While most Majority members remain cowed by minority violence, the "hard hats" of the craft unions, many of them belonging to Assimilable Minorities, have dared to fight Unassimilable Minority street gangs with their own weapons on their own ground. The aggressiveness of the construction workers in attacking "peace" demonstrators on Wall Street in 1970 not only dealt another mortal blow to Marxist theory, but revealed that the American Legion and the Daughters of the American Revolution no longer have a corner on patriotism.

On the debit side these same hard hats are staunchly committed, as are most other union members, to the wage-price spiral which has made big business and big labor synonymous with monopoly and inflation. Only the most affluent corporations are now able to afford the ballooning wages, free medical care, accident insurance, retirement pensions, long vacations, multiple rest periods, absenteeism, slowdowns, and walkouts that are inevitably associated with union contracts.

Unable to meet these rising costs, small business is edging toward the red and small agriculture is being forced out of the economy.[12] The old-time American entrepreneur, the store owner, the wildcatter, the prospector, the rancher with a small

---

11. It is logical for American labor organizations to strive for higher living standards and better working conditions for their members. If the end result, however, is a labor force half-heartedly working thirty-five hours or less a week, while the labor force of an aggressive superpower—where piecework and production quotas flourish and strikes are forbidden—is averaging forty to fifty hours a week, how secure is the national security of the country with the better working conditions?

12. The United States had 6,097,799 farms in 1940; in 1974, 2,314,013. *1980 World Almanac*, p. 136.

cattle spread, the dirt farmer [13]—all those engaged in the traditional Majority occupations—are joining, or facing the prospect of being compelled to join, the ranks of the proletariat.

"The true hallmark of the proletarian," Toynbee has written, "is neither poverty nor humble birth but a consciousness—and the resentment which this consciousness inspires—of being disinherited from his ancestral place in Society and being unwanted in a community which is his rightful home; and this subjective proletarianism is not incompatible with the possession of material assets." [14] To apply Toynbee's words to the United States of 1980, the Majority proletarian is a casualty in the ongoing racial confrontation. His body may be unscarred, but his mind and his will have been temporarily or permanently scathed. And as a proletarian, as one who has been racially neutralized, he may be easily persuaded to sign up with the forces that have brought him low.

Proletarianization often reaches as high as the skyscraper offices of corporate management, where Majority executives, caught up in an octopean mass of government regulations, labor contracts, taxes, Affirmative Action, and administrative red tape, have become as much the faceless cogs of a soulless economy as the lowliest workers on the production line. Their six-figure incomes, their overgenerous expense accounts, and their imposing titles hardly compensate for the frustration of losing command, of giving fewer orders and taking more, and of bowing and bending incessantly to the demands of troublesome shareholders and bumptious union shop stewards. They have lost or are losing the authority to fire, and are beginning to lose the authority to hire. The union shop has abrogated the former, and union rules and obligatory racial quotas are abrogating the latter.[15]

The separation of ownership from management in big business and the growing difficulty of retaining ownership in small business have transformed once hard-working Majority executives into a nomadic bureaucratic caste that moves from company to company in an unending, nonsensical circular migration. In many corporations the corner-cutting, whip-cracking chief executive—in some

---

13. The number of Negro farms has been declining at an even greater rate than white farms.

14. *A Study of History*, Vol. V, p. 63.

15. See pp. 409–410.

cases the man who built the company from scratch, in most cases the only man who can get things moving—has been replaced by an accountant, with the result that quality mass production, the great invention of Majority business genius, has been made subservient to finance.[16] Even more humiliating to old-school Majority decision-makers is that many critical company policies are no longer formulated by management, but by "public opinion." [17]

In its day-in, day-out attack on the Majority business community, the liberal-minority intelligentsia adds insult to injury by constantly raising the specter of a "military-industrial complex," which is depicted as a sort of wholesale conspiracy against the American people by WASP military brass and WASP industrial leaders.[18] Since all it takes is a stroke of the presidential pen to remove any officer from the armed services, the presidents themselves must have been privy to the plot. As the complex supposedly feeds on war, it must have been much better nourished under the Democratic administrations which engaged the Unites States in World Wars I and II and the Korean and Vietnam conflicts. To put it another way the military-industrial complex, if it exists at all, must be partly the brainchild of its critics. That such powerful plotters get such a bad press, and that any topflight television commentator, newspaper editor, or columnist wields ten times

---

16. Robert McNamara, ex-president of the Ford Motor Company and later secretary of defense, began his business career as an accountant, not joining Ford until he was thirty. *Current Biography*, 1961, p. 292. Today, the boards of directors of Detroit's "Big Three" automobile companies have some members who probably don't know how to change a tire.

17. Monroe J. Rathbone, when president of Standard Oil of New Jersey, stated, "We never do anything of importance without first considering in great detail the public relations aspects." *Wall Street Journal*, Vol. LXVII, No. 99, p. 1.

18. The phrase first appeared in President Eisenhower's valedictory address at the end of his second term, a speech ghostwritten by Malcolm Moos. *Nation*, April 28, 1969, p. 525, and *U.S. News & World Report*, Sept. 19, 1958, p. 17. As head of the University of Minnesota in 1969, Moos preferred no disciplinary charges against 70 Negro students who seized a building for 24 hours and did $5,000 damage. *New York Times*, Oct. 26, 1969, p. 59. The closest thing to a military-industrial complex first made its appearance during World War I, when Bernard Baruch regimented American industry to meet the requirements of total warfare. It was revived in World War II as part of the Industrial Mobilization Plan developed by Louis Johnson, assistant secretary of war, and approved by President Roosevelt. *New York Times*, March 22, 1970.

the influence of a big corporation executive or a Pentagon general, would seem to militate against the likelihood of such a conspiracy.

The military-industrial complex is merely one of many semantical bugbears—an updated version of bourgeois exploiter, capitalist monster, economic royalist, Zurich gnome, Wall Street bloodsucker, fascist, Nazi, and other liberal and Marxist pejoratives—by which the Majority is divided into classes, into rich and poor, business and labor, advantaged and disadvantaged. It is all part of the grand strategy of assigning man to economic instead of genetic categories, a very handy and very effective strategy for minorities who wish to overcome majorities.

Labor leaders know better than anyone that the most direct route to the human heart is the appeal to self-interest, which in the best union tradition includes both the carrot of the pay raise and the stick of joblessness. They also know that there is a bit of the proletarian in everyone and that their job is to maximize it and bring it to the surface. What they do not know, or pretend not to know, is that when man is reduced to economic man he becomes an animal that preys on his own kind.

CHAPTER 27

The Fiscal Battlefront

O N THE SURFACE, taxation is a means of defraying the cost of government and—in this Keynesian age—of regulating the economy. Beneath the surface, taxation is a means of capturing and keeping control of the state, of choosing the occupants of the seats of power. In the past it was the habit of the conquerors of a nation to exempt themselves from taxation and place the tax burden entirely on the subjugated population. Taxation, consequently, was the price of defeat. With the coming of economic and social democracy, little has changed. The purpose of taxation has been extended from the tapping of wealth to its equalization and redistribution. Not surprisingly, these new tax functions, which under the name of "tax reform" have presented Americans with a soaring income tax bill, have had a peculiar attraction for the liberal-minority coalition.

The taxes that lend themselves most readily to the art of fiscal warfare are individual and corporate income taxes and inheritance and gift taxes. Unlike property, excise, and sales taxes, these "selective" taxes have a sliding (some would call it a crushing) scale. The overwhelming share of all federal tax revenues now comes from the individual and corporation income tax and the "social insurance taxes"—taxes which did not even exist at the turn of the century.[1]

---

1. In fiscal 1977 the federal individual income tax brought the Treasury Department almost $157 billion; the corporation income tax almost $55 billion; social security taxes, retirement and unemployment contributions more than $108 billion; excise taxes (alcohol, tobacco, fuel, etc.), custom duties, and estate and gift taxes close to $36.6 billion. *1980 World Almanac*, p. 77.

It was the Democratic administration of Woodrow Wilson which inaugurated the federal income tax in 1913, the same year the 16th Amendment became law.[2] The rate was a flat 1 percent on income above $3,000 (single) and $4,000 (married) with surtaxes of from 1 to 6 percent on taxable income above $20,000. By World War I, income taxes had risen to 6–12 percent with surtaxes of up to 65 percent.[3]

It was another Democratic administration, that of Franklin Roosevelt, which raised individual income taxes to savings-destroying rates that ranged from 23 percent minimum to 94 percent maximum, and the corporation tax, which was 1 percent in Wilson's day, to 52 percent.[4] Since World War II there have been some reductions of the individual and corporate income tax, but few of great significance except for some important cuts at the high side of the tax bracket. For the Americans who profit from investments or speculation (the Internal Revenue Service makes little distinction between the two), there is a capital gains tax designed to take away much of whatever has not been swallowed up by the income tax. As salaries are raised to keep up with the mounting cost of living caused by inflation, the taxpayer is moved to higher tax brackets and consequently must pay a disproportionately higher income tax. Meanwhile forty-five states and at least forty cities now have their own income tax.[5]

In its present form the income tax discriminates against the American Majority for many subtle and many not-so-subtle reasons. The historical record shows that the income tax, a Northern European fiscal institution, only functions effectively in countries where Northern Europeans or descendants of Northern Europeans predominate.[6] In Latin nations, for example, cheating on income taxes is so widespread that income tax regulations are

---

2. There was a federal income tax for ten years during and after the Civil War and another in 1894, which was found to be unconstitutional by the Supreme Court.

3. *Ency. Brit.,* Vol. 12, p. 136.

4. Ibid.

5. *1980 World Almanac,* pp. 56–59, 61.

6. "Credit for the establishment of the first major successful income tax in the world is usually given to Great Britain. The British tax was first introduced in 1779. . . ." *Ency. Brit.,* Vol. 12, p. 136.

virtually unenforceable.[7] It is unnecessary to add that the taxpaying habits of Old World peoples have not been radically altered by their descendants in the new.

A review of the tax fraud cases in the United States in recent years reveals an unusually high proportion of minority names.[8] The days of the medieval burghers of Bremen who, without benefit of tax collectors or tax laws, paid their taxes "in honest assessment of one's ability to pay and in voluntary fulfillment of an honorary duty" have long passed.[9] But it is fair to say that the Majority is still underrepresented in the list of tax dodgers who, according to an Internal Revenue Service estimate, annually bilk the United States Treasury of $4 billion.[10] The Mafia, of course, pays little or no taxes on its annual $30 billion "take." [11]

Since it is precisely at either end of the American wealth spectrum that the minorities are concentrated, the tax load has fallen oppressively on the middle of the spectrum, the Majority center. Tax loopholes and exemptions help the very rich and the very poor, but not the white-collar and blue-collar worker, the junior executive and the engineer. Withholding taxes make it impossible for salaried people to escape the tax collector, but medical and legal fees, the emoluments received by the minority-crowded professions, are more difficult to trace. As for tax revision, which all politicians insist is an absolute necessity, it usually takes the form of a hue and cry against the oil depletion allowance, oil being a Majority-dominated industry, while nothing is said about the tax-deductible contributions that are financing Israeli expansion in the Middle East.

In addition to being weighted against the Majority's pocketbook, the graduated income tax is also weighted against the Majority's

---

7. In Italy people are often taxed for their "apparent" rather than their real income. For this reason they keep their sports cars in their garages in the days preceding income tax assessment.

8. See Chapter 30.

9. Wilhelm Röpke, *A Humane Economy*, Henry Regnery, Chicago, 1960, p. 133.

10. Internal Revenue estimate from *New York Times Magazine*, April 15, 1962, p. 70.

11. If the Mafia paid taxes on its illegal profits, there could be a 10 percent tax reduction for everyone. *Reader's Digest*, Jan., 1969, p. 225.

work habits. When taxes get too high, they destroy incentive, discourage saving, and encourage spending—economic behavior which adds up to a repudiation of the Protestant Ethic, the traditional guideline of Majority work habits. Centuries of religious indoctrination plus some possible genetic influences make it more difficult for Majority than minority members to adjust to the new Prodigal Ethic of expense accounts, credit cards, and limitless installment buying—the fly-now, pay-later mores of a spendthrift economy. Perhaps the hardest hit by this turn of events is the Majority entrepreneur, who even at the earliest stages of business growth is forced by high taxation to find outside capital in order to survive. Nowadays the more successful a company becomes, the more quickly its creator loses his independence.

The heirs of those Majority fortunes which have not yet been squandered still keep most of their holdings in the large corporations founded by their forebears. The income from these fortunes has now become the target of a double taxation system, whereby corporation profits are taxed at roughly 50 percent and the dividends paid out of the remaining profit again taxed as ordinary income. Even more detrimental to the conservation of Majority capital are the steadily rising inheritance and gift taxes (federal and state),[12] which are chiefly responsible for the creation of the monumental tax dodge known as the tax-exempt foundation.

In the late 70s there were 28,000 private foundations in the United States, of which the 3,138 largest (all tax-exempt) have assets of $32.4 billion and annually disburse $2.2 billion.[13] The six richest were (in millions): Ford, $2,291; Johnson (Robert Wood), $863; Kellogg (W. K.), $827; Mellon (Andrew W.), $776; Rockefeller, $739; Pew Memorial Trust, $604.[14] By establishing these huge institutions, Majority millionaires have managed to keep their wealth out of the reach of the Internal Revenue Service, but they have not prevented it from falling into the hands of those whose political and economic philosophies are far removed from their own.

---

12. Federal estate taxes go as high as 70 percent and state estate taxes may increase the tax bite many additional percentage points.

13. *The Foundation Directory*, The Foundation Center, New York, 1979, pp. xii, xvi, and *Statistical Abstract of the U.S.: 1979*, p. 361.

14. *The Foundation Directory*, p. xv.

Practically all the large foundations are now administered by liberals and are generally slanted toward liberal and minority causes.[15] One might well imagine Henry Ford's reaction if he discovered that his Ford Foundation, the world's richest, is headed by a Negro lawyer, Franklin Thomas. He might even be more perplexed to learn that his foundation once gave $175,000 to the Congress of Racial Equality to elect Cleveland's first black mayor, Carl Stokes,[16] and subsidized the writing and production of black racist melodramas, many of whose characters do nothing but mouth imprecations against everything white.[17] As a onetime anti-Semite, however, Ford might have been amused when his foundation financed a New York City school decentralization experiment which precipitated a bitter racial split between Negro parents and Jewish teachers.[18]

Small foundations are likely to have an even more pronounced minority slant than the larger ones. An increasing number are being set up by minority millionaires who are quite specific that their money be used solely to advance minority causes. The minority rich are also more apt to take the alternate path of avoiding inheritance taxes by leaving their estates directly to "charitable organizations"—organizations strictly devoted to the domestic or overseas interests of their own minority.[19]

---

15. Alger Hiss once headed the Carnegie Endowment for International Peace. Another Carnegie foundation, the Carnegie Corporation, financed Gunnar Myrdal's *An American Dilemma*. Among the few Majority-oriented foundations are the MacArthur Foundation, the Pioneer Fund, and the Foundation for Human Understanding.

16. *Time*, Jan. 19, 1968, p. 16.

17. The plays sponsored by the Ford Foundation were not quite as bad as those put on by the Black Arts Theater School with $44,000 of federal anti-poverty funds. Even Sargent Shriver, a brother-in-law of the late President Kennedy, who was ultimately responsible for the allocation of such funds, had to admit that they were "vile, racist plays." *New York Times*, Feb. 38, 1966, p. 11, and March 9, 1966, p. 24. In 1951 the Ford Foundation set up the Fund for the Republic, which among its other projects spent a small fortune attacking the House Committee on Un-American Activities. Goodman, *The Committee*, p. 379.

18. *Wall Street Journal*, Feb. 18, 1969, p. 16.

19. Of the 107 tax-exempt foundations in Maryland in 1967, fifty-seven were Jewish, almost all with specifically Jewish objectives. *The Foundation Directory*, pp. 315–28. The Jewish proportion of the Maryland population in 1970 was approximately 5 percent.

It is ironic that Majority members, whose ancestors were the first to develop the revolutionary concept that taxation should derive from the consent of the taxpayer and whose war cry in the struggle against King George III was "no taxation without representation," should have given up their tax prerogatives so easily. Theoretically, members of Congress still determine the national tax structure. Practically, government spending has become so enormous that, when tax bills are rushed through to meet it, there is often nothing Congress can do but rubberstamp them.[20] Also, as in other areas of legislation, Majority representatives are so sensitive to liberal-minority lobbying that they frequently vote for taxes which discriminate directly against their own constitutents.

Taxation, however, is only one aspect of the fiscal war being waged against the Majority. Welfare is another. The duties and obligations of society to the destitute, sick, aged, and unemployed were once assumed by the family, the village, private charity, and the church. Today these functions are being taken over by federal, state, and local governments. Here again, the benefits are not distributed proportionately. The poor, who are disproportionately nonwhite, can have as many children as they want, since they receive free medical and hospital care, as well as bigger welfare checks for each additional child. Middle-income Americans, most of whom still insist on paying their own way, cannot afford large families anymore.

Now that charity no longer begins at home, national, state, and local governments are spending, according to one study, $362 billion a year on welfare.[21] The Aid to Dependent Children program for 3,500,000 families (fiscal 1979) cost $10.5 billion, and overpayments exceeded $1 billion.[22] The number of mothers with illegitimate children rises as their dependent daughters have their

---

20. The most publicized tax cuts are strictly political and seldom keep pace with increases in payroll deductions for social security.

21. Urban League study entitled, "The Myth of Income Cushions for Blacks." *The Oregonian,* Oct. 1, 1980, p. A23. A more conservative set of statistics states that in 1977 all government (federal, state, and local) welfare totaled $49.5 billion, plus $144.1 billion in social security and retirement benefits. *Statistical Abstract of U.S.: 1979,* p. 553.

22. *New York Times,* March 13, 1980, Sec. II, p. 10.

own children, thereby putting three generations of the same family on welfare.[23] In one New York City tenement, "Every girl . . . over the age of 13 was pregnant, or had delivered a baby. [At] 18 they could expect to receive their own crisp, IBM-processed public-assistance check." [24]

Relief is made more difficult by the work attitudes of America's proliferating indigent class. An unemployed person can consider a job "menial," refuse it, and still qualify for unemployment insurance. Yet these so-called menial positions are the only ones for which most of the jobless are qualified.[25] The unemployment problem, consequently, has social as well as economic roots. It may also have genetic roots. The "disadvantaged" population groups in America have always been "disadvantaged" in whatever countries they happened to live, including their native countries. To permit and even to encourage this indigent class to reproduce at a much faster rate than the rest of the population [26] is simply to compound the relief crisis and force the allocation of an ever greater share of the gross national product to nonproducers.

At present, welfare wears the dress of humanitarianism, but its political slip is showing. The basic purpose of welfare, it is reasonable to assume, is to insure a decent standard of living and a decent life to those incapacitated by age, ill health, or accidents. But the most active proponents of the welfare state talk about cradle-to-grave security, guaranteed incomes for every adult and, occasionally, capital levies to redistribute the wealth. They go far, but often in the wrong direction. They look for the economic and social causes of poverty, but shun the genetic causes. They demand slum clearance, but do not demand an end to the

---

23. *Wall Street Journal,* Feb. 7, 1964, p. 1.

24. Ibid. As quoted from a magazine article by a consultant to the New York State Senate.

25. In 1964 unemployment cost the nation about 75,600,000 lost work weeks, even though there were 2,000 state-supported employment offices to help the jobless find work. In the same year California had to import tens of thousands of Mexicans to harvest the crops. George Pettitt, *Prisoners of Culture,* Scribner's, New York, 1970, pp. 140, 142.

26. A cretin class is also making its appearance. In 1965 there were 1,117,800 mentally retarded children, 972,000 mentally disturbed children, and 486,000 children with learning difficulties. Ibid., p. 221.

overbreeding largely responsible for creating and perpetuating the slums.

The political nature of welfare and the inherent antihumanitarianism of prominent welfare advocates are best revealed by the black minority's tepid acceptance—both in practice and in theory—of birth control as one solution of the poverty problem. As a high-ranking NAACP official stated, blacks "need to produce more babies, not less" to acquire more political clout.[27]

The welfare state contains the seeds of its own destruction in the underwriting of inflation as a means of meeting ever increasing government expenditures. In order to keep the votes rolling in and make good on their campaign promises of more sizable and more frequent federal subsidies, the politicians of welfare—a category which now includes major political figures in both parties—must resort to the device of deficit spending. As the national debt goes up, the value of the dollar shrinks. As unions force business to pay higher wages, business forces consumers to pay higher prices.

It is all very Keynesian and very clever and, predictably, hurts the Majority, the most stable element of the population, more than any other group. It is the Majority, which out of habit and tradition—sometimes even out of patriotism—prefers savings accounts, life insurance, and government bonds, the "safe" investments that depreciate most during inflation, to the speculations and peculations which make fortunes for financial plungers in times of currency debasement. And it will be the Majority, clinging forlornly to the last shreds of the Protestant Ethic, which will doubtless continue to take this economic drubbing until the American dollar, presently decreasing in value at the rate of 12 percent per annum (Sept. 1980), starts imitating the German mark, which in late 1923 was collapsing at the rate of 50 percent an hour.[28]

The poison of inflation is slow-acting. It does not destroy an economy as swiftly and dramatically as the ravaging venom of a stock market debacle or a military occupation. But in the long run it is just as deadly. That a day of judgment will certainly

---

27. *Time*, July 25, 1969, p. 21.

28. Postage for a local letter in Germany cost 100 billion marks at the end of 1923. Salaries were often paid daily so wage earners could purchase their necessities instanter. If they kept their money overnight, they might only be able to buy half as much the next day.

come for the liberal-minority inflationists should offer the Majority scant comfort. By then it will be too late—just as it was too late for Aesop's grasshopper when winter came.

Inflation can be slowed by making every increase in wages contingent on an increase in production. But this must be preceded by far-reaching changes in the thinking and composition of the monetarist and pump-priming hierarchy which presently directs American economic policy. The welfare system, which now starves the spirit as it feeds the body, can be redeemed by continuing to assist the needy, but ceasing to reward the idlers, the delinquents, and the brood mares of the ghettos. The power of taxation can be reclaimed by restricting it to defraying the costs of government. Tax laws should have a higher purpose than providing the legal cover for arbitrary and selective assessments which encourage one population group to live off another. If there are to be tax loopholes, let them benefit the farmer, the manufacturer, the production worker, the engineer, and the artist—the makers of civilization, not the freeloaders.

But none of these vital reforms will be accomplished as long as they are regarded as purely fiscal matters. Fiscal policies are not the expressions or trademarks of an economic system. They are the expressions of how different peoples measure the input they expect to give society and the output they expect to receive from it. When the work force in Detroit was of European descent, the American automobile industry led the world in motor car production. As the work force darkened, as accountants and salesmen replaced entrepreneurs and engineers as chief executives, as the minority-oriented unions tightened their grip, the lead passed to the Germans and Japanese.[29]

The question boils down not to economics, but to race.[30] There are those who view work as an end in itself, who conceive of

---

29. "From 1947 to 1965, U.S. productivity increased by 3.4 percent a year, but the growth rate dipped to 2.3 percent in the following decade, then dropped to below 1 percent in the late 1970s and down to —.9 percent in 1979. (Japan's productivity growth, by contrast, has been climbing at an average annual rate of about 7.3 percent.)" *Time*, Dec. 8, 1980, p. 73.

30. Today the West Germans operate the white world's most successful capitalistic economy; the East Germans the most successful Communist economy. Yet economists carefully avoid mentioning biology when called upon to explain this phenomenon.

America, the world, and even the cosmos as an infinite series of frontiers offering infinite possibilities of work. Let them know that the frontiers are numbered, that the last ones are coming into sight, and their incentive and initiative will all but vanish.

Then there are those who think of work as a means, as a hardship, often as a curse. Their America is a closed circle, an economic project that can and must be completed so that all human labor will be reduced to the barest minimum. Their world and their imagination are finite.[31] Even their universe is circumscribed by the Einsteinian curvature of space.

The present rulers of the American economy are not moving the nation into the future. They are marching it backward to conform to an age-old philosophy of work that is not the Majority's.

---

31. "The more important fundamental laws and facts of physical science have all been discovered and these are now so firmly established that the possibility of their ever being supplanted in consequence of new discoveries must be looked for in the sixth place of decimals." Albert A. Michelson, 1894, in the dedication of the Ryerson Physical Laboratory, University of Chicago. Another example of the static mind is the argument of the Boas school of anthropology, voiced most loudly by Margaret Mead, that no one should waste his time searching for the origins of culture, a question upon which "there is not and cannot be any valid evidence." Leslie A. White, *The Evolution of Culture*, McGraw-Hill, New York, 1959, p. 71.

PART VIII

The Legal Clash

CHAPTER 28

The Adulteration of the Law

MUCH ATTENTION has been paid in this study to the adroitness shown by the Unassimilable Minorities in adapting Majority institutions to their own advantage. Nowhere has this talent been more dramatically displayed than in the field of jurisprudence. The results have been so shattering that a few preliminary words on the nature and origin of law may help present a clearer picture of what has taken place.

Laws have their origins in the customs of the tribe. The first laws probably arose from crude attempts to formalize the social norms of primitive living. They were probably a simple list of things not to be done. In time, certain knowing tribal members, all too aware of their kinsmen's fear of the supernatural, received direct instructions from otherworldly voices concerning rules of behavior. Accordingly, laws were given a religious sanction. Even when the lawgiver claimed no heavenly connection, as in the cases of Lycurgus and Hammurabi, he was quickly elevated to semi-divine status. The canon law was the best proof of the early and persistent relationship between lawyer and priest.

As social systems grew more complex, laws were codified and began to spin their web throughout the length and breadth of human activity. In more sophisticated societies laws became the rules of the game of civilization. As respect for the law diminished, laws proliferated or rather degenerated into masses of contradictory regulations. Tacitus described the cause and effect relationship in one of his neater epigrams, "When the state is most corrupt, the laws are most abundant." [1]

---

1. "et corruptissima re publica plurimae leges." *Ab Excessu Divi Augusti*, I, xxvii.

Nevertheless an established body of law has a conservative influence on society. The older the laws, the more inertia they acquire and the more difficult they are to change, particularly when they have the combined support of custom, religion, and practicality. It is a truism that these triple foundations of an effective legal system are far more common in homogeneous than in heterogeneous societies. A diversity of peoples means a diversity of customs, which create basic contradictions in the law from the very beginning. As Matthew Arnold once noted, "the mixture of persons of different race in the same commonwealth, unless one race had a complete ascendancy, tended to confuse all the relations of human life, and all men's notions of right and wrong. . . ." [2]

In his article on English Law in the *Encyclopaedia Britannica,* Frederic Maitland takes a similar approach to the subject by stating, "Law was a matter of race." [3] The law of Northern Europeans was in fact the Germanic law, which later evolved into the Anglo-Saxon or common law and is still being practiced in Britain, the British Dominions, and the United States. It was unique among sophisticated legal systems because it was based on precedent rather than on written codes. In criminal cases it considered an accused person to be innocent until pronounced guilty by a jury of his peers. [4]

The relationship of the law to the other symbols of state authority is as important as the law itself. De Tocqueville said that the stability of England had been largely due to the alliance between the aristocracy and the bar. He attributed the instability of France to the fact that the Bourbons had snubbed French lawyers as a class, thereby provoking their enduring resentment. [5] Edmund Burke agreed with de Tocqueville when he criticized the French Revolutionary Assembly for being composed "of the inferior, unlearned, mechanical, merely instrumental members of the legal

---

2. As quoted by Walter Bagehot, *Physics and Politics,* pp. 29–30.

3. Volume 8, p. 547.

4. Trial by jury of one's peers was brought to England by the Normans and probably originated in Scandinavia, where the judicial number of 12 was always held in great veneration. William Forsyth, *History of Trial by Jury,* John Parker, London, 1852, p. 4.

5. *De la démocratie en Amérique,* Tome I, pp. 275–76.

profession. . . . the whole train of the ministers of municipal litigation. . . ." [6]

In the United States, according to de Tocqueville, there was no aristocracy for the lawyers to either oppose or join, so they created their own and became a *rang à part,* a veritable *noblesse de robe.* Describing the American legal profession as a powerful barrier against the vagaries of democracy, de Tocqueville came to the conclusion that it represented a power which was scarcely noticed, caused no great fear, bent quietly to the needs of the time, and took a willing part in all the movements of the body politic, all the while penetrating deeply into every economic class, working in secret, and acting unceasingly to mold society according to its wishes. [7]

De Tocqueville's somewhat ethereal, somewhat conspiratorial view of American lawyers had a certain relevancy in the days of Patrick Henry, Thomas Jefferson, and even Abraham Lincoln— attorneys one and all. Today, such a characterization of the legal profession would seem absurd. There still remains, however, de Tocqueville's conspiratorial component—conspiratorial not in the manner of soldier lawyers Alexander Hamilton and John Marshall, who conspired with pen and gun to free the colonies from their British overlords, [8] but in the manner of union lawyer (and on-again, off-again Supreme Court Justice) Arthur Goldberg, who specialized in pitting labor against business, and of the late lawyer-agitator Saul Alinsky, [9] who specialized in pitting blacks against whites. As for those other contemporary members of the legal profession—including the swarms of divorce attorneys, ambulance chasers, Mafia mouthpieces, and other assorted shysters whose principal functions are breaking up families for extortionate fees, filing million-dollar negligence suits, and generally making certain the guilty go free—they have by and large reduced a once great

---

6. *Reflections on the Revolution in France,* p. 54.

7. This paragraph loosely summarizes the subchapter, "De l'esprit légiste aux Etats-Unis," in de Tocqueville's *De la démocratie en Amérique,* Tome I, pp. 274–81.

8. The ratio of lawyers to non-lawyers in the First Continental Congress was 24/45; in the Second, 26/56; in the Constitutional Convention, 33/55. Beard, *The Rise of American Civilization,* Vol. 1, p. 101.

9. *Time,* March 2, 1970, pp. 56–57.

body of law to mere word games and litigious byplay.[10] Meanwhile the few Majority lawyers who still cling to the tradition of a *noblesse de robe* have for the most part walled themselves up in walnut-paneled skyscraper suites where they defend their corporate clients against "class actions" for not hiring or promoting enough women, blacks, and Hispanics.

Legal statistics for 1979 show 450,000 lawyers in the United States, perhaps as many as 300 in Congress, and 40,000 in Washington, D.C., working for and against government.[11] Twenty-five attorneys were found guilty of Watergate-related crimes. The ratio of lawyers to the American population is one to 500; in Britain, one to 1,500; in West Germany, one to 2,000; in Japan, one to 10,500. Nationwide, 20 percent of all lawyers are Jewish—in New York City, 60 percent. In the top law schools Jews now account for almost a third of the entering class. At Harvard, the most influential law school of all (25 percent of the nation's law professors are Harvard alumni), almost half the faculty is Jewish.

The more minority influence has been brought to bear on the American legal system, the more its breakdown is becoming apparent. The English common law, which derived from Northern Euro-

---

10. If these are harsh words, it should be recalled that even Jesus Christ lost his equanimity when discussing the legal profession. "Woe unto you also, ye lawyers! for ye lade men with burdens grievous to be borne, and ye yourselves touch not the burdens with one of your fingers. . . . ye have taken away the key of knowledge. . . ." Luke 11:46,52. Shakespeare was probably venting his own personal feelings when Dick the Butcher advises Jack Cade that come the revolution, "The first thing we do, let's kill all the lawyers." Cade readily agreed, wondering why it was "that parchment being scribbled o'er, should undo a man?" II Henry VI, act 4, sc. 1. Harold Laski, who qualifies as an expert on the subject, has said that in every revolution the lawyers lead the way to the guillotine or the firing squad. Fred Rodell, *Woe Unto You, Lawyers!*, Pageant Press, New York, 1957, p. 17.

11. Facts and figures in this paragraph are taken from Martin Mayer, *The Lawyers*, Harper & Row, New York, 1967, pp. 11–16, 84, 87, 93, 97–98, *U.S. News & World Report*, March 25, 1974, pp. 23–24, *Washington Post*, Aug. 27, 1980, p. A25. Perhaps the most ominous statistic is the rapid rate of lawyer proliferation. In 1963 there were 43,000 law students; in 1978, 125,000. The legal profession, it might be added, is now costing Americans $25 billion annually.

pean folk law,[12] functioned adequately, at times superbly, in the United States as long as the nation was dominated by people of English and Northern European descent. But when minorities became an important element in both the law-making and the law-breaking process, American law underwent a deep transformation. The legal system which used to be principally concerned with the *intra*group relations of Majority members was now being forced to turn its attention to the *inter*group relations of increasing numbers of alien elements.

Theories of legal absolutism to the contrary, the law is not an abstract set of principles equally applicable to all men, but an organic part of a people's culture, with a style and form uniquely its own. The English and American common law eventually came to rest on the axiom of individual responsibility and on commonly held moral attitudes and commonly shared ideas about life and property. The notion of collective rather than personal guilt and the habit of blaming society rather than the individual for criminal acts rub sharply against the grain of both the substance and practice of American jurisprudence. Neither Jewish nor Oriental law, neither Negro tribal "courts" nor Negro mores ever demonstrated any substantial legal protection for the individual, whose interests were always put below those of the nation or tribe. This collective approach is clearly evident in contemporary law where more emphasis is being placed on minority rights than on individual rights.

The liberal-minority dilution of the bloodlines of Anglo-Saxon law was demonstrated in the Nuremberg trials (1945–46), which the late Senator Robert Taft characterized as "a blot on the American record that we shall long regret." The verdicts, Taft stated, "violate that fundamental principle of American law that a man cannot be tried under an *ex post facto* statute." He added that the purpose of the trials was to "clothe vengeance in the form of legal procedure." [13]

The press, it goes without saying, gave the Nuremberg trials

---

12. Hardly any Welsh, Irish, or Roman traces can be found in the old Anglo-Saxon laws, which seem to have predominately Frankish (Teutonic) origins. *Ency. Brit.,* Vol. 8, pp. 546, 548.

13. *New York Times,* Oct. 6, 1946, p. 1.

almost unanimous support, as it did the Eichmann trial in 1960, in which the accused was condemned to death by hostile judges in a juryless trial for a crime which existed in no recognized body of international law when he allegedly committed it. Eichmann, who was kidnapped from Argentina by Israeli agents, had to rest his case without testimony from his most important defense witness, to whom the Israeli government had refused to issue a safe-conduct.[14]

Of all American legal institutions the one which has suffered the most in recent years has been trial by jury. It is one thing to be judged by one's neighbors and peers. It is quite another to get a unanimous verdict out of twelve people of widely varying intelligence levels, economic status, and racial and cultural backgrounds. It is even more difficult when racially mixed juries sit in cases that already have racial implications or into which unscrupulous attorneys can inject such implications. In a San Francisco trial, for example, ten white jurors who voted to convict a Negro "sit-in" demonstrator were actually threatened with violence by the predominantly Negro audience in the courtroom, while the two Negro jurors who voted to acquit were applauded as heroes.[15] In a murder trial in Los Angeles, no verdict could be obtained because two minority jurors (a Negro and a Mexican) felt they had been victims of racial slurs from white jurors.[16] In the murder and conspiracy trials that arose from Black Panther violence and from the 1968 Chicago riots, civil rights lawyers managed to make race the major issue and justice the minor.[17] In a Washington,

---

14. Yosal Rogal, *The Eichmann Trial,* Center for Study of Democratic Institutions, Santa Barbara, Calif., 1961, p. 28. The pamphlet (p. 25) contrasts retroactive laws with the traditional Western attitude of *nullum crimen sine lege, nulla poena sine lege.*

15. *San Francisco Chronicle,* May 21, 1964, p. 16.

16. *Life,* March 28, 1960, p. 76. The admission of Negroes to Southern juries has produced another strange legal perversion—the illiterate juror. The foreman of one all-Negro jury signed a statement declaring the defendant innocent although he and the rest of the jury had actually found him guilty. *Time,* Aug. 27, 1965, p. 40.

17. William Kunstler, who is Jewish, is probably the foremost civil rights lawyer. It was he who led the defense in the so-called "Chicago 7" trial in 1970, in which the defendants, their lawyers, and the judge, almost all minority members, nearly succeeded in wrecking the legal process. After being sentenced to

D.C., case a seventeen-year-old black youth was set free by an all-black jury after he had attempted to rape one eighteen-year-old white girl and had succeeded in raping another white girl of the same age, both on the same day. Later the judge admitted the defendant had voluntarily confessed his crimes to the police, but because of Supreme Court decisions the confession could not be admitted in evidence.[18]

Today, jury selection in the United States has been developed into a fine art. If the prosecutor wants to throw the book at a white defendant, he will try to stack the jury with blacks. That was the secret of so many Watergate convictions. The trials were held in the nation's capital, where juries are overwhelmingly black. On the other hand, if defense attorneys want to get the best break for black criminals, they demand the inclusion of black jurors and, if they don't get enough of them, they ask for a new trial. In "sensitive" cases, a battery of minority social scientists and specially trained minority lawyers are called in by the defense to screen jury lists and jurors with the use of census data, computers, telephone surveys, and anthropological studies of "body language" and dress styles.[19]

In the past, the presence of different racial and cultural elements within the same society was solved by the establishment of several legal systems. The ancient Jews had one set of laws for themselves and another for the Gentiles in their midst.[20] The Romans reserved the *jus civile* for Roman citizens and used the *jus gentium* for disputes between non-Romans of different provinces. Local statutes were only preempted by Roman law and imperial edict when the security of the empire was at stake.[21] In the Middle Ages, England

---

four years in prison for contempt, Kunstler went on a nationwide lecture tour. When he finished a wildly irresponsible speech at the University of California at Santa Barbara, some of his listeners staged a one-night insurrection, during which they burned down the local branch of the Bank of America. *New York Times*, Oct. 1, 1969, p. 30, and Feb. 27, 1970, p. 1. Kunstler has never spent a day in jail.

18. *Miami Herald,* Dec. 6, 1972, p. 7-A.

19. *Miami Herald,* Aug. 5, 1973, p. 16-A.

20. Deut. 15:3 and 23:6–20. Perhaps the most celebrated example of this legal double standard is the law which permitted Jews to lend money at interest to strangers, but not to each other.

21. *Ency. Brit.,* Vol. 19, pp. 447–48.

had its common law, but it also had a special law for Jews and
foreign merchants.

The United States, although it has never formally recognized
separate legal systems for its minorities, does not interfere too
zealously when Indians settle internal problems according to old
tribal laws. Since slaves did not come under the common law, a
whole corpus of special codes, some originating from the judicial
fiats of plantation owners, grew hand in hand with slavery and
reflected not only white attitudes, but Negro customs brought
over from Africa. Even after Negroes were officially included in
the American legal system by the 13th, 14th, and 15th Amendments, even after the full legal equality given them in recent decades, criminal justice is still geared to Negro "differences." In
the South, minor violations committed by Negroes against each
other are frequently overlooked.[22] In the North, overtly seditious
appeals by Negro militants for arson, the shooting down of "white
pig cops," and armed insurrection are frequently ignored.

If the United States has the legal flexibility to acknowledge
the *Code Napoléon* as the state law of Louisiana, might it not also
recognize the need for separate legal systems for the Unassimilable Minorities—a need for laws tailored to the different attitudes
these groups have always displayed toward property, family relationships, business dealings, and citizenship? Apart from ending
the impracticality and the injustice of imposing the law of one
people on another, the purpose would be twofold—to preserve
the racial and cultural identity of *all* Americans and to stop the
immense psychological damage being wrought by aggressive cultural overlap. Certainly, protecting one population group against
the cultural monopoly of another is as fundamental a human right
as protecting it against financial monopoly.

Meanwhile, even the most obtuse American is beginning to
understand that no system of law is big enough or broad enough
to encompass both the urban militant who considers "the law"
his mortal enemy and the Pennsylvania farmer who, working the
same land his forebears cleared eight generations ago, has an

---

22. A Georgia businessman who had given a lifetime to jury duty once said:
"In all my experience in the courts I have never seen a Negro get justice. What
he got was mercy." Putnam, *Race and Reality*, p. 168.

almost genetic affinity for Anglo-Saxon jurisprudence. Herding widely different population groups into one mammoth legal super-system, one vast noetic corral of incomprehensible statutes, incoherent regulations, and unobservable rules is as unrewarding and as dangerous a task as any other kind of forced integration. The way out of the impasse is in exactly the opposite direction—minority laws for minorities and Majority law for the Majority.

An ethnic departmentalization of the American legal system would return to the minorities the laws they have lived by for thousands of years, while removing them from the jurisdiction of laws they have never learned to live by. The national law would be the *Salus populi suprema est lex* [23] of the Romans, which would take precedence in disputes *between* not *within* population groups. It would not be Majority law as such, but it would be administered by the Majority, the *national* population group. Majority law would be the common law restored to a climate of reason, respect, and responsibility and ready to focus once again on its primary purpose—guarding and expanding the Majority's freedom of action.

---

23. The supreme law is the safety of the people.

CHAPTER 29

The Legislating Judiciary

IT WAS FORESEEABLE that the main wave of the legal attack against the Majority would come from the judicial branch of government. Overriding the will of the greatest number of Americans is more easily accomplished by nine men appointed to office and responsible to no one, not even to each other, than by legislators who are subject to periodic electoral review. The rulings of the liberal and minority Justices of the Supreme Court offered anti-Majority factions a quasi-legal means of achieving societal goals that could never have been obtained through the normal legislative process.

The charter of the Supreme Court is the Constitution, a document whose very existence violated Anglo-Saxon legal tradition. The Founding Fathers' English ancestors had become quite skeptical toward written recipes for government and had decided, according to Walter Bagehot, that "most of them contain many errors . . . the best of them are remarkable for strange omissions . . . all of them will fail utterly when applied to a state of things different from any which its authors ever imagined." [1] That the American Constitution did not remain unwritten, as did its British counterpart, was partially due to the influence of such Franco-philes as Franklin and Jefferson who, during their stay in Paris, had caught the contractual fever of the French Enlightenment.[2] Fortunately, the Constitution, despite its massive institutional in-

---

1. *Bagehot's Historical Essays,* Anchor Books, New York, 1965, pp. 348–49.
2. One Frenchman, who was not of the Enlightenment, had an English view of constitutions, "Dès que l'on écrit une constitution," wrote Joseph de Maistre, "elle est morte."

ertia, can be amended, and has been—twenty-six times. It can also be changed by the Supreme Court's interpretative function, which in itself is a form of legislation, as former Chief Justice Earl Warren has freely admitted.[3]

Today, the Constitution has become an object of special veneration to conservatives, who look upon it as a stumbling block to modern liberalism, concentrating their wrath on what the Supreme Court has tried to make of the Constitution rather than on the document itself. They have apparently forgotten that some of the great American conservatives of the past were very unhappy about the Constitution. Alexander Hamilton, who did as much as anyone to get it adopted, called it a "frail and worthless fabric." [4] Patrick Henry was even more pessimistic. "I look upon that paper as the most fatal plan that could possibly be conceived to enslave a free people." [5]

In their often quoted written and verbal debates, the framers of the Constitution refused to let their thoughts be dominated by racial issues. Reading John Jay, one would hardly think that minorities of any kind existed in the new nation. "Providence," he wrote in the second *Federalist* paper, "has been pleased to give this one connected country to one united people—a people descended from the same ancestors, speaking the same language, professing the same religion, attached to the same principles of government, very similar in their manners and customs. . . ." [6]

Even though Indians and Negroes composed a higher proportion of the total population than they do today, the Constitution treated them with studied indifference. Slaves were described as "other persons" and for purposes of apportionment were counted as three-fifths of a white man, while untaxed Indians were treated as nonpersons and not counted at all.[7] The troublesome issue of slavery itself was carefully bypassed—with two exceptions. The slave trade was permitted until 1808, and the return of fugitive slaves was made mandatory.[8]

---

3. As stated in a television interview on WNET, Sept. 8, 1969.
4. Frank Donovan, *Mr. Madison's Constitution*, Dodd, Mead, New York, 1965, p. 1.
5. Ibid., p. 2.
6. *The Federalist Papers*, Mentor books, New York, 1961, p. 38.
7. Art. I, Sec. 2, Par. 3.
8. Art. I, Sec. 9, Par. 1, and Art. IV, Sec. 2, Par. 3.

The Constitution's "neutrality" on slavery provoked Abolitionists to the limits of invective. William Lloyd Garrison stumped
the North, demanding nothing less than the annulment of this
"covenant with death," "agreement with hell," and "refuge of
lies." [9] Southerners slowly rallied to its defense. Chief Justice
Taney, a Maryland planter's son, climaxed the verbal stage of
the controversy by his ruling in the Dred Scott case (1857) that
Negroes were "beings of an inferior order and altogether unfit
to associate with the white race . . . so far inferior that they had
no rights which the white man was bound to respect. . . ." [10]

The Constitution took on an entirely different aspect after the
Civil War when it was updated to conform to the vengeful mood
of the Northern victors. The 13th, 14th, and 15th Amendments
abolished slavery and guaranteed citizenship rights to Negroes
although reiterating that "Indians not taxed" were not to be
counted in the apportionment of representatives to Congress.
That these amendments were necessary—theoretically they had
already been spelled out in the Bill of Rights—again proved that
the Constitution in its original form was never intended to apply
to nonwhites. After Reconstruction came to an end and Northern
occupation troops were withdrawn, none of these amendments
was seriously enforced in the South. Meanwhile, once again reversing itself, the Supreme Court produced two landmark decisions
which seemed to sanction non-enforcement: *Civil Rights* (1883),
in which it ruled that Congress could not stop whites from discriminating against Negroes in public places, and *Plessy* v. *Ferguson*
(1896), which set forth the historic "separate but equal" doctrine.

The Court welcomed its first minority member with Woodrow
Wilson's appointment of Louis Brandeis in 1916. Together with
Oliver Wendell Holmes, a constitutional and legal relativist, Brandeis racked up the all-time Court record for dissents. Though a
millionaire several times over, he fought hard against the "curse
of bigness," by which he meant the Majority corporations. He
fought equally hard for what he called "his brethren," going to
great anthropological lengths to establish their biological distinc-

---

9. Carl Becker, *The Declaration of Independence*, Knopf, New York, 1956, p.
242. The parents of Garrison, an apprentice shoemaker, came from the British
province of New Brunswick.

10. Bernard Steiner, *Roger B. Taney*, Williams and Wilkins, Baltimore, 1922,
p. 347.

tiveness. "The percentage of foreign blood in Jews today is very low," he stated. "Probably no important European race is so pure." Brandeis, now acclaimed as one of the Supreme Court greats, used the prestige of his high office to urge young American Jews "to be trained in Zionism . . . to know their ancestors' great past [so that] when they grow up, they, too, shall be equipped for the harder task of Palestine building. . . ." [11]

After the appointment of Brandeis broke the bonds of custom, the concept of a permanent "Jewish seat" on the Supreme Court began to capture the imagination of editorial writers. When Justice Holmes resigned in 1932, Herbert Hoover, a Republican president, named Benjamin Cardozo, a liberal Democrat, to fill the vacancy. Cardozo, who made his mark as a negligence case lawyer, had no difficulty winning Senate confirmation because the press unanimously agreed to suppress the unpleasant fact that his father had been a member of the corrupt Tweed Ring and had been forced to resign as a New York Supreme Court Justice during one of New York City's perennial political scandals. [12]

Cardozo died in 1938, and a year later Felix Frankfurter was appointed to the Court. Frankfurter was the Vienna-born Harvard law professor who managed to get his first big publicity break as the result of his zealous agitation on behalf of Sacco and Vanzetti, two world savers who were canonized by the liberal press and executed by the State of Massachusetts for their part in a 1920 Boston murder-holdup. [13] Frankfurter, one of the founders of the American Civil Liberties Union, aspired to the label of

---

11. *Brandeis on Zionism*, Zionist Organization of America, Washington, D.C., 1942, p. 77.

12. *Dictionary of American Biography*, Vol. XXII, Supplement Two, Scribner's, New York, 1958, p. 94.

13. In an article he wrote for the *Atlantic Monthly* (March 1924), Frankfurter called Judge Thayer's ruling in the case "a farrago of misquotations, misrepresentations, suppressions and mutilations." If a professor of law had made such a statement in England concerning a case on appeal, he would not only have lost his position but would have been sent to jail. *Times Literary Supplement*, July 26, 1963, p. 546. The quotation was taken from Francis Russell's *Tragedy in Dedham*, McGraw-Hill, New York, 1962, p. 343. Twelve months before Pearl Harbor, Frankfurter, while a Supreme Court Justice, sent a "Personal Secret" cable to Winston Churchill urging him to "butter up" Roosevelt as a means of bringing the United States into World War II. Jack Anderson column, Oct. 19, 1973.

conservative in his later years.[14] He quit the Court in 1962 at age eighty, making way for Arthur Goldberg, a labor lawyer for the CIO. Goldberg resigned in 1965 to become ambassador to the United Nations, whereupon President Johnson appointed Abe Fortas to succeed him.

When Johnson tried to promote Fortas to chief justice, the Senate refused to go along. Although the media raged, the senators were well advised. In 1969, after the truth came out about his financial dealings with swindler Louis Wolfson, Fortas had to quit the Court.[15] Thurgood Marshall, the first Negro justice, was nominated and confirmed in 1967.

The votes of these Unassimilable Minority members, when added to those of the liberal justices, were sufficient to generate the far-reaching decisions which have so drastically reordered American society.[16] The three Majority members most responsible for the Court's transvaluation of the American way were Chief Justice Warren and Associate Justices Black and Douglas. Some clues to the motivations of these men have already been given.[17] Others may be pieced together by scanning certain of the darker paragraphs of their voluminous biographies.

Earl Warren was a second-generation American, both of his parents having been born abroad. His Norwegian father, Erik

---

14. One authentically conservative Supreme Court Justice, James McReynolds, was accused by Frankfurter of "primitive anti-Semitism." *Felix Frankfurter Reminisces,* Reynal, New York, 1960, p. 101.

15. See pp. 432–33.

16. The Court's impact on crime and the rights of criminals will be examined in Chapter 30. According to Warren, his and his colleagues' most important decision was *Baker* v. *Carr* (one man, one vote). Next was *Brown* v. *Board of Education* (school desegregation). Then came *Gideon* v. *Wainwright* (free legal counsel for the indigent accused), *Mapp* v. *Ohio* (inadmissibility of illegally seized evidence), *Escobedo* v. *Illinois* (suspect's right to legal counsel during interrogation) and *Miranda* v. *Arizona* (duty of police to warn the accused of his rights). Warren apparently did not consider the following decisions to be significant enough for comment: the 1963 decision barring prayers and Bible readings from public schools, the pornography rulings, the unconstitutionality of compulsory registration of Communist party members, the overturning of Virginia's miscegenation law, the definition of libel as malicious and reckless untruth rather than disregard for the truth. For a thumbnail epitome of the Warren Court's record, see *Time,* July 14, 1969, pp. 62–63.

17. See Chapter 11.

Methias Varran, whose education ended in the seventh grade, was an impecunious mechanic, who later became a prosperous California landlord. In 1938 he was bludgeoned to death with an iron pipe—a murder that was never solved.[18] Earl, a local district attorney at the time, is said to have shared a $177,653 estate with his sister.[19]

In 1942, as attorney general of California, Warren advocated one of the most unconstitutional acts in American history—the incarceration of masses of Japanese Americans in various Western "relocation centers."[20] Two years later this czarist approach to internal security was given the official approval of the Supreme Court in *Korematsu* v. *United States,* Justice Black writing the majority opinion and Justice Douglas concurring.[21] In 1952, having progressed to the governorship of California and having failed to secure the presidential nomination himself, Warren swung his delegation to Eisenhower at a critical moment in the Republican convention. A year later, when Chief Justice Vinson died, Warren received his reward, although Eisenhower would never admit there had been a political payoff.

On being notified of the assassination of President Kennedy in 1963, Warren in a national news release described the murderer, in so many words, as a right-wing bigot.[22] In spite of pre-

---

18. Luther A. Huston, *Pathway to Judgment,* Chilton, Philadelphia, 1966, pp. 13, 15.

19. John D. Weaver, *Warren,* Little, Brown, Boston, 1967, p. 50. Another Warren biographer says he only inherited $6,000. Huston, op cit., p. 17.

20. See pp. 107, 206.

21. Weaver, op. cit., pp. 105–6. Robert Jackson was one of the three justices who could not stomach *Korematsu,* although he later took a leave of absence to become chief prosecutor in the Nuremberg trials. Another Supreme Court Justice, Tom Clark, who in 1942 as a Department of Justice official helped direct the roundup of Japanese Americans, said in 1966: "I have made a lot of mistakes in my life, but there are two that I acknowledge publicly. One is my part in the evacuation of the Japanese from California . . . and the other is the Nuremberg Trials. I don't think they served any purpose at all. . . ." Ibid., p. 113.

22. *New York Times,* Nov. 23, 1963, p. 8. The news media's attempt to make the Kennedy assassination a white supremacist plot failed lamentably when Warren's own commission conceded that, prior to gunning down the president, Oswald had taken a shot at right-wing General Edwin Walker. *Report of the President's Committee on the Assassination of President John F. Kennedy,* U.S. Government Printing Office, Washington, D.C., 1964, pp. 13–14.

judging the case—and prejudging it incorrectly—Warren was put in charge of the commission appointed by President Johnson to investigate Kennedy's murder. When asked by a reporter if all the facts would ever be made public, Warren replied, "Yes. . . . But it might not be in your lifetime." [23]

The *Warren Report,* despite its length, had gaps. The investigation seemed to cool down perceptibly when it came to Jack Ruby's gangster background and the strange coincidence of his Cuban trip, to the part played by high government officials in arranging for the defector Oswald's return to America, and to the connections of Marina Oswald's family with the Russian secret police.[24] The Commission ignored Ruby's statement that he had murdered Oswald because "he wanted the whole world to know that the Jews had guts." [25]

Even Warren's most ardent supporters have had to agree that he displayed a broad streak of inconsistency. He was more responsible for school desegregation than any other American, yet he never sent any of his own four children (one adopted) to an integrated school. He climbed to the political heights as a Republican, yet always acted like a Democrat and was even described as one by President Truman.[26] Certain decisions of the Warren Court should have rested at least partly on the scientific evidence, but Warren was exceedingly reluctant to consider such evidence, perhaps because he had almost failed science in high school.[27]

---

23. Leo Katcher, *Earl Warren,* McGraw-Hill, New York, 1967, p. 458. A prominent member of the Warren Commission, Senator Richard Russell of Georgia, was convinced that more than one person was involved in the assassination. "There were too many things—the fact that he [Oswald] was at Minsk, and that was the principal center for educating Cuban students . . . some of the trips he made to Mexico City and a number of discrepancies in the evidence . . . caused me to doubt that he planned it all by himself." *Human Events,* Jan. 31, 1970, p. 2.

24. *Hearings Before the President's Commission on the Assassination of President Kennedy,* Vol. 1, p. 278. Marina Oswald's uncle, with whom she had lived for many years, was a Soviet security officer.

25. Melvin Belli, *Dallas Justice,* David McKay, New York, 1964, p. 167. Belli was Ruby's chief counsel in the murder trial. After losing the case for his client, Belli blamed his failure in part on the fact that Dallas was "anti-Semitic." *New York Times,* March 16, 1964, p. 23.

26. WNET television interview, Sept. 8, 1969.

27. Huston, op. cit., p. 25. Also see footnote 21, p. 291, of this study and Putnam, *Race and Reality,* Chapter IV.

Never one to be hamstrung by precedent, legal or otherwise, Warren did not become a crusader for the rights of the accused until he had taken his seat on the High Bench. In his early days as a headline-making California district and state attorney, he had achieved a certain notoriety for his arbitrary handling of suspects, occasionally holding them overnight without bail.[28] Today, however, Warren stands as the prophet emeritus of that school of criminal procedure that believes the accused should not only be afforded every benefit of the doubt, but every technicality of the law. Only in the area of religion did Warren, who may be fairly described as a latitudinarian, maintain a certain consistency. As one of his biographers stated, "Warren, a quondam Methodist married to a devout Baptist whose children . . . have drawn no line in their marriages between Catholic and Protestant, Gentile and Jew, has never been one to make a public display of piety.[29]

Warren's rationale for his Supreme Court record was the same as that of his other liberal colleagues. He insisted he was simply spelling out the Bill of Rights for all Americans instead of some. His legal philosophy might be understandable if the legal institutions laboriously developed by one people could be moved bag and baggage across the centuries and made to function efficiently for a population mix of many peoples without undotting an "i" or deleting a comma. Unfortunately they cannot. One people's right to life, liberty, and the pursuit of happiness may be another people's right to crime. Rights *earned* by one group become curiously transformed in text and context when they are *donated* to another group. It is for this reason that the alteration of custom by judicial fiat is one of the more noxious forms of tyranny.

Warren is the classic example of the political operator who surfaces at the highest levels of government in a time of decline and disintegration—a man clever enough to swim beautifully with the political tides, but not intelligent enough to probe the deepwater evolutionary currents. The secret of such a person's success is a delicate blend of ignorance, overweening ambition, and an

---

28. Huston, op. cit., p. 47. When the Senate Judiciary Committee was debating Warren's appointment as chief justice, the person who produced the most charges against him, a certain R. J. Wilson, was arrested after leaving an executive session of the committee at the telegraphed request of the San Francisco police chief. He was later released for lack of evidence. Ibid., p. 99.

29. Weaver, op. cit., p. 268.

acute sensitivity to the wishes and moods of those who control public opinion. In one of the most ironic twists in the saga of human endeavor, Warren's fame rests on his almost total misconception of the one-to-one relationship between law and culture.[30]

Although it violates the bounds of permissible caricature both with respect to the Warren Court and Warren's role therein, the late Justice Hugo Black may be categorized as Warren's John the Baptist. Black, who "went to law school . . . because he was too poorly educated to go anywhere else," [31] was not born a liberal. Like Warren he accumulated liberalism at the same rate he accumulated power. In 1923–24, he was a dues-paying member of the Georgia Ku Klux Klan, a stern prohibitionist, and an affluent attorney who specialized in personal injury cases. When he ran for the United States Senate in 1926, Black felt it politic to drop his Klan membership. But after winning his senatorial seat, he was given the Klan's Grand Passport, which he gratefully accepted in a public ceremony. [32]

Black was appointed to the Supreme Court in 1937, having convinced Roosevelt that he was an authentic, un-Klannish New Dealer. How as a Supreme Court Justice he dispensed his newly acquired liberalism has been noted in the reference to the *Korematsu* decision. He went even further in *Yamashita* (1946), when he upheld the death sentence given a Japanese general in a "war crimes" trial which had violated almost every article and paragraph of the Bill of Rights, the very document of which Black was supposed to be the champion.[33] In 1967 the learned justice, who in his metaphysical exaltation of due process and social permissiveness had helped to push the law of the land to the threshold of anarchy, dismayed his liberal-minority claque by upholding the

---

30. Other Warren misconceptions were equally appalling. In an extreme example of illiteracy in high places, aired over a public television station, he gave his unstinting approval to the "Roman democracy" which, he explained, lasted "one thousand years" because of Roman proficiency in self-government—a statement, needless to say, that would have been news to Marius, Sulla, Julius Caesar, and Elagabalus. WNET television broadcast, Sept. 8, 1969.

31. John P. Frank, *The Warren Court*, Macmillan, New York, 1964, p. 42.

32. Leo Pfeffer, *This Honorable Court*, Beacon, Boston, 1965, pp. 326–27.

33. Rocco J. Tresolini, *Justice and the Supreme Court*, Lippincott, Philadelphia, 1963, Chapter VIII.

sentences of street demonstrators found guilty of underscoring their protests with violence.[34] As the end days of his judicial career drew near, Black seemed dimly aware of what he had done to the law and what had to be undone to prevent it from collapsing entirely.

Associate Justice William Douglas, like Black a product of the Majority Split in the Ranks, was a vigorous mountain climber, long-distance hiker, world traveler, conservationist, and *bon vivant,* who often out-liberaled Black himself. As much of a libertine as a liberal, at the age of sixty-seven he married his fourth wife, a twenty-two-year-old college coed.[35] A few months later it was discovered that Douglas was receiving $12,000 annually from something called the Albert Parvin Foundation, the income of which derived principally from mortgages on a Las Vegas hotel and gambling casino.[36] Douglas refused to give up this gratuitous supplement to his already large income (Supreme Court salary, expenses, lecture fees, book royalties) until it was further discovered that Albert Parvin had once been named as a co-conspirator with Louis Wolfson in one of the latter's many sordid financial dealings.[37] Though Douglas's relationship with Wolfson's friend was just as unethical as Fortas's relationship with Wolfson, Douglas refused to resign his seat.[38] In 1970, after the Senate Judiciary Committee's hearings to determine whether impeachment proceedings should be initiated against him, Douglas was given the expected whitewash by eighty-two-year-old Committee Chairman Emanuel Celler. The liberal-minority coalition protects its own.

Whatever the cause of Douglas's extreme strenuosity, whether glandular or compensation for a childhood attack of infantile pa-

---

34. Weaver, op. cit., pp. 337–40.
35. *Time,* July 29, 1966, p. 17.
36. *San Francisco Examiner,* Oct. 16, 1966, p. 1.
37. *Time,* June 6, 1969, p. 23.
38. Among his other peccadilloes, Douglas sold an article in 1969 for $350 to the magazine, *Avant Garde,* whose publisher, Ralph Ginzburg, had been given a five-year sentence for pornography. Earlier, when Ginzburg's case had come before the Supreme Court and the verdict upheld, Douglas had been the lone dissenter. In 1970 Douglas's book, *Points of Rebellion,* was published. In it he warmly encouraged law-breaking demonstrations, writing that "violence may be the only effective response" to present-day American problems. *Human Events,* Feb. 14, 1970, p. 4, and March 14, 1970, p. 3.

ralysis, he was without doubt the most energetic of the 101 Supreme Court Justices. He was also one of the most dissenting justices until he was able to join the liberal majority which emerged after Warren's appointment. In the *Cramer* decision (1945), which had its roots in an abortive wartime German sabotage operation, the Supreme Court threw out a death sentence for treason, since the Constitution specifically provides that "no person shall be convicted for treason unless on the testimony of two witnesses to the same overt act." [39] Though there were two witnesses, neither gave evidence of any overt act. Nevertheless, Douglas dissented sharply by insisting that the mere presence of Cramer in the company of two German saboteurs was sufficient to warrant conviction.[40]

Having failed to get a pro-German electrocuted, Douglas, who later posed as the archenemy of capital punishment, failed in another dissent to save a pro-Russian from prison. In *Dennis* v. *United States* (1950) his minority opinion defined Communist appeals to revolution as strictly within the law.[41] In view of his libertarian tilt it came as no surprise that, when the Court refused to review the Rosenberg atomic spy case in 1953, the defense attorneys turned directly to Douglas, who at the last minute took it upon himself to stay the Rosenbergs' execution.[42] Douglas again exhibited his partiality for the totalitarian left when, swept up in the anti-McCarthy hysteria, he enthusiastically joined the Court majority in *Watkins* (1957), which attempted to curb the power of congressional investigations by freeing a close-mouthed fellow traveler from a contempt citation issued by the House Un-American Activities Committee.[43]

Other members of the Warren Court included William Brennan, whose father was born in Ireland and who worked his way up from coal shoveler to union agent before becoming a lawyer; Byron White, a devoted Kennedy backer, who was the highest-paid professional football player in the nation in 1938; and John M. Harlan, a Wall Street corporation lawyer, whose grandfather

---

39. Art. III, Sec. 3, Par. 1.
40. Frank, op. cit. pp. 60–61.
41. Ibid., pp. 58–59.
42. Pfeffer, op. cit., pp. 374–76.
43. Katcher, op. cit., pp. 365–68.

when serving on the Supreme Court uttered the celebrated aphorism, "The Constitution is color blind." Of all the Warren Court
justices, only Potter Stewart occasionally evinced concern for the
rights of the Majority. The lone dissenter in the school prayer
decision, he was the only one to recognize the real issue in the
case, as demonstrated by his comments that the ruling was just
as much an assault on the "religious traditions of our people"
as it was on religion itself.[44]

When Richard Nixon assumed the presidency in 1973, he made
it known he was going to reverse the leftward drift of the Court.
Although the two conservative Southern judges he nominated
were both rejected by the Senate, his nomination of Warren
Burger as chief justice was confirmed, as were his appointments
of Lewis Powell, William Rehnquist, and Harry Blackmun. With
Warren retired, Black dead, Douglas ailing, and Fortas having
resigned in disgrace, the country was primed for a legal backlash.

What the country got, however, was more of the same. The
Burger Court proved to be more ideologically attuned to the liberal-minority coalition than to Nixon. There was some tightening
up of the criminal justice system, some loosening of restrictions
on suing the government, a few reductions in the privileges of
the press, but in regard to Majority interests the Burger Court
did as much as Warren to skew the Constitution. The Burger
Nine's three most infamous decisions: (1) *Bakke* (1978), which
ordered a medical school to admit a qualified white applicant
who had been turned down in favor of less qualified Unassimilable
Minority members, while at the same time ruling that race could
be considered a factor in admissions policy; (2) *Weber* (1979),
where the Court agreed that a 50 percent quota for blacks in a
company training program was legal; (3) *Fullilove* (1980), in which
the court ruled that it was quite constitutional for the government
to specify that 10 percent of the contracts in a federal public
works program be awarded to minority contractors.

Despite its down-the-line liberal rulings on school desegregation, pornography, criminal rights, and voting rights, the Warren

---

44. Most of the biographical items in this paragraph were taken from the
chapter-length profiles of the justices in John Frank's *The Warren Court*. For
other remarks of Justice Stewart on the school prayer case, see p. 272 of this
study.

Court never went so far as to introduce the notion of racial quotas in its decisions. It left this unfinished business to the so-called moderates and conservatives of the Burger Court, who treated the American public to the spectacle of the highest tribunal in the land standing the law on its head. Congress had solemnly affirmed in the 1964 Civil Rights Act (Title VII) that there would be no racial discrimination in employment or employment opportunities. The Court brazenly sabotaged or abrogated this law in *Bakke, Weber,* and *Fullilove.*[45]

Since the one usually goes with the other, the dearth of justice displayed by the Supreme Court in the latter half of this century was accompanied by a dearth of dignity. The latter began in 1949 when Justices Frankfurter and Reed appeared in a federal court in New York City as character witnesses for Alger Hiss.[46] Since then, the internal squabbling of the justices, their lecture-circuit moonlighting, their political partisanship, and their moral cowardice have done little to restore the public's waning confidence in what used to be the most prestigious branch of American government.[47]

---

45. It is only fair to say that Justices Burger and Rehnquist dissented from most of the decisions favoring racial quotas.

46. *New York Times,* June 23, 1949, p. 1. Hiss started out as one of Frankfurter's Happy Hot Dogs at the Harvard Law School. Before he went to the State Department he had been Justice Reed's law clerk. Reed himself had clerked for Brandeis.

47. The justices of the Warren and Burger Courts have been and will be judged on their record. They will also be judged by their behavior as individuals.

Item. Fortas on the payroll of a notorious swindler. Douglas on the payroll of a gangster. Brennan involved in shady real-estate deals with Fortas.

Item. Brennan flaunting a grotesque mask of Nixon in his chambers. Marshall breaking off a lunch on "dirty movie" Monday so he wouldn't miss viewing the hardcore exhibits of obscenity cases. White appending "Some man!" to a Burger memo about Richard Speck, who raped and killed eight women.

Item. The Court reversing Muhammad Ali's conviction for draft dodging on a technicality for fear of arousing black resentment.

Item. The nearly blind Harlan running his chambers from his hospital bed and signing his bedsheet instead of a legal brief. The half-paralyzed Douglas insisting on sitting on the bench after he had resigned and when he could no longer stay awake in his wheelchair for more than an hour or two.

Item. Marshall's unwillingness to do his homework to the point where he knew nothing of the contents of some of the opinions his clerks had written for him.

Item. Marshall voting to force Nixon to turn over his tapes to Judge Sirica

Wallowing in the deceptive glow of the liberal-minority *Weltan-schauung*, the Warren and Burger courts attempted to transform the organic law of Majority America into a code of moral and racial imperatives as inapplicable to the crucial issues of the day as they were unenforceable. By its ill-timed and ill-conceived reinterpretation of the Bill of Rights and other constitutional guarantees, the Supreme Court has in effect usurped the legislative function of Congress—a gross abuse of the judicial power as defined by the Constitution. Before they addressed themselves to the impractical task of changing men by changing laws, the justices might have pondered the words of Savigny (1779–1861), who wrote in his *Theory of Organic and Natural Law:*

> Law is no more made by lawyers than language by grammarians. Law is the natural moral product of a people . . . the persistent customs of a nation, springing organically from its past and present. Even statute law lives in the general consensus of the people.[48]

Some have proposed that the best means of bringing a runaway Supreme Court to heel is by the complicated and little-used process of impeachment. But this would not eliminate the disease—only a few of the carriers. If the Court is to be fought seriously, it must be fought with its own weapons and on its own ground. That which perverts the law can be controverted by the law. The Court, one need not point out, exists and acts on the sufferance of the Constitution. One simple amendment could limit its power, narrow its functions, transfer its authority to state courts, or abolish it altogether.

When history hands down its final verdict on the Warren Court, it will be found guilty on many counts, none more serious than

---

while admitting he would not want his own taped conversations with President Johnson made public. Powell hiring a Harvard Jewish radical for his law clerk to prove he wasn't an old fuddy-duddy.

Item. William Kunstler throwing his arms around Nixon appointee Blackmun after he had supported a lower court's ruling against the Philadelphia police department.

For all the above—and more—see Bob Woodward and Scott Armstrong, *The Brethren,* Simon and Schuster, New York, 1979.

48. As quoted from Carl Becker, *The Declaration of Independence,* Knopf, New York, 1942, p. 264.

its tampering with the criminal law. Criminal justice was originally intended to protect society from the lawbreaker. By the time the Warren Court had finished with it, its chief function was to protect the lawbreaker from society. Moreover the Court's exaggerated magnification of criminal rights worked directly to the advantage of the minorities that shelter criminal castes within their ranks. With batteries of expensive lawyers at their beck and call, organized criminals, whether they belong to the Mafia, black revolutionary cadres, anti-Soviet Jewish terrorist units, or bomb-planting student gangs, stand to gain much greater benefits from legal permissiveness than the criminal loner. Also, by arousing false expectations of immediate economic gain and by seemingly agreeing that Negro poverty and underachievement were entirely the fault of past and present discrimination on the part of malevolent whites, the Court actually raised racial tensions. When to the tom-tom beat of media demands for "redressing wrongs" the enemy is officially identified by nine venerable black-robed justices, he is not hated less, but more.

As will be seen in the next chapter, the Supreme Court has opened a Pandora's box which may not be closed again without repressive measures that will put criminal justice, and much else of what remains of American jurisprudence back several centuries. Only the complete repudiation and reversal of the Supreme Court's major rulings on criminal rights will provide the necessary legal machinery for weeding out the blight that has all but ended Western civilization in wide areas of America's largest cities. Meanwhile, as crime grows beyond all endurance, so does the catalog of criminals and of those who work hand in glove with criminals. This catalog is now so large and so replete with famous names that it is beginning to resemble *Who's Who in America.*

CHAPTER 30

The Minority Underground

THE LEAST SAVORY dimension of the conflict being waged against the Majority is the underground war, which the media euphemistically call a crime wave. The extent and ferocity of this war is revealed by the number of casualties released periodically by the Federal Bureau of Investigation in the form of crime statistics. Responsible for some of this lawbreaking are the criminal elements present in every society and in every race. But an increasing share of it is due to the calculated efforts of minority groups and minority individuals.

In the period 1960–72, crime in the United States went up 191.7 percent while the population increased about 14 percent. Although this dismaying trend fell off somewhat during the rest of the 70s, there were 12,152,730 reported crimes in 1979, of which 1,178,539 were categorized as violent. Violent crimes broke down into 21,456 murders and non-negligent manslaughter cases (up 34.1 percent from 1970); 75,989 forcible rapes (up 100 percent); 466,881 robberies (up 33.4 percent); 614,213 aggravated assaults (up 83.4 percent). Nonviolent crime accounted for: 3,299,484 burglaries (up 49.6 percent from 1970); 6,577,518 larceny-thefts (up 55.7 percent); 1,097,189 motor vehicle thefts (up 18.2 percent). Altogether these figures indicate one violent crime every 27 seconds and one property crime every 3 seconds. Of the 16,955 offenders identified with 15,040 murders, 49 percent were white, 48 percent black, 3 percent "other races." Fifty percent of those arrested for forcible rape were white, 48 percent black.[1] The race of the rape victims was not specified. It is possible

---

1. *Crime in the United States (1972)* and *(1979)*, Uniform Crime Reports, Federal Bureau of Investigation, Washington, D.C. The racial picture of contemporary

half a million forcible rapes occurred in 1979, since some criminologists say only one out of seven rape victims goes to the police. Consequently rape, no matter how it is counted, is increasing faster than any other crime. With regard to other criminal offenses, a presidential crime commission has stated that less than half are reported.[2] But merely on the basis of reported crimes, it is a mathematical probability that a criminal act will be committed against one out of every five American families every year.[3] According to former Senator Kenneth Keating of New York, "Every one in this land can expect to be a victim of a major crime at least once in his lifetime if he lives to be sixty years old." [4]

Correlated with the crime explosion, and a major contributory factor, were several Supreme Court rulings against standardized methods and practices of bringing criminals to trial. In *Gideon* v. *Wainwright* (1963) the Court upheld the right of the accused to counsel, if necessary at the taxpayers' expense. In *Escobedo* v. *Illinois* (1964) it held that a suspect may not be prevented from seeing his lawyer during police interrogation. In *Miranda* v. *Arizona* (1966) the Court stated that police must warn the suspect of his right to remain silent and to be represented by counsel before being questioned.[5] Since all these decisions were retroactive, their effect on already crowded court calendars and on already overburdened law enforcement officers was disastrous. After *Gideon,* in Florida alone 976 prisoners were set free and excused from retrial, while 500 more had to be arraigned a second time.[6]

For the Court to indulge in such a sweeping extension of due

American crime is perhaps better illustrated by the table in Appendix B (see p. 568).

2. *San Francisco Examiner,* June 4, 1963, p. 1. Only about one-tenth of shoplifting incidents are reported. Retailers say they could lower prices 15 percent across the board if shoplifting was halted. *New York Times Magazine,* March 15, 1970.

3. As stated by Earl Morris, president of the American Bar Association. *U.S. News & World Report,* Feb. 5, 1968, p. 50.

4. *Wall Street Journal,* Vol. LXV, No. 68, p. 1.

5. *Time,* July 4, 1969, p. 63. Escobedo, who was freed while serving a murder sentence as a result of the Supreme Court's ruling that bears his name, was later rearrested for selling 11 grams of heroin. *San Francisco Chronicle,* Aug. 4, 1967, p. 2.

6. Anthony Lewis, *Gideon's Trumpet,* Random House, New York, 1964, p. 205.

process at the very moment it was becoming impossible for millions of American citizens to walk the streets of their own cities at night was sheer judicial irresponsibility. Again, as it had in the miscegenation, school desegregation, and school prayer rulings, the Court was playing favorites. Again, as in nearly all its landmark decisions, it ruled in favor of plaintiffs represented by minority lawyers in appeals financed largely by minority organizations.

Although the marked increase in crime could be attributed in part to the breakdown of law enforcement caused by the Court's coddling of criminals, it was due in larger part to the appearance of a new criminal type. Not that there was anything new about minority crime in America. As Samuel Eliot Morison wrote, the "alliance between urban politicians, the underworld of gambling and prostitution, and the foreign vote was already established in 1850." [7] But the invasion of the cities by an army of Negro looters, arsonists, and snipers a century later raised minority crime to the level of urban warfare.

The property loss and death toll caused by Negro insurrections in major cities in 1964–68 have been given previously.[8] In 1969, while white businesses were still counting their losses in the larger metropolitan slums, Negroes turned their attention to the ghetto commercial areas in the middle-sized cities. Concurrently, there was a mounting incidence of attacks on white policemen. No longer a common thief or mugger but a self-appointed revolutionary, the Negro criminal began to be looked upon by his own people, and by more than a few whites, as a kind of twentieth-century Robin Hood.[9] The armed takeover of college buildings

---

7. Morison, *The Oxford History of the American People,* p. 487.

8. See p. 220.

9. Most leading Negro militants acquired a criminal record long before they became revolutionaries. Malcolm X was a convicted pimp, dope peddler, and robber; Eldridge Cleaver, a convicted rapist; H. Rap Brown, a convicted burglar. The crimes committed by Bobby Seale and others in the line of their revolutionary services for the Black Panthers overshadowed their earlier lawbreaking. The hero worship of these individuals by the Negro community and by many white liberals and white minority leaders was probably as great an incentive to Negro crime as the orders of white mayors forbidding the police to shoot looters. Summing up the attitude of Negro slum dwellers, a weekly news magazine reported, they "not only passively accept crime, but also actively admire the crimi-

by black students and the armed invasion of a state legislature by swaggering black commandos were greeted as acts of liberation.[10] There remained, of course, considerable black-on-black crime. But as white city dwellers and suburbanites were learning firsthand, more and more violent crime was becoming black on white.[11]

Negro lawbreaking has been militarized in the sense that much of it is committed against "the enemy," in the sense that many victims do not bother to report offenses to the police but simply become "casualties" and silently await further attacks by foraging bands from the inviolate sanctuaries of metropolitan ghettos, where white Americans are no safer than they would have been in a Viet Cong stronghold. Negro crime has also been tribalized in that it is becoming an initiation rite and a proof of bravery. In 1972 members of a black group called De Mau Mau were charged with killing nine whites in Illinois.[12] In the 1973 Zebra murder rampage in California, a Negro gang named the Death

---

nals—especially if their victims are white." *Time,* Feb. 14, 1969, p. 60. Charles Evers, a Southern Negro politician widely praised by the media and his black constituents, is a former pimp who has frequently neglected to pay his income taxes. Ronald Reagan was pleased to receive Evers's endorsement in the 1980 presidential campaign.

10. In 1967 a group of Negroes with loaded rifles marched into the state capitol at Sacramento, Calif., while the legislature was in session. Punishment was meted out lightly or not at all. *New York Times,* May 3, 1967, p. 24.

11. A 1970 government report stated that urban blacks are arrested eight to twenty times more often than whites for homicide, rape, aggravated assault, and robbery. Since a large proportion of the victims of black crime are blacks, the report concluded that no racial factors were involved. *New York Times,* Sept. 8, 1970, p. 1. That one particular race has a crime rate several times higher than other races may not have any racial connotations to government bureaucrats, but it has many such connotations to whites attacked by Negro muggers. If 60 to 70 percent of black crimes are committed against blacks, that still leaves tens of thousands of violent crimes each year to be committed by blacks against whites. In Washington, D.C., for example, in 1959–65, nine out of ten rapists were black and 59 percent of the white women attacked were victims of Negroes. *San Francisco Chronicle,* Jan. 4, 1967, p. 2. Another ominous trend is the kidnapping of young white women in broad daylight. One blonde housewife was abducted from a Birmingham bus station and taken to a black-operated house of prostitution. After three days she managed to escape by jumping out of a second-story window. *Birmingham News,* June 10, 1980, p. 1.

12. *Miami Herald,* Oct. 16, 1972, p. 2-A.

Angels murdered twenty-three whites, torturing one for almost a day before cutting him up into small pieces, wrapping the remains in a plastic bag, and dumping them on a nearby beach. A reporter who wrote a book about the grisly racial killings said the white death toll really amounted to 135 males, 75 females, and 60 children. Gang members received special promotions and commendations from their leaders for the murder of white children.[13] Something similar happened in Michigan. The leader of a gang of young Negroes told a twenty-two-year-old member: "Prove yourself a black warrior. Bring in the ears of a white man." The young black obeyed, leaving a sixteen-year-old white youth not only earless but dead.[14] In the 1980 Miami riot whites unfortunate enough to blunder into the riot area were mutilated both before and after being killed.

It is true there has been some backlash of white violence, some evidence of white vengeance on blacks, such as sniper killings in various cities in 1980. But the number of blacks killed or wounded has been minuscule compared to the number of white casualties. Although black criminals have been gunned down while threatening the lives of police officers or while fleeing from the scenes of crimes, the number of white policemen gunned down by blacks has been substantially greater. From 1970 to 1979, 1,143 law enforcement officers have been killed, 89 percent of them white. The murderers were divided about equally: 792 whites and 779 blacks. Seventeen criminals were slain by law enforcement officers in 1979, compared to 106 law enforcement officers killed, 93 of them white, 10 black.[15] At the rate indicated above, it will not be long until the number of white police officers killed by blacks will equal the number of blacks killed by Southern lynch mobs. According to the *Encyclopaedia Britannica*, 4,730 persons were lynched in the United States from 1882 to 1951: 1,293 whites and 3,437 Negroes.[16]

---

13. Clark Howard, *Zebra*, Richard Marek Publishing, New York, 1979, see especially pp. 34, 173–81.

14. The youth group, it might be added, had received financial support from the "respectable," tax-exempt Urban League. *New York Times*, March 4, 1970, p. 31.

15. *Crime in the United States (1979)*.

16. *Ency. Brit.*, Vol. 14, p. 526.

"Police brutality," whether real or imagined, has been developed into a standard excuse for Negro rioting and looting. As a result, police officers in most cities have been ordered to use minimum force against black lawbreakers. The ever present threat of black rioting has also caused judges and juries to lean over backwards to give accused blacks every benefit of the law and the lightest possible sentences. A stiff sentence in a well-publicized trial can cause a city tens of millions of dollars in damaged, burned-out, and looted property. The same exaggerated leniency extends to capital punishment. As of early 1981, only three criminals had been executed in the United States since 1967. All three were white, although death rows teem with blacks.

Black-on-white crimes have been committed against every stratum of white society. A white judge was shot dead in his courtroom in California by blacks. A black robber seriously wounded Senator John Stennis outside his home in Washington, D.C. But by and large most white victims have been the owners or employees of fast-food stores, gas stations, and small retail establishments. All too often, after the cash register has been emptied, the robbers kill the robbed.

Meanwhile the other large criminal caste,[17] the Cosa Nostra, has grown less militant and even semi-respectable as it has scaled new heights of prosperity, its members having given up their white neckties and broad-brimmed hats for conservative Brooks Brothers styles. Some of the ceremonial claptrap has been waived, but the blood oath remains, as does the basic requirement for membership, the racial test of Southern Italian or Sicilian parentage.[18]

This racial test has only been suspended for Jews, who have supplied the Mafia with most of its legal and financial brains. Indeed the Mob's leadership, according to Ralph Salerno, former New York City Police Department crime expert, has always been a "happy marriage of Italians and Jews." Meyer Lansky, for many

---

17. Gypsies may also be defined as a criminal caste. The Latin-American gangs who are taking over much of the drug trade are more accurately described as "families." Hasidic Jews, who traditionally engage in jewel smuggling, do not consider their occupation a crime because it is only against "Gentile Law." Yaffe, op. cit., p. 120. In regard to Jewish crime in general, Yaffe has written, "Nobody, no matter how reprehensible, ever gets completely read out of the Jewish community." Ibid., p. 277.

18. *Time*, Aug. 22, 1969, pp. 19, 21.

decades the Cosa Nostra's financial director, said with some understatement, "We're bigger than U.S. Steel." Since Mafia gross revenues are estimated at over $30 billion a year with annual profits of from $7 billion to $10 billion, he could have included a few more corporations.[19] The wealth of some Mafiosos is almost beyond belief: $521,000 in cash was found in a suitcase belonging to the son of Buffalo's Boss Magaddino; New York's Boss Gambino and his adopted family had real estate holdings valued at $300 million; Philadelphia's Boss Bruno, when asked to produce collateral for a business venture, came up with a certified check for $50 million.[20]

The Cosa Nostra flourishes because of what might be described as political protection in depth. At one time mobsters exercised varying degrees of control over some twenty-five congressmen as well as thousands of lesser political figures at state and local levels.[21] The servile relationships of certain New York City and Chicago judges to Mafia leaders are too well known to need documentation. According to *Look* magazine, Mayor Alioto of San Francisco had direct connections with the underworld and even arranged a series of loans totaling $105,000 for notorious Cosa Nostra killer, Jimmy Fratianno.[22] Frank Sinatra, an associate of leading mob figures,[23] was for years one of the chief fund raisers of the Democratic party before he offered his talents to the Repub-

---

19. Ibid., p. 18.   20. Ibid., p. 21.

21. Ibid., p. 19. As excerpted by *Time* from the book, *The Crime Federation* by Ralph Salerno. New Jersey Cosa Nostra leader Joe Zicarelli, according to Salerno, wielded such power over Congressman Cornelius Gallagher that he could summon him from the floor of the House of Representatives to answer his phone calls. Gallagher was a member of the House Government Operations Committee, which watches over the federal agencies which in turn watch over the Mafia. In 1972 he pleaded guilty to evading $74,000 in income taxes. *Miami Herald*, Dec. 22, 1972, p. 36-A.

22. *Look*, Sept. 23, 1969, p. 17. Alioto's libel action as a result of *Look's* article ended in two mistrials. Fratianno later became a government witness against his former Mafia associates.

23. Sinatra was a personal friend of Lucky Luciano, once the nation's top-ranking gangster, and owned 9 percent of the Mafia-controlled Sands Hotel in Las Vegas before Howard Hughes bought it. Ed Reid and Ovid Demaris, *The Green Felt Jungle*, Pocket Books, New York, 1964, pp. 56, 74–76, 198. Sinatra's gaming license, revoked in 1963 because of his association with gangster Sam Giancana, was restored in modified form in 1981 by the Nevada Gaming Control Board.

licans. For his work in organizing and directing the 1961 pre-Inaugural Ball in Washington, Sinatra received the profuse thanks of President Kennedy and the first dance with the First Lady.[24] Even Barry Goldwater, who despite his many failings was at least considered one of the most honest presidential candidates in decades, was quite close to two important underworld members. Of gangster Gus Greenbaum, who died with his wife in a macabre gangland double murder in Phoenix on Dec. 3, 1958, Goldwater said, "I knew him all my life." Goldwater was also a good friend of Willie Bioff, a convicted panderer and gangland extortionist, whom the Arizona senator piloted back from Las Vegas to Phoenix in his own plane only two weeks before Bioff was blown to fragments when he tried to start his car.[25]

Although the Cosa Nostra buys most of its protection, some of it is furnished free of charge in the form of Italian-American solidarity. After the confessions of Joseph Valachi, a renegade Mafioso, had been written at the request of the Department of Justice, twelve prominent Italian Americans, including four Congressmen, met with Attorney General Katzenbach and demanded publication be stopped. The Justice Department obediently started action to prevent Peter Maas, a writer working with Valachi, from "disseminating or publishing" the manuscript.[26]

Mario Procaccino, the Democratic candidate in the 1969 New York City mayoralty race, was equally sensitive about the Mafia. Although Procaccino was not known to have any direct ties to gangsters, he nevertheless repeatedly refused to condemn the Cosa Nostra, even while going to great pains to stress the "law and order" theme in his campaign. "I don't know any Mafias," he declared. "I never have and I never will. Don't talk about the Mafia to me because I think it's insulting. . . . "[27] The Italian-

---

24. Victor Lasky, *JFK, The Man and the Myth*, Macmillan, New York, 1963, p. 14.

25. Reid and Demaris, op. cit., pp. 43, 144, 202.

26. It took a long court battle to get permission to publish the material, finally entitled *The Valachi Papers*. In the interim Valachi tried to commit suicide. *Reader's Digest*, January 1969, pp. 224–25.

27. *New York Times Magazine*, Aug. 10, 1969, p. 62. Many years earlier, Frank McGee, the noted TV commentator, had taken the same line as Procaccino by asserting on Aug. 29, 1958, "we have come to the conclusion that the Mafia

American Civil Rights League, founded by Joseph Colombo, Sr., the head of a Mafia family, also denied the Mafia's existence and persuaded the Justice Department to stop referring to the Mafia or Cosa Nostra by name.[28] Since both Procaccino and the League were based in New York City, it would seem incredible that the Mafia had escaped their attention, particularly after a well-known New York political figure, James L. Marcus, was sentenced to jail for dividing a kickback from a municipal reservoir project with a leading Cosa Nostra gangster.[29]

Other gangster links to the highest levels of government can be detected in the executive pardons issued frequently to important gangsters. Lucky Luciano, who succeeded Al Capone at the top of the Mafia hierarchy and who was a specialist in narcotics, murder, and prostitution, was given a full pardon by New York Governor Thomas Dewey in 1946.[30] Luciano's influence was so global that, working through the American army in World War II, he actually helped reestablish the Mafia in its original Sicilian homeland where it had been stripped of most of its power during the Mussolini era. At his direction American planes dropped special packages to the world Mafia chieftain, Don Calo Vizzini, in the town of Villaba.[31]

President Kennedy gave a presidential pardon to another gangster, Jake (the Barber) Factor, who was scheduled for deportation by the Department of Justice but made a citizen after he contributed $10,000 to the Democratic party.[32] Factor repaid the favor

---

in this country is a foolish and distracting myth." Musmanno, *The Story of the Italians*, p. 202. In spite of, or perhaps because of, his Mafia blindness, McGee remained at his influential job until his death in 1974.

28. *Time,* July 12, 1971, pp. 14–15.

29. It was the Cosa Nostra's loan shark operations which drew Marcus, whose wife was the daughter of former Connecticut Governor John Cabot Lodge, into the net. He could not afford the 104 percent yearly interest, so he tried to repay gangster Anthony Corallo in other ways. *Time,* Aug. 22, 1969, p. 20. The Cosa Nostra, it might be added, is also in the loan *receiving* business. The Small Business Administration admitted in 1969 that it had loaned more than $1,000,000 to the ANR Leasing Corp., a Mafia-controlled trucking concern in the Bronx. *New York Times,* April 27, 1969, p. 1.

30. *New York Times,* Feb. 9, 1946, p. 19.

31. *Times Literary Supplement,* June 18, 1964, p. 534.

32. *New York Times,* Dec. 29, 1963, p. 4.

by increasing his donations, and in 1968 he was revealed to be the largest financial contributor to the Democratic party's presidential campaign.[33] Another questionable pardon was given by President Truman to movie mogul Joseph Schenck, after he had been sent to prison for lying about his Mafia associations.[34]

There is no more visible sign of national decay than the continuing success story of the Cosa Nostra, an organization which, among other things, sold $350,000,000 worth of heroin a year way back in the 60s, before hard drugs had become big business.[35] Majority and minority politicians and public figures are still shocked and horrified by Nazi misdeeds decades after the fact, but neither they nor the news media are half so upset about atrocities practiced by Mafia thugs upon thousands of Americans. Though Cosa Nostra leaders have moved to exclusive suburbs and now greet each other in public with handshakes instead of kisses, some still boast about sending their victims to Mafia-owned wholesale meat houses, from which they are distributed to restaurants in the form of "manburgers." [36] While the media still concentrate on Nazi or Soviet brutality, the Mafia has refined a particularly painful murder technique in which death is accomplished by inserting the end of a home fire extinguisher in the condemned man's ears.[37] Police tapped and taped one Mafia telephone conversation in which a giggling gangland executioner described in minute detail the last three days of a man who had been hung on a meat hook and who "flopped around . . . screaming" when tortured with an electric prod.[38]

As two veteran crime reporters have summed it up:

> Slowly, but inexorably, the Mafia has assumed a position of supremacy that is total and absolute. . . . Every Mafioso, young or old, truly believes that he has an inalienable right to traffic in dope

---

33. *San Francisco Sunday Examiner and Chronicle, This World,* Jan. 12, 1969. Factor and his wife allegedly donated or loaned $350,000 to various Humphrey-Muskie organizations.

34. *San Francisco Chronicle, This World,* Oct. 25, 1961, p. 22. Schenck died a multimillionaire in his penthouse suite at the Beverly Wilshire Hotel.

35. Donald Cressey, *Theft of the Nation,* Harper & Row, New York, 1969, pp. 91–92.

36. *Saturday Evening Post,* Nov. 9, 1963, p. 21.

37. Ibid.

38. *Time,* Aug. 22, 1969, p. 22.

and prostitution, to plunder and murder. The laws of organized society do not bind him.[39]

Collective or organized crime having become a minority monopoly, the law of averages would predict that most of the "independent" criminals, most of the criminal loners, would be Majority members. But such is not the case. Here again, the minority overrepresentation is incontestable. The fact is, whenever a Majority member, particularly a well-known Majority public figure, is haled into court, it is surprising how often his partner or associate is a minority member.

The following roster of peculations, embezzlements, tax evasions, serious crimes, petty thefts, conflicts of interest, or betrayals of public trust is restricted to people of national or local importance. Occasionally the catalog of wrongdoing includes crimes in which the minority connection is tenuous or nonexistent. In such cases the intention is to demonstrate the moral degradation of Majority leaders in an era of minority domination—a degradation that has been both a cause and an effect of such domination.[40]

To begin at the top, one of the ugliest aspects of American crime has been its frequent appearance in the ambit of the presidency. Not one administration in recent decades has remained unscathed. Most, if not all, presidents or presidential candidates have engaged at one time or another in highly questionable conduct or have had known lawbreakers as friends, advisers, or fund raisers. A typical example was President Truman's close association with the flamboyantly corrupt Pendergast machine, which sponsored his entry into politics. In 1939 Boss Tom Pendergast, one of Truman's closest friends, went to jail for income tax evasion. In 1945, when Truman was vice-president, Pendergast died. Truman immediately flew to St. Louis and lent the dignity of

---

39. Reid and Demaris, op. cit., pp. 186–87. Members of the Mafia, according to C. D. Darlington, are prisoners of their genes: "[P]eople for whom there is no possibility of coercion, correction or conversion. Nothing on earth will make them come to terms with the general body of society. They are a race apart." *The Evolution of Man and Society,* p. 611.

40. Different races and population groups seem to have different propensities for crime—the Negro for crimes of violence, the Mediterranean for crimes of passion, the Jew for financial crimes. Generally speaking, the unassimilated or partly assimilated have less of a built-in crime deterrent because they have fewer emotional and personal attachments to the state and to the law of the state.

the second highest office in the land to the last rites of a convicted felon. A few months later, when he became president, Truman pardoned fifteen Pendergast henchmen who had been jailed for stuffing ballot boxes.[41]

It was Truman who pardoned Mayor Curley of Boston for a previous criminal conviction and reduced Curley's jail sentence for mail fraud.[42] It was Truman who appointed Mayor O'Dwyer of New York, a friend of gangster Frank Costello, ambassador to Mexico, and spirited him out of the country just in time to escape being arrested on charges of graft.[43] Truman made a further attempt to obstruct the course of justice, when he called the Alger Hiss case, months before it came to trial, a "red herring." [44]

The mink coat and deep freeze payoffs to Truman cronies made many headlines during the Truman administration. But it was not known until after Truman had left office that his commissioner of internal revenue, Joseph Nunan, Jr., had been evading income taxes as well as collecting them, and that his assistant attorney general in charge of the Justice Department's Tax Division, T. Lamar Caudle, had been conspiring with men like Abraham Teitlebaum, a former lawyer for Al Capone, to avoid tax payments.[45] Nunan went to jail in 1957, and Caudle, who served only six months of his three-year sentence, was imprisoned in 1960.[46] Even J. Howard McGrath, Truman's attorney general, had a brush with the law as the result of mail fraud charges against the International Guaranty and Insurance Co., of which he and Jake Ehrlich, the headline-hunting criminal lawyer, were trustees.[47]

---

41. Jules Abels, *The Truman Scandals,* Henry Regnery, Chicago, 1956, pp. 22–23.

42. Ibid., p. 32.

43. Ibid., p. 36.

44. Although he later changed his mind about Communists, Truman, following the pattern established by Franklin Roosevelt, retained in office several key bureaucrats whom the FBI had certified as bona fide Soviet agents, among them Assistant Secretary of the Treasury Harry Dexter White. Chambers, *Witness,* pp. 68, 510.

45. *New York Times,* May 24, 1957, p. 17 and May 5, 1960, p. 29.

46. *New York Times,* Oct. 30, 1960, p. 81.

47. *New York Times,* Nov. 25, 1961, p. 1, and March 30, 1963, p. 7. Both McGrath and Ehrlich signed their names to the very brochure for which Stewart

President Eisenhower's administration produced little to compare with the scandals of the Truman era, although Sherman Adams, Eisenhower's chief assistant, was forced to resign when it was revealed he had received various gifts and subsidies from Bernard Goldfine. Jailed in 1961 for dodging taxes to the amount of $7,838,298,[48] Goldfine was paroled in less than two years after serving a good part of his sentence in a hospital.[49] Eisenhower himself accepted expensive gifts from well-wishers, but unlike Adams did not exert any influence on their behalf with federal agencies. Senator Payne of Maine, who received more of Goldfine's largesse than Adams, was resoundingly defeated in his try for reelection in 1958.[50]

The enormous Billie Sol Estes swindle began in the Eisenhower years, but climaxed in the Kennedy administration. Estes, with high connections in Texas and national politics, managed to defraud the Department of Agriculture of $500,000 by falsifying inventory records. He was finally sent to prison, but no one has yet been able to discover how he managed to bilk so many important government officials, not just once but again and again. When the investigation started, the ranking Department of Agriculture official in Texas, Hilton Bates, "committed suicide" by the astonishing feat of shooting himself five times with a bolt-action rifle. The Department of Agriculture official who bore the chief responsibility for the payments to Estes turned out to be Under Secretary Thomas Murphy, who had been appointed through the efforts of Estes's friend, Lyndon Johnson, at that time senator from Texas.[51]

President Kennedy's administration, aside from the Estes affair and being beholden to people like Frank Sinatra, was relatively clean—or so it appeared at the time. Later it was discovered that Kennedy, an inveterate womanizer, had had a banal affair with a Mafia moll named Judith Exner. He entertained her frequently

---

Hopps, the promoter of the insurance company, was convicted of mail fraud. Both McGrath and Ehrlich got off scot-free.

48. *New York Times,* Jan. 30, 1962, p. 12, and June 6, 1961, p. 20.

49. *New York Times,* Feb. 21, 1963, p. 10.

50. *New York Times,* Sept. 9, 1958, p. 1.

51. Clark Mollenhoff, *Despoilers of Democracy,* Doubleday, New York, 1965, Chapters 7–9.

in the White House when his wife was absent and made many long-distance phone calls to her in Chicago while she was sitting beside Mafia Boss Sam Giancana.

The black sheep of the Kennedy family, excluding father Joseph Kennedy who made millions in Wall Street by selling short at the start of the depression,[52] is Senator Ted. Ted was expelled from Harvard in 1951, after he had persuaded a fellow student to take a Spanish exam for him.[53] Family influence got him reinstated two years later, though students who had committed much lesser offenses were expelled permanently. In the summer of 1969, on the night before two Americans landed on the moon, Kennedy drove his car off a bridge, drowning his young female passenger, Mary Jo Kopechne. A few days later the senator, who had waited ten hours before notifying the police, was given a two-month prison sentence (suspended) for leaving the scene of an accident. After the inquest, which had been held in secret, Judge James Boyle accused Kennedy of driving "negligently" and of having "contributed to the death" of Miss Kopechne.[54]

While her husband was president, Jacqueline Kennedy, whose mechanical charm and artistic affectations, however galling, were at least an improvement on the dowdiness of her immediate predecessors, took an extended Mediterranean cruise on the yacht of Aristotle Onassis, the Greek shipping magnate indicted in 1953 for conspiracy to defraud the United States. To escape being arrested the next time he visited his New York office, Onassis had to pay a $7,000,000 fine.[55] Even in the reigns of the most depraved emperors it would have been unthinkable for a first lady of Rome to consort publicly with a man who had admittedly defrauded

---

52. A typical Kennedy operation was the Libbey-Owens-Ford pool, in which he and the banking house of Kuhn, Loeb had the biggest interest. The group got control of 1,000,000 shares of the company's stock, forced down the price by selling short, and then bought in before the shares went up. Kennedy got $60,805 for his part in the transaction. No one invested a penny. Frank Cormier, *Wall Street's Shady Side*, Public Affairs Press, Washington, D.C., 1962, pp. 3, 9.

53. *New York Times*, March 31, 1962, p. 1.

54. *The Inquest*, EVR Production, Inc., New York, 1970, p. 126.

55. Using dummy corporations, Onassis bought wartime Liberty ships, which by federal law were reserved for sale to American citizens in order to build up the postwar American merchant marine. *New York Times*, Feb. 26, 1963, p. 2, Feb. 9, 1954, p. 1, and Dec. 22, 1955, p. 47.

the empire. It would have been doubly unthinkable that, when she became a widow, she would marry him. The Kennedy-Onassis wedding in 1967, however, was not too surprising from a racial perspective. Jacqueline's paternal great-grandfather was a carpenter from Southern France. Her father, who had a darker Mediterranean coloration than Onassis, bore the nickname of "Black Jack." [56]

The Kennedy administration ended with the crime doubleheader of the century, the assassination of the president by Lee Harvey Oswald and the subsequent murder of the assassin in front of millions of television viewers by Jack Ruby (Rubenstein), a petty mobster and strip-tease entrepreneur. A racial motivation for Ruby's act has already been noted,[57] but Oswald's motives have never been satisfactorily explained. Many establishment intellectuals have struggled heroically to make the assassination the deed of a cowardly Southern white supremacist against a heroic minority president. Barbara Garson, a Jewish playwright, wrote a play, *MacBird,* which proposed that Johnson arranged Kennedy's death so he could succeed him in the presidency.[58] But the thesis of a right-wing, racist plot was laughable in view of Oswald's Communist affiliations and his minority background.[59]

The assassination in 1968 of Kennedy's brother, Robert, had

---

56. *Time,* May 16, 1969, p. E7.

57. See pp. 404.

58. It ran nearly a year in an off-Broadway theater. In 1972, a movie called "Executive Action" attributed the assassination to the machinations of a right-wing Texas plutocrat.

59. Little is known about Oswald's father, who died before his son was born. Oswald's mother (née Claverie) may have come from a Cajun family since she said her father was French and spoke French in his home. *Hearings Before the President's Commission on the Assassination of President Kennedy,* Vol. 1, pp. 252, 437. The conspiracy weavers had an easier time with the assassination of Martin Luther King, Jr., in 1967. Nevertheless James Earl Ray, the guilty party, had minority as well as Majority connections. He was born north of the Mason-Dixon line and his mother "came from a devout Irish-Catholic family." *New York Daily News,* March 11, 1969, p. 4. Not many people, however, found any plot in the slaying of George Lincoln Rockwell, American Nazi leader, by John Patsalos, a Greek American. *New York Times,* May 31, 1970, p. 8. The family origins and political connections of Arthur Bremer, the would-be assassin of George Wallace, are extremely obscure. The FBI duly certified that he was not a part of any conspiracy, though millions of Americans disagreed.

explicit instead of implicit minority connotations. In his delayed candidacy for the Democratic presidential nomination, Kennedy demanded the reduction of the American commitment to Vietnam, but insisted on maintaining the American commitment to Israel. It was after he had emphasized this point on a television broadcast that an Arab American from Palestine was sufficiently aroused to shoot him down in the basement of a Los Angeles hotel. If Kennedy had concentrated more on Majority interests and less on the interests of a minority that was not even his own, he might have become the 37th president.

As attorney general in his brother's administration, Robert Kennedy had shown some commendable zeal for law enforcement and had instituted the legal proceedings against Teamster James Hoffa which ultimately sent the boss of the nation's biggest union to jail for eight years for jury tampering.[60] Robert's refusal to pamper criminals, however, did not prevent brother John from giving a presidential pardon to convicted arms smuggler Hank Greenspun, a Las Vegas publisher and former publicity agent for gangster Bugsy Siegel.[61] Greenspun took advantage of his restored civil rights to run unsuccessfully in the Republican primary for governor of Nevada.[62]

No president has been as tainted with minority-related malfeasance and scandal as Lyndon Johnson. The most fateful and agonizing moments in Johnson's political life came in the 1948 Texas senatorial primary when he ran what almost amounted to a dead heat with his opponent, Coke Stevenson. At the very last minute, when it appeared that Stevenson was winning by 100 votes, 203 votes for Johnson were suddenly discovered, after the official counting had come to an end, in a South Texas district run by a political boss named George Parr. These 203 votes gave Johnson an 87-vote edge, the final count being 494,191 to 494,104.[63]

A preliminary investigation showed that most of these votes

60. *Facts on File*, 1967, p. 78. Also see footnote 7, p. 371, of this study.

61. The nature of Greenspun's criminal activities may explain Kennedy's leniency. See footnote 18, p. 501.

62. *Time*, Aug. 31, 1962, p. 18.

63. Harry Provence, *Lyndon B. Johnson*, Fleet, New York, 1964, pp. 81, 83–84, 86. The Mexican American who was put in charge of this vote rigging later confessed his crime on television.

came from Mexican Americans, many of whom had been so inspired by Johnson's senatorial qualifications that they had actually
risen from their graves to vote for him. When an official inquiry
began, the 203 ballots suddenly disappeared in an "accidental"
fire.[64] In the end, Johnson's political career was assured when
the state investigation was quashed and when Associate Judge
Hugo Black blocked a Court order to reopen it. It is noteworthy
that during this crucial time in Johnson's life, Abe Fortas was
his chief troubleshooter in Washington.[65]

Johnson overcame another embarrassing crisis when the Bobby
Baker case came under the halfhearted scrutiny of a Senate investi-
gating committee. Baker, while secretary to the Senate Democratic
Majority, had been a business associate of such men as Las Vegas
casino operator Ed Levinson and Miami gambler Benny
Siegelbaum.[66] Baker had also been a political protégé of Johnson,
who called him "my strong right arm" and "the last man I see
at night, the first one I see in the morning." It was no surprise
that Fortas quickly materialized as Baker's legal counsel.[67] Finally
in 1967, after Fortas had withdrawn from the case, Baker was
given a one- to three-year jail sentence for income tax evasion,
theft, and conspiracy.[68]

In his role of perennial political fixer, Fortas had previously
been ordered by the president to suppress the Jenkins scandal,
which cropped up in the middle of the 1964 presidential campaign.
Walter Jenkins, Johnson's most trusted assistant, who as secretary
of the National Security Council had access to almost every important classified document in Washington, was arrested for perversion in a YMCA men's room. Even though Jenkins, a Baptist
who converted to Catholicism, had been arrested once before for
similar activities, Johnson kept him on. Fortas, together with
Clark Clifford, later secretary of defense, called on various newspaper editors to blue-pencil the story. Some agreed, but when the

64. Robert Sherrill, *The Accidental President*, Grossman, New York, pp. 28–29,
114.

65. Roland Evans and Robert Novak, *Lyndon B. Johnson*, New American Library,
New York, 1966, p. 25.

66. *New York Times*, Jan. 14 and 15, 1964, p. 1.

67. *Esquire*, June 1965, p. 86.

68. *New York Times*, April 8, 1967, p. 1.

United Press broke the news, the censorship plot miscarried.[69]

In the matter of the probity and the close minority relationships of recent also-ran presidential candidates, Goldwater's close friendship with gangsters Gus Greenbaum and Willie Bioff has already been mentioned. Adlai Stevenson, the Democratic presidential candidate who lost to Eisenhower in 1952 and 1956, was the "political find" of lawyer Louis Kohn and Jacob Arvey, retired boss of the venal Chicago Democratic machine.[70]

Despite the financial backing of Majority corporations, much of it illegal, President Nixon went begging for campaign money from minority peculators like Robert Vesco, whose $200,000 cash contribution led to the criminal trials of former cabinet members John Mitchell and Maurice Stans. Both were leading actors in the Watergate affair, which unloosed the greatest wave of media paranoia since the attack on Senator Joseph McCarthy.[71] In an effort to make the Nixon administration a sinkhole of Majority corruption, the press carefully emphasized the German and WASP origins of some participants, while ignoring the minority background of other important wire-pullers.[72] Henry Kissinger, James Schlesinger, Caspar Weinberger, William Safire, Leonard Garment, and other Jewish members of the Nixon administration were given clean bills of health. In fact, Kissinger and Schlesinger stayed on as cabinet members in the Ford administration, while three Majority cabinet members—Maurice Stans, John Mitchell, and Richard Kleindienst—were all found guilty of various offenses, and Mitchell was sent to jail.

In one sense Watergate (and related events) was a liberal-minor-

---

69. *Life*, May 9, 1969, p. 34, and *Time*, Oct. 23, 1964, pp. 19–23.

70. Kenneth S. Davis, *The Politics of Honor*, Putnam, New York, 1967, p. 178. Stevenson, as revered by the liberal-minority coalition as was Ted Kennedy many years later, was also involved in a death incident. As a boy, he unwittingly shot and killed Ruth Merwin, a young girl who was visiting his family during the Christmas holidays. Eleanor Ives Stevenson and Hildegarde Dolson, *My Brother Adlai*, Morrow, New York, 1956, p. 72.

71. One phase of Watergate, the operation of the White House "plumbers," was triggered by the late J. Edgar Hoover, who would not permit a full-scale investigation of Ellsberg, the purloiner of the Pentagon Papers, in deference to his friendship for Louis Marx, Ellsberg's millionaire father-in-law.

72. *The Washington Post*, so bitter about the Watergate coverup, had willingly participated in the Jenkins coverup during the Johnson era.

ity purge of an entire presidential administration. Before getting rid of the president himself, Nixon's opponents found it necessary to remove Vice-President Spiro Agnew, an equally despised enemy. This was accomplished by persuading minority members who had surrounded him while he was governor of Maryland to testify about kickbacks. With Agnew safely out of the way, the media turned all their guns on Nixon, who had been the principal punching bag of the intellectual establishment ever since his election victories over Congressman Jerry Voorhis and Senator Helen Gahagan Douglas and his prominent role in the downfall of Alger Hiss. Actually, Nixon had done no more or less than several other presidents in violating his oath of office. Wiretapping the telephone of a political opponent and stealing the files of a psychiatrist, while certainly unbecoming actions for a president to condone and cover up, hardly compared to the vote fraud that put President Johnson on the political map or the semi-treasonable misdeeds of Franklin D. Roosevelt in entangling America in World War II. But as the Vietnam War demonstrated, the media had now become all-powerful. Even though Nixon had just been reelected in one of the greatest landslides in American history, in less than two years he was brought down in disgrace and forced to resign, largely by the *Washington Post* and the unblinking, all-seeing, unforgiving eye of the television tube. If there is any question as to where the real power lies in America, one has only to recall that Daniel Ellsberg, the man who stole important military secrets from the Pentagon, and the editors of the *New York Times* who published them went unpunished, while the White House agents, Gordon Liddy and E. Howard Hunt, who attempted to "get the goods" on Ellsberg, spent years behind bars. The spy went free. The spy chasers were jailed.

The administration of Gerald Ford, the first appointed president of the United States, was relatively free of scandal except for the presidential pardon accorded Nixon. The return of a Democratic administration to Washington was accompanied by a new outburst of political chicanery: the financial high jinks of President Carter's good friend and short-term budget director, Bert Lance; the involvement of several White House aides in drug use; the large "loans" made by the government of Libya to brother Billy Carter. The Carter years were also noted for multifarious crimes of congressmen, some of whom actually pocketed bribes in front of hidden TV cameras. Even though convicted of felonies and sex-related crimes, several representatives were actually reelected and returned to their seats in the House. The Reagan presidency started out with Frank Sinatra as the entertainment director of the inaugural festivities, with a Mafia-connected Teamster official on the transition team, and with the president's son the target of a securities investigation. Not a very auspicious start for what the nation hoped would be a relatively honest administration.

The decline of morality in high places is perhaps best illustrated by the careers of the four sons of Franklin Delano Roosevelt. James Roosevelt, a congressman from Los Angeles, the city with the second highest concentration of Jews in the United States, served as a kind of "minority spokesman" in Washington and after a succession of marital mishaps moved to Switzerland as an executive of a minority-owned overseas investment company.[73] Franklin D. Roosevelt, Jr., delinquent in his 1958 income taxes to the amount of $38,736, was an attorney for dictator Rafael Trujillo of the Dominican Republic.[74] John Roosevelt, the youngest brother, spoke at a 1961 Miami Beach Teamsters' Convention in support of the reelection of President James Hoffa, even then in deep difficulty with the law.[75] Elliott Roosevelt, whose five wives had made him the most married and divorced of all FDR's sons, was handpicked for mayor of Miami Beach by Louis Wolfson,[76] the celebrated corporate raider and former inmate of the federal penitentiary at Atlanta, Georgia.[77] It was this same Wolfson who,

---

73. It was in Switzerland, while working for Bernard Cornfeld, that Roosevelt was stabbed by his third wife as he was preparing to undertake his fourth marriage. *Time*, Oct. 10, 1969, p. 98. Worth $150,000,000 until the collapse of his Investors Overseas Service, Cornfeld was charged with attempted rape and indecent assault while on a visit to London in 1973. *Miami Herald*, Feb. 10, 1973, p. 9-A. After a short stint in a Swiss jail, Cornfeld moved to Beverly Hills, where he proceded to host lavish parties for the show business demimonde.

74. *New York Times*, May 23, 1963, p. 1. Franklin's third wife was Felicia Sarnoff, granddaughter of Jacob Schiff.

75. John Roosevelt was a partner in an investment counseling firm which handled a considerable amount of Teamsters' Union pension funds. Clark Mollenhoff, *Tentacles of Power*, World Publishing, Cleveland, 1965, pp. 345–46.

76. Patricia Roosevelt, *I Love a Roosevelt*, pp. 134, 251, 328, 377, 379.

77. *San Francisco Sunday Examiner and Chronicle, This World*, Dec. 15, 1968, p. 5.

when under government investigation for stock fraud, arranged to have his tax-exempt foundation pay Associate Supreme Court Justice Fortas $20,000 a year for life.[78]

Lesser minority political fry or influence peddlers who have done little to help the country that gave their immigrant forebears the first taste of freedom they had ever known include: Morris Shenker, one of Hoffa's lawyers, who paid Senator Edward Long of Missouri $48,000 while the latter's Senate subcommittee was investigating wiretapping, a method of criminal sleuthing abhorrent to Hoffa; [79] Marvin L. Kline, former mayor of Minneapolis, given a ten-year sentence for grand larceny for stealing from the Sister Kenny Foundation, a charitable organization for infantile paralysis victims; [80] Victor Orsinger, Washington lawyer, found guilty of stealing $1,500,000 from an order of Catholic nuns; [81] John Houlihan, former mayor of Oakland, California, convicted of stealing $95,000 from a trust fund of which he was the executor; [82] Hugh Addonizio of Newark, New Jersey, another ex-mayor, sentenced to ten years in prison for receiving kickbacks while in office.[83] The leading gubernatorial criminal of recent times was Marvin Mandel of Maryland, who received his under-the-table payments from racetrack operators. Perhaps the worst case of influence peddling involved House Speaker John McCormack, in whose office two political fixers, Nathan Voloshen and Martin Sweig, operated for years, sometimes even using the speak-

---

78. See Chapter 29. Fortas kept the first $20,000 installment for almost a year, long after Wolfson was formally indicted. In the meantime, he received $15,000 for a few lectures at American University's Washington College of Law. Later it was discovered the fee had not been paid by the university, but by such personages as Maurice Lazarus, department store magnate, and Gustave Levy and John Loeb, two of the world's richest private bankers. The money could be interpreted as the gift of friends or as the means by which the international banking community is able to keep a Supreme Court Justice on the payroll. *Time*, May 23, 1969, p. 23, and *Life*, May 23, 1969, pp. 38–39.

79. *Facts on File*, 1967, p. 460.

80. *New York Times*, Sept. 14, 1963, p. 10.

81. *Washington Post*, June 4, 1970, p. B4.

82. After being indicted, but before going to jail, Houlihan served a three-month stint as consultant to the Center for Study of Democratic Institutions, Santa Barbara, Calif. *New York Times*, April 30, 1966, p. 28, and Sept. 8, 1968, p. 21, and *Oakland Tribune*, June 3, 1966, p. 22.

83. Associated Press report, Sept. 23, 1970.

er's name. When Sweig and Voloshen were brought to trial, McCormack, one of the canniest politicians in Washington, claimed he was unaware of his friends' actions.[84]

With the exception of Lowell Birrell, whose father was a Protestant minister, Estes, Baker, Robert Trippet, and a few others, every notorious financial con man since World War II has been a minority member. One of the biggest swindlers, Anthony De Angelis, incredibly cheated his friends, business associates, and the United States Treasury out of some $219,000,000 in a soy bean fraud.[85] Compared to De Angelis, Eddie Gilbert, who fleeced his stockholders out of $1,900,000 and then ran off to Brazil, was a piker.[86] Another stock manipulator was Morris Schwebel who, with a few other operators, kited the price of Canadian penny stocks to five dollars a share. Later the shares turned out to be almost worthless, and the public lost $16,000,000.[87] A more vi-

84. *Life*, Oct. 31, 1969, p. 52, and *New York Times,* Jan. 13, 1970, p. 1. Representative John Dowdy of Texas and Senator Daniel Brewster of Maryland were two members of Congress involved with minority criminals. Dowdy was convicted of taking a bribe from Nathan Cohen to block a government investigation. Brewster was given two to six years for taking money from Spiegel, a mail order house.

85. *Time,* June 4, 1965, p. 20. The biggest tax dodger of them all was Samuel Cohen of Miami Beach, who, according to the Internal Revenue Service, neglected to report $25,578,000 in taxable income for the single year of 1967. Gannett News Service report, July 11, 1971. The second biggest tax dodger was Allen Glick, a gambling house operator in Nevada and Teamsters' Union associate, who owes $9,500,000 to the Internal Revenue Service in back taxes and fraud penalties, *New York Times,* June 19, 1977. Also in the running and also Jewish is Edward Krock, who was notified of his indictment for defrauding the government of $1,400,000 in taxes while taking a leisurely summer cruise on his 150-foot yacht.

86. *New York Times,* April 24, 1964, p. 1, and April 28, 1967, p. 1. Gilbert later came back and surrendered. Although Benjamin Javits, the brother of New York Senator Jacob Javits, represented him, Gilbert was sent to jail. Gilbert's rich mother then paid a large sum of money to Speaker John McCormack's fixer co-worker, Voloshen, to get her son out of jail.

87. In his trial, Schwebel was represented by former Federal Judge Simon Rifkind who explained that the defendant was a philanthropist and a religious and community leader, adding that both Schwebel and his wife had recently had heart attacks. Schwebel was fined $15,000 and sentenced to a year and a day in prison. The sentence was later suspended. *New York Times,* June 7, 1964, p. 60 and Aug. 26, 1964, p. 24.

cious type of financial predator was international banker Serge Rubinstein, who supplemented his monetary operations with draft dodging and was later murdered in gangland style.[88]

Louis Wolfson was relatively subtle in his financial dealings and leaned heavily on high government officials for support. With the help of ultraliberal Senator (now Representative) Claude Pepper of Florida and millionaire contractor Matt McCloskey, both high in Democratic party councils, Wolfson made his first killing by buying an American naval shipyard, which cost the taxpayers $19,262,725, for $1,926,500.[89] Like Wolfson, Leopold Silberstein went to jail for violating the rules of the Securities and Exchange Commission. Even the assistance of former Secretary of the Interior Oscar Chapman was unable to save him.[90] Other notorious wheeler-dealers were: David Graiver, an Argentine Jew who looted $40 million from the American Bank & Trust Co., who was chief banker for Argentina's Marxist terrorists, and who may or may not have died in an airplane crash in Mexico as he was fleeing New York police; Robert Vesco, the inheritor of Bernard Cornfeld's crumbling financial empire, who managed to filch $224,000,000 from four mutual funds; Michele Sindona, a Sicilian, who precipitated the failure of the Franklin National Bank, the biggest bank crash in American history, by misusing $45,000,000 of its funds; Rabbi Bernard Bergman, who defrauded Medicare of $1,200,000 and was given a four-month jail sentence; Eli Black, president of United Brands, who jumped from his forty-fourth floor office after being involved in a million-dollar bribery scandal; [91] and Stanley Goldblum of Equity Funding, who supervised the forging of $200,000,000 worth of insurance policies.[92]

Last, but not least, there is Roy Cohn, who has recently spent a great deal of his life in court defending himself—so far successfully—against an apparently never ending series of charges ranging from conspiracy and mail fraud to bribery, extortion, and

---

88. *Time,* May 6, 1946, p. 84, and Feb. 7, 1955, pp. 16–17.

89. Leslie Gould, *The Manipulators,* David McKay, New York, 1966, pp. 5–6.

90. Benjamin Javits was also Silberstein's lawyer. Ibid., p. 53.

91. For Graiver, see *New York Times,* Nov. 28, 1972, p. 1; Vesco, *Wall St. Journal,* April 13, 1978, p. 13; Sindona, *Village Voice,* Jan. 21, 1980, p. 27; Black, *New York Times,* Feb. 4, 1975, p. 1; Bergman, UPI report, June 18, 1971.

92. *Miami Herald,* April 22, 1973, p. 7-E.

blackmail.[93] If Jewish lawyer Abe Fortas symbolizes the corruption of the liberal-minority coalition, Jewish lawyer Cohn, former aide to the late Senator Joseph McCarthy, is the symbol of the spiritual desiccation of so-called American conservatism. In 1964, after Cohn had won acquittal in one trial, he received congratulations from Cardinal Spellman, Senator Dirksen, and Senator Eastland.[94] Among Cohn's other friends are Senator Edward Long of Missouri, whose relationship with Hoffa was mentioned previously, and William F. Buckley, Jr.[95]

But Cohn's most important connections were Lewis Rosenstiel, the multimillionaire founder of Schenley Industries, and Louis Nichols, former assistant to the director of the FBI. Both men were extremely close to FBI head J. Edgar Hoover. Rosenstiel was the largest single contributor to the J. Edgar Hoover Foundation and Rosenstiel's own foundation helped subsidize two books on the FBI, one of which was authored by Hoover.[96] Cohn is also known to have been friendly with Congressman Emanuel Celler, chairman of the House Judiciary Committee, Congressman Cornelius Gallagher, who was openly accused of close association with the Cosa Nostra, and Edwin Weisl, President Johnson's financial adviser and personal ambassador to New York's Democratic party.[97] It was on Cohn's yacht that ex-Tammany Boss and convicted extortioner Carmine DeSapio and other Democratic bigwigs chose a slate of judges for the 1969 New York City election.

A month before the 1968 presidential race, Cohn gave three checks amounting to $9,000 to Republican candidates. In return he was allegedly assured that Chairman Manuel Cohen of the Securities and Exchange Commission and Robert Morgenthau, federal attorney for the Southern District of New York, his alleged

---

93. *New York Times*, Dec. 14, 1969, p. 74.

94. *Life*, Sept. 5, 1969, p. 28.

95. Cohn arranged for a Chicago bank in which he had an interest to give Senator Long a $100,000 unsecured loan. Cohn also got a $60,000 loan for Buckley, who used it to buy a 60-foot sloop. *Life*, Sept. 5, 1969, pp. 28–29.

96. *Life*, Sept. 5, 1969, pp. 29–30.

97. Ibid., pp. 28–29. Weisl was also a director of Cenco Instruments Corp., controlled by Alfred E. Strelsin, one of the country's wealthiest and most dedicated Zionists. Cenco was banned from the New York Stock Exchange for inventory fraud in 1975.

"persecutors," would be removed if Nixon won. After the election Cohen was replaced forthwith, and Morgenthau fired a few months later.[98] The involvement of the Nixon administration with such shabby promoters as Cohn was not an isolated incident. Later, Walter Annenberg, the Philadelphia publisher who was once indicted for income tax evasion, was appointed ambassador to England.[99]

Crime has penetrated so deeply into the minority-dominated entertainment industry that it has become an underworld jungle. Gangsters control the juke boxes, own many of the nation's nightclubs, and put up much of the money for Broadway productions. As the result of the gangster hold over gambling, practically every big name in the entertainment world has at one time or another received Mafia money for appearing in Las Vegas. Several leading show business and television personalities have even established criminal records of their own. The late Jack Benny, one of the nation's highest-paid comedians, was convicted of diamond smuggling in New York, but it never seemed to hurt his ratings.[100] David Begelman, president of Columbia Pictures, although he confessed in 1977 to forging the names of prominent Hollywoodians to five-figure checks, never spent a day in prison and two years later was appointed head of M-G-M's film company at $500,000 per annum plus expenses. Winston Burdett, a smooth-talking television news reporter, was a spy for the Red Army in Finland when Russia was trying to overrun that small nation in the winter of 1939–40. After Burdett had confessed all to a congressional committee, his employer, the Columbia Broadcasting System, kept him on the payroll as if nothing had happened.[101]

In the world of print, obscenity is now so much the thing that when magazine publishers have been arrested for pornography, as have Hugh Hefner of *Playboy* and Ralph Ginzburg of *Eros*, their

---

98. Ibid., p. 26. Cohn's three checks bounced for some time before they were finally covered. He once wrote $50,000 worth of checks against a non-existent account. Ibid., p. 30.

99. Annenberg's father, Moses, went to jail for two years for evading income taxes in the amount of $1,200,000. Walter was never brought to trial. *Washington Evening Star,* Jan. 7, 1969, p. 1.

100. *New York Times,* Oct. 12, 1940, p. 19.

101. *New York Times,* June 30, 1955, p. 1.

reputations have been enhanced. After Ginzburg received a five-year prison sentence, he managed to solicit contributions for a new magazine, *Fact,* from such notables as Bertrand Russell, Mary McCarthy, Linus Pauling, and Robert Hutchins.[102]

Other writers, almost all belonging to minorities, were not only involved with criminals but were criminals in their own right. The dean of this literary breed is Harry Golden, who, before becoming the bestselling author of anti-Southern homilies and the owner-publisher of the influential *Carolina Israelite,* served almost five years in Sing Sing under his real name, Herschel Goldhurst.[103] Norman Mailer, who received $400,000 for his denigrating series of essays on the moon landing, was arrested in New York in 1961 on a charge of wife-stabbing.[104] A less scatological author, literary critic Leslie Fiedler, aged fifty, was picked up by police with Mrs. Fiedler, his son, and two teenagers in 1967 for maintaining premises where narcotics were used.[105] Timothy Leary, former Harvard instructor, writer, and guru, was found guilty and given a thirty-year sentence (later reversed) for smuggling drugs into the country from Mexico.[106] Pearl Buck, the noted liberal who was born in China and won the Nobel Prize in literature, was forbidden by the State of Pennsylvania to solicit any

---

102. *Time,* April 3, 1964, p. 59, and *New York Times,* June 26, 1963, p. 26. Although convicted in June 1963, Ginzburg never saw the inside of a jail until 1972. An equally adept prison dodger was Saul Birnbaum, an accountant convicted of bribing an Internal Revenue Service agent in 1961. Birnbaum did not go to jail until May 1970, and then only as the result of some unfavorable publicity. *New York Times,* May 27, 1970, p. 26.

103. Nixon restored Golden's civil rights in 1973.

104. *New York Times,* Jan. 13, 1961, p. 58; Jan. 31, 1961, p. 13; Nov. 14, 1961, p. 45.

105. *New York Times,* April 30, 1967, p. 78.

106. *New York Times,* March 12, 1966, p. 1, and Oct. 21, 1966, p. 1. Leary, who was later jailed on another drug charge and then broke out of prison, is probably as responsible as anyone for influencing a considerable portion of an entire generation of Americans to experiment with or take up drugs. The last time that drug addiction reached similar proportions was in early twentieth-century China. The radical left in the United States either favors or is tolerant of drugs, yet Mao Tse-tung, the late Chinese Communist leader who remains a hero of the radical left, made not only drug peddling but even the slightest use of drugs a major crime. Today the drug scourge has all but disappeared from China.

more money for her foundation because of its mishandling of charitable funds.[107] Topping them all was literary forger Clifford Irving.

The police records of leading black militant writers have already been referred to, but it is appropriate to mention that LeRoi Jones, the prominent Negro playwright, was arrested in New York in 1966 for assault and robbery.[108] Arthur Miller, the most honored contemporary Jewish playwright, was cited for contempt of Congress in 1956.[109] Ten leading Hollywood film writers, minority members with one or two exceptions, had been previously jailed for the same offense.[110]

The emphasis on minority criminals in this chapter has not been intended to imply that there is no crime where there are no minorities. It is worth repeating that every race and every society have their criminals. But multiracial societies have more crime, and the multiracial society in which the struggle for power becomes a blatantly racial struggle has the most crime. Furthermore there are some offenses which could only occur in heterogeneous societies. In 1964 thirty-eight people in a New York suburb watched for one hour and a half out of apartment windows as a young white woman, Kitty Genovese, repeatedly calling for help, was slowly murdered in the courtyard beneath them. The murderer, a Negro necrophile, climaxed the gruesome exhibition by raping her when she was dead. Still, not a single person lifted a finger to stop him, or raised his or her voice, or picked up the telephone to call the police.[111]

---

107. *Time,* July 25, 1969, p. 60. In 1965 the foundation's board of governors included Art Buchwald and Sargent Shriver.

108. Allen Ginsberg, the poet, put up the $500 bail. *New York Times,* July 31, 1966, p. 55.

109. *Facts on File,* 1956, p. 441, and *New York Times,* June 10, 1950, p. 3, June 30, 1950, p. 1, Sept. 28, 1950, p. 20. Miller probably escaped jail because he was married at the time to actress Marilyn Monroe, whose overexploitation by film magnates led to a pathetic suicide.

110. The most serious offenses committed by these movie trenchermen were the treacly, moronic potboilers they cranked out for salaries of up to $1,000 a week.

111. *Time,* June 26, 1964, pp. 21–22. A similar occurrence took place in Rochester, New York. Hundreds of cars passed a ten-year-old girl being assaulted beside a freeway. Not one car stopped, even when the girl momentarily escaped

Such an event could never have happened in a homogeneous society. A sense of community and kinship, not to speak of the moral commands of a commonly shared religion, would have forced the onlookers to intervene. Also, in a homogeneous society the chances of the occasional minority criminal being present would have been less. Even if he had contemplated such an act, he would have been aware of the fierce community reaction it would have aroused—an awareness which alone might have proved a decisive deterrent. For example, it is doubtful that the Boston Strangler, Albert DeSalvo, would have been able to murder eleven women in the closely knit society of Southern Italy, where his family originated. For one thing he would not have been tempted by the presence of women of other races. Predictably, there was not one Italian name in the roster of his butchered victims.[112] Neither was there a Mexican name among the twenty-five persons killed by Juan Corona north of San Francisco. All were Americans of Anglo-Saxon background except for one Negro, who was buried in a separate grave.[113] There were even racial connotations in the incredible mass suicide of Negroes in Guyana ordered by the Reverend Jim Jones, who was almost certainly part Indian, and the mass murders in California ordered by Charles Manson, whose father was probably a mulatto.[114] On the other hand, homosexually motivated mass murders in Texas and Chicago were committed by a Majority member and an ethnic, though it must be remembered that the heterosexual and the homosexual permissiveness encouraged by the courts, the federal government, the minority media, and minority social scientists create an atmosphere where perverts can stalk their prey with little fear of the law or social condemnation. Here it might be

---

from her attacker and waved frantically for help. Her body was found two days later in a ditch. Associated Press report, Nov. 28, 1971. Winston Mosely, the murderer of Kitty Genovese, after being sent to Attica, escaped from a prison hospital in Buffalo where he was being treated for a self-inflicted wound. He raped a housewife and terrorized an entire neighborhood until persuaded to surrender to FBI agents. *Time*, March 29, 1968, p. 41.

112. Gerold Frank, *The Boston Strangler*, New American Library, New York, 1966, pp. 157–58.

113. *Miami Herald*, Oct. 12, 1973.

114. Vincent Bugliosi, *Helter Skelter*, W. W. Norton, N.Y., 1974, pp. 410–11.

pointed out that First Lady Rosalynn Carter had her photograph taken with both Rev. Jim Jones and John Gacy, the Democratic party ward heeler who killed more than thirty young white males in the Chicago area.

As racial crime becomes one of the commonest forms of crime in America, American law refuses to distinguish it from other criminal offenses.[115] Where everyone is still equal before the law and entitled to the same legal safeguards, the minority criminal thrives. Yet he no more deserves the protection and benefits of due process than an enemy soldier captured in battle. Both the enemy soldier and, increasingly, the minority lawbreaker feel their crimes are not crimes in the real sense but simply acts of justifiable violence against an oppressor. This is why the odds against the racial criminal's rehabilitation in prison are so high. To most minority inmates the modern American prison is a prisoner-of-war camp—albeit a strange and incomprehensible one from which prisoners are released while the war is still in progress and where the troops of both sides are incarcerated together, as they continue at close quarters the racial conflict being waged outside.[116]

Humanitarianism, which is the extension of familial love to all mankind,[117] was the chief architect of the present-day prison system. Until recently most civilized countries fined, branded, mutilated, enslaved, or killed their criminals, when they did not exile them or organize them into large work gangs. The herding of large numbers of men into vast prison complexes is a relatively new development in criminology. Long prison sentences cause immeasurable psychological damage to inmates by wasting their lives away in useless and profitless pursuits, while the soaring

---

115. A new crime on the books—violation of a citizen's civil rights—favors the Unassimilable Minorities in their war against the Majority. Civil rights violations allow federal law enforcement agencies to intrude in the state's prosecution of Majority members, even to the extent of putting them in double jeopardy.

116. The United States has a higher proportion of its population in jail than any other country—178 per 100,000, as against Japan's 89 per 100,000 and Britain's 65. Simpson and Yinger, *Racial and Cultural Minorities*, p. 217. The United States also has a much higher crime rate. In 1971 there were 113 murders and 135 rapes in London. In the same year there were 1,691 murders and 3,271 rapes in New York City.

117. Arnold Gehlen, *Moral und Hypermoral*, Athenäum Verlag, Frankfurt am Main/Bonn, 1970, pp. 79, 123, 142.

costs of prison upkeep place a heavy financial penalty on those who observe the law. And as jails become more crowded, they become more insufferable. In many prisons white inmates are now almost totally at the mercy of black criminals, since the latter make up most of the prison population. The homosexual acts and terrorism to which youthful Majority prisoners are forced to submit represent one of the most cruel and hideous ordeals in the history of punishment.[118]

It is obvious that the answer to this lapse into barbarism is not the legal permissiveness which has clogged the courts to such a degree that many criminals commit two or three more offenses while out on bail awaiting trial for earlier crimes. Such permissiveness promotes rather than diminishes crime, as noted early in this century by Vilfredo Pareto, the Italian sociologist:

> The effect of the probation law extends beyond the criminal whom it protects. The population at large grows accustomed to thinking that a first crime may be committed with impunity; and if that manner of thinking becomes ingrained in sentiment, diminishing the aversion for crime that the civilized human being instinctively feels, criminality may increase in general. . . . The wholehearted punishment of crimes that took place over long periods of time in centuries past has contributed to the maintenance of certain sentiments of aversion to crime. . . . Those nations which are nowadays indulging in an orgy of humanitarianism are acting like the prodigal son in frittering away the fortune he had inherited from his father.
>
> Mild laws in general . . . the extreme mercifulness of courts and juries; the kind-hearted patience of magistrates who allow criminals to show contempt for them in public court, and sometimes to utter personal insults and ridicule the penalties with which they are threatened . . . the mitigation of penalties already mild; frequent commutations and pardons—all such things allow a large

---

118. In three Pennsylvania jails, in which Negroes comprised 80 percent of the inmates, there were 2,000 sexual assaults over a two-year period. Half of these assaults were directed against whites. *Time*, Sept. 20, 1968, p. 48. Often the only way a young Majority member can get by in jail is to debase himself by becoming the "punk" of a hardened minority criminal, who then protects him against gang assaults. In spite of this appalling situation, the Supreme Court upheld a lower court decision forbidding the segregation of prisoners by race to avoid violence. *1969 World Almanac*, p. 49.

number of individuals to think lightly of crime and punishment of crime. . . .[119]

Crime in America will almost certainly continue to escalate until criminologists and social scientists are willing to consider the genetic ramifications of the problem. So far only one prominent American anthropologist has had the courage to assert that crime is largely the result of physical and racial factors. After conducting an anthropological study of 13,873 male prisoners in ten states, the late Earnest Hooton declared that the country's "criminal stock" must be eliminated. He further observed that the only way to check the growth of criminality was to breed a better race.[120]

As expected, the equalitarian prejudices of Boas and Ashley Montagu have provided most of the anthropological guidelines for contemporary criminology. Montagu himself has stated, "There is not the slightest evidence to believe that anyone ever inherits a tendency to commit criminal acts." [121] There is, of course, in addition to Hooton's work, a wealth of such evidence. Studies of glandular disorders and chromosome defects and the correlation of body types to delinquency all indicate the indisputable biological origin of certain criminal tendencies.[122]

Because of crime's genetic component, crime prevention should start in the home or, more properly, in the bedroom. There are already too many Americans and many too many criminal Americans. For those criminal elements who not only insist on multiplying, but multiplying much faster than noncriminal elements, the only alternative is sterilization. According to Professor H. S. Jennings, denying the right of reproduction to habitual criminal of-

---

119. Vilfredo Pareto, *The Mind and Society*, trans. Andrew Bongiorno and Arthur Livingston, Harcourt Brace, New York, 1935, Vol. 3, pp. 1284–85.

120. Harry Elmer Barnes and Negley K. Teeters, *New Horizons in Criminology*, Prentice-Hall, Englewood Cliffs, N.J., 1959, pp. 131–32.

121. Ashley Montagu, "The Biologist Looks at Crime," *The Annals of the American Academy of Political and Social Sciences*, Vol. 217, p. 55.

122. The history of the Jukes family, which produced hundreds of criminals in six generations, is further evidence of the genetic basis of much crime. Lothrop Stoddard, *Revolt Against Civilization*, pp. 95–96. More recently the inherited XYY chromosomal defect has been tentatively linked to criminal and antisocial behavior. Also see William H. Sheldon, *Varieties of Delinquent Youth*, Harper & Row, New York, 1949.

fenders would eliminate some 11 percent of the mental defectives (including the criminally insane) in each successive generation.[123] Professor Samuel J. Holmes has stated that the sterilization of 10 percent of the population would get rid of most of America's hereditary defectives.[124]

The psychic backwash of crime and its deadening and cynical effect on reciprocity, self-denial, and other moral prerequisites of civilized man are beyond the scope of this study. Here it will be merely pointed out that a citizenry which must devote an ever larger portion of its time and resources to personal security is neither in the mood nor in the position to care much about national security. Crime, in other words, has a direct bearing on America's defense capability. The stark, humiliating daily record of the ongoing orgy of American crime is a searing proof of national division and disunity. As such, it stimulates the neutralist propensities of allies, while encouraging the aggressive instincts of enemies.

In ways too subtle for most historians or political analysts to grasp, one of the principal products of the minority underground has been the etiolation of American foreign policy.

---

123. Barnes and Teeters, op. cit., p. 137. It is estimated that there have been as many as 70,000 involuntary sterilizations of mental patients in thirty states since 1900. As far as can be ascertained, this form of negative eugenics has now been ended for several reasons, one being the threat of lawsuits by organizations such as the American Civil Liberties Union. UPI report, March 24, 1980. Many, if not most, voluntary sterilizations are dysgenic in that they are performed on healthy, intelligent persons who do not want any—or any more— children.

124. Ibid., p. 137.

PART IX

The Foreign Policy Clash

CHAPTER 31

The Denationalization of Foreign Policy

THE FOREIGN POLICY of the United States or of any nation is the vector addition of the internal forces which shape its domestic policy and the external forces brought to bear by the foreign policies of other nations. Since American domestic policy has reflected a consistent liberal-minority bias throughout most of this century, American foreign policy, differing infinitesimally as Democratic and Republican presidents have seesawed in and out of power, has been cast in the same ideological mold. As a consequence, it tends to favor those states and governments which appeal to the taste of modern liberalism and to the emotions of America's more powerful minorities. As a further consequence, contemporary American foreign policy does not serve the interests of the nation as a whole, but rather of certain segments of the nation.

Democratic theory assumes that the foreign policy of a democracy is a truer and more faithful image of the people's attitudes, needs, and desires than that of a monarchy, aristocracy, or dictatorship. This might be true of a democratic country with a relatively homogeneous demographic base. But the theory hardly fits large multiracial states where there is no "people," where there is only a conglomerate of separate peoples, each with its own divergent and often divisive demands upon foreign relations.[1]

---

1. De Tocqueville, the great analyst and friend of American democracy, exhibited grave doubts about the ability of democratic governments in the field of foreign affairs, believing that the qualities which distinguish democracies in the conduct of domestic affairs were the opposite of those needed for the proper handling of foreign affairs. "La politique extérieure n'exige l'usage de presque

447

American foreign policy was born and nurtured in the isolation-
ism so ineluctably appropriate to the new nation's remoteness
and limited resources and so succinctly set forth in Washington's
Farewell Address.[2] The young country, although bursting at the
seams with an energy that anywhere else would have been subli-
mated into a riotous imperialism, was at first forced by the demands of geography to turn the martial instincts not reserved
for the preservation of its liberties to the more humble pursuits
of wilderness clearing and land reclamation.

But once the crisis of independence had been surmounted and
the War of 1812 had ended in a draw, America dropped its isolationist mask and embraced the entire Western Hemisphere with
the pronouncements of the Monroe Doctrine. As most Europeans
and Latin Americans correctly diagnosed it, the Monroe Doctrine
was only a diplomatic euphemism for infectious American expansionism. Another word for it was Manifest Destiny, which, though
it did not become an article of faith until somewhat later, was
in the wind from the time of the original settlements along the
Eastern seaboard.

It is hard to estimate when and where the territorial aggrandize-
ment would have stopped had American energies not been dissipated in the Civil War. If there had been no slavery issue, it is
quite possible that Canada, Mexico, Central America, and the
Caribbean islands would be additional stars in the American flag.
After Appomattox, after the wounds had been bound (but long
before they had healed), the imperialistic *Drang* was renewed. In
1898–99 Cuba was "liberated" from Spain and America took over
the Philippines. Then came Theodore Roosevelt, the last of a
breed, the last of the *national* imperialists, with his big stick, his
world-circumnavigating fleet, his Panama blitz, and his aggressive
arbitration of the Russo-Japanese War.

The twin forces of liberalism and minority racism did not secure

---

aucune des qualités qui sont propres à la démocratie." In the preceding paragraph de Tocqueville wrote, "c'est dans la direction des intérêts extérieurs de
la société que les gouvernements démocratiques me paraissent décidément in-
férieurs aux autres." *De la démocratie en Amérique,* Tome I, p. 238.

2. Washington, it should be emphasized, was not against expansion and empire. He was simply opposed to meddling in European politics and taking sides
in European wars.

a firm foothold in the formulation of American foreign policy until the Wilson administration. America's greatest classical liberal, Thomas Jefferson, had been as isolationist as Washington and, against his will, as expansionist as Theodore Roosevelt.[3] It had been the extreme elements among Jefferson's followers who tried to sweep the United States into a European war on the side of revolutionary France. Later the Abolitionists, another faction that put ideology above country, sabotaged the national interest wherever it meant an increase in slaveholding territory.[4] But by and large, until the inauguration in 1913 of Woodrow Wilson, American foreign policy remained largely unresponsive to liberal-minority pressures. Washington's advice, although frequently ignored, had never been repudiated.

The grand turnabout in American foreign policy was signaled by America's entry into World War I. At the war's outbreak the Majority was neutral or mildly favorable to England; the less assimilated Germans and most German Jews mildly pro-German; the Eastern European Jews strongly anti-Russian (because of czarist anti-Semitism); and the more unassimilated Irish vehemently anti-British. The other white minorities, although some of their homelands were directly involved, were either unconcerned or were unable to drum up nationwide sympathy. The nonwhite minorities were generally mute and dormant.

Since minority pressures more or less canceled each other out during the initial stages of World War I, the forces of intervention came from three sectors: (1) those who were still conscious of their Anglo-Saxon ancestry or were induced to become conscious of it by pro-British newspapers; (2) those who believed in the superiority of Anglo-American political institutions and felt they

---

3. In his first inaugural address Thomas Jefferson, although he had always entertained a very great affection for France, called for "entangling alliances with none . . . absolute acquiescence in the decision of the majority." It was the southern and trans-Appalachian farmers, Jefferson's cherished yeomen, who furnished most of the support for American expansion. Much to Jefferson's consternation his negotiation of the Louisiana Purchase transformed him, willy-nilly, into America's foremost imperialist. Beard, *The Rise of American Civilization,* Vol. 1, Chapter IX.

4. The Abolitionists favored seceding from the Union if there was no other way of ending slavery. The annexation of Texas was their most decisive political defeat. Ibid., pp. 581, 595.

were being threatened by goose-stepping militarists; (3) those who had a direct economic interest in a British victory, as the result of the close financial alliance which had sprung up between Wall and Threadneedle Streets after the British blockade of Germany.

To make their case the interventionists embellished the British-French-Russian cause with favorite liberal shibboleths—democracy, human rights, self-determination of peoples—and blackened the German cause with favorite liberal pejoratives—tyranny, man's inhumanity to man, Teutonic supremacy. But despite the national furor over the sinking of the *Lusitania* in 1915, the propaganda made little headway. There was hardly a modicum of truth in the allegorization of the war as a battle between Good and Evil, democracy and absolutism, unless Czar Nicholas II was to be accepted as a good democrat. The Anglo-Saxon and financial connections, while admittedly there, were not considered worth dying for. Britain, on the brink of defeat in 1916, had to look for a more powerful lodestone to draw the United States into war.

One such magnet had been taking shape in America since the beginning of the New Immigration. Britain's ambassador to Washington, Cecil Spring-Rice, had unwittingly discovered it when he reported to his government on the increasing influence of American Jews. He wrote in one dispatch, "a Jewish deputation came down from New York and in two days 'fixed' the two houses so that the President had to renounce the idea of making a new treaty with Russia." [5] At almost the same time in London, Chaim Weizmann, the leader of the world Zionist movement, had been expounding on the strength of world Jewry and promising its full support to Britain in return for the British endorsement of a Jewish homeland in Palestine.[6] The British government paid particular heed to Weizmann's proposal because as a prominent chemist he had greatly aided the British war effort by developing a process for the synthesis of acetone, a vital ingredient in the production of explosives.[7]

---

5. William Yale, *The Near East,* University of Michigan Press, Ann Arbor, 1958, p. 267. Yale, an American university professor, spent several years in the Near East on State Department assignments.

6. Ibid. Also see Sachar, *The Course of Modern Jewish History,* pp. 372–73.

7. Sachar, op. cit., p. 372. Jewish work on high explosives and the tangible rewards accruing to Jewish causes therefrom are a recurring theme of modern

The British and French apparently decided to proceed with Weizmann's homeland idea in 1916. Samuel Landman, an influential British Zionist who had been transferred to the British Propaganda Ministry in accordance with Weizmann's wishes, has written that Mark Sykes, under-secretary to the British War Cabinet, and Georges Picot and Jean Gout of the French Foreign Office were convinced by 1916

> that the best and perhaps the only way (which proved so to be) to induce the American President to come into the War was to secure the co-operation of Zionist Jews by promising them Palestine, and thus enlist and mobilise the hitherto unsuspectedly powerful forces of Zionist Jews in America and elsewhere in favour of the Allies on a *quid pro quo* contract basis. Thus, as will be seen, [to] the Zionists, having carried out their part, and greatly helped to bring America in, the Balfour Declaration of 1917 was but the public confirmation of the necessarily secret "gentlemen's" agreement of 1916. . . .[8]

In March 1917, the last formidable obstacle to enlisting the support of American Jews for the Allies was removed when a revolution overthrew the czar and brought a provisional government to power in Russia. One of the new regime's first acts was to assure the world that czarist anti-Semitism was a thing of the past and that Russian Jews would now have the same rights as all other Russians.[9] On April 2, Woodrow Wilson, who had been reelected president the preceding November on the campaign slogan, "He kept us out of war," asked Congress to declare war on Germany.[10] Within weeks, British Foreign Minister Arthur Balfour arrived in the United States. Almost immediately after seeing Wilson, he had a long conference with Justice Louis Brandeis, the leading American Zionist.

A few months later Henry Morgenthau, Sr., and Felix Frankfurter, who were slightly below Brandeis in the American Zionist hierarchy, persuaded the State Department to send them on a

---

Jewish history. See Chapter 38 of this study for the Jewish role in the development of the fission and fusion bombs.

8. Yale, op. cit., p. 267. The quotation and reference are from Samuel Landman's book, *Great Britain, the Jews and Palestine*, New Zionist Press, London, 1936.

9. *New York Times*, March 21, 1917, p. 1, and April 3, 1917, p. 9.

10. American Zionists then held a convention and sent their formal congratulations to Wilson. *New York Times*, April 11, 1917, p. 8.

secret mission to Europe to try to obtain a separate peace from Turkey. Chaim Weizmann headed them off at Gibraltar, convincing them that an early end to hostilities with Turkey would damage the Zionist cause. Palestine was then a Turkish possession, and Weizmann explained that a thoroughly defeated Turkey would not be able to offer much resistance to the foundation of a Zionist state. Morgenthau and Frankfurter agreed and returned to the United States, their mission uncompleted.[11]

It will probably never be ascertained if Zionism was the blast of wind that knocked the already teetering United States off the tightrope of neutrality. Although the evidence is sketchy and circumstantial, it is not altogether unconvincing. The matter certainly deserves further study and should be rescued from the historical deep freeze in which overcautious historians have stored it.[12] If

---

11. Yale, op. cit., p. 241, and Louis Gerson, *The Hyphenate in Recent American Politics and Diplomacy*, University of Kansas Press, Lawrence, 1964, pp. 91–92.

12. There are many other bits and pieces of historical evidence to strengthen the case that Zionism was an important cog in the wheel of American intervention in World War I. Lloyd George went on record as stating that the Balfour Declaration would have an important influence on world Jewry outside Russia and be in the best interests of Jewish financial circles. Leonard Stein, *The Balfour Declaration*, Simon and Schuster, New York, 1961, p. 575. In America, Lloyd George pointed out, the Declaration would have a special value when the Allies had exhausted their gold reserves and negotiable securities. Ibid., p. 575. There was a French government mission to American Jews in 1915; in 1916 the British Foreign Office urged British Jews to interest American Jews in the Allied cause. Ibid., pp. 218–19. French Zionists openly admitted attempts to influence public opinion in France, even to the extent of using government channels of information. Ibid., p. 375. It is possible that Wilson assured prominent New York City Zionists of his true intentions toward intervention in return for support in the 1916 presidential election. Ibid., p. 227. Brandeis at the time was receiving Zionist communications by British diplomatic courier. Ibid., p. 377. A year later he publicly agreed that Zionists stood to benefit from the Russian Revolution. Ibid., p. 382. After Wilson had endorsed the Balfour Declaration in a letter dated August 31, 1918, Brandeis "declared that opposition to Zionism could henceforth be considered disloyalty to the United States." Gerson, op. cit., p. 94. Almost the very moment the Revolution in Russia began, the Rothschilds, who had refused to loan money to the czarist regime, telegraphed one million rubles to the new government. Frederic Morton, *The Rothschilds*, Atheneum, New York, 1962, p. 175. The Turkish Revolution (1908–9), which helped weaken Turkey's hold over Palestine, "had been organized from Salonica, where the Jews, together with crypto-Jews known as Dönmeh, formed a majority of the

nothing else, the diplomatic attention given Palestine proved that minority racism was beginning to exert a dominating and self-serving influence in some sectors of American foreign policy. In the case of the Morgenthau-Frankfurter mission, it was clear that Zionists were already conducting a second American foreign policy of their own.

After an outpouring of treasure such as only the world's most opulent nation could afford, the United States ended its first military incursion into Europe and celebrated its victory by retreating pell-mell to the New World, where American foreign relations were again deflated to their traditional hemispheric range. At the inglorious peace conference at Versailles, Wilson's utopian hopes of a liberal world community had gone up in the smoke of nationalism, irredentism, and revolution. What's more, the president had to suffer the final humiliation of having his own brainchild, the League of Nations, repudiated by the United States Senate. By the time of his death in 1924, it was generally conceded that, in direct contradiction to America's most trumpeted war aim, World War I had imperiled democracy everywhere by piling the Ossa

---

population." Stein, op. cit., p. 35. British Prime Minister Asquith wrote in 1914, "it is a curious illustration of [Disraeli's] favourite maxim that 'race is everything' to find this almost lyrical [Zionist] outburst proceeding from the well-ordered, methodical brain of H.S." Stein, op. cit., p. 112. Asquith was referring to Herbert Samuel, one of Britain's most powerful Jews and a member of the British Cabinet. Later, a still more powerful Jew, Lord Reading (Rufus Isaacs), who had been a bankrupt stock speculator and the subject of Kipling's vitriolic poem *Gehazi*, was sent to America, first as chief of a British financial mission, then as British ambassador. H. Montgomery Hyde, *Lord Reading*, Farrar, Straus and Giroux, New York, 1967, p. 188. Reading was a good friend of Colonel House, Wilson's closest adviser, and his "influence with Lloyd George [was] greater perhaps than any other man's in England." Hyde, op. cit., p. 229. Samuel Gompers, a Jew and the head of the American Federation of Labor, seemed to synchronize his changing attitude toward the war with the shift in the Zionist position. In 1914 Gompers was all for neutrality. But in February 1917, he called a meeting of the AFL Executive Council and came out with a strong declaration against Germany. Ronald Radosh, *American Labor and U.S. Foreign Policy*, Random House, New York, 1969, p. 8. As for the average American's desire to enter World War I, Senator La Follette declared that if the issue had been submitted to a referendum the vote would have been ten to one for nonintervention. Beard, op. cit., Vol. 2, p. 635. It might be noted that the Sedition Act of May 1918 made most criticism of intervention illegal. Ibid., p. 640.

of fascism on the Pelion of communism. Almost every thoughtful American, no matter what his politics, was ready to agree that intervention in Europe had been a disaster and must never happen again.

It happened again in less than a quarter century. This time the interventionists, despite the embarrassment of having to recant their most solemn promises and renege on their most steadfast resolutions, had a much easier task. Before World War II, Hitler had established himself as the archenemy of liberalism, Marxism, and Jewry—precisely the three driving forces of the liberal-minority coalition that had ridden into power with Franklin Roosevelt's New Deal. Capitalizing on the ready-made anti-Nazism, the media soon became rabid. By 1940 it was hard to find a liberal or minority intellectual—give or take a few Old Believers—who was not a raging interventionist.[13] The few Majority leaders who tried to make their voices heard above the martial clangor were discredited by charges of anti-Semitism.[14]

As Charles Beard ably demonstrated by a mass of documentation, America entered World War II long before Pearl Harbor and the Axis declaration of war.[15] It had, in fact, been unofficially committed by November 1940, when Roosevelt, repeating Wil-

---

13. Sidney Hillman, the minority labor chieftain, was so incensed at Hitler that he personally directed the breaking of a 1940 strike at North American Aviation in Inglewood, Calif. Radosh, op. cit., p. 19. The man who had made a career out of the union movement wanted no slowdown in the production of war materials, even though it meant betraying a union local.

14. After he had made a brief mention of the specifically Jewish agitation for intervention, the press reduced Charles Lindbergh from the status of epic hero to Nazi hireling. Lindbergh remained a nonperson for many years thereafter. New Republic, Sept. 22, 1941, pp. 360–61, and Time, Sept. 22, 1941, p. 17. In 1970, Lindbergh published his Wartime Journals, in which he insisted that his noninterventionist stand had been fundamentally correct and that the United States had actually lost the war, since it had merely destroyed a lesser menace to help establish a greater one. He particularly stressed the irreparable genetic loss suffered during the war by the Northern European peoples. Lindbergh's written words repeated, and did not modify, his 1941 accusation that Jews had been a major force in involving the U.S. in World War II. See footnote 34, p. 163, of this study and The Wartime Journals of Charles A. Lindbergh, Harcourt Brace Jovanovich, New York, 1970, pp. xv, 218, 245, 404, 481, 538–39, 541, 545.

15. Beard, President Roosevelt and the Coming of the War, 1941.

son's feat, was reelected after solemnly promising to keep the United States out of war.[16] Even before his reelection Roosevelt had transferred fifty American destroyers to Britain. After reelection he persuaded Congress to adopt the Lend-Lease Act, which placed a large part of the war's financial burden on the American taxpayer. He then ordered in quick succession: (1) American naval escort of British convoys; (2) open warfare on German naval vessels; (3) the occupation of Iceland; (4) the drawing up of secret defensive agreements with Britain; (5) an ultimatum to Japan which demanded the removal of Japanese troops from China and tightened the American steel and oil embargo.[17] The official entry of the United States into the war came almost as an anticlimax.

If there was some difficulty in identifying the forces of intervention in the initial stages of American embroilment in World War II,[18] there was none when the guns stopped firing. The policy of unconditional surrender, the Morgenthau Plan,[19] the abandonment of Eastern Europe to Russia, the German war crimes trials, and the denazification purges clearly proved that the United States had not been by any stretch of the imagination engaged in a war of survival, as newspaper editorials proclaimed, but rather in a war to destroy Hitler.[20]

---

16. In his celebrated campaign address in Boston (Oct. 30, 1940), Roosevelt stated: "I have said this before, but I shall say it again and again and again: Your boys are not going to be sent into any foreign wars."

17. Beard, op. cit., pp. 68, 97, 108, 134, 140, 239, 241, 356, 435, 453.

18. British Prime Minister Neville Chamberlain apparently shared some of Lindbergh's views as to the origins of the conflict. According to Ambassador Joseph Kennedy, Chamberlain told him, "America and the world Jews had forced England into the war." But Chamberlain's statement was not made known until 1951. *The Forrestal Diaries,* edited by Walter Millis, Viking, New York, 1951, p. 122.

19. Introduced at the Second Quebec Conference (1944) by Secretary of the Treasury Morgenthau and authored by Harry Dexter White, assistant secretary of the treasury (later identified as a Soviet agent), the plan called for the dismantling of all German industry and the reduction of Germany to an agrarian state. Churchill originally agreed to the plan in return for an extension of Lend-Lease. *Current Biography,* 1944, p. 724, *Time,* August 9, 1948, p. 15, and John M. Blum, *From the Morgenthau Diaries,* Houghton Mifflin, Boston, 1967, Vol. III, p. 373.

20. To some it was purely and simply a war of racial revenge. Secretary Morgenthau, in discussing the postwar treatment of Germany, said: "The only thing

There was no American retreat from Europe when World War II ended. Had there been, Western Europe would have followed Eastern Europe into the Soviet orbit. By force of circumstance American foreign policy was now converted into an impromptu defense mechanism on the grand scale, an infinite series of on-the-spot reactions and counteractions to Communist acts of aggression, both in Europe and Asia. This containment policy, as it came to be called, made it necessary for Americans to pay for the rebuilding of the very same industries they had recently destroyed, for American soldiers to join forces with the very enemy they had recently been ordered to kill. The West was saved, at least temporarily, but at the cost of another fearful outpouring of America's human and industrial resources.[21] The East, or at least the greater part of the East, was lost.

During and after World War II, American foreign policy alternately went far beyond and fell far short of the national interest. As if in penance for not joining the League of Nations, the United States became the founder and principal shareholder of the United Nations.[22] But the UN was no better at keeping the peace than

---

. . . I will have any part of, is the complete shut-down of the Ruhr. . . . Just strip it. I don't care what happens to the population. . . . I would take every mine, every mill and factory and wreck it . . . why the hell should I worry what happens to [the] people?" That such a policy would have starved thirty million Germans to death was beside the point. Morgenthau persisted in his plan even though New York Governor Thomas Dewey stated that the Morgenthau Plan brought about a sharp increase in German resistance. It is needless to speculate how many deaths and casualties on both sides were caused by Morgenthau's Old Testament vengeance. Blum, op. cit., Vol. III, pp. 354, 378.

21. The United States, as of 1978, is still owed $25,730,992,168 from unpaid World War I loans. *1980 World Almanac,* p. 334. In World War II, American Lend-Lease to the Allies amounted to $49 billion, of which only a fraction has been repaid. The Marshall Plan for European recovery accounted for $8.6 billion. *Ency. Brit.,* Vol. 4, p. 834. In the postwar period (fiscal 1946 through fiscal 1977), 139 nations and 8 territories received $143.4 billion in foreign aid. Another $46 billion was handed out in the form of loans. *Orlando Sentinel Star,* May 31, 1978, Charles Reese column. Foreign aid is now running at approximately $7 billion a year. *1980 World Almanac,* p. 604.

22. The United States pays one-third of the operating budget and 70 percent of its total expenditures. The Soviet Union has three votes in the General Assembly, as against one for the United States. Nations with about 5 percent of the earth's population control a majority of votes in the General Assembly.

the League. Almost singlehandedly the United States assumed the defense of the West.

In Asia, America was on the losing side in China and then was drawn, in defiance of all military common sense, into Asiatic land wars it could only have won with the help of nuclear weapons or dedicated allies. In the Middle East once friendly Moslem nations began to entertain grave doubts about the United States after America's sponsorship of Israel and the Shah of Iran. The radical Arab states invited the Soviet Union into the area as arms suppliers and military advisers, while the moderate states sharpened their oil weapon. Revolutionary Iran turned anti-American, as Egypt entered into a semi-alliance with Washington in the hope that the Camp David accords would force Israel to permit the creation of a Palestinian state. In Africa the emerging black nations were given lavish financial and ideological support, while the white governments of South Africa and Rhodesia were condemned and sanctions imposed on the latter. In Latin America the blindness of one American president helped install Castro; the blindness of a second allowed the Pearl of the Antilles to become a Russian military base; the blindness of a third allowed the establishment of at least one Soviet-tilted revolutionary regime in Central America.

Prestige and power, the twin sources of respect, are an invincible combination in winning the friendship and support of foreign peoples and governments. Not so long ago America and Americans had the respect of most of the world, a universal esteem that made the formulation and implementation of foreign policy relatively easy. Today, the nation which is still on paper the most powerful or second most powerful on earth is so shorn of respect that any fifth-rate banana dictatorship, Communist client state, tribal military junta, or fanatic mullah is able to humble and humiliate it at will.

The nation that went to war with Spain over the sinking of the battleship *Maine* froze into inaction and impotence when Israeli torpedo boats and Mirage jets bombed and strafed the *U.S.S. Liberty,* killing 34 and wounding 171 Americans; when North Korea captured the naval vessel *Pueblo* with its entire crew; when foreign gunmen assassinated the American ambassadors to Guatemala, Sudan, and Afghanistan; when Venezuelans stoned the American vice-president; when hijacking terrorists commandeered American airliners to Cuba with impunity; when radical students supported by the Iranian government seized and held 52 American hostages for more than a year; when American prisoners of war in Asia were brainwashed, tortured, and shot; when American citizens in the Congo were raped and cannibalized; when American installations overseas were routinely looted and gutted; when the nation which once proclaimed "Millions for defense, but not one cent for tribute" [23] paid $53 million ransom to a posturing Caribbean Mussolini for the release of 1,113 prisoners captured in the Bay of Pigs fiasco.[24]

As the above incidents illustrate, the new-style American diplomacy in which the strong surrender to the weak—or buy protection from the weak in the form of foreign aid—has not produced many stirring successes.[25] In fact whatever solid gains American foreign policy has achieved since World War II must be largely attributed to two crucially important factors for which the nation's policy makers can take hardly any credit at all. These are America's nuclear preponderance, now reduced to nuclear parity, and the internal breakup of the Communist world. That the movers and shakers of America did not sufficiently exploit these two fateful foreign policy windfalls is a diplomatic failure of the first magnitude, one that will weigh heavily on future generations.

But what else could be expected from a foreign policy that has been put through the grinder of denationalization? When diplomacy becomes a shuttlecock of every special interest group and every minority bloc that can afford a Washington lobbyist, Allies and friends of long standing are neutralized or turned into

---

23. Spoken by Charles Pinckney in 1797, when American minister to France.

24. *1965 World Almanac*, p. 371.

25. George Kennan, one of the few creative minds in the diplomatic corps, has been highly critical of what he calls the "histrionic futility" of American statesmanship. The addiction of American politicians to injecting extraneous considerations into American foreign policy makes it, according to Mr. Kennan, "ineffective in the pursuit of real objectives in the national interest, allowing it to degenerate into a mere striking of attitudes before the mirror of domestic political opinion. Until the American press and public learn to detect and repudiate such behavior, the country will not have a mature and effective foreign policy worthy of a great power." George Kennan, *Memoirs, 1925–1950*, Little, Brown, Boston, 1967, p. 54.

enemies, while professional diplomats, forced to sit on the sidelines, grow more cynical and more helpless every hour. The State Department may pretend to be the agency that directs or implements American foreign policy, but it is little better than an information center and message service. One single editorial in the *New York Times* carries more weight than the dispatches of twenty ambassadors.

A denationalized foreign policy has many heads and hearts, but no soul. It supports imperialism in one part of the world and opposes it in another. It upholds human rights in some areas; in others it honors and rewards the violators of these rights. It gives money and arms to anti-American governments but boycotts pro-American governments. It is against Soviet aggression in Eastern Europe and Afghanistan but tolerates it in Cuba, from whose airfields Communist bombers can be over Florida in fifteen minutes.

Not only America but most of the world has lived to regret the day the Majority lost control of American foreign policy.[26] There is nothing more dangerous in international relations than misdirected energy, nothing more tragic than a great nation that expends its greatness blindly. Until the special interests of the minorities and the special enthusiasms of liberals are again made subservient to the national interest, American foreign relations will stagger from crisis to crisis and from war to war.

---

26. June 8, 1915, when William Jennings Bryan resigned as secretary of state in protest against the first real signs of the Wilson administration's bristling interventionism, is as good a date as any to mark the end of nationalism as the guiding light of American foreign affairs.

CHAPTER 32

The United States and Western Europe

Nothing points up the impermanency of the human condition so poignantly as the tragic deterioration of Western Europe in the twentieth century.[1] As the century began, Western Europe was the lord of the earth, the fountainhead of world industry, technology, and military power—the headquarters of nine empires.[2] In the latter half of the century Western Europe was a power vacuum, a buffer zone between the Soviet Union and the United States. The great empires, either vanished or reduced to a fraction of their size, now had to depend on a transatlantic power for their defense. Slavic troops stood on the Elbe, from which they had been driven more than a millennium earlier by Charlemagne.[3] The Western European land space, a peninsula of a peninsula, beckoned the Russians as a divided, strife-torn Greece had once beckoned Alexander, while Western Europeans themselves felt less and less comforted by America's protective nuclear canopy.

---

1. Western Europe is here designated as that part of Europe west of the Slavic lands and the Balkans.

2. British, French, German, Austro-Hungarian, Italian, Dutch, Belgian, Spanish, and Portuguese.

3. Describing conditions in Europe in the seventh century A.D., a modern Scandinavian historian has written: "In these dark centuries, the center of Europe's cultural life shifted so far west that the once-vital barter between Scandinavia and the South could take place only on the Rhine and along the Atlantic coast. The 'West' had been just as menacingly reduced and narrowed down as it is today." Eric Oxenstierna, *The Norsemen*, New York Graphic Society, Greenwich, Conn., 1965, p. 26.

America and Russia are children of Western Europe in the sense that both countries have looked to it for most of their cultural nourishment and both were founded by the race that has been dominant in Western Europe, or at least in Northwestern Europe, since the beginning of recorded history.[4] A great unresolved question of the future is whether one of these unruly offspring, semi-barbaric Russia, will attempt to claim the patrimony defended by the other sibling, America, itself now sinking into semi-barbarism. Or will the parent revive, mend his self-destructive ways, and reassert his authority?

As yet there are few signs of the latter possibility. Only the Germans still exhibit the traditional Western European dynamism. But the West German defense forces, armed with foreign weapons, their numbers restricted by law and pacifism, their ranks demoralized by heavy doses of defeatism and modern liberalism, could hardly, even with the help of their American and NATO allies, roll back a conventional military attack by the Russians and would have little chance of surviving an all-out nuclear one. It is true that the West German economy is now as healthy as any in the world. But if not used to shore up German defenses, economic prosperity can only make the Federal Republic more attractive to the foreign predator.

Today, Western Europe is wracked by many of the same diseases tearing at the vitals of America. Western European nations have their own minority problems, their own liberal "public opinion" mills,[5] and their own insurrectionary Marxist cabals, both pro- and anti-Russian. When the cultural and political output of New York and Beverly Hills is added, there is probably almost the same disproportionate Jewish influence in the arts, news media, and government.[6]

---

4. See pp. 72–74.

5. "If all the books written about the European Left were laid end to end, they might stretch halfway around the globe. Books on the European Right would more likely not stretch a mile. . . ." *Times Literary Supplement,* May 14, 1970, p. 1.

6. Beside the century-old Jewish wealth represented by the Montagus, Mocattas, and Rothschilds in Britain stand such pound millionaires as Isaac Wolfson and Lord Sieff (department stores); Sir Samuel Salmon and Isidore Gluckstein (restaurants and hotels); Siegmund Warburg and Baron Swaythling (banking); Baron Melchett (chemicals); Marquess of Reading (steel); Viscount Bearsted

Britain has some 410,000 Jews and upwards of 2,000,000 non-whites, the latter increasing at the rate of 100,000 a year.[7] Nevertheless those who call for greater safeguards for the British gene pool are excoriated as mercilessly as their American counterparts. Though Prime Minister Margaret Thatcher promised to tighten immigration policy, nonwhites still arrive in droves. Enoch Powell, a professor of Greek before he worked his way up in the Conservative party hierarchy, has been treated as an illiterate blackguard.[8] For its stentorian opposition to immigration, Britain's small National Front has been labeled by the British media as a Nazi organization.

The alien influx into other Western European countries is of a lighter coloration than Britain's Negro-Pakistani mix. France

---

(oil); Sir Louis Sterling (record players); Lord Grade, Lord Bernstein, and Jeremy Isaacs (commercial television); Sir Bernard Delfont (electronics); Sir James Goldsmith (financier and magazine publisher); Sir George Weidenfeld (book publisher); Sir Joseph Kagan (garment manufacturer), a close friend of former Labour Prime Minister Harold Wilson. Kagan was jailed in 1981 for violating Britain's export laws. Sir Eric Miller (real estate), another friend of Wilson's, committed suicide while under investigation for fraud. Sir Keith Joseph is the éminence grise of the Conservative party; Lord Lever the éminence grise of the Labour party. Arnold Weinstock heads the British equivalent of General Electric; Sir Derek Ezra, the National Coal Board. In 1981 there were 32 Jewish Members of Parliament (21 Labour, 11 Conservative). Jewish academicians include Sir Isaiah Berlin, Max Beloff, and David Daiches. At least half the leading British playwrights are Jewish—Bernard Kops, Arnold Wesker, Harold Pinter, and Peter Shaffer. Stephen Spender leads the contingent of Jewish poets. See Chaim Bermant, *Troubled Eden, an Anatomy of British Jewry*, Valentine, Mitchell, London, 1969; Sachar, *The Course of Modern Jewish History*, pp. 497–98; the British *Who's Who*. In France, the French branch of the Rothschild family still has a hold on the nation's purse strings. Marcel Dassault, the aviation magnate who converted to Catholicism, is reputed to be worth $1 billion. Prominent Jewish publishers and pundits include Jacques Servan-Schreiber, Raymond Aron, and Pierre Lazareff, B. H. Lévy, and André Glucksmann. Pierre Mendès-France, René Mayer, Michel Debré, Maurice Schumann, and Mme. Simone Veil, first president of the European Parliament, are or were among the most influential politicians. Leading intellectuals and literary lights like André Malraux, Jacques Maritain, and Louis Aragon have or had Jewish wives. In Italy the richest man is probably Arrigo Olivetti, the Jewish typewriter magnate.

7. London *Daily Telegraph*, Jan. 22, 1977.

8. A Gallup Poll claimed 74 percent of the British population supported Powell's opposition to colored immigration. *San Francisco Chronicle*, May 8, 1968, p. 14. Powell predicts there will be 5 to 7 million Afro-Asians in Britain by the year 2000, if his country's immigration laws are not completely revised.

has its 1 or 2 million North Africans and its 650,000 Jews. Though only 35,000 Jews remain in West Germany, the country now has 4,000,000 foreign residents (guest workers) and their dependents, most of whom came from Southern Europe and the Middle East. Some 8,500,000 Swedes now have 1,250,000 non-Swedes in their midst. Holland has experienced several outbreaks of violence from its South Moluccan community. And so it goes. What is most frightening is that the birthrate of the more Nordic Western Europeans has fallen well below the replacement level—in West Germany far below it—while the foreign non-Nordics in Western Europe still maintain relatively high birthrates. For this reason in a few German cities non-German births are accounting for more than a quarter of all births. It appears that if nuclear war does not destroy Western Europe, race suicide will. In 1800 Europe had 20 percent of the world's population. Today it has 9 percent. Unless the increasing demographic imbalance is radically corrected, it will have 4 percent in 2075.[9]

Britain has already experienced its first American-style race riot in Bristol (1980), and racial "incidents" on the American model are cropping up in West Germany, France, the Low Countries, even in Scandinavia. There are many other examples of what Europeans call Americanization, as if Americans as a whole were responsible for what has been emanating from a few academic, literary, and entertainment sinkholes in Manhattan, Washington, and West Los Angeles. Americans have suffered as much as Europeans from the childish pop art, the banal television sitcoms, the Ziegfeld tinsel, hardcore pornography, venal media, minority literati, and African syncopation. The truth is, the same species of culture vulture feathers its nest on both sides of the North Atlantic.

The only effective resistance to this blight in Western Europe comes from the gray, heavy-handed cults of Marxism, the neofascist parties in Spain and Italy, oldtime nationalists in every country, and the New Right in France.[10] The latter, with its manifestos and preachments against the Judeo-Christian heritage, religious

9. *Chicago Sun-Times*, Aug. 10, 1980, p. 44. In 1980 East German women were averaging 1.89 children each; British women, 1.7; Dutch, 1.6; Swiss, 1.5; Austrian, 1.4 or 1.5; West German, 1.4. Bangladesh, a miasma of poverty and ignorance, now produces more babies annually than Western Europe.

10. For an overview of French New Right thought, see Alain de Benoist, *Vu de droite*, Copernic, Paris, 1977.

and secular totalitarianism, democracy, and racism of every variety (including minority racism), offers the brightest prospect to minds deadened by orthodox liberalism and equalitarianism. But the Nouvelle Droite is meeting increasing intolerance, oppression, and violence from the leftist establishment and Zionist fellow travelers. Race relations laws in France, as elsewhere in Western Europe, make objective criticism of the ruling liberal-minority ideology extremely difficult. Any spoken or written word that can be interpreted as racist exposes the speaker or author to heavy fines or imprisonment.[11]

In World War I the United States assumed Britain's traditional role of preventing European unification by calling into play the "balance of power." The organization of coalitions against the strongest and most aggressive European nation or nations was simply the politics of Polycrates on the grand scale (cut the tallest stalk of wheat down to size). As a long-range strategy, it was not too destructive as long as Western Europe was so strong that even divided it could dominate the world. But carried to its ultimate conclusion in 1939–45, it demolished Western European military primacy, perhaps for all time, leaving the entire region a client state of the United States and the helpless target, if American forces should fold up their nuclear umbrella and withdraw, of Soviet imperialism.

It is unlikely that any single Western European nation will soon again be able to qualify as a world power. Only a unified Western Europe would have the capability of equaling or surpassing the American or Russian military machines, and the keystone of any such European confederation would have to be West Germany or, better, a reunited Germany. France and Italy proved conclusively in World War II that they can no longer fulfill any important military mission beyond serving as a theater of operations and a source of supplies and auxiliary troops for allies. The smaller Western European nations have developed a tradition of neutrality or instant surrender which, with the possible exception of Sweden

---

11. The West German government is so nervous about anti-Semitism that it has paid the largest war reparations in history to Jews (see p. 500). Germans have been punished with jail sentences or large fines merely for selling copies of *Mein Kampf*, for questioning the Holocaust or the *Diary of Anne Frank*, or for making anti-Semitic remarks in public.

and Switzerland, would make their military contributions meaningless. The Spanish soldier is brave, but has few weapons and little European consciousness. Even the fighting ability of the British is currently open to question. No great people ever gave up so great an empire so effortlessly.[12]

Building Western European unity around a German nucleus would seem to offer the only long-term assurance of keeping the Russians quarantined in Eastern Europe. In a united Western Europe the Germans and other Northern Europeans would perform the same function as a resurrected American Majority in the United States and the now almost completely rehabilitated Russian Majority in the Soviet Union. They would supply the racial backbone, the physical stamina, the dynamism, and the organizational drive that a modern superpower must require of its dominant population group.

The unification of Western Europe would relieve the United States of furnishing most of the money, arms, and men for repelling a Russian attack, a burden that puts a severe strain on both the American military and the American economy. American troops could be safely withdrawn from Europe because advanced missile technology now makes it almost as simple to mount a nuclear counterstrike from New World installations and ocean-ranging submarines as from Old World land bases. With much less chance of being involved in a thermonuclear war, Western Europe would utter a sigh of relief. Also disbanded would be the North Atlantic Treaty Organization, which makes its Western European military contingents seem like American mercenaries. A Western European defense force under a single flag and a single command would attract the best soldiers from the nations whose own armies no longer have any real fighting potential. From a military standpoint, the whole would prove to be greater than the sum of its parts.

As a final step, the United States of America and the United States of Western Europe would join in an alliance based not on shifting political and economic dogmas, tactical opportunism,

---

12. In 1921 the British Empire had 524,000,000 inhabitants. In 1966, when the Colonial Office was closed down, Britain had only twenty-one overseas possessions left, most of them remote islands, and the total number of people living under the British flag was 56,000,000.

or extraneous minority pressures, but on the more enduring foundation of a common culture and a common desire to raise Western civilization to new summits of achievement. Such an alliance would help prevent the recurrence of the political, economic, and social failures brought about by centuries of "balance-of-power" diplomacy. America could hardly afford another $350 billion war (two or three times that much at current prices).[13] Western Europe could scarcely survive a deeper Soviet penetration of its frontiers, another 12,000,000 dispossessed refugees from the East, and another genocidal round of class and racial confrontations and saturation bombings.[14]

Most important, a formal acknowledgement of the racial and cultural basis of the alliance might stifle any renewed outbreak of the brutalized statesmanship which reduced the peacemaking of two global wars to the level of a lynching bee. The unconscionable Allied demand of unconditional surrender prolonged World War II, perhaps as long as eighteen months, by playing directly into Hitler's immolation tactics and by cutting away popular support for an anti-Nazi uprising.[15] It also gave Stalin time to seize all of Eastern Europe, most of the Balkans, and a large part of Germany.

A child seeing two school bullies locked in a knock-down, drag-out fight would know better than to help one bully overcome the other. Incomprehensibly America, whose armed forces did

---

13. *Ency. Brit.,* Vol. 23, p. 793R. The $350 billion figure is the estimated amount the U.S. spent between 1939 and 1946 on its own armed forces and on war materiel sent to the Allies.

14. According to one historian, the total cost of World War II to all nations was $4 trillion and the total number of dead, 40,000,000. Martha Byrd Hoyle, *A World in Flames,* Atheneum, New York, 1970, pp. 323–24.

15. Major General J. F. C. Fuller, *A Military History of the Western World,* Funk & Wagnalls, New York, 1954, Vol. 3, pp. 506–9, 538–39. The type of mentality directing the American war effort can be judged by the following remarks of President Roosevelt at the 1943 Casablanca conference. When he first uttered the phrase, "unconditional surrender," Roosevelt congratulated himself by saying, "Of course it's just the thing for the Russians. They couldn't want anything better. Unconditional surrender! Uncle Joe might have made it up himself." Ibid., pp. 506–7. In the final pages of his book, General Fuller asked, "What persuaded them to adopt so fatal a policy?" The only explanation he could give was "blind hatred." Ibid., p. 631.

not land in the European mainland until after the battle of Stalingrad, the turning point of the war, devoted the major share of its military effort to the annihilation of an enemy who was already beaten.[16] Hitler, who had never been able to defeat Russia and Britain, was replaced by a rocket-rattling Stalin with only America's nuclear might standing between him and an easy march to the Atlantic. If this march ever takes place, the United States will go down in history as the gravedigger rather than the liberator of Western Europe.[17]

---

16. The battle of Stalingrad ended in February 1943 with the surrender of an entire German army. American troops did not land in Italy until September 1943 and in France until June 1944.

17. It should be pointed out that the unification of Western Europe stressed in this chapter is limited to military and economic unification, without which no effective defense can be mounted against Russian expansionism. While advocating more organization at the top of the European community, the author at the same time urges less organization in the middle and much more at the bottom. By this is meant a deemphasis on the nationalism which has kept Europe divided for so many centuries and a reemphasis on the regional and provincial divisions, the seedbeds of the great flowerings of Western civilization. For example, France might be restructured to give full cultural and partial political autonomy to Normandy, Brittany, Provence, Alsace-Lorraine; a reunited Germany to grant autonomy to Bavaria, Saxony, Prussia, and the Rhineland; the United Kingdom to give semi-independence to England, Wales, Scotland, and Ulster. Devolution, as it is now called in Britain, might also revive the glories of the great city-states of Florence, Venice, Weimar, etc. The same process is recommended for the United States. See "The Utopian States of America" in Wilmot Robertson's *Ventilations*.

CHAPTER 33

The United States and the Soviet Union

Most Americans are aware of the differences, especially the ideological differences, between their country and the Soviet Union. They are also aware of some of the similarities—the extended land mass, the advanced space technology, the vast industrial and natural resources. But there is one striking resemblance which is not so well known and which should be clearly comprehended before undertaking any serious discussion of Soviet-American relations. This is the analogous fate the twentieth century had in store for both the American Majority and the Russian Majority.

The Russian Majority is composed of Great Russians, the Russians proper,[1] who as Slavs were originally Nordic in race, but centuries ago were brachycephalized into Alpines.[2] While this racial transmutation was taking place, small quantities of Nordic genes were added back by the Scandinavian Varangians who founded the Russian state,[3] by the intermingling of the Russian and Teutonic aristocracies, and by the agents of the thousand-year German commercial, technical, and cultural penetration of Russia. For all these reasons the Russian Majority, like the American Majority, belongs to the lighter-complexioned segment of the white race, with members of the American Majority tending on the average to be somewhat blonder, taller, and longer-headed due to their higher incidence of Nordicism.

---

1. As shown in Table V, p. 64, the American Majority represents 59 percent of the population of the United States.
2. See p. 74.   3. See pp. 72–73.

THE POPULATION OF THE SOVIET UNION (1970) BY NATIONALITY GROUP

	Population (000's)	% of total		Population (000's)	% of total
Great Russians	129,015	53.37	Tatars	5,931	2.45
Ukrainians	40,753	16.86	Cossacks	5,299	2.19
Byelo-Russians	9,052	3.74	Azerbaijanians	4,380	1.81
Poles	1,167	.48	Chirvashians	1,694	.70
Lithuanians	2,665	1.10	Tajiks	2,136	.88
Latvians	1,430	.59	Turkomans	1,525	.63
Moldavians	2,698	1.11	Kirghis	1,452	.60
Romanians	119	.05	Bashkirs	1,240	.51
Germans	1,846	.76	Georgians	3,245	1.34
Estonians	1,007	.42	Chechen-Ingush	613	.25
Karelians	146	.06	Armenians	3,559	1.47
Finns	85	.03	Others	6,899	2.86
Jews	2,151	.89			
Uzbeks	9,915	4.10	TOTAL	241,720	100.00

Note: The 1979 Soviet census shows a population of 262,442,000. At this writing, the new figures for nationality groups and their percentages of the total population were not available. An estimate in *Air Force Magazine* (Oct. 1979) indicates a slight decline of the Great Russians to 52 percent of the total, a decline of the Jewish population because of emigration to Israel and the West, and an increase of nonwhites in the Central Asian republics. Because of disparate birthrates it is expected that the Great Russians will represent less than 50 percent of the population by the end of the century. Even so, the Great Russians will remain by far the largest component of a Slavic majority comprising 70 percent of the total Soviet population.

From the racial standpoint the differences between the Slavic-speaking Russian Majority and the Slavic-speaking minorities (Ukrainians, Byelo-Russians, Poles) are minor. They are less than those which set the American Majority apart from the Assimilable Minorities and much less than those that set it apart from the white Unassimilable Minorities. The great separator of the Soviet Union's Slavic population groups is not race but culture. Each speaks its own particular Slavic language, has its own distinct brand of nationalism, and inhabits its own particular territory. The non-Slavic minorities are equally regionalized—the blond East Baltic peoples in the northwest, the Mediterranean and part-Mediterranean Georgians, Armenians, and Romanians in the south, and the Mongolian and other nonwhite minorities in the east.[4]

In comparison with the American population, the Soviet Union

---

4. Only in some Siberian areas and perhaps in Moscow are the various Soviet peoples mixed together on the same scale as population groups in the United States.

has a smaller Mediterranean component and a larger proportion of Mongolians. Russia has fewer Jews than the United States, but, as in America, they are concentrated in large urban centers and in white-collar occupations. The one overwhelming difference in the racial makeup of the two countries is that Russia has no Negroes.

The Russian and American Majorities are somewhat similar in racial composition. They are more similar in number and in their proportion to the total population of their respective countries. They are very similar in their recent historical experience. Both have known the humiliation of dispossession, the endless bowing and scraping to new control groups, the self-abasement and frustration of working for the greater good of one's detractors. In contrast to the slow decomposition of the American Majority, however, the Russian Majority was dispossessed all at once in the 1917 revolutionary holocaust.

The racial factors underlying the Bolshevik uprising have already been discussed,[5] but not the Russian Majority's return to favor, which began after the German attack on the Soviet Union in the summer of 1941. Since no country can long survive a massive invasion when its strongest and most numerous population group has been alienated and proletarianized, the Soviet government was quickly forced to renounce many of the key assumptions of Communist dogma or face the prospect of total collapse.

On November 6, 1941, as the German Wehrmacht stood before the gates of Moscow, Stalin tore up the Marxist-Leninist rule book by describing Hitler's onslaught, not as an assault on the citadel of world communism, the Holy Land of Marxism, but as a war of extermination against the Slavs. No more were the German invaders portrayed as last-ditch capitalists trying to root out socialism from the face of the earth. Historical materialism, economic determinism, the class struggle, all the sacred pillars of Communist ideology crumbled into dust as the Soviet news media revived the racial glories of Mother Russia, even going so far as to invoke the ghosts of long-departed czarist heroes and Orthodox saints.[6]

---

5. See pp. 360–61.

6. Hans Kohn, *Pan-Slavism,* Vintage Books, New York, 1960, p. 292. "Stalin understood intuitively that his government and his social system could not with-

The result is history. On May 24, 1945, seventeen days after Germany had been defeated, Stalin proposed an almost heretical toast at a Kremlin banquet of Red Army commanders:

> I should like to drink to the health of our Soviet people . . . and first of all to the health of the Russian people . . . because it is the most outstanding nation of all the nations forming the Soviet Union. . . . It has won in this war universal recognition as the leading force in the Soviet Union among all the peoples of our country. . . .[7]

On March 15, 1954, *Izvestia* stated in a leading article:

> Every people in the Soviet Union understands perfectly well that the main decisive role in the achievement of victory over the enemy in the Great Patriotic War . . . was played by the Great Russian people. For this reason the prestige of the Russian people is so immeasurably high among the other peoples; for this reason the peoples of the USSR bear toward it boundless confidence and a feeling of tremendous love and gratitude.[8]

It is not necessary to point out that the American Majority received no such glowing tribute, either from the American government or the American press, for its "main decisive role" in America's military victory in World War II or, for that matter, World War I.

The rehabilitation of the Russian Majority was accompanied by a revival of anti-Semitism.[9] The Russian people had never been happy about the disproportionate number of Jews in the Revolution, nor about Jewish responsibility for the murder of the Romanovs. Yurovsky, a Jewish member of the secret police, working under the orders of the secretary of the Party's Central Committee, Sverdlov, another Jew, supervised the massacre of the czar, the

---

stand the blows of the German Army unless they leaned for support on the age-old aspirations and ethos of the Russian people." Djilas, *Conversations with Stalin*, p. 48.

7. Kohn, op. cit., p. 297.

8. Ibid., p. 299.

9. Russian anti-Semitism, it must be remembered, had a long and uninterrupted history and was never considered as "unrespectable" as it was in the West. Dostoyevsky, for example, had proudly expatiated on his anti-Semitism, as had some other famous Russians.

czarina, their four daughters, Olga (twenty-two), Tatiana (twenty), Maria (seventeen), Anastasia (fifteen), and Aleksei, the czarevitch (thirteen).[10]

Although anti-Semitism was entered in the law books as a capital crime when Communists took over the government, it still simmered in non-Jewish party cadres, flaring up sharply when Dora Kaplan tried to assassinate Lenin, an act from which he never fully recovered.[11] But rather than taking the classical form of pogroms, anti-Semitism, as it developed into a fine art under Stalin, became an important tool in the struggle for control of the Communist party. In the 1930s, Stalin killed or jailed most of the important Soviet Jews, while Hitler was content to let thousands of prominent German Jews escape, along with hundreds of thousands of the less prominent. (Only after the invasion of Poland in 1939 did Nazis begin to herd non-German Jews into concentration and work camps.) However, the part Jews played in the receiving end of the Great Terror, as Stalin's pre-World War II purges are now known, was never mentioned in the Soviet press.[12]

It was not until a few years after the war that Stalin decided to bring his sub-rosa anti-Semitism out into the open.[13] In 1948,

---

10. The murders took place in an Ekaterinburg cellar in 1918. Yurovsky shot some of the Romanovs himself. Also shot were the family doctor, three servants, and Anastasia's dog. Nobel Franklin, *Imperial Tragedy*, Coward-McCann, New York, 1961, p. 156, and Gleb Botkin, *The Real Romanovs*, Fleming Revell, New York, 1931, p. 236. A meticulously documented bestseller on the Romanov tragedy neglected to mention the Jewish backgrounds of Sverdlov and Yurovsky, even though the non-Russian origins of the soldiers who helped carry out the murders were carefully noted. Robert Massie, *Nicholas and Alexandra*, Dell, New York, 1967, pp. 511–15.

11. Litvinoff, *A Peculiar People*, p. 74. Although a Jewish woman nearly killed Lenin, "Jewish revolutionaries were to be found in every branch of [his] administration." Jews were also in the forefront of the fight against Christianity. Emelian Yaroslavsky, a prominent Jewish Bolshevik, was the leader of the League of Militant Atheists. Ibid., pp. 73–76.

12. For some Jewish victims of Stalin's purges, see Robert Conquest, *The Great Terror*, Macmillan, New York, 1968, pp. 76–77, 430, 498, 512, 538–39.

13. Stalin's daughter, Svetlana Alliluyeva, has made several pointed references to her father's chronic antipathy toward Jews. "To this [the rebirth of Russian anti-Semitism] my father not only gave his support; he even propagated a good deal of it himself." She said it developed from her father's fight with Trotsky. When she married her first Jewish husband—of her five husbands two were

he closed down all Jewish cultural enterprises, prohibited the teaching of Hebrew, and halted the construction of new synagogues. He imprisoned and shot hundreds of Jewish writers and artists, all the while raising a great hue and cry against "cosmopolitans," who were invariably identified as Jews by the Soviet press.[14] The campaign climaxed in 1953, when nine top-ranking doctors, at least six of them Jewish, "confessed" to the murder of an important Soviet official, A. A. Zhdanov, and to plotting the elimination of high-level army officers.[15]

Stalin died as the plot was being unraveled, and his successors, perhaps in response to the violent reaction from abroad, swept the whole affair under the rug. But as no Jew, or at least no admitted Jew, has been a member of the Politburo, the inner sanctum of Soviet officialdom, since the expulsion of Kaganovich in 1957,[16] it can be assumed that present-day Russian policy to-

---

Jewish—her father told her, "The Zionists put him over on you." In regard to Rosa Kaganovich, widely heralded as Stalin's third wife by the Western press, Svetlana said that no such person existed. *Twenty Letters to a Friend*, Harper & Row, New York, 1967, pp. 68, 159, 181, 186, 196, and *Only One Year*, Harper & Row, New York, 1969, pp. 152–55, 168, 382.

14. *The Saturday Evening Post*, June 16, 1962, pp. 15–17. Also see *Ency. of Russia and the Soviet Union*, p. 259.

15. Some were accused of belonging to an American intelligence agency; others of having contacts with an American-Jewish charity organization. Ibid., p. 133. The Doctor's Plot was faintly reminiscent of the Lopez affair in which a Portuguese-Jewish physician was hanged for allegedly trying to poison Queen Elizabeth in 1597.

16. According to the *American Jewish Yearbook* (1967), pp. 383–84, the only Jew to retain an important government post was Benjamin Dimschitz, one of the several deputy premiers, and only five Jews were to be found among the 1,517 members of the two chambers of the Supreme Soviet. No Jews held an important position in the army or diplomatic corps. A report published in the *Richmond Times-Dispatch* (Oct. 4, 1965, p. 19), stated 41.1 percent of the deputies of the Supreme Soviet were Jewish before World War II, but by 1958 the figure had dropped to 0.25 percent. As to Jewish personalities, Molotov's wife was Jewish, but her husband could not or would not save her from arrest and transportation to Siberia. Khrushchev had a Jewish daughter-in-law, and there were well-known Jewish names in artistic, literary and scientific circles—ballerina Maria Plissetskaya, violinist David Oistrakh, some writers, a few of whom had been in and out of prison for years, and one or two noted physicists and economists. Litvinoff, op. cit., p. 91. A wire service has reported that Brezhnev's wife is Jewish. *Gainesville Sun*, Gainesville, Florida, Dec. 10, 1977, p. 2A.

ward Jews has not deviated too far from the established Stalinist line.[17] Zionism is still a crime against the state. Jews are still listed as Jews in Soviet passports. Novels, histories, at least one prime-time television documentary, and various official and underground publications have raised anti-Zionism to a pitch where it can hardly be distinguished from anti-Semitism.[18] The U.S.S.R. has become the protector, so to speak, of the radical Arab world and has

17. Anti-Semitism hit the satellite countries particularly hard in the Stalin era. East Germany was forbidden to make any reparations to Israel for confiscation of Jewish property by Nazis. *New York Herald-Tribune*, Nov. 11, 1962, p. 25. Of the fourteen prominent Czechoslovak Communists whom Stalin brought to trial in Prague in 1952, eleven were Jews. It was at this trial that a wife denounced her husband as a "traitor to his party and his country" and a son demanded the death penalty for his father. The son wrote the presiding judge: "Only now do I see that this creature, whom one cannot call a man . . . was my greatest and vilest enemy . . . hatred toward my father will always strengthen me in my struggle for the Communist future of my people." Edward Taborsky, *Communism in Czechoslovakia*, Princeton University Press, Princeton, N.J., 1961, pp. 95, 106.

18. The list includes *Judaism Without Embellishment* by Trofim Kichko (1963, 191 pages, 60,000 copies, later withdrawn from sale after its crude anti-Jewish cartoons drew Western protests); *Judaism and Zionism* by Kichko (1968, charges Jewish messianism was responsible for the massacre of Palestinians); *Caution: Zionism!* by Yuri Ivanov (1969, hundreds of thousands of copies translated into English, style and content somewhat reminiscent of *Protocols of the Elders of Zion*); *In the Name of the Father and the Son* by Ivan Shevtsov (1970, 369 pages, 65,000 copies, attacks Jews for their liberalism, abstract art, and pornography); *Zionism and Apartheid* by Valery Skurlatov (1975, criticizes the Jewish-Protestant hold on American capitalism); *Invasion Without Arms* by Vladimir Begun (1977, 150,000 copies, concerns a Jewish-Zionist plot to achieve world domination); *Wild Wormwood* by Tsezar Solodar (1977, 200,000 copies, a novel accusing Jews of trading in "feminine flesh"); *International Zionism: History and Politics* by V. I. Kiselev et al. (1977, 26,000 copies, Marxist interpretation of Jewish control of international banking); *Love and Hate* by Ivan Shevtsov (1978, 400,000 copies, Jewish villain is a pervert, sadist, dope peddler, and murderer). *The Covert and the Overt*, a film only shown to officers of the armed services, labels Trotsky a Jewish traitor and blames Jewish capitalists for Hitler's rise to power. *Traders of Souls*, a 1977 network television presentation, depicts furtive Zionist agents passing out money to anti-Soviet demonstrators in London. See the *New York Review*, Nov. 16, 1972, pp. 19–23; *Publishers Weekly*, Sept. 18, 1978, p. 126; *New Statesman*, Dec. 15, 1978, pp. 814–18; Chicago *Jewish Sentinel*, Oct. 12, 1978, p. 27; London *Jewish Chronicle*, July 25, 1980, p. 19; "Anti-Zionism in the U.S.S.R." by William Korey, *Problems of Communism*, Nov.–Dec. 1978, U.S. Information Service, Washington, D.C., pp. 63–69.

armed Israel's most hostile neighbors, Iraq and Syria. Jews have left the Soviet Union in record numbers since 1968 when the doors were first opened—perhaps as many as 250,000.[19] But the clinching argument for Soviet anti-Semitism has been the establishment of quotas for Jews, not only in government but in the universities. They used to crowd higher education as disproportionately as they do in the United States. Today, Jews account for only 1.3 percent of the students in Soviet higher education, as compared to 13 percent in 1935.[20]

The tottering position of Soviet Jewry and the almost complete domination of the Politburo by members of the Russian Majority are signs that the fifth and final stage of the Russian Revolution is now running its course. These five stages, which bear certain resemblances to other revolutions, can be characterized as follows:

1. The Majority, divided and anesthetized by massive injections of liberalism, partially proletarianized by class agitation, and left helpless by its own decadent leadership, is dispossessed by a coalition of minorities.

2. The triumphant minorities and their Messianic Leader, so talented in undermining the old state, find their revolutionary gifts of little avail in organizing a new state and turn their frustrations and failures on themselves.

3. The Minority Strongman [21] emerges, establishes the Terror, and liquidates the dissident and discordant minority leaders, once his partners and political allies, but now his most effective and most dangerous opponents.

4. His regime in shambles, under military attack from abroad, and pushed to extremes by increasing social and economic anarchy at home, the Strongman initiates the counterrevolution by abandoning proletarian dogma and building a new power base on the Dispossessed Majority, whom he woos with appeals to patriotism, racism, and tradition.

---

19. Associated Press report, Oct. 9, 1980.

20. *Jewish News*, Detroit, Michigan, Dec. 9, 1977.

21. After the death of Messianic Leader Lenin, it took Minority Strongman Stalin more than a decade to consolidate his power. If the sequence holds true for China, the long life of Messianic Leader Mao (he died at 83) has delayed the appearance of the Strongman, who in China's case may not be a minority member because of the country's racial homogeneity.

5. In his latter years the Strongman identifies himself almost totally with the Majority [22] and at his death the state slowly reverts to Majority control.[23]

Expansionism, which seems to be a common obsession of czars and commissars, has been one of the two principal determinants of Soviet-American relations. America first felt the hot breath of Russian imperialism in the middle of the nineteenth century, when the Russians, who had occupied Alaska, extended their fur-trading empire as far south as Fort Ross in Northern California, seventy miles above San Francisco. But Russia's unfortunate experience in the Crimean War (1854–56) led to a worldwide retrenchment. The Russians first pulled back to Alaska, then in 1867 sold "Seward's Icebox" to the United States for $7,200,000. There were no other significant contacts between the two nations until 1905, when President Theodore Roosevelt indulged his passion for high politics by becoming the mediator of the Russo-Japanese War. The lesson of this conflict, the first in modern times in which a nonwhite country defeated a white country, was not lost on the world's colonial peoples.

The second principal determinant of Russo-American relations has been Russian anti-Semitism. The public outcry against the

---

22. Stalin's daughter had this to say concerning her father's Russification. "I have no idea whether or not my mother could sing, but it is said that once in a long, long while she would dance a graceful Georgian *lezghinka*. Otherwise, however, we paid no special attention to anything Georgian—my father had become completely Russian." Svetlana Alliluyeva, *Twenty Letters to a Friend,* p. 31.

23. When the above scenario is applied to other countries, fascist or military counterrevolutions may upset it at stage 2, before the proletarian forces have been able to consolidate their victory. In this case the role of Minority Strongman is usurped by a Majority Strongman, whose Majority pedigree, however, may leave a lot to be desired. Hitler was an Austrian and Napoleon a Corsican. Since Stalin was a Georgian, the three leading revolutionary or counterrevolutionary figures of modern European history all came from their countries' southern periphery. If this should prove to be a law of history, the future American strongman will be a Southerner—an hypothesis given some credibility by the premature strivings of Huey Long and George Wallace. In Mediterranean countries the Strongman seems to come from the North. Mussolini and Franco were born in the septentrional regions of their countries. Castro is the illegitimate son of a Spaniard from Galicia in northern Spain.

pogroms and other anti-Semitic acts of czarist governments was first raised in the heyday of the New Immigration, as hundreds of thousands of Russian and Polish Jews were introduced into the American body politic.[24] Almost from the moment they landed, they joined with the more established and more restrained German and Sephardic Jews in demanding that the American government take official steps to protect the millions of other Jews still remaining in the Russian Empire. As a result American relations with Russia became so strained that in the summer of 1915, when British and French officials approached Wall Street bankers for a war loan, Jacob Schiff, senior partner of Kuhn, Loeb, refused to let his firm participate unless the British and French finance ministers gave their assurance in writing that "not one cent of the proceeds of the loan would be given to Russia." [25]

The overthrow of Czar Nicholas II in 1917 completely reversed the attitude of American Jews toward Russia. As the chaos within Russia increased, Russo-American relations grew proportionately warmer, so warm that Woodrow Wilson hailed the Menshevik Revolution in March as a kind of political second coming and used it as one of his several justifications for American intervention in World War I. That part of Wilson's war message to Congress dealing with the Russian situation can be considered as the first high-level outpouring of the blind mendacity, blind stupidity, and blind idealism which poisoned the wells of information about Russia for the next half-century. Wilson orated:

---

24. Total number of Jewish immigrants (to 1930) was 2,400,000, of which perhaps 5 to 7 percent arrived before 1880 and were largely of German and Sephardic origin. Davie, *World Immigration*, pp. 144–45.

25. This was not the first time that Jacob Schiff had brought minority racism to bear on the fate of Russia. During the Russo-Japanese War, when London banking circles were skeptical of Japan's chances, Schiff raised $30,000,000 for the Japanese. As his daughter, Frieda, later wrote, it was "his hatred of Imperial Russia and its anti-Semitic policies that prompted him to take this great financial risk." Later J. P. Morgan, George F. Baker, and the Rockefeller-Stillman interests joined Schiff in three massive loans to the Japanese and the door was opened for Japanese conquests in Asia and the Pacific. In 1905, after a series of anti-Semitic outbursts in Odessa, Schiff went directly to Theodore Roosevelt and demanded presidential action against the czarist government. Roosevelt obediently wrote a personal letter to the czar. Stephen Birmingham, *Our Crowd*, Harper & Row, New York, 1967, pp. 282, 317.

Does not every American feel that assurance has been added to our hope for the future peace of the world by the wonderful and heartening things that have been happening within the last few weeks to Russia? Russia was known by those who knew it best to have been always in fact democratic at heart. . . . The autocracy . . . was not in fact Russian in origin, character or purpose; and now it has been shaken off and the great, generous Russian people have been added in all their naive majesty and might to the forces that are fighting for freedom in the world, for justice, and for peace. Here is a fit partner for a league of honor.[26]

After the war the "league of honor" was quickly dissolved. Totalitarian ukases outraged traditional American attitudes toward individual freedom and private property. Conversely, the arrival of American troops in Archangel and Vladivostok to aid the anti-Bolshevik forces offended as many non-Communist as Communist Russians. During the 1921–22 famine in the Ukraine, one of the world's most fertile farm belts, American financial aid and food shipments saved perhaps 10,000,000 lives. But since the Communist party did its best to keep the news secret, relations were not much improved.[27]

Until the coming of the New Deal, the Soviet Union remained unrecognized by the United States, although the appeal of communism to American minorities and to the more dogmatically inclined liberals made Russia, the most backward of the great powers, an intellectual Mecca for wayward American minds. In the 1930s a strong conspiratorial streak developed in Russo-American relations as the Comintern intensified its intercontinental espionage and as numerous American Communists and crypto-Communists covertly organized a formidable pro-Russian lobby. Ultimately, owing to the fears aroused by the Spanish Civil War and Hitler's lengthening shadow, pro-Communist bias reached a fever pitch of religiosity among liberal and minority intellectuals, who came to look upon Stalin as an anti-fascist Gabriel sent to destroy the Archfiend. It was both tragic and comic that at the very moment this idolatry reached its peak, the Soviet dictator, with his purges, massacres, institutionalized torture, show trials, and slave labor

26. George Kennan, *Russia and the West Under Lenin and Stalin*, Little, Brown, Boston, 1961, p. 19.

27. Ibid., p. 180.

camps, was busily destroying almost the entire Communist party hierarchy and state apparatus.[28] No political leader in history had so ruthlessly exploited and so cleverly duped his following.

The Russo-German Nonaggression Pact (1939) came as a traumatic shock to those who received their intellectual nourishment from the Communist party line. Bewildered, benumbed, and betrayed, liberals and minority members, particularly Jews, began to desert the Communist cause in droves. But the German invasion of Russia two years later drove some of the strays, at least temporarily, back into the corral. While there, they helped restore the Communist party to its prewar level of prestige and influence. Party members and fellow travelers were again appointed to several key posts in government departments and agencies.[29] In fact,

---

28. Of the 1,966 delegates to the XVIIth Party Congress (January 1934), 1,108 were shot on Stalin's orders within the next few years. Of the 139 members and candidate members of the Central Committee, 98 persons or 70 percent were later arrested and shot (mostly in 1937–38). From the army Stalin purged three out of five marshals, 13 out of 15 army commanders, 57 out of 87 corps commanders, 110 out of 195 division commanders, 220 out of 406 brigade commanders. In all, there were some 700,000 "legal" executions, about 1,-000,000 secret executions, and some 12,000,000 deaths in the prison camps themselves. Counting the 5,500,000 who died in the forced collectivization of agriculture in the late 30s and the man-made famine which accompanied it, Stalin can be credited with a grand total of 20,000,000 dead victims. According to some commentators, this figure is 50 percent too low. It only includes the period 1930–50, not the last years of Stalin's activities during which the slave labor camp population numbered at least 10,000,000. Conquest, *The Great Terror,* pp. 36–38, 527–28, 533; Hugh Seton-Watson, *From Lenin to Malenkov,* Praeger, New York, 1955, p. 170. It might be noted that during the Stalin purges, the worst of which took place before the outbreak of World War II, the communications media in the West gave Stalin a much better press than Hitler. Very little news of the mass liquidation of a sizable fraction of the Russian population was ever published and, when it was, it was attacked as false and unfounded by many of the West's leading intellectuals. The almost complete blackout for two decades of one of the greatest crimes in history lends substance to those who claim the near total corruption and venality of the world press. Typical was the observation of Professor Harold Laski: "Basically I did not observe much difference between the general character of a trial in Russia and in this country [Britain]." Conquest, op. cit., p. 506. Sartre once said the evidence about the Soviet forced labor camps should be ignored. Ibid., p. 509.

29. The most important Communist concentrations were in the Departments of State, Agriculture, and Treasury. The roster of names includes Hiss, Currie, Ware, Pressman, Abt, Silverman, Collins, Duggan, Witt, Perlo, Reno, White,

if Roosevelt had not had a last-minute change of heart in the 1944 Democratic convention and replaced his vice-president, Henry Wallace, with Harry Truman, a fellow traveler would have become president on Roosevelt's death in 1945.[30] It is true that Wallace finally recanted and admitted the error of his ways. But even as late as 1948 he was the presidential candidate of the Progressive party, which was almost totally dominated by Communists and leftist appeasers of Stalin.[31]

As the cold war progressed, however, and as Communist inroads into various sectors of American life were made public, America's close wartime associations with Russia were severed and dealings between the two countries took on an icy formality—interrupted by occasional hot flashes of hostility (Berlin airlift, U-2 incident, Cuba) and one joint peace-keeping venture (the halting of the 1956 British-French-Israeli blitz on Egypt). At a slower pace Soviet support of the Arab world against Israel and continuing revelations of Soviet anti-Semitism were reducing the once overwhelming Jewish enthusiasm for Russia to the vanishing point.

Toward the middle of the 1950s, after the hysterical liberal-minority reaction to Senator Joseph McCarthy's flailing attack against the Stalinist apparatus had subsided,[32] anti-communism,

---

Remington, Wadleigh, Field, and Gompertz. Chambers, *Witness*, especially pp. 466–69.

30. In 1944 Henry Wallace and Professor Owen Lattimore visited a Russian slave labor camp at Magadan, Siberia. This was part of a complex in which the death rate among prisoners was about 30 percent per annum, where outside work was compulsory until the temperature reached −50°C, where it was difficult to live on camp rations for more than two years, and where the fate of many inmates followed the inexorable pattern of "sickness, self-mutilation, suicide." The food rations of prisoners were reduced to the starvation level when they did not fulfill work quotas. Yet Wallace found the camp idyllic and Lattimore considered it a great improvement over the czarist system. By temporarily removing watchtowers, segregating the prisoners in huts, and peopling a model farm with girl swineherds who belonged to the secret police, the camp commandant successfully duplicated the feat of Potemkin. Conquest. op. cit., p. 350.

31. Wallace's apologia was issued in the form of a magazine article in *Life*, May 14, 1956. He admitted that he had misunderstood Russian intentions and that Communists had exerted a commanding and deleterious influence on his presidential campaign. Senator McGovern, it might be noted, was a delegate to the 1948 Progressive party convention.

32. McCarthyism, the media intoned, had made America a land of fear and trembling. But just who was fearful? In academia and in media country it always

at long last, became respectable in the United States. But the respectability was assumed in large part by the very intellectuals who had been most distinguished for their apodictic communism in the past and who, as unreconstructed Marxists, had shown their true colors by blaming the failures of communism not on the animadversions of Lenin but on the perversions of Stalin. As for anti-liberal Americans who had known what had been happening in the U.S.S.R. all along, they were given scant credit for their prescience and were still beyond the intellectual pale. Many conservatives among them deserved their fate because they insisted on confusing the external Soviet threat with an internal Communist threat that had long since passed. Their dogmatic obtuseness prevented them from understanding that those who represented the real internal threat—the coalition of liberals and minority racists—had now become as anti-Russian, though by no means as anti-Marxist, as themselves.

By the end of the 1970s it was safe to say that Russian nationalism, militarism, imperialism, and Great Russian racism, not Russian communism, comprised the greatest external menace to American national security. Internally, the United States was becoming more revolutionary than the Soviet Union. Now more than sixty years old, the world's first Communist state had destroyed its creators and produced a bureaucratic, military, managerial caste that is probably the most conservative ruling group of any great power. To the present masters of the Soviet Union, Marxism is no longer the article of faith it was to the Old Bolsheviks. In private it is derided as an obsolescent grab bag of empty phrases and empty thoughts. In public it is used as a shibboleth to strengthen their grip on the state and to advance Soviet power abroad.

From the standpoint of numbers there are still many Communists spread over the face of the earth—a grand total of 45,200,000 members in eighty-eight parties.[33] But as their recent divisions, revolts, and defections have shown, the hearts and minds of most Communists no longer belong to Moscow. Some Communist parties, such as the Chinese, are more frantically anti-Russian than

---

took much more courage to say a good word for McCarthy than to denounce him.

33. *Time*, June 13, 1969, p. 28.

the most rabidly reactionary parties of the West. It is not overstating the case to say that today the chief binding force of the Soviet branch of world communism is nothing more or less than the presence or potential presence of the Red Army.

So far, the United States has had little to fear from the U.S.S.R. economically. With more people, land, and resources than America, the Soviet Union has a gross national product only 48 percent of America's.[34] One American farmer still works four times the land that a Russian works on a collective farm, uses five and a half times more power, and gets twice as much yield for five to sixteen times less labor.[35] As for consumer products and services, the Soviet Union has lagged far behind the West. But since America's economic and technical superiority over Russia is due to the American Majority's superior capabilities in these fields, America's lead will narrow as the dispossession of the American Majority continues and as the Russian Majority, its dispossession ended, comes into its own.

If Americans should ever adopt a policy of self-interest in their dealings with the U.S.S.R., they might start by abandoning détente and the SALT agreements, which only give the Soviet leaders time to catch up and surpass the United States militarily, and begin to do unto the Russians as the latter have been long doing to the West. With lavish outpourings of Communist propaganda and subversion, the Soviet Union has sought, often only too successfully, to weaken Western nations from within by divisive appeals to class and race, and from without by jingoist appeals to the nationalism and anti-colonialism of the have-not countries. Why isn't the U.S.S.R. a fertile field for similar subversive activities by the United States? Many Soviet minorities have never forgiven or forgotten czarist and Bolshevik tyranny.[36] The peoples of the Soviet satellite states, if given the chance, would break away from Russian domination with only the slightest regret. America should

---

34. *Wall Street Journal,* Dec. 31, 1968, p. 18.

35. *Ency. of Russia and the Soviet Union,* pp. 10–12. The U.S. has 6,000,000 people engaged in agriculture—Russia, 45,000,000.

36. Hitler might possibly have defeated Russia if he had handled the Russian minorities less roughly. Until they came to know them better, the Ukrainians treated the German invaders as liberators. J. F. C. Fuller, *A Military History of the Western World,* Vol. 3, p. 447.

also back to the hilt the manifestos of the writer-hero, Solzhenitsyn, who wants Russia to turn inward, give up imperialism and "political gigantism," and concentrate on the development of the Russian Northeast, by which he means northern European Russia, and most of Siberia.[37]

Although the Soviet Union must never be allowed to grow so strong that it can engulf Western Europe, it must never be permitted to become so weak that it cannot guard Europe against Mongolian inroads from the Asiatic steppes. To obviate the real possibility of the Russification of Europe, Russian nationalism must be prevented from coalescing into Pan-Slavism. There are, as indicated in the beginning of this chapter, perhaps 136,000,000 Great Russians. But, including the Great Russians, there may be as many as 260,000,000 Slavs.[38] The emergence of a latter-day Ivan the Terrible at the helm of a race-conscious Slavic imperium—in which the Slavic minorities in Russia and the Slavic populations in the Russian satellite states are raised to first-class citizenship and inspired with a common racial fervor—would present the West with an almost irresistible concentration of military strength. In such an event, in the words of Stalin, "No one in the future will be able to move a finger. Not even a finger!" [39]

It is, in brief, not the Soviet Union of Lenin that the United States and the West have to fear. It is the Russia of the Pan-Slav Dostoyevsky, a far greater genius with a much sharper eye for the shape of tomorrow.[40]

---

37. Aleksandr Solzhenitsyn, *Letter to the Soviet Leaders,* Harper & Row, New York, 1975, especially p. 55. Solzhenitsyn, however, is unheroic when it comes to space exploration, to which he is opposed.

38. In addition to the Great Russians, Ukrainians, and Byelo-Russians, Slavs include Poles, Czechs, Slovaks, Serbs, Croats, Slovenes, and some Macedonians and Bulgarians.

39. Djilas, *Conversations with Stalin,* p. 114.

40. The ban on Dostoyevsky, whose novel *The Possessed* (published in 1871) was an uncanny preview of twentieth-century Russian history, has now been lifted in the Soviet Union—one more proof of the resurgence of the Russian Majority.

CHAPTER 34

The United States and the Far East

Nowhere in the last hundred years has American foreign policy wobbled so wildly and gone through so many ups and downs as it has in the Far East. Take China, for instance. At the start of the twentieth century, Americans stood considerably higher in Chinese esteem than the other foreign devils who had been beleaguering the moribund Celestial Kingdom. The United States, though committed to extraterritorial rights and the conversion of the heathen, was probably the least active of all Western nations in concession hunting, lease grabbing, opium smuggling, and similar manifestations of Western financial privateering.[1] It was Secretary of State John Hay's Open Door Policy in 1899 that helped tone down some of the bolder forms of plundering by shoring up Chinese sovereignty. After the collapse of the Manchu dynasty in 1911–12, American ideas and practices of constitutional government inspired Sun Yat-sen, China's first modern hero, to set up a republic. When Japan attacked Manchuria in 1931, the United States protested more loudy than any other Western nation.

China was an ally of the United States in World Wars I and II. In the latter conflict American military aid to Chiang Kai-shek played a considerable part in preventing Japanese armies from overrunning all China. When World War II ended, the Chinese

---

1. One nineteenth-century lapse in American neutrality was Commander Josiah Tattnall's rescue (1859) of a badly battered British naval force off the Chinese coast. His excuse was the now almost forbidden proposition that "blood is thicker than water." Tattnall later skippered the Confederate ironclad *Virginia* (formerly *Merrimack*) after her battle with the *Monitor*. *Webster's Biographical Dictionary*, Merriam, Springfield, Mass., 1966, p. 1448.

were particularly grateful for United States support since no territorial or financial favors were asked in return. But while the Nationalist Chinese and the Chinese Communists had been fighting the Japanese, they were both preparing for a renewal of the bitter civil strife which had begun in the 1920s and which had been temporarily postponed by the Japanese invasion. As expected, the Carthaginian struggle between the Communists and Nationalists flared up again when the common enemy surrendered.

In 1949 Chiang Kai-shek and the rags and tatters of his Nationalist forces ignominiously fled to Formosa where they were sheltered from the triumphant Communists by the United States Navy. American aid to Chiang had not been sufficient to prevent his defeat, but more than sufficient to embitter the victors, who proceeded to make the United States the chief scapegoat for all China's ills, past and present, foreign and domestic, real and illusory. America's relations with China reached their lowest point in 1950 when American troops in the Korean War, having forced the North Koreans to retreat to the Chinese border, were in turn surprised, mauled, and driven back to South Korea by 200,000 Chinese "volunteers." The Korean war ended with the reestablishment of the tenuous *status quo ante.* In spite of 57,000 American casualties, it was the second war in United States history to end in a stalemate.

One of the principal reasons for the collapse of Sino-American relations had been America's refusal to consider and understand the racial factors which had been shaping the momentous changes in modern China. For one thing China is fundamentally a monoracial state. While the Northern Chinese are taller and have larger heads than the brachycephalic Southern Chinese, almost all Chinese are Mongoloids and belong to a race that is less differentiated than the Caucasian.[2]

Although American liberals have made much of the indignities heaped upon Chinese immigrants in California, the Chinese themselves have a long history of racism. Even the highest foreign dignitaries, classified by imperial edict as "outside barbarians,"

---

2. Coon, *The Living Races of Man.* pp. 148–50. Only about 6 percent of the inhabitants of China can be properly described as belonging to minorities, and most of these live in China's frontier regions. Amrit Lal, "Ethnic Minorities of Mainland China," *Mankind Quarterly,* April-June, 1968.

had to perform the kowtow in the emperor's presence. In a formal communication to King George III in 1807, the Chinese emperor employed slurs that would have been insulting to the denizens of skid row.[3]

The intensity of Chinese racism, however, does not mean that Western influences are no longer at work in China or that divisions do not exist within the Communist regime. The cultural distinctions between Chinese provinces are often pronounced, and there is such a variety of languages and dialects that some Chinese communicate with each other in English. Ironically, the anti-Western and antiwhite Mao Tse-tung in his grandiose effort to communize more than one billion people sanctified the teachings of the Western Jew, Karl Marx. But China's ancient ways, its ancestor worship, and its family-centered provincial life still place massive inertial constraints on enduring proletarianization.

Although few history books say so, the principal Chinese Communist dynamic has not been Marxism but xenophobia. The hated white had to be expelled from Chinese territory, and he was. Even the Russians, who were supposed to be permanently joined to the Chinese in the fraternal embrace of worker solidarity, were driven out and damned as heretics.[4]

As to the future, Mao envisioned a new kind of class war— the countryside, with the peasantry in the role of the proletariat, versus the city. Ruralized Africa, Asia, and Latin America would surround and strangle urbanized North America and Western Europe, the last stronghold of the moneygrubbing capitalists and bourgeoisie, corrupt labor unions, and decadent Communist revisionists. The war would be won by guerrilla tactics à la Vietnam, with a little help here and there from China's swelling nuclear arsenal.[5]

Mao's successors will probably never make good his threats or live up to his aphorisms.[6] Nevertheless American foreign policy

---

3. Nathaniel Peffer, *The Far East*, pp. 51–54.

4. The last Russians left in 1960. All that remains of white rule in China are the small and precarious enclaves of British Hong Kong and Portuguese Macao.

5. A. Doak Barnett, *China After Mao*, Princeton University Press, Princeton, N.J., 1967, pp. 59–60, 75, 77.

6. "Politics is war without bloodshed while war is politics with bloodshed. . . . War can only be abolished through war, and in order to get rid of the

gained little by cultivating the Formosan nettle in China's eastern flank. American backing of Taiwan only strengthened the Communist position in China. The United States Seventh Fleet patrolling the Chinese coast and 600,000 Nationalist troops in training one hundred miles off the Chinese mainland fitted neatly into the Communist propaganda picture of blood-thirsty imperialists readying a mass assault to recapture their lost financial hegemony. Also there was nothing like a good invasion scare to take Chinese minds off the monumental problems besetting the home front.

Totally misunderstanding the racial nature of the Chinese revolution, American foreign policy experts were convinced that any Communist state would become, ipso facto, a Russian ally. The truth is that, in times of revolution, race or nationality takes precedence over class. As Yugoslavia, Albania, Communist Vietnam, Communist Cambodia, and China itself have amply demonstrated, Communist states are just as proficient as anti-Communist states in developing and promoting anti-Russian, anti-Chinese, or neutralist foreign policies. Reds, it has come to pass, have no greater enemies than other Reds.

America has been wise to continue to mend its diplomatic fences with China. By doing so the United States can fully restore its traditional friendship with the world's most populous nation. Renewed American neutrality in Far Eastern affairs could well be strengthened by acting as the middle man in the reunification of Formosa and mainland China, much as Theodore Roosevelt increased American prestige immeasurably in the Orient by mediating the end of the Russo-Japanese war. Now that Chiang Kai-shek and Mao are both dead, it is time to take the inevitable first steps to make the two Chinas one. Whatever happens, no ideological affection for Taiwanese capitalism, no guilt feelings about an abandoned ally, and no ideological hostility toward the convulsive Communist Chinese economy should be allowed to furnish a pretext for China to revive its short-lived alliance with

---

gun it is necessary to take up the gun. . . . The more books a person reads the more stupid he becomes . . . I do not mean to close down the schools. What I mean is that it is not absolutely necessary to go to school. . . . Not to have a correct political point of view is like having no soul." *Quotations from Chairman Mao Tse-tung,* Bantam Books, New York, 1967, pp. 32, 35, 69, 78. Also see *New York Times,* March 1, 1970, p. 26.

the Soviet Union. One of the greatest assurances of American and Western European security lies in the continuing hostility of Peking and Moscow, a hostility that shrewd American diplomacy should keep simmering as long as the Soviet Union has designs on the West.

American foreign policy has an easier task in the Far East than anywhere else. In East Asia the United States does not need to establish a military counterweight to the U.S.S.R. The counterweight already exists. For the foreseeable future China is the one nation in the world that has the will, the manpower, and the resources to fight the Soviet Union single-handedly in a conventional war. Moreover it may soon be able to give a good account of itself in a nuclear war. That the United States should pursue anything but a friendly policy toward China, the only nation that can effectively oppose Soviet expansion in the Far East, is schizoid diplomacy at its worst. History, geography, culture, race—all indicate an eventual clash between China and the Soviet Union.

This is not to say the United States should enter such a war on the side of China, as no doubt will be proposed by the growing anti-Soviet faction of the liberal-minority coalition. America helped destroy Germany, the Western bastion against Slavdom, in 1945. It would be a worse tragedy if America helped China destroy Russia, the white bastion against the yellow race.

Moving the discussion to Japan, one might begin by saying it would have been better for all concerned, especially the Japanese, if Commodore Perry had never landed in Yedo Bay in 1854. By forcing Japan to give up its 400-year isolation, the United States was unwittingly sowing the dragon's teeth which sprouted into the fanatic and dedicated military machine it would meet eighty-seven years later at Pearl Harbor. Since Japanese geography precluded regional and cultural fractionation on the Chinese model, Japan was able to convert to Western technology much faster and more efficiently, and without China's revolutionary turmoil.

Racially the Japanese are a Mongoloid people from the Asiatic mainland with an admixture of prehistoric migrants from Southeast Asia. Having experienced little immigration in the last thousand years, Japan boasts one of the most homogeneous populations on earth, which partially accounts for its citizenry's fierce sense of race. Like the Chinese, the Japanese were outraged by American immigration restrictions against Orientals, although Japan itself had practiced racial exclusiveness for centuries. The original inhabitants of Japan were the Ainus, a Caucasoid stock, perhaps the remnants of a white race that once dominated Northern Asia. The Ainus have now been pushed back to the northernmost areas of Japan, where they have been undergoing a process of biological and cultural absorption that is rapidly destroying their racial identity. Another important minority in Japan has not fared much better. During the 1923 earthquake, there was a pogrom of Koreans in Tokyo.[7]

Article IX of Japan's postwar constitution contains the widely acclaimed clause renouncing war as a "sovereign right of the nation" and stating that "land, sea and air forces, as well as other war potentials, will never be maintained." This is a rather startling reversal for a country which had developed the military way of life to a fine art (Bushido) and whose social hierarchy consisted of the soldier, artisan, peasant, and merchant in that order.[8] No other nation, not even Sparta, has ever produced anything like the incredible heroics of the Kamikaze pilots of World War II.

The constitution notwithstanding, Japan now has a "Self-Defense Force" of 268,000 men, 800 military aircraft, 46 destroyers, and 44 submarines.[9] With an increasingly militarized China a few missile minutes away, with the Soviet Union poised on the southern half of Sakhalin Island (Stalin's prize for entering the Pacific war five days before it ended), the Japanese have little reason to cling much longer to their uncharacteristic experiment in disarmament. Japan has the world's third largest economy, yet it only devotes one percent of its GNP to defense. It depends almost entirely on Arabian and Iranian oil, yet relies on America to keep open the shipping lanes of the Persian Gulf. Its cars, cameras, watches, TV sets, and electronic gear are causing severe economic dislocation and unemployment in the industrial nations of the West, yet it bristles at the thought that others might adopt the protectionism with which it defends its own industries.

---

7. Peffer, *The Far East,* p. 341.
8. Ibid., p. 34.
9. *Whitaker's Almanack 1981,* p. 889.

Unfortunately for the Japanese business community, America can no longer afford to be the guardian angel of a nation that is putting it out of business. American troops stationed in Japan, always a source of friction in Japanese-American relations, will almost certainly be withdrawn in one or two decades, along with the nuclear umbrella. No one, least of all the Japanese, seriously believes that the United States would expose its own cities to devastation by using thermonuclear bombs to defend Japan against Soviet aggression. At any rate it is more to China's interest than to America's to prevent an attempt by the U.S.S.R. to "Finlandize" Japan by means of nuclear blackmail.

With a population of 115,000,000 (1978 estimate) packed into an area only slightly smaller than California, only one-sixth of it arable,[10] Japan is in for some rough sledding in the twenty-first century. Once the most isolationist of nations, Japan has lost much of its unique character and its highly developed aesthetics in its mad rush to dominate world trade. A considerable reduction in the size of the Japanese population by a nationwide birth-control program, accompanied by a considerable measure of de-industrialization, would rescue Japan from its headlong rush toward Western-style materialism, while eliminating a hideous, unlivable urban sprawl like modern Tokyo. Fewer Japanese and fewer Japanese products would not only benefit the rest of the world by saving the precious natural resources consumed by Japan's voracious industry, but might also prove to be the salvation of the threatened Japanese ethos.

If an American withdrawal from Japan endangers the independence of South Korea, so be it. The United States cannot overextend itself indefinitely guaranteeing the freedom of Far Eastern client states. All such countries have been occupied so long by other nations that they have almost forgotten the meaning of independence. When it is thrust upon them, they have even less chance of achieving it.

Elsewhere in the Far East, the policy of the United States, at least until quite recently, seems to have been the protection of the unprotectable. American intervention in Vietnam has starkly underlined what happens to a hamstrung, unmotivated, magnifi-

---

10. Peffer, op. cit., p. 40.

cently equipped modern military machine when it meets a determined, highly motivated, poorly equipped fighting force of guerrillas and regulars. If the makers of American foreign policy had
understood that the antiwhite feelings of the Vietnamese were
so intense that the mere presence of American troops on one
side would immeasurably boost the morale and will to fight of
the other, they might not have been so eager to send a large
American army to replace the departed and defeated French.[11]

The primary mistake of those responsible for America's military
involvement in Vietnam was their ignorance of the racial dynamics
at work in Southeast Asia. The secondary mistake was to engage
American armed forces in a war which, from the very first day,
they were not permitted to win. Recent history has proved that
the United States can only be aroused to a proper fighting pitch
when the war objectives correspond to the goals of the liberal-
minority coalition. Unless such "objectives" can be established
or invented, the media are likely to remain indifferent or even
hostile. If North Vietnam had had a fascist dictator instead of
the patriarchal "Uncle Ho," [12] if it had mistreated Jews and
Negroes [13] instead of Vietnamese peasants, the theater of opera-

---

11. Americans themselves would not be likely to hold any party or faction
in high respect that invited the Vietnamese army into the United States to help
defend it from an attack by other Americans. The appearance of foreign troops
on either side in the Civil War would certainly have stiffened the resistance of
the other. One reason Americans were able to escape defeat in Korea was that
there were many fewer North Koreans than South Koreans, a proportion which
did not prevail in Vietnam. The North Koreans had to call in the Chinese to
save them, thereby robbing their propaganda of some of its nationalist, anti-
foreign appeal. South Korea's population is 29,000,000; North Korea's 12,-
000,000. In contrast North Vietnam's population is 20,000,000; South Vietnam's
16,000,000. The ethnic differences of the two nations should also be kept in
mind. According to Darlington, the frontier between North and South Vietnam
is "one of the great racial boundaries of the world." *The Evolution of Society,* p.
615.

12. The late Drew Pearson, who was syndicated in 650 papers, twice as many
as any other columnist at the time, compared Ho Chi Minh to George Washington. *San Francisco Chronicle,* June 2, 1965, and *Time,* Sept. 12, 1969, p. 82.

13. Many Negro soldiers in Vietnam had special war aims of their own. Almost
half of those questioned said they would use arms to gain their rights when
they returned to the States. There were several military skirmishes between
white and black troops during the course of the war and nearly 800 attacks

tions would have been extended to North Vietnam and the war quickly won. The American experience in Korea had already demonstrated the coldness and opposition of liberal and minority intellectuals to a conflict which did not have the proper ideological ingredients.

The collapse of South Vietnam after Henry Kissinger's counterfeit peace, for which he had the gall to accept the Nobel Peace Prize, the imperialism of the Communist Vietnamese after their conquest of the South, Communist Vietnam's racial purge of its ethnic Chinese,[14] the horrors of the Communist revolution in Cambodia, followed by the Vietnamese invasion and occupation, the military punishment of Vietnam by China—all these events prove conclusively that there is as much disunity and strife among Marxist states in the second half of the twentieth century as there was among capitalist states in the first half.

The most and the best that America can do for the nations of Asia is to leave them alone. For many of the smaller countries neutrality is the surest protection against invasion or revolution. When America retires from the Far East, the chances are that other nations in the area, such as the Philippines, will eventually experiment with communism. If they do, it is to be hoped—and it is a well-founded hope—that they will turn against the neighboring Communist states rather than against America and the West. The United States spent more than $40 billion and lost more than 58,000 lives in an unsuccessful attempt to prevent the fall of South Vietnam, which the domino theorists said would make Southeast Asia part of a worldwide, monolithic Communist imperium. When the smoke had cleared away, the feared monolith broke apart into bitterly hostile fragments, just as it had in Eurasia after the Communist revolution in China.

There are only two countries in the Far East—or more correctly in Australasia—with which the United States should maintain the firmest military ties. These are Australia and New Zealand. Here

---

on officers and sergeants with fragmentation grenades, resulting in 101 deaths. *Miami Herald*, Nov. 10, 1972, p. 2A, *Time*, Sept. 19, 1969, p. 22, and Jan. 23, 1971, p. 34, and *Dallas News*, April 2, 1977.

14. Much as the economic success of Jews gives rise to anti-Semitism in the West, the affluence of Chinese minorities provokes outbursts of anti-Sinicism in Southeast Asia.

the American commitment should transcend the usual materialistic and ideological considerations of strategy, anti-communism, self-determination, and democracy, and rest on the more permanent and solid foundations of biological and cultural affinity. Australia and New Zealand, inhabited by more than 17,000,000 people of largely British descent, are the last frontier of the Northern European, who is never really happy unless he has a frontier. Since there were no Asians, only a few Stone Age aborigines, on the Australian land mass when the whites arrived, Chinese, Japanese, and other Orientals can hardly accuse Australians of being white exploiters of the yellow man.[15] The Maoris have a slightly better case against the New Zealanders because they were there first—by nine centuries—and account for 8 or 9 percent of the present population.

Australia had a selective immigration policy that was intended to double or triple the country's population by the end of the century without, however, altering its basic racial composition.[16] This sensible plan of homogeneous growth was dashed by the 1972 election victory of the Labor party, which immediately renounced the "white Australia" policy for one of accepting all colors and creeds. Since then some 25,000 nonwhites a year have been entering the country, making a grand total to date (1980) of about 250,000. The Conservative party's return to power in 1978 did little to resist the seeping equalitarianism of the West, against which 10,000 miles of ocean had been no protection. New Zealand, on the other hand, much smaller (1977 population estimate, 3,110,000) and with only 3,803 Jews, has so far attracted a much smaller, though significant, amount of Third World overflow.

Today Australasia still remains one of the whitest spots in the

---

15. Australia's aboriginal minority now totals 50,000 plus 150,000 half-castes. The aborigines belong to the separate Australoid race, have a coloration that ranges from sooty black to brown and are distinguished by their beetling brows, sloping foreheads and projecting jaws. Coon, *The Living Races of Man*, pp. 12, 310. Their low place on the human evolutionary scale makes it difficult for even the most equalitarian-minded anthropologist to credit them with the same mental abilities as whites or Mongoloids.

16. In 1978 Australia had an estimated population of 14,250,000. The *1981 World Almanac* says there are 70,000 Jews in Australia, one of whom is Governor-General Zelman Cowen. Prime Minister Malcolm Fraser is half-Jewish.

increasingly mottled population map of Western civilization. If any nation should erect strict immigration barriers against non-whites, it is Australia, an underpopulated continent which faces the southeast corner of the world's most populated continent. If Australia does manage to stay white, it may eventually be the center of the most advanced and authentic expression of Western life, a final port of call for those Majority Americans and Northern Europeans who allowed their own countries to become minority-ridden bedlams. Should it follow current Western population trends, however, Australia in the words of its great poet, A. D. Hope, may become "the last of the lands, the emptiest . . . where second-hand Europeans pullulate timidly on the edge of alien shores."

CHAPTER 35

The United States and the Middle East

THE EXACT GEOGRAPHICAL makeup of the Middle East has never been authoritatively defined or agreed upon by mapmakers, historians, or experts in foreign affairs. Here it will be demarcated, perhaps too inclusively, as Iran, Iraq, Jordan, the Arabian peninsula, and those countries contiguous to the Eastern Mediterranean ranging clockwise from Turkey through Morocco. It was in the Middle East that man is supposed to have invented civilization. It is in the Middle East that warring Jews, Arabs, Iranians, or oil-thirsty outsiders may provoke a nuclear confrontation which could bring much of civilization to an untimely end.

The United States was involved in Middle Eastern matters as far back as 1805 when Captain William Eaton, directing a land attack on the ports of the Barbary Pirates, marched a handful of American marines, Greeks, Bedouins, and Arab camel drivers 500 miles across the desert from Egypt to the eastern edge of present-day Libya, where he captured the city of Derna.[1] Ten years later Stephen Decatur with the help of an American naval squadron forced the Dey of Algiers to stop levying tribute on American vessels and holding American seamen for ransom.[2]

For more than a century thereafter, American relations with Middle Eastern nations were, on the whole, economic in nature, of small historical import, and friendly. It was only after World

---

1. Henry Adams, *History of the U.S. during the First Administration of Thomas Jefferson,* Boni and Liveright, N.Y., 1930, Book II, pp. 432, 488.

2. Kendrick Babcock, "The Rise of American Nationality," *The Historians' History of the United States,* Putnam, New York, 1966, p. 458.

War II, when the United States was drawn into the void left by the imploding British Empire, that the Middle East drew the serious attention of American diplomacy. The Truman Doctrine (1947), in response to Stalin's resurrection of czarist designs on Constantinople, allocated part of a $400,000,000 aid program to Turkey. In return for arms, money, and full-scale military assistance in the event of a Russian invasion, Turkey gave the United States the right to construct air bases and became an American ally.

Then, in 1948, the liberal-minority coalition succeeded in shifting the fulcrum of America's Middle Eastern policy from Turkey to Israel. The Balfour Declaration, by means of which the British government bought the support of world Jewry in World War I, has been mentioned earlier.[3] It must now be added that, while promising British backing for a Jewish homeland in Palestine, Britain had two years earlier, in 1915, made similar promises to the Arabs to enlist them in the fight against Turkey, Germany's ally in the Middle East.[4] The Palestinian Arabs, whose country had been ruled by Turkey for 400 years, did not need much urging. But when the war had come to an end, when Turkey had lost all its Arab lands, when the League of Nations had given Britain the Palestinian mandate, the British government made no effort to make good its word to either side, beyond allowing an ominous increase in Zionist immigration. Britain had in effect sold a house it did not own to two different buyers, the prior sale having been to its Arab occupants.

The size and rate of Zionist immigration is the key to all that followed. In World War I, Jews comprised 10 percent of Palestine's population. By 1940 there were 456,743 Jews in Palestine—one-third of the inhabitants. The remaining two-thirds consisted of 145,063 Christians and 1,143,336 Moslems, whose ancestors

---

3. See pp. 450–51.

4. Britain's high commissioner to Egypt gave formal assurances regarding Arab independence in the Middle East to the emir of Mecca, later the king of Hejaz, in what has come to be known as the McMahon-Hussein correspondence. It might be noted that the World War I hero and desert fighter, T. E. Lawrence, was deeply indignant at his country for what he considered its later betrayal of the Arab cause. Sachar, *The Course of Modern Jewish History*, pp. 370–71, and Yale, *The Near East*, pp. 243–44, 320.

had lived in Palestine for a hundred generations.[5] After an absence of nearly 2,000 years, it was the Jews who were the newcomers.

The Nazi persecution of European Jewry stimulated a worldwide Zionist effort to make the glowing dream of Israel an immediate reality. An unprecedented, intercontinental lobbying campaign, seasoned with mounting acts of Jewish terrorism,[6] finally drove the British to hand Palestine over to the United Nations and withdraw. The Zionists were ready. On the very day the last British high commissioner left Palestine (May 14, 1948), Israel was proclaimed an independent state. President Truman recognized it exactly ten minutes later,[7] despite President Roosevelt's written pledge to King Ibn Saud of Saudi Arabia (April 5, 1945) that the United States would take no action which might prove hostile to the Arab people.[8]

Russia also hastened to recognize Israel, knowing that turmoil between Arab and Jew would smooth the entrance of Soviet communism into a sun-drenched, oil-rich southland long coveted by the czars. Even the United Nations ultimately welcomed Israel as its fifty-ninth member (1949), although an Israeli gang had assassinated the UN mediator, Count Bernadotte, and although the use of terror in the creation of Israel was in total violation of the letter and spirit of the UN charter.

A month before the birth of the Zionist state, the skirmishing that had been going on for years between Jews and Arabs erupted into war. The Jewish terrorist attack on Deir Yassin on April 9, 1948, in which 254 Arab women, children, and old men were indiscriminately slaughtered,[9] precipitated an Arab exodus which

---

5. Population statistics from *Ency. Brit.*, Vol. 17, pp. 133–34.

6. The Stern and Irgun terrorist gangs, armed with American Lend-Lease weapons stolen by the truckload, ran wild through Palestine, shooting down British soldiers. In July 1946, they set off a bomb in a Jerusalem hotel, killing ninety-one people, mostly civilians. *Ency. Brit.*, Vol. 17, p. 136.

7. Sachar, *The Course of Modern Jewish History*, p. 479.

8. Yale, op. cit., p. 402.

9. Alfred Lilienthal, *The Zionist Connection*, Dodd, Mead, New York, 1978, p. 254. It is not known if the soldiers who committed this massacre were ever punished. Most of those who took part in another atrocity—the machine-gunning of forty-nine Arab villagers returning to the hamlet of Kafr Kassim (Oct. 29, 1956), fourteen of them women with children in their arms—went scot-free after standing trial. A few, however, were given prison sentences of one year.

eventually totaled 2,700,000 displaced persons (the original refugees, their children born in exile, and the refugees from the 1967 war).[10] Since most Palestinian Arabs and Arabs of neighboring states had barely progressed beyond the feudal stages of society, they were no military match for the Westernized Jews—whose highest-ranking officers, both mentally and physically, were often closer to the Northern European than to any Jewish stereotype.[11]

Today the Palestinian and Jewish proportions of the population of Israel are almost the exact reverse of what they were fifty years ago. Half of the 3,200,000 Israeli Jews (1980 estimate) are *Schwarzim*, dark Jews from North Africa and Asia who arrived after World War II [12] and who are rapidly outbreeding the lighter European

---

These sentences were somewhat lighter than those given Nazi defendants at the Nuremberg trials, a decade earlier. Interestingly, there was not the slightest outcry from the news media against the Israeli war criminals. *San Francisco Chronicle*, Jan. 10, 1962, and Alfred Lilienthal, *The Other Side of the Coin*, Devin-Adair, New York, 1965, pp. 219–20. Within Israel, however, there has been some distress over the eventual repercussions of military adventurism. After an Israeli terrorist attack on Jordan in February 1951, four Hebrew University professors asked: "Is this the Jewish tradition on which we believe the state of Israel was founded? Is this the regard for human life on which the Jewish people stood when they were not yet a political nation? Is this the way of proving to the world that our nation upholds the principle of justice?" See William Ernest Hocking's article on Israel in *Christian Century*, Sept. 19, 1951. One of the worst and most incomprehensible acts of the Israelis was the looting of the Old City of Jerusalem in the 1967 war, described by Evan Wilson, the U.S. consul general and minister at Jerusalem, in his book, *Key to Peace*, The Middle East Institute, Washington, D.C., 1970, p. 111.

10. A 1981 count of Palestinians showed 530,600 in Israel proper, 818,300 in the occupied West Bank, 476,700 in the occupied Gaza Strip, 1,160,800 in Jordan, 347,100 in Lebanon, 215,500 in Syria, 278,800 in Kuwait, 127,000 in Saudi Arabia, 34,700 in the United Arab Emirates, 22,500 in Qatar, 10,200 in the U.S., and 218,000 elsewhere. *Economist* (London), March 25, 1981, p. 50.

11. The toughest stratum of European Jewry went to Palestine in the turn-of-the-century pioneering days, when most Jews were going to New York. Sabras, native-born Jewish Palestinians, evince their own particular "inside racism" by insisting that they are Israelis, not Jews. The infrequency of recognizable Jewish physical traits in Israel is illustrated by the popularity of a favorite Israeli anecdote—the reply of the tourist when asked how he liked Israel. "Fine," he said, "but where are the Jews?" Robert Ardrey, *The Territorial Imperative*, Atheneum, New York, 1966, p. 310.

12. J. Robert Moskin, "Prejudice in Israel," *Look*, Oct. 5, 1965, pp. 56–65. The *Schwarzim* charge European Jews with discrimination because the latter hold

elements.[13] Immigration is not helping to redress this racial imbalance nor doing much to build up the population as a whole. Since 1948, 1,700,000 Jews have immigrated to Israel, including a large number of the 250,000 who left the Soviet Union. But today almost as many are leaving Israel as are arriving. Soviet Jews often prefer to go to America, even to Germany.[14] As many as 400,000 Israelis now reside in the United States.

Almost totally dedicated to Israel in spirit, American Jews have nevertheless preferred to support the Jewish homeland by opening their purses rather than by dodging Arab bullets. Only 100 American Jews (as of 1969) were serving in the Israeli armed forces.[15] Financially, however, the contributions of American Jews to Israel have been staggering. So have the contributions of the American government. Speaking in 1980, Deputy Assistant Secretary of State Michael Sterner said the United States had provided the Jewish state with $20 billion in military and economic aid since 1948.[16] On May 19, 1978, Vice-President Walter Mondale asserted:

> In the last four years (1974–1978) alone, the U.S. has allocated $10 billion in military and economic assistance to Israel, more than

---

most of the important state jobs. As in America, the darker-skinned members of the population have started a few riots to emphasize their displeasure and frustration.

13. The orientalization of Israel does not disturb Foreign Minister Abba Eban. "[Our] cultural future," he stated, "lies in the victory of the existing culture, which is European in its roots and Hebrew in its garb." Ibid.

14. In 1980, despite intense pressure from American Jewry, Jewish emigration from the Soviet Union, after reaching a high of nearly 51,000 in 1979, was expected to fall to 36,000. Associated Press report, Oct. 9, 1980. Congress has appropriated tens of millions of dollars to pay Soviet Jews' traveling expenses and continues to withhold most-favored nation status for Soviet trade until the U.S.S.R. opens its exit gates for Jews much wider.

15. World Press Review, WNET, New York, Nov. 3, 1969. American Jews can join the Israeli army and still retain their American citizenship.

16. Much of the financial and military aid has been involuntary. Most American taxpayers would never have approved the tax deductibility of the private gifts to Israel or many of the congressional grants. Quite a few members of the United Auto Workers and the Teamsters disagree with the large purchases of low-interest Israel bonds by the directors of union pension funds. They wonder why part of their dues is being invested in a country that is practically bankrupt, that has an immense and unmanageable national debt, and has, at this writing, an annual inflation rate of 130 percent.

to any other nation in the world. . . . Of all American security assistances proposed in next year's budget, 42 percent of our supporting assistance and 48 percent of military sales credits and 56 percent of all military grants are distributed to the single nation of Israel. And repayment on half of those credits, which total $1 billion, is systematically waived by the U.S. That's a benefit enjoyed by no other nation on earth.

Mondale's financial statement did not include the $3.1 billion owed to Israel as a result of the Camp David accords. Nor did it include the billions of dollars raised by the sale of Israel bonds (without fully complying with SEC regulations), nor the tax deductible billions poured into Jewish organizations and then transferred to Israel, nor the hundreds of millions, if not billions, derived from special import privileges, preferred customer status for buying from government stockpiles, and patent and licensing agreements.

Practically unknown to the American public are the huge reparations paid to Israel and Jews everywhere by West Germany—the *Wiedergutmachung* that will amount to almost 90 billion marks before the reparations program ends in 1984–85.[17] In the course of these payments—unmatched in history both in size and in the amount awarded to individuals—the mark ranged in value from 23¢ to 56¢. When the financial outlays from the rest of world Jewry are added to the American and West German contributions, it is no exaggeration to say that close to $75 billion has been given in a little more than three decades to a nation equal in size to Massachusetts with a population equal to Tennessee's.

In the manifold discussions and debates about the "dollar drain" and "tax loopholes," there has been very little mention of American financial aid to Israel, one of the most important sources of the dollar drain and one of the widest of the tax loopholes. The purchases of American tourists abroad are limited and the oil depletion allowances reduced. Tax shelters are bitterly attacked. But tax-free money still flows in torrents to Israel with hardly a murmur of criticism—money that not only escapes the United States Treasury, so that every American is taxed a little more, but money that escapes the country altogether, so that

---

17. Chicago *Sentinel,* Dec. 25, 1980, p. 6.

the dollar is weakened and the balance of payments worsened.

The Internal Revenue Service is not the only government agency that has exceeded the bounds of its authority in helping the cause of Zionism. In the hectic days just preceding Israel's creation, the FBI winked at the establishment of a clandestine Zionist radio station on the Eastern seaboard and at the rash of gunrunning and other violations of American neutrality laws.[18] Rudolph Sonneborn, the millionaire head of Witco Chemical, set up in New York City what amounted to the American branch of Haganah, the Zionist underground organization. Five hundred American and Canadian flyers, many of them non-Jews, pieced together the Israeli Air Force while Palestine was still under British rule. Three United States Army officers were serving in Haganah under the command of Chief of Staff Yaacov Dori when the Zionists opened their military attack against the British occupation troops. Members of the Office of Strategic Services taught Zionist agents the use of ciphers and codes in a secret New York City espionage school.[19] It was all very gallant and exciting, except that it ended in the expulsion of a peaceful, agricultural population from its ancient homeland and created a festering international sore that will take decades, if not centuries, to heal.

While many of these events were taking place, James Forrestal, secretary of defense in the Truman administration, was the only cabinet member who spoke out publicly against Zionism. In the manner of Cassandra and with equal effect, he warned of the geopolitical consequences of American sponsorship of an anachronistic imperialism and colonialism that brought back memories of pith helmets and swagger sticks to Third World nations—the

---

18. After two Zionist agents were arrested at the Canadian border for arms smuggling, Robert Nathan, a White House assistant, got them a personal interview with FBI Director J. Edgar Hoover, who offered them his cooperation. Leonard Slater, *The Pledge*, Simon and Schuster, New York, 1970, pp. 75–76. Hank Greenspun, a Las Vegas publisher, was convicted of stealing cases of rifle barrels for Israel from a U.S. Naval Supply Depot in Hawaii, yet neither he nor any other American Jewish gunrunner guilty of similar charges ever spent a day in jail. The only one who did go to prison for illegally obtaining arms for Israel was Charlie Winters, a Protestant. William Horowitz, who was deeply involved in these unlawful operations, is now a banker and a member of the Yale Corporation, the governing body of Yale University. *Ibid.*, p. 59.

19. *Ibid.*, pp. 22, 101–3, 117, 309.

very nations then being assured by the State Department of America's peaceful, anti-imperialist, anti-colonialist intentions. The vituperation Forrestal received from press and radio was one of the factors which led to his suicide.[20]

Dean Acheson, at that time under secretary of state and extremely active in foreign affairs, chose not to support Forrestal and obediently executed Truman's pro-Israeli policy, although he later frankly admitted it was against the "totality of American interest" in the Middle East.[21] Some twenty years after the fact, Acheson also explained that Truman did not, as British Foreign Minister Bevin had charged, commit the United States to Israel in order to woo the Jewish vote. According to Acheson, Truman's pro-Israel stance was explained by his friendship with Eddie Jacobson, his erstwhile partner in a short-lived haberdashery business in Kansas City.[22]

From the birth of Israel up to the present, a blind, unquestioning pro-Zionist ideology has so permeated and dominated American thought that, whenever the discussion has turned to the Middle East, leaders in every walk of public life abandon all reason and judgment, not to mention their intellectual integrity.[23] The same

---

20. See footnote 42, p. 324.

21. Dean Acheson, *Present at the Creation,* Norton, New York, 1969, p. 169. The news media never criticized Acheson for his pusillanimity in refusing to fight for the Middle Eastern policy he believed in. But it hailed him for his courage when he made the memorable statement, "I will not turn my back on Alger Hiss."

22. Ibid. A leading Jewish scholar does not exactly agree with the Acheson theory. Howard Sachar asserts that Truman was also attracted to the Israeli cause by the pressure of such important American Jews as Governor Herbert Lehman of New York, Jacob "Jake" Arvey, the Chicago political boss, and David Niles, Roosevelt and Truman's special assistant for minority affairs. *The Course of Modern Jewish History,* p. 471.

23. As one writer put it, "Zionist propaganda in this country has been so powerful, so contemptuous of constraints . . . that the few voices raised in criticism of it have scarcely been heard." *San Francisco Examiner, Book Week,* May 23, 1965, p. 15. Perhaps the most effective of these "few voices" is that of the tireless anti-Zionist Jew, Alfred Lilienthal. The most outspoken Jewish anti-Zionist group, the American Council for Judaism, lost 80 percent of its membership a year after Israel was founded. In June 1967, most of its prominent members were supporting Israel as devotedly as the most fervent Zionists. Yaffe, op. cit., pp. 186–88, and *Commentary,* August 1967, p. 70. The leitmotiv of Jewish

educators who insist on the desegregation of American schools have solidly supported Israel, which has segregated schools for its Arab minority. The same churchmen and laymen who preach the separation of church and state, the equality of the sexes, and opposition to any racial or religious tests for marriage have stood four-square for Israel, where church and state are one, where interfaith marriages are forbidden, and where women who worship in Orthodox synagogues are segregated behind screened-off galleries.

The same "One Worlders" who founded the United Nations have had only good things to say for the Zionist diplomacy that has flaunted almost all UN resolutions on Israel.[24] The same "decent" liberals who believe in the self-determination of peoples and the peaceful arbitration of international disputes have given their unstinting approval to a nation founded on old-fashioned, blood-and-iron tactics of conquest and the military dispersion of the natives. The same editorial writers who adulate leaders of anti-colonialist and socialist nations transformed Egypt's late President Nasser, the anti-colonialist, socialist leader par excellence, into a latter-day Hitler. The same opinion makers who called South Vietnam's Vice-Premier Ky a butcher applauded—whenever Israeli foreign policy so dictated—the archreactionary King Hussein of Jordan when his Bedouin mercenaries laid down artillery barrages on Palestinian refugee camps. The same writers, painters, and musicians who are horrified at the slightest restriction of artistic expression have had nothing but praise for a country which officially banned the music of Wagner and Richard Strauss.[25] The same pacifists who fought the draft so bitterly in the United States clamorously applaud a government which not only drafts all able-bodied males between eighteen and twenty-six for twenty-six months, but unmarried women of the same age for twenty months.

As the 1967 replay of the periodic Arab-Israeli conflict approached, the liberal-minority establishment seemed to lose all contact with logic and rationality and lapsed into a kind of babbling

anti-Zionism springs from the fear that Zionism in the long run will augment rather than diminish anti-Semitism.

24. When the UN turned sharply against Israel in the "Zionism equals racism" vote, American liberals obediently turned against the UN.

25. *San Francisco Chronicle*, June 18, 1966, p. 34.

schizophrenia. The nation's foremost advocate of nonviolence, Martin Luther King, Jr., demanded America use force, if necessary, to keep open the Strait of Tiran, which Nasser had ordered closed to ships bringing strategic war materials to the Israeli port of Elath.[26] Members of peace groups threw down their placards and demonstrated with war groups.[27] Senator Wayne Morse, the Senate's leading dove, stood up and said the United States Navy should sail into the Gulf of Aqaba "with flags flying." [28] The late Robert Kennedy, although busy establishing an antiwar image for the 1968 presidential race, came on almost as strongly. The ideological reversal of America's most prominent intellectuals and politicians was so complete, the Orwellian double-think and double-talk so incredible, that it could not altogether escape the attention of the less fanatical news organs.

The warm feelings of American Jews toward Israel are understandable. But their totalitarian dedication to Zionism has created a grave conflict of interest in regard to their duties and responsibilities as American citizens. French and Soviet officials, who are allowed some free expression on the issue, have already called into question the split loyalty of their Zionists and Zionist supporters.[29] In America, however, the following questions must still be asked—and answered—in silence: How American is the American citizen who has forced through a foreign policy that in a few short years has made the United States, once their firm friend, the enemy of most of the world's 130,000,000 Arabs and many of the world's 546,000,000 Moslems? [30] How American is

---

26. *New York Times*, May 28, 1967, p. 4. Both sides of the strait, which separates the Red Sea from the Gulf of Aqaba, were Arab territory.

27. *Time*, June 2, 1967, p. 11.   28. Ibid.

29. In an article in *Le Monde*, René Massigli, former French ambassador to London, wondered about the loyalty of French Jews, particularly after their indifference to the attack on French President Pompidou by American Jews. *New York Times*, March 2, 1970, p. 15.

30. Although anti-Semitic acts are not tolerated in the U.S., anti-Arabic acts are. In 1966, King Faisal of Saudi Arabia, one of America's few remaining friends in the Middle East, was officially snubbed during a visit to New York City. Mayor Lindsay refused to give him an official reception for fear of offending his Jewish constituency. *New York Times*, June 24, 1966, p. 1. Lindsay was even more discourteous during the visit of French President Pompidou in early 1970. He not only refused to greet Pompidou, but ran off to Washington and remained there

the American citizen who has knowingly promoted and financed a program of military adventurism that gives Communist propaganda mills an unheard-of opportunity to discredit America in the Middle East, an area that contains two-thirds of the world's proven oil reserves?

Today, as a consequence of American connivance in the genesis and growth of Israel, the Soviet Union can pretend to be the champion and friend of the Arabs, once the most anti-Communist people on earth. The Soviet navy, with almost as many vessels as the United States Sixth Fleet, patrols the Eastern Mediterranean and has penetrated the Red Sea and the Indian Ocean. As one report stated in 1968:

> The defeat of the United Arab Republic by Israel, jubilantly treated as a defeat for Russia, actually has proved also to be a disguised blessing for Moscow. The Soviets are now gradually taking over both the Republic of Yemen and the larger Republic of South Yemen created by Britain's walkout from Aden . . . the United States is going to discover with astonishment that it has lost its entire power structure from the Mediterranean to Southeast Asia.[31]

The policy which has already cost America the friendship of most of the Arab world and the respect of the Moslem world may also carry a much higher price. It was pointed out earlier that the liberal-minority coalition will only lend its full support to a war in behalf of liberal goals and minority interests. As these two necessary requirements are now present in the Middle East, American intervention is not only possible but probable.

The news media are already geared for the task and behind the news media stand the war lobbies and their political acolytes. The B'nai B'rith, which describes itself as a religious and charitable organization and which exists on tax-deductible contributions, works around the clock to see that every member of the executive

---

while the French president was in New York. In Chicago, Madame Pompidou was spat upon, jostled, and cursed by Jewish pickets who were not afraid to create a serious incident with America's oldest ally in order to vent their spleen on France for selling fighter bombers to Libya. *New York Times*, March 3, 1970, p. 28. When Premier Golda Meir of Israel arrived in New York in late 1969, Lindsay treated her to a modern version of a Roman triumph.

31. *San Francisco Examiner and Chronicle*, April 7, 1968, Sec. A, p. 11.

and legislative branch of the American government stands unreservedly behind Israel. Other official or unofficial Zionist lobbies keep up a constant propaganda barrage, not only on the politicians, but on prominent Americans in all walks of life. Senators, who have received tens of thousands of dollars for speaking at Jewish fund-raisers, vote vast giveaways of American treasure to Israel.[32] In the old days this would have been called bribery. Today it is called smart politics.

A preview of what Jewish pressure groups have in store for the American people in the approaching Middle Eastern showdown was provided by the media's coverage of the 1967 "Six-Day War." [33] Even though the Israelis launched a combined air, land, and sea blitz on Egypt on the morning of June 5, 1967, it was several days before the American public was told who attacked whom. There were press, radio and television correspondents all over the Middle East, all primed for the outbreak of hostilities. Still no one seemed to know what was taking place.[34] The strategy was quite obvious. Israeli aggression was to be concealed as long as possible, so Israel could conquer as much territory as possible. On the other hand, when Egypt and Syria were the first to attack in 1973, the media immediately branded the Arabs as the aggressors.

---

32. In 1973 alone, the following senators received the following amounts from organizations such as the United Jewish Appeal, B'nai B'rith, and the Development Corporation of Israel: Birch Bayh, $21,500; Hubert Humphrey, $27,500; Henry Jackson, $9,700; Edmund Muskie, $14,650. Between 1971 and 1974 Jackson received $41,000 for addressing Zionist groups. Lilienthal, *The Zionist Connection*, p. 263.

33. It was a six-day battle or a six-day campaign, but the Arab-Israeli war was already twenty-one years old when it took place. If present-day headline writers had been alive in the fourteenth century, and had been as pro-English as they are now pro-Zionist, they probably would have described the battle of Crécy, which opened the Hundred Years' War between England and France, as a "One-Day War."

34. To this day many Americans actually believe that the Egyptians started the battle. Both during and after the June 1967 fighting, few stories of Arab suffering appeared in the press, even though the city of Suez was practically destroyed by bombs, artillery shells, and napalm and its population of 268,000 reduced to 10,000. In Ismailia nearly every building was leveled and almost the entire population of 100,000 forced to vacate. *Time*, May 17, 1971, p. 28. One can well imagine what the media would have done if the agony of Ismailia had been visited upon Tel Aviv or Haifa.

The early successes of the Egyptian forces in the 1973 war evoked another cyclic outburst of hysteria from the American Jewish community. The public was treated to the spectacle of Bella Abzug, the superdovish congresswoman from New York City, waving a handful of atrocity photographs to promote Israel's war effort and of Senator Edward Kennedy voting to give the Zionist state the same napalm and antipersonnel bombs that had so outraged him when they were used in Vietnam.[35]

Although President Nixon had been specifically warned by the Arab world that American military aid to Israel during the war would lead to an oil embargo, vast amounts of weapons and materiel were sent to Israel in one of the largest airlifts of all time. The subsequent Arab oil cutoff caused the loss of half a million American jobs, reduced the American GNP by $35 to $45 billion, and accelerated the worldwide inflation rate.[36] Today, when America is importing approximately half its oil, compared to 35 percent in 1973–74, another military intervention of the United States on the side of Israel would provoke another embargo which this time would probably bring large areas of the American economy to a grinding halt. Yet presidential, congressional, and media support of Israel is still at fever pitch, though it must be admitted that the temperature has dropped a few degrees.

The Camp David agreements, hailed by the Carter administration as one of the great achievements of modern American foreign policy, are little more than a delaying action that infuriated many of the Arab states and gave Egypt, which temporarily deserted the always divided Arab cause, some late-model weaponry for its armed forces and billions of dollars for its creaking economy. Camp David cannot possibly achieve its lofty goals because Israel will never accept a truly autonomous Palestinian state on its borders, and the Palestinian leadership, no matter what it promises, will never give up its hope of driving the hated oppressor into the sea.

Camp David might have worked if the United States had been permitted to put pressure on Israel and to be even-handed in its dealing with Israelis and Arabs. But America could hardly play the role of "honest broker" in the Middle East when the Jewish

---

35. *Miami Herald,* Dec. 26, 1975, 7A.
36. *Christian Science Monitor,* May 17, 1977, p. 3.

lobby refused to let American officials speak to the Palestinian Liberation Organization. How does one arbitrate a dispute when it is forbidden to speak to one of the disputants? Indeed, when UN Ambassador Andrew Young had a conversation with a PLO official, he was peremptorily fired (ordered to resign), even though he was the symbol of President Carter's all-important political link with American blacks. Better than a thousand newspaper stories or magazine articles, the dismissal of Young spelled out the relative power in America of the Jewish and Negro minorities.

Two months before the Camp David accords were finalized in March 1979, Israel suffered a setback when Iran expelled the Shah, who had supplied the Jewish state with oil, and replaced him with a clique of anti-Zionist mullahs led by Ayatullah Khomeini. A year later, however, the Soviet move into Afghanistan was a short-term boon for Israel, as was the Iranian-Iraqi war, because both events diverted the Arab states and the PLO from their campaign against Zionism.

One of the great roadblocks in the way of stabilizing the Middle East has been the behavior of the American media. In 1967 the press and television gave conclusive proof of their cringing Zionist bias by soft-pedaling the deliberate Israeli assault on the *Liberty*, an unarmed American communications ship. Thirty-four Americans were killed and 171 wounded in repeated bomb, rocket, napalm, and torpedo attacks on a bright, sunlit day while the easily identifiable ship was flying an oversize American flag.[37] After the facts had come to light, not more than one or two important public figures raised their voices in protest, a strange and unique silence in a nation which used to be so concerned with the freedom

---

37. The *Liberty* was an electronic surveillance vessel sent to monitor the Israeli assault on Egypt, which apparently had been agreed to by President Johnson. Seizure of Syrian territory, however, went beyond the agreement. Since the Israelis wanted to keep their designs on Syria secret, they decided to destroy the one source of communications in the area that would have revealed their battle plans before they were consummated. Having been outwitted, deceived, and betrayed so brazenly by a so-called ally, President Johnson nevertheless decided to cover up this most shameful episode in American naval annals, even going so far as to recall American jets speeding to the assistance of the *Liberty*. James M. Ennes, Jr., *The Assault on the Liberty*, Random House, New York, 1980, and Jim Taylor, *Pearl Harbor II*, Mideast Publishing House, Washington, D.C., 1980.

of the seas and the safety of its shipping. As has been noted, the sinking of the *Maine* in Havana harbor in 1898 was a *casus belli.* The attack on the *Chesapeake,* which cost only three American lives, led to Jefferson's embargo on all foreign commerce.[38] The sinking of the British-owned *Lusitania,* which carried 139 Americans to the bottom, almost brought about a declaration of war against Germany. But a direct attack against an American naval vessel by a foreign power in 1967 produced neither indignation nor retaliation.

The American press was equally reticent in its handling of the "Lavon Affair." In 1954 Israeli secret agents were preparing to bomb and burn down various American installations, including the American library, in Cairo, Egypt, and blame the Egyptians. The idea was to further poison American-Arab relations and manufacture more American sympathy for Israel. The plot was uncovered in time and the principal agents arrested. Eventually the Israeli cabinet had to admit Israel's involvement, whereupon, it underwent some reshuffling.[39] But still the America news media and the State Department did not consider the plot worthy of serious or extended comments. The Lavon Affair was just an early, though unsuccessful, example of the Israeli cloak-and-dagger diplomacy that drove German missile scientists out of Egypt with letter bombs, hijacked a uranium cargo on the high seas, stole uranium from a nuclear materials company in Pennsylvania, and blew up a French-built reactor just before it was to be delivered to Iraq. As a result of all this derring-do, Israel managed to accumulate an arsenal of fission bombs (and possibly a few fusion bombs) that qualified it as a mini-superpower.[40]

As for acquiring other advanced military technology, the Israelis have a rather easy time of it. According to *Newsweek* magazine (Sept. 3, 1979, p. 23):

> "They have penetrations all through the U.S. Government. They do better than the KGB," says one U.S. intelligence expert. With the help of American Jews in and out of government, Mossad looks

38. *Ency. Brit.,* Vol. 22, p. 761.

39. Nadev Safran, *The United States and Israel,* Harvard University Press, Cambridge Mass., 1963.

40. Lilienthal, *The Zionist Connection,* pp. 329–33, 364–66, 370; *The Economist* (London), Oct. 18, 1980, p. 54; *Inquiry,* Nov. 13, 1978, pp. 20–22.

for any softening in U.S. support, and tries to get any technical intelligence the Administration is unwilling to give to Israel. "Mossad can go to any distinguished American Jew and ask for his help," says a former CIA agent.

If there were ever a reason for the American Majority to regain control of American foreign policy, it would be to undo the catastrophic damage that Zionism has inflicted upon American relations with the Middle East. By aligning itself with Israel, a state created by wholesale evictions of Palestinians, the United States, so frequently reproached in the past for moralizing and overmoralizing its foreign policy, revealed itself to be a nation of immoralists.

The hypocrisy of the American ambassador to the United Nations, Arthur Goldberg, himself a Jew and a Zionist,[41] abstaining and temporizing during the 1967 Israeli *coup de main*, while the overwhelming majority of delegates were calling for a cease-fire and the withdrawal of all troops to the pre-attack frontiers, will not be quickly forgotten, particularly by those who once believed that the United States stood for the rights of all peoples, including Arabs, to self-determination. Neither will President Johnson's solemn promise a few days before the renewed outbreak of hostilities that America would oppose any change in the frontiers of Middle Eastern nations.[42]

After the frontiers of three Arab countries had again been pushed back by armed force—Egypt's all the way to Suez—Johnson did not bother to eat his words. He simply chose to ignore them. Just as conspicuously silent were the Protestant and Catholic churches, even though additional thousands of Arab Christians now swelled the ranks of those who had already been driven from their homes by previous Israeli aggression.[43] Christian attitudes toward the Holy Land were not exactly those of the Crusades.

What has happened in the Middle East since the end of World War II offers a valuable object lesson on the nature and extent

---

41. Goldberg was a Zionist supporter while in private law practice. Litvinoff, *A Peculiar People*, p. 59.

42. *Time*, June 2, 1967, p. 11.

43. The young Sirhan Sirhan was one of these refugee Arab Christians. The young presidential aspirant Robert Kennedy was one of the leading American Christians. The two met in the basement of the Hotel Ambassador in Los Angeles at 12:16 A.M., June 5, 1968.

of minority power in the United States. The national interest required the safeguarding of the oil fields, the encouragement of areawide political stability to restrain Russian military and economic penetration, and the presence of friendly, pro-American, anti-Communist governments.[44] But all this has been given up for the sake of a numerically inconsequential American minority. Even Turkey, once America's strongest friend in the Middle East, is having second thoughts about NATO and the American alliance as the United States puts more and more of its strategic eggs in the basket of Israel, a nation whose very presence keeps the region in constant ferment and disequilibrium. In a pusillanimous act of deference to Greek Americans, Washington actually embargoed arms to Turkey after a Turkish takeover of part of Cyprus.

The seizure of American Embassy personnel in Iran was the delayed aftermath of another serious miscalculation of American diplomacy in the Middle East—the CIA's heavy-handed installation and support of the Shah. America's reaction to the hostage crisis—most of the blacks and women were let go, the remaining fifty-two were held for 444 days—was what might have been expected from an indecisive White House: one ineffective pourparler after another, a failed and botched rescue mission with eight dead, and payment of ransom in the form of releasing frozen Iranian assets and previously ordered military equipment. In this connection it might be noted that no modern or Third World country has as yet taken any Russian hostages, perhaps because it is generally understood that the Soviet reaction would be sharply different from America's.

In the conquest and settlement of Palestine the Israelis have imitated the work of their remote forebears by making the desert bloom and transforming vast stretches of sandy waste into fertile farm lands and fruitful orchards. Their brilliantly executed desert campaigns, which will rank in military history with those of Joshua, Tancred, Saladin, Lawrence, Allenby, Montgomery, and Rommel, have come close to the fulfillment of Biblical prophecy. All that is lacking is the Messiah.

---

44. Even as late as 1970 no Arab state permitted the existence of a Communist party within its borders. Israel has a Communist party.

But those who are caught up in desert politics—not only American Jews but Zionists and Zionist supporters everywhere—should beware of mirages. For the first time since A.D. 135, Jews have become a majority in a Jewish state—and those who make up this majority have been transformed into something which is almost the opposite of the historic Jewish image. Also transformed is the ex-majority of Palestine. After years of exile, poverty, and defeat, the Palestinian Arabs, the Middle Eastern "wretched of the earth," are as racist, as hungry for heroism, and as obsessed about their homeland as their Zionist counterparts. These Palestinian exiles and the populations of the neighboring Arab countries which shelter them may be far behind the Westernized Zionists technically and economically. But they are not spear-carrying natives. They may not be able to make their own advanced weapons, but they know where to buy them, and they have the money to buy them.

And so the Mideast crisis deepens—for Jews, for Arabs, for Moslems, and for the world. Jewish nationalism begets Arab nationalism, Jewish racism begets Arab racism, Zionism begets anti-Zionism, Semitism begets anti-Semitism.[45] At best, the conflict will smolder for decades, using up the physical, if not the spiritual, resources of the entire area. At worst, it might detonate a nuclear war, in which minuscule Israel could hardly escape annihilation.

For the United States to have aided and abetted the dispossession of the greater part of the Palestinian population is an act of barbarism. For American Jews to continue to edge the United States into the Middle Eastern imbroglio, where America has everything to lose and nothing to gain, is an act of sheer ingratitude to the nation which has given them more wealth, freedom, and

---

45. A century before the birth of modern Israel, Dostoyevsky provided an inkling of present-day events in the Middle East by speculating on what would happen if the Jewish minority in Russia became the majority. "How would they [the Jews] treat them [the Russians]?" he asked. "Would they permit them to acquire equal rights? Would they permit them to worship freely in their midst? Wouldn't they convert them into slaves? Worse than that: wouldn't they skin them altogether? Wouldn't they slaughter them to the last man, to the point of complete extermination, as they used to do with alien peoples in ancient times, during their ancient history?" The Diary of a Writer, trans. Boris Brasol, Scribner's, New York, 1949, Vol. 2, pp. 644–45.

power than any other in the long sinusoidal curve of their history.[46]

In 1973, J. William Fulbright publicly stated: "Israel controls the Senate. The great majority of the Senate of the U.S.—somewhere around 80 percent—are completely in support of Israel; anything Israel wants." [47] This was a sensational charge, coming as it did from the respected chairman of the Senate Foreign Relations Committee, and he was duly defeated when he ran for reelection.

In the winter of 1973–74, when long lines began to form in front of gas pumps and thousands of American workmen were laid off their jobs, the politicians continued to vote for "anything Israel wants." Everyone but the real culprit was blamed for the oil shortage. Every solution but the obvious one was recommended. The media cooperated fully in this massive deception, which was an unforgettable example of totalitarian mind-bending.

It was a pathetic and shameful sight to watch Americans being duped into accepting sacrifice after sacrifice, even the possibility of the supreme sacrifice, for a racial dream that was not their own.

Moreover it was not really a Jewish dream. Jews paid for it and plotted for it, but most are unwilling to live it. Consequently the American beachhead on the west edge of Asia—the tail that wags the dog—is as tenuous as South Korea, the beachhead on the east edge—the tail that doesn't. The fate of both, unless America withdraws its commitment to the former and its troops from the latter, will probably be as tragic and humiliating as what occurred in Vietnam, that other American beachhead in Asia.

America's role in the Middle East should be absolute noninterference in any country's internal affairs, as it should be in the

---

46. Israel refused to sign the 1975 Sinai agreement unless American technicians were interposed between the Israeli and Egyptian armies, thereby setting the scene for an incident which could get the United States into a war on Israel's side with minimum resistance and maximum speed.

47. *Miami Herald*, April 22, 1973, p. 32A. Congress had or has very few members like Fulbright. Senator James Abourezk of South Dakota, a politician of Arab descent, spoke up for the Palestinians, but he only served one term. Representative John Rarick, for years the only outspoken anti-Zionist in the House, was defeated in his reelection race in 1974. Congressman Paul Findley, who has had several meetings with PLO leaders, whose cause he supports, managed to overcome a ferocious media and Zionist attack and won reelection in 1980.

rest of Asia. The sheik in your pocket today may be the imam who declares war on you tomorrow. In the short term America may have to keep the sea lanes open for the oil, which Americans and Britons, not Allah or the faithful, discovered, drilled, pumped out of the desert sand, refined, distributed—and, once upon a time, owned. But in the long term the United States must go nuclear and go beyond nuclear if it wants to work itself free of present and future oil cartels. Everyone understands that the mountains of currency flowing into Middle Eastern coffers are economically disrupting to the West. But few understand that these torrents of cash are culturally corrupting to the sellers.

Arabs are probably too "racially spent" to again become a world power, as they were in the great days of Islam. But at the very least they should drop their old rivalries and join together to protect their way of life, their religion, and their lands from Soviet and Israeli encroachment. Here again the watchword should be more organization at the top—a strong, united Arab federation; less organization in the middle—the slow dissolution of the nations artificially created from the provinces of the defunct Ottoman Empire; and more organization at the bottom—a reinvigoration of the regional Arab cultural clusters within their natural frontiers.

CHAPTER 36

The United States and Africa

O F ALL THE SEVEN continents, with the exception of Antarctica, Africa should be of the least concern to the United States. Far removed in time and space, no African nation or combination of nations could possibly offer a serious military threat to America now or in the future. The possession of parts of Africa by the Soviet Union and its Cuban mercenaries certainly doesn't strengthen Western defenses, but it does provide the new imperialists with debits as well as credits. African nations have been known to expel their Soviet friends as quickly as they welcomed them, and in the long run decolonialized blacks think all armed white intruders look alike. As does the U.S.S.R., the United States casts a greedy eye on Africa's abundance of uranium, diamonds, gold, chrome, tin, vanadium, manganese, platinum, cobalt, oil, and rubber—all of which America would have difficulty finding elsewhere or producing artificially. Nevertheless, these strategic materials can be procured more easily by normal trade practices than by meddling diplomacy, military threats, or expeditionary forces. Yet in spite of these perfectly good reasons for keeping a proper distance, the United States is being steadily drawn deeper into African affairs. The causes, as in the Middle East, are Soviet expansionism and domestic minority racism, with the emphasis on the latter. But this time the racism is of a different and darker vintage.

Before World War I, Africa could be accurately described as a wholly owned subsidiary of Europe. After World War II, when Europe was weary and bleeding, when the anti-imperialist promises of the Atlantic Charter and the United Nations had come home to roost, when liberalism was triumphant throughout the West, Africans, white and black, decided the time had come to strike for self-government. They were more surprised than anyone when the colonial powers capitulated. In some cases the transition was peaceful; in others it took a war of attrition or excessive doses of terrorism. At any event, by 1980 European domination had been almost totally erased from the continent.

Africa's pigmentation spectrum, viewed geographically from north to south, is sallow or dark white at the top, black in the center and black, brown and white at the bottom. Little will be said in this chapter about Egypt and the other Arab and Moslem nations of North Africa. They are only African by geography. Their religion, culture, history, and racial composition—as well as their anti-Zionism—make them a part of the Middle East.

Africa today is the home of forty-seven Negro states, all but two born after World War II. These infant nations, whose frontiers rarely correspond to tribal boundaries,[1] have not produced an enviable record of political stability. An unending succession of political and military coups, tribal feuds, and genocidal wars [2] has done nothing to disprove the Negro's historic incapacity for self-government.[3] Once a tribal chief or ambitious army officer or noncommissioned officer takes over, he inevitably follows the familiar diplomatic pattern of playing the West against the East (the Soviet Union, its satellites, and China) in order to squeeze every last penny out of foreign aid. Having removed whites from political control, having made it extremely difficult to carry on business and commerce, having made the growth of heavy industry all but impossible, black leaders have no choice but to persuade whites to remain or return if the new governments are to be saved from economic ruin. Without whites, most of Black Africa

---

1. There are 2,000 tribes in black Africa.

2. In the Nigerian civil war 1,000,000 members of the Ibo tribe of Biafra were killed between 1967 and 1969. *New York Times,* Nov. 23, 1969, p. 1.

3. Black African states were the scene of seven military takeovers, two bloody army coups, a tribal massacre, the murder of 100,000 civilians, and the flight of a million refugees—all in the year 1966. *San Francisco Sunday Examiner, This World,* Jan. 8, 1967, p. 22. So far not more than a handful of the new black governments have been voted out of office, although almost all the new states make some pretense of democracy. *Time,* March 31, 1967, p. 29.

would quickly revert, as is already happening in many areas of the Congo,[4] to the primitive cultural level in which it languished before the advent of European colonialization.

Now that they have achieved independence—a purely nominal independence that has "hardly touched the personal life of most Africans"[5]—the black nations seem more interested in imitating white nations than in developing their own gifts and competencies. African art is in a state of steep decline,[6] and despite impassioned statements about *négritude* (American Negroes call it "soul"), the black elite builds ornate homes and government buildings in the Western style, speeds around in late-model Cadillacs, satiates itself on the cheaper and coarser forms of Western culture, occasionally marries European women, and leaves the African masses to shift for themselves.[7] The late philosopher of African nationalism, Frantz Fanon, could not abide this new Negro bourgeoisie and accused it of almost as many crimes as he attributed to the white colonialists.[8]

Rhodesia was the last British outpost in Africa to throw in the towel. Having watched the disestablishment of the whites in Kenya and 75,000 other whites in Northern Rhodesia (now Zambia), 220,000 white Southern Rhodesians, a 5 percent minority in a total population of 4,530,000, seceded from Britain and asserted their independence. A pariah among nations, abandoned by its mother country, and subjected to sanctions and boycotts

4. A gruesome, sardonic overview of this reversionary process is furnished in Shiva Naipaul's *North of South*, Simon and Schuster, New York, 1979.

5. John Hatch, *A History of Postwar Africa*, Praeger, New York, 1965, p. 404.

6. Traditionally, African artists have concentrated on sculpture. Today most of the wood carving and bronze casting is "clumsy, imitative and mass-produced." The decorative arts have also deteriorated. There is some literature—in European languages or newly grammaticized African dialects—but almost no reading public. Smith Hempstone, *San Francisco Chronicle, This World*, Feb. 4, 1962, pp. 21–22.

7. A highly informative description of day-to-day living in new African nations is found in Thomas Molnar, *Africa: A Political Travelogue*, Fleet, New York, 1965.

8. Frantz Fanon, *The Wretched of the Earth*, trans. Constance Farrington, Grove Press, New York, 1963. See especially the chapter, "The Pitfalls of National Consciousness." Fanon, a Negro psychiatrist from Martinique, was so anti-American he criticized the "jazz howl" of American Negroes and described the United States as a "monster in which the taints, the sickness and the inhumanity of Europe have grown to appalling dimensions." Ibid., pp. 243, 313.

imposed by most of the world's white and colored nations,[9] Rhodesia managed to endure until 1979, when mounting terrorism, plus British and American arm-twisting, induced the whites to surrender to "majority rule," which in this case meant handing over the government a year later to Robert Mugabe, a Marxist revolutionary.[10] By the beginning of 1981 whites were fleeing Zimbabwe, as it was now called, in droves. All the thousands of white hopes had been dashed; all the millions of white man-hours had been wasted. The Western presence in southern Africa was now bounded on the north by Kipling's "great, grey-green, greasy Limpopo River, all set about with fever trees."

The next and final target of the anticolonialist crusade is South Africa, where 4,400,000 whites, an 18 percent minority in a population of 23,900,000,[11] direct the destiny of Africa's most modern, most prosperous, and only remaining Western nation.

The story of South Africa began in 1652 with the landing of the first Dutch pioneers. In many ways the country's development paralleled that of the United States. The settlers were Protestants of Northern European descent who usually brought their families with them. For this reason, except at the earliest pioneering stages, there was a minimum of racial mixing. The enemy of the colonists was not the native African but the British, who harried them almost from the very beginning and took the colony from Holland by force during the Napoleonic wars when the Dutch were active allies of France. Forty years later, to escape from British rule, 12,000 Dutch-descended Afrikaners went northward in the 1835 "Great Trek," a march which compares in heroism and fortitude to the Mormon migration to Utah. The low point in Afrikaner

---

9. In 1972 the Rhodesian team, after being invited to the Olympic games, was ejected because of a threatened black boycott. A few days earlier General Idi Amin of Uganda had ordered 50,000 Asians to quit his country in 90 days. The Uganda team stayed in the Olympics.

10. A black Marxist head of state, although so far he has been more pro-Chinese than pro-Soviet, is always a hopeful sign to the Kremlin. Soviet influence, often backed up by thousands of Cuban mercenaries, is now paramount in Ethiopia, Angola, Zambia, Mozambique, and Botswana.

11. The nonwhite population is comprised of 16,200,000 blacks, 2,500,000 coloreds and 778,000 Asians. *U.S. News & World Report*, Oct. 8, 1979, p. 68. The Afrikaners represent more than half of the white population; South Africans of British descent less than half. There are approximately 100,000 Jews.

fortunes came in the Boer War (1899–1902), a war for independence that failed.

But the Afrikaners' defeat was not final. Overcome on the battlefield, they retreated to the ballot box, and, as South Africa moved
from colonial to commonwealth status, their political hopes
brightened. In 1948 the Afrikaners outvoted the English-speaking
whites and set up a white supremacist government. In 1961 they
led South Africa out of the British Commonwealth and made it
an independent republic.

South Africa hopes to solve its almost insoluble racial problems
by means of apartheid or the separate development of races, a
milder approach than *baaskap,* which is absolute domination by
whites.[12] The blacks, forbidden to intermarry with whites and
living in segregated communities, are eventually to have their
own homelands with full cultural and some political freedom.[13]
Their contacts with whites will be limited to the economic sector.
South Africa's white liberal element, largely of British and Jewish
origin, opposes apartheid and favors giving full rights, including
the voting franchise, to nonwhites.[14] The Communists, now under-

---

12. Drury, op. cit., p. 98.

13. Ten such homelands already exist, though only three have asked for or
been given independence. In 1980 the South African government, to placate
the Western media, hinted it was going to soften and change some apartheid
and homeland policies.

14. South African racial politics is both similar and dissimilar to American
racial politics. There is the same liberal-minority coalition with affluent Jews
at the top, impecunious Negroes at the bottom, and whites of British descent
playing the liberal role. One great difference is that the dominant Afrikaner
population group votes en bloc. Another great difference is that South African
Negroes, who vastly outnumber whites, cannot vote, whereas American Negroes,
vastly outnumbered by whites, can. Though they have less political power than
American Jews, South African Jews wield as much financial power. There is
no restriction in the cash flow to Israel, and Harry Oppenheimer, chairman of
Anglo American Corp., is probably the world's richest Jew. Oppenheimer's De
Beers Consolidated Mines and Diamond Trading Co. produces and sells 85
percent of the world's rough, uncut diamonds. "In these modern times, when
price-controlling cartels have been outlawed in other industries, the survival
of the De Beers monopoly is astonishing." *McCall's,* March 1969, pp. 167–68.
The best gem diamonds come from Sierra Leone where a company broke the
De Beers monopoly for a brief period in the early 1960s, until Oppenheimer
persuaded the Sierra Leone Parliament to shut down the competition. Israel's

ground or working with black terrorist groups outside the country, advocate an armed black uprising.[15]

Americans have been indoctrinated to regard South African blacks, who did not arrive in any numbers until the late eighteenth century—150 years after the Dutch—as the country's rightful owners. Unlike American Negroes, the blacks who came to South Africa came voluntarily, first in search of land, then in search of jobs. South African blacks further differ from American blacks in that they speak several different languages and are divided by fierce tribal loyalties which impede the organization of a united anti-white political front.

In the past several decades the United States, under pressure from liberal-minority lobbies and the news media, has developed a deep and disturbing concern for South African blacks, as it has for blacks in every part of Africa. The concern is described as disturbing because previous American efforts in behalf of African Negroes have been, to say the least, counterproductive. Before the Civil War, white Americans founded the state of Liberia on Africa's west coast to serve as a national homeland for emancipated slaves. Small groups of ex-slaves made the voyage to Liberia, where they formed the country's aristocracy, numbering 20,000 when last counted in 1945. But Liberia had little or no attraction for American Negroes generally, whether slave or free, and after the Civil War the migratory trickle came to an end.[16] Sixty-five years later Liberia was formally censured by a League of Nations committee for permitting the existence of slavery and forced labor. Both the president and vice-president had to resign in the ensuing scandal.[17]

Although pretending to be a democracy, modern Liberia has

---

ties to South Africa are rather close, considering that the Zionist state votes against South Africa whenever the latter's racial "misbehavior" comes up before the United Nations. South Africa has plenty of uranium and Israel a lot of nuclear technology. The combination of the two will certainly improve the nuclear capability, both military and industrial, of both countries.

15. Drury, op. cit., pp. 96–97, and Molnar, op. cit., pp. 166–67. Joe Slovo, a Lithuanian Jew who works out of Maputo, the capital of Mozambique, is generally thought to be the brains of the 4,000-man black guerrilla band dedicated to imposing black rule on South Africa.

16. *Ency. Brit.*, Vol. 13, pp. 994–96.

17. *New York Times*, Dec. 6, 1930, p. 38, and June 7, 1931, p. 5.

actually been governed by a succession of president-dictators,[18] and the constitution has racial qualifications that restrict citizenship to Negroes only.[19] Liberia also happens to be one of the most backward African states, principally because it was never a colony and consequently only rarely exposed to white political organization and modern technology.[20]

In the aftermath of World War II the power and influence of American "public opinion" was a great source of encouragement to the native African's precocious demands for independence. Belgium was forced to give up the Congo before there were nearly enough qualified Negroes to administer it. As the country sank back into barbarism, the United States contributed 40 percent of the $400,000,000 spent by the United Nations "peace-keeping" mission (1960–1963). In the course of the almost interminable bush wars and insurrections which ravaged the Congo for two decades, both loyal and rebel Congolese troops mutilated, butchered, and occasionally cannibalized more than a few Americans, including missionaries and nuns.[21] Even so, the American press continued to support the occasionally pro-Russian, always black racist Congolese government and carried on a bitter editorial and headline campaign against Moise Tshombe, the one pro-Western Congolese politician of stature. Tshombe, after being driven into exile, was kidnapped and flown to an Algiers prison, where he was probably murdered.

In the light of recent events and present trends, it must be said that Darkest Africa is becoming darker than ever, and Ameri-

---

18. The most recent, William Tolbert, was murdered in 1980 in a military revolt that was followed by a series of gory public executions.

19. *Ency. Brit.*, Vol. 13, p. 996.

20. Almost as backward is part-black Ethiopia, the one other nonwhite country in Africa with a fairly continuous history of independence, only briefly interrupted in recent times by the Italian occupation (1936–1941). Molnar, op. cit., p. 223, and Hatch, op. cit., pp. 185–86.

21. "The Congolese government denied charges that its troops had killed at least 11 Europeans and raped 30 white women, but its own interim minister made the most astonishing charge of all—that Congolese had eaten several white settlers in Lubumbashi, formerly Elisabethville." *Life,* July 21, 1957, p. 34. It might be added that some cannibals were not primitive natives wearing loincloths, but "men and women schooled and dressed in the European way." Molnar, op. cit., p. 30.

can foreign policy is hastening the process. The plantations, industrial installations, public utilities, mining companies, and large commercial establishments only remain in operation as long as there is white supervision and white money. The blacks who are trying—with scant success—to replace the white technocrats are Western-trained intellectuals, a species of imitation white men scorned by their own people and ridiculed by their former European masters. The real Africa and the only authentic black culture are not to be found within the city limits but out in the bush in the tribal compounds. If white liberals, white churchmen, white capitalists and Communists, Cuban Hessians, and the black intelligentsia would leave the black tribesman to his own devices, he would be free to pursue and develop the way of life which suits him best and makes the best use of his uniquely different cultural and artistic gifts.

But they will not leave him alone. Western nations continue to receive, indoctrinate, and return to their native countries a black elite which, wittingly or unwittingly, carries home a colonialism of white thought, white attitudes, and white institutions that weighs more heavily on the black soul than did the economic colonialism of the white imperialists. Even the Arab and Moslem states of North Africa attempt to meddle with black destinies by proposing a continental pan-Africanism, apparently forgetting that many blacks have more animosity toward Arabs than toward European whites. It was the Arabs who managed the African slave trade long before the arrival of the Europeans, and it was the Arabs who kept it alive long after the Europeans had outlawed it.

Highly sensitive to liberal and black lobbying, the United States keeps aiding, abetting, and financing "Western-model" African republics which invariably turn out to be travesties of the political, economic, and social institutions they laboriously mimic. Although Joseph Conrad's *Heart of Darkness* probably offers the best clue to the black African's future, America prefers to base its African policy on Marxist prophecy, the antiwhite palaver of the late Jean-Paul Sartre, and the racial fantasies of the late Frantz Fanon.[22]

---

22. Sartre's preface to Fanon's tract, *The Wretched of the Earth,* is one of the most vituperative and extensive slurs in the history of racial invective. It is a sign of the times and of the pressures of the times that the most rabid perpetrators of antiwhite racism are accepted as respectable members of the white intellectual fraternity.

Ignored is the historical record which is replete with evidence that Negroes in Africa, Haiti, the United States, and South America have a congenital aversion to the higher expressions of Western civilization, including Western styles of government.

Apart from the Middle East, there is no area on earth where American foreign policy is as rigged against the American Majority as it is in Africa. Instead of normalizing relations with South Africa, whose resources, military capability, and political stability make it the only nation on the continent worthy of the name, the United States deliberately adopts a policy that ranges from moral indignation to an arms embargo. Rhodesia, an oasis of Northern European civilization in an almost totally black environment, might have expected some sympathy from the United States, if only because white Rhodesians were English-speaking and of British descent. But America helped plant the dagger in Rhodesia's back, and Rhodesia devolved into Zimbabwe.

Unbelievable as it may seem, the more a population of any African nation differs racially and culturally from the American Majority, the more that nation is likely to receive American support and American largesse. The more the population approaches the racial composition of the Majority, the more coolly it will be treated, often to the point of open enmity. The white (Mediterranean) racial layer of North Africa has fallen under the ban imposed on anti-Zionist Arabs, though a temporary waiver has been granted to Egypt and its mulatto leader, Sadat. The white (Northern European) racial component of South Africa has fallen under the ban imposed for more than a century on the American South.

CHAPTER 37

The United States and the
Western Hemisphere

G EOGRAPHICALLY, THE Western Hemisphere is divided into two
continents, North and South America. Geopolitically, it is
divided into Latin America (South America, Central America, and
Mexico) and Anglo America (the United States and Canada). Latin
America is primarily tropical or subtropical in climate; Catholic
in religion; Spanish, Portuguese, or Indian in language; Latin,
Indian, or Negro in culture (in varying proportions); and Mediterranean, Mongoloid, or Negroid in race (in varying mixtures). The
mid-1980 population estimate for Latin America (thirty independent nations, plus a few European dependencies, mostly in the
Caribbean) is 363,600,000, as compared to 252,400,000 for Anglo
America.[1] In 1975–80 Latin America's population increased by
44,000,000; Anglo America's by 8,600,000.[2]

In the time of Columbus there were 16,000,000 Indians in the
New World, 15,000,000 in Latin America.[3] When their palefaced
conquerors arrived, they were subjected to two different ordeals
and styles of conquest. The English, Dutch, Germans, and Scandinavians parleyed and traded with the Indians, before they fought
them, killed them, and drove the remainder west, ultimately onto
reservations. But they rarely mated with them and hardly ever
married them. This sexual abstinence could be attributed to strong
feelings of racial solidarity, accentuated by the color differences,
and to the fact that many were settlers who had brought along
their wives and families.

---

1. *World Population Estimates,* The Environmental Fund, Washington, D.C.,
1980.
2. Ibid.   3. *Ency. Brit.,* Vol. 12, pp. 200, 203.

A much higher proportion of the Spanish and Portuguese migration, whose members were more concerned with military glory and fortune-hunting than farming, were bachelors. Of a darker shade and noticeably shorter than the Northern Europeans, they were less separated from the Indians by physical traits.[4] They also happened to be confronted with a greater number of Indians, who were more attractive and more civilized than the nomadic redskins of the northern plains and forests. When the slave ships unloaded their human cargoes, Latins persisted in their miscegenation while Northern Europeans, with some exceptions, notably in the American South and French Canada, remained true to their segregated mating habits.[5]

Centuries of racial blending in Latin America have produced many different population groups. In Mexico and Peru, where there were advanced Indian cultures, the mestizo element is Spanish-Indian. In Brazil considerable numbers of Negroes as well as Indians generated more complex racial shadings—Portuguese-Indian, Negro-Indian, Portuguese-Negro, and Portuguese-Indian-Negro. In the West Indies, where Negro slaves replaced the Indians who died off in the sixteenth century, many islands are almost totally black. In Cuba and Puerto Rico the mulatto share of the population is predominant with pure Negroes and pure whites in the minority.[6]

In the more remote Andean nations, Ecuador and Bolivia, and in Guatemala, pure Indian strains are still in the majority. In Paraguay, Guarani, an Indian dialect, is an official state language. In Argentina, Uruguay, and Costa Rica, where the paucity of mineral

---

4. The reference here is to the racial type of most of the soldiers, prospectors, administrators, and priests from Spain and Portugal. Their leaders, the *conquistadores,* exhibited many Northern European physical traits. See p. 77.

5. In contrast to the practice in Latin America, the mixed offspring of Southerners were hardly ever legitimized.

6. Both the capitalist census takers in Puerto Rico and the Communist census takers in Cuba seem somewhat color blind. In the early 1960s less than 20 percent of the Puerto Rican population was classified as nonwhite, and in Cuba one-eighth of the population was described as Negro and one-seventh as mulatto. Any visitor to either country can quickly gauge the reliability of these statistics, whose exaggerated pro-white bias is additional proof of the social value attached to the white label. In Cuba "the proportion of the population with some Negro ancestry is much higher than the figures indicated," states the *Ency. Brit.,* Vol. 6, p. 875.

resources drew settlers instead of prospectors, the population is overwhelmingly white. Complicating the racial picture throughout Latin America are enclaves of Germans and Japanese in Brazil; Germans in Chile; Jews in Argentina; [7] Dutch and East Indians in Suriname; French in French Guiana, Martinique, and Guadeloupe; and Indians (from India) in Guyana, formerly British Guiana.

Economic wealth and social prestige in Latin America generally vary according to the whiteness of one's skin. In Central America, Costa Rica, the only white nation, is by far the most advanced and most prosperous. Haiti, with the longest continuous history of independence of any Negro country anywhere, is the least prosperous and least advanced of any New World nation, except for a few new black independencies in the smaller Caribbean islands. In South America, Chile, Uruguay, and Argentina, in spite of the Latin penchant for dictatorship or army rule, are on a higher plane of civilization than states where Negro or Indian elements predominate.

Whatever aristocracy remains in Latin America is based almost entirely on an unsullied and uncontaminated white family tree. Politics in many areas has long since passed into the hands of mestizos, but mestizos on the light side, who marry on the light side, and whose descendants eventually qualify for "certificates of whiteness." Although there is no official or legally sanctioned racial discrimination in Latin America, it can be seen, felt, and sensed everywhere.

Neither the Indians nor the Negroes played any considerable part in the early stages of Latin American independence movements.[8] It was the Creoles, the native-born whites—some with

---

7. The Migdal brothers, Lithuanian Jews, ran the vicious and lucrative white slave trade in Argentina, which was finally brought to an end by the Jewish community itself. Argentine inflation has raised havoc with Jewish small business, but the 400,000 Jews in Argentina still represent the richest and most influential Jewish minority in Latin America. Sachar, *The Course of Modern Jewish History*, pp. 510–18. Among the 150,000 Jews in Brazil are Israel Klabin, mayor of Rio de Janeiro, and Adolpho Bloch, the country's leading publisher.

8. Juárez, the famed Indian revolutionary of Mexico, did not come to prominence until the middle of the nineteenth century, almost four decades after two white priests, Hidalgo and Morelos, had launched the drive for Mexican independence.

a few mestizo genes—who in almost every case first organized and led the armies that fought the Spanish regulars.[9] There was a moment in the 1820s when the new Latin American states might have banded together in a federation on the United States model. But the two principal leaders, Bolívar and San Martín, fell out. From that day on, Latin America has been divided by petty provincialism and a never ending succession of revolutions, military dictatorships, clerical and anti-clerical juntas, and men on horseback. Venezuela has had more than a hundred revolutions in 150 years; Bolivia 179 changes of government in 126 years. Paraguay had thirty-nine different heads of state between 1870 and 1954.[10] It was this ceaseless political and economic ferment that caused Latin America, once a century or more ahead of Anglo America, to fall more than a century behind.

Latin America, it should be recalled, once included Florida, Louisiana and its vast hinterland, and almost limitless expanses of geography in the American Southwest and Far West. After acquiring Louisiana by purchase and parts of Florida by force, the United States attempted to erect a diplomatic wall around the remainder of the Western Hemisphere in the form of the Monroe Doctrine (1823).

In solemnly proclaiming that the New World was closed to further colonization by European powers, America helped to safeguard the newly acquired freedom and independence of the Latin American countries which had seceded from Spain. But as American aggression against Mexico increased and as Texas, New Mexico, Arizona, California, and parts of Colorado and Wyoming were incorporated into the United States, Latin Americans could be pardoned for equating the Monroe Doctrine with Yankee imperialism. It appeared as if the United States wanted to isolate the Western Hemisphere from Europe, not for the high-minded purpose of protecting the New World against the machinations of

---

9. Many Creole leaders inherited the courage of the *conquistadores* but not their attitudes. Bolívar, who had a touch of Indian, married his sister to a Negro general. San Martín, who had black hair, eyes, and olive skin, once publicly announced he was an Indian. O'Higgins, the liberator of Chile, was the illegitimate son of an Irishman and a Chilean woman of mixed ancestry. Gunther, *Inside South America*, pp. 134–37 and 332–33.

10. Ibid., p. xvi.

the Old, but to treat Latin America as Britain, France, and a few other European nations were beginning to treat Africa.[11]

Not until the 1930s did Franklin Roosevelt's Good Neighbor Policy attempt to soothe the ruffled feelings and hurt pride resulting from Latin America's century-long exposure to "gringo" dynamism. The expropriation of hundreds of millions of dollars of American investments and property by Mexico's revolutionary government was forgiven and forgotten, and a new soft-key approach to Latin American relations inaugurated. In the late 1940s the Organization of American States was formed, of which the United States was only one of twenty-three (now twenty-eight) member nations, each with an equal vote. Two decades later President Kennedy's Alliance for Progress added grants and loans to American investments as a means of building up Latin America's lagging economy. Despite these conciliatory steps, an era of hemispheric good feeling was as far away as ever.

Meanwhile the United States was forced to take cognizance of stepped-up Soviet activity south of the border. The Russian subversion of Guatemala was checkmated by an American-instigated uprising which sent Jacobo Arbenz, the first Soviet puppet of stature in the New World, packing in 1954. But Cuba was a different matter. The failure of the United States to prevent the Sovietization of the richest, most important, and most populated West Indian island stands as one of the gigantic blunders in American diplomatic history. The events represent a classic cautionary tale of how American national security is damaged when the liberal-minority coalition impinges its political and social dogmas upon the conduct of foreign affairs.

Until the *New York Times* discovered him and his small band of ragtag guerrillas in Cuba's remote Sierra Maestra mountains

---

11. In tune with the expansionist mood, William Walker, doctor, lawyer, editor, freebooter, and native of Nashville, Tennessee, briefly carved an independent "republic" out of Mexico's Lower California and Sonora. Later, with fifty-six followers, he took over Nicaragua. If he had not crossed the path of Cornelius Vanderbilt's economic interests—the Commodore wished to build a Nicaraguan canal—Walker might have eventually become the emperor of Central America instead of dying before a Honduran firing squad in 1860. Albert Carr, *The World and William Walker*, Harper & Row, New York, 1963.

in 1957, Fidel Castro was an unknown, clownish, and down-at-heel revolutionary. Then, in a series of interviews, *Times* correspondent Herbert Matthews, whose reporting of the Spanish Civil War had been a monument of non-objectivity,[12] painted a heroic portrait of Castro as an idealistic, "anti-Communist" patriot with "no animosity toward the United States and the American people." [13] Matthews' prettifications also contained the flat statement, "But there is no communism to speak of in Castro's 25th of July movement. . . ." [14] Earl Smith, who was America's ambassador to Cuba at the time, stated that after Matthews' interviews were published, arms, money, and support for Castro poured in from all sides.[15]

Inevitably, President Eisenhower himself fell under the *Times*'s spell,[16] refusing to sell the legitimate Cuban government badly needed arms even when Castro's insurrection assumed threatening proportions.[17] Ambassador Smith was ordered to urge President Batista, the Cuban strongman, to retire.[18] On January 1, 1959, Batista fled to Portugal, and the Castro forces triumphantly entered Havana. American diplomacy had incomprehensibly taken the lead in replacing a sworn friend with a sworn enemy.

After Castro had seized control of Cuba, prominent liberals rushed into print to add further touches to Matthews' panegyrics. William Benton, one of the most influential members of the Democratic party and onetime senator from Connecticut, wrote that

---

12. For Matthews' pro-Loyalist bias, see Hugh Thomas, *The Spanish Civil War*, pp. 233, 388.

13. Quotations from Matthews' front-page stories in *New York Times*, Feb. 24–26, 1957.

14. Ibid.

15. Herbert Dinsmore, *All The News That Fits*, Arlington House, New Rochelle, N.Y., 1968, p. 185.

16. Ibid., p. 177. At a press conference at Grinnell College (May 13, 1965), Eisenhower made it clear that "Herbert Matthews . . . almost single-handedly made Castro a national hero." He went on to say that John Kennedy, when senator, had told him that Castro was following in the footsteps of Bolívar.

17. The delivery of fifteen airplanes which Cuba had already bought and paid for was stopped by the State Department. M. Stanton Evans, *The Politics of Surrender*, Devin-Adair, Old Greenwich, Conn., 1966, p. 380.

18. Ibid., p. 379. For a full discussion of the general situation by a Cuban participant, see Mario Lazo, *Dagger in the Heart—American Foreign Policy Failures in Cuba*, Funk & Wagnalls, New York, 1968.

Latin America appeared to be the "area of the world least menaced by a Soviet or Chinese military threat (even through Cuba)." [19] C. Wright Mills, one of the nation's leading sociologists, wrote, "Fidel Castro's no Communist and never has been." [20] Mills then went on to say that Castro would never allow Russia to set up bases in Cuba and, besides, Russia did not want such bases.[21]

In 1961, when Castro announced publicly that he had always been a Marxist-Leninist and had only concealed his Communist ties in order to grease the wheels of revolution,[22] Matthews was still writing about Cuba for the *Times,* later being promoted to chief editorial writer for Latin American affairs. In this post his supervisor was John Oakes, *Times* editorial director and son of George Ochs-Oakes, founder Adolph Ochs's brother.[23] Even after Castro had expropriated more than $1 billion in American property and had set up an orthodox Communist state, complete with mass purges and forced collectivization of agriculture, the liberal-minority arbiters of foreign policy kept evincing their friendship for the Cuban Revolution, although they were having doubts about Castro himself.

Since the very men who had been most mistaken about Castro

---

19. From the preface of Benton's book, *The Voice of Latin America,* Weidenfeld & Nicolson, London, 1961, p. xii. If Benton was so unknowing about foreign affairs, he had no business serving as an assistant secretary of state in 1945–47. The multimillionaire publisher of the *Encyclopaedia Britannica,* which was cited by the Federal Trade Commission for using deceptive pricing and bargain claims (Associated Press report, July 1, 1961), Benton started his career as a radio huckster. His deodorant commercials set a standard for banality seldom matched in the history of the advertising profession.

20. *Listen, Yankee!* Ballantine Books, New York, 1960, p. 103.

21. Ibid., pp. 94–95.

22. *Ency. Brit.,* Vol. 5, p. 44. It must have been galling for William Benton to have read in his own publishing venture a complete refutation of his predictions concerning Russian intervention in Cuba.

23. Dinsmore, op. cit., p. 179. In 1967 Matthews grudgingly admitted that Castro was a Communist, but said that he became one in 1960, a statement which does not agree with Castro's. Matthews, who as a foreign correspondent in Europe in the 1930s affected a gray fedora, beige gloves, matching spats, and Malacca walking stick, remained on good terms with his employers until the very end. Mrs. Arthur Sulzberger was the godmother of his only son. Gay Talese, *The Kingdom and the Power,* 1969, p. 463–64.

and most insistent in forcing their mistaken views on the government were, in the Kennedy administration, raised to important decision-making positions, it is not astonishing that American-Cuban relations proceeded from bad to worse. The White House specialist in Latin American affairs was the minority intellectual, Richard Goodwin, a Kennedy speech writer. Another minority intellectual who had much to do with diplomatic dealings with Castro was Arthur Schlesinger, Jr., the author of the administration's 1961 White Paper on Cuba. In an outburst of ringing clichés, Schlesinger described how the "hemisphere rejoiced at the overthrow of the Batista tyranny, looked with sympathy on the new regime, and welcomed its promises of political freedom and social justice for the Cuban people." [24]

There followed a farce of contradictions. On April 17, 1961, the White House intellectual general staff, suddenly reversing itself, sent a force of 1,500 American-trained and American-equipped Cuban exiles to invade Cuba. But at the very climax of the Bay of Pigs landing, the Kennedy administration, overly concerned about the cool reaction of the news media, lost its nerve and canceled all but the first of the covering air strikes.[25]

The nuclear confrontation with Russia, which came after this shameful exhibition of American indecision and weakness, culminated in what the press regarded as a Kennedy "victory," although no conclusive proof has been offered that the Russians ever removed *all* their missiles and warheads from Cuba. On the contrary, there is evidence that many missiles remain, along with other advanced Soviet weapons, in the vast network of Cuba's underground installations.[26] Kennedy's diplomatic triumph, it

---

24. Evans, op. cit., p. 381.

25. Ibid., pp. 385–86.

26. In a 1964 interview Castro's sister, Juanita, said, "In Cuba there are long-range ballistic missiles which are well camouflaged." A year before, Representative Donald Bruce of Indiana stated, "there are forty or more Soviet missiles still in Cuba today and the highest officials in the U.S. government know it." Evans, op. cit., pp. 403–6. It is not clear what type of missile Representative Bruce had in mind. There is no question that Soviet SA-2 anti-aircraft missiles are present in Cuba—144 of them according to *Time,* July 27, 1970, p. 17. But Washington is more concerned about the installation of such missiles in the Middle East than in Cuba. According to *U.S. News & World Report* (March

so happened, did not include the right of on-site inspection.

There is also little doubt that Kennedy made a secret agreement with Khrushchev concerning the inviolability of Cuba. By allowing the installation of a permanent Soviet military base only ninety miles from Florida and by promising not to invade Cuba,[27] the president did not pigeonhole or abrogate the Monroe Doctrine; he turned it upside down. The United States, once committed to preventing European intervention in the New World, had in effect become the protector of a Russian satellite sate in the strategic Caribbean area. That Cuba was also a training camp for revolutionary cadres whose mission was to spearhead armed Communist uprisings in Latin America and later to send tens of thousands of mercenaries to Africa to set up pro-Soviet regimes made Kennedy's Cuban policy all the more inexcusable.[28]

Since dominant population groups of Northern European descent are not to be found in Latin American countries, the racial ingredient of representative or genuinely democratic government is missing. It follows that whatever political and economic stability exists will probably continue to be provided by dictators, benevolent or malevolent. Among them will certainly be a number of Castros, who will ride into power on the misery, ignorance, and superstition of the illiterate masses, using the tested Communist strategy of playing on racial animosity in the name of class war.

The United States helped an unfriendly Castro assume power by withdrawing support from a friendly dictator, Fulgencio Batista. The CIA participated in the assassination of the friendly Dominican dictator, Rafael Trujillo, which precipitated so much chaos that President Johnson had to order in 24,000 Marines. More recently President Carter abandoned friendly dictator Anastasio Somoza and allowed the pro-Soviet and pro-Castro Sandinistas

---

9, 1970, p. 48), there are 165 Soviet combat planes in Cuba, 500 anti-aircraft missiles, 300 tanks, 100 self-propelled guns, and 200 troop carriers. A Soviet army brigade has been stationed in Cuba for more than a decade.

27. In 1964 Castro declared: "There is to be no invasion of Cuba by the U.S. That is formal. It is binding on the U.S. government under any president, any government. . . . When Khrushchev proposed that there be no invasion of Cuba, Kennedy said yes." Evans, op. cit., p. 401.

28. Ibid., pp. 406–7.

to take over Nicaragua. Since Carter was not decent enough to grant him permanent exile in the United States, Somoza fled to Paraguay, where he was assassinated by left-wing terrorists.

Countries friendly to the Soviet Union may be weaned from Moscow, as Egypt and Somalia proved when they expelled their Russian "advisers." But in the Western Hemisphere, where no country is in the dangerous position of having to share a frontier with the U.S.S.R., it would be wiser and much less costly to prevent a pro-Soviet regime from taking over in the first place. Today the top of the agenda for America's Western Hemisphere policy is to stop the creeping Russian penetration of Central America in its tracks, to repossess the Panama Canal, and by clever diplomacy, economic finesse, or brute force to remove Cuba from the Soviet orbit. The Monroe Doctrine should be rescued from the diplomatic dead file and dusted off, but only implemented in the event of direct foreign interference in Latin American affairs and never again used as a pretext for old-fashioned Yankee intervention. Whatever else the United States does in Latin America, it should no longer be identified with the losing side in civil wars and revolutions. There being very little possibility that an American-style economy will ever operate successfully in the quasi-feudal conditions of Latin America, the United States should be resigned to an endless parade of collectivist regimes. Rather than pick and choose between them according to the liberal-minority formula that totalitarians of the left are to be favored over totalitarians of the right, American diplomacy should endeavor to see that all Latin American states, whatever their politics, remain loyal to the Western Hemisphere.

Utopians have often envisioned a Pan-American Union, in which the United States is an equal partner, as the ideal instrument for resolving hemispheric problems and maintaining hemispheric defense. But the United States has such an overwhelming industrial and financial edge over the other New World countries that it can hardly avoid the responsibility and stigma of domination. Latin American politicians may complain about American imperialism, but certainly their own countries, either alone or jointly, do not have the strength to defend the New World against Old World predators. Latin American capitalists and Marxists may denounce the Yankee business colossus, but the economy of their countries would be much the worse for wear if American firms shut their doors and went home.[29]

Pavlovian cries of "gringoism" should not be allowed to conceal a much more dangerous form of aggression that is now taking place in the Western Hemisphere. This is the aggression that is pointing north, not south. With much of Texas and the American Southwest reverting to a Spanish-speaking Mexican culture, with Puerto Ricans breeding faster than Negroes in New York, with Cuban refugees [30] crowding into Florida, it is possible that Latin Americans will soon reconquer their lost North American territories by default. The northward extension of Latin America can only weaken hemispheric security by further reducing the power of the American Majority, on whose shoulders any effective defense of the two continents must ultimately rest. Deprived of the leadership and fighting strength of the American Majority, the New World might once again become the possession of the Old.

Turning finally to Canada, it must be recognized at the outset that from a racial and cultural standpoint Canada is two nations, not one. The truth is that British and French Canada are as socially differentiated in the Western Hemisphere as Britain and France are in Europe. In fact British-descended and French-descended Canadians distrust each other more than the French in France distrust Perfidious Albion and vice versa. There is no English Channel to keep them apart, and the religious differences are sharper, French Canadians being more intensely Catholic and British Canadians more pronouncedly Protestant than the French and British in Europe.

As the original white settlers of Canada, French Canadians like to think of themselves as the true Canadians. They have expressed

---

29. As of 1969, American business employed 2,000,000 Latin Americans, accounted for 12 percent of Latin America's Gross National Product and one-third of its exports, and paid more than one-fifth of its taxes. *Time*, July 11, 1969, p. 26.

30. The 1980 wave of 120,000 Cubans which washed ashore in Florida had a large component of criminals, homosexuals, and retardates. By injecting these diseased elements into the American population, Castro won another victory in his cold war against the United States.

these sentiments with Molotov cocktails, bombs, kidnappings, and murder—a form of political activity unnerving to English-speaking Canadians. Deliberate attempts by France, particularly in the de Gaulle era, to arouse separatist feelings and promote French culture did nothing to ameliorate the situation. In 1976 the separatist Parti Quebecois come to power in Quebec, and three years later a referendum calling for outright separation was defeated, but not decisively. Today Canada is held together largely because of the conciliatory attitude of English-speaking Canadians, who, manipulated by the liberal-minority media and the political legerdemain of perennial Prime Minister Pierre Trudeau, have leaned over backwards in granting the strident demands of 5,880,000 French Canadians for ever more autonomy.

British Canada, as distinct from French Canada, has a racial mixture that approximates that of the white population of the United States. Canadians of British origin number approximately 14,122,800; Italian origin, 484,000; German, 476,700; Ukrainian, 282,000; Indian/Eskimo, 133,000; Chinese, 132,500; Portuguese, 126,500; Other, 1,347,700.[31] In the last category are 305,000 Jews (two in the cabinet) and a growing Negro minority that numbers perhaps 200,000. Some of the latter are descendants of fugitive slaves who escaped from the United States shortly before the Civil War.[32] As Negroes everywhere, Canadian blacks are at the bottom of the social and economic ladder, even though they have had the vote and the full protection of the law, including integrated education, for more than a hundred years.[33] As Jews everywhere, Canadian Jews are concentrated in a few of the larger cities, principally Montreal and Toronto, and have a disproportionate share of the country's wealth.

The idea has now lost most of its fire, but the annexation of Canada once received a great deal of serious consideration from those few politicians in American history who deserve the name of statesmen. Over the strong objections of tens of thousands of American Loyalists who had fled north across the border, Benja-

---

31. *1981 World Almanac*, p. 508. Since the classification is by "Mother Tongue," the British figure evidently includes Canadians of Irish descent.

32. Many of these returned after the war ended. John Hope Franklin, *From Slavery to Freedom*, Knopf, New York, 1969, p. 377.

33. Ibid., pp. 376, 380–81.

min Franklin tried to persuade the British to give up Canada in the peace talks which ended the War of Independence. Another wave of annexation fever swept the United States in the early years of Manifest Destiny,[34] some of it reciprocated by the Canadians, at that time still British colonials. Even as late as 1911 the speaker of the House, Champ Clark of Missouri, was hailing "the day when the American flag will float over every square foot of British North American possessions clear to the North Pole." [35] Today the anti-imperialism of United States politics, except in the Middle East, coupled with Canada's intensified economic nationalism and lingering resentment over the Vietnam War,[36] have postponed all thought of union.[37]

But this does not mean the thought will not come up again. Americans have invested more money in Canada, $37 billion, than in any other country. Moreover Canada is by far America's best customer, and the United States buys approximately 75 percent of all Canadian exports. Since the two nations are so economically interwoven and since Canada's English-speaking Majority has such a close biological and cultural relationship with the American Majority, it seems inevitable that the two Majorities, no matter how intensely the minorities in both countries oppose it, will draw closer together.

---

34. Before the outbreak of the War of 1812, Henry Clay told the House of Representatives, "The militia of Kentucky alone are competent to place Montreal and Upper Canada at your feet." Another nineteenth-century hawk, John Calhoun, prophesied, "I believe that in four weeks from the time a declaration of war is heard on our frontier, the whole of upper Canada and a part of lower Canada will be in our power." Beard, *The Rise of American Civilization*, Vol. 1, p. 416.

35. Samuel Flagg Bemis, *A Diplomatic History of the U.S.*, Holt, Rinehart, and Winston, New York, 1955, p. 735.

36. In 1969 Canada served as a refuge for 53,000 American draft dodgers and deserters. *Times Literary Supplement*, Aug. 28, 1969, p. 2.

37. During World War II, 24.4 percent of the Americans interviewed in an opinion poll desired the annexation of Canada, and 23.3 percent of the Canadians shared their view. *Fortune*, April, 1942, p. 112.

PART X

Prospects and Perspectives

CHAPTER 38

Nuclear Hypnosis

NOWHERE IN THIS STUDY, except for a few passing references in the foreign policy chapters, has any serious note been taken of that awesome new tool of warfare, the nuclear-tipped missile. The omission was deliberate. The very word *nuclear* raises semantical perturbations which tend to emotionalize and obscure rather than clarify the meaningful discussion of any topic, particularly international relations. Secondly, in spite of its horror, nuclear war is still war and as such can best be studied in a military context. Even the non-military implications of nuclear weapons— for example, the nuclear hypnosis which blocks all realistic approaches to foreign policy—rightfully belong under the heading of psychological warfare.

Incongruously, the immediate military results of the discovery of nuclear weapons, at least up to the present writing, have been to channel war into more conventional paths.[1] In order to keep the fission and fusion bombs safely deactivated, the nuclear and non-nuclear powers which have engaged in post-World War II conflicts have held a tighter rein on their military operations than might normally have been expected. The existence of sanctuaries,[2]

---

1. A rather tortuous way of making good another brilliant "prophecy" of Engels. In 1878 he wrote that military technology "had reached such a state of perfection that further progress which would have any revolutionizing influence is no longer possible. . . . all further improvements are more or less unimportant for field warfare. The era of evolution is therefore, in essentials, closed in this direction." *Anti-Dühring*, p. 188.

2. Hanoi and its port, Haiphong, were notable examples of unbombed or unblockaded sanctuaries during most of the Vietnam War. Even when air raids

the taking of hostages, the holding of prisoners for ransom, and the renewed popularity of guerrilla warfare all point to a step backward into the military past.[3]

It was in the early days of World War II that the same liberals and equalitarians who later posed as the fiercest opponents of atomic warfare actually started the nuclear arms race. Indeed it is understating the case to say that the concept, design, development, and production of the world's first atomic bomb was from beginning to end a minority labor of love. The chronology begins with Lise Meitner, a refugee German scientist, who went to Denmark in 1938 and handed physicist Niels Bohr the data of a successful fission experiment recently performed in Berlin. Bohr passed the information along until it reached Einstein, whereupon the latter, then in Princeton, wrote a personal letter to President Roosevelt urging that America immediately start a full-scale bomb development program. The first letter was delivered by banker Alexander Sachs and contained the allegation (which was false) that the Germans were building an atomic bomb. As World War II progressed, Fermi, Bethe, and Szilard worked out the details of the A-bomb, which was constructed under the direction of Oppenheimer. Teller and von Neumann, after assisting on the A-bomb, went on to develop the H-bomb. Meanwhile Rosenberg, Greenglass, and Sobell stole various bomb schematics and gave them to the Russians.[4]

That the atomic bomb, as well as the espionage that grew up around it,[5] was basically a minority idea is demonstrated by the

---

were permitted and a sea blockade was established, the United States Air Force and Navy were restricted to purely military targets. In the Korean War the supply lines of the Chinese "volunteers" were off limits to General MacArthur, whose warplanes were forbidden to fly over Red China.

3. The exception may be the Soviet Union's supposed use of poison gas in the war against Afghanistan.

4. Facts, names, and dates have been taken, in most part, from Robert Jungk, *Brighter than a Thousand Suns*, Harcourt, Brace, New York, 1958.

5. One of the excuses offered by those who came to the defense of the atomic spies—and there were many who came—was that Soviet scientists would have sooner or later penetrated the mysteries of nuclear energy by themselves. In answer, it might be stated that the secret formula for Greek fire was successfully guarded from the seventh to the ninth centuries by the Eastern Roman Empire. To reveal any knowledge of it was not only considered treason but sacrilege.

roster of names in the preceding paragraph. Every single person is Jewish with the exception of Roosevelt and Fermi, an Italian with a Jewish wife. German anti-Semitism had provoked a prodigious reaction from the world Jewish community, which included a number of high-ranking nuclear physicists, almost all of them educated at Germany's University of Göttingen. But it was Einstein, still considered a model of humanitarianism by the media, who was most responsible for "selling" the bomb to the American government. As the foremost promoter of the deadliest weapon of all time, the expounder of Relativity played a role in the history of warfare that had previously been ascribed to Basil Zaharoff, the Krupps, and the other "merchants of death" who have become stock characters in liberal-minority demonology.

The bomb was not completed in time to drop it on Germany. But the fraternity of atomic scientists who built it had few compunctions about using it against Japan, the ally of Hitler. The final decision, of course, was President Truman's. The scientist who opposed the project most adamantly was Ernest Lawrence, a Majority member.[6]

The racial motivations of the minority scientists who conceived and produced the A-bomb were made perfectly clear after the war when Oppenheimer, the most influential American nuclear physicist, attempted to stop the development of the H-bomb at the very moment the Russians had begun a crash program to build their own. Oppenheimer explained his change of heart by appealing to established liberal and pacifist principles. He emphasized his desire to give up "the devil's work."[7] But since he and practically all his colleagues had been pacifistic, liberal, and even ultraliberal before the appearance of Hitler, their second change of heart within a decade could more logically be attributed to a

---

It was Greek fire that helped the Byzantine government repulse the Arab attack on Constantinople, thereby, according to Will Durant, "saving Europe" and prolonging the life of the Eastern Roman Empire for nearly 800 years. *The Age of Faith,* pp. 424–25.

6. Jungk, op. cit., p. 186n. A later development, the neutron bomb, which was designed specifically to kill people, was the brainchild of Samuel T. Cohen, a California scientist. The bomb's greatly reduced blast does little damage to property. *Newsweek,* April 17, 1978, p. 36.

7. Ibid., p. 333.

change of enemy. That Oppenheimer would have been so diligent about building bombs if Hitler had not been anti-Semitic, and so quick to give up his bomb work if he had not had the typical minority intellectual's soft spot for Marxism, is open to doubt.[8]

It took a great deal of effort on the part of the American government to override Oppenheimer's opposition to the H-bomb, backed up as it was by the most influential portion of the news media.[9] Of all the top-tier minority scientists, only Edward Teller and John von Neumann seemed to perceive the dangers of allowing America's nuclear technology to fall behind Russia's. Both Teller and von Neumann had had first-hand experience with communism in their native Hungary. It was the vigorous, opinionated Teller, far in advance of his colleagues in detecting Stalin's shift to nationalism and anti-Semitism, who fought most doggedly for the H-bomb program—often in the face of waves of vilification from the press.[10] As it turned out, the United States beat Russia to the H-bomb by only ten months.

Having failed to take America out of the nuclear arms race, the disarmament lobby proposed a mutual Soviet-American ban on all nuclear weapons. The Russians evinced their willingness, but refused to permit on-site inspection. Incredibly, liberal and minority intellectuals were prepared to grant this concession. Fortunately, the Joint Chiefs of Staff and a bare majority of Congress were not.

In the years immediately following World War II, the arguments for nuclear disarmament were based on fear, pacifism, defeatism, and vainglorious proposals for world government. The old liberal-minority fixation on Russia as the birthplace of communism and equalitarianism was an important motivating force, as illustrated in part by the well-publicized slogan, "Better Red than dead."

---

8. Oppenheimer had many Communist connections, which eventually cost him his security clearance amid a press hullabaloo that brought back memories of the Dreyfus affair.

9. When the Special Committee of the National Security Council finally ordered the H-bomb program to proceed at full speed, the vote was two to one. David Lilienthal, the only minority member and the first chairman of the Atomic Energy Commission, voted no. Ibid., pp. 284–85.

10. At first Teller was treated as an outcast by his fellow Jews. Today, as the Jewish establishment turns against Russia, he is rapidly returning to favor.

A great deal of the disarmament propaganda originated in the White House itself. Such influential minority presidential consultants as Seymour Melman, Jerome Wiesner, and Walt W. Rostow proposed policies which were all to the ultimate military advantage of the Soviet Union.[11]

Nowhere in recent years has the downgrading of American national security been more effective than in the area of civil defense. In the event of a nuclear war with the Soviet Union, the ability of American manpower and industry to survive devastating H-bomb attacks will represent victory or the closest thing to victory. In plain words, if there is no lack of nuclear weapons on either side, as is now the case, the country whose people and industrial plants are more widely scattered and more deeply "dug in" will have the better chance of avoiding total defeat. Largely as the result of America's indifference and at times open enmity to the whole concept of civil defense, the Soviet Union's elaborate civil defense system is far ahead. Sixty million members of DOSAAF, a kind of Soviet National Guard, each receive twenty hours of compulsory civil defense training a year. By 1985 blast resistant shelters are expected to shield from 15 to 30 percent of the entire Soviet population. The United States spends $100 million a year on civil defense; the U.S.S.R., $2 billion. The United States has 4,150 full-time and 2,300 part-time personnel in civil defense; the U.S.S.R., 100,000. Each summer at 55,000 Pioneer Camps, Soviet children between the ages of seven and fifteen receive lessons in constructing air raid shelters, removal of chemical and radioactive contamination, nerve gas antidotes, and the proper use of gas masks.[12]

It is not necessary to be a general or an admiral on the Joint Chiefs of Staff to know that surprise gives an overwhelming edge in nuclear war. Yet an American president, John Kennedy, went on record with the statement that the United States will never be the first to launch a nuclear attack [13]—a gratuitous and comforting promise to an enemy which has different ideas. The late Mar-

---

11. For a concise but comprehensive survey of the activities of the Disarmament Lobby, including sketches of the principal lobbyists, see the chapter of the same name in Evans, op. cit.

12. *Tulsa World,* Aug. 13, 1980.

13. Evans, op. cit., pp. 262–63.

shal Grechko, Soviet minister of defense, said in 1970: "The Americans are fooling themselves. The only war to fight, to win, is an atomic one, and it is what we should be prepared for." [14] A mysterious Russian intelligence officer, Colonel Oleg Penkovskiy, who may or may not have had close connections with the CIA, stated categorically that the Soviet Union had built its nuclear strategy on a first strike against the United States. He also asserted that the Soviet General Staff is not at all convinced that both sides would be destroyed in a nuclear war, believing it quite possible to win such a war, provided it is short and does not degenerate into a grinding conflict of attrition. Soviet strategists, he added, count on total surprise and the widespread radioactive fallout produced by Russia's bigger and dirtier bombs to mount an attack of paralyzing proportions.[15] Perhaps half the American population and most of the American industrial complex would be exposed to thermonuclear destruction, and it is not comforting to think that Americans are relying on poor Russian marksmanship rather than on a highly organized system of civil defense for the survival of their families and their factories. Meanwhile, with its key personnel and many of its key defense plants safely underground, Russia would be well braced for retaliatory strikes by the United States.

Is the Soviet Union, bedeviled from within by an irrational economic system and from without by increasingly restless and unhappy satellites, ready for this horrendous gamble? Will it ever be ready, even when its nuclear arsenal bulges much larger than America's? One sign the Kremlin might be thinking in that direction would be a preventive strike on Chinese missile bases and atomic installations, for it is hard to believe that the Soviet Union will follow the American pattern and permit its greatest and most threatening enemy to build up a lethal nuclear stockpile. Far too fast for Russia's satisfaction, China is becoming a principal member of the world's nuclear club, which includes Britain, France, India, Israel, and possibly South Africa. Other nations, particularly

---

14. *Reader's Digest,* Oct., 1970.

15. "When circumstances are favorable for delivering the first nuclear strike, the Soviet Union will deliver this strike under the pretense of defending itself from an aggressor. In this way it will seize the initiative." Oleg Penkovskiy, *The Penkovskiy Papers,* Avon Books, New York, 1966, pp. 72–73, 250–54.

Iraq and Pakistan, would also like to belong and are working hard at it. That the two superpowers, having agreed to stop their own atmospheric testing, permit China and France to continue theirs shows a disturbing lack of concern not only for the security of America and the Soviet Union but for the security of the world.

If liberal-minority domination of American "public opinion" had not been so complete in the aftermath of World War II, mankind might never have had to worry about the possibility of thermonuclear war. From 1945 to 1949 the United States had an absolute monopoly in nuclear weapons. It had produced an atomic bomb four years ahead of Russia, and was even further ahead in the development and production of carrier systems. At any time during a five-to ten-year period, the United States, without any fear of effective retaliation, could have presented the Soviet Union with an ultimatum demanding the immediate dismantling of all its nuclear installations, thereby bringing Russia's nuclear buildup to a dead halt. If Russia had ignored the ultimatum, the United States could have accomplished the dismantling on its own initiative by a massive preventive strike, not against the Soviet population but against Soviet nuclear facilities and missile sites. The same preemptive measures could have later been applied to any other nation foolish enough to start building a nuclear arsenal.

All during the critical first decade of the Atomic Age, there were many sensible and realistic Americans who advocated such a policy—a policy which was humanitarian in the highest sense of the word because it might eventually have saved hundreds of millions of lives. But these Americans were either never heard or, if heard, were mercilessly pilloried and then silenced. The liberal-minority cacophony of unilateral disarmament and accommodation with Russia at any price, including the sharing of American atomic research, would admit no debate.

As suggested in the beginning of this chapter, the present nuclear balance of power between Russia and the United States may actually have a calming and restraining effect on war by localizing and limiting conflicts and placing a renewed importance on such old-fashioned weapons as the rifle and such old-fashioned tactics as hand-to-hand combat. But if it does not, and if nuclear war should erupt, it is not likely that all civilization—despite the dire predictions of the doomsayers—will be utterly blotted out.[16]

Mankind has already survived a few ordeals which come close to the horror predicted for a future nuclear war. Carthage could not have been demolished more completely by an H-bomb than it was by Roman legions. Genghis Khan is reported to have killed 1,600,000 men, women, and children in Herat. Not one person was left alive when Tamerlane passed through Baghdad.[17] The Black Death wiped out one-fourth of Europe's population in 1348–50.[18] Men have fought many wars in which no prisoners were taken and lost many sieges in which all the besieged, regardless of age or sex, were slain. Although megaton hydrogen bombs are up to a thousand times deadlier than the kiloton atomic bombs dropped on Hiroshima and Nagasaki, it is noteworthy that both of these cities are now more populated and more flourishing than they were before the atomic attacks.

Even conceding that a full-scale nuclear war would annihilate the entire population of Europe, North America, and Asia, any one country such as New Zealand or Argentina would be quite able to carry on twentieth-century civilization with scarcely an interruption. When it is remembered that the population of Athens was only 130,000 [19] in the Age of Pericles, human quality would seem to be a more basic ingredient of civilization than human quantity. In fact a cynic or a hardened social Darwinist might say that a nuclear war could actually save civilization by attacking the enemies which are threatening to extinguish it— the urban blight, the excessive industrialization, the exponential birthrate of the genetically impoverished, and all the other ecological and dysgenic disasters of the present era.

What is to be feared even more than nuclear war is the nuclear hypnosis to which the American public has been subjected for the last several decades. First, Americans are told to produce

16. Prophets of death and desolation have been in vogue since the days of the flood and Sodom and Gomorrah. The invention of the sling, the spear, the bow and arrow, and gunpowder may have been as terrifying in their day as chemical, biological, and nuclear weapons have been to people of the present era.

17. *Ency. Brit.*, Vol. 12, p. 1001.

18. *Scientific American*, Feb. 1964, p. 114. As late as 1970, 300,000 to 600,000 East Pakistanis died in a Bay of Bengal cyclone. *Time*, Nov. 30, 1970, p. 16.

19. Only 50,000 of these Athenians were citizens. See p. 236.

atomic bombs, then to drop them on two undefended cities in a nation already on the verge of defeat,[20] then to forfeit the A-bomb's immense strategic advantages by sharing America's atomic research with Russia, then to agree to nuclear disarmament without inspection, then to scrap the H-bomb at the very moment Russia was building its own and, finally, in the name of a Strategic Arms Limitations Treaty to guarantee the Soviet Union a lead in nuclear-tipped intercontinental ballistic missiles.

But this is by no means the end. Since the nuclear policy of the liberal-minority coalition is not as selflessly humanitarian as it pretends, further shifts and reverses may be expected. Let Russian commissars start imitating the pogroms of the czars, let there be the glimmerings of an Israeli Dunkirk in Palestine, let South Africa defend itself with nuclear weapons against black and white invaders from the north, let a massive Fascist uprising take place anywhere in the Western world, let any one of these events occur and the disarmament lobby will quickly drop its pacifist mask and be the first to demand the thermonuclear incineration of the "enemy." [21]

The somnambulism that has surrounded the formulation of America's nuclear strategy will vanish as soon as it is acknowledged that nuclear weapons are not an ideological issue. They are not to serve as whipping posts or chess pieces in a game of racial politics. Since each warhead on each missile is a Damoclean sword over the head of every foreign potentate with aggressive designs

---

20. The atomic attacks on Hiroshima and Nagasaki will always be considered a blot on American history and will be blamed on the American people as a whole instead of the minority scientists who invented and built the bomb and the liberal-minority "humanitarians" who ordered and applauded the bombing. It was the same group that supported and applauded the 1945 air assault on Dresden, which killed 150,000 people in one night, most of them war refugees, the advance guard of the 13,000,000 Germans who fled westward from the depredations of the Red Army and the retributions of the Poles and Czechs. *Time,* June 21, 1963, pp. 30, 95–96.

21. One sign of what may be expected was a little-publicized incident which happened during the 1967 flare-up of the Arab-Israeli war. SANE (Sane Nuclear Policy Committee), which had always been in the forefront of every attempt to limit and weaken America's nuclear capability, had to cancel a peace march because so many of its members were getting ready to demonstrate for more military assistance to Israel. Dinsmore, *All The News That Fits,* p. 323.

on the New World, nuclear weapons are nothing more and nothing less than the principal line of American defense.

The best way to avoid a nuclear war is to recognize that it is not nuclear preparedness which increases the chances of an H-bomb strike against America, but the defeatism, divisiveness, and discord promoted by a minority-dominated mass media. The aim seems to be to destroy America's will to resist while chipping away at the primary means of resistance, the all-important nuclear deterrent. Those whose ideas and activities encourage a guerrilla war within the United States extend a standing invitation to totalitarian militarists overseas to inch their fingers closer to the nuclear button. Those who do not understand that hydrogen warfare calls for the modification not the abandonment of age-old concepts of tactics and strategy may one day invite a nuclear attack from those who do. Those who assert there can be no such thing as victory in a nuclear war are making such a victory possible—for the other side.

A Majority-dominated America would be relatively impervious to the selfish interests and special pleading which have recently involved the United States in so many fruitless and profitless foreign crusades. The national effort would be withdrawn from the worldwide defense of degenerate political regimes and outmoded ideologies, and focused on the well-being of America. And America's well-being, in a nuclear context, means an unshakable commitment to the proposition that war is the final court of appeal, not for the protection of foreign investments and foreign homelands, not for glory-seeking Gracchites or racist Messiahs in equalitarian clothing, but for a society faced with the immediate threat of disintegration and oblivion.

CHAPTER 39

Northern European Ingathering

IT IS NOT, however, to America's nuclear defenses that the Majority must look for deliverance and regeneration but to the defenses of the mind. There will be no end to its dispossession until the Majority learns to reject *all*, repeat *all*, the main currents of modern liberal thought, and there can be no such rejection until the true nature of the illiberal forces which engender and direct modern liberalism are clearly understood. The absurdities, fallacies, and contradictions of Marxism, Freudianism, the equalitarian anthropology of Boas, and contemporary social democracy are not important in themselves. What is important is how and why they have been developed and synthesized into the most unbending intellectual absolutism since medieval scholasticism.

To understand what has happened to the Majority it is first necessary to realize that the deterioration of power is as much the result of success as it is of failure. The hard-pressed society knows better than to let down its guard. It cannot afford to ignore the motives and acts of its opponents. It is aware that any abrogation of its possessions, tangible or intangible, is a loss that can only be recovered by the most prolonged and arduous efforts. Conversely, the successful or affluent society, by virtue of its surplus of life's necessities, has the time to turn away from the grindstone of daily existence. Less touched by the existential forces of the human condition, its members have the rare and dangerous opportunity of stretching their individualism well beyond the normal societal breaking point.

Measured by any yardstick of material progress toward the good life, history has never recorded a more successful society than

549

the United States from the end of the Civil War to the late 1920s. Even the incapable and incapacitated elements of the population, those genetically or culturally unsuited to participate fully and voluntarily in a Western-style, progress-oriented industrial society, were moving ahead, albeit slowly. Even the lowliest newcomers from Europe, compared to those they left behind, were immensely better off the minute they planted their feet on American soil. And all the while every American of whatever background and at whatever stage of assimilation was being exposed to undreamed-of possibilities of self-fulfillment and self-realization by the soaring vitality of Majority imagination and enterprise.

The successful can afford to share their success, and the Majority did so with indiscriminate prodigality. With few qualifications or conditions, the laboriously accumulated privileges of Majority institutions were distributed gratis to members of other races and cultures, who accepted them almost as a matter of course, often with a show of ingratitude, and then used them for purposes entirely different from those for which they had been intended. The new Americans began to vote, not as individuals but as members of blocs. Although many of them prospered greatly in an unfettered economy, they spent much of their wealth on group projects that were often opposed to the national interest. They reveled in the freedom they had never been able to win for themselves; but instead of treating it respectfully and guarding it responsibly, they looked upon it as a gift, as their rightful and permanent possession, whether or not they deserved it, worked to acquire it, or struggled to maintain it. Their children thronged to the free public schools of a matchless educational system, where they learned enough about American civilization to criticize it, but not enough to uphold and advance it.

At first many Unassimilable Minority members did try to fit into the overall Majority pattern. But how could they be good democrats when democracy had always been foreign to their historical experience? How could they begin supporting an establishment when they had always been against all establishments? Many were learned in the law—their religion was often their law—but how remote such theological exercises were from the Anglo-Saxon common law! As for assimilation, how could they mix with others when the whole secret of their survival had been standing apart?

They toyed a little with the American Dream, but it eluded

them. Their intellectuals read Locke, Jefferson, Emerson, and Mill, but later came to prefer such Old World kinsmen as Marx, Freud, and Boas. The Old Testament apocalyptics of Marxism had a familiar and agreeable ring. The anthropomorphic symbolism of Freud sat well with a religious people looking for a replacement for a dying, anachronistic faith. It was a godsend when Boas obligingly declared that all races were equal. The Declaration of Independence had so intimated, but now it was a "scientific fact."

It did not take long to discover that these new theories were much more than intellectual playthings. They comprised a vast stockpile of doctrinal weapons made to order for a strategy of *divide et impera*. Marx had separated men, not into races but into exploiters and exploited, upper classes and lower classes—and the Majority was so separated. Freud had changed men into mindless animals—and the Majority was so animalized. In the matter of the great guideposts of Majority rule, the New Testament and the Constitution, by adding a little here and subtracting a little there, by emphasizing some words and reinterpreting others, both could be turned against the Majority and used to produce further divisions in its already divided ranks.

Meantime, Majority members went blindly about their business, convinced that America would remake the strangers in its midst, not the other way around. Only a prescient handful rejected these environmentalist fantasies and warned of what was really taking shape behind the smokescreen of proletarian rhetoric and "progressive" legislation. But Henry Adams, Madison Grant, Lothrop Stoddard, Henry Ford, Ezra Pound, Charles Lindbergh, and Carleton Putnam were voices crying in an echo chamber. All that was heard was the million-throated, liberal-minority chorus of calumny stigmatizing them as eccentric crackpots or murderous racists or both. Ezra Pound, the bitterest and most poetic of these voices, was singled out for more spectacular chastisement. For weeks the man described as "a principal founder and moving spirit of modern poetry in English" [1] was exposed in an iron cage in Pisa and then locked up for twelve years in a District of Columbia insane asylum.[2]

---

1. *Who's Who in America,* 1969–70.

2. "It was an incredible barbarity for Americans to conceive and execute." Charles Norman, *Ezra Pound,* Macmillan, New York, 1960, p. 397. The aging

Even in the 1960s and 70s, when the liberal-minority grip on the nation had tightened to a stranglehold, Majority members still could not believe they had become a people of little or no account in their own country. Most still had a home, a late-model car, and a loaded deep freeze. But they no longer had preachers or teachers to defend the Majority cause, no literature, no theater, no press, no television, no nationwide forum of expression. As its ascendancy was efficiently blotted out, the Majority was transformed into a swarm of middle-class drones, still permitted certain physical comforts but carefully isolated and quarantined from the vantage points of decision-making and opinion-molding. Majority industrial magnates were given a few more years or decades of limited independence within the narrow confines of their corporations—someone had to turn the wheels—but they were to keep their mouths and their minds shut. As for Majority politicians and intellectuals, they were still safe, provided they voted right and obeyed their masters' voices.

Yet all was not clear sailing for the minority side. Equalitarianism, a contagious dogma of epidemic potential, was getting out of hand. It was predictable that the ruling race, having been reduced to equality, were scheduled for a further loss in status. It was understandable that the subject races, having been raised to equality, would try to climb higher, particularly after learned professors had flattered their genes and whetted their ambitions with allusions to racial superiority. It was logical that blacks, having been told they were equal or superior to whites, would blame their social disadvantages not on any innate limitations but on a devilish white conspiracy. It was inevitable that some blacks, having come to this conclusion, would feel they had a perfect right to avenge themselves and burn down cities and "get whitey." But the problem was that "whitey" was often a member of another Unassimilable Minority, the Jew who owned most of the ghetto tenements and retail shops.

Pound, it might be added, was held incommunicado in his Pisan cage, allowed no mail, and forced to sleep on the cement floor. Compare this treatment to that accorded Jane Fonda and Ramsey Clark, who trafficked with the enemy in Hanoi during the Vietnam war. Ex-Attorney General Clark, while a member of the law firm of Paul, Weiss, Goldberg, etc., was a *defense witness* in the trial of the New Left hit man whose bomb killed a Majority student at the University of Wisconsin.

So the Jewish dime-store owners and the less affluent Jewish retirees were sacrificed to the muggers and arsonists in urban no-man's lands, the latter often working under the table with the slum lords, while Jewish New Leftists, holed up safely in suburbia, drew up manifestos denouncing the Ku Klux Klan and nuclear power and demanding heavier doses of forced busing and Affirmative Action. As if nothing had happened, millionaire Gracchites and Jewish Old Leftists, some now calling themselves neo-conservatives, continued to foot most of the bills. After all, it was war, and a few minor betrayals and casualties should not be allowed to detract from a victory already in sight. In any event everyone was too committed to go backward—and a slowdown might give the Majority time to reorganize.

Time certainly was of the essence. Sensitive ears were beginning to hear rumblings and grumblings in the hinterland, in the heartland, in the South and Southwest, and, most forebodingly, in the sacred groves of academe, where the Arthur Jensens and Edward Wilsons were raising their voices. Incredibly, the Majority was finally starting to rouse itself. To smash these stirrings of resistance, the liberal-minority general staff opened up all the old stops, the mind-deadening cacophony of Marxist and liberal dogma and the sly equalitarian appeals to minority racism, as well as a few new stops—drugs, pornography, homosexuality, the generation gap, and women's liberation. As usual, the big guns blasted at the weakest spots in the Majority's defenses—the students and the young women. But they were also zeroing in on the prime target, the Majority's last redoubt, the family.

Now, to save itself from spiritual extinction, the Majority had no choice but to quickly unlearn every lesson it had been taught since the beginning of its dispossession. The dignity of the individual? The triumph of reason? The rights of man? The Majority's ancestors had been the first to develop these concepts and apply them to society. In their perverted modern form they were the killers of society. Democracy, genuine liberalism, the common law, the free play of the imagination, the technological breakthroughs, all the great political, social, and scientific achievements of Western man were now the spoils of non-Western man. History, once it had been "restructured" by the liberal-minority intelligentsia, not only became bunk but a deliberate fraud, the basic strategy of a war in which truth was the first casualty. Environment, climate, geography, economics, religion, and blind chance were solemnly proclaimed to be the only possible (and permissible) creators of the past and future. Race was still the unspeakable historical determinant, although the loudest denouncers and deniers of race were, as always, the biggest racists.

The very desperation of the denials lent substance to the claim that history clusters about race; that race is written large in every obscure paragraph and every radiant page of the human record; that where there is no race consciousness there is no historical consciousness, and where there is no historical consciousness there is chronology but no history; that archaeological diggings and today's headlines both testify that the essence of history is the rise and fall of races.

To the racial historian race is the being and the becoming of organized humanity. As race has been the controlling factor of much of the human past, so it will assume even greater importance in the future. Man's fate has now become the world's fate. Supreme efforts are necessary to put a stop to the devastation of the environment—and supreme efforts can only be undertaken by large groups of men with similar political and social reflexes, by great teams not great mobs, specifically by great races. Race, the highest manifestation of the team spirit, may be nature's way of organizing men for the accomplishment of the unaccomplishable.

Just as the body rejects transplanted organs, races have the habit of rejecting transplanted ideologies. They may accept them temporarily, but the buildup of "antibodies" is unceasing. The only ideology acceptable to all races would seem to be the grand design of evolution, which will ultimately select one of them to give birth to a new species, the better-than-man.

In an age beginning to uncover the mysteries of the gene, whose frequencies and combinations are the fundamental units of character and intelligence, both of individuals and of races, the race most likely to raise the *hominidae* another notch in the evolutionary scale will be the one that concentrates on the penetration of the genetic riddle. It will certainly not be the race that dissipates its energies on doctrinal crusades, seeking its salvation outside itself, allowing itself to become a hostage to fortune. This is the way back to the primeval ooze and the plasma—the way of devolution.

As the twentieth century winds down, the race best suited to shoulder the main weight of the evolutionary burden would appear to be the Northern European. Equally adept at physics and metaphysics, induction and deduction, theory and application, equally at home in the macrocosm and the microcosm, Northern European man has managed to soar a little higher above the animal kingdom than the other divisions of mankind. For the time being, two devastating intraracial wars in the first half of the century and the dispossession of the American Majority, the largest reservoir of Northern European genes, have grounded him. Permanently or temporarily, it is too early to know.

To put Northern Europeans back on the evolutionary track—to rekindle the Northern European efflorescence—is a project of monumental complexity. Of all the Northern European peoples, only a rehabilitated American Majority, mindful of the history it has made and is about to make, would have the strength and the resources to bring about a Northern European ingathering—not merely a political and economic clustering cemented by treaties and trade agreements and by the common nationality and citizenship which might come in time, but an ingathering of race consciousness, the most lasting and tenacious of all social binding forces.

Should this pooling of the work and thought of a highly gifted but widely dispersed people ever be effected, there would be such a preponderance of power that no external predator would dare so much as touch the remotest corner of the Northern European living space, either in Europe, Anglo America, or Australasia. The minorities within this living space, no longer able to prosper from the divisions of their hosts, might finally learn to look to themselves for sustenance. Forced into unaccustomed self-sufficiency, they might well rebuild their own depleted cultures—and gain from the experience.

Such is the shimmering prospect of a Northern European ingathering, a Pax Euramerica, a world order more encompassing than the Pax Romana and more enduring and more constructive than the Pax Britannica. The Pax Romana, though Rome was ruled in its expansionist days by patricians of Northern European descent, was never willing or able to reach far enough north to envelop the peoples of Germany and Scandinavia. Consequently the first and best chance for European unity was lost.

The Pax Britannica, which kept the peace so long throughout so much of the nonwhite world, while establishing new white worlds in newly discovered continents, was dysgenically disastrous to Northern Europeans everywhere. Britain's balance-of-power diplomacy which divided and exhausted Europe for hundreds of years was one direct cause of the ill-fated twentieth-century conflicts that so significantly lowered the genetic quality of all but the neutral European states—with the British gene pool eventually suffering the greatest damage of all. Also, at the very crest of empire, Britain lost her most important possessions in North America, a racial setback of the most serious consequences. If the secession of the thirteen colonies could have been prevented—not an impossible feat for subtle eighteenth-century statesmanship—the Pax Britannica might still be the mainstay of Western politics. Instead, present-day Britain is a weary little island kingdom, whose recovery awaits a new upsurge of the unquenchable British spirit.

The Germans brought down the Pax Romana by their victories and the Pax Britannica by their defeats. At almost any time since the Middle Ages, Britain could have dampened German militarism by supporting, not opposing, the historic German mission of defending the West against the inroads of the East. But Britain appointed herself the archenemy of European union, the same European union which would have nipped Bolshevism in the bud and forbidden the presence of Russian armies on the banks of the Elbe.

The Northern European ingathering, its primary task the consolidation, security, and advancement of the Northern European peoples, would be the first world order whose geographical frontiers matched its racial frontiers, once the minority elements were separated out and either sent back to their old homelands or established in new ones. Such a genetically based intercontinental confederation, a radically new way of bringing a scattered people together, might overcome or alleviate some of the dangers to mankind which the crypto-racism of proletarian politics seems to multiply. There would be room in it for Russians and other Slavs of Northern European descent, when and if the cumbersome Soviet complex fell apart of its own weight or was broken up by an invasion from the Asiatic steppes. There would emphatically be no place for the old-style exploitation of nonwhites or for the forcible adaptation of autochthonous civilizations to Northern European cultural norms.

But everything hangs on the fate of the American Majority. If its dispossession is not stopped and reversed, there will be no Northern European ingathering, no racial consolidation, no halt to the decline of the West, no giving the lie to Spengler. In fact there will soon be no America. History is insistent on pointing out that when the dominant population group goes, the country goes. As is daily becoming more apparent, the dying fall of the American Majority is the dying fall of America itself.

Appendixes

APPENDIX A

Explanation of Racial Census

During the debate on immigration quotas in the early 1920s, an attempt was made to determine the proportion of white Americans originating from various Old World and a few New World countries. The results, as published in *Immigration Quotas on the Basis of National Origin,* 70th Congress, 2d Session, Senate Document 259, p. 5, are given on the following pages. The right-hand columns of the table contain estimates of the racial composition of the mother country made by Carl Brigham, an associate professor of psychology at Princeton University. Brigham wanted to correlate the voluminous results of Army World War I intelligence tests with race. His findings were severely challenged, not so much for his racial estimates, but because he used them to help "prove" the intellectual superiority of American Nordics. See Carl Brigham, *A Study of American Intelligence,* Princeton University Press, Princeton, N.J., 1923, pp. 160, 190.

Brigham later recanted his hypothesis of Nordic intellectual superiority, but not his racial allocations, which are similar to those of Carleton Coon in *The Races of Europe,* the notable exception being Ireland. Here, Brigham seemed to go completely astray. He failed to include the large Irish Alpine component and apparently decided, in contradiction to most other anthropologists, that the Keltic element was more Mediterranean than Nordic. The percentages in the United Kingdom entry are Brigham's racial estimates for England. He had separate figures for the racial composition of Scotland (85 percent Nordic; 15 percent Mediterranean) and Wales (40 percent Nordic; 60 percent Mediterranean). He also had two categories for Turkey—Turkey (in Europe) and Turkey. His figures for the former are given in the table. As for the percentages omitted by Brigham, they can be obtained from Coon's *The Races of Europe* or from racial studies by European anthropologists.

561

TABLE A
WHITE POPULATION OF U.S. BY COUNTRY OF ORIGIN AND RACE

Country of Origin	% of White Population		% LIGHT WHITE Nordic	% WHITE Alpine	% DARK WHITE Medit.
	1790	1920			
Austria	*	0.9	10	90	
Belgium	1.5	0.8	60	40	
Czechoslovakia	0.1	1.8			
Denmark	0.2	0.7	85	15	
Estonia	. . .	0.1			
Finland	*	0.4			
France	1.9	1.9	30	55	15
Germany	7.4	16.3	40	60	
United Kingdom	77.0	41.4	80		20
Greece	. . .	0.2		15	85
Hungary	. . .	0.6	10	90	
Ireland	4.4	11.2	30		70 **
Italy	. . .	3.6	5	25	70
Latvia	. . .	0.2			
Lithuania	. . .	0.2			
Netherlands	3.3	2.0	85	15	
Norway	0.2	1.5	90	10	
Poland	*	4.1	10	90	
Portugal	0.1	0.3	5		95
Romania	. . .	0.2		100	
Russia	*	1.8	5	95	
Spain	1.0	0.2	10	5	85
Sweden	0.5	2.1	100		

TABLE A (cont'd)
WHITE POPULATION OF U.S. BY COUNTRY OF ORIGIN AND RACE

Country of Origin	% of White Population		% LIGHT WHITE Nordic	% WHITE Alpine	% DARK WHITE Medit.
	1790	1920			
Switzerland	0.9	1.1	35	65	
Syria, Lebanon	. . .	0.1			
Turkey	. . .	0.1		60	40
Yugoslavia	. . .	0.5			
All Other	*	0.2			
Canada	1.6	4.3			
Newfoundland	*	0.1			
Mexico	0.7	1.2			
West Indies	*	0.1			
All Other	*	*			

(*) Less than 0.1%.   (**) See p. 561.

Given the above table, it is now possible to obtain a very rough approximation of the number of Nordics, Alpines, and Mediterraneans in the United States. The method is as follows:

1. Multiply the 1980 Census Bureau count of the white population (173,991,893) by the 1920 percentage given for each nationality group (second column, Table A). The arithmetic will produce an up-to-date figure for the population of the particular nationality group.

2. Multiply this number by the appropriate percentages given in the three right-hand columns of Table A. Percentages may be given for one, two, or all three races, as the case may be. The result will approximate the number of Nordics, Alpines, or Mediterraneans within the specific nationality group.

3. Add up all the Nordic, Alpine, and Mediterranean components in all the nationality groups to obtain the total number of the three races.

To illustrate this projection method, the Alpine component of Americans of German extraction can be determined as follows: In Table A it is found that 16.3 percent of the white population in 1920 was contributed by Germany. Taking 16.3 percent of the 1980 white population (0.163 × 173,991,893) produces a figure of 28,361,000, which represents the present number of Americans of German origin. In the Alpine column of the table, 60 percent of the German population is estimated to be Alpine in race. Taking 60 percent of the number of living Americans of German extraction (0.6 × 28,361,000) yields 17,017,000 as the number of American Alpines of German origin.

The projection method, however, presents a few problems. Some of the nationality groups in Table A are not broken down into racial percentages. The racial divisions of some others are obviously inaccurate or poorly defined. In some cases, better racial percentages can be obtained from Carleton Coon's *The Races of Europe* than from Table A. Frequently, it is more accurate to rely on a direct count of the population groups, as given in such reference sources as the *Harvard Encyclopedia of American Ethnic Groups* or *One America,* than to multiply the 1920 percentage of the white population by the 1980 Census count of the white population. When statistics for national origin groups are taken from reference sources, they are either multiplied by Table A or Coon's racial percentages, whichever seems more accurate, to obtain the approximate racial count. When these are not available or are too vague, the author of this study will introduce his own estimates.

In Table B on the following page the various methods and procedures outlined above will be used to obtain a census of the 1980 American white population by race. The Nordic component will be omitted, however, since the Nordic count can be obtained more easily by subtracting the Alpine and Mediterranean totals from the white total. The sources and methods used to obtain the figures in Table B are given in the right-hand column. The first line indicates the source of the total population within the national origin group. The second line will show method used to arrive at the racial figure. When *The Dispossessed Majority* is cited as a source, the page number is given so the reader can find the primary source of the figure given for the nationality group.

The Nordic component of the American white population can be obtained by subtracting the Mediterranean and Alpine totals in Table B from the white population total in Table I, p. 64—173,791,893 minus 60,429,000 equals 113,362,893. No total has been given for the population figures in the first column of Table B because not all the national origin groups have been included. Since the sole purpose of Table B is to obtain some rough figures for the Alpine and Mediterranean components of the white population, there is no Nordic column. When some of the national origin groups listed in Table B have a Nordic component, no figure is given for the Nordics. Also, some nationality groups, such as those from the United Kingdom, Sweden, and Canada, have been

ALPINE AND MEDITERRANEAN RACIAL ALLOCATIONS

	TOTAL	ALPINE	MEDITER-RANEAN	SOURCE
ALBANIANS	70,000	70,000		HE, p.23 RE, pp.601–4
ARABS *	1,000,000		1,000,000	HE, p.128 RE, pp.507–8
ARMENIANS	400,000	134,000	266,000	HE, p.136 RE, p.629
AUSTRIANS	1,564,000	1,408,000		PM RP
BELGIANS	1,390,000	556,000		PM RP
BULGARS	70,000	28,000	42,000	HE, p.187 RE, pp.611–12
CUBANS	850,000 **		425,000	DM, p.149 AE
CZECHO-SLOVAKS	1,000,000	1,000,000		HE, pp.261,928,934 RE, pp.560–62
DANES	1,217,000	183,000		PM RP
DUTCH	3,456,000	518,000		PM RP
ESTONIANS	200,000	120,000		HE, p.340 RE, p.354, AE
FINNS	400,000	150,000		OA, p.206 RE, p.351, AE
FRENCH	5,300,000	3,392,000	530,000	DM, pp.141–42 RE, p.522
GERMANS	28,328,000	16,997,000		PM RP
GREEKS	1,400,000	210,000	1,190,000	HE, p.430 RP
HUNGARIANS	310,000	295,000		DM, p.141 RE, pp.585–86
IRANIANS	75,000		75,000	HE, p.523 RE, p.418
IRISH	16,000,000	9,040,000	48,000	DM, pp.129–30 RE, pp.375–76, AE

(cont'd on next page)

ALPINE AND MEDITERRANEAN RACIAL ALLOCATIONS

	TOTAL	ALPINE	MEDITER-RANEAN	SOURCE
ITALIANS	8,764,000	1,753,000	7,011,000	DM, p.146 RE, pp.555–56, AE
JEWS	5,781,000	5,203,000	578,000	DM, p.152 RE, pp.639–46, AE
LATVIANS	86,000	60,000		HE, p.638 RE, pp.362–65, AE
LITHUANIANS	331,000	265,000		HE, p.665 RE, pp.365–68, AE
NORWEGIANS	2,607,000	261,000		PM RP
POLES	5,100,000	3,825,000		HE, p.787 RE, pp.563–67 AE
PORTUGUESE	435,000		435,000	HE, p.813 RE, p.495
ROMANIANS	90,000	54,000	36,000	HE, p.881 RE, pp.614–16, AE
RUSSIANS	350,000	315,000		OA, p.130 RE, pp.573–74, AE
SPANISH	225,000 ***		125,000	DM, p.149 RE, pp.489–95, AE
SWISS	1,912,000	1,243,000		PM RP
TURKS	100,000	60,000	40,000	HE, p.992 RE, pp.576–84, AE
UKRAINIANS	488,000	488,000		HE, p.998 RE, pp.569–71
YUGOSLAVS	1,000,000	1,000,000		HE, p.918 RE, pp.587–95
TOTAL		48,628,000	11,801,000	

(*)   Syrians, Lebanese, Palestinians, Iraqis, Saudis, and members of Arab population groups from the Middle East.

(**)   Total number. About half the Cubans are Negroes or mulattoes.

(***)   Including 100,000 Old Immigration Spaniards who have now been completely assimilated, largely by intermarriage.

KEY: For population totals: PM (Projection Method from Table A); HE *(Harvard Encyclopedia of American Ethnic Groups)*; OA *(One America)*; DM *(The Dispossessed Majority)*.

       For racial allocations: RP (Racial percentages from Table A); RE *(Races of Europe)*; DM *(The Dispossessed Majority)*; AE (Author's estimate).

omitted because Americans who originated from these countries have been defined as overwhelmingly Nordic, one exception having been made for French Canadians, who have been included in the French category.

Finally, there is no Hispanic column in Table B. Only a very small percentage of Hispanics are white and the few whites among them would have to be allocated to the Mediterranean column.

APPENDIX B

Urban Racial Crime

		White Victim		Negro Victim	
Crime	All Offenses	White Offender	Negro Offender	White Offender	Negro Offender
Murder & non-negligent man-slaughter	100.0	24.0	6.5	3.8	65.7
Aggravated assault	100.0	23.9	8.4	1.8	65.9
Forcible rape	100.0	29.6	10.5	0.3	59.6
Armed robbery	100.0	13.2	46.7	1.7	38.4
Unarmed robbery	100.0	17.9	43.9	1.1	37.1

Race of Victim & Offender, by Type of Violent Crime: 1967 (for 17 major cities, in %)

Source: National Commission on the Causes and Prevention of Violence, *Crimes of Violence,* Vol. 11, 1969.

Bibliography

Bibliography

Adams, Henry, *The Education of Henry Adams,* Modern Library, New York.

Adams, Henry, *History of the U.S. During the First Administration of Thomas Jefferson,* Boni & Liveright, New York, 1930.

Allegro, John, *The Chosen People,* Doubleday, New York, 1972.

Ardrey, Robert, *The Territorial Imperative,* Atheneum, New York, 1966.

Arnold, Matthew, *Culture and Anarchy,* Cambridge University Press, Cambridge, England, 1961.

Bacon, Francis, *New Atlantis,* Great Books, Chicago, 1952.

Baker, John R., *Race,* Oxford University Press, New York, 1974. Reprinted in 1981 by Foundation for Human Understanding, Athens, Ga.

Beard, Charles, *President Roosevelt and the Coming of the War, 1941,* Yale University Press, New Haven, 1948.

Beard, Charles and Mary, *The Rise of American Civilization,* Macmillan, New York, 1930.

Benoist, Alain de, *Vu de droite,* Copernic, Paris, 1977.

Boman, Thorleif, *Hebrew Thought Compared with Greek,* Norton, N.Y., 1970.

Brown, Lawrence, *The Might of the West,* Joseph J. Binns, Washington, D.C., 1979.

Carrel, Alexis, *Man the Unknown,* Harper & Row, New York, 1935.

Cattell, Raymond B., *A New Morality from Science: Beyondism,* Pergamon Press, New York, 1972.

Coon, Carleton, *The Origin of Races,* Knopf, New York, 1962.

Coon, Carleton, *The Races of Europe,* Macmillan, New York, 1954.

Cuddihy, John M., *The Ordeal of Civility,* Dell Publishing, New York, 1976.

Darlington, C. D., *The Evolution of Man and Society,* Allen and Unwin, London, 1969.

Darwin, Charles, *The Origin of Species,* Modern Library, New York.

Davie, Maurice, *World Immigration,* Macmillan, New York, 1949.

Dostoyevsky, Fyodor, *The Possessed,* Modern Library, New York.

Drury, Allen, *A Very Strange Society,* Pocket Books, New York, 1968.

Dunlap, Knight, *Personal Beauty and Racial Betterment,* C. V. Mosby, St. Louis, 1920.

Eibl-Eibesfeldt, Irenäus, *Ethology, the Biology of Behavior,* Holt, Rinehart & Winston, New York, 1970.

Eibl-Eibesfeldt, Irenäus, *Love and Hate,* Holt, Rinehart & Winston, New York, 1972.

Eliot, T. S., *Notes towards the Definition of Culture,* Harcourt Brace, New York, 1949.

Ellenberger, Henri F., *The Discovery of the Unconscious,* Basic Books, New York, 1970.

Ellis, Havelock, *Studies in the Psychology of Sex: Sexual Selection in Man,* F. A. Davis Co., Phila., 1906.

Emerson, Ralph Waldo, *English Traits,* E. P. Dutton, New York, 1932.

Fogel, Robert William, and Engerman, Stanley L., *Time on the Cross,* Little, Brown, Boston, 1974.

Fuller, Major General J. F. C., *A Military History of the Western World,* Funk & Wagnalls, New York, 1954.

Galton, Francis, *Hereditary Genius,* Peter Smith, Gloucester, Mass., 1972.

Gehlen, Arnold, *Moral und Hypermoral,* Athenäum Verlag, Bonn, 1969.

Gibbon, Edward, *Decline and Fall of the Roman Empire,* Modern Library, New York.

Gobineau, Arthur de, *Essai sur l'inégalité des races humaines,* Librarie de Firmin-Didot, Paris, 1884.

Gradmann, Hans, *Das Rätsel des Lebens,* Ernst Reinhardt, Munich, 1962.

Gross, Martin L., *The Psychological Society,* Random House, New York, 1978.

Harvard Encyclopedia of American Ethnic Groups, Stephan Thernstrom, ed., Harvard University Press, Cambridge, 1980.

Heidegger, Martin, *Sein und Zeit,* Max Niemeyer Verlag, Tübingen, 1977.

Hoffer, Eric, *The True Believer,* Harper's, New York, 1951.

Hooton, E. A., *Twilight of Man,* C. P. Putnam's Sons, New York, 1939.

Huntington, Ellsworth, *The Character of Races,* Scribner's, New York, 1925.

Keith, Arthur, *A New Theory of Human Evolution,* Peter Smith, Gloucester, Mass., 1968.

Kroeber, A. L., *Anthropology,* Harcourt, Brace, New York, 1948.

Lawrence, D. H., *Studies in Classical American Literature,* Viking Press, New York, 1964.

Le Bon, Gustave, *The Crowd,* Viking Press, New York, 1973.

Lemberg, Eugen, *Nationalismus,* Rowalt, Stuttgart, 1950.

Lilienthal, Alfred, *The Zionist Connection,* Dodd, Mead, New York, 1978.

Lorenz, Konrad, *On Aggression,* Harcourt, Brace, New York, 1963.

Lynn, Richard, *Personality and National Character,* Pergamon, N.Y., 1971.

Macaulay, Thomas, *History of England from the Accession of James II*, Macmillan, London, 1914.

Mahieu, Jacques de, *Le grand voyage du dieu-soleil*, Edition Spéciale, Paris, 1971.

Monod, Jacques, *Chance & Necessity*, Knopf, New York, 1971.

Ney, John, *The European Surrender*, Little, Brown, Boston, 1970.

Nietzsche, Friedrich, *The Portable Nietzsche*, Viking Press, New York.

Novak, Michael, *The Rise of the Unmeltable Ethnics*, Macmillan, New York, 1972.

One America, Francis J. Brown and Joseph S. Roucek, eds., Prentice-Hall, Englewood Cliffs, N.J., 1962.

Ortega y Gasset, José, *La rebelión de las masas*, Espasa-Calpe, Madrid, 1966.

Pareto, Vilfredo, *The Mind and Society*, Harcourt, Brace, New York, 1935.

Pendell, Elmer, *Why Civilizations Self-Destruct*, Howard Allen Enterprises, Cape Canaveral, Fl., 1977.

Putnam, Carleton, *Race and Reality*, Howard Allen Enterprises, Cape Canaveral, Fl., 1980.

Putnam, Carleton, *Race and Reason*, Howard Allen Enterprises, Cape Canaveral, Fl., 1977.

Raspail, Jean, *The Camp of the Saints*, Sphere Books, London, 1975.

Ripley, W. Z., *The Races of Europe*, Appleton, New York, 1910.

Schoeck, Helmut, *Envy*, Harcourt, Brace, New York, 1970.

Schrag, Peter, *The Decline of the Wasp*, Simon & Schuster, New York, 1971.

Schumpeter, Joseph A., *Capitalism, Socialism and Democracy*, Harper & Row, New York, 1962.

Sheldon, William, H., *Varieties of Delinquent Youth*, Hafner, Darien, Ct., 1949.

Shuey, Audrey M., *The Testing of Negro Intelligence*, Foundation for Human Understanding, Athens, Ga., 1966.

Solzhenitsyn, Aleksandr, *Letter to the Soviet Leaders*, Harper & Row, New York, 1974.

Sorokin, Pitirim A., *Contemporary Sociological Theories*, Harper & Row, New York, 1964.

Spanuth, Jürgen, *Atlantis*, Grabert-Verlag, Tübingen, 1965.

Spengler, Oswald, *The Decline of the West*, Knopf, New York, 1957.

Strode, Hudson, *Jefferson Davis*, Harcourt, Brace and World, 1955–64.

Swartzbaugh, Richard, *The Mediator*, Howard Allen Enterprises, Cape Canaveral, Fl., 1973.

Thornwald, Jürgen, *Das Gewürz*, Droemer Knaur, Locarno, Switzerland, 1978.

Tiger, Lionel, *Men in Groups*, Vintage Books, New York, 1970.

Tocqueville, Alexis de, *Democracy in America,* trans. George Lawrence, Harper & Row, New York, 1966.

Tolstoy, Nikolai, *The Secret Betrayal, 1944–1947,* Scribner's, New York, 1977.

Unamuno, Miguel de, *Del Sentimiento Trágico de la Vida,* Las Americas Publishing Co., New York, 1966.

Unwin, J. D., *Sex and Culture,* Oxford University Press, London, 1934.

Weber, Max, *The Protestant Ethic and the Spirit of Capitalism,* Allen and Unwin, London, 1930.

White, Leslie A., *The Evolution of Culture,* McGraw-Hill, New York, 1959.

Williams, Duncan, *Trousered Apes,* Arlington House, New Rochelle, N.Y., 1971.

Wilson, Edward O., *Sociobiology,* Harvard University Press, Cambridge, Mass., 1975.

Worthy, Morgan, *Eye Color, Sex and Race,* Droke House/Hallux, Anderson, S.C., 1974.

Yaffe, James, *The American Jews,* Random House, New York, 1968.

Yale, William, *The Near East,* University of Michigan Press, Ann Arbor, 1958.

Zayas, Alfred de, *Nemesis at Potsdam,* Routledge & Kegan Paul, London, 1979.

Index